AN ANNOTATED SECONDARY BIBLIOGRAPHY SERIES ON ENGLISH LITERATURE IN TRANSITION

1880–1920

W. EUGENE DAVIS

GENERAL EDITOR

JOSEPH CONRAD

THOMAS HARDY

E. M. FORSTER

JOHN GALSWORTHY

GEORGE GISSING

D. H. LAWRENCE

H. G. WELLS

WALTER PATER

G. B. SHAW

CONTRIBUTORS

J. C. Almaric   *Université Paul Valéry*
Werner Bies   *Universität Trier*
Masahiko Masumoto   *Nagoya University*
Mary DeJong Obuchowski   *Central Michigan University*
J. P. Wearing
David Welsh   *University of Michigan*

ASSOCIATE CONTRIBUTORS

Eugene Steele   *University of Jos*
Peter Obuchowski   *Central Michigan University*

G. B. Shaw

AN ANNOTATED
BIBLIOGRAPHY
OF WRITINGS
ABOUT HIM

VOLUME I: 1871–1930

COMPILED AND EDITED BY

J. P. WEARING

NORTHERN ILLINOIS UNIVERSITY PRESS

DEKALB, ILLINOIS 1986

J. P. Wearing is co-founder and former editor (1972–1986) of the journal, *Nineteenth Century Theatre Research*. His books include *the Collected Letters of Sir Arthur Pinero* (1974), *The London Stage 1890–1899: A Calendar of Plays and Players* (1976), *English Drama and Theatre, 1800–1900* (1978), *American and British Theatrical Biography: A Directory* (1979), *The London Stage 1900–1909* (1981), *The London Stage 1910–1919* (1982), and *The London Stage 1920–1929* (1984).

Library of Congress Cataloging-in-Publication Data
Wearing, J. P.
George Bernard Shaw: an annotated bibliography
of writings about him.
(Annotated secondary bibliography series on
English literature in transition, 1880–1920)
Includes indexes.
Contents: v. 1. 1871–1930.
1. Shaw, Bernard, 1856–1950—Bibliography.
I. Title.   II. Series.
Z8814.5.W4   1986   (PR5366]   016.822'912   86-8649
ISBN 0-87580-125-0 (v. 1)

Preface

The purposes of the Annotated Secondary Bibliography series, delineated by its founding editor (the late Helmut E. Gerber), are well worth reiterating here because they have provided the major guidelines for the scope of the present volume. Those purposes are (1) to provide scholars with a comprehensive record of everything that has been said, in any language, about a given author; (2) to eliminate duplication of scholarship on selected authors; (3) to eliminate long hours of fruitless research; (4) to make available some scholarship that is not readily accessible (for example, work in obscure journals or in foreign languages unfamiliar to most scholars); (5) to provide a ready reference to materials for studies of the history of taste in a limited period for scholars concerned not with individual authors but with cultural history; (6) to provide, by means of five indexes, a reference work that will simplify studies in an author's reputation (generally or in a particular nation), a periodical's critical position, a particular critic's criteria for judging literary works, and the like; and (7) to provide intrinsically other information that can be used for varied and diverse purposes. Within that context, this present volume on Shaw covers the years 1871 (the year of the earliest item on Shaw located) through 1930 (when, it can be fairly stated, Shaw had written most, if not all, his major work). Thus, this bibliography focuses on Shaw's growing reputation and eventually his establishment as a major figure, while two other volumes cover later years and developments in his career and reputation.

Unfortunately, when the general purposes and principles are applied to the early Shaw, the task of the bibliographer becomes utterly monumental and, ultimately, impossible (which may well account for the absence, until the present endeavor, of any truly extensive bibliography of Shaw criticism). Quite literally, it would be possible to spend an entire lifetime tracking down and recording the incalculable number of items written on Shaw throughout the world during 1871-1930. Moreover, such a bibliography (apart from being economically unfeasible from a publishing point of view) would require the services of numerous people with access to perfect collections of all the kinds of sources in which Shavian criticism appeared—books, newspapers, periodicals, and assorted ephemera. Clearly, that is not a realistic proposition, and I seriously doubt whether the labor expended on such an ideal task would be worthwhile. I also doubt whether the impression gained of Shaw in this present, more circumscribed bibliography, would be radically altered.

Nevertheless, even with those sorts of limitations, I think this bibliography does offer a sound base of information, valuable both in itself and as the foundation for subsequent research and discoveries. The focus here has been to exhaust, as nearly as possible, all current standard reference sources and to track down additional materials connected with, for example, stage productions and revivals. Indeed, one of the strengths of the bibliography is its coverage of Shaw's developing reputation in the theatre, particularly in London and New York—incidentally, a fertile ground for future research on Shaw. However, it has still not proved possible to include every item on Shaw, and readers will find many helpful suggestions elsewhere, particularly in three works published after work on this bibliography was essentially complete: Dan H. Laurence, BERNARD SHAW: A BIBLIOGRAPHY, 2 vols (Oxford: Clarendon Press, 1983); István Pálffy, "George Bernard Shaw's Reception in Hungary; The Early Years, 1903-1914," THEATRE HISTORY STUDIES, IV (1984), 101-13; and, Rodelle Weintraub, ed., SHAW: THE ANNUAL OF BERNARD SHAW STUDIES: VOLUME FIVE: SHAW ABROAD (University Park & Lond: Pennsylvania University Press, 1985). Similarly, innumerable potential leads could be generated by an inquisitive reading of Shaw's own letters, of which there are three volumes to date, also edited by Dan H. Laurence.

In common with other bibliographies in this series, I have omitted reference to portraits of Shaw, reviews of books about Shaw, and such items as excerpts of Shaw's own writings. However, I have varied the usual series practice by frequently grouping under one item number several articles of related interest in the same newspaper or journal: if each item were entered separately, it would be dispersed throughout the bibliography. A glance at item 271 will demonstrate this practice—numerous items from the NEW YORK TIMES concerning the controversy surrounding the production of Mrs. Warren's Profession are all listed together. (The various indexes will help readers locate any individual item inadvertently buried.) Consequently, there are actually many more items in the bibliography than the 3676 recorded numerically.

The aim of the annotations is objectivity; any critical comment, supplementary information, or précis has been bracketed. All items not specifically seen or read have been clearly marked "not seen." Entries are listed under the date of first publication; within the listing for each year all entries are alphabetized either by author or, where there is no author, by title. Finally, I have, of course, endeavored to provide complete bibliographical information for each item. In some cases, for various reasons, this has not proved possible, but I have given as much information as is available, which may help others locate the item and so preserve it from oblivion.

ACKNOWLEDGMENTS

While I am responsible for the vast majority of the English language entries (and a few of the foreign language ones), I have received valuable assistance in the compilation of this bibliography from several people. Werner Bies handled virtually all the German language items, as the late David Welsh did for Polish and Russian (as well as other assorted languages). Similarly J. C. Almaric and Masahiko Masumoto provided items in French and Japanese respectively. Other foreign language items were handled by Eugene Steele (Italian and Roumanian), J. S. Tedesco (Italian and French), and Mario Curreli (Italian). I am grateful to Asela Rodriguez de Laguna for making available to me her bibliographies of Hispanic items on Shaw. Mary DeJong Obuchowski assisted with a considerable number of English language items. I have also received valuable assistance from Peter Obuchowski, Willard Wolfe, Larry L. Bronson, Elsie B. Adams, Donald C. Haberman, Ethelyn Wuertz, Teresa Shaw, and Karl H. Schoeps. Judy Johnson has generated the camera-ready copy for this volume with a serenity that defies comprehension, and I am truly grateful for her many months of extremely hard work.

Contents

NOTE ON ENTRY STYLE

Titles of Shaw's books are underlined; titles of his short works are in quotation marks. Titles of books by other authors, collections of stories and letters edited by other writers, and names of periodicals and newspapers appear in all capital letters. The translations appearing in parentheses are confined to meanings of the phrases; however, it should be noted that the titles of translations are seldom literal ones.

A Checklist

I. DRAMA

A. SEPARATE WORKS

Widowers' Houses. Lond, 1893.
Mrs. Warren's Profession. Lond, 1902.
Man and Superman. Lond, 1903; NY, 1904.
Passion, Poison, and Petrifaction. NY, 1905; Lond, 1907.
How He Lied to Her Husband. Berlin, 1906 [German translation].
The Doctor's Dilemma. Berlin, 1909 [German translation].
Press Cuttings. Lond & NY, 1909.
The Shewing-up of Blanco Posnet. NY, 1909.
Getting Married. Berlin, 1910 [German translation].
Misalliance. Berlin, 1910 [German translation].
Fanny's First Play. Berlin, 1911 [German translation].
Pygmalion. Berlin, 1913 [German translation]; NY, 1914.
Androcles and the Lion. Berlin, 1913 [German translation].
Great Catherine. Berlin, 1919 [German translation].
Back to Methuselah. NY & Lond, 1921.
Saint Joan. Lond & NY, 1924.
Translations and Tomfooleries. NY & Lond, 1926.
The Apple Cart. Berlin, 1929 [German translation]; Lond, 1930;
 NY, 1931.

B. COLLECTED EDITIONS

Plays Pleasant and Unpleasant [Vol I: Unpleasant Plays: Widowers'
 Houses, The Philanderer, Mrs. Warren's Profession; Vol II: Pleasant
 Plays: Arms and the Man, Candida, The Man of Destiny, You
 Never Can Tell]. Lond & NY, 1898.
Three Plays for Puritans [The Devil's Disciple, Caesar and Cleopatra,

Captain Brassbound's Conversion]. Lond & NY, 1901.
John Bull's Other Island and Major Barbara. NY & Lond, 1907.
The Doctor's Dilemma, Getting Married, and The Shewing-up of Blanco Posnet. Lond & NY, 1911,
Misalliance, The Dark Lady of the Sonnets, and Fanny's First Play. Lond & NY, 1914.
Androcles and the Lion, Overruled, Pygmalion. NY & Lond, 1916.
Heartbreak House, Great Catherine, and Playlets of the War. NY & Lond, 1919.
The Plays of Bernard Shaw: Pocket Edition [Translations and Tomfooleries, Jitta's Atonement, The Admirable Bashville, Press Cuttings, The Glimpse of Reality, Passion, Poison, and Petrifaction, The Fascinating Foundling, The Music-Cure]. Lond, 1926.
The Works of Bernard Shaw: Collected Edition. Lond, 1930-38; NY, 1930-32.

II. FICTION

SEPARATE WORKS

Cashel Byron's Profession. Lond & NY, 1886.
An Unsocial Socialist. Lond, 1887; NY, 1900.
Love Among the Artists. Chicago, 1900; Lond, 1914.
The Irrational Knot. NY & Lond, 1905.

III. ESSAYS AND MISCELLANEOUS WRITINGS

The Quintessence of Ibsenism. Lond & Bost, 1891.
The Perfect Wagnerite. Lond, 1898; NY, 1899.
The Common Sense of Muncipal Trading. Lond, 1904; NY, 1911.
Dramatic Opinions and Essays. NY, 1906; Lond, 1907.
The Sanity of Art. Lond & NY, 1908.
Socialism and Superior Brains. Lond, 1909; NY, 1910.
Common Sense About the War. Lond, 1914.
Peace Conference Hints. Lond, 1919.
The Intelligent Woman's Guide to Socialism and Capitalism. Lond & NY, 1928.

Abbreviations

OF SELECTED PERIODICAL AND BOOK TITLES

Amalric	Jean-Claude Amalric, BERNARD SHAW: DU REFORMATEUR VICTORIEN AU PROPHETE EDOUARDIEN (Paris: Didier, 1977)
AROUND THEATRES	Max Beerbohm, AROUND THEATRES, 2 vols (Lond: Heinemann, 1924 [not seen]; NY: Knopf, 1930)
ATH	ATHENAEUM
CUR LIT	CURRENT LITERATURE (NY)
CUR OP	CURRENT OPINION (NY)
DC	DAILY CHRONICLE (Lond)
DN	DAILY NEWS (Lond)
DT	DAILY TELEGRAPH (Lond)
Evans	T. F. Evans, ed, SHAW: THE CRITICAL HERITAGE (Lond, Henley & Bost: Routledge & Kegan Paul, 1976)
FORT REV	FORTNIGHTLY REVIEW (Lond)
Hood	Samuel Stevens Hood, ed, ARCHIBALD HENDERSON: THE NEW CRICHTON (NY: Beechhurst, 1949)
ILN	ILLUSTRATED LONDON NEWS
LAST THEATRES	Max Beerbohm, LAST THEATRES 1904-1910 (Lond: Hart-Davis, 1970)
LIT DIG	LITERARY DIGEST
Litto	Fredric M. Litto, AMERICAN DISSERTATIONS ON THE DRAMA AND THE THEATRE: A BIBLIOGRAPHY (Kent: Kent State UP, 1969)

MacCarthy	Desmond MacCarthy, SHAW (Lond: MacGibbon & Kee, 1951)
MORE THEATRES	Max Beerbohm, MORE THEATRES 1898-1903 (NY: Taplinger, 1969)
MPOST	MORNING POST (Lond)
NEW REP	NEW REPUBLIC
NSTATE	NEW STATESMAN
NYH	NEW YORK HERALD
NYT	NEW YORK TIMES
NYTTR 1886-1895	THE NEW YORK TIMES THEATER REVIEWS 1886-1895 (NY: NEW YORK TIMES & Arno, 1975)
NYTTR 1896-1903	THE NEW YORK TIMES THEATER REVIEWS 1896-1903 (NY: NEW YORK TIMES & Arno, 1975)
NYTTR 1904-1911	THE NEW YORK TIMES THEATER REVIEWS 1904-1911 (NY: NEW YORK TIMES & Arno, 1975)
NYTTR 1912-1919	THE NEW YORK TIMES THEATER REVIEWS 1912-1919 (NY: NEW YORK TIMES & Arno, 1975)
NYTTR 1920-1926	THE NEW YORK TIMES THEATER REVIEWS 1920-1970: VOLUME I: 1920-1926 (NY: NEW YORK TIMES & Arno, 1971)
NYTTR 1927-1929	THE NEW YORK TIMES THEATER REVIEWS 1920-1970: VOLUME II: 1927-1929 (NY: NEW YORK TIMES & Arno, 1971)
NYTTR 1930	THE NEW YORK TIMES THEATER REVIEWS 1920-1970: VOLUME III: 1930-1934 (NY: NEW YORK TIMES & Arno, 1971)
OBS	OBSERVER (Lond)
PMG	PALL MALL GAZETTE
REV OF REVS	REVIEW OF REVIEWS
Rodriguez (MD)	Asela Rodriguez-Seda, "Shaw in the Hispanic World: A Bibliography," MODERN DRAMA, XIV (Dec 1971), 335-39

ABBREVIATIONS

Rodriguez (MS)	Asela Rodriguez de Laguna, Unpublished bibliography of Hispanic items on Shaw, provided to the author
SAT REV	SATURDAY REVIEW (Lond)
STIMES	SUNDAY TIMES (including SUNDAY TIMES AND SUNDAY SPECIAL) (Lond)
TIMES	TIMES (Lond)
TLS	TIMES LITERARY SUPPLEMENT
Weintraub	Stanley Weintraub, ed, SAINT JOAN FIFTY YEARS AFTER: 1923/24-1973/74 (Baton Rouge: Louisiana State UP, 1973)
WEST REV	WESTMINSTER REVIEW

Introduction

T. F. Evans in the introduction to his SHAW: THE CRITICAL HERITAGE (1976) has already provided a judicious and reasonably detailed survey of Shaw's growing reputation during the period covered by this bibliography. My remarks here, therefore, are necessarily briefer than they might have been otherwise, and should be regarded as merely supplemental to Evans's.

Although Shaw was being written about from 1871 onward, and although he began to establish himself politically and in other ways in the 1880s, it was not until 1892, with the production of Widowers' Houses, that his own work attracted any significant attention. The mixed nature of the early critical responses was to be repeated every time Shaw produced a new work: critics, generally, were either pro-Shaw (with perhaps some reservations) or anti-Shaw (with perhaps some grudging praise). Only occasionally does one find a critic who occupies some middle ground with equanimity.

The positive qualities of Widowers' Houses were its wit and humor, against which were balanced its faulty dramaturgy and the influence of Ibsen, as evidenced in its pronounced thesis. Interestingly, two later revivals, in 1909 and 1922, generated equally mixed reviews: the play was seen simultaneously as an early one; not dated; completely Shavian; flimsy and unconvincing; and Shaw's best work because it is lean, tense, and has no superfluous dialogue. Virtually the same process was repeated with such plays as Arms and the Man and Mrs. Warren's Profession. Arms and the Man enjoyed several productions (for example, in 1894, 1908, 1911, 1915, 1919, and 1930) and was seen as fresh, anachronistic, avante-garde, silly, unsuited to wartime production, and absolutely right about war. Mrs. Warren's Profession, whose progress to the stage was ever surrounded by controversy, was viewed as didactic, Ibsenesque, doctrinal, not harmful, and almost mid-Victorian. However, the play also marked the beginning of one of the dominant criticisms of Shaw's plays—characters who lack individuality, possess no inner life, and who are mere reflections of Shaw himself.

That kind of recurrent criticism seems to me a more profitable way of assessing Shaw's development through 1930, rather than to simply catalogue and summarize the reactions to individual works (reactions that can be easily located in the bibliography itself). And Shaw's apparent inability to fully flesh out his characters was indeed something even his supporters would concede. William Archer [item 253] deemed the characters in Major Barbara mere "animated points of view," a description echoed in a later criticism of Overruled with its mechanical puppets. Even the moderately successful Caesar and Cleopatra was seen as being peopled by characters no more than vehicles for Shaw's wit. By 1916, Philip Littell, in the NEW REPUBLIC [1696], thought it was about time a new, younger dramatist demonstrated to Shaw that there were other ways of classifying people rather than by opinion. Even Joan in the highly successful Saint Joan drew blame for lacking an inner life [2360]. The same writer thought all Shaw's characters "exist in virtue of the thought they express rather than in virtue of the feeling they communicate."

Of course, from another point of view, such means of characterization could be and were seen as innovative. Many times Shaw was dubbed the innovator of the era—the iconoclast (a favored description) who was helping to shatter many of the existing traditions, both philosophically as well as dramaturgically. However, at the same time, Shaw's strong dramatic roots in nineteenth-century theatrical traditions were also recognized (both favorably and adversely). Max Beerbohm [383] could fault a revival of Captain Brassbound's Conversion because of its traditional conventions, although the parody in The Devil's Disciple of nineteenth-century melodrama was found to be a positive asset.

Given Shaw's indebtedness to nineteenth-century theatrical dramaturgy (a topic excellently explored in Martin Meisel's 1963 book, SHAW AND THE NINETEENTH-CENTURY THEATRE), it might at first glance seem somewhat curious that his plays were often thought to be more readable than playable. (Nineteenth-century plays are playable but far from eminently readable.) This view of Shaw became quite common once the published versions of the plays (with their lengthy prefaces) began to achieve general circulation. On one level this is easily explained by Shaw's innovative use of extremely detailed, almost novelistic stage directions, which do indeed make the printed versions more nearly resemble literature than do those of Pinero or H. A. Jones (as Clayton Hamilton pointed out [1777]). Perhaps, too, Shaw's inclination towards philosophy, propaganda, and preaching (see for example, 177, 252) results in works better read than acted. Or, perhaps, we should synthesize all these views and criticisms and see that the prefaces, stage directions, and plays constitute a radically new or different art form that suits the conventional theatre only indifferently at best. (William Archer, in a somewhat paradoxical review of You Never Can

Tell [85], did suggest that Shaw should have stood in the pit and read out his own stage directions during the performance.) What does appear to have been recognized in some quarters [886] is that Shaw and his dramaturgy are really sui generis.

While that may be true of Shaw's resultant style and methods, his indebtedness to others (over and above the nineteenth-century theatrical traditions already noted) was frequently pointed out. Indeed, the list of names of those whose works and ideas influenced Shaw is remarkably long—Ibsen, Nietzsche, Henry George, Schopenhauer, Voltaire, Anatole France, Tolstoy, Chekhov, Darwin, Pushkin, Smollett, Swift, and even Charlie Chaplin and Mack Sennett. Sometimes Shaw was perceived as adding virtually nothing to his sources or influences [354], yet a sprawling play such as Back to Methuselah could be viewed as molding a new visionary religion out of earlier formative influences [2149, 2152].

One figure who, I think it can be fairly said, did not influence Shaw (for all his jesting self-comparisons with him) is Shakespeare. In that comparison can be detected, I believe, a basic defect in Shaw as a dramatist, a defect picked out early in a NEW YORK TIMES review of Plays Pleasant and Unpleasant, namely, "the fault of Shaw as a dramatist is his lack of poetry" [58]. The drama is much more compressed and suggestive than Shaw realized; he wanted to render everything in his plays explicit and fixed (hence the prefaces, stage directions, and his propensity to debate every facet of any topic to the point of exhaustion). Concommitant with that failing is another discerned by St. John Ervine [1918], Shaw's inability to understand "the beauty and fascination of mere irrelevancy" and natural beauty (the latter despite Shaw's love of hiking). This criticism is fully and best summarized by Joseph Wood Krutch [3577], whose objection is worth quoting at some length:

> The Apple Cart is a remarkable play if judged only as a part of contemporary literature, but if the time ever comes when the wit and satire of Shaw's plays are no longer enough by themselves to justify their claim upon the attention of an audience, then I suspect that this play will be found wanting along with the rest, and that its defect will be the same defect of the others. In each there comes a moment when the author must transcend in a mystical flight the logic which he has seemed to follow; a moment when . . . a vision and a faith are necessary to supply a link that is not there in the chain of reason; but the enraptured eloquence which would enable him to leave common sense behind never quite breaks free. The thing which he wants most to say is something which no prose, not even his, can communicate, and thus there is always one point in every play where he fails of complete success because he is not a poet.

While Shaw was accruing all this blame and praise as a writer, he was acquiring also a wide public reputation that he aided and abetted with his own public persona. Most frequently (and more times than it is almost possible to cite) Shaw was dubbed a self-publicizing charlatan, buffoon, humbug, or jester (or all four). Naturally his supporters sprang to his defense against such attacks, pointing to his underlying, ever-serious purposes. However, Shaw, either directly or indirectly, was not above propagating any and every perception of himself that helped to keep him in the public eye. Thus he would write letters to the editors of various newspapers and journals on all sorts of topics and issues—small pox (from which he had suffered), Henry Irving's knighthood, spelling reform, land nationalization, vivisection, censorship, force-feeding, whipping, cremation, and a host of socialist issues, to name but a fraction. Moreover, the controversies some of his works created added fuel to the furnace of publicity. Mrs. Warren's Profession was banned (in London) or closed down (in New York); his books were banned, at least temporarily, in New York; and The Shewing-up of Blanco Posnet suffered from censorship, was produced in Dublin (away from the reach of English law), played to packed houses, and subsequently considered a storm in a theatrical teacup. Additionally the word bloody in Pygmalion served as excellent publicity even though Shaw was not the first to use it on stage. The play also generated further interest since Shaw allowed it to be produced first outside England because of the allegedly hostile treatment meted out to his work by the London theatre critics. He repeated the process with Heartbreak House and The Apple Cart (plays with distinctively English themes), and in all three instances newspapers reported the events fully and thereby added to Shaw's notoriety.

Of course, Shaw needed suitable accomplices to wittingly or unwittingly assist him as a "self-advertizer." The most obliging individual was Archibald Henderson whose devotion to writing on and about Shaw has surely never been surpassed by any other Shavian devotee. A corporate accomplice emerged in the form of the NEW YORK TIMES, which, unlike the TIMES (London), began to report the least item of news about Shaw, frequently on its front page. My own favorite "silly news" items are those on Shaw learning to dance the tango [1665, 2859], but equally frivolous silliness can be found in items 1637, 2886, 3029, 3037, 3225, 3230, 3351, 3454, and 3518, or by perusing the index of the titles of secondary works under "Shaw." Probably no other literary or theatrical figure of the period was the focus of quite so much public attention.

Other forms of publicity (and its attendant legitmate step-relation, reputation) also attached to Shaw. Most notable, perhaps, was the Nobel Prize, awarded to Shaw in 1925, a year in which he produced no significant work—a fact to which he readily and typically drew attention. With equal panache (and publicity) he gave the prize money away so that the Anglo-Swedish Literary Foundation could be formed. He also received distinctive recognition in having at least twenty major critical works devoted to his writings. In itself that distinction is somewhat ambiguous: some of the critics were reasonably eminent (H. L. Mencken, Holbrook Jackson, G. K. Chesterton, P. P. Howe, and Gilbert Norwood), while others were either mediocre or outrightly adulatory. Personally, I find none of the book-length studies particularly insightful or stimulating, though others may well challenge that assessment.

Some facts about Shaw's developing reputation, however, are clear. First, by 1900–1901 it is safe to say that any work by Shaw would be reviewed extensively. Second, virtually twice as much was written on Shaw between 1920 and 1930 as had been written in the preceding fifty years—quite staggering statistics even given that they are based on the present, fallible bibliography. Third, Shaw's overall reputation was always subject to change, depending on which critic was providing the assessment. Thus he could be the equal of Sheridan, Molière, or Aristophanes or deader than Tennyson and much more inferior than Thomas Hardy. Perhaps, however, the Malvern Festival, established in 1929, places this paradox in perspective. Set well away from London (the theatrical center of Britain), that sleepy Worcestershire town became host to what was really a Shaw festival to which all the London critics (and many international) theatre critics dutifully came. It, and Shaw, simply could not be ignored.

G. B. Shaw

AN ANNOTATED BIBLIOGRAPHY

OF WRITINGS ABOUT HIM

VOLUME I

The Bibliography

1871

---

1 "Editorial Replies," VAUDEVILLE MAGAZINE, I (Sept 1871), 16.
"You [Shaw] should have registered your letter; such a combination of wit and satire ought not to have been conveyed at the ordinary rate of postage. As it was, your arguments were so weighty that we had to pay <u>twopence</u> extra for them."

1872 — 1874

[No entries for these years.]

1875

---

2 H., W. C. "Correspondence: Messrs. Moody and Sankey," PUBLIC OPINION, XXVII (10 April 1875), 453-54.
[This letter forms part of a debate on the qualities of the American evangelists, Moody and Sankey, which had been opened in the correspondence columns of PUBLIC OPINION by "J. R. D." on 27 March 1875, p. 390. Shaw, as "S.," contributed a letter on 3 April 1875, p. 422 which was referred to by "W. C. H." as evincing proof "of the reality of the conversions at Dublin." Additional correspondence was provided by Edward R. Whitby, "Vox," "G. W. B.," and George Barlow on 10 April 1875, p. 454; "R.," "E. D. I. N.," Ernest Davies, Philip O. S. Fair, Robert L. McAdam, "Oxford," "Diakonos," 17 April 1875, pp. 486-87; William Mathew, Edward R. Whitby, "Tweed," Alexander

1

Mackenzie, Richard Robinson, "T. M.," 24 April 1875, pp. 518-19.]

1876—1884

[No entries for these years.]

1885
---

3 Wicksteed, Philip H. "The Jevonian Criticism of Marx: A Rejoinder," TODAY, April 1885; rptd in BERNARD SHAW & KARL MARX: A SYMPOSIUM 1884-1889 (NY: Richard W. Ellis/Georgian Press for Random House, 1930), pp. 91-99.
Shaw has a faulty notion of the exchange values of commodities, and his Marxian theories are based on literary rather than arithmetical experience.

1886
---

4 M., W. "Review," COMMONWEAL (Lond), II (17 July 1886), 126.
Cashel Byron's Profession is an indictment of our sham society and criticizes contemporary follies incisively.   The atmosphere is fantastic, and the characters are Shaw's puppets.   But scenes are depicted accurately, "more after the manner of a painter than a dramatic writer." It is a conscientious and artistic work.

5 R., J. "Cashel Byron's Profession," OUR CORNER, VII (1886), 301-05.
Cashel Byron's Profession is a new type of fiction which is realistic, satiric, and idealistic.   Shaw has Dickens' humorous imagination, but a far wider intellectual grasp.   The dialogue is vivid and vigorous, the style elastic and varied.   Shaw's weaknesses are that Lydia Carew is a mechanical rather than a real woman, and that Shaw dazzles rather than wins over his audience.

1887
---

6 Hyndman, H. M.   "Correspondence: Marx's Theories," PMG, XLV (11 May 1887), 11.
It is difficult to know whether Shaw's defense of Marx's economic and

historical theories is serious or a mere jest. He should substantiate his position. [Shaw's comments appeared as "Correspondence: Marx and Modern Socialism," PMG, XLV (7 May 1887), 3. For further details of the debate see: Shaw, 12 May 1887, p. 11, and Hyndman, 16 May 1887, p. 2.]

7 "New Publications: Cashel Byron's Profession," NYT, 5 Jan 1887, p. 10.
Shaw writes with great familiarity about boxing.

1888

8 [The British Association], TIMES, 8 Sept 1888, p. 7.
[Brief mention of Shaw reading a paper on "The Transition to Social Democracy."]

1889—1890

[No entries for these years.]

1891

9 Archer, William. "The Quintessence of Ibsenism: An Open Letter to George Bernard Shaw," NEW REVIEW, V (Nov 1891), 463-69; rptd in Thomas Postlewait, ed., WILLIAM ARCHER ON IBSEN: THE MAJOR ESSAYS, 1889-1919 (Westport, CT & Lond: Greenwood, 1984), pp. 29-34.
There is less jargon in the published version of The Quintessence of Ibsenism than in an earlier draft, and Shaw's "analyses of [Ibsen's] plays are little masterpieces of dialectical and literary dexterity." However, he is frequently and wantonly obscure, and the jargon disguises a lack of originality.

1892

10 A[rcher], W[illiam]. "The Theatre: Widowers' Houses," WORLD, No. 963 (14 Dec 1892), 14-15; rptd in Evans, pp. 48-53.
Widowers' Houses is quite competent and entertaining, although Shaw has an imperfect concept of stagecraft. His theories are paramount, and his not quite credible characters indulge in lengthy diatribes.

3

[Archer's criticism is prefaced by an account of his collaboration in the play.]

11 "Drama: The Week," ATH, No. 3399 (17 Dec 1892), 865.
Widowers' Houses "aims to show with Zolaesque exactitude that middle-class life is foul and leprous," and reveals Shaw's indebtedness to Ibsen.

12 Grein, J. T. "The Independent Theatre," DT, 13 Dec 1892, p. 3; rptd in Evans, pp. 46-47.
Shaw is undoubtedly a brilliant man, and it was far better for the Independent Theatre to produce Widowers' Houses (a flawed success) than "a triumph by a safe mediocrity."

13 "The Independent Theatre," TIMES, 10 Dec 1892, p. 5.
Widowers' Houses bears similarities to Scandinavian drama, and is clever but perverse. Some dialogue is amusing and the characters are plausible, although the audience was not totally appreciative.

14 "London Theatres: The Royalty," STAGE, 15 Dec 1892, pp. 12-13.
Widowers' Houses possesses wit and characterization, but other dramatic ingredients are missing. The Fabians' view of society is not everyone's.

15 M[assingham], H. W. "A Realist Play," ILN, CI (17 Dec 1892), 770; rptd in Evans, pp. 53-54.
Widowers' Houses is a "Socialist criticism of life" which Shaw has rendered very plausibly.

16 "Royalty Theatre," DT, 10 Dec 1892, p. 3; rptd in Evans, pp. 41-44.
Shaw's avowed intention in Widowers' Houses is to lecture upon the morality of the middle classes. This he does pugently, as well as exaggerating Ibsen's dramaturgical traits and overstating his case. Some dialogue is witty, together with incipient good characterization.

17 [Thomas, W. Moy]. "The Drama: Royalty Theatre," DN, 10 Dec 1892, p. 5; rptd in Evans, pp. 44-46.
Widowers' Houses reveals the marks of a first-rate dramatist, particularly so far as characterization is concerned.

18 "Undergraduates' Practical Joke at Oxford," TIMES, 23 Feb 1892, p. 8.
Shaw was the victim of a practical joke while visiting Magdalen College.

19 W[alkley], A. B. "The Drama: Widowers' Houses," SPEAKER, VI (17 Dec 1892), 736-37; rptd in Evans, pp. 55-58.
Widowers' Houses possesses many brilliant qualities, but it fails when judged by dramaturgical standards.

20 Walkley, A. B. PLAYHOUSE IMPRESSIONS (Lond: T. Fisher Unwin, 1892), pp. 5-6.
Shaw's critical standards are unattainably high, and he refuses to recognize genuine advances. He dislikes the theatre because it is theatrical.

21 "Widowers' Houses," ERA, 17 Dec 1892, p. 8.
Widowers' Houses is non-dramatic and didactic, with contemptible characters. The dialogue is "pungent and pointed." We trust he will write more plays, but not plays with a purpose.

1893

---

22 Walkley, A. B. "Some Plays of the Day," FORT REV, LIX (April 1893), 473-74.
Widowers' Houses has a more important place in the evolution rather than the history of the theatre. Shaw is a courageous, lucid, remorselessly logical thinker, and is bound to leave his mark; but the invasion is not a conquest yet.

1894

---

23 A[rcher], W[illiam]. "The Theatre: Arms and the Man," WORLD, No. 1034 (25 April 1894), 22-23; rptd in THE THEATRICAL "WORLD" OF 1894 (Lond, 1895; rptd NY: Blom, 1971), pp. 109-18; rptd in THE ENGLISH DRAMATIC CRITICS: AN ANTHOLOGY, 1660-1932, ed. James Agate (Lond: A. Barker, 1932; rptd NY: Hill & Wang, n.d.), pp. 223-28; rptd in A. C. Ward, SPECIMENS OF ENGLISH DRAMATIC CRITICISM XVII-XX CENTURIES (Lond: Oxford UP, 1945), pp. 190-97; rptd in George Rowell, VICTORIAN DRAMATIC CRITICISM (Lond: Methuen, 1971), pp. 304-07; rptd in Evans, pp. 61-65.
Arms and the Man is really a "fantastic, psychological extravaganza" in which Shaw explores the "seamy side" of his characters.

24 "Arms and the Man: Richard Mansfield Sings," NYT, 18 Sept 1894, p. 5; rptd in NYTTR 1886-1895, [n. p.].
Although Arms and the Man was well received, some people will object to having irony and satire forced on them so blatantly.

25 "At the Herald Square," NYH, 18 Sept 1894, p. 9.
Arms and the Man "is essentially an entertainment for dramatic epicureans, for people who are satiated with plots, nauseated with climaxes, disgusted with farcical fun, and who visit the playhouse only when something is offered that can make them forget it."

26 "Avenue Theatre," DT, 23 April 1894, p. 3.
In Arms and the Man Shaw induces sympathy for a character, only to later mock that character. Tone and characterization change frequently, but there are signs of promise here if Shaw can be more consistent and give more dramatic point to his work.

27 "Avenue Theatre," TIMES, 23 April 1894, p. 3.
Arms and the Man is a burlesque in which Shaw pours ridicule on numerous subjects in his own cynical spirit. The characters are grotesque.

28 "The Avenue Theatre: Arms and the Man," OBS, 22 April 1894, p. 5.
Arms and the Man tells a good story, but is full of unrelieved cynicism and satire. The play is unengaging and will not be popular.

29 "Avenue Theatre: Production of Arms and the Man," STIMES, 22 April 1894, p. 5.
Arms and the Man is clever, with real life characterizations. Shaw sees the worst in mankind, and although he says much that is true about warfare, it is not the whole truth. The play should have been edited by an experienced dramatist.

30 "The Drama: Arms and the Man," CRITIC (NY), XXV (22 Sept 1894), 194.
Arms and the Man is keen, bright, entertaining satire. The characters are an effective vehicle for Shaw's satire on "all kinds of humbug." The piece is reminiscent of W. S. Gilbert.

31 "Drama: The Week," ATH, No. 3470 (28 April 1894), 550.
Arms and the Man is a farce with a touch of satire and burlesque. It is saucy and impertinent, and Shaw's characters are "the shallowest imposters ever seen."

32 "Fabian, Critic, Dramatist," NYT, 27 May 1894, p. 20.
Shaw is not well-known in America, but he should be after the forthcoming production of Arms and the Man.

33 "The London Theatres: The Avenue," ERA, 28 April 1894, p. 9.
Arms and the Man is both a comedy of manners and a Gilbertian satire. "It is by no means a great or a strong play, but it is smart, humorous, clever, and eccentric."

34 "London Theatres: The Avenue," STAGE, 26 April 1894, pp. 12-13.
Arms and the Man is full of perverse cleverness, biting humor, and realistic characterization. It is an "ironic extravaganza" which burlesques theatrical forms and characters.

35 Mallock, W. H. "A Socialist in a Corner," FORT REV, LXI (May 1894), 693-704.

Shaw misrepresents my position on socialism, capital and ability: labor is <u>not</u> the sole producer of wealth. Shaw's contentions about human motives in accruing wealth are also wrong and reveal his ignorance of human nature and the entire socialist doctrine.

36 "Spectator." "Avenue Theatre: <u>Arms and the Man</u>," STAR, 23 April 1894, p. 1; rptd in Evans, pp. 60-61.
<u>Arms and the Man</u> is an "amalgam of burlesque, farce and comedy," and is much better than <u>Widowers' Houses</u> because Shaw knows more about playwriting now.

37 "The Stage," ACADEMY, No. 1156 (30 June 1894), 541.
<u>Arms and the Man</u> is characteristically Shavian, provokes sympathetic laughter, but leaves a doubt whether it is a serious work.

38 W[alkley], A. B. "The Drama: <u>Arms and the Man</u>," SPEAKER, IX (28 April 1894), 471-72; rptd in Evans, pp. 66-68.
Unlike W. S. Gilbert, Shaw seeks to show that current ideals are bad and need rejecting. <u>Arms and the Man</u>, therefore, embodies "a criticism of conduct, a theory of life."

1895

---

39 D., E. A. "The Theatrical Week," NYT, 28 April 1895, p. 12.
Shaw remains unpopular and unsuccessful in America, which is hardly surprising when account is taken of his paradoxical views and his "sentimental socialism."

40 "Mr. Mansfield's Theatre," NYT, 24 April 1895, p. 4; rptd in NYTTR 1886-1895, [n. p.].
<u>Arms and the Man</u> is a smart, satirical, ironically witty play which surely can be understood by theatregoers, despite W. D. Howells' recent contention to the contrary.

41 "Opens Its Doors as the Garrick," NYH, 24 April 1895, p. 9.
<u>Arms and the Man</u> has received a generally excellent production.

42 "The Theatrical Week," NYT, 16 June 1895, p. 13.
It is futile to attempt to argue against Shaw's preposterous comments about Elizabethan dramatists.

1896

---

43 Archer, William. "Shaw <u>v</u>. Shakespeare and Others," WORLD, 27 May 1896 [not seen]; rptd in THE THEATRICAL "WORLD" OF 1896 (1897; rptd NY: Blom, 1971), pp. 159-69.

Shaw's attacks on Shakespeare should be directed against the play-wright and not on the performers of his work. Shaw has yet to real-ize he really dislikes Shakespeare.

44 Filon, Augustin. LE THEATRE ANGLAIS: HIER—AUJOURD'HUI—DEMAIN (Paris: C. Levy, 1896), p. 266.
Shaw has made a lot of noise as a drama critic in support of Ibsen.
[In French.]

45 "(P)Shaw! A Page from an Interviewer's Log-book," PUNCH, CXI (1896), 180.
[A satire on Shaw declaring his disdain for Shakespeare in the SAT REV.]

46 Rook, Clarence. [Interview], CHAP-BOOK (Chicago), V: 12 (1 Nov 1896); rptd in INDEPENDENT SHAVIAN, IV: 1 (Fall 1965).
[Biographical.]

1897

---

47 Beerbohm, Max. "Chromoconanography," SAT REV, LXXXIV (1897), 31-32.
Shaw's picture of Napoleon in The Man of Destiny is not perfect, but at least Shaw gives him something to do.

48 "Candida," ERA, 7 Aug 1897, p. 11.
In Candida Shaw refrains from his pet socialist theories (though they are present). Instead he presents a "fantastic" group of characters who are given satirical, paradoxical and brilliant dialogue.

49 Dithmar, Edward A. "The Devil's Disciple," NYT, 10 Oct 1897, part IV, p. 4; rptd in NYTTR 1896-1903, [n. p.].
The Devil's Disciple reveals Shaw is a real dramatist, although he needs to prepare his audience more for some of the later develop-ments in the play. Otherwise they seem rather melodramatic.

50 "The Drama: The Devil's Disciple," CRITIC (NY), XXXI (9 Oct 1897), 209.
Although playgoers may be puzzled by the meaning of The Devil's Disciple, its thesis is really familiar: an unreligious man may be good and a religious one may be a hypocrite. This is a lively production; Dudgeon and the Andersons are well conceived; the scenes at the Anderson home are particularly fine; the court martial scene is not so successful.

51 "Her Majesty's Theatre: Candida," ABERDEEN JOURNAL, 31 July 1897, p. 4; rptd in Evans, p. 69.
Candida is reasonably successful, although Shaw is working on famil-

iar lines. There are some "smart sayings throughout the play, but on the whole it lacks robustness. A little more of the butterman and a and a trifle less of the poet would be a decided improvement."

52 "London Theatres: The Grand, Croydon," STAGE, 8 July 1897, p. 6.
The Man of Destiny would "gain much and lose nothing by judicious pruning."

53 "The Man of Destiny," ERA, 3 July 1897, p. 17.
The Man of Destiny is "capitally written" and provides good acting opportunities.

54 "Provincial Productions: Candida," STAGE, 5 Aug 1897, p. 9.
Shaw's Fabian socialism does not dominate Candida as might have been expected. Instead the play is a pleasant satire with "crisp, racy, and pungent" dialogue.

1898

---

55 Beerbohm, Max. "Gibiesse Oblige," SAT REV, LXXXV (1898), 482-83; rptd as "G. B. S. Oblige," in MORE THEATRES, pp. 17-21.
Shaw's contempt for artistic talent is readily apparent in his praise of William Heinemann's SUMMER MOTHS. Shaw's thesis is that a natural aptitude for drama is "baneful" and that a bad play is really a good play. He should reconsider his views on artistic talent.

56 Beerbohm, Max. "Mr. Shaw's Profession," SAT REV, LXXXV (1898), 651-52, 679; rptd in SHAW REVIEW, V (Jan 1962), 5-9; rptd in MORE THEATRES, pp. 21-27; rptd in Evans, pp. 76-80.
The problem with Mrs. Warren's Profession is that, despite other virtues, Shaw cannot create "human characters." Here, and in his other plays, his "men are all disputative machines . . . and the women [are] . . . rather more self-conscious than the men."

57 [Beerbohm], Max. "Why I Ought not to have Become a Dramatic Critic," SAT REV, LXXXV (1898), 709-10; rptd in AROUND THEATRES, pp. 3-7.
Shaw may have had numerous faults as a drama critic of SAT REV, but he is "the most brilliant and remarkable journalist in London."

58 "Bernard Shaw's Plays," NYT, 18 June 1898, Saturday supp, p. 397.
In Plays, Pleasant and Unpleasant Shaw is smart and glib, and Widowers' Houses, You Never Can Tell, and The Philanderer are not worth performing. "The fault of Shaw as a dramatist is his lack of poetry."

59 Blathwayt, Raymond. "What Vegetarianism Really Means: A

Talk with Mr. Bernard Shaw," VEGETARIAN, 15 March 1898 [not seen]; rptd in INDEPENDENT SHAVIAN, VIII: 2 (1969-70), 17-19.
[Shaw's views on vegetarianism; biographical.]

60 "Book Reviews Reviewed," ACADEMY, LIII (4 June 1898), 613-14.
[Selected extracts of various reviews of Plays, Pleasant and Unpleasant, including those by William Archer and W. P. James.]

61 [Elton, Oliver]. "The Independent Theatre: Miss Janet Achurch and Mr Charles Charrington in Candida," MANCHESTER GUARDIAN, 15 March 1898, p. 8; rptd in Evans, pp. 70-73.
Candida, with its mixture of humor and paradox, renders Shaw "eminent among dramatic judges." Marchbanks is a triumphant creation, possibly owing something to Dostoievsky's THE IDIOT.

62 Hale, Edward E., jr. "The Drama as Literature," DIAL, XXV (16 July 1898), 43-45.
Plays, Pleasant and Unpleasant indicates Shaw's attitude that plays can be read as well as seen; the chief characteristics of Shaw's plays are not precisely dramatic; they might also appear in novels because Shaw's plays are "almost conventional farce." Mrs. Warren's Profession, Widowers' Houses and The Philanderer are problem plays; Candida, Arms and the Man, and You Never Can Tell have no problems and hence are superior. Candida has the most depth and more "earnest searchingness, or searching earnestness."

63 [Knight, Joseph]. "Drama," ATH, No. 3683 (28 May 1898), 703-04; rptd in Evans, pp. 81-82.
Plays, Pleasant and Unpleasant is amusing, "quaint, whimsical, unreal, saucy, cynical, perverse" and didactic. Shaw's main purpose is satire, and his prefaces are customarily clever and paradoxical.

64 "Mr. Bernard Shaw's Plays," CRITIC (NY), XXXIII (1898), 81-83.
Shaw is "ingenuously egotistical" in his preface to Plays, Pleasant and Unpleasant which is not without merit. The plays are "eminently readable, if not playable." Shaw's aversion to old romantic drama is clear, but if his own work is realistic in places, his dialogue is "too good to be true to life."

65 [The Perfect Wagnerite], ATH, No. 3714 (31 Dec 1898), 938.
In The Perfect Wagnerite, Shaw's purpose is to analyze the philosophy of THE RING OF THE NIBELUNGS. Occasionally his explanations are forced and he is far from being a perfect Wagnerite. The pamphlet is, however, clever and very readable.

66 "Personal," NYT, 22 June 1898, p. 6.

Now Shaw is married to a wealthy woman, he will no longer be compelled to write "either slashing criticisms or plays in which he rails at
human nature."

67 "Plays, Pleasant and Unpleasant," NATION (NY), LXVII
(1898), 36-37.

Plays, Pleasant and Unpleasant leaves an impression of "mingled
melancholy and indignation at the spectacle of so much wasted
natural ability and perverted talent." Shaw is really observant, witty,
and accomplished, but he needs to exercise a greater sense of proportion and show more sanity.

68 R[ook], C[larence]. "Mr. Shaw's Future: A Conversation,"
ACADEMY, LIII (30 April 1898) [not seen]; rptd in INDEPEN-
DENT SHAVIAN, XII: 2 (Winter 1973), 17-18.
[An interview.]

69 [Street, G. S.]. "Socrates as Playwright," ACADEMY, LIII
(30 April 1898), 461-63 and (7 May 1898), 490-92.

Plays, Pleasant and Unpleasant shows Shaw is a romantic who is con-
sumed by a passion for reform and who uses some of Socrates'
methods. The Philanderer, even though it lacks humanity, is "more
really dramatic" than Widowers' Houses because Shaw handles his
material more easily. Mrs. Warren's Profession is much better than
either because Shaw the preacher recedes considerably. The preface
to the pleasant plays is "nobly and touchingly eloquent." Arms and
the Man is witty and interesting, Candida is Shaw's "masterpiece in
human drama," while You Never Can Tell (because of its narrow
interest) flags when Shaw's vitality and spirits droop.

70 Sullivan, T. R. "George Bernard Shaw and His Plays,"
BOOKBUYER (NY), XVI (July 1898), 502-05.
[An overview of Shaw's plays and career to date.]

71 Wilstach, Paul. "The Pleasantries of an Unpleasant Man,"
BOOKMAN (NY), VII (July 1898), 416-17.

The tone of Plays, Pleasant and Unpleasant is querulous, although
much amusement can be derived from this work. The Philanderer is
an enjoyable, satiric comedy; the hypothesis of You Never Can Tell is
not necessarily unpleasant; Mrs. Warren's Profession is nasty, and
Widowers' Houses is full of bitter truths. Arms and the Man is
"amusingly iconoclastic" while The Man of Destiny is the closest
thing to a real play.

1899

---

72 Archer, William. STUDY & STAGE: A YEAR-BOOK OF
CRITICISM (Lond: Grant Richards, 1899), pp. 1-22.

Plays, Pleasant and Unpleasant contains Shaw's most beautiful play, Candida, and his basest (The Philanderer); perhaps in the future he will show more discretion. It is also very easy to reconstruct Shaw's own personality from the characters in his plays, something quite impossible to do with Shakespeare. Philanderer is full of persiflage and is "steeped in an atmosphere of bloodless erotics that is indescribably distressing." Mrs. Warren's Profession is a powerful play, both intellectually and dramatically. In Arms and the Man Shaw uses the Gilbertian trick of self-analysis and exposure; the play is a brilliant extravaganza, but not realistic drama. You Never Can Tell is cast in a similar mold. Candida is full of beauty, humor, ingenuity and tenderness; here Shaw creates good characters and situations which make it a play of "rare genius."

73 [Beerbohm], Max. "'G. B. S.' at Kennington," SAT REV, LXXXVIII (1899), 453-54; rptd in AROUND THEATRES, pp. 50-54; rptd in George Rowell, VICTORIAN DRAMATIC CRITICISM (Lond: Methuen, 1971), pp. 308-10.
The Devil's Disciple is an irresistible romantic melodrama which Shaw has written in spite of himself. The last, farcical act gives one the opportunity of releasing all the laughter which builds up and simmers during the first two.

74 "The Devil's Disciple," ERA, 30 Sept 1899, p. 11.
Shaw now joins the ranks of professional dramatists. His earlier works have been clever but exotic; however, with The Devil's Disciple he has infused new life into old melodramatic forms and succeeded well.

75 "The Devil's Disciple," NYT, 19 Dec 1899, p. 3; rptd in NYTTR 1896-1903, [n. p.].
The Devil's Disciple continues to wear well, although imperfections in stagecraft leave some people confused.

76 Dukat, Vladoje. "George Bernard Shaw i njegove drame" (George Bernard Shaw and His Plays), NARODNE NOVINE (Zagreb), 173 [not seen].
[Cited in Rudolf Filipović, ENGLESKO-HRVATSKE KNJIŽEVNE VEZE (English-Croatian Literary Connections) (Zagreb: Liber, 1972), p. 287. In Croatian.]

77 "Kennington Theatre," TIMES, 27 Sept 1899, p. 8.
The Devil's Disciple is not a sympathetic play, being replete with biting satire, an air of insincerity, and mere posing. Shaw appears unable to take his own work seriously.

78 Kirk, John Foster. "Shaw, George Bernard," A SUPPLE-MENT TO ALLIBONE'S CRITICAL DICTIONARY OF ENGLISH LITERATURE AND BRITISH AND AMERICAN AUTHORS: VOLUME II (Phila: Lippincott, 1899), p. 1336.

[Bibliographical details of two of Shaw's novels.]

79 Payne, William Morton. "Musical Matters, and Others," DIAL, XXVI (1899), 342.
The Perfect Wagnerite is an example of the new provocative music criticism and shows Shaw appreciates Wagner's greatness.

80 "The Perfect Wagnerite," BOOKMAN (Lond), XV (Feb 1899), 150-51.
In The Perfect Wagnerite, Shaw, with his overwhelming cleverness and remarkable ingenuity, shows us how wrong we have been about Wagner. He thinks the perfect Wagnerite is a revolutionist, a mildly, persistently subversive Fabian. As an isolated treatise on public morality, Shaw's work is admirable; as a commentary, it is a piece of serious-minded impertinence.

81 "The Princess of Wales's, S. E.," STAGE, 28 Sept 1899, pp. 18-19.
Every aspect of The Devil's Disciple is paradoxical, and, although there are some dramatic scenes, it is clumsily constructed.

82 "A Valuable Study of Wagner," NYT, 6 May 1899, Saturday supp, p. 302.
Despite the various reactions his sundry works have provoked, Shaw's The Perfect Wagnerite belongs in the first rank of Wagner literature.

83 Walkley, A. B. FRAMES OF MIND (Lond: Grant Richards, 1899), pp. 37-49.
All Shaw's ideas in Plays, Pleasant and Unpleasant have appeared before; now they just happen to take what appears to be dramatic form. But theses are not really plays, only amusing games. Arms and the Man is a very remarkable play and in a droll, fantastic and farcical way presents us with a theory of life.

1900

---

84 Archer, William. "The Theatre," WORLD, No. 1382 (26 Dec 1900), 25-26; rptd in Evans, pp. 89-91.
Captain Brassbound's Conversion does not conform to the formulae demanded by West-End theatre managers, but is nevertheless a delightful mixture of comedy, melodrama, philosophy and farce. Not his best play, but the product of a thinker.

85 Archer, William. "The Theatre: You Never Can Tell," WORLD, No. 1349 (9 May 1900), 28-29.
You Never Can Tell acts better than it reads because it carries its audience with it as Shaw defies all the laws of logic and plausibility. Shaw should have stood in the pit and read out his own stage

directions.

86 "Arms and the Man: Mr. Mansfield's Engagement," NYT, 9 Jan 1900, p. 5; rptd in NYTTR 1896-1903, [n. p.].
Arms and the Man is a "very smart comedy" which exposes the falsity of traditional views of warfare. Shaw's clearly stated views may be made unfairly, however.

87 Bax, E. Belfort. "Correspondence: Socialism and Republicanism," SAT REV, XC (1900), 552-53.
Shaw has confused the distinctions between "socialistic legislation" and "socialism," and generally appears to have a simplistic view of what practical socialism entails. [For the complete exchange of correspondence between Bax and Shaw, see SAT REV, XC (1900), 493, 519-20, 618-19, and item 88.]

88 Bax, E. Belfort. "Socialism and Republicanism," SAT REV, XC (1900), 648-49.
What Shaw and Bland call the "Old Guard" is really the socialist party. Shaw and the Fabians are a muddle-headed lot and of only passing significance.

89 [Beerbohm], Max. "Captain Brassbound's Conversion," SAT REV, XC (1900), 818-19; rptd in MORE THEATRES, pp. 335-38.
Captain Brassbound's Conversion is not a good dramatic play, although it is entertaining and thoughtful. Shaw jumbles several methods--farce, comedy, melodrama—so that there is no continuity of manner.

90 [Beerbohm], Max. " 'Quo Vadis' and 'Nil Praedicendum,' " SAT REV, LXXXIX (1900), 585.
Commercial theatre managers should play Shaw for all he is worth because his plays "have qualities which delight the public." You Never Can Tell is a mixture of the serious and the farcical, and needs to be acted extravagantly.

91 Bland, Hubert. "Correspondence: Socialism and Republicanism," SAT REV, XC (1900), 586.
Both Bax and Shaw are too long-winded, and their views of socialism are simply quite different. Bax's socialism "is a more or less cut-and-dried political and economic system; [Shaw's] is an attitude of mind." [see items 87, 88.]

92 "Cashel Byron at the Herald Square," NYT, 28 Dec 1900, p. 6; rptd in NYTTR 1896-1903, [n. p.].
Cashel Byron's Profession tries the patience of audiences with the "vast and wearisome conversational powers of up-to-date pugilists."

93 "Drama: The Week," ATH, No. 3785 (12 May 1900), 603-04.
You Never Can Tell is thoroughly enjoyable, although it is difficult to discover when Shaw is being serious or what the objects of his satire

are.

94 K., H. A. "Plays and Players," STIMES, 6 May 1900, p. 6.
You Never Can Tell is an entertaining play, although Shaw occasionally makes the mistake of treating trivial matters seriously.

95 "A New Play Tried," NYH, 28 Dec 1900, p. 11.
Cashel Byron's Profession is interesting but slow and the "hero does
not appeal strongly to one's sympathies."

96 Newton, H. Chance.   "Bernard Shaw and Shaw-ism,"
    SKETCH, XXX (2 May 1900), 70.
For all his extreme views, Shaw generally provokes sympathy because
of his opposition to suffering and his support of the weak and
helpless.   You Never Can Tell is a clever play and "anything but a
conventional comedy."

97 "A Novel by Bernard Shaw," NYT, 23 June 1900, Saturday
    supp, p. 419.
An Unsocial Socialist is adequately constructed, smart, buoyant and
scintillating. "What all his writings seem to lack is genuine sympathy
with human nature."

98 "The Playhouses," ILN, CXVII (1 Dec 1900), 797.
Forbes Robertson, an unlikely choice for a Shaw play, takes full
advantage of Shaw's sardonic humor in The Devil's Disciple. The play
is an audacious parody of the archetypal situations found in sensational dramas.

99 "The Playhouses," ILN, CXVII (29 Dec 1900), 966-67.
Captain Brassbound's Conversion is full of the usual Shavian paradoxes and absurdities, but Shaw's ends are now achieved through
action rather than aphorism—a distinct advance in his dramaturgy.

100 Rist, Charles.   "Correspondence: Socialism and Repub-
    licanism," SAT REV, XC (1900), 619-20.
Shaw's ideas are correct in theory, but no Frenchman believes that
the economic views of Jaures and Millerand are not associated with a
particular form of government.   For them socialism and republicanism go hand in hand. [In French.]

101 "The Strand," STAGE, 3 May 1900, p. 15.
Although You Never Can Tell is supposed to be a concession to the
average playgoer's tastes, it is still characteristically Shavian.   It
possesses eccentric humor and is highly improbable.

102 "The Strand Theatre," TIMES, 3 May 1900, p. 11.
The English theatre may be dying because of intellectual starvation,
but Shaw and You Never Can Tell will not save it because Shaw has
"too much intellect."

103 "Strand Theatre: You Never Can Tell," DT, 3 May 1900,

p. 7.

You Never Can Tell should be shorter. Shaw's whimsical and extravagant characters and conversations are amusing; his verbal fireworks bombard the audience constantly.

104 Street, G. S. "Sheridan and Mr. Shaw," BLACKWOOD'S MAGAZINE, CLXVII (June 1900), 832-36; rptd in Evans, pp. 86-88; rptd as "Mr. Shaw," CUR LIT, XXIX (Aug 1900), 145.

You Never Can Tell reveals Shaw's major weaknesses. His plays have too many ideas in them; he pours forth all his philosophy all the time so that the audience feels it is listening to a lecture. Shaw ignores character and experience. Nevertheless, his work is enjoyable even if it is not dramatic.

105 Tarpey, W. Kingsley. "English Dramatists of To-Day," CRITIC (New Rochelle), XXXVII (Aug 1900), 124.

Shaw has yet to join the ranks of the regular dramatists; indeed, he is not by nature a dramatist, rather a "preacher and satirist." He is "essentially a moral force."

106 "Theatre Gossip: You Never Can Tell at the Strand Theatre," SKETCH, XXX (9 May 1900), 131.

Critics appear to disapprove of You Never Can Tell despite the fact that both they and audiences laugh at it enormously. It is a mixture of the comical and farcical; some characters are seriously drawn and played, others are purely farcical.

107 "The Whimsical 'G. B. S.,'" CRITIC (New Rochelle), XXXVII (Aug 1900), 114-16.

[An exchange of correspondence between Shaw and Harper & Brothers concerning royalty payments for Cashel Byron's Profession.]

108 "You Never Can Tell," ERA, 5 May 1900, p. 13.

Shaw would get a better response to You Never Can Tell and his other plays if he stopped drawing attention to his own cleverness. Superficially the play appears trivial, but there is a purpose.

109 "You Never Can Tell at the Strand," ILN, CXVI (12 May 1900), 662.

In You Never Can Tell Shaw is attempting to humanize fashionable sentimental comedy with its hackeneyed topics. This he achieves by "unhackeneyed and lifelike characterization."

1901

---

110 [Beerbohm], Max. "A Cursory Conspectus of G. B. S.," SAT REV, XCII (1901), 556-57; rptd in AROUND THEATRES, pp. 217-21.

Cashel Byron's Profession, an early work, is really mature although superficialities makes it appear otherwise. It is Shavian in its desire to press viewpoints, usually through characters who are thin disguises of Shaw himself. Shaw's humor saves him whenever he threatens to become too serious. But such work will not last because it is really a form of public speaking; Shaw is not a "strict artist."

111 [Beerbohm], Max. "Mr. Shaw Crescent," SAT REV, XCI (1909), 107-08; rptd in AROUND THEATRES, pp. 148-53.
It is still too early to pass judgment on Shaw; Three Plays for Puritans shows him stepping outside the Ibsenesque mode, at which he was not good. Captain Brassbound's Conversion is not "masterly," The Devil's Disciple is praiseworthy, while Caesar and Cleopatra is by far the best of Shaw's work.

112 [Bennett, Arnold]. "George Bernard Shaw: An Equiry," ACADEMY, No. 1501 (9 Feb 1901), 127-28; rptd in SHAW REVIEW, XII (1969), 77-79, 85; rptd in Evans, pp. 92-96.
Shaw is a "born debater" who cuts down his opponents. He lacks emotion, is unsympathetic to works of art, and his judgments are half true. Three Plays for Puritans reveals why he writes prefaces—because he neglects dramatic technique and cannot say what he wants in the plays themselves. His plays lack any hint of creative power.

113 "The Comedy," STAGE, 4 April 1901, p. 12.
Shaw may not always be understandable, but he is always interesting. In The Man of Destiny he is "eminently amusing," using "good-humoured banter."

114 "Comedy Theatre," TIMES, 30 March 1901, p. 14.
The Man of Destiny proves that it is possible to listen to Shaw's string of rhetoric. The best joke here is that this one-act melodrama is suffused with philosophy and rhetoric.

115 Dorman, Marcus R. P. "Vaccination Statistics," TIMES, 10 Oct 1901, p. 5.
Shaw in his letter [TIMES, 8 Oct 1901, p. 5] is really twisting the statistics on smallpox vaccination in order to suit his own purposes.

116 "Drama: Three Plays for Puritans," ATH, No. 3824 (9 Feb 1901), 186-87.
Although Shaw's plays have yet to be staged extensively, Three Plays for Puritans shows that his work possesses dramatic qualities. He is also a humorist, and, if he protested less, it might be possible to believe him a serious dramatist.

117 Huneker, James. [Three Plays for Puritans], MUSICAL COURIER (NY), XLII (15 May 1901), 22 [not seen]; rptd in Evans, p. 97.
Shaw, in Three Plays for Puritans, is not an original thinker but a

17

radical preacher. However, he should not use an art form as a propagandistic medium.

118 "Inquirer." "Vaccination Statistics," TIMES, 10 Oct 1901, p. 5.
Shaw in his letter [TIMES, 8 Oct 1901, p. 5] is correct in his attitude towards what smallpox vaccination statistics tell us.

119 "The Irrepressible Dramatist," DIAL, XXX (1901), 343.
Three Plays for Puritans is, on balance, good, although not Shaw's best work. The Devil's Disciple is interesting only in the final act; Captain Brassbound's Conversion becomes better as it progresses; Caesar and Cleopatra provides a welcome stimulant.

120 "The Man of Destiny," ERA, 30 March 1901, p. 13.
The Man of Destiny is one of Shaw's cleverest plays and demonstrates he can invent situations, characters and dialogue. Shaw's view of history is debatable, and the neatly constructed piece is marred by the typically Shavian verbosity assigned to the characters.

121 "Medical Officer of Health." "Smallpox in London," TIMES, 25 Sept 1901, p. 5.
Shaw has indulged in his usual paradoxes in his attitude towards various approaches to controlling smallpox. [In response to Shaw's letter, TIMES, 21 Sept 1901, p. 12.]

122 Norman, Florence. "George Bernard Shaw," ACADEMY, LX (1901), 192-93.
Parts of You Never Can Tell and The Devil's Disciple have more genuine feeling in them than most dramas currently being produced in London. Candida demonstrates Shaw's technical abilities, where his technique embodies the expression admirably.

123 Patrick, David, and J. Liddell Geddie, and J. C. Smith. CHAMBERS'S CYCLOPAEDIA OF ENGLISH LITERATURE (1901; rvd ed Phila & NY: Lippincott, 1938), pp. 705-06, 722.
[Brief biographical details with cryptic comments on the works.]

124 Perry, Jennette Barbour. " 'G. B. S.' and His Environment," CRITIC (NY), XXXVIII (1901), 453-55.
Shaw's novels are really plays in which the main interest lies in the plot, situation and scene. "The characters are mere pieces in the game."

125 Power, J. Danvers. "Smallpox in London," TIMES, 25 Sept 1901, p. 5.
Shaw's suggestions for the control of smallpox would create a worse state of affairs. [In response to Shaw's letter, TIMES, 21 Sept 1901, p. 12.]

126 R., V. "Novel Notes: An Unsocial Socialist," BOOKMAN (NY), XII (Jan 1901), 519-21.

In An Unsocial Socialist Shaw both expounds his pet theory and demonstrates its weaknesses and impracticality. Really, he has written a burlesque of socialism.

127 Ratcliffe, S. K. "From Our Readers: 'G. B. S.' and the Language of Cockayne," MORNING LEADER, 17 Aug 1901, p. 4.

Shaw has wrong-headed notions about the dialect of uneducated Londoners, as is plainly obvious in what he puts into the mouth of Drinkwater in Captain Brassbound's Conversion. [In response to Shaw's letter, "Spelling Reform v. Phonetic Spelling," MORNING LEADER, 16 Aug 1901, p. 4, which itself was provoked by William Archer's article on this topic on 10 Aug 1901, p. 4. Additional correspondence ensued, see: E. B. Lloyd, 17 Aug 1901, p. 4; W. F. Dunton, 19 Aug 1901, p. 4; A. A. Mitchell, 20 Aug 1901, p. 4; Shaw, 22 Aug 1901, p. 4; S. K. Ratcliffe, W. F. Dunton, R. I. Close, "Londoner," 23 Aug 1901, p. 4; William Archer, W. C. Carter, "Cosmo," 24 Aug 1901, p. 4; F. Rockell, 26 Aug 1901, p. 4; W. Scotcher, jr, E. Jones, Henry Hassall, "J. T.," 27 Aug 1901, p. 4.]

128 "Theatrical and Musical Gossip: Mr. G. Bernard Shaw's Book of Plays," SKETCH, XXXIII (30 Jan 1901), 77.

Shaw himself probably does not know why he entitled this volume Three Plays for Puritans, although he attempts to offer an explanation in his "lengthy, interesting, weird preface." He still isn't taken seriously; nevertheless, this collection is "irritating," "alluringly perverse," "amazingly clever and astoundingly wrong, and, above all, so deliciously amusing."

129 [Three Plays for Puritans], ACADEMY, 2 Feb 1901, pp. 97-98.

Three Plays for Puritans reveals Shaw's methodology. "What Mr. Shaw does is to tesselate his ideas into the form of a play, and then he takes to himself seven devils of theory and writes a preface."

130 "Three Plays for Puritans," NATION (NY), LXXII (1901), 460.

Shaw is amusing but not instructive. Why does a man of obvious abilities allow his fantasy to lead him into "all sorts of intellectual bogs and morasses"?

131 Van Westrum, A. Schade. "Recent Fiction," BOOK BUYER (NY) XXII (Feb 1901), 58.

Love Among the Artists is an "amusing tale without much plot" which concerns itself with the Bohemian's disdain for the Philistine. There are some good descriptions, but there is "no logical ending. After entertaining its readers through nearly 450 pages, it stops." Shaw provides a whimsical introduction.

1902

132 Archer, William. "The Theatre," WORLD, No. 1437 (15 Jan 1902), 25-26.
Mrs. Warren's Profession has a radical defect—its "terrible, insistent didacticism that permeates every scene and conditions every character." It is well-built, but Shaw lacks sufficient tact in presenting his subject.

133 [Beerbohm], Max. "Mr. Shaw's Tragedy," SAT REV, XCIII (1902), 139-40; rptd in AROUND THEATRES, pp. 244-48.
Mrs. Warren's Profession is a "failure with elements of greatness." It is in the Ibsen mode but Shaw fails to keep to his point; such irrelevancy epitomizes Shaw's genius. The play fails because Shaw is a comedian trying to be tragic.

134 "Bernard Shaw Explains," NYT, 22 Jan 1902, p. 2.
Shaw believes the Governor of Jamaica, Sir Alexander Swettenham, did what he thought polite with regard to American offers of assistance.

135 Brandes, Georg. "Bernard Shaws Teater" (Bernard Shaw's Theatre), POLITIKKEN (Copenhagen), 22 Dec 1902 [not seen].
[In Danish.]

136 Brooks, J. Harley. "Vaccination," TIMES, 20 Feb 1902, p. 10.
Recent figures on smallpox vaccination will not be palatable for Shaw since they do not support his contentions. [See also Shaw's reply, TIMES, 22 Feb 1902, p. 4, and Brooks' rejoinder, 27 Feb 1902, p. 12.]

137 "Capt. Brassbound's Conversion," ERA, 17 May 1902, p. 10.
Shaw's whimsicality in Captain Brassbound's Conversion is much more important than the story itself. Lady Cicely is a "superlative achievement"; Brassbound is a melodramatic figure on whom most of Shaw's satirical humor is exercised; Drinkwater embodies much of Shaw's humor.

138 "Captain Brassbound's Conversion at the Queen's," MANCHESTER GUARDIAN, 13 May 1902, p. 12.
Because of his elaborate stage directions and his prefaces, Shaw is more appropriate to the study than the stage. The events of Captain Brassbound's Conversion suffer from Shaw's irony and the play is dominated by his personality. It is generically mixed, being comedy, melodrama, farce and masquerade.

139 Clapp, John Bouvé, and Edwin Francis Edgett. PLAYS OF THE PRESENT (NY: Dunlap Society, 1902; rptd NY: Blom, 1969), pp. 12-14, 36, 85-88, 193-94, 232-33.

[Production histories and details of <u>Arms and the Man</u> and <u>The Devil's Disciple</u>.]

140 "The Drama," WEST REV, CLVII (March 1902), 344-47.
<u>Mrs. Warren's Profession</u> is a "study in actuality," but Shaw dramatizes "in communities rather than in individuals" which is reflected in his lack of character development. It is an interesting but imperfect play.

141 "Drama: The Week," ATH, No. 3872 (11 Jan 1902), 60.
<u>Mrs. Warren's Profession</u> is a clever and aggressive play, although there are ethical questions surrounding its production. Shaw is an adept dramatist, and some scenes are both dramatic and thrilling.

142 Grein, J. T. DRAMATIC CRITICISM: VOL. III: 1900-1901 (Lond: Greening, 1902), pp. 293-96; rptd in DRAMATIC CRITICISM: VOL. IV: 1902-1903 (Lond: Eveleigh Nash, 1904), pp. 7-11; rptd in George Rowell, VICTORIAN DRAMATIC CRITICISM (Lond: Methuen, 1971), pp. 311-13.
<u>Mrs. Warren's Profession</u> is not sufficiently realistic to be educative, and as a play it is unsatisfactory "because the characters have no inner life, but merely echo certain views of the author." The piece belongs in the study not on the stage. In any case, Shaw's treatment of the topic is not worthwhile; he has dealt with a dangerous subject half earnestly, half jestingly.

143 "Microbe." "Mr. Bernard Shaw and Vaccination," TIMES, 4 April 1902, p. 9.
Shaw really should have stopped to think before he discoursed on vaccination and smallpox.

144 "Mr. Bernard Shaw on Plays," MANCHESTER GUARDIAN, 13 May 1902, p. 12.
A conversation with Shaw on his plays is a dazzling, almost bewildering experience. [With lengthy extracts of the conversation.]

145 "Monocle" [E. F. Spence]. "The Book and Its Author: <u>Mrs. Warren's Profession</u>," SKETCH, XXXVIII (11 June 1902), 303.
The preface is the cleverest part of Shaw's book, although he is wrong in claiming that the production of <u>Mrs. Warren's Profession</u> created a sensation in London. Shaw is, unconsciously, a humbug who uses the charlatan's methods of self-advertisement. He also suggests, wrongly, that his is a lone voice crying out against stage censorship.

146 "<u>Mrs. Warren's Profession</u>," ERA, 11 Jan 1902, p. 15.
In <u>Mrs. Warren's Profession</u> Shaw uses a Pre-Raphaelite technique of sublimating and extracting everything from his material which could be undramatic or insignificant. His method is frequently photographic. Much in the play is not amusing or expedient, and Shaw is too much the doctrinal socialist.

147 "Music and Drama: A New and Original Play at the Queen's," MANCHESTER CITY NEWS, 17 May 1902, p. 3.
Captain Brassbound's Conversion is typically Shavian in its unconventionality, sparking dialogue, and ironic wit. It is well constructed, and fortunately does not depend on the "eternal sex problem."

148 "The Playhouses," ILN, CXX (11 Jan 1902), 39.
Mrs. Warren's Profession provides "intellectual stimulus rather than aesthetic satisfaction." Shaw's subject matter cannot be quarrelled with, and he has a serious purpose.

149 "Provincial Productions: Captain Brassbound's Conversion," STAGE, 15 May 1902, p. 10.
Captain Brassbound's Conversion lacks "true dramatic force and intensity." Shaw's perverse humor and cynicism abound in this "quaint mixture of melodrama and comedy, with a tinge of tragedy."

150 Seaman, Owen. BORROWED PLUMES (NY: Holt, 1902), pp. 179-88.
[A parody of Shaw's style and ideas.]

151 "Shaw—Cashel Byron's Profession," CRITIC (NY), XL (1902), 179-80.
People who relish Shaw's humor will welcome this reprint of Cashel Byron's Profession; however, there are few people who take Shaw seriously.

152 "A Short Exposure of George Bernard Shaw," SKETCH, XXXVII (12 March 1902), 302-03.
Shaw is a many-sided person, and has achieved distinction in various fields through sheer hard work. Until recently his achievements have been limited to a few people, and his theatrical successes have been in America.

1903

---

153 Archer, William. "Mr. Shaw's Pom-Pom," DAILY CHRONICLE, 24 Aug 1903, p. 7; rptd in CRITIC (New Rochelle), XLIII (Oct 1903), 310-12.
Every page of Man and Superman bristles with wit, although it is not overflowing with thought. It is a symbolic extravaganza which reworks elements of Shaw's earlier, more promising drama.

154 Archer, William. "Study and Stage Mr. Shaw and Mr. Pinero," MORNING LEADER, 22 Aug 1903, p. 4.
While Shaw was a drama critic, he possessed an inveterate hatred of the new dramatic movement led by Pinero, and had he been more influential he might have destroyed that movement. Shaw was really

objecting to Pinero not writing the sort of play Shaw would have written. [See Shaw's rebuttal, 28 Aug 1903, p. 4.]

155 Austin, L. E. "The Employment of Children on the Stage," TIMES, 26 May 1903, p. 13.
Shaw's views of child actors [TIMES, 25 May 1903, p. 4] are the result of his freakish fantasy; they will not persuade anyone else.

156 Beerbohm, Max. "LITTLE MARY," SAT REV, XCVI (1903), 423-24; rptd in MORE THEATRES, pp. 595-99.
"There are two ways of expressing a peculiar self through an art-form. One way is Mr. Barrie's. [Shaw's] way is to have no innate sense for the art-form which you select and to disdain any effort at mastery of it."

157 Beerbohm, Max. "Mr. Shaw's New Dialogues," SAT REV, XCVI (1903), 329-30; rptd in AROUND THEATRES, pp. 343-48; rptd in Evans, pp. 102-105.
Man and Superman, in book form, is Shaw's masterpiece so far; the thought is clear, the dialectic razor sharp, and the humor abundant.

158 Beerbohm, Max. "A Triple Bill," SAT REV, XCV (1903), 744-45; rptd in MORE THEATRES, pp. 580-84.
The Admirable Bashville should be a full-length play, even though Shaw's work is formless and unpolished.

159 "Bernard Shaw's Candida," NYT, 9 Dec 1903, p. 6; rptd in NYTTR 1896-1903, [n. p.].
Candida, a delightful play, can mystify with its "convention-breaking force of character drawing . . . spiritual depth . . . intellectual intentions . . ." and wit.

160 [Bettany, F. G.]. "Drama," ATH, No. 3961 (26 Sept 1903), 422-23; rptd in Evans, pp. 106-07.
"In Man and Superman [Shaw] carries his theories to extremes, and incurs something more than a risk of begetting weariness in those he has been accustomed to exhilarate."

161 Broutá, Julio. "El Teatro de Bernard Shaw" (Bernard Shaw's Theatre), REVISTA CRÍTICA, No. III (April 1903), 12-43 [not seen].
[Cited in Rodríguez (MD), p. 335. In Spanish.]

162 Chesterton, G. K. "Man v. the Superman," DN, 22 Aug 1903, p. 8; rptd in Evans, pp. 98-101.
Man and Superman is a good play but it betrays Shaw's weakness of not seeing things as they really are. Shaw "has to understand . . . there is such a thing as being fond of humanity."

163 Corbin, John. "Candida," NYT, 13 Dec 1903, part III, p. 25; rptd in NYTTR 1896-1903, [n. p.].
Candida is a superior play both technically and spiritually. Shaw is

more stimulating than either H. A. Jones or Pinero because he looks to the future while they are based on the past.

164 "Drama: The Week," ATH, No. 3946 (13 June 1903), 763.
The Admirable Bashville is a piece of topsy-turvydom which amusingly portrays Shaw's well-known and characteristic views. It ranks below Shaw's best work.

165 Dukat, Vladoje. "George Bernard Shaw," VIENAC (Zagreb), 1903, p. 325 [not seen].
[Cited in Rudolf Filipović, ENGLESKO-HRVATSKE KNJIŽEVNE VEZE (English-Croatian Literary Connections) (Zagreb: Liber 1972), p. 292. In Croatian.]

166 "Just Two Hours of Bernard Shaw," NYH, 9 Dec 1903, p. 9.
Candida is a conscientious play "mainly in the form of dialogue on abstruse sociological subjects." There is too much talk and the play's morality is twisted.

167 [Kraus, Karl?]. "Literatur" (Literature), DIE FACKEL, IV: 129 (11 Feb 1903), 12-23.
[Discusses attacks on translations of Shaw by Siegfried Trebitsch. In German.]

168 Maude, Cyril. THE HAYMARKET THEATRE: SOME RECORDS & REMINISCENCES, ed by Ralph Maude (Lond: Grant Richards, 1903), pp. 210-17; rptd as "G. B. S. on Bernard Shaw in a Moment of Anonymity," NYT, 1 March 1914, part VII, p. 7.
The whole experience of rehearsing and producing You Never Can Tell was disastrous and best forgotten. Shaw did his best to unnerve everyone.

169 "Mr. Bernard Shaw and the Borough Councils," TIMES, 30 May 1903, p. 10.
Shaw has discoursed humorously and eloquently on various aspects of local government.

170 "Mr. Bernard Shaw's New Play," TLS, No. 84 (21 Aug 1903), 247.
The published version of Man and Superman will reinforce the common man's opinion that Shaw is a brilliant author, even if all Shaw's sallies go over his head and he cannot believe that what is presented in the play is a realistic portrayal of life as he knows it. Shaw's wit also confuses because serious plays are not expected to be amusing as well.

171 "Musings without Method: Man and Superman," BLACKWOOD'S MAGAZINE, CLXXIV (Oct 1903), 532-35.
Shaw is always the revolutionary who wishes to save the world by means of whatever recent fad he has encountered. In Man and

<u>Superman</u> he is now to be found tub-thumping Nietzsche and his philosophy.

172 Pierson, Edgar. "Bühnentelegraph: Dresden" (Telegraph of the Stages: Dresden), BÜHNE UND WELT, VI: 1 (1903-04), 258-59.
<u>Candida</u> resembles a novelette in the form of dialogues rather than being a play. It is original, but not suitable for a large audience. [In German.]

173 Ryan, W. P. "Literary London: The One and Only G. B. S.," MUNSEY'S MAGAZINE, XXIX (1903), 612-13.
Shaw is a serious social reformer as well as a wit.

174 "Shaw's <u>Candida</u> Played," SUN (NY), 9 Dec 1903, p. 5.
<u>Candida</u> is potentially a great play, "but contains no smart speeches or so-called dramatic situations." Some call Shaw paradoxical, but he is very earnest.

175 S[pence], E. F. "The Stage from the Stalls," SKETCH, XLII (17 June 1903), 306.
The <u>Admirable Bashville</u> is a clever but uneven <u>jeu d'esprit</u>. It is mechanical and flat in places, but shows Shaw could write a great satirical play.

176 S[pence], E. F. "The Stage from the Stalls: <u>Man and Superman</u>," SKETCH, XLIII (2 Sept 1903), 232.
Without the preface and the Don Juan sequence, <u>Man and Superman</u> is a very clever farce. However, the whole book is a deeply philosophical problem play with a vivid and effective denunciation of society.

177 "The Stage Society," ERA, 13 June 1903, p. 11.
The topsy-turveydom of <u>The Admirable Bashville</u> is worthy of W. S. Gilbert at his best.

178 "The Stage Society," STAGE, 11 June 1903, p. 14.
The <u>Admirable Bashville</u> is a "delightfull piece of extravagant nonsense, brimful of wit and satire in Mr. Shaw's best vein."

179 Stümcke, Heinrich. "Von den Berliner Theatern 1903/04" (About the Berlin Theatres 1903/04), BÜHNE UND WELT, VI: 1 (1903-04), 471-74; 520-23.
The <u>Man of Destiny</u> reads like a parody of Carlyle's ON HEROES, HERO-WORSHIP, AND THE HEROIC IN HISTORY. The plot of <u>Candida</u> is ridiculous, and the play seems to be a travesty of Ibsen's BRAND and THE LADY FROM THE SEA. [In German.]

180 Symons, Arthur. PLAYS, ACTING AND MUSIC (Lond: Duckworth; NY: Dutton, 1903), pp. 150-52.
<u>Mrs. Warren's Profession</u> is "brilliantly clever . . . [and] made up of merciless logic and unanswerable commonsense." However, the play

does not represent life but rather discusses it.

181 Walkley, A. B.   [Shaw], LE TEMPS, 18 July 1903, pp. 2-3.
Shaw's comedies are not "theatre." [In French.]

1904

---

182 Adams, W. Davenport, A DICTIONARY OF THE DRAMA: A GUIDE TO THE PLAYS, PLAYWRIGHTS, PLAYERS, AND PLAYHOUSES OF THE UNITED KINGDOM AND AMERICA, FROM THE EARLIEST TIMES TO THE PRESENT: VOL. I: A-G (Lond: Chatto & Windus, 1904) [no more published].
[Useful entries on Candida, The Devil's Disciple, Caesar and Cleopatra.]

183 Archer, William.   "The Theatre: Candida," WORLD, No. 1557 (3 May 1904), 752.
Candida may be wrong, absurd and fantastic, but it is brilliant. It is the product "of an admirable, but somewhat too self-willed and self-conscious, talent." It is Shaw's most human play in which he succeeds in hiding himself behind his puppets.

184 Archer, William.   [The Theatre: John Bull's Other Island], WORLD, No. 1584 (8 Nov 1904), 771; rptd in Evans, pp. 127-29.
John Bull's Other Island is not as dramatic as Candida or The Devil's Disciple because both the story and plot are buried in discussion and generalizations.

185 "At the Play," OBS, 1 May 1904, p. 7.
Candida is undeniably original in its humor, but its social satire is too subtle to be appreciated by the average playgoer.

186 "At the Play," OBS, 6 Nov 1904, p. 6.
John Bull's Other Island reveals Shaw as a professional jester, but it is too long, does not have a worthwhile story, and is full of characters who are variations of Shaw himself.

187 B[aughan], E. A. "Royal Court Theatre: John Bull's Other Island," DN, 2 Nov 1904, p. 8; rptd in Evans, pp. 126-27.
John Bull's Other Island is a "formless piece of excellent fooling" and "the tragedy of Mr. Shaw's creative life is that his constitutional wit stands in his way."

188 Beerbohm, Max.   [Bernard Shaw], STAGE SOCIETY NEWS, 11 May 1904 [not seen]; rptd in LAST THEATRES, pp. 9-10.

Shaw is no longer a critic but a creative artist, and just as a schoolboy cannot abide his master, so Shaw cannot stand critics. He does
not mind criticism, but abhors praise.

189 Beerbohm, Max. "Mr. Shaw at His Best," SAT REV, XCVIII
(1904), 608-09; rptd in AROUND THEATRES, pp. 453-58; rptd
in Evans, pp. 130-33.

John Bull's Other Island does not conform to the critics' prescribed
formula, because it contains a great deal of talk and not much else.
Nevertheless it is a play, and in Broadbent we have a "masterpiece of
observation and of satire."

190 "Bernard Shaw," NYT, 18 June 1904, Saturday supp, p. 414.
The publication of Man and Superman yields another amusing and
unique Shavian work. The dialogue is delightful, brilliant and racy.

191 "Bernard Shaw on Incomes," NYT, 23 Dec 1904, p. 8.
Shaw's lecture in London on "Socialism for the Upper Classes" provoked considerable amusement in the audience whose response disgusted Shaw.

192 "Bernard Shaw Turned Briton," NYT, 28 Sept 1904, p. 9;
rptd in NYTTR 1904-1911, [n. p.].

How He Lied to Her Husband is characteristically Shavian, but incor-
porates the sort of humor found in H. J. Byron or Maddison Morton.

193 "Bernard Shaw's Plays," ERA, 14 May 1904, p. 19.
Shaw is a rather abrasive man, "a master of the art of verbal attack,"
whose conceit tends to be amusing. His failing is that he preaches
through his characters and dehumanizes them. An exception to this
is Lady Cicely Waynefleete.

194 "Candida," ERA, 30 April 1904, p. 15.
Shaw's plays often read better than they act, perhaps because Shaw
is, as an artist, too personal and too self-conscious. This is true of
Candida.

195 "Candida Well Played," NYH, 5 Jan 1904, p. 12.
For a change, both players and audience understood Candida with its
unique Shavian philosophy.

196 Cary, Elisabeth Luther. "Apostles of the New Drama,"
LAMP (NY), XXVII (Jan 1904), 593-98.
Although they are unlike in mind and temperament, Shaw and W. B.
Yeats share a disapproval concerning the modern stage. Each agrees
that the theatre is on a low plane, pandering mostly to the "theatre
of commerce." Shaw is "chiefly concerned with lifting the veil from
popular morality," as is seen in Candida which is a realistic and
meaningful play. It also possesses "poetic divination, the gift of
reading messages from the invisible world."

197 Colby, F[rank] M[oore]. "A Clever Man," BOOKMAN

(NY), XIX (Aug 1904), 609-10.
Shaw is clever and always attempts to set himself apart from common people. In Man and Superman he attacks conventions simply because they are conventions. If people began adhering to Shaw and his ideas, he would simply strike out in a new direction.

198 Colby, Frank Moore. IMAGINARY OBLIGATIONS (NY: Dodd, Mead, 1904; rptd 1913), pp. 142-44.
Shaw wants people to listen to his message although he does not always understand human nature. He is more entertaining than other contemporary dramatists, and only pales when compared with the absolute greats.

199 Colby, F[rank] M[oore]. "Mr. Shaw and The Man of Destiny," BOOKMAN (NY), XIX (April 1904), 160.
Shaw places too much emphasis on his brilliant wit, but he has forgotten that the world expects serious men to be dull at times. However, with Napoleon in The Man of Destiny, he has taken more care with his character and shows some degree of sympathy for him.

200 Corbin, John. "THE COLLEGE WIDOW, How He Lied to Her Husband, THE TEMPEST," NYT, 9 Oct 1904, part III, p. 4; rptd in NYTTR 1904-1911, [n. p.].
Shaw's "satirical clods and cabbages" in How He Lied to Her Husband are "directed by an entire misconception of the nature of his vogue" in New York. His satirical armor is easily pierced by intelligence.

201 Corbin, John. "Shaw without the 'P.,'" NYT, 14 Feb 1904, part III, p. 24; rptd in NYTTR 1904-1911, [n. p.].
The production of Candida and The Man of Destiny appear to mark the beginning of a Shaw boom in America. Both plays are better received in America because the audiences are distanced from Shaw's audacious, paradoxical attacks on sacred British prejudices.

202 "The Court," STAGE, 3 Nov 1904, pp. 14-15.
John Bull's Other Island is a "collection of mutually antagonistic and destructive political diatribes [rather] than a play proper." It lacks good construction and is undramatic, though Shaw's wit dazzles.

203 "Court Theatre," DT, 27 April 1904, p. 11.
Shaw burlesques domestic drama so much in Candida that he is in danger of destroying the theatre by antagonizing his audience. Is he a serious dramatist or merely a jester?

204 "Court Theatre," TIMES, 27 April 1904, p. 12.
It is surprising the general public has had to wait so long for a performance of the delightful Candida.

205 [Court Theatre: Candida], STAGE, 1 Dec 1904, p. 17.
It is always difficult to know how seriously Shaw should be taken, but Candida reveals his determination to tackle the perennial question of

what is love.

206 "Daly in a New Shaw Drama," SUN (NY), 10 Feb 1904, p. 9.
The Man of Destiny contains some superfluous but brilliant dialogue.
Shaw is particularly vulnerable to a dull company or audience.

207 "The Drama: Candida," TLS, No. 120 (29 April 1904), 133.
Shaw is a "stimulating fantasist" who travesties life by removing
everything except pure intelligence. In Candida he renders the
traditional eternal triangle into something new, exciting and strange.

208 "Drama: The Week," ATH, No. 3992 (30 April 1904), 570.
Candida has real merits, even if it is somewhat trifling. It amuses,
stirs feelings, and is a mixture of impertinence and moral lesson.

209 "Drama: The Week," ATH, No. 4019 (5 Nov 1904), 631-32.
John Bull's Other Island is long, amorphous, illogical, inconsistent,
and unsympathetic. However, it is also brilliant, intellectually
stimulating, and "wholly nondescript."

210 "Dramatic Notes," ACADEMY, LXVI (7 May 1904), 528.
Candida is a fine play without a "trace of impishness." The characters are well developed, the plot is "simple and natural."

211 Dunbar, O. H. "The Acute Mr. Shaw and His Shawness,"
CRITIC (New Rochelle), XLV (Aug 1904), 186-87.
Man and Superman is an undramatic work written for a "pit of phil-
osophers." Shaw's individuality and ideas will attract his followers.

212 Ellis, Havelock. "The Prophet Shaw," WEEKLY CRITICAL
REVIEW, 15 Jan 1904 [not seen]; rptd in VIEWS AND
REVIEWS: A SELECTION OF UNCOLLECTED ARTICLES 1884-
1932: FIRST AND SECOND SERIES (1932; rptd Freeport, NY:
Books for Libraries, 1970); rptd as "Bernard Shaw," in FROM
MARLOWE TO SHAW: THE STUDIES, 1876-1936, IN ENGLISH
LITERATURE, ed by John Gawsworth (Lond: Williams &
Norgate, 1950), pp. 291-96.
Shaw is a prophet who combines the artist, scientist, and moralist.
He has the prophet's problem of longing to be "dragged to the stake"
while the public, hearing only the pleasant artistic voice, merely
smiles and applauds. To be a prophet one must be a scientist to see
things as they are, but to buffet things as they are contradicts
scientific objectivity.

213 Farrer, Reginald. "Salted Pap," SPEAKER, XI (19 Nov
1904), 184; rptd in part in Evans, pp. 134-35.
What does Shaw mean to say in John Bull's Other Island, since we
cannot sympathize with either Broadbent or Larry? Shaw lacks sincerity and is completely destructive in his attacks on characters and
institutions.

214 Fitzgerald, C. C. Penrose. "Flogging in the Navy," TIMES,

9 Sept 1904, p. 6.

Shaw's anti-flogging views clearly render him wiser than Solomon, although many will disagree with him. [See Shaw's letters, 2 Sept 1904, p. 5, 15 Sept 1904, p. 8, and 11 Oct 1904, p. 9. Responding correspondence came from "A Believer in Discipline," 20 Sept 1904, p. 9; C. C. Penrose Fitzgerald, 24 Sept 1904, p. 8; Harold R. Wintle, 29 Sept 1904, p. 8.]

215 Goodman, Eckert. "The Drama: Mr. George Bernard Shaw, Dramatist," CUR LIT, XXXVII (Aug 1904), 165-67.

It is difficult to know if Shaw is in earnest, but he must be taken seriously or not at all. There are similarities between Shaw and Ibsen; both men strike repeatedly at hypocrisy, especially self-hypocrisy. However, Ibsen uses metaphysical approaches, whereas Shaw is a psychologist attacking idealism, that is, romanticism.

216 Grein, J. T. "Premieres of the Week," STIMES, 1 May 1904, p. 6.

Shaw has an amazing ability to do the unacceptable, and frequently defies all normal logic. Yet Candida persuades us he is right and knows the nature of men.

217 Grein, J. T. "Premieres of the Week," STIMES, 6 Nov 1904, p. 4.

Shaw is the most brilliant, daring and subtly humorous dramatist. In John Bull's Other Island he directs his satire at numerous subjects, but it is clear, too, that his characters are only types.

218 Henderson, Archibald. "Arnold Daly and Bernard Shaw: A Bit of Dramatic History," ARENA (Bost), XXXII (Nov 1904), 489-96.

After much difficulty, Arnold Daly managed to stage Candida successfully. Shaw himself is versatile, clever, and brilliant; he is full of modern ideas, and catches the audience's attention by attacking "its sense of order and propriety."

219 Henderson, Archibald. "The Duel of Sex," DIAL, XXXVII (16 July 1904), 33-34.

Man and Superman reinforces Shaw's views that audiences want plays which will make them think. It is a play of ideas and affirms that the Life Force is found supremely in woman. Thus romanticism is abolished in favor of realism in sexual matters.

220 Henderson, Archibald. "George Bernard Shaw: A Brilliant Literary Sinner," DAILY OBSERVER (Charlotte, NC), 28 Aug 1904, p. 12 [not seen].

[Cited in Hood, p. 223.]

221 Henderson, Archibald. "The Present Vogue of Mr. Shaw," READER MAGAZINE (Indianapolis), IV (June 1904), 49-53, 89; rptd in BOSTON TRANSCRIPT, 20 May 1904, p. 11.

Shaw enjoys greater popularity in America than in England. He is bent on serious reform, and realizes that theatrical reform must come from within by writing realistic plays containing ideas instead of romanticism. His plays "teem with ideas, scintillate with cleverness, live in the invigorating air of modernity," and are always in quest of genuine realism.

222 Henderson, Archibald. "Two Irish Dramatists: William B. Yeats and George B. Shaw," DAILY OBSERVER (Charlotte, NC), 17 April 1904, p. 15 [not seen].
[Cited in Hood, p. 223.]

223 Henderson, Archibald. "Voices of a New Century," DAILY OBSERVER (Charlotte, NC), 16 Oct 1904, p. 12 [not seen].
[Cited in Hood, p. 223.]

224 Hoffsten, Ernest Godfrey. "The Plays of Bernard Shaw," SEWANEE REVIEW, XII (1904), 217-22.
At the moment Shaw is a "comparative nonentity." However, he has a "keen intellect," and is a good satirist, although his satire overpowers his plays. He "dominates his characters," but has good wit and humor. His plays are effectively constructed.

225 Huneker, James. "The Truth about Candida," METROPOLITAN MAGAZINE (NY), XX (Aug 1904), 632-36.
Candida is really a womanly woman whom Shaw presents as outmoded and worthy of our contempt and ridicule. Marchbanks realizes life is nobler than the picture Candida paints and so he leaves.

226 "John Bull's Other Island," ERA, 5 Nov 1904, p. 15.
Shaw is both incorrigible and impossible. He has perception, humor and imagination, but persists in writing plays like John Bull's Other Island.

227 Jones, Henry Arthur. THE FOUNDATIONS OF A NATIONAL DRAMA (1904; rvd 1913; rptd Freeport, NY: Books for Libraries, 1967), pp. 288-89, 297-98, 315.
[Passing references to Shaw and censorship.]

228 Kobbé, Gustav. "A Personal Sketch of George Bernard Shaw," HARPER'S WEEKLY (NY), XLVIII (27 Aug 1904), 1317.
[Biographical details as a result of a personal visit to Shaw.]

229 Lee, Elisabeth. "Echo des Auslands. Englischer Brief" (Echo from Abroad. English Letter), DAS LITERARISCHE ECHO, VII: 6 (15 Dec 1904), columns 429-31.
In John Bull's Other Island Shaw favors a melting of the English and Irish races. The play cannot compete with Candida in quality. [In German.]

230 Lewis, Austin. "The Point of View of Bernard Shaw," OVERLAND MONTHLY (San Francisco), ns XLIII (Jan 1904),

43-46.

Man and Superman serves to reinforce Shaw's career as "one of the greatest of literary curiosities." In addition to his position as a socialist, he has also taken on the impossible task of trying to educate the British public "in the whimsicalities of Nietzsche"—all with great humor. He is not, however, a mere jester.

231 "London Theatres: The Court," STAGE, 28 April 1904, p. 14.
Shaw's intentions in Candida are somewhat obscure; Morell could be a fine man or a windbag. There are some passages of "charming delicacy" and "genuine feeling."

232 "Man and Superman," INDEPENDENT (NY), LVII (11 Aug 1904), 335-36.
Man and Superman, with its preface and appendix, is "delightfully witty and paradoxical," and Shaw's fantastic genius has probably never had better testimony.

233 "Man and Superman," NATION (NY), LXXIX (1904), 486.
Man and Superman is written with the avowed intention of converting everyone to the dogma of eugenics. It is interesting sociologically, but is undramatic.

234 "The Man of Destiny," NYT, 10 Feb 1904, p. 9; rptd in NYTTR 1904-1911, [n. p.].
The Man of Destiny is brilliant in its "sublimated theatricism," although it is "less profound emotionally than Candida."

235 Meyerfeld, Max. "Bernard Shaw und sein Dolmetsch" (Bernard Shaw and His Interpreter), ENGLISCHE STUDIEN, XXXIII (1904), 143-56.
[A book review of Plays, Pleasant and Unpleasant, Three Plays for Puritans, Cashel Byron's Profession, and Siegfried Trebitsch's translations of Candida, Arms and the Man, The Devil's Disciple which were published together as Drei Dramen von Bernard Shaw (Three Dramas by Bernard Shaw). In German.]

236 "Mr. Bernard Shaw on Municipal Trading," TIMES, 19 Jan 1904, p. 5.
Shaw has led a debate on municipal trading with an audience of largely working-class men.

237 "The Playhouses," ILN, CXXV (5 Nov 1904), 643.
John Bull's Other Island is not a play but a series of loosely connected scenes. Shaw is impartial to both England and Ireland; the play is cynical, amusing, and profound.

238 "The Playhouses: Candida Revived at the Court," ILN, CXXV (3 Dec 1904), 840.
Nearly all Shaw's plays can be viewed as travesties, and Candida is a

burlesque of the problem-play. Shaw has never troubled to invent new dramatic forms for his ideas.

239 "The Quintessence of Ibsenism," NATION (NY), LXXIX (1904), 282.
Shaw sets out to explain Ibsen's moral doctrine, and his essay should at least arouse his readers' curiosity.

240 S., C. K. "George Bernard Shaw—A Conversation: Concerning Mr. Shaw's New Play, John Bull's Other Island," TATLER, No. 177 (Nov 1904), 242-43.
[Title describes.]

241 "Shaw, George Bernard," THE AMERICANA (NY: Scientific American, 1904-06), XIII.
[Encyclopedia entry covering the works and life to date.]

242 S[pence], E. F. "The Stage from the Stalls," SKETCH, XLVI (4 May 1904), 88.
Candida is serious, moving and dramatic. As a "sex drama" it is weak, but as a study of conflicting temperaments it is thrilling and powerful.

243 S[pence], E. F. "The Stage from the Stalls," SKETCH, XLVIII (9 Nov 1904), 122.
John Bull's Other Island is entertaining, formless, plotless, and largely irrelevant.

244 Szini, Gyula. "Shaw elveiröl" (On Shaw's Principles), PETSI NAPLO (Budapest), 8 Dec 1904 [not seen.]
[In Hungarian.]

245 "This Liar Made a Decided Hit," NYH, 27 Sept 1904, p. 7.
How He Lied to Her Husband is an instant success in New York, and one of the "most brilliant dramatic trifles" in a long time.

246 Varona, Enrique José. "Una Transfiguración de Rosina y Querubín" (A Transfiguration of Rosina and Cherubin) [originally published 1904; not seen]; rptd in DESDE MI BELVEDERE (From My Viewpoint) (Havana: Papeleria de Rambla y Bouza, 1907), pp. 253-58 (rptd Havana: Edicion Oficial Cultural, 1938), pp. 190-93.
The characters of Beaumarchais' LE MARRIAGE DE FIGARO, Cherubin and Rosine, become Marchbanks and Candida in Shaw's play. Moreover, some of Shaw's situations and expressions closely resemble scenes and dialogue in Beaumarchais, a fact which points to a possible influence on Shaw. [In Spanish.]

247 [Walkley, A. B.]. "Court Theatre: John Bull's Other Island," TIMES, 2 Nov 1904, p. 6; rptd in DRAMA AND LIFE (1908; rptd Freeport, NY: Books for Libraries, 1967), pp. 219-23; rptd in Evans, pp. 125-26.

John Bull's Other Island is good in its satiric attacks and dialectic, but is poorly constructed with characters wandering aimlessly on and off stage.

1905

---

248 "The Actors' Orphanage Fund," TIMES, 15 July 1905, p. 8.
[A descriptive account of Passion, Poison, and Petrifaction.]

249 Archer, William. "Study and Stage: America and Mrs. Warren," MORNING LEADER, 4 Nov 1905, p. 4.
The banning in New York of Mrs. Warren's Profession puts Shaw in his element—at the center of controversy. This prohibition proves America is as Anglo-Saxon in its moral attitudes as is Britain.

250 Archer, William. "The Theatre," WORLD, No. 1598 (14 Feb 1905), 273.
John Bull's Other Island is good for people who can think and laugh at the same time. Shaw's dialogue is brilliant.

251 Archer, William. "The Theatre," WORLD, No. 1601 (7 March 1905), 385.
How He Lied to Her Husband is "pure delight from first to last" and possesses unequalled wit and invention for a play of this length.

252 Archer, William. "The Theatre," WORLD, No. 1613 (30 May 1905), 914-15; rptd in Evans, pp. 116-19.
Shaw is a tripartite composite of dramatist, philosopher, and wit—but the dramatist is the weakest element, as Man and Superman proves yet again.

253 Archer, William. "The Theatre," WORLD, No. 1640 (5 Dec 1905), 971-72; rptd in Evans, pp. 151-53.
We are used to Shaw dispensing with plot, but in Major Barbara he also dispenses with characterization: "there are only animated points of view." The incidents are incredible.

254 "At the Play: Mr. Shaw's Major Barbara," OBS, 3 Dec 1905, p. 5.
Major Barbara "is an odd blend of intellectual farce distinctly brilliant in its irresponsible humour and of low-life drama very painful in its realistic brutality."

255 B[aughan], E. A. "Royal Court Theatre: Bernard Shaw's View of Women," DN, 24 May 1905, p. 4; rptd in Evans, pp. 108-09.
Despite his virtues, Shaw has a narrow mind, as Man and Superman demonstrates. He has a particular view of women which is exacerbated by humor.

256 Beerbohm, Max. "Dramatic Translation," SAT REV, XCIX (1905), 76-77; rptd in LAST THEATRES, pp. 121-124.
[An answer to Shaw's challenge in SAT REV, XCIX (1905), 48 to provide a guide to translating foreign plays.]

257 Beerbohm, Max. "Mr. Shaw's Position," SAT REV, C (1905), 745-46; rptd in AROUND THEATRES, pp. 528-34; rptd in Evans, pp. 155-59.
The imputations of blasphemy in Major Barbara are as utterly wrong as Shaw's use of Barbara's execration is completely and dramatically right. Every other critical objection to Shaw, such as an inability to characterize, is also answered in this play.

258 Beerbohm, Max. "THE NEW FELICITY," SAT REV, C (1905), 14; rptd in LAST THEATRES, pp. 167-71.
Shaw has already spawned his imitators (such as Alma Tadema's THE NEW FELICITY), but they have none of his powers.

259 Beerbohm, Max. "THE RETURN OF THE PRODIGAL," SAT REV, C (1905), 463-64; rptd in AROUND THEATRES, pp. 506-10.
St. John Hankin's THE RETURN OF THE PRODIGAL clearly shows the influence of Shaw, but there is only a technical and superficial similarity. Had Shaw written the play he would have harangued us with "delicious comedy."

260 Beerbohm, Max. "THE VOYSEY INHERITANCE," SAT REV, C (1905), 620-21; rptd in AROUND THEATRES, pp. 518-23.
Harley Granville-Barker's THE VOYSEY INHERITANCE demonstrates how strong Shaw's influence is with certain dramatists. Granville-Barker's young female characters are exactly like Shaw's.

261 Beers, Henry A. "The English Drama of To-Day," NORTH AMERICAN REVIEW, CLXXX (May 1905), 746-57.
Shaw is the Sheridan of the modern stage. Arms and the Man is effective. Shaw has described his heroine in Candida as a most unprincipled woman, but his stage directions tell us otherwise. All his stage directions are explicit and profuse, containing full character analyses. The plays are really novels overflowing on to the stage. Shaw detests both sentiment and romance and champions realism; the latter reveals Ibsen's influence. Emancipated women populate Shaw's plays, although he satirizes them in The Philanderer. Shaw shares Ibsen's "impatience of heroics, cant, social lies, respectable prejudices, the conventions of a traditional morality." His favorite characters are audacious and irreverent young men and women who delight in shocking their elders.

262 "Bernard and Demi Shaw," SUN (NY), 6 Sept 1905, p. 7.
With Man and Superman Shaw is finally enjoying the fruits of his labors, and is helping to elevate the position of the theatre.

263 "Bernard Shaw Bumps Poetry," SUN (NY), 27 Oct 1905, p. 4.

[A facetitious account of Edwin Earle Purinton, "poet of womanhood," and his lecture attacking Shaw.]

264 "A Bernard Shaw Comedy," ERA, 11 Feb 1905, p. 16.

John Bull's Other Island is full of clever cynicism and shrewd criticism, although Shaw does not expect us to take him seriously all the time.

265 "Bernard Shaw, the Socialist Politician," CUR LIT, XXXIX (Oct 1905), 451-53.

[A largely biographical account of Shaw's Fabian and socialist activities.]

266 Bernstein, Eduard. "Ueber Bernard Shaw" (About Bernard Shaw), SOZIALISTISCHE MONATSHEFTE (Marz), 1905 [not seen].

[In German.]

267 "A Brilliant Company in a Brilliant Comedy," NYT, 6 Sept 1905, p. 7; rptd in NYTTR 1904-1911, [n. p.].

Shaw can be denounced as being inconsistent, but we enjoy seeing him erect edifices which he later tears down. Such is the case with Man and Superman.

268 Chesterton, G. K. HERETICS (Lond & NY: John Lane, 1905), pp. 54-67.

Shaw, despite popular opinion, is remarkably consistent in his views and insists on telling the truth about everything. The truth is so strange that we think Shaw is continually jesting. Where Shaw errs is in his unreasonable demands: it is impossible for man to achieve the sort of progress Shaw requires. Hence we should not seek out a superman, but rather a new philosophy.

269 Coleridge, Stephen. "The Late Sir Henry Irving and Mr. Bernard Shaw," MPOST, 8 Dec 1905, p. 7.

It is now abundantly clear that Shaw was wrong in asserting that Irving demanded a knighthood and that his productions were subsidized by wealthy women.

270 Coleridge, Stephen. "Sir Henry Irving's Knighthood," TIMES, 26 Oct 1905, p. 8.

As usual, Shaw has reacted in his fanciful manner to the facts surrounding Irving's knighthood. [See also Shaw's letters, 25 Oct 1905, p. 8, 27 Oct 1905, p. 8, 8 Dec 1905, p. 8; and Coleridge's letters 7 Dec 1905, p. 6, 9 Dec 1905, p. 10.]

271 "Comstock at it Again," NYT, 25 Oct 1905, p. 1.

Anthony Comstock, head of the Society for the Supresion of Vice, has warned Arnold Daly against producing Mrs. Warren's Profession.

[For additional information surrounding this controversy, see the following items in NYT: "Comstock vs. Shaw Again," 26 Oct 1905, p. 8; "Comstock Won't See Bernard Shaw's Play," 26 Oct 1905, p. 9; "Shaw Play Arouses New Haven Audience," 28 Oct 1905, p. 9; "Daly's New Shaw Play Barred in New Haven," 29 Oct 1905, p. 1; "Stage Morals and Stage Money," 30 Oct 1905, p. 8; "Pencil on Shaw's Play," 30 Oct 1905, p. 9; "Shaw's Play Unfit; The Critics Unanimous," 31 Oct 1905, p. 9; "Shaw's Play Stopped; The Manager Arrested," 1 Nov 1905, p. 1; "Daly to Make a Fight to Give Shaw's Play," 2 Nov 1905, p. 9; "Ten Commandments Before Shaw--M'Adoo," 3 Nov 1905, p. 6; "Arnold Daly Held for His Shaw Play," 15 Nov 1905, p. 13; "Arnold Daly Held for Trial," 24 Dec 1905, p. 3.]

272 Cortissoz, Royal. "George Bernard Shaw," OUTLOOK (NY), LXXXI (1905), 732-36.
Shaw's talents need more control. He could employ some Gilbertian humor, learn more about stagecraft, show more sense of proportion and taste, and be more urbanely ironic.

273 "The Court," STAGE, 4 May 1905, pp. 15-16.
You Never Can Tell is full of Shaw's "quips and cranks and wiles."

274 "The Court," STAGE, 30 Nov 1905, p. 17.
The torrents of ideas on every conceivable topic cloaked in Shaw's typically witty dialogue mask the fact that Major Barbara is only occasionally dramatic.

275 "Court--Major Barbara," ATH, No. 4075 (2 Dec 1905), 772.
Major Barbara is a discussion and is not dramatic or humorous. But there are well-devised characters and touching scenes, together with clever and paradoxical dialogue.

276 "Court Theatre," DT, 1 March 1905, p. 11.
In How He Lied to Her Husband Shaw burlesques himself and Candida quite effectively, and the play is a good mixture of travesty, farce and comedy.

277 "Court Theatre," DT, 24 Oct 1905, p. 11.
Man and Superman is witty, clever, and flaunts theatrical conventions.

278 "The Court Theatre," PMG, LXXXI (29 Nov 1905), 9; rptd in Evans, pp. 142-43.
Major Barbara is witty play, though perhaps not witty enough for three hours of discussion. Shaw has no religious sense and wants to irradicate human nature.

279 "Court Theatre," TIMES, 1 March 1905, p. 11.
How He Lied to Her Husband is a piece of fun and its idea can be found in a score of plays.

280 "Court Theatre," TIMES, 24 Oct 1905, p. 6.

Man and Superman is not an easy play to find amusing; the humor lies in what is said, not in situations or plot.

281 "Court Theatre," TIMES, 29 Nov 1905, p. 10.
Major Barbara shows Shaw "has no dramatic skill, has apparently no dramatic instinct, but he is a thinker."

282 "Court Theatre: Major Barbara," MPOST, 29 Nov 1905, p. 9; rptd in Evans, pp. 144–46.
The satire in Major Barbara is esoteric and caters to an intellectual coterie.

283 "Court Theatre: Major Barbara: Mr. Bernard Shaw's Ideas," DT, 29 Nov 1905, p. 7.
Major Barbara is full of destructive cleverness and endless paradoxes. Some characters are repulsive because Shaw "treads remorselessly upon all our feelings and instincts."

284 Crosby, Ernest. "The Bernard Shaw Philosophy," COSMOPOLITAN, XL (Dec 1905), 247–48.
In Man and Superman Shaw's thoughts are all wrong. He believes fallaciously that marriage is only a business affair, that "romance, poetry, religion, have nothing to do with it," and that falling in love "is an irrational, a lunatic condition."

285 Daly, Arnold. "Impressions of Bernard Shaw," HARPER'S WEEKLY, XLIX (20 May 1905), 732-33 [not seen].
[Cited in Amalric, p. 470.]

286 "Dr. Adler Calls Shaw a Literary Anarchist," NYT, 6 Nov 1905, p. 6.
Shaw is "not all bad, but has chosen a cheap road to notoriety."

287 "Drama: The Week," ATH, No. 4036 (4 March 1905), 284.
How He Lied to Her Husband is Shavian absurdity, humorous, witty, extravagant, infinitely diverting. It is also assertive and vainglorious.

288 "Drama: The Week," ATH, No. 4045 (6 May 1905), 571.
In You Never Can Tell Shaw is a master creator of characters.

289 "Drama: The Week," ATH, No. 4048 (27 May 1905), 667-68.
Man and Superman is enlivened with so much humor and paradox that its "trumperiness" is overlooked.

290 E., H. C. "Book Reviews: The Common Sense of Municipal Trading," YALE REVIEW, XIV (1905-06), 441-442.
Although Shaw's aim in The Common Sense of Municipal Trading is not always clear, every reader will find it a stimulating work.

291 "Fiction: The Irrational Knot," TLS, No. 197 (20 Oct 1905), 350.
Shaw rightly attacks the weak points of society's view of marriage as a matter of convenience. But Shaw's views are trite and common-

place, and one suspects this old novel is published now only because Shaw has become a literary figure.

292 Filon, Augustin. "M. Bernard Shaw et Son Théâtre" (Mr. Bernard Shaw and His Theatre), REVUE DES DEUX MONDES, XXX (15 Nov 1905), 405-33.

Shaw found nineteenth-century theatre poor and dying. In his own plays Shaw is aggressively good humored and shows a perpetual disrespect for everything. Caesar and Cleopatra, The Devil's Disciple, and The Man of Destiny have scarcely any historical meaning. Only the first act of Arms and the Man is excellent. Lady Cicely is a charming and exceptional character. In Widowers' Houses Shaw shows that the typical English gentleman is honorable only to a certain point. Mrs. Warren's Profession is impossible to stage and painful to read. You Never Can Tell is funny. In Man and Superman the idea of a misogynous Don Juan is a nice one, but why should he be a socialist? Candida is Shaw's masterpiece. The exchange of ideas in John Bull's Other Island is a rare intellectual treat. Shaw charms intellectuals, but disappoints playgoers. Overall his dialogue is brilliant, his gallery of women astonishing, but his situations are lacking. His plays are a campaign against ancient institutions and long-established principles: marriage, property, morality, duty. [In French.]

293 Ford, James L. "Shaw's Influence on Our Embryo Dramatists," HARPER'S WEEKLY (NY), XLIX (25 Nov 1905), 1712.

The danger of Shaw's witty cleverness is that fledgling dramatists will attempt to ape his style, believing that is what makes drama. But there is only one Shaw, and the novices should realize drama is composed largely of action.

294 France, Wilmer Cave. "The Philosophy of Bernard Shaw," BOOKMAN (NY), XXI (June 1905), 428-31.

Shaw does not write for art's sake; rather, he is an aggressive philosopher who "desires nothing less than the destruction of the ideals and of the culture of his race."

295 "Free Libraries Bar Bernard Shaw's Books," NYT, 21 Sept 1905, p. 9.

Arthur E. Bostwick, head of the circulation department of the New York Free Lending Libraries, thinks Shaw's books are bad for children and has removed them from the open shelves. [For further details of this incident see the following in NYT: "Bernard Shaw Resents Action of Librarian," 26 Sept 1905, p. 1; "Ban Off Shaw's Books," 27 Sept 1905, p. 1; "George Bernard Shaw" [Editorial], 27 Sept 1905, p. 8.]

296 "George Bernard Shaw," REV OF REVS, XXXI (1905), 745.

Shaw now seems to be the most talked about dramatist, and he is being written about seriously in the significant periodical press.

297 Grein, J. T. "Premieres of the Week," STIMES, 5 March 1905, p. 6.

Much of the humor of How He Lied to Her Husband is forced, and the play should be shorter.

298 Grein, J. T. "Premieres of the Week," STIMES, 3 Dec 1905, p. 4.

Major Barbara is a great play; the only fault is the use of physical brutality in act two. Shaw is clearly a colossal, universal thinker, and not a mere jester.

299 Gwynn, Stephen. "Mr. G. B. Shaw and the British Public," CORNHILL, XCI (April 1905), 503-12.

You Never Can Tell and Captain Brassbound's Conversion have thrilled Stage Society audiences; both plays thoroughly amuse, but only if one is prepared to think. Shaw is probably not a popular success because "you can never be sure that he will not make you feel uncomfortable." His comedy stems from "the clash of ideas" rather than anything else.

300 "The H. B. Conway Matinee," STAGE, 25 May 1905, p. 10.

J. B. Fagan's SHAKESPEARE V. SHAW depicts Shaw being arraigned for libelling Shakespeare. Shaw is called as a witness and contends he is better than Shakespeare because he is still alive while Shakespeare is dead.

301 Hale, Edward Everett, jr. DRAMATISTS OF TO-DAY: ROSTAND, HAUPTMANN, SUDERMANN, PINERO, SHAW, PHILLIPS, MAETERLINCK: BEING AN INFORMAL DISCUSSION OF THEIR SIGNIFICANT WORK (1905; 6th ed NY: Holt, 1911), pp. 112-47, 215, 223, 231, 263-65.

Shaw's wit and paradox make him appear frivolous, but he is really serious. Stagecraft is not his strong point, and his success is the result of other elements. Chief of these are his radical, revolutionary, socialist ideas which reveal he is the champion of a different order of society. Candida is his best play where the reformer is sometimes lost in the dramatist, and it is full of flashes of reality. Man and Superman is more a play of ideas; it is extravagant, full of clever dialogue and abstruse ideas—the essence of Shaw, ideas in dialogue.

302 Henderson, Archibald. "You Never Can Tell," DAILY OBSERVER (Charlotte, NC), 28 May 1905, p. 17 [not seen].

[Cited in Hood, p. 223.]

303 [Howells, W. D.]. "Editor's Easy Chair," HARPER'S MONTHLY (NY & Lond), CXI (Sept 1905), 633-35.

[Largely a discussion of Shakespeare in the light of Shaw's assertion that he could if he chose write as good or better poetic drama as Shakespeare.]

304 Huneker, James. "Bernard Shaw and Woman," HARPER"S BAZAAR (NY), XXXIX (June 1905), 535-38.
Although Shaw did not invent the "unpleasant girl," he is the first writer to make her a prominent figure in all his plots. His unpleasant girls are so fascinating because they are drawn from life.

305 Huneker, James. ICONOCLASTS: A BOOK OF DRAMATISTS (NY: Scribner's, 1905), pp. 233-68.
Shaw's literary pedigree is "W. S. Gilbert out of Ibsen," although his plays are "full of modern odds and ends." He is very versatile, and a man of many masks practicising a great comedic wit with the persistent objective of telling the truth at all costs. The Philanderer is true Shavian comedy. You Never Can Tell, Arms and the Man, Candida, and The Devil's Disciple "are a quartet difficult to outpoint for prodigal humour and ingenious fantasy." Man and Superman has a promising beginning, a thin second act, and a third act which recalls a Gilbert farce and is talk, talk, talk.

306 "An Irish Bull in the China Shop," INDEPENDENT (NY), LIX (1905), 1060-61.
Mrs. Warren's Profession speaks too plainly, and shocks, not because it is immoral but because it is not immoral in the conventional way.

307 [The Irrational Knot], ACADEMY, LXVIII (21 Oct 1905), 1094.
The characters in The Irrational Knot are rigid and inflexible. They are the creation of a "youth who in his revolt against old conventions has already rushed into grooves of his own."

308 [The Irrational Knot], NATION (NY), LXXXI (1905), 368.
The Irrational Knot is inferior to Cashel Byron's Profession and less repulsive than An Unsocial Socialist and Love Among the Artists. Shaw's own preface forestalls criticism, but Irrational comprises little more than a "gallery of prigs."

309 "Is Bernard Shaw a Menace to Morals?" CUR LIT, XXXIX (Nov 1905), 551-52.
[Details of the controversy surrounding Shaw's works being placed on the restricted list of the circulating department of New York Public Library.]

310 "Is Shaw Sincere?" NYT, 23 Oct 1905, p. 9.
Members of the New York Playgoers' Club have divided opinions on Shaw's sincerity.

311 "The Jester to the Nation," SPECTATOR, XCV (9 Dec 1905), 970-71.
Shaw's considerable achievements warrant him the title of "jester to the nation," a position which requires "a certain complex mixture of character." He has been of great service to England, and has been more than "merely witty and entertaining."

312 "John Bull's Other Island," NYT, 15 Oct 1905, part III, p. 10; rptd in NYTTR 1904-1911, [n. p.] .

John Bull's Other Island helps repudiate the notion that the theatre is no place for ideas. Ideas should be foremost and theatrical craftsmanship can come later.

313 "John Bull's Other Island," SUN (NY), 11 Oct 1905, p. 8.

John Bull's Other Island reflects Shaw at his characteristically best and worst. Best are his ideas; worst is his lack of broad appeal.

314 Lee, Elisabeth. "Echo des Auslands. Englischer Brief" (Echo from Abroad. English Letter), DAS LITERARISCHE ECHO, VII: 18 (15 June 1905), columns 1354-57.

At last Shaw's plays are accepted by the British public. [In German.]

315 Lewis, Austin. "The Nemesis of Bernard Shaw," OVERLAND MONTHLY (San Francisco), XLVI (Oct 1905), 369-71.

Man and Superman represents Shaw's climax as a writer and the "probable conclusion of his influence as a moulder of opinion." Shaw actually longs to be a leader, a role of which he is incapable because the English do not take him seriously.

316 Lodge, Sir Oliver. "Major Barbara, G. B. S., and Robert Blatchford," CLARION, No. 734 (29 Dec 1905), 5; rptd in Evans, pp. 160-62.

While the second act of Major Barbara is one of the best pieces of dramatic art—full of tension—the third is flat and "diabolically cynical" in that it preaches poverty is the only crime we should care about.

317 "London & Suburban Theatres: Court Theatre," ERA, 16 Sept 1905, p. 12.

John Bull's Other Island proves Shaw is becoming one of the most popular dramatists of the age.

318 "London Theatres: The Court," STAGE, 2 March 1905, p. 16.

How He Lied to Her Husband is whimsical, irresponsible fooling, apparently designed as an ingenious advertisement for Candida.

319 "London Theatres: The Court," STAGE, 25 May 1905, p. 14.

Man and Superman is whimsical, brilliantly argumentative, and profoundly serious.

320 "London Theatres: The Court," STAGE, 14 Sept 1905, pp. 16-17.

John Bull's Other Island is "tommy-rot . . . with its irresponsible hitting-out all around."

321 "London Theatres: The Court," STAGE, 26 Oct 1905, p. 18.
Man and Superman appears to prove, in revival, that Shaw has caught on with the better class of playgoer.

322 "M'Adoo Talk on Virtue Stirs Y. M. C. A. Men," NYT, 9 Oct 1905, p. 4.
New York Police Commissioner sees Shaw as a new Oscar Wilde.

323 "Major Barbara," ERA, 2 Dec 1905, p. 17.
Major Barbara is consistently dramatic with a progressive purpose and shape. It is a discussion embellished with quips and fantastic irony, including the Gilbertian notion of the foundling inheriting the armaments factory.

324 "Man and Superman," ERA, 27 May 1905, p. 13.
"Man and Superman is Shaw in excelsis—Shaw on the stump, with philosophical topsy-turvydom run mad. The audacious heterodoxy of the whole thing is delicious."

325 "Manchester," STAGE, 28 Sept 1905, p. 3.
The Admirable Bashville reveals Shaw in his finest epigrammatic mood, coupled with abundant wit and satirical raillery at society.

326 Masterman, C. F. G. IN PERIL OF CHANGE: ESSAYS WRITTEN IN TIME OF TRANQUILLITY (Lond: T. Fisher Unwin, 1905), pp. 190-96, 211-12.
Shaw is now at a stage of life where he finds himself disillusioned with many things. He is also in a state of revolt, and calls for a superman to show a new path for man (as Man and Superman and John Bull's Other Island demonstrate).

327 Mencken, H. L. GEORGE BERNARD SHAW: HIS PLAYS (Bost & Lond: J. W. Luce, 1905; rptd New Rochelle, NY: E. V. Glaser, 1969)
The best and easiest way to view Shaw is to treat his plays simply as dramas; the latter lose their comprehensibility if he is seen as a doctrinaire preacher. As plays many of his works "pass the test," although some are woefully lacking. Mrs. Warren's Profession is Shaw's "most remarkable play" in which the hidden nuances of human nature are explored to a "superlative degree." Arms and the Man, an exuberant comedy replete with abundant humor and excellent characterization, is not among Shaw's best work. Most of the drama of The Devil's Disciple occurs in Act One and the remainder of the play is largely "commonplace melodrama." Widowers' Houses is not a masterpiece, but had the virtue of introducing Shaw to the public (although the play derives from Pinero and H. A. Jones). The Philanderer is described as a "topical comedy," though it is "archaic" and really a "comic opera libretto in prose." Captain Brassbound's Conversion combines excellent interaction of characters with finely spun humor (which has not always been appreciated), although the

exposition is verbose. Shaw's <u>Caesar and Cleopatra</u> is a recon-struction in modern terms of Shakespeare's characters and hence, to modern audiences, they do appear more human and logical than Shakespeare's. <u>The Man of Destiny</u> is a bravura piece and remarkable in many aspects—characterization, craftsmanship, incident and dialogue. Although <u>Candida</u>, an "essay in feminine psychology," has been widely misunderstood, it reveals Shaw's mellowed genius and exhibits many assured touches. <u>How He Lied to Her Husband</u> is a slight piece of foolery. <u>You Never Can Tell</u> was written to order and follows the commercial theatrical formula of the day. The result is irresistible humor, though with a nasty undercurrent reminiscent of that in <u>Widowers' Houses</u>. <u>Man and Superman</u> is an encyclopedic tract and bulks as Shaw's magnum opus in which he appears to have written to purge himself of numerous "disquieting doctrines." It would have been better as two plays. <u>John Bull's Other Island</u> is a political satire and Shaw at his most humorous, and, charac-teristically, he gives all views an impartial airing. [With chapters on the novels, biography, and Shakespeare and Shaw. Each chapter is brief and suggestive but not exhaustively persuasive.]

328 Mendez, Britz. "Correspondencia: Carta de Londres" (Correspondence: London Letter), LA LECTURA, Año V, Tomo I (1905), 52-55 [not seen].
[Cited in Rodríguez (MS). In Spanish.]

329 "Might Supplement <u>You Never Can Tell</u> with 'I Told You So,' " NYT, 10 Jan 1905, p. 5; rptd in NYTTR 1904-1911, [n.p.].
The major failing of <u>You Never Can Tell</u> is that Shaw has not clearly delineated the purposes of the characters and situations.

330 "Mr. Daly Scores in Shaw Comedy," NYH, 10 Jan 1905, p. 11.
<u>You Never Can Tell</u> bubbles with epigrams and witty quips, and drives Shaw's remorseless logic home. Shaw preaches sermons in satire.

331 "Mr. Shaw's 'Shocker,' " ERA, 11 Nov 1905, p. 21.
The Chief Commissioner of Police in New York has a perfect right to ban <u>Mrs. Warren's Profession</u> because the play outrages the American public instinct.

332 "<u>Mrs. Warren</u> Professes," SUN (NY), 31 Oct 1905, p. 7.
<u>Mrs. Warren's Profession</u> "is, in fact, little more than the drama-tization of a tract of the social evil, with much socialistic discussion of the right of women to labor and be paid living wages." It is difficult to see why there is any controversy. [For details of the controversy surrounding the New York production see the following items in SUN: "M'Adoo's Eye on Shaw Play," 31 Oct 1905, p. 7; "M'Adoo Stops the Shaw Play," 1 Nov 1905, p. 6; "Court Hearing on Shaw Play," 2 Nov 1905, p. 9; "M'Adoo on <u>Mrs. Warren</u>," 3 Nov 1905, p. 9; John Corbin, "Dramatic Censor M'Adoo," 5 Nov 1905, part II,

p. 6; "Felix Adler Arraigns Shaw," 6 Nov 1905, p. 7.]

333 "Music and Drama: Arms and the Man," MANCHESTER CITY NEWS, 23 Sept 1905, p. 6.
A week of Shavian drama, including The Admirable Bashville and Arms and the Man, has not been successful because Shaw is still not widely known with playgoers of all types.

334 "Music and the Drama: Notable Plays of the Month: Mrs. Warren's Profession," CUR LIT, XXXIX (1905), 660-61.
[An account of American productions of Mrs. Warren's Profession with extracts of criticism.]

335 "Music, Art and Drama," INDEPENDENT (NY), LIX (1905), 925-28.
[A favorable survey of Candida, Man and Superman, and John Bull's Other Island.]

336 "Musings without Method," BLACKWOOD'S MAGAZINE, CLXXVII (July 1905), 133-35.
Shaw has finally found fame and can be regarded as almost the rival of Pinero and H. A. Jones. Despite his disciples, his clowning, his desire to be his own philosopher and critic, Shaw is a "dramatist from first to last." His morals are rather antiquated, but his construction and characterization are unsurpassable.

337 "New Novels: The Irrational Knot," ATH, No. 4069 (21 Oct 1905), 539.
Much of the dialogue of The Irrational Knot may seem "unreadable vulgarity" to some, while others will see it as being as good as anything Shaw has done. His preface is a "perfect piece of criticism."

338 "A New Old Shaw Book," NYT, 17 June 1905, part II, p. 409.
The Irrational Knot is apparently dear to Shaw's heart, and he has added a delightful preface.

339 "New Shaw Play a Masterpiece of Satire," NYT, 11 Oct 1905, p. 11; rptd in NYTTR 1904-1911, [n. p.].
John Bull's Other Island demonstrates Shaw's "humor is so scintillant, his wit so dazzling, his intellectuality so enveloping, that he defies all the ordinary processes."

340 "New Shaw Play is Outrageous," NYH, 28 Oct 1905, p. 16.
Mrs. Warren's Profession is "shockingly indecent" and a "shameful social study."

341 "Opening of the Dramatic Season in New York," CUR LIT, XXXIX (1905), 542.
[A summary and anthology of criticisms of Man and Superman.]

342 "Passages in Man and Superman that Provoke Laughter or Invite Criticism," NYT, 1 Oct 1905, part III, p. 2.
[Title describes.]

343 "The Playhouses: Major Barbara at the Court," ILN, CXXVII (9 Dec 1905), 845.
Major Barbara is the product of a fearless thinker, which for two acts contains cutting satire. Then the play falls apart. Shaw's nimble intellect makes us think and laugh, but not feel.

344 "The Playhouses: Man and Superman at the Court," ILN, CXXVI (27 May 1905), 739.
Man and Superman is the apotheosis of the current Shaw season, and represents Shaw's views on woman as the eternal hunter.

345 "The Playhouses: Man and Superman at the Court," ILN, CXXVII (28 Oct 1905), 595.
Shaw's popularity boom continues. Man and Superman "cannot be described as much more than a very little, if very witty and exhilarating, piece of topsy-turvy comedy."

346 "The Playhouses: Mr. Bernard Shaw's Vogue at the Court," ILN, CXXVI (20 May 1905), 702-03.
Shaw's plays have become very fashionable, even among society playgoers who laugh as though they understood Shaw's caustic wit.

347 [Prevost, Francis]. "The Plays of Mr. Bernard Shaw," EDINBURGH REVIEW, CCI (April 1905), 498-523; extract rptd in Evans, pp. 135-38.
Shaw's work has not received much theatrical exposure, and this is perhaps because "he is a dramatist because he is a moralist. For art's sake he would have nothing to do with art." Also, as a socialist, he is interested in a new order of things. His published plays help reveal what we have missed and his stage directions show a true novelistic instinct. He may produce greater work, but "it must be conceived by a less contentious spirit and wrought in a serener air."

348 "Prince of Advertisers, Says Page of Shaw," NYT, 24 Oct 1905, p. 9.
Thomas Nelson Page believes that Shaw is a self-advertiser, insincere, Man and Superman is rotten, and that Shaw will not alter the world's morals.

349 "The Queen's Bounty and Mr. Shaw," SAT REV, C (1905), 647-48.
Shaw is right in saying that more than the Queen's (and other people's) charity is needed to solve the unemployment question.

350 "A Review of the Season's Fiction," REV OF REVS, XXXII (Dec 1905), 759.
The Irrational Knot should prove popular, even though it lacks a

moral.

351 "The Rise and Decline of Bernard Shaw," CUR LIT, XXXIX (Dec 1905), 664-66.
[A small anthology of critical opinions which support the idea that Shaw is past his peak and that his influence is waning.]

352 "Royal Court Theatre," TIMES, 3 May 1905, p. 10.
Shaw's purpose in You Never Can Tell is to delight audiences; it is next to impossible to pin down any single thematic idea.

353 "Sentiment in New Shaw Play," NYH, 11 Oct 1905, p. 12.
John Bull's Other Island has little plot, is full of Shaw's usual satire, and, surprisingly, contains sentiment.

354 [Shaw], NYT, 26 Jan 1905, p. 6.
After all Shaw's sources, such as Henry George, Nietzsche and Schopenhauer, are removed, "what remains . . . but his quips and his cleverness?"

355 "Shaw at His Worst," NYT, 14 Oct 1905, p. 682.
Shaw does not take his readers seriously as the evidence of The Irrational Knot demonstrates.

356 "Shaw in Intellectual Farce," SUN (NY), 10 Jan 1905, p. 7.
You Never Can Tell is just plain intellectual farce, although there are moments when it suggests other genres.

357 "Shaw on Shakespeare," NYT, 28 April 1905, p. 8.
Shaw's lecture, in London, on Shakespeare contained some characteristically Shavian remarks.

358 "Shaw Play Arouses New Haven Audience," NYT, 28 Oct 1905, p. 9; rptd in NYTTR 1904-1911, [n. p.].
Some lines in Mrs. Warren's Profession almost provoked some audience members to vocal protest, and many wondered whether they should sit out the play.

359 "Shaw Play Full of Plain Speech," NYH, 6 Sept 1905, p. 10.
Shaw keeps Broadway on its toes in terms of sophistication, and Man and Superman out-Shaw's earlier work. The play is full of frank talk, some of it unwholesome

360 "Shaw Play the Limit of Stage Indecency," NYH, 31 Oct 1905, pp. 3, 5; rptd in Montrose J. Moses and John Mason Brown, THE AMERICAN THEATRE AS SEEN BY ITS CRITICS, 1752-1934 (NY: Norton, 1934), pp. 163-67; rptd in Evans, pp. 139-41.
Mrs. Warren's Profession, despite some alterations, is "wholly immoral" and has no redeeming features. A "morbidly curious audience" was present to see the "superabundance of foulness." The play is literary muck which insults New Yorkers' moral intelligence. [For

more detail surrounding the controversy see the following items in NYH: "Dooley Sees Daly in Banned Play," 30 Oct 1905, p. 4; "Police Stop Shaw Play, Make Arrest," 1 Nov 1905, p. 4; "Fights to Prove Shaw Play Moral," 2 Nov 1905, p. 8; "M'Adoo Deplores Evil in Shaw Play," 3 Nov 1905, p. 8; "Managers, Playwrights and Actors Discuss Stage Morals," 5 Nov 1905, part III, p. 14; "Bernard Shaw Defends Play," 7 Nov 1905, p. 9.]

361 "Shaw's Play Unfit: The Critics Unanimous," NYT, 31 Oct 1905, p. 9; rptd in NYTTR 1904-1911, [n. p.].
Mrs. Warren's Profession has no place in the theatre, either as a sociological treatise or as the ill-conceived drama it is. It has created a considerable furor and the critics are generally hostile.

362 Simpson, Herman. "Shaw as Playwright and Philosopher," INDEPENDENT (NY), LIX (1905), 34-38.
The secret of Shaw's success is that his plays violate all normal rules, deal with popular ideas, and have a serious purpose (disguised in comic form).

363 S[pence], E. F. "The Stage from the Stalls," SKETCH, XLIX (15 Feb 1905), 166.
John Bull's Other Island proves Shaw is "profoundly sane and deeply in earnest." It is truly the only political play of the times.

364 S[pence], E. F. "The Stage from the Stalls," SKETCH, XLIX (8 March 1905), 266.
How He Lied to Her Husband was written to demonstrate Shaw "is not gulled by his own sophistries."

365 S[pence], E. F. "The Stage from the Stalls," SKETCH, LII (6 Dec 1905), 238.
Major Barbara is theatrical propaganda. The characters talk as though they were reading from pamphlets. The play is amusing and paradoxical, but any real consequence is missing.

366 S[pence], E. F. "The Stage from the Stalls: 'G. B. S.' and the Pending Theatre Trust," SKETCH, LI (9 Aug 1905), 114.
Shaw should discover how inimical his and the proposed Trust of American Managers' real objectives are to the English theatre.

367 Strachey, Lionel. "The Popularity of Bernard Shaw," CRITIC (NY) XLVII (Nov 1905), 415-23.
Shaw's independence from dramatic conventions, his wit, the worsting of age by youth, and the submission of man to woman make him popular in America. Shaw's treatment of domestic and matrimonial life commands approbation. However, he is not for people with "good, plain, sound, common sense."

368 "Theatre Royal: The Admirable Bashville," MANCHESTER GUARDIAN, 23 Sept 1905, p. 8.

The Admirable Bashville is the cleverest literary parody there has ever been.

369 "Theatrical Garden Party," ERA, 22 July 1905, p. 10.
Passion, Poison, and Petrifaction was an oustanding feature of the garden party; it lasts ten minutes and was repeated six times.

370 "Theatrical Garden Party," STAGE, 20 July 1905, p. 13.
Passion, Poison, and Petrifaction is a "startling, original, pathetic, blood-curdling, and entrancing tragedy in one act and ten mechanical effects."

371 Thompson, Alex M. "The Sur-Passing Shaw: An Account of Major Barbara," CLARION, No. 731 (8 Dec 1905), 3; rptd in Evans, pp. 154-55.
Major Barbara is an "audacious propagandist drama" which urges people to discard their obsolete creeds and morality and to set about developing a superman. Parts of the play are verbose and nebulous.

372 Vedrenne, J. E. "Major Barbara," MPOST, 1 Dec 1905, p. 7.
Shaw's plays in general and Major Barbara in particular are playing to wider audiences than some reviews have implied.

373 "A Vedrenne-Barker Matinee," ERA, 4 March 1905, p. 19.
How He Lied to Her Husband is not a travesty of Candida and does not absurdly exaggerate the latter's sentiment.

374 W. "Hall Caine Caught by a Caricaturist," NYT, 1 Oct 1905, part III, p. 5.
The subject of Major Barbara is more appropriate for Hall Caine to write about. Caine also believes Shaw is a "man of deep emotional feeling."

375 [Walkley, A. B.]. "The Drama: Man and Superman," TLS, No. 176 (26 May 1905), 170; rptd in DRAMA AND LIFE (1908; rptd Freeport, NY: Books for Libraries, 1967), pp. 224-232; rptd in Evans, pp. 110-15.
Man and Superman is an unsatisfying play because its construction is weak and the plot trivial.

376 Walkley, A. B. [Shaw], LE TEMPS, 28 Aug 1905, pp. 1-2.
Shaw has become a successful playwright; however, he is not a born dramatist but a born iconoclast. [In French.]

377 "Who's Bernard Shaw? Asks Mr. Comstock," NYT, 28 Sept 1905, p. 9.
Anthony Comstock, head of the Society for the Suppression of Vice, is unaware of Shaw and will investigate him. [See also in NYT: "Shaw and Comstock" [editorial], 29 Sept 1905, p. 8; "A Lesson for Mr. Shaw" [editorial], 2 Oct 1905, p. 8; "Chicago 'Comstockery'" [editorial], 6 Oct 1905, p. 8; "Get Out, Says Pool to Anthony

49

Comstock," 7 Oct 1905, p. 12.]

378 "The 'Women Wooers' of Bernard Shaw's Plays," CUR LIT, XXXIX (1905), 81-82.
Unlike Shakespeare's varied women, Shaw's are remarkably similar as can be seen in Blanche Sartorius, Julia Craven, Gloria Clandon and Ann Whitefield.

379 "The Yellow Dramatist," OUTLOOK, LXXXI (1905), 701.
Mrs. Warren's Profession proves Shaw likes to make fools out of his audiences. He is not a buffoon or prophet, but simply a "yellow journalist on the stage."

1906

380 A., M. "Spelling Reform," TIMES, 27 Sept 1906, p. 10.
Shaw is correct in asserting the alphabet needs to be expanded to accomodate all the various sounds. [See also in TIMES: W. F. Kirby, "Spelling Reform," 2 Oct 1905, p. 9; Avary H. Forbes, "Spelling and Pronunciation," 8 Oct 1905, p. 11; Shaw's letter, 25 Sept 1906, p. 6.]

381 Balfour, Edith. "Shaw and Super-Shaw," NATIONAL REVIEW, XLVI (Feb 1906), 1040-45.
Major Barbara painfully reveals Shaw's deficient vision of life; "he does not suggest the mysterious presence of life, but only dissects its manifestations." The play mocks its audience unfairly.

382 Barnicoat, Constance A. "Mr. Bernard Shaw's Counterfeit Presentiment of Women," FORTNIGHTLY (NY), LXXXV (March 1906), 516-27; rptd in LIVING AGE, CCXLIX (14 April 1906), 67-75.
With the exception of Candida and Major Barbara, Shaw presents a gallery of unlovable, foolish, unpleasant women in his plays. [Discusses the women in Mrs. Warren's Profession, Man and Superman, Captain Brassbound's Conversion, You Never Can Tell, Widowers' Houses, The Devil's Disciple, Candida, The Philanderer, Major Barbara and John Bull's Other Island.]

383 Beerbohm, Max. "A Great Dear," SAT REV, CI (1906), 360; rptd in LAST THEATRES, pp. 242-45.
Captain Brassbound's Conversion does not seem as good a play as when it first appeared. Then Shaw had not found his particular dramatic method and was simply using old conventions.

384 Beerbohm, Max. "Languishing Theatres," SAT REV, CII (1906), 42-43; rptd in LAST THEATRES, pp. 252-55.
The theatre is in a parlous state, and the apparent success of Shaw's plays at the Court Theatre is not evidence of improvement. Shaw has

become fashionable, but his work is not appreciated.

385 Beerbohm, Max. "Mr. Shaw's RODERICK HUDSON," SAT REV, CII (1906), 639-40; rptd in AROUND THEATRES, pp. 567-71; rptd as "Jacobean and Shavian" in Leon Edel, ed, HENRY JAMES: A COLLECTION OF CRITICAL ESSAYS (Englewood Cliffs, NJ: Prentice-Hall, 1963), pp. 18-22.
The themes of The Devil's Disciple and Henry James's RODERICK HUDSON are generally similar, but the artistic methods are completely different. "The hand of the artist in [James] is held tightly over the mouth of the preacher. In Mr. Shaw, the preacher is ever vocal."

386 "Bernard Shaw in Hungary," NYT, 29 April 1906, p. 7; rptd in NYTTR 1904-1911, [n. p.].
The Devil's Disciple has met with very flattering critical reviews in Budapest.

387 Beswick, Harry. "G. B. S.—The Orator," CLARION, 26 Oct 1906 [not seen] ; rptd in SHAW REVIEW, VIII (1965), 25-28.
[An account of Shaw as a platform speaker.]

388 Blum, Jean. "George Bernard Shaw," REVUE GERMANIQUE, X (Nov-Dec 1906), 634-55.
Shaw was first a music and drama critic, and a diffuser of socialist propaganda—hence his mastery of the art of dialogue and his knowledge of the language of various classes. Shaw is a comic poet; his social criticism is Ibsenesque. He attacks romantic and respectable ideals, and has created a new religion and philosophy of the superman who will be a better, wiser man, free from prejudices. [In French.]

389 Braby, Maud Churton. "G. B. S. and a Suffragist: An Intimate Interview," TRIBUNE, 12 March 1906 [not seen] ; rptd in INDEPENDENT SHAVIAN, XII (Fall 1973), 1-3.
[Title describes.]

390 "Caesar amd Cleopatra," ERA, 17 Nov 1906, p. 15.
Shaw's paradoxical wit in Caesar and Cleopatra accords with the American sense of humor. This is a "clever compound of truth, travesty, and satire."

391 "Caesar and Cleopatra," NYT, 4 Nov 1906, part IV, p. 2; rptd in NYTTR 1904-1911, [n. p.].
Although Caesar and Cleopatra is overloaded with dialogue, just the one scene of Caesar meeting Cleopatra is better than six other plays put together.

392 "Caesar and Cleopatra an Artistic Triumph," NYT, 31 Oct 1906, p. 9; rptd in NYTTR 1904-1911, [n. p.].
Caesar and Cleopatra may flag at times, but generally it is "pure fun with such amazing touches of true dignity and tenderness." Shaw's

intepretation of history does not much matter.

393 "Captain Brassbound's Conversion," ERA, 24 March 1906, p. 17.
Captain Brassbound's Conversion is interesting, but not as "sparkling" as some of Shaw's later works, and it begins rather tamely.

394 "Cashel Byron's Profession is Dramatized for Gentleman Jim," NYT, 2 Jan 1906, p. 9; rptd in NYTTR 1904-1911, [n. p.].
After Mrs. Warren's Profession Shaw has rehabilitated himself with Cashel Byron's Profession.

395 Castren, Gunnar. G. BERNARD SHAW (Helsinki: Forlagsaktiebolaget Helios, 1906) [not seen].
[In Finnish.]

396 "Catty Cleopatra and Bald Caesar," NYH, 31 Oct 1906, p. 9
Caesar and Cleopatra is Shaw's "serio-comic extravaganza, which is made a vehicle for clever paradoxes and cynical witticisms."

397 "Cesar i Kleopatra od Bernarda Sava" (Caesar and Cleopatra by Bernard Shaw), PRAVDA (Belgrade), III (1906), 104, 3 [not seen].
[In Serbian.]

398 Chesterton, G. K. [Shaw the Puritan], INDEPENDENT REVIEW (Lond), VIII (1906), 81-87.
A profound flaw in Shaw's philosophy is that his intellectual Puritanism, which refuses to idealize anything, causes him to miss the basic truth that if "things are to be real at all, they must be romantic." [Reference to Major Barbara, Candida, The Philanderer and Man and Superman.]

399 Chilton, Carroll Brent. "Shaw Contra Mundum," INDEPENDENT (NY), LX (1906), 550-56.
Shaw, a lesser Nietzsche, turns everything upside down and asserts that the reverse of everything is really true. He is a "professed profaner of man, who . . . cleverly employs the 'hydrostatic paradox of controversy.' "

400 "Corbett and the Shaw Boom," SUN (NY), 9 Jan 1906, p. 7.
In Cashel Byron's Profession Shaw has worked, for once, with his eyes rather than his brain, and has provided some "first rate fun."

401 Corbett, Ex-Champion, has a Go at Shaw," NYT, 9 Jan 1906, p. 9; rptd in NYTTR 1904-1911, [n. p.].
Cashel Byron's Profession is an undramatic story with specious pleading. It is without incident and contains superfluous dialogue.

402 "Corbett Knocks Out Bernard Shaw," NHY, 9 Jan 1906, p. 12.
Former boxing champion Jim Corbett dominates both Cashel Byron's

Profession and Shaw.

403 "The Court," ERA, 22 Sept 1906, p. 13.
Shaw's subtleties and brilliant satire are now appreciated, as a revised John Bull's Other Island shows.

404 "The Court Approves Bernard Shaw's Play," NYT, 7 July 1906, p. 7.
Mrs. Warren's Profession has been ruled legally not indecent, even though there are repellent things in it. [See also in NYT: "Bernard Shaw's Profession" [editorial], 8 July 1906, p. 8; "Won't Revive Mrs. Warren: Too Much Notoriety, Says Arnold Daly," 29 July 1906, p. 9.]

405 "Court Theatre," TIMES, 30 Oct 1906, p. 10.
There is a certain deliberate coarseness to Man and Superman which makes the bourgeois sit up and take notice.

406 "Court Theatre: Captain Brassbound's Conversion," DT, 21 March 1906, p. 11.
Much of Captain Brassbound's Conversion is dull; interest revives only with Lady Cicely, which owes much to Ellen Terry's acting.

407 "Court Theatre: Mr. Bernard Shaw's New Play," MPOST, 22 Nov 1906, p. 4; rptd in Evans, pp. 165-67.
Original, amusing, intellectual and mostly unintelligible, The Doctor's Dilemma also deliberately annoys its audiences. The doctors appear as puppets.

408 "The Current Plays," THEATRE MAGAZINE (NY), VI (Dec 1906), 312-13.
Caesar and Cleopatra has no sentiment and portrays only highly superficial emotions. Shaw is a skilful dramatist, and his satire on history is readily acceptable.

409 D., M. "A Doctor on The Doctor's Dilemma," SKETCH, LVI (28 Nov 1906), 200.
Shaw has his medical facts right in The Doctor's Dilemma, but his medical characters are merely types. Any realism is sacrificed to other considerations.

410 "Daly's: Cashel Byron's Profession," THEATRE MAGAZINE (NY), VI (Feb 1906), v.
Cashel Byron's Profession is not sufficiently Shavian to be a distinctive Shaw play; it leans too much towards the romantic mode.

411 Davis, P. R. "George Bernard Shaw," AFRICAN MONTHLY, I (Dec 1906), 52-59.
Cashel Byron's Profession is a "capital book," though Shaw is better as a revolutionary dramatist.

412 D[awson], A[lbert]. "Mr. G. Bernard Shaw on Religion, Including His Own," CHRISTIAN COMMONWEALTH, XXVII (29

Nov 1906), 149-50.
Shaw's lecture, "The Religion of the British Empire," was less shocking than many Christians might think, and he revealed himself as "a
man of strong and definite religious conviction." [See also a subsequent sermon on Shaw's lecture: Rev. R. J. Campbell, "The Modes of
God," CHRISTIAN COMMONWEALTH, XXVII (6 Dec 1906), 165-66.]

413 Dickinson, G. Lowes. "Shakespeare, Ibsen and Mr. Bernard
Shaw," LIVING AGE, CCL (1906), 437-40; rptd in INDEPEN-
DENT REVIEW (Lond), X (1906), 83ff [not seen].
The reason modern dramatists have turned away from Shakespeare's
kind of drama is that "they have a different vision of life, determined
by the circumstances of our age." Shaw sees Ibsen as a prophet
because of his revolutionary views, but we need poetry as well as
social criticism in drama.

414 "The Doctor's Dilemma," DT, 21 Nov 1906, p. 9.
Shaw provides a solid scientific scaffolding for The Doctor's
Dilemma, but also reveals that, for once, he can write scenes full of
emotion and tenderness.

415 "Drama: The Week," ATH, No. 4126 (24 Nov 1906), 665.
The Doctor's Dilemma is really a satiric burlesque rather than the
tragedy it purports to be. There is some sort of plot, and Shaw creates "a world of topsy-turvydom and unreason" which his characters
inhabit appropriately.

416 Fitzgerald, Percy. SIR HENRY IRIVING (Lond: T. Fisher
Unwin, 1906), pp. 241-42.
Shaw was wrong in asserting that Irving had actually applied for his
knighthood.

417 "Forbes Robertson Dilates on the Modest Bernard Shaw,"
NYT, 28 Oct 1906, part IV, p. 1.
[An assortment of sundry comments by Johnston Forbes-Robertson
on Shaw and his plays, including Caesar and Cleopatra and Man and
Superman. It focusses particularly on the relationship between
Forbes-Robertson and Shaw in a theatrical context.]

418 Fyfe, H. Hamilton. "The Theatre," WORLD, No. 1691 (27
Nov 1906), 1062.
With The Doctor's Dilemma Shaw has changed his tack, and adopted a
more serious mode; so he is criticized for not adhering to his role of
jester.

419 Fyfe, H. Hamilton. "The Theatre: Brieux and Bernard
Shaw," WORLD, No. 1659 (17 April 1906), 694-95.
Shaw is better than Brieux because he does not bow to the conventions of story telling. He is a discussion–dramatist; any development
in a play takes place in the audience's minds.

420 Fyfe, H. Hamilton. "The Theatre: You Sometimes Can Tell," WORLD, No. 1672 (17 July 1906), 150-51.
Gradual and continued exposure to Shaw's work reveals that there is a purpose behind his paradoxical and wayward humor, as You Never Can Tell proves.

421 "G. B. Shaw May Visit US," NYT, 24 July 1906, p. 7.
Shaw may possibly visit America.

422 "G. Bernard Shaw," OUTLOOK, LXXXIV (1906), 1082.
Dramatic Opinions and Essays is "provokingly quotable" and full of daring paradoxes. Shaw's opinions are impressive in their analysis.

423 "G. Bernard Shaw Sues to Get Book Royalties," NYT, 15 April 1906, p. 22.
[Details of Shaw's suit for $25,000 against his American publishers.]

424 "George Bernard Shaw," ERA, 18 Aug 1906, p. 13.
Shaw's outrageously funny plays amuse, but are not taken seriously. He points out the misery of the oppressed, and asks whether technological progress has improved people. He demolishes such illusions as romance, patriotism and idealism.

425 "German Artists' Exhibition," TIMES, 23 May 1906, p. 5.
Shaw responded to the toast to drama at an inaugural dinner for the German artists' exhibition.

426 Godley, Eveline [C.]. "Drama," THE ANNUAL REGISTER 1905 (Lond: Longmans, Green, 1906), part II, pp. 98-101.
Shaw has suddenly been recognized as a "leading dramatist" and, with Harley Granville-Barker, is one of the most important theatrical men of the year. [References to Man and Superman, How He Lied to Her Husband, You Never Can Tell, and Major Barbara.]

427 Grein, J. T. "Premieres of the Week," STIMES, 25 March 1906, p. 4.
Captain Brassbound's Conversion is "merely a series of debates with incidental melodramatic interludes" which are only padding. The central characters hold our interest.

428 Grein, J. T. "Premieres of the Week," STIMES, 25 Nov 1906, p. 4.
The death scene in The Doctor's Dilemma is a mistake because Shaw's handling of such a solemn event inspires only aversion. The play finally runs awry and ends in a powerful sneer.

429 Greville, Eden. "Bernard Shaw and His Plays," MUNSEY'S MAGAZINE, XXXIV (March 1906), 765-68.
Shaw is a brilliant writer, but not a great playwright because of the careless construction of his plays. [An overview including comments on Widowers' Houses, You Never Can Tell, Candida, Captain Brassbound's Conversion, Mrs. Warren's Profession, Arms and the

Man, The Devil's Disciple, and Man and Superman.]

430 Hankin, St. John. "Puritanism and the English Stage," FORT REV, LXXXVI (Dec 1906), 1055-64; rptd in THE DRAMATIC WORKS OF ST. JOHN HANKIN, 3 vols (Lond: Martin Secker; NY: Mitchell Kennerley, 1912), III, 131-48.

[Passing references to Shaw. Mrs. Warren's Profession is a "courageous statement of a terrible social problem," and Shaw is "almost our only 'serious dramatist.'"]

431 Harrison, Austin. "Mr. Bernard Shaw's New Play," OBS, 25 Nov 1906, p. 11.

The Doctor's Dilemma is a real play marred by "self-conceit, bathos, and errors of good taste . . . Death is always wrong; to use it as a stuffing to cram incongruous pantaloonery down the throats of Philistine Suburbia is wrong artistically."

432 Huneker, James. "A Word on the Dramatic Opinions and Essays of Bernard Shaw," DRAMATIC OPINIONS AND ESSAYS WITH AN APOLOGY BY BERNARD SHAW, vol I (NY: Brentano's, 1906), ix-xix.

Shaw's theatre criticism maintains its vitality, and Shaw himself is that rarity known as an honest man. His prose is buoyant and represents the best of the work, "the very pith of the man."

433 Hunt, Bampton, ed. THE GREEN ROOM BOOK; OR, WHO'S WHO ON THE STAGE (Lond: T. Sealey Clark; NY: Frederick Warne; 4 eds, 1906-09). [Vols for 1908-09 ed by John Parker.]

[Each edition includes a biographical entry on Shaw with other incidental factual information.]

434 "I." "Mr. Shaw's 'Caesar' and the 'Comic Relief,'" HARPER"S WEEKLY, L (17 Nov 1906), 1650.

Caesar and Cleopartra is audaciously daring in its presentation of the two eponymous characters and in its dramatic range.

435 "Impressions of the Theatre: Captain Brassbound's Conversion," REV OF REVS, XXXIII (April 1906), 361-63.

Captain Brassbound's Conversion is a "subtle satire upon the omnipotence of the monopolist" and shows the "potency of indifference."

436 "Impressions of the Theatre.--XIV. (26.)--Mr. Bernard Shaw's Major Barbara," REV OF REVS, XXXIII (Jan 1906), 37-40.

Shaw wants to be a prophet but cannot help being a jester as well: "the soul of Jeremiah is re-incarnated in the body of Grimaldi." Major Barbara is very witty, though marred by some farcical caricatures.

437 "Interesting Shaw Revival," ERA, 14 July 1906, p. 19.

In You Never Can Tell Shaw's "flippancy and superficiality are redeemed by his spontaneous fun, his fertility of invention, his comic side-issues."

438 Judson, Leonard. "Moralizing in the Drama: An Apology for George Bernard Shaw—His Preaching," NYT, 6 April 1906, p. 10.
[Title describes.]

439 Krnic, Ivan. "Bernard Shaw kao dramaticar" (Bernard Shaw as Dramatist), SAVREMENIK (Zagreb), I: 1 (1906), 104-15.
Shaw is either accepted or rejected. He delights by aggressive mockery and disrespect, and spares nobody and nothing. However, he beams with optimism when referring to himself. Shaw's historical plays are entirely modern. He is a literary anarchist, and his "system" consists of no system at all. He stumbles over theatrical conventions, although his dialogue is easy and natural, his invention witty, and his gallery of women admirable. However, his situations are poor, and his characters are undeveloped. [In Croatian.]

440 "Land Nationalization," TIMES, 15 Oct 1906, p. 4.
Shaw has spoken in a debate on the nationalization of land.

441 "Law of Compensation as Applied to Entertainment," NYT, 4 Nov 1906, part IV, p. 2.
Shaw's plays are full of humor and ideas, although they would gain from greater conformity to theatrical rules.

442 "Lecture by Mr. Bernard Shaw," TIMES, 29 June 1906, p. 5.
Shaw has given a lecture entitled "Poisoning the Proletariat."

443 "Literature: [The Irrational Knot]," INDEPENDENT (NY), LX (1906), 1042-43.
Only Shaw could dream up such a revolting denouement as is in The Irrational Knot. He is a "typical mushroom genius. He grows upon what is bad."

444 "THE LITTLE FATHER OF THE WILDERNESS, THE STRENGTH OF THE WEAK, Arms and the Man," NYT, 22 April 1906, part IV, p. 1; rptd in NYTTR 1904-1911, [n. p.].
Arms and the Man is the "merriest of Shaw's comedies" and benefits from good acting.

445 "London Theatres: The Court," STAGE, 22 March 1906, p. 16.
Captain Brassbound's Conversion is typically Shavian, less contentious than Man and Superman or John Bull's Other Island, and is perhaps less amusing as a result.

446 "London Theatres: The Court," STAGE, 12 July 1906, p. 14.
You Never Can Tell is delightfully entertaining, a "characteristically Shawesque mixture of chaff and ethical disquisitions."

447 "London Theatres: The Court," STAGE, 22 Nov 1906, p. 16.
The Doctor's Dilemma lacks dramatic form, balance, perspective, and
is baffling to those who would take Shaw seriously.

448 Loraine, Robert. "Where Does Shaw Leave You?"
COSMOPOLITAN, XL (Jan 1906), 339-44.
Shaw is an iconoclast with wit, humor and insight. His plays create
"utter desolation" as idols are smashed, and existing institutions are
attacked. Man and Superman ends in marriage because "custom is
commonly too strong for the most resolute resolver."

449 MacCarthy, Desmond. "At the Court Theatre: Mr. Bernard
Shaw," SPEAKER, ns XV (24 Nov 1906), 226-27; rptd in Evans,
pp. 168-72.
The Doctor's Dilemma is interesting, amusing, shocking, and irritating. Shaw's satire on the medical profession is not as good as
Molière's because he satirizes what are essentially "contemporary and
temporary types."

450 "Man and Superman," NYT, 7 Jan 1906, part IV, p. 3; rptd
in NYTTR 1904-1911, [n. p.].
Shaw is helping to make the conventionally constructed play outmoded (as with Man and Superman), and he is bringing thought into
the theatre.

451 "Miss Herne's Hit in Shaw Play," NYH, 17 April 1906, p. 9.
[On a revival of Arms and the Man, focussing mainly on the acting.]

452 "Mr. Bernard Shaw on Religion," TIMES, 30 Nov 1906, p.
10.
Shaw has lectured on "Some Necessary Repairs to Religion" to an
audience including G. K. Chesterton, whose questions Shaw answered.

453 "Mr. Bernard Shaw on the Drama," TIMES, 8 March 1906, p.
10.
Shaw has delivered a lecture on drama at a meeting chaired by A. B.
Walkley.

454 "Mr. Bernard Shaw's Play in America," TIMES, 7 July 1906,
p. 8.
An American court has ruled Mrs. Warren's Profession is not indecent
and does not violate the penal code.

455 "Mr. Churchill on Mr. Bernard Shaw," TIMES, 23 Oct 1906,
p. 6.
Shaw's views are rather like a volcano exploding, full of pyrotechnics
with the occasional worthwhile golden glimmer.

456 "Mr. G. B. Shaw and Vivisection," TIMES, 11 May 1906,
p. 9.
Shaw has given an address in which he regards vivisection as a crime.

457 "Mr. Shaw has a New Plan," NYT, 25 Oct 1906, p. 8.
There is a certain charm to Shaw's idea that "nobody has a right to live at all who cannot prove that he does more for the world than the world does for him."

458 Moss, Mary. "Notes on New Novels," ATLANTIC MONTHLY, XCVII (1906), 56.
The Irrational Knot "is the raw, inexperienced venture of an immensely witty person, formless in a way, full of pith, full of promise."

459 "Music and the Drama," DC, 10 Nov 1906, p. 8.
[An interview with Yorke Stephens which details the many roles he has played in Shaw's works.]

460 "Music and the Drama: Bernard Shaw's 'Discussion'—Major Barbara," CUR LIT, XL (Feb 1906), 191-93.
An overview of critical responses to Major Barbara demonstrates Shaw is able to stir up intellectual unrest.

461 "Music and the Drama: Notable Plays of the Month: Caesar and Cleopatra," CUR LIT, XLI (Dec 1906), 651-53.
Caesar and Cleopatra is a triumph, although critical opinion is divided as to whether it is a serious play or merely a clever tour de force.

462 "Not for Shaw, Thank You," NYT, 15 Sept 1906, p. 9.
Marc Klaw has been unsuccessful in attempting to induce Shaw to visit America.

463 "The Playhouses: Captain Brassbound's Conversion at the Court," ILN, CXXVIII (31 March 1906), 442-43.
Without Lady Cicely and Drinkwater, two of Shaw's "most subtly observed and entertaining" characters, Captain Brassbound's Conversion would be a second-hand play. It is a burlesque of hackneyed romantic melodrama.

464 "The Playhouses: You Never Can Tell at the Court," ILN, CXXIX (14 July 1906), 70.
You Never Can Tell is "perhaps the merriest and most exhilarating little comedy" Shaw has ever written.

465 "Plays: Pleasant and Unpleasant," INDEPENDENT (NY), LXI (1906), 396-97.
Shaw's published plays read better than anyone's; however, "unpleasant" is a misnomer for plays which tackle social problems.

466 "The Religion of the British Empire," CHRISTIAN COMMONWEALTH, 29 November 1906 [not seen]; rptd in THE RELIGIOUS SPEECHES OF BERNARD SHAW, ed by Warren Sylvester Smith (University Park, PA: Pennsylvania State UP, 1963), pp. 1-8.
[A report of Shaw's speech.]

467 "Revival at the Court," ERA, 3 Nov 1906, p. 17.
In none of his comedies has Shaw drawn more amusing characters than he has in Man and Superman; the dialogue is brilliant, too.

468 Rhoades, Winfred Chesney. "Is Bernard Shaw among the Prophets?" BIBLIOTHECA SACRA, LXIII (July 1906), 528-41.
Shaw is a destroyer of ideals who becomes a cynic because he cannot find his ideals in the world. Although he has tremendous social passion, he has a hating nature. He fails both as a preacher and as a literary artist. [Brief mention of Mrs. Warren's Profession, "The Revolutionist's Handbook," Man and Superman, Widowers' Houses, The Philanderer, and Candida.]

469 Rogers, Joseph M. "Some Aspects of George Bernard Shaw," LIPPINCOTT'S, LXXXVIII (Oct 1906), 444-53.
Shaw is "sarcastic, audacious and questionable." He sees things jokingly, while his emotionless characters are mere vehicles for his ideas. Shaw emerges as a teacher who plays the clown in order to heard.

470 "Royal Court Theatre," TIMES, 10 July 1906, p. 10.
You Never Can Tell has really good roles.

471 "Says Shaw's Plan Won't Do," NYT, 26 Sept 1906, p. 1.
Shaw's ideas for spelling reform are impractical. [See also in NYT: "An Attack from the Flank" [editorial], 26 Sept 1906, p. 8; W. L. D. O. 'G., "New York—How?" 27 Sept 1906, p. 8.]

472 "Serves Us Right—Shaw," NYT, 27 Aug 1906, p. 7.
Shaw's opinion on American spelling has been sought and given.

473 "Shaw and Forbes Robertson," SUN (NY), 31 Oct 1906, p. 9.
Caesar and Cleopatra is a mixture of dramatic genres and can be tedious at times, especially "much of the talk [that] is out of the Pshaw windbag."

474 "Shaw on Christian Wealth," NYT, 22 Aug 1906, p. 1.
Shaw does not believe that Christians should make fortunes.

475 S[pence], E. F. "The Stage from the Stalls," SKETCH, LIII (28 March 1906), 336.
"Captain Brassbound's Conversion might well be used as a means of breaking-in people to an appreciation of Mr. Shaw, for of all the works of G. B. S., it has the smallest proportion of wilful 'startlers' and the greatest amount of form and story."

476 S[pence], E. F. "The Stage from the Stalls," SKETCH, LV (18 July 1906), 14.
In You Never Can Tell Shaw, like J. M. Barrie, often risks the quality of his work in order to be original. Shaw never stops asking his audience to think.

477 S[pence], E. F. "The Stage from the Stalls," SKETCH, LVI (7 Nov 1906), 110.
Man and Superman, in its abbreviated form, is a "capital farce," although Shaw's works tend to begin to be hackneyed.

478 S[pence], E. F. "The Stage from the Stalls," SKETCH, LVI (28 Nov 1906), 210.
The Doctor's Dilemma is badly proportioned. With Ridgeon and Dubedat Shaw has aimed at subtlety and gone too far; he revels in being misunderstood and in writing puzzling scenes.

479 Walkley, A. B. "Court Theatre," TIMES, 21 Nov 1906, p. 11; rptd in DRAMA AND LIFE (1908; rptd Freeport, NY: Books for Libraries, 1967), pp. 239-244; rptd in THE ENGLISH DRAMATIC CRITICS: AN ANTHOLOGY, 1660-1930, ed by James Agate (Lond: A. Barker, 1932; rptd NY: Hill & Wang, nd), pp. 261-65; rptd in George Rowell, VICTORIAN DRAMATIC CRITICISM (Lond: Methuen, 1971), pp. 316-19.
The Doctor's Dilemma is thoroughly Shavian—stimulating, amusing, distressing, and bewildering.

480 Welch, Catharine. "An Hour at Home with George Bernard Shaw," NYT, 30 Dec 1906, part IV, p. 1.
[An interview.]

481 "Where Barrie and Bernard Shaw Fail," CUR LIT, XL (May 1906), 524.
Shaw and J. M. Barrie are emphemeral because of their sundry shortcomings and limitations.

482 "Young Playgoer." "Grandeur et Décadence de Bernard Shaw" (Grandeur and Decadence of Bernard Shaw), CORNHILL, XCIII (Feb 1906), 237-50.
Although Shaw has contributed greatly to British drama, his plays have serious weaknesses. He purports to deal with major ideas, but the plays really exhibit only two: that women pursue men only for the purpose of having fit fathers for their children, and the reformation of society.

483 Z., X. Y. "The Doctor's Dilemma," SAT REV, CII (1906), 678.
The issue of The Doctor's Dilemma is that an amoral or immoral genius is of infinite worth.

1907

---

484 Alexander, W. F. "A Lord of Misrule," CONTEMPORARY REVIEW (NY), XCII (Nov 1907), 659-71.

Shaw is modern, lacking ancient loyalties and superstitions; he is practical and scientific. As a dramatist, he is serious and satiric. In Candida he attacks the convention that "the poetry of life floats" apart from practical reality. Arms and the Man deflates the image of courage and heroism in war, but not completely successfully. There is wisdom in John Bull's Other Island, while Widowers' Houses and Mrs. Warren's Profession both lack taste and logic. Shaw tends to use the same two characters (himself and a conventional person) repeatedly: Sergius, Valentine, Tanner, Octavius Robinson, and Don Juan are really the same person.

485 Archer, William. "About the Theatre: G. B. S. on the Warpath," TRIBUNE (Lond), No. 372 (23 March 1907), 2.
Shaw has, at last, recognized that as a drama critic he was advocating that playwrights should produce the sort of plays he wanted.

486 Archer, William, and H. Granville Barker. A NATIONAL THEATRE: SCHEME & ESTIMATES (1907; rptd Port Washington, NY & Lond: Kennikat, 1970), pp. ix, xi, 44.
[Shaw, along with some other contemporary dramatists, is excluded from a specimen repertory of plays for a national theatre because his work is "disreputable."]

487 "Art, Music and the Drama: The Playhouses," ILN, CXXXI (30 Nov 1907), 792.
The Devil's Disciple continues to popularize Shaw's theatre of ideas. But not every character is a medium for his views, and some are very human.

488 "At the Play," OBS, 1 Dec 1907, p. 4.
Caesar and Cleopatra is a "pot-pourri of anachronisms, tragedy, burlesque, talk, whimsicality, wit, bathos, snuff-box philosophy, crocodile humour, Fabian platonics, platitude, heroics, and pretty, pretty Cleopatastric pantaloonery, more or less brilliant, weak and indifferent."

489 "At the Play: Don Juan in Hell at the Court," OBS, 9 June 1907, p. 11.
Don Juan in Hell is a provocative "freak of wit," but not a play, merely a "battle of dialectics." The Man of Destiny is too long and verbose.

490 B[aughan], E. A. [Caesar and Cleopatra], DN, 26 Nov 1907, p. 7 [not seen] ; rptd in Evans, pp. 182-83.
Caesar and Cleopatra is dull and foolish but with moments of greatness. It is pure burlesque.

491 Baumann, Arthur A. "Mr. Shaw Run to Waste," SAT REV, CIV (1907), 662-63.
Shaw's view of history in Caesar and Cleopatra is perfectly acceptable.

492 Beerbohm, Max. "G. B. S. Again," SAT REV, CIII (1907), 713; rptd in LAST THEATRES, pp. 296-99.
Don Juan in Hell reveals all Shaw's genius and agility of mind. The Man of Destiny is a careless piece of work and tedious.

493 Beerbohm, Max. "G. B. S. Republished," SAT REV, CIII (1907), 518-19; rptd in LAST THEATRES, pp. 292-95.
In Dramatic Opinions and Essays Shaw makes every word tell forcibly, even if ultimately his essays must be judged as journalism only.

494 Beerbohm, Max. "Mr. Vedrenne," SAT REV, CIV (1907), 508-10; rptd in AROUND THEATRES, pp. 618-22.
The Devil's Disciple remains as fresh as ever, "as witty a comedy, as vigorous a melodrama, as wayward and jolly an ebullition of Mr. Shaw's peculiar genius."

495 Beerbohm, Max. "The Philanderer," SAT REV, CIII (1907), 166; rptd in AROUND THEATRES, pp. 576-79.
The Philanderer belongs to either the 1890s or the 1920s; at the moment it is dull, flat, stale, and lifeless.

496 "Bernard Shaw as Dramatic Critic," CUR LIT, XLII (Jan 1907), 71-72.
The publication of Dramatic Opinions and Essays shows what a remarkable and startling drama critic Shaw was.

497 "Bernard Shaw Makes a Discovery," NYT, 9 June 1907, part III, p. 1.
Shaw has declared that charity wastes millions and what the poor suffer from is poverty.

498 "Bernard Shaw Nearer in Spirit to Americans than to Englishmen," NYT, 18 Aug 1907, part V, p. 7; rptd in NEWS AND OBSERVER (Raleigh, NC), 25 Aug 1907 [not seen].
[An account of Archibald Henderson's impressions of Shaw.]

499 "Bernard Shaw on American Women," COSMOPOLITAN, XLIII (Sept 1907), 557-61.
[An interview.]

500 "Bernard Shaw's Latest," NYT, 13 July 1907, pp. 437-38.
In Major Barbara Shaw is a true seer and radical, who employs paradox to make his point.

501 "Bernard Shaw's Religion," CUR LIT, XLII (Feb 1907), 198-200.
Shaw's address from the pulpit of London's City Temple demonstrated his moral seriousness.

502 "Bernard Shaw's Solution to the Problem of Evil," CUR LIT, XLIII (Aug 1907), 191-92.
Shaw, who is always paradoxical and puzzling, has now posed the

question of whether God is attempting to produce something higher (rather than lower) than Himself.

503 Boynton, H. W. "Mr. Shaw as Critic," ATLANTIC MONTHLY, XCIX (1907), 553-60.
Dramatic Opinions and Essays reveals Shaw's sincerity and integrity, and it cannot be dismissed out of hand however much people may dislike other aspects and characteristics of the man.

504 Broutá, Julio. "Bernard Shaw," DE ARMAS TOMAR (To Take Arms) (Madrid: Velasco, 1907), pp. 5-13 [not seen].
[Cited in Rodríguez (MS). In Spanish.]

505 Broutá, Julio. "Prefacio" (Preface), NON OLET (Madrid: Velasco, 1907), pp. v-vi [not seen].
[Cited in Rodríguez (MS). In Spanish.]

506 Broutá, Julio. "Prefacio" (Preface), TRATA DE BLANCAS (White Slavery) (Madrid: Velasco, 1907), pp. v-viii [not seen].
[Cited in Rodríguez (MS). In Spanish].

507 "Caesar and Cleopatra: Savoy Theatre," DT, 26 Nov 1907, p. 12.
Caesar and Cleopatra is bleak and arid in spirit, avoids romance and sentiment, and does not adhere to history. Its purpose is serious.

508 "The Case of the Poets versus Shaw," CUR LIT, XLIII (July 1907), 81-83.
Shaw, who for so long has scorned the drama of poets as romantic and untrue, is now being attacked by such poets as Richard Le Gallienne, Arthur Symons, and Alfred Noyes.

509 "The Constructive Side of Bernard Shaw's Philosophy," CUR LIT, XLIII (Dec 1907), 647-50.
Shaw usually wears a comic mask, but behind that lies an all-pervasive thinker and philosopher.

510 "Coronet Theatre," TIMES, 17 Sept 1907, p. 7.
Captain Brassbound's Conversion is full of characters drawn from life.

511 "Court Theatre: The Philanderer," DT, 6 Feb 1907, p. 6.
If The Philanderer proves anything it is that the Ibsenites were rather silly and the older generation quite sane.

512 Dawson, Albert. "Day by Day: Mr. G. Bernard Shaw's New Theology," CHRISTIAN COMMONWEALTH, XXVII (30 May 1907), 618.
It is difficult to accept Shaw's theology of a benevolent but fallible force behind the cosmos. However, it is clear that Shaw is genuinely religious and profoundly earnest.

513 "Dinner to Mr. Vedrenne and Mr. Barker," TIMES, 8 July

1907, p. 11.
Shaw responded to the toast to the authors of the Court Theatre.

514 "Don Juan in Hell," ERA, 8 June 1907, p. 13.
Shaw "can apparently use any theme for his favourite pursuit of
baiting the Briton, and the more audaciously he brings the weaknesses
of his audiences before them the greater is the welcome extended to
their portrayal." Both Don Juan in Hell and The Man of Destiny prove
very popular.

515 "Drama and Music." NATION (NY), LXXXV (1907), 19-20.
The prefaces to John Bull's Other Island and Major Barbara are worth
reading for what they reveal about Shaw's mental processes. However, the book has more bulk than substance.

516 "The Drama: Don Juan in Hell," TLS, No. 282 (7 June 1907),
181.
Don Juan in Hell is altogether too long; The Man of Destiny is also
too prolix.

517 "Drama: The Week," ATH, No. 4137 (9 Feb 1907), 175.
The Shaw cult is waning: The Philanderer is outdated and its brilliant
dialogue cannot gloss over the play's lack of meaning.

518 "Drama: The Week," ATH, No. 4169 (21 Sept 1907), 344.
You Never Can Tell is the most humane and merry piece in the Shaw
repertory.

519 "Drama: The Week," ATH, No. 4179 (30 Nov 1907), 699.
Caesar and Cleopatra is really opera-bouffe which runs away with
itself.

520 [Dramatic Opinions and Essays], DIAL, XLII (1907), 13.
Shaw's theatre criticism was sparkling when written, but hardly
substantial enough to warrant publication in permanent form.

521 "Ellen Terry as the Shaw Man," SUN (NY), 29 Jan 1907, p.
7.
Captain Brassbound's Conversion is superficially realistic and
scientific, but in fact it mingles "picturesque, improbable adventures
and farcically topical, deliciously exaggerated, wit."

522 "Ellen Terry Welcomed in Comedy by Shaw," NYT, 29 Jan
1907, p. 9; rptd in NYTTR 1904-1911, [n. p.].
Captain Brassbound's Conversion is a satire on the British judiciary
and could benefit from more conformity to dramatic rules.

523 E[llis], Anthony L. "The Theatre," WORLD, No. 1719 (11
June 1907), 1063.
Don Juan in Hell is a remarkable, if excessively lengthy, discussion
which lacks "dramatic energy." The Man of Destiny's worth is nulli-
fied by poor acting.

524 Ellis, Anthony L. "The Theatre," WORLD, No. 1744 (3 Dec 1907), 942.

Caesar and Cleopatra is better to read than to see largely because of the omission of a whole act.

525 "England's Railway Crisis," NYT, 22 Sept 1907, part III, p. 4.

Shaw has taken to task the directors of the railroads for their imbecilic and discourteous attitude during the current crisis.

526 Farr, Florence. "G. B. S. and New York," NEW AGE I: 4 (May 1907), 57.

There are certain affinities between Shaw and New York City, both can be aggressive, brutal, and poetic.

527 "Femina." [Shaw], LE FIGARO, 3 Oct 1907.

Shaw's function is to make people think after making them laugh. He offers sincere discussion of problems. [In French.]

528 Fyfe, H. Hamilton. "Dr. Shaw's Black Draught," WORLD, No. 1702 (12 Feb 1907), 268.

The Philanderer is an amusing and a depressing play, but it does force people to examine carefully their behavior in their relationships with others.

529 Fyfe, H. Hamilton. "The Theatre," WORLD, No. 1734 (24 Sept 1907), 505.

Shaw, in You Never Can Tell, provides amusing, ingenious, thought-stimulating characters, but they can hardly be called life-like. Rather they are so many "little Bernard Shaws."

530 Fyfe, H. Hamilton. "The Theatre," WORLD, No. 1738 (22 Oct 1907), 668.

The Devil's Disciple is as remote from reality as any melodrama, but the ideas are provocative and unconventional.

531 "G. B. Shaw's View of His Biography," NYT, 17 Aug 1907, p. 7.

[Details of Archibald Henderson interviewing Shaw for his biography.]

532 "Gentility Fatal to Progress—Shaw," NYT, 18 Aug 1907, part III, p. 3.

Shaw believes that the Labour Party's Members of Parliament are becoming perfect gentlemen and thereby hindering progress.

533 Gilman, Lawrence. "Mr. Shaw's New Volume of Plays," NORTH AMERICAN REVIEW, CLXXXVI (1907), 284-88.

John Bull's Other Island (and other plays) shows Shaw is poetic, intense, sensitive, and a moralist with an "inextinguishable sense of comedy."

534 Godley, Eveline C. "Drama," THE ANNUAL REGISTER 1906 (Lond: Longmans, Green, 1907), part II, 100-04.
The Doctor's Dilemma is not as good a play as Major Barbara or John Bull's Other Island. Shaw has apparently determined to "use the most hackneyed devices of stage pathos and work them triumphantly into an original effect."

535 Grein, J. T. "Premieres of the Week," STIMES, 10 Feb 1907, p. 4.
The Philanderer is outdated, and even "when it was topical it was a play of little account—Shaw's only and complete failure."

536 Grein, J. T. "Premieres of the Week," STIMES, 9 June 1907, p. 4.
If people fail to understand Shaw in Don Juan in Hell, the fault is their's not his. He knows what he is talking about.

537 Grein, J. T. "Premieres of the Week," STIMES, 20 Oct 1907, p. 4.
The Devil's Disciple, with its varying styles, shows Shaw is never fettered by any particular convention.

538 Grein, J. T. "Premieres of the Week," STIMES, 1 Dec 1907, p. 4
Caesar and Cleopatra attempts to dethrone classical romantic tragedy and replace it with the new drama. However, this burlesque fails when the printed words are transferred to the theatre.

539 H[ankin], St. J[ohn]. [John Bull's Other Island and Major Barbara], ACADEMY, LXXII (29 June 1907), 621
Both John Bull's Other Island and Major Barbara are badly constructed and too long.

540 Hankin, St. John. "Mr. Bernard Shaw as Critic," FORTNIGHTLY REVIEW (NY), LXXXVII (June 1907), 1061-66; rptd in THE DRAMATIC WORKS OF ST. JOHN HANKIN, 3 vols (Lond: Martin Secker; NY: Mitchell Kennerley, 1912), III, 149-70; rptd in part in Evans, pp. 173-74.
In Dramatic Opinions and Essays Shaw proves himself to be one of the ablest critics of the theatre. He is likewise "as acute a critic of his own works as he is of the works of others," and "his dramatic criticisms are sermons," not the work of a jester. His weaknesses as a critic were that he was interested in only one kind of play, and unfair to those which did not interest him. His stance as a reformer and propagandist led to biased opinions because of his intolerance towards theatre which merely entertained.

541 Harrison, Austin. "At the Play," OBS, 10 Feb 1907, p. 4.
The Philanderer is out of date and so somewhat tiresome, if amusingly so. It is essentially a well-constructed British comedy full of talk.

542 H[arrison], A[ustin]. "The Devil's Disciple: Mr. Shaw's 'Diabolonian' Play at the Savoy," OBS, 20 Oct 1907, p. 4.
The Devil's Disciple is the closest thing to a conventional play Shaw has written and is potentially a melodrama in the vein of Sardou.

543 "Hearty Greeting to Miss Ellen Terry," NYH, 29 Jan 1907, p. 10.
Captain Brassbound's Conversion is not a brilliant play, being full of long speeches and not very good humor.

544 Henderson, Archibald. "George Bernard Shaw," NORTH AMERICAN REVIEW, CLXXXV (1907), 293-305; rptd in DEUTSCHE REVUE, XXXII (Aug 1907), 180-85.
There is now a wide range of evidence to demonstrate Shaw is "the most versatile and cosmopolitan genius in the drama of ideas that Great Britain has yet produced."

545 Henslowe, L[eonard]. "George Bernard Shaw as a Vegetarian," GOOD HOUSEKEEPING, XLV (Oct 1907), 370-73 [not seen].

546 Henslowe, Leonard. "Just What Mr. Bernard Shaw Eats & Drinks," HEALTH AND STRENGTH, 28 November 1907 [not seen].

547 "Herald Square: Widowers' Houses," THEATRE MAGAZINE (NY), VII (April 1907), 90, xii.
Widowers' Houses still provokes, pretends to point a moral, but does not. Shaw indicates the ills in society but fails to give a remedy.

548 "I." "Mrs. Warren, and the Klondike," HARPER'S WEEKLY, LI (30 March 1907), 472.
Mrs. Warren's Profession is no longer the cause of sensation and everyone knows its theme. The latter is really unsuitable for dramatic presentation.

549 "Ireland," TIMES, 11 Oct 1907, p. 12.
In a speech in Dublin, H. B. Tree has called Caesar and Cleopatra a play of a great Irishman who, as a dramatist, always dares to tell the truth.

550 Jackson, Holbrook. BERNARD SHAW (Lond: Grant Richards, 1907).
Shaw is an unconventional, grown-up enfant terrible who is both sincere and witty, even though he does possess a bewildering egotism. In practical politics he is a Fabian socialist, although he cannot be rigidly pigeonholed as such. He believes that socialism can be achieved through the fabric of society without the need for bloody revolution. His Fabian tracts reveal his whimsical sense of humor being applied to a factual and commonsense view of social problems. But he is out of patience with modern economics.

Shaw is a philosopher-preacher first and foremost, and an artist second. Art for him is good workmanship, and his plays are the modern equivalent of the medieval morality plays. He is critical of society and believes that the theatre is the temple of life. Drama, for Shaw, should embody genuine human action and express life realistically, without any romantic illusions. Mrs. Warren's Profession and Widowers' Houses are dramatized social science, while in You Never Can Tell and Candida Shaw creates beings who both embody and interpret ideas. But Shaw is always philosophizing, and his characters tend to be merely extensions of himself. Discussion is the main ingredient in his plays (e.g., Major Barbara) and there is little action.

Shaw thinks of himself as a philosopher, and his originality lies in the organic relationship between his ideas and the actions of ordinary men and women. He believes philosophy must be applied to life to have any meaning. Central to his philosophy is the Life Force which is a "world willing itself towards ampler certainty of its end." Shaw has faith in this somewhat blundering force, which depends on man, and therefore should be assisted by man. But Shaw also revolts against the way life treats man, and this is profoundly sane. Man must realize the trend of the life force because this will make man valuable. All in all, Shaw is benevolent and human. [Descriptive rather than critical or analytical.]

551 [Knight, Joseph]. "Drama: John Bull's Other Island," ATH, No. 4161 (27 July 1907), 107-08; rptd in Evans, pp. 175-76.
Shaw's prefaces are "but journalistic essays." The plays, for example John Bull's Other Island, Major Barbara, The Philanderer, live only by their ideas, and when those lose their topicality, Shaw the revolutionary may become old fashioned.

552 Krans, Horatio S. "Three Distinguished Critics," PUTNAM'S MONTHLY, I (March 1907), 754-55.
Dramatic Opinions and Essays demonstrates Shaw is no Lessing, but his views are frank and honest, and as a dramatic critic Shaw is sui generis.

553 "Leeds: Grand Theatre," ERA, 21 Sept 1907, p. 10.
[Largely an account of the accomplished acting in Caesar and Cleopatra.]

554 "London has a New Mystery," NYT, 15 Feb 1907, p. 10.
Shaw has lent his support to the suffragettes in London, but their current course of action is not entirely clear.

555 "London Theatres: The Court," STAGE, 7 Feb 1907, p. 16.
The Philanderer now seems stale and "less brilliantly witty and entertainingly paradoxical" than Candida or John Bull's Other Island.

556 "London Theatres: The Court," STAGE, 6 June 1907, p. 16.
Don Juan in Hell is full of speechifying, and the only really dramatic moment comes when Dona Ana accustoms herself to Hell. The Man of Destiny is much more like a play.

557 "London Theatres: The Savoy," STAGE, 28 Nov 1907, pp. 17-18.
Caesar and Cleopatra is a "huge and tortuous joke"; it also attempts to humanize the historical play, to remove the artificial and conventional elements from such pieces. Shaw's prejudices creep in with his handling of Cleopatra.

558 M., C. E. "The Playgoers' Theatre," MANCHESTER GUARDIAN, 8 Oct 1907, p. 6.
Widowers' Houses is Shaw's least successful play and no longer scandalizes.

559 MacCarthy, Desmond. THE COURT THEATRE 1904-1907: A COMMENTARY AND CRITICISM (Lond: A. H. Bullen, 1907), pp. xi-xiii, 5-6, 8-9, 14, 16, 47-118, 123-25, 127, 129, 131-32, 135-40, 143, 145-46, 151, 154-55, 158-59, 161-62, 168-69; pp. 47-118 rptd in MacCarthy, pp. 3-24, 28-40, 44-72, 77-79, 84-89; rptd in part in George Rowell, VICTORIAN DRAMATIC CRITICISM (Lond: Methuen, 1971), pp. 314-16.
Shaw's characters are exceptionally varied and vivid, and capture the essence of real people. He demonstrates that people are basically ruled by the same impulses and that these stem from social circumstances. His characters possess a lyrical quality of temperament which is infused with excitement and urgency, and Shaw uses this often to express sexual emotion. However, "his principal intellectual failing . . . is to exaggerate the stupidity of mankind." Candida is one of Shaw's best plays because it has a sustained focus. Although it adheres to no theatrical rules, John Bull's Other Island is also very successful. You Never Can Tell has no story, and the interest lies solely in its characters. Man and Superman is Shaw's most brilliant piece of work, while the merit of Captain Brassbound's Conversion consists of its ability to provoke serious thought and laughter simultaneously. How He Lied to Her Husband is unimportant, and The Man of Destiny is too mechanical in its psychology. The Doctor's Dilemma, despite some delightful satire, fails to maintain plausibility and so weakens Shaw's purpose. The Philanderer is a "queer piece of work," while in Major Barbara Shaw reveals his impatience by abandoning persuasion for bullying. [With detailed discussion of plots and reproductions of playbills of the Court Theatre productions.]

560 "Man and Superman Revived," ERA, 1 June 1907, p. 15.
Even without the "Don Juan in Hell" episode, Man and Superman is "Shaw on the stump."

561 Manager (TIMES Book Club). "Books and the Public,"

TIMES, 24 Sept 1907, p. 6.
The TIMES Book Club acted in good faith towards John Bull's Other Island, despite Shaw's charges [in TIMES, 23 Sept 1907, p. 6].

562 "The Meek and Lowly Shaw," NYT, 17 Nov 1907, part III, p. 1.
Shaw has declared he will write no more plays for two years and then produce his masterpiece.

563 "Meeting of the Authors' Society," TIMES, 21 March 1907, p. 11.
[An account of the meeting to discuss a dispute between the TIMES and publishers and booksellers. Shaw's, and others', comments recorded. See also Shaw's letter, TIMES, 25 March 1907, p. 12.]

564 Michaud, Régis. "Bernard Shaw," LA REVUE DE PARIS (Sept-Oct 1907) [not seen].
[In French.]

565 "Misadventure to Mr. Bernard Shaw," TIMES, 10 Sept 1907, p. 8.
Shaw got lost while hiking in Wales and spent the night wandering the hills.

566 "Mr. Bernard Shaw and Dr. Nordau," JEWISH WORLD, LXIX (20 Dec 1907), 6.
Shaw is really sympathetic towards Jewry, despite recent reports to the contrary. [Also includes details of correspondence between Shaw and Max Nordau.]

567 "Mr. Bernard Shaw and Female Clerks," TIMES, 22 Nov 1907, p. 8.
Shaw has addressed a meeting (largely of women) in support of greater financial and political security for women.

568 "Mr. Bernard Shaw and the Jews," TIMES, 20 Dec 1907, p. 9.
Shaw has written to defend himself against charges of anti-Semitism brought by Dr. Max Nordau.

569 "Mr. Bernard Shaw's Dramatic Criticisms," SPECTATOR, XCVIII (13 April 1907), 567-68.
Dramatic Opinions and Essays shows how Shaw brought about change in the theatre. His principles are clear, although one could not have forecast his manner of applying them to other playwrights such as Pinero and H. A. Jones.

570 "Mr. Bernard Shaw's Philanderer at the Court," ILN, CXXX (9 Feb 1907), 202.
The Philanderer contains no thematic surprises as Shaw reworks his Schopenhauerian theories of woman as the eternal hunter of man.

571 "Mr. Forbes-Robertson in Leeds: Caesar and Cleopatra," YORKSHIRE POST, 17 Sept 1907, p. 6; rptd in Evans, pp. 177-79.

Shaw's portrayal of Caesar in Caesar and Cleopatra is sacrilegious, and many of his speeches end in mere bathos. The play is really comic opera, and Shaw is constantly ironic and merely manipulates his puppets for satirical purposes.

572 "Mr. G. Bernard Shaw's New Play," MPOST, 26 Nov 1907, p. 7; rptd in Evans, pp. 183-84.

The chief flaw of Caesar and Cleopatra is Shaw's portrayal of Caesar which is simply not credible.

573 "Mr. Shaw and the Censorship," ERA, 23 Nov 1907, p. 21.

Shaw argues well about stage censorship, but gets his facts wrong.

574 "Mr. Shaw as Dramatic Critic," TLS, No. 274 (12 April 1907), 117-18.

Although the drama of the 1890s is largely forgotten, Shaw's Dramatic Opinions and Essays brings them back to life, albeit through Shaw's biased eyes. The reviews are earnest and sane, with an air of religious fervor.

575 "Mrs. Warren's Profession," NYT, 10 March 1907, p. 9; rptd in NYTTR 1904-1911, [n. p.].

A revival of Mrs. Warren's Profession has failed to produce the excitement of its American premiere.

576 "Mrs. Warren's Profession," SUN (NY), 10 March 1907, part I, p. 5.

Mrs. Warren's Profession is neither wicked nor diverting.

577 Mulliken, Clara A. "Reading List on Modern Dramatists; D'Annunzio, Hauptmann, Ibsen, Maeterlinck, Phillips, Rostand, Shaw and Sudermann," BULLETIN OF BIBLIOGRAPHY, V (Oct 1907), 52-53; rptd and revd as Mrs. Clara Norton [Mulliken], Frank K. Walter, and Fanny Elsie Marquand, MODERN DRAMA AND OPERA: A READING LIST ON THE WORKS OF D'ANNUNZIO, HAUPTMANN, IBSEN, JONES, MAETERLINCK, PHILLIPS, PINERO, ROSTAND, SHAW, SUDERMANN AND OF DEBUSSY, PUCCINI, RICHARD STRAUSS (Bost: Boston Book Co, 1911), pp. 61-66.

[A critically annotated bibliography of primary and secondary works.]

578 "Music and the Drama: Major Barbara—Bernard Shaw's New Apotheosis of Money," CUR LIT, XLIII (Aug 1907), 193-98.

[A plot synopsis with extracts of the text.]

579 "National Art Collections Fund," TIMES, 26 April 1907, p. 9.

Shaw has spoken on the inadequacy of the National Art Collections Fund which suffers from underfinancing.

580 N[ewton], H[enry] C[hance]. "Mr. Forbes-Robertson on the Censor, and Caesar, and Other Matters," REFEREE, No. 1581 (1 Dec 1907), 2.
[An interview with Forbes-Robertson, who thought Caesar and Cleopatra a remarkable, though not well-made play, full of brilliant thoughts.]

581 Nordau, Max. "Open Letter to Bernard Shaw," FRANKFURTER ZEITUNG, 24 Nov 1907 [not seen].
[Shaw's reply printed 14 Dec 1907.]

582 Noyes, Alfred. "Mr. Shaw's Antics" [source unknown; 1907]; rptd BOOKMAN (Lond), LXXXVII (Dec 1934), 206-07.
[A very hostile review of Dramatic Opinions and Essays.]

583 Payne, George Henry. "George Bernard Shaw as Critic" NY TELEGRAM, 6 April 1907 [not seen]; rptd INDEPENDENT SHAVIAN, XI: 1 (1973), 4.
Shaw seems radical and brilliant when first read, but almost false in retrospect—as the publication of Dramatic Opinions and Essays shows.

584 "Pendennis." "Arnold Daly to Promote Theatre of Ideas," NYT, 18 Aug 1907, part V, p. 7.
[An account of Arnold Daly's planned repertoire which included several of Shaw's plays.]

585 "The Philanderer," ERA, 9 Feb 1907, p. 15.
The Philanderer depends on its amusing ideas; the Ibsen allusions are somewhat stale.

586 "The Playhouse," TIMES , 29 Jan 1907, p 10.
[Brief mention of The Interlude at the Playhouse.]

587 "The Playhouse Opening," ERA, 2 Feb 1907, p. 17.
The Interlude at the Playhouse is a clever and amusing duologue.

588 "The Playhouse: Opening of Mr. Maude's Theatre," STAGE, 31 Jan 1907, p. 17.
The Interlude at the Playhouse is characteristically cynical.

589 "The Playhouses: A Bernard Shaw Afternoon at the Court," ILN, CXXX (8 June 1907), 862.
Don Juan in Hell is mental gymnastics, lacking drama and emotion. This witty discussion is interesting in the study but not the theatre.

590 "The Playhouses: Caesar and Cleopatra at the Savoy," ILN, CXXXI (30 Nov 1907), 778.
Caesar and Cleopatra is "an amusing but odd sort of entertainment."

591 "The Playhouses: The Devil's Disciple at the Savoy," ILN, CXXXI (19 Oct 1907), 546.
The Devil's Disciple is a burlesque melodrama which parodies stock romantic and sentimental situations.

592 "The Playhouses: You Never Can Tell at the Court," ILN, CXXX (16 Feb 1907), 246.
Only John Bull's Other Island can compete with You Never Can Tell; the latter is a "merry little play" and the most humane of Shaw's works.

593 "The Playhouses: You Never Can Tell at the Savoy," ILN, CXXXI (21 Sept 1907), 402.
You Never Can Tell is Shaw's brightest comedy.

594 "Prevention of Infant Mortality," TIMES, 2 July 1907, p. 8.
Shaw contributed a letter and his support to a conference on the prevention of infant mortality.

595 "Provincial Productions: Caesar and Cleopatra," STAGE, 19 Sept 1907, p. 22.
Although Caesar and Cleopatra is a historical play, it seems more like a burlesque. "Shaw has surpassed himself in the matter of flippancy, and extravagance of motif."

596 "Sardou and Shaw Plays Presented," NYH, 8 March 1907, p. 10.
Although Widowers' Houses may not be a protypical Broadway play, its grim theme is leavened with humor and benefits from an excellent cast.

597 "The Savoy," STAGE 19 Sept 1907, p. 18.
You Never Can Tell is "one of the lightest and most genuinely entertaining" of Shaw's plays.

598 "The Savoy," STAGE, 17 Oct 1907, pp. 18-19.
The Devil's Disciple is an "odd piece in which [Shaw] wrapped in a coating of old-style heroic melodrama his patent pills of satirical extravaganza or ironic burlesque."

599 "Savoy—The Devil's Disciple," ATH, No. 4173 (19 Oct 1907), 492.
The Devil's Disciple is a parody of melodrama.

600 "Savoy Theatre," TIMES, 17 Sept 1907, p. 7.
You Never Can Tell is "madcap fun" even if there is just a little too much of it.

601 "Savoy Theatre," TIMES, 15 Oct 1907, p. 9.
The form of The Devil's Disciple is old-fashioned melodrama, but everything else is new and unfamiliar.

602 "Savoy Theatre," TIMES, 31 Dec 1907, p. 8.

Shaw has gone a long way since writing Arms and the Man, but nothing he has produced is more exhilarating and light-hearted.

603 "Savoy Theatre: Caesar and Cleopatra," TIMES, 26 Nov 1907, p. 5; rptd in Evans, pp. 178-81.
Caesar and Cleopatra is very similar to an Offenbach comic opera and, for all its modernity, is really the "old, old burlesque producing its old laughs in its old way."

604 "Savoy Theatre: The Devil's Disciple," DT, 15 Oct 1907, p. 6.
The Devil's Disciple may have "subtle and elusive psychology" in it, but it remains a melodrama "tempered by exuberant farce." The plot could be convincing if Shaw refrained from interjecting his own personality into the play.

605 "Shakespeare and Caesar," ERA, 30 Nov 1907, p. 23.
Caesar and Cleopatra is amusing, but contains no new philosophy, and in itself refutes Shaw's attacks on Shakespeare.

606 "Shaw Admits Guilt as Man of Wealth," NYT, 20 Oct 1907, part III, p. 3.
Shaw says he is guilty about his wealth, but promises to dispose of it according to socialist principles—if the socialists ever gain control.

607 "Shaw and Melodrama," ERA, 20 April 1907, p. 19.
In Dramatic Opinions and Essays Shaw is sometimes coarse and sometimes "amusingly slangy." Shaw has a limited vision because he fails to realize how small is his audience of philosophers. What draws people to his plays is the sight-seer's curiosity.

608 "Shaw and Super-Shaw," DT, 5 June 1907, p. 13.
Don Juan in Hell is a long rambling philosophical treatise on numerous subjects, and is a debate or sermon rather than a play. The Man of Destiny, if judiciously cut, would be an admirable curtain-raiser.

609 "Shaw and the Slum Landlord," SUN (NY), 8 March 1907, p. 9.
Widowers' Houses's theme is still timely for New York, but the characters are contemptible. Moreover, it lacks the mixture of Shaw's humor and satire.

610 "Shaw at the Savoy," ERA, 20 July 1907, p. 19.
A Shaw season at the Court Theatre will be interesting because Shaw is a phenomenon. Shaw's philosophy may be contemptible to some, but now that W. S. Gilbert has retired Shaw is the only dramatic humorist.

611 "Shaw at the Savoy," ERA, 19 Oct 1907, p. 17.
The Devil's Disciple shows Shaw has studied American history carefully. His serious characters are "boldly and spiritedly drawn,"

while the lighter ones prove amusing.

612 "Shaw Attacks the Selfish Landlord," NYT, 8 March 1907, p. 9; rptd in NYTTR 1904-1911, [n. p.].
Widowers' Houses is less theoretical than most Shaw plays, and his incidents and characters are more generally recognizably human.

613 "Shaw Encounters His Biographer," NYT, 23 June 1907, part III, p. 3.
[Details of Shaw's encounter with Archibald Henderson.]

614 "Shaw Leads His Disciples a Chase," NYT, 15 Sept 1907, part III, p. 3.
[An account of Shaw getting lost in the Welsh mountains.]

615 "Shaw Meets Twain and Explains Him," NYT, 19 June 1907, p. 1.
[An account of the meeting between Shaw and S. L. Clemens.]

616 "Shaw's Imitation of Shaw," CUR LIT, XLII (Jan 1907), 69.
In The Doctor's Dilemma Shaw succeeds only in producing a poor imitation of his earlier dramaturgical powers.

617 "Shaw's Next Play to be on Marriage," NYT, 22 Sept 1907, part III, p. 2.
[Title describes, with other brief details of productions of Shaw's plays.]

618 "Shaw's Plans for a Queer New Party," NYT, 25 Aug 1907, part III, p. 1.
Shaw has outlined his plans for setting up a new political party.

619 Simpson, H. "Bernard Shaw's Political Allegory," BOOKMAN (NY), XXVI (Nov 1907), 307-09.
In Major Barbara Shaw again uses an improbable plot merely as a vehicle for his "peculiar ideas." It is an allegory for the successive shifts in political/class power in England.

620 "The Socialist Movement," TIMES, 18 Oct 1907, p. 8.
Shaw has discoursed on "How the Middle Class is Fleeced."

621 "Society of Authors," TIMES, 9 May 1907, p. 11.
Shaw responded to the toast to the Drama at the Society's annual dinner.

622 S[pence], E. F. "The Stage from the Stalls," SKETCH, LVII (13 Feb 1907), 140.
Shaw has progressed a long way since the first production of The Philanderer.

623 S[pence], E. F. "The Stage from the Stalls," SKETCH, LVIII (12 June 1907), 266.
Don Juan in Hell is "merely a kind of costume quartet-lecture," full

of ideas and "living thoughts." The Man of Destiny is clever, injudicious and tiresome.

624 S[pence], E. F. "The Stage from the Stalls," SKETCH, LX (23 Oct 1907), 42.

We should be grateful for the merits of The Devil's Disciple and overlook its faults. Shaw tries to introduce human nature into the play, but fails, and the piece "displays the ill-balanced genius of a man of ideas."

625 Spender, J. A. "Mr. Shaw's Prefaces," NINETEENTH CENTURY, LXII (1907), 852-64.

In his prefaces to John Bull's Other Island and Major Barbara, Shaw often strains his argument by attempting to balance one paradox with another. They contain many admirable passages, but Shaw's ironic spirit forces him, regrettably, to encompass less worthy causes.

626 "A Sprightly Preface by Mr. Shaw," NYT, 13 July 1907, p. 442.

"First Aid to Critics" [Major Barbara] reveals a new sincere Shaw who does not suffer fools gladly, and who indulges in less levity.

627 "Theatre Royal: Mr. Forbes Robertson's Visit," MANCHESTER COURIER, 19 Nov 1907, p. 8.

Caesar and Cleopatra is a curious amalgam of history and farce combined with Shavian philosophy. It is rather long and needs judicious cutting.

628 "Theatrical Censorship," NYT, 9 July 1907, p. 6.

Shaw's proposed system of theatrical licensing has some merits.

629 "Three New Shaw Plays," INDEPENDENT (NY), LXIII (1907), 879-80.

Readers of Shaw's plays have the advantage of Shaw's long and witty prefaces.

630 "Vedrenne-Barker at the Savoy," ERA, 21 Sept 1907, p. 17.

You Never Can Tell is a "series of trivial episodes illustrated by many excellent jokes, its want of form and purpose being more than compensated for by the delicious subtlety of its comedy scenes."

631 V[engerova?], Z. "Bernard Shaw: John Bull's Other Island and Major Barbara," VIESTNIK EVROPY (St. Petersburg), XLII: 5 (1-15 Sept 1907), 411-20.

Shaw is popular in England, although he does not submit to public taste—quite the contrary, he is "fashionable." One may or may not agree with his views, but they are always interesting. He is a keen psychologist and satirist. The conflicts in his plays are always much the same: a dreamer against a strong individual. The former are in the right, but so are those who have practical aims and achieve them. [With detailed plot synopses of John Bull's Other Island, and Major

Barbara. In Russian.]

632 Webb, Sidney. "Socialist 'Facts,' " TIMES, 22 Oct 1907, p. 4.
[Webb supports Shaw's statistics on Londoners and their expenditures, given at a recent lecture. See also, "Your Reporter," TIMES, 22 Oct 1907, p. 4.]

633 "Woman Suffrage," TIMES, 27 March 1907, p. 10.
Shaw seconded a motion calling for the franchise to be extended to women.

634 "You Never Can Tell," PLAY PICTORIAL, X: no. 62 ([1907]), 109-18.
[Production photographs, with excerpts of the text, and a letter from Shaw on the heroic actor.]

635 "Z." "Sham and Super-Sham," BLACKWOOD'S MAGAZINE, CLXXXI (June 1907), 825-30; rptd in LIVING AGE, CCLIV (6 July 1907), 32-36.
Shaw is a professionally clever person, puffed up with his own conceit, who has managed to achieve a following by skillful self-advertising. However, his works are bad, shallow, and fatuous.

1908

---

636 "At the Play," OBS, 17 May 1908, p. 5.
Getting Married does not solve the marriage question; rather, Shaw's witty and mordant conversation seeks to provoke numerous questions. It follows few accepted theatrical conventions.

637 Barker, J. Ellis. BRITISH SOCIALISM: AN EXAMINATION OF ITS DOCTRINES, POLICY, AIMS AND PRACTICAL PROPOSALS (Lond: Smith, Elder, 1908), pp. 418-24, 486-87.
[Passing references to Shaw in connection with the Fabian Society.]

638 Beerbohm, Max. "Arms and the Man." SAT REV, CV (1908), 9-10; rptd in AROUND THEATRES, pp. 632-34; rptd in Richard A Cassell & Henry Knepler, eds. WHAT IS THE PLAY (Glenview, IL: Scott, Foresman, 1967), pp. 687-88.
Arms and the Man still has the ring of truth to it; nevertheless, it is narrow and shallow in comparison with Shaw's mature work.

639 Beerbohm, Max. "Getting Married," SAT REV, CV (1908), 657-58; rptd in AROUND THEATRES, pp. 655-60.
Getting Married is rather like trying to follow an oral delivery of Plato's SYMPOSIUM—almost impossible. Shaw also tends to bore us because his fun is not an integral part of the play.

640 BERNARD SHAW ET SES TRADUCTEURS FRANCAIS, AUGUSTIN ET HENRIETTE HAMON (Bernard Shaw and His French Translators, Augustin and Henriette Hamon) (Paris: R. Munier [1908]).
[Biographical information on Shaw and his French translators, and how the latter became acquainted with him, and why he chose them. In French.]

641 "Bernard Shaw shi" (Mr. Bernard Shaw), TAIYO (Tokyo), XIV: 15 (Nov 1908), 169-74.
Shaw is representative of modern British drama. [In Japanese.]

642 "Bernard Shaw's Discovery of a Supertramp," CUR LIT, XLV (Sept 1908), 294-96.
[An account of Shaw's support of W. H. Davies, for whose AUTOBIOGRAPHY OF A SUPER-TRAMP Shaw wrote a preface.]

643 Besant, Annie. ANNIE BESANT: AN AUTOBIOGRAPHY (Lond: T. Fisher Unwin, 1908), pp. 303, 311, 319, 336.
[Biographical details of Shaw the socialist.]

644 Bidou, Henry. [Candida], LE JOURNAL DES DEBATS, 11 May 1908.
Candida is an interesting play, but difficult to understand. [In French.]

645 Bordeaux, Henry. [Candida], LA REVUE HEBDOMADAIRE, June 1908 [not seen]; rptd in LA VIE AU THEATRE (Paris: Plon-Nourrit, 1910), pp. 199-208, 329-30.
Shaw is something of an Ibsenesque author, whose work is meant to be read as well as seen. Candida is a strange, realistic play, with touches of caricature. [In French.]

646 Borsa, Mario. THE ENGLISH STAGE OF TO-DAY. Trans & ed Selwyn Brinton (Lond & NY: John Lane/Bodley Head, 1908), pp. 110, 120-66, 261. [Originally published as IL TEATRO INGLESE CONTEMPORANEO (Milan: Treves, 1905).]
Shaw may be the most original and amusing character in England. His career has two sides to it. Mrs. Warren's Profession, Candida, and The Devil's Disciple, although flawed, are genuine drama and works of art because Shaw gives us real human types and situations. But after that Shaw allowed his gifts to atrophy, and he has produced only discussions and homilies. He could have painted "a living and realistic picture of the society of his own times," and it is a pity not to have that.

647 Brisson, Adolphe. [Shaw], LE TEMPS, 11 May 1908.
Shaw is a reformer, revolutionary, realist, pessimist, and moralist. An understanding of Shaw's philosophy is necessary to appreciate his plays; his characters are urged by a life force. [In French.]

648 Browne, Walter, & E. de Roy Koch. WHO'S WHO ON THE STAGE 1908 (NY: B.W. Dodge), pp. 394-95.
[Biographical reference source.]

649 Bruggen, C. J. A. van. GEORGE BERNARD SHAW (Haarlem: [no publisher], 1908) [not seen].
[In Dutch.]

650 "Candida," COMOEDIA, 9 May 1908, p. 3.
Candida is considered a masterpiece in England, but not France. Shaw is a prophet only in England. He should read more Wilde and less Ibsen if he wants to please the French. [In French.]

651 Carson, L[ionel], ed. THE STAGE YEAR BOOK (Lond: Carson & Comerford, 1908-28).
[A good source of factual information concerning Shaw's work on the London stage. Appropriate volumes include cast-lists of plays, other performance details, and annual essays surveying the dramatic season.]

652 Chassé, Charles. [Shaw], LA REVUE, Nov 1908.
Shaw is not a philosopher; he wants a nation of supermen, but is on his way to collectivism. He awakens men's minds, but is not a prophet. [In French.]

653 "Chronicle and Comment: A Desultory Combat," BOOK-MAN (NY), XXVII (Aug 1908), 541-45.
[An account of an exchange of correspondence between Lord Alfred Douglas and Shaw as a result of the former's review of Getting Married, ACADEMY, 23 May 1908; see item 660.]

654 "Chronicle and Comment: Bernard Shaw's Reasons," BOOK-MAN (NY), XXVII (June 1908), 331-33.
Shaw has been involved in a controversy over royalties with COLLIER'S MAGAZINE. The only interest in this is that it proves Shaw is not a thinker but merely a stimulator of thought.

655 "Chronicle and Comment: Other Stage Books," BOOKMAN (NY), XXVIII (Nov 1908), 199-201.
[Brief comment on Ellen Terry's REMINISCENCES, with references to Shaw.]

656 "THE CLERK," TIMES, 2 Jan 1908, p. 10.
A new monthly publication, THE CLERK, contains some characteristic reminiscences by Shaw of his own early life.

657 "Clerks, Moralists and Bernard Shaw," INDEPENDENT (NY), LXIV (1908), 164-65.
Shaw can always be depended upon to provoke controversy, and this is again true with his remarks about clerks and their function in society.

658 Cornwallis-West, Mrs. George. THE REMINISCENCES OF

LADY RANDOLPH CHURCHILL (NY: Century, 1908; rptd NY: Kraus, 1972), pp. 381-82.
[A brief reminiscence, with a telegram and letter by Shaw.]

659 Davison, R. C. "Bernard Shaw in Portrait and Caricature," IDLER, XXXIII (1908), 236-45.
[Largely biographical. Sees Shaw as first and foremost a socialist.]

660 Douglas, Lord Alfred. "For Shame, Mr. Shaw!" ACADEMY, 23 May 1908, p. 806; rptd in SHAW REVIEW, IX (1966), 66-68.
Getting Married is a tedious undramatic conversation; Shaw may be witty and brilliant, but he is not a deep thinker. [Douglas's review sparked a controversy with Shaw; see ACADEMY: "Can You Not Manage?" 30 May 1908, p. 830; "The Shaving of Patshaw," 6 June 1908, p. 855; both rptd in SHAW REVIEW, IX (1966), 68-74.]

661 "Drama: The Week," ATH, No. 4184 (4 Jan 1908), 23.
Arms and the Man, in addition to Shaw's philosophy, has more story, action, character and geniality than most of his later works.

662 "Drama: The Week," ATH, No. 4204 (23 May 1908), 647.
Only Shaw's wit and humor prevent Getting Married—a plotless, actionless play—from being boring. In parts it is commonplace and lacks inspiration.

663 "Editorial Bulletin," COLLIER'S, XLI (25 April 1908), 7, 11.
[A tongue-in-cheek editorial reply to a letter by Shaw protesting the double payment he received for his short story, "Aerial Football—The New Game," which appeared in COLLIER'S on 23 Nov 1907.]

664 Florence, Jean. [Shaw], LA PHALANGE, 15 July 1908.
Shaw's uncompromising conscience makes Shaw a kind of Beaumarchais whose mind would have been matured by the lessons of the Revolution. [In French.]

665 Fowke, V. de S. "Regicide as Accident de Travail," SAT REV, CV (1908), 204-05.
Shaw's remarks on the dangers of political assassination for monarchs [SAT REV, CV (1908), 172] applies equally to other kinds of heads of state. There is also a danger socialism will destroy the notion of the sacredness of human life.

666 Fyfe, H. Hamilton. "The Theatre: Getting Married," WORLD, No. 1768 (20 May 1908), 919; rptd in Evans, pp. 190-93.
Shaw is fascinated by the subject of marriage to the extent that he is becoming boring. Getting Married is dull because Shaw is "so tremendously in earnest" and too intellectual.

667 "G. B. Shaw Loses on Appeal," NYT, 7 March 1908, p. 8.
Shaw has lost a law suit for copyright infringement.

668 "George Bernard Shaw as One of His Own Puppets," HARPER'S WEEKLY, LII (18 July 1908), 29.
[Shaw in a production photograph of Getting Married.]

669 "Getting Married," ERA, 16 May 1908, p. 17.
Shaw has given Getting Married two amusing acts and a third which tries the patience of even his most fervent admirers.

670 "Getting Married: Mr. Shaw's 'Conversation': Paradox and Prolixity," DT, 13 May 1908, p. 9.
Shaw makes his characters talk exactly like himself, and he revels in turning conventional morality upside down. However, there is a growing tendency for his plays to be really over long before Shaw himself is ready to bring down the curtain.

671 Godley, Eveline C. "Drama," THE ANNUAL REGISTER 1907 (Lond: Longmans, Green, 1908), part II, pp. 95-99.
The Philanderer does not stand the test of time, although Caesar and Cleopatra and The Devil's Disciple fare somewhat better.

672 Grein, J. T. "Premieres of the Week," STIMES, 17 May 1908, p. 4.
Getting Married is an orgy of words, which at first delights and then palls. Shaw lacks a sense of proportion.

673 Grendon, Felix. "Shakespeare and Shaw," SEWANEE REVIEW, XVI (1908), 168-83.
[A comparison of Shaw and Shakespeare, with unrestrained approbation given to the former. With marginal notes by Shaw.]

674 "The Growing Garrulousness of Bernard Shaw," CUR LIT, XLV (July 1908), 83-85.
John Bull's Other Island and Major Barbara were both talkative plays, but Shaw's growing tendency towards garrulousness becomes unbearable in Getting Married.

675 Hamon, Augustin. "Un Noveau Molière: A French View of Bernard Shaw," NINETEENTH CENTURY, LXIV (July 1908), 48-63.
Shaw's originality arises from the fact he is not indebted to the romantic drama of the French school, and he disregards all the supposed rules of art. Shaw's plays are "eminently beautiful and artistic," and amusing with excellent style and character. Shaw and Molière share a common comic approach, often developing into buffoonery, farce, and burlesque tinged with a deep bitterness. Shaw is rigorously anti-romantic, and unlike other playwrights (including Molière), he criticizes not people, but social principles such as greed and individual property. Shaw's drama is determinist: characters behave according to the influence of various kinds of environment upon them, especially the "economico-political conditions of the social environment." Shaw and Molière's plays suffer from the

common fate of being misuderstood and hence ridiculed or severely criticized. Because of Shaw's Irish wit, his plays will undoubtedly prove popular in France.

676 "The Haymarket," STAGE, 14 May 1908, p. 18.
Getting Married is excessively repetitive; its ideas have been expounded in earlier plays.

677 "Haymarket Theatre," TIMES, 13 May 1908, p. 13.
Getting Married demonstrates Shaw's passion for ideas and justice, and is in the form of a symposium.

678 Henderson, Archibald. "Bernard Shaw kein Vampyr?" (Bernard Shaw No Vampire?) DER DEUTSCHE VORKÄMPFER, II: 9 (Sept 1908), 27 [Not seen].
[Cited in Hood, p. 224. In German.]

679 Henderson, Archibald. "La Carrière de Bernard Shaw" (Bernard Shaw's Career), LA SOCIETE NOUVELLE, IV, 2nd series (May 1908), 186-205 [not seen.]
[Cited in Hood, p. 224. In French.]

680 Henderson, Archibald. "The Real Bernard Shaw," MUNSEY'S MAGAZINE, XXXVIII (Jan 1908), 452-56.
[Biographical.]

681 Hirata, Tokuboku. "Bernard Shaw no Akugeki" (Bernard Shaw's Unpleasant Plays), TOKYO NIROKU SHINBUN, 19-29 Oct 1908.
Although he uses the dramatic form to propagate his socialistic ideas, Shaw is a dramatic poet. He is not superior to Ibsen, but a much better dramatist than Pinero. Mrs. Warren's Profession, Candida, and Caesar and Cleopatra are his masterpieces. [In Japanese.]

682 "Ireland," TIMES, 8 Oct 1908, p. 10.
Shaw has agreed to present Rodin's bust of him to the Dublin Municipal Gallery of Modern Art.

683 Jackson, Holbrook. "Bernard Shaw in Portrait and Caricature," IDLER, XXXIII (1908), 227-36.
Shaw is well-known but not popular as a writer. His views are witty but quixotic, and he is seen as an egotist. It is interesting to compare Shaw the man with portraits of him. [Numerous portraits reproduced and analyzed.]

684 Kerr, Alfred. "Korrekturbogen über Shaw" (Proof-sheets on Shaw), DIE NEUE RUNDSCHAU, XIX: 1 (1908), 138-45.
A definite note of social protest is a common characteristic of The Quintessence of Ibsenism, The Perfect Wagnerite, and Mrs. Warren's Profession. Shaw is angry with the happy few rather than kind to the underprivileged. He is a European in his plays, a London man in his essays. [In German.]

685 "London Theatres," STAGE, 2 Jan 1908, p. 20.
Arms and the Man now seems a bit silly and feeble, since Shaw's ideas in this play have been expressed subsequently with greater force.

686 "M. Charles Chasse Investigates Bernard Shaw's Philosophy," NYT, 13 Dec 1908, part VI, p. 6.
[Biographical interview.]

687 Mencken, Henry L. THE PHILOSOPHY OF FRIEDRICH NIETZSCHE (Lond: T. Fisher Unwin, 1908), pp. 272-79.
Shaw is the most influential contemporary English dramatist and his plays embody Nietzsche's philosophy absolutely. Characters such as Tanner, Bluntschli, and Undershaft spout this philosophy without almost any changes, although Shaw has attempted to deny this.

688 Meyerfeld, Max. "Shaws erster Monograph" (Shaw's First Monograph), DIE NEUE RUNDSCHAU, XIX: 1 (1908), 316-18.
[A description of Meyerfeld's visit to Shaw.] Shaw's wit is chameleon-like. [In German.]

689 "Mr. Bernard Shaw in Liverpool," TIMES, 16 Nov 1908, p. 6.
Shaw delivered a closing address at a book exhibition held in Liverpool.

690 "Mr. Bernard Shaw on Socialism," TIMES, 26 March 1908, p. 4.
Shaw's address on socialism to the Fabian Society was received cordially.

691 "Mr. Shaw Explains His Religion," FREETHINKER, XXVIII (1 Oct 1908), 689 [not seen].
[Cited in David S. Thatcher, NIETZSCHE IN ENGLAND (Toronto: University of Toronto Press, 1970).]

692 "Mr. Shaw Expounds Art," NYT, 11 Oct 1908, part III, p. 1.
Shaw has "delivered a sermon on literature and art."

693 "Mr. Shaw's New Play: His Revenge on the Critics," STIMES, 10 May 1908, p. 4.
Getting Married is to be all talk and will appear to consist of nothing but Shaw himself.

694 "Mordred." "On Getting Married: Mr. Bernard Shaw Talks: A 'Conversation' at the Haymarket," REFEREE, No. 1605 (17 May 1908), 2.
Shaw is going too far in his unashamed self-advertising. His ideas in Getting Married are not particularly new or original.

695 Mozley, J. Kenneth. "Modern Attacks on Christian Ethics," CONTEMPORARY REVIEW (Lond), XCIII (1908), 423-35; rptd in LIVING AGE, CCLVII (1908), 358-62.
Shaw is a genuinely humane man, a socialist who wants to raise all

men to the level of the Superman (this latter creation is to be achieved by careful breeding). His ideas are at odds with, for example, the Christian view of the sacrament of marriage.

696 "Music and the Drama: The Gallic Genius of Bernard Shaw," CUR LIT, XLV (Oct 1908), 429-31.
[A synopsis of item 675.]

697 Osanai, Kaoru. "Vedrenne Barker Gomei Engeki" (The Vedrenne-Barker Management), SHINSHOSETSU (Tokyo), XIII: 11 (Nov 1908), 27-39; rptd in OSANAI KAORU ENGEKIRON ZENSHU (The Collected Works of Kaoru Osanai's Dramatic Theory), vol I (Tokyo: Miraisha, 1964), pp. 366-73.
The new dramatic movement in Japan should follow the Vedrenne-Barker management in its footsteps. [Describes in detail the Vedrenne-Barker venture; references to Shaw. In Japanese.]

698 "The Playhouses: Arms and the Man Revived at the Savoy," ILN, CXXXII (4 Jan 1908), 2.
People have learned to understand Shaw since Arms and the Man was first produced. Shaw's ideas and attitudes are now familiar.

699 "The Playhouses: Mr. Bernard Shaw's Conversation: Getting Married at the Haymarket," ILN, CXXXII (16 May 1908), 730.
Getting Married is really one long conversation and lacks action, situations, and plot. However, it is no use complaining Shaw breaks dramatic conventions since he wilfully flouts the rules and yet keeps his audience amused and locked in thought.

700 Rageot, Gaston. "A French Estimate of George Bernard Shaw," BOOKMAN (NY), XXVII (July 1908), 474-77.
Shaw's Irishness has caused him to perceive the unctuous "moralising genius of the 'nation of shopkeepers' " and to expose it with the satirist's eye. His style and wit resemble Voltaire and Anatole France, although he has clearly been influenced by Ibsen, Tolstoy, and Nietzsche.

701 Salter, William Mackintire. "Mr. Bernard Shaw as a Social Critic," INTERNATIONAL JOURNAL OF ETHICS (Phila), XVIII (July 1908), 446-58.
Although Shaw is difficult because we do not know how to take him and because he often shocks us, he is a significant and social critic. Shaw uses the preacher's overemphasis and absolutism as well as the mountebank's gyrations; he sometimes flouts ideals, but is idealistic. He is not a pessimist, rather an audacious optimist who is a sensitive and moral socialist.

702 "The Savoy," ERA, 4 Jan 1908, p. 15.
Arms and the Man is one of Shaw's "cleverest and soundest" works, and its theme of deromanticizing war is an excellent one.

703 "Shaw and Irving," ERA, 19 Sept 1908, p. 21.
Shaw always manages to get his facts wrong, but succeeds in his self-advertising. Ellen Terry's THE STORY OF MY LIFE refutes Shaw's earlier claims that Henry Irving actively sought to produce The Man of Destiny.

704 "Shaw as Shown to Europe by an American, NYT, 1 Nov 1908, part V, p. 10.
[An account of Archibald Henderson's biographical endeavors with Shaw.]

705 "Shaw in Parliament," NYT, 6 April 1908, p. 6.
Shaw should stand for Parliament as he would be an undoubted acquisition and bring much needed wit and humor to that institution.

706 "Shaw on Man's Cowardice," NYT, 5 Jan 1908, part III, p. 1.
Shaw has delivered a characteristic discourse on cowardice where one of his targets is English middle-class clerks. [See also "Clerks," NYT, 6 Jan 1908, p. 6.]

707 "Shop Assistants and Living-in," TIMES, 12 Feb 1908, p. 12.
Shaw has spoken for improved living and working conditions for shop assistants.

708 "Society of Authors," TIMES, 21 March 1908, p. 14.
[A report of Shaw's and other's comments on the inaction of the Dramatic Committee over theatrical censorship.]

709 S[pence], E. F. "The Stage from the Stalls," SKETCH, LXII (20 May 1908), 170.
Shaw should have combined with Pinero in writing Getting Married—then the play would have had a sound dramatic foundation. Shaw is clever, but he cannot prevent his piece from becoming monotonous.

710 Taylor, G. R. S. LEADERS OF SOCIALISM PAST AND PRESENT (Lond: New Age, 1908), pp. 90-99.
Shaw's socialist message is really "sheer commonsense," and commonsense and socialism are one and the same thing. However, Shaw chooses to remain rather in the background of the Fabian Society.

711 "Temperance and Social Reforms," TIMES, 20 March 1908, p. 13.
Shaw has urged restraint in statements made about the liquor trade by temperance reformers.

712 Terry, Ellen. "From Lewis Carroll to Bernard Shaw," McCLURE'S MAGAZINE, XXXI (1908), 565-76.
[Passing references to Shaw, especially pp. 572-74, and the dealings between Terry and Shaw particularly concerning Terry's appearance in Captain Brassbound's Conversion.]

713 Terry, Ellen. THE STORY OF MY LIFE: RECOLLECTIONS

AND REFLECTIONS (NY: McClure, 1908), pp. 345-47, 353-54, 397.
[Brief details of Terry's associations with Shaw.]

714 Van Vorst, Mrs. John. "Rodin and Bernard Shaw," PUTNAM'S, III (Feb 1908), 534-35.
[A brief discussion of Rodin's bust of Shaw.]

715 W., J. "The Stage from the Stalls," SKETCH, LX (8 Jan 1908), 394.
Arms and the Man remains as fresh as ever, although Shaw's wit and satire seems a trifle less forceful nowadays.

716 Walkley, A. B. [Getting Married], LE TEMPS, 31 Aug 1908, pp. 1-2.
Getting Married lacks dramatic form; it is a long, boring discussion on marriage. Shaw is too much of a puritan to discuss the sexual problem in fundamental terms. [In French.]

717 Wilstach, Paul. RICHARD MANSFIELD: THE MAN AND THE ACTOR (NY: Scribner's, 1908), pp. 259-61, 264-65, 282-86, 439.
[Details of Mansfield's career in Arms and the Man and The Devil's Disciple.]

1909

---

718 "Abbey Theatre: The Shewing-up of Blanco Posnet," IRISH TIMES, 26 Aug 1909, p. 7.
The Shewing-up of Blanco Posnet proves anti-climactic; as soon as Shaw verges on the shocking he moves on to another topic. The philosophy is second-rate, and only the play's infamy ensured its production.

719 "The Admirable Bashville; or, Constancy Unrewarded," ERA, 30 Jan 1909, p. 17.
The Admirable Bashville is one of Shaw's "drollest things" with "strong, telling blank-verse" and "cleverly-turned sentences."

720 "The Afternoon Theatre," STAGE, 28 Jan 1909, p. 18.
The Admirable Bashville is "merely a . . . rather cheaply facetious satire on prize-fighting and burlesque of Shakespeare's blank verse."

721 "At the Play," OBS, 11 July 1909, p. 6.
There is no conceivable reason why Press Cuttings should have been banned on political grounds.

722 "At the Play," OBS, 29 Aug 1909, p. 4.
The Shewing-up of Blanco Posnet is obvious satire, crude melodrama,

and blatant sermonizing. However, there is Shaw's wit, and more humanity to be found here than often in his work.

723 "At the Play," OBS, 12 Dec 1909, p. 8.
The Shewing-up of Blanco Posnet is not as important or interesting as the pre-production publicity led people to believe.

724 Bab, Julius. DER SCHAUSPIELER UND SEIN HAUS (The Actor and His Theatre) (Berlin: Oesterheld, 1909), pp. 35, 36-38.
Shaw is able to see the ambiguity of things in his social criticism. [In German.]

725 Benavente, Jacinto. EL TEATRO DEL PUEBLO (The Theatre of the Town) (Madrid: Fernando Fé, 1909), pp. 75-78.
Shaw does not use the theatre solely as theatre; it is also a place for his propaganda. Caesar and Cleopatra is a major work by a unique English dramatist. [In Spanish.]

726 "Bernard Shaw in Shakespeare's Shoes," CUR LIT, XLVII (Sept 1909), 318-19.
Shaw's use of blank verse in The Admirable Bashville proves he is unworthy to walk in Shakespeare's shoes.

727 "Bernard Shaw is Ill," NYT, 23 Jan 1909, p. 1.
[Title describes. See also "Mr. Shaw's Unguarded Utterance," NYT, 26 Jan 1909, p. 8 (an editorial on Shaw's remark "tell them I'm dead").]

728 "Bernard Shaw's New Four-Hour Play," NYT, 15 Dec 1909, p. 2.
Shaw has announced the completion of his latest opus.

729 Birmingham, George A. "The Showing Up of Blanco Posnet," SPECTATOR, CIII (4 Sept 1909), 340.
The Shewing-up of Blanco Posnet is a "remarkably orthodox sermon" on a great but not original theme (the working of the Divine Spirit on an unwilling man's soul). The title character is the play's great achievement.

730 Broutá, Julio. "Prefacio" (Preface) to CESAR Y CLEOPATRA (Caesar and Cleopatra) (Madrid: Velasco, 1909), pp. v-ix [not seen].
[Cited in Rodríguez (MS). In Spanish.]

731 "Carados." "Dramatic Gossip: A Shakespeare Memorial," REFEREE, No. 1657 (16 May 1909), 2.
Shaw is a showman and a humbug who attracts attention by his antics rather than his talents.

732 "The Censor Censured," LITERARY DIGEST, XXXIX (1909), 347-48.
[Brief mention of Shaw's role in the theatrical censorship debate.]

733 Chesterton, Gilbert K. GEORGE BERNARD SHAW (Lond & NY: John Lane, [1909], 1910); pp. 34-53 rptd in Kenneth Robinson, et al, ESSAYS TOWARD TRUTH (NY: Holt, 1924), pp. 189-95.

Before writing about Shaw, it is necessary to delineate the three traditions which have influenced him, and these may be called "The Irishman," "The Puritan," and "The Progressive." Shaw is Irish in that he seeks for the truth in a direct, honest manner which is difficult for the more devious English to understand. Irish, too, is his "intellectual chastity" and "fighting spirit." With Swift, Shaw shares the quality of "inhumane humanity" and would knock someone down for his own good. Shaw is a puritan in his fierce and total concentration on matters; he is never frivolous or irresponsible. Similarly he is a great wit, not a humorist, because wit is always connected with truth, humor with trickery. Shaw's pro-gressive stance is reflected in his ability to give "fresh and personal arguments" for modern, revolutionary notions, and thus he startles people with his ideas. As a critic, Shaw has said "many impudent things" pleasantly and agreeably (as if inviting a dialogue); he has also revolted against current artistic ethics which rule on behalf of art for art's sake.

Arms and the Man demonstrates Shaw's use of bathos and "savage sincerity"—one of the keys to his work. Moreover, he possesses the ability to stand the universe on its head, as is brilliantly exemplified by the final scene of Candida. The Philanderer, far more important than The Man of Destiny, is "full of fine strokes and real satire." You Never Can Tell is "the work." However, the rationalistic method of Widowers' Houses leads to its failure as a drama. Mrs. Warren's Profession is a fine play because of the controversy it caused and because of the ensuing censorship debate. The Devil's Disciple has great, but incidental, merits. Captain Brassbound's Conversion, a charming piece, turns on "the idea of the vanity of revenge." Caesar and Cleopatra belongs to the more important group of plays, and it seems inevitable that Shaw should write about Caesar, the only great historical figure to whom his theories apply. The failure of the play is a common weakness in all of Shaw—his inability to use a joke merely for its own sake without pretending to a higher significance. With Man and Superman "Shaw has become a complete and colossal mystic," and its philosophy helps rebut the notion he writes paradoxical, socialistic, problem plays. His philosophy can be summed up as "Schopenhauer standing on his head" with life being the primary thing.

734 "Clarence, Reginald" [H. J. Eldridge]. "THE STAGE" CYCLOPAEDIA: A BIBLIOGRAPHY OF PLAYS (Lond: THE STAGE, 1909).

[Arranged alphabetically by play title. Provides production details.]

735 Clarke, Joseph I. C. "Conditions on the Stage and Their Causes," NYT, 14 Feb 1909, part V, p. 8.
[A survey of some "degenerative" trends on the American stage, with references to Mrs. Warren's Profession.]

736 "The Coronet Theatre," TIMES, 8 June 1909, p. 12.
Widowers' Houses is "made of well-known fibres—a social question, a Shavian woman, and a battery of wit."

737 "The Coronet, W.," STAGE, 10 June 1909, p. 17.
The characters in Widowers' Houses "cannot be wholly sympathetic and convincing, as they are used simply as the means of delivering clever and effective sallies."

738 "Drama: The Week," ATH, No. 4240 (30 Jan 1909), 143.
The Admirable Bashville is little more than a joke, and its unsubtle satire does not hit its target.

739 "Drama: The Week," ATH, No. 4264 (17 July 1909), 79.
Press Cuttings is amusing, but the burlesque element is so strong that there is only a glimpse of Shaw's ideas. Often the language is inappropriate to the characters.

740 "Dramatic Gossip," ATH, No. 4271 (4 Sept 1909), 276.
The Shewing-up of Blanco Posnet is primitively sentimental, contains effective situations and vivid dialogue, but is not a very serious work.

741 "Dramaticus." "The Censor's Revenge," GRAPHIC, LXXX (3 July 1909), 22.
Press Cuttings has been banned by the Lord Chamberlain because two of the characters suggest public figures. "You may satirize politicians in comic papers, but not on the stage."

742 "Dramaticus." "The Play: Press Cuttings," GRAPHIC, LXXX (24 July 1909), 126.
Press Cuttings is "just a harmless skit written to poke fun at current topics."

743 Dunsany, Lord. "A Note on Blanco Posnet," SAT REV, CVIII (1909), 254.
The Shewing-up of Blanco Posnet is a very moral and successful play which is not at all blasphemous.

744 "The Dynamic Drama," ERA, 20 Feb 1909, p. 21.
Shaw has advertised himself and mesmerized the critics with his "impudent eccentricity coupled with rare ability." However, Shaw is only really popular with a vocal minority of playgoers.

745 [Editorial], IRISH TIMES, 26 Aug 1909, p. 6.
The Shewing-up of Blanco Posnet is not a scandalous, shocking play; rather it is "well-intentioned" and "pious."

746 "Election Intelligence: Portsmouth," TIMES, 27 Nov 1909, p. 8.
Shaw was the principal speaker at an election meeting in Portsmouth.

747 "The Fabian Essays," NYT, 10 April 1909, part II, p. 206.
Shaw's preface is characteristically forceful and direct, and he makes his usual misstatements of facts.

748 Fagan, James Bernard. "Dramatic Censorship," TIMES, 1 June 1909, p. 6.
Shaw's comparisons of Granville-Barker's WASTE with Fagan's THE EARTH demonstrate his perversion of the substance of each play in his desire to prove censorship is based solely on private prejudice. [See also Shaw's letter, TIMES, 29 May 1909, p. 10.]

749 Florence, Jean. "Bernardo Shaw, orador" (Bernard Shaw, Orator), LA LECTURA (Spain), Año IX, tomo I (1909), 130-31 [not seen].
[Cited in Rodríguez (MS). In Spanish.]

750 Frohman, Charles. "National and Repertory Theatres," TIMES, 11 May 1909, p. 8.
Shaw's fears [letter, TIMES, 10 May 1909, p. 12] about the effects of Frohman's repertory theatre on the plans for a national theatre are unfounded.

751 Fyfe, H. Hamilton. "The Theatre," WORLD, No. 1850 (14 Dec 1909), 1043.
The Shewing-up of Blanco Posnet presents a spiritual, puritan view of things. It blusters, is "crude melodrama," but the strongest of Shaw's works because Shaw is here at his most sincere and straightforward.

752 Fyfe, H. Hamilton. "The Theatre: Mr. Bernard Shaw's New Skit," WORLD, No. 1828 (13 July 1909), 69.
The production of Press Cuttings highlights the stupidities surrounding the law of censorship, for it is an innocuous play.

753 Garnett, Edward. "The Censorship of Public Opinion," FORT REV, ns LXXXVI (1909), 137-48.
Shaw's plays avoid censorship because they are all witty talk and no one knows if he is serious or not. However, he has not been lucky with Mrs. Warren's Profession or The Shewing-up of Blanco Posnet.

754 Garnett, Edward. "Drama: The Repertory Theatre in England," NATION (NY), LXXXIX (1909), 125-26.
[Brief mention of Shaw's role in the repertory theatre movement.]

755 Godley, Eveline C. "Drama," THE ANNUAL REGISTER 1908 (Lond: Longmans, Green, 1909), part II, pp. 94-98.
Getting Married is aptly named a "conversation," and Shaw's unorthodox ideas are presented "in extraordinarily natural and well-chosen

language."

756 Grau, Robert. FORTY YEARS OBSERVATION OF MUSIC AND THE DRAMA (NY & Baltimore: Broadway Publishing, 1909), pp. 68, 133.
[Passing references to Shaw's plays and performers in them.]

757 Gregory, A[ugusta]. "The Shewing Up of Blanco Posnet," IRISH TIMES, 25 Aug 1909, p. 7.
Despite various reports of the contrary, the text of The Shewing-up of Blanco Posnet to be performed is exactly as Shaw wrote it originally.

758 [Gregory, Augusta, & W. B. Yeats]. "Mr. Shaw's Play: Letter of Protest," DT, 27 Aug 1909, p. 6.
[The text of a letter protesting the conditions under which Gregory and Yeats were obliged to produce The Shewing-up of Blanco Posnet, and asserting the outcome of the production has justified their position.]

759 Grein, J. T. "Premieres of the Week," STIMES, 12 Dec 1909, p. 4.
The Shewing-up of Blanco Posnet is not good Shaw, and without his name would probably be regarded as American melodrama.

760 Grendon, Felix. "Some Misconceptions Concerning Shaw," POET LORE, XX (1909), 376-86.
Shaw was not discovered by America: he had a big reputation long before his work was produced on the American stage. Nor is it true that he believes he is a better dramatist than Shakespeare, that he is not to be taken seriously, that he does not write plays at all.

761 Gruber, M. "Bernard Shaw. Portret engleskog dramatičara" (Bernard Shaw. Portrait of the English Playwright), NARODNE NOVINE (Zagreb), LXXV (1909), 257-58 [not seen].
[In Croatian.]

762 Hamilton, Clayton. "Pleasant and Unpleasant Plays," FORUM (NY), XLI (March 1909), 213-14.
The reason why the pleasant plays, such as Candida, are more successful than the unpleasant ones, such as Mrs. Warren's Profession, is because they appeal to both the intellect and the emotions. The unpleasant plays appeal only to the cold intellect.

763 Hankin, St. John. "Dramatic Censorship," TIMES, 2 June 1909, p. 13.
Shaw's letter [TIMES, 29 May 1909, p. 10] demonstrates clearly "some of the practical difficulties of a dramatic censorship."

764 Hasegawa, Tenkei. "Riso wa kamennari" (Ideals are Masks), TAIYO (Tokyo), XV: 16 (Dec 1909), 153-60.

[Defends naturalistic literary movements in Japan on the authority of The Quintessence of Ibsenism. In Japanese.]

765 Henderson, Archibald. "The Career of Bernard Shaw," ARENA, XLI (1909), 2-17.
[Biographical overview.]

766 Henderson, Archibald. "The Philosophy of Bernard Shaw," ATLANTIC MONTHLY, CIII (Feb 1909), 227-34.
Every aspect of Shaw and his work is the result of his socialism; his characters are a product of the social environment which molds their fate. Shaw believes that life should be pursued for its own sake and is an idealistic optimist. "He regards man as divine because actually he is the last effort of the will to realize itself as God."

767 "His Majesty's Theatre," TIMES, 27 Jan 1909, p. 8.
The Admirable Bashville is a diversion and as recognizably Shavian as any of Shaw's other works.

768 "How Shaw Makes Enemies," LITERARY DIGEST, XLIX (1909), 631-32.
G. K. Chesterton has put his finger on why Shaw makes enemies—he makes people feel they are being fooled by his erratic levity.

769 "How to be Happy though Married: Mr. Belasco to the Rescue," GRAPHIC, LXXX (1909), 286.
[Brief mention of the censorship controversy surrounding The Shewing-up of Blanco Posnet.]

770 "Imperial Colonial Club," TIMES, 25 May 1909, p. 8.
Shaw addressed a few remarks to the Imperial Colonial Club, indicating his pro-German sympathies.

771 "Ireland: Mr. Shaw's Play in Dublin," TIMES, 24 Aug 1909, p. 8.
[Various details, including letters, concerning the controversy surrounding the production of The Shewing-up of Blanco Posnet in Dublin.]

772 "Irish Notes," LAW TIMES (Lond), CXXVII (28 Aug 1909), 409.
[A brief discussion of Irish law relating to the theatre in connection with the Irish Literary Society and The Shewing-up of Blanco Posnet.]

773 "Irish Notes," LAW TIMES (Lond), CXXVII (4 Sept 1909), 425.
The Shewing-up of Blanco Posnet is really a study in jurisprudence, and Shaw's presentation of rough justice is "instructive, though not alluring."

774 Joyce, James. "La Battaglia fra Bernard Shaw e la

Censura" (Bernard Shaw's Battle with the Censor), IL PICCOLO DELLA SERA (Trieste), 5 Sept 1909 [not seen]; rptd in Ellsworth Mason & Richard Ellman, THE CRITICAL WRITINGS OF JAMES JOYCE (NY: Viking, 1959), pp. 206-08; rptd in Evans, pp. 197-99.

Shaw is a "born preacher," and The Shewing-up of Blanco Posnet is like a "dialogue novel." The play does not convince as either sermon or drama.

775 Kawashima, Fūkotsu. "Bernard Shaw to sono gekihyo" (Bernard Shaw and His Dramatic Criticism), SHINCHO (Tokyo), X: 3 (March 1909), 43-46; rptd as "Bernard Shaw ni tsuite" (On Bernard Shaw), TEIKOKU BUNGAKU (Tokyo), XV: 10 (Oct 1909), 1220-25.

Shaw does not have much sympathy with dramatic poetry, nor with immanent criticism. His distinctive character as a critic is to defend one play at the cost of another, rather than to make an objective evaluation of them. [In Japanese.]

776 Kellner, Leon. DIE ENGLISCHE LITERATUR IM ZEITALTER DER KÖNIGIN VIKTORIA (English Literature in the Victorian Age) (Leipzig: Bernhard Tauchnitz, 1909), pp. 8, 14, 26, 169, 496, 551, 647-51, 668-72.

[A biographical sketch, with an assessment of Shaw's personality, and a survey of the plays.] Two human types are characteristic of Shaw's plays: the "impudent fellow" and the servant (the lackey by profession). In everything he does Shaw is the exact opponent of the average Englishman. [In German.]

777 Kerr, Alfred. "Thoma—Wedekind—Shaw, "NEUE RUNDSCHAU, XX: 1 (1909), 137-42.

Shaw is the "immortal poet of the immortal The Doctor's Dilemma," which contains a kind of religion by which all religion becomes unnecessary. Shaw destroys the horrors of death. [In German.]

778 "The Labour Party and the Tsar," TIMES, 26 July 1909, p. 6.

Shaw addressed a meeting in Trafalgar Square to protest the visit of Tsar Nicholas II.

779 "Labour Party Conference," TIMES, 29 Jan 1909, p. 10.

Shaw attended and spoke at the annual conference of the Labour Party.

780 "Lyric: THE CHOCOLATE SOLDIER," THEATRE MAGAZINE (NY), X (Nov 1909), xiii.

Many Shawisms have been lost in the transformation of Arms and the Man into THE CHOCOLATE SOLIDER.

781 "The Lyric—THE CHOCOLATE SOLDIERS," HAMPTON'S MAGAZINE (NY), XXXIII (Nov 1909), 700.

There is very little of <u>Arms and the Man</u> in THE CHOCOLATE SOLDIER.

782 M., C. E. "Gaiety Theatre: Mr. Shaw's <u>Press Cuttings</u>," MANCHESTER GUARDIAN, 28 Sept 1909, p. 7.
Shaw's wit is more economical in <u>Press Cuttings</u>, a topical and popular piece, than in his other works; but, although thinner, his humor produces the desired effect—corrosive satire.

783 Mallock, W. H. "Mr. Bernard Shaw on Mr. Mallock," TIMES, 6 Feb 1909, p. 12.
Shaw's views of W. H. Mallock's treatment of socialism are completely irrelevant. [See also in TIMES: "Layman," "Mr. Mallock and Mr. Bernard Shaw," 8 Feb 1909, p. 10; and Shaw's letter, 5 Feb 1909, p. 7.]

784 Maude, Aylmer. "Dramatic Censorship," TIMES, 11 June 1909, p. 12.
Shaw's disapproval of dramatic censorship is justified, although his factual grasp of some censored plays is faulty.

785 Metcalfe, J. S. "Drama: The Bill of Fare for the New Theatre," LIFE, LIV (23 Sept 1909), 412-13.
Although <u>Arms and the Man</u> and its musical version, THE CHOCOLATE SOLDIER, are very different from each other, both pieces are excellent.

786 "Miss Marlowe Again—ZAZA in Two Tongues," NYT, 14 Feb 1909, part V, p. 14.
[An interview with Shaw in which he discusses intimate theatre.]

787 Mr. Bernard Shaw and the Censorship," TIMES, 17 June 1909, p. 12.
Shaw has addressed the Poets' Club on the topic of theatrical censorship.

788 "Mr. Bernard Shaw on Photography," TIMES, 19 Oct 1909, p. 13.
Shaw has given a lecture on photography.

789 "Mr. Bernard Shaw on Socialist Politics," TIMES, 1 Feb 1909, p. 8.
Shaw addressed a very large meeting at Portsmouth on socialist politics.

790 "Mr. Bernard Shaw on the Medical Profession," TIMES, 17 Feb 1909, p. 10.
Shaw took part in a discussion of the medical profession at a meeting of the Medico-Legal Society.

791 "Mr. Bernard Shaw on Unemployment," TIMES, 6 March 1909, p. 12.

Shaw presided at a meeting of the Fabian Society on unemployment. He made some remarks and introduced Sidney Webb.

792 "Mr. Shaw and the Censor," LITERARY DIGEST, XXXIX (7 Aug 1909), 206.
Shaw's Press Cuttings has been banned by the censor, and this action has created much debate.

793 "Mr. Shaw and the Censor," TIMES, 24 May 1909, p. 12.
Shaw has declared he will allow The Shewing-up of Blanco Posnet to be performed in America and Europe, and will also publish it.

794 "Mr. Shaw's New Play in Dublin," TIMES, 26 Aug 1909, p. 8.
The Shewing-up of Blanco Posnet "is like a story by Berte Harte dramatized by a mind of very different quality from Harte's," but is not up to Shaw's highest standards.

795 "Mr. Shaw's New Play is Heard in Dublin," NYH, 26 Aug 1909, p. 10.
There is grim humor in The Shewing-up of Blanco Posnet, but it is difficult to understand why it was suppressed in London.

796 "Mr. Shaw's Play in Dublin," IRISH TIMES, 21 Aug 1909, p. 7.
The Lord Lieutenant has taken certain precautions which would enable him to close the production of The Shewing-up of Blanco Posnet should disturbances be provoked by the first-night performance.

797 "Mr. Shaw's Play: Piece not to be Withdrawn," IRISH TIMES, 23 Aug 1909, p. 7.
None of the protests about The Shewing-up of Blanco Posnet has caused the directors of the Abbey Theatre to consider withdrawing the play. Shaw's play is a "high and weighty argument upon the working of the Spirit of God in man's heart" and deserves to be staged.

798 "Mr. Shaw's Play: Press Cuttings: A Topical Sketch," DT, 10 July 1909, p. 12.
Press Cuttings is a humorous, "somewhat incoherent piece of badinage" with a very slight story.

799 "Mr. Shaw's 'Skit,'" ERA, 17 July 1909, p. 15.
[Largely lengthy extracts from Press Cuttings, given at a private performance.]

800 "A National Theatre," TIMES, 1 Dec 1909, p. 14.
Shaw has presided at a lecture given by Harley Granville-Barker.

801 Osanai, Kaoru. "Grein no Dokuritsu Gekijo" (Grein's Independent Theatre), KABUKI (Tokyo), No. 105 (April 1909), 22-26; rptd in OSANAI KAORU ENGEKIRON ZENSHU (The Collected Works of Kaoru Osanai's Dramatic Theory), vol I

(Tokyo: Miraisha, 1964), pp. 360-62.
The existence of the Independent Theatre is well justified with the production of Widowers' Houses, even if it did not venture anything else. [In Japanese.]

802 Osanai, Kaoru. "Suteiji Sosaiechi" (The Stage Society), KABUKI (Tokyo), No. 106 (May 1909), 62-68; rptd in OSANAI KAORU ENGEKIRON ZENSHU (The Collected Works of Kaoru Osanai's Dramatic Theory), vol I (Tokyo: Miraisha, 1964), pp. 362-65.
[Evaluates highly the activities of the Stage Society, with special mention of various productions of Shaw's works. In Japanese.]

803 Osanai, Kaoru. "Ze Kooto Shiata no Jigyo" (The Achievements of the Court Theatre), KABUKI (Tokyo), No. 107 (June 1909), 91-94, No. 108 (July 1909), 80-84, No. 112 (Nov 1909), 68-71; rptd in OSANAI KAORU ENGEKIRON ZENSHU (The Collected Works of Kaoru Osanai's Dramatic Theory), vol I (Tokyo: Miraisha, 1964), pp. 374-79.
[A detailed description of the Vedrenne-Barker management of the Court Theatre, with special reference to Shaw. In Japanese.]

804 "Parliamentary Committee," TIMES, 31 July 1909, p. 10.
[A report of Shaw's evidence before the Parliamentary committee on dramatic censorship, with cross-questioning.]

805 "The Playhouses: Mr. Bernard Shaw's Banned Sketch: Press Cuttings," ILN, CXXXV (17 July 1909), 108.
Press Cuttings can be regarded as either a topical farce or a strong plea for the suffragist cause. Either way it is a "topsy-turvy fantasy, a rare bit of stage journalism."

806 "The Playhouses: Mr. Shaw's Admirable Bashville at the Afternoon Theatre," ILN, CXXXIV (30 Jan 1909), 146.
The Admirable Bashville "is at once a skit on Elizabethan poetic drama and a parody of Mr. Shaw's own juvenile composition."

807 Poland, Harry B. "Dramatic Censorship," TIMES, 3 June 1909, p. 12.
Shaw is rather confused about how the Theatres Act of 1843 (censorship) is actually enforced and operated. [See also in TIMES: Shaw's response, 4 June 1909, p. 8, and Poland's rebuttals, 5 June 1909, p. 6., 10 June 1909, p. 12.]

808 "The Poor-Law," TIMES, 13 Oct 1909, p. 7.
Shaw has spoken at a meeting of the National Committee to Promote the Break-up of the Poor Law.

809 "Premijera Zanat gospode Warren" (First Night of Mrs. Warren's Profession), HRVATSKA POZORNICA (Zagreb), XIX (1909-10), 1-3 [not seen].

[In Croatian.]

810 [Press Cuttings], BERLINER TAGEBLATT, 8 July 1909 [not seen].
[Apparently contains references to the banning of Press Cuttings, with comments on an anti-German war scare. In German.]

811 "Press Cuttings," ERA, 2 Oct 1909, p. 15.
Press Cuttings is not a play,; it is merely a topical sketch, which was originally banned because of its satire on well-known figures.

812 "Press Cuttings," STAGE, 30 Sept 1909, p. 15.
At the first public performance of Press Cuttings there were some changes in the script in order to meet the censor's requirements.

813 "The Progressive League," TIMES, 12 Oct 1909, p. 4.
Shaw was one of several speakers at a meeting of the Progressive League to which several hundred people could not gain admittance.

814 Quimby, Harriet. "What New Yorkers are Seeing behind the Footlights," LESLIE'S WEEKLY, CIX (30 Sept 1909), 318.
THE CHOCOLATE SOLDIER does not possess the energy and drive of Arms and the Man, and is generally "dull and commonplace."

815 Redford, G. A. "Dramatic Censorship," TIMES, 5 June 1909, p. 6.
Shaw is confused about Redford's actual job title, which is "Examiner of Plays." [See also Shaw's response, TIMES, 7 June 1909, p. 8.]

816 "Repertory at the Coronet," ERA, 12 June 1909, p. 15.
Widowers' Houses has not dated, and Shaw expresses his theme in typically witty fashion.

817 REPORT FROM THE JOINT SELECT COMMITTEE OF THE HOUSE OF LORDS AND THE HOUSE OF COMMONS ON THE STAGE PLAYS (CENSORSHIP), (1909); rptd in BRITISH SESSIONAL PAPERS: HOUSE OF COMMONS 1731-1949, ed by Edgar L. Erickson (NY: Readex Microprint), VIII, 459-905.
[On censorship generally, with Shaw's evidence and cross-examination.]

818 Ross, Robert. MASQUES & PHASES (Lond: Arthur L. Humphreys, 1909), pp. 224-47, 252-53.
[Parodies and satires entitled, "Shavians from Superman," "Some Doctored Dilemma," and "The Jaded Intellectuals."]

819 "Royal Court Theatre," TIMES, 10 July 1909, p. 12.
Press Cuttings does not pretend to be a play; it is a witty, farcically funny conversation.

820 Scott, Temple. "The Terrible Truthfulness of Mr. Shaw," [written October 1909]; rptd as "Temple Scott on Bernard Shaw: An Unpublished Article," SHAW REVIEW, XXIII (1980),

21-26.
[Attacks Shaw's views on photography.]

821 "The Select Committee on the Censorship," TIMES, 2 Aug 1909, p. 6.
[A letter from Shaw and a description of his evidence before the Parliamentary committee on theatrical censorship.]

822 Semar, John. "The Censor and THE MASK," MASK, II (1909-10), 49-52.
The censor should allow Shaw's plays to be produced because any good influence in them will survive. If they are mere sideshows nothing will happen. Either way there is not much to lose.

823 Semar, John. "Mr. Bernard Shaw and the Censor," MASK, II (1909-10), 40.
Because Shaw lacks nobility of spirit he creates works of mischief. "The Censor is a blessing . . . he saves us from the infection of Mr. Shaw's most lurid plays."

824 Sharp, R. Farquharson. A SHORT HISTORY OF THE ENGLISH STAGE FROM ITS BEGINNINGS TO THE SUMMER OF THE YEAR 1908 (Lond & NY: Walter Scott, 1909), pp. 183, 196, 225-27, 229.
[Unanalytical details of stage productions.]

825 "Shaw Describes Frohman," NYT, 10 May 1909, p. 1.
Shaw characterizes Frohman favorably and supports his scheme for a repertory theatre in London. [See also "Mr. Shaw on Mr. Frohman," NYT, 11 May 1909, p. 8.]

826 "Shaw Play on Suffrage," NYT, 24 May 1909, p. 7.
Press Cuttings, like The Shewing-up of Blanco Posnet, is controversial in its subject matter. [See also "Another New Shaw Play," NYT, 30 May 1909, part III, p. 2.]

827 "Shaw Taken Ill as His Play Fails," NYT, 31 Jan 1909, part III, p. 2.
Shaw has taken to his bed after the poor reception of The Admirable Bashville.

828 "Shaw will not Visit Us," NYT, 6 Dec 1909, p. 8.
[Humorous editorial on Shaw being better at a distance.]

829 "Shaw would be Censor," NYT, 11 Oct 1909, p. 1.
Shaw believes theatrical censorship should be abolished, but, if it is to be retained, he should be the censor.

830 "The Shewing-up of Blanco Posnet," IRISH TIMES, 24 Aug 1909, p. 7.
[Several extracts of letters by Shaw, Lady Gregory, and the Lord Lieutenant of Dublin on the controversy surrrounding the production

of The Shewing-up of Blanco Posnet. The issues include censorship, altering the text to suit Irish conditions, and the power of the Lord Lieutenant in the matter generally.]

831 "The Showing-up of Blanco Posnet," ERA, 28 Aug 1909, p. 19.

[Largely a plot description.]

832 "The Showing-up of Blanco Posnet," STAGE, 2 Sept 1909, p. 19.

The Shewing-up of Blanco Posnet heightens the current debate over theatrical censorship. The play also has Shaw's usual perverse wit, but the "manipulator of puppets contrives for once to keep himself largely out of sight."

833 S[pence], E. F. "The Stage from the Stalls: The Censored Shaw," SKETCH, LXVIII (15 Dec 1909), 294.

If the Irish authorities had not made so much fuss, The Shewing-up of Blanco Posnet would not have attracted the attention it did. Some may find the religious expletives blasphemous, but the play is undeniably moral.

834 S[pence], E. F. "The Stage from the Stalls: The Prohibited Shaw," SKETCH, LXVII (21 July 1909), 46.

In Press Cuttings Shaw is a "sort of Aristophanes in a hurry"; the play needs judicious cutting.

835 [Spencer, Arthur W.?]. "Mr. Bernard Shaw Poses as a Commonplace Person," GREEN BAG, XXI (Oct 1909), 537-38.

The Shewing-up of Blanco Posnet is a study in jurisprudence, more noteworthy for its imprudence.

836 Spiller, G. "Super-Man or Super-Society?" ETHICAL WORLD, III (15 July 1909), 99-100.

Shaw's advocacy of eugenics in "The Revolutionist's Handbook" is flawed because it appears to be founded on a fear of democracy.

837 "The Stage Society," STAGE, 9 Dec 1909, p. 19.

The Shewing-up of Blanco Posnet is a very moral sermon; the censorship fuss is essentially a trivial one.

838 "The Stage Society," TIMES, 7 Dec 1909, p. 10.

The Shewing-up of Blanco Posnet is one of Shaw's "happiest, wittiest . . . most human, inventions."

839 "Stage Society: Mr. Shaw's Blanco Posnet and Others," DT, 7 Dec 1909, p. 6.

The Shewing-up of Blanco Posnet is indeed a crude melodramatic sermon, "full of lurid and coarse language," However, it possesses some force and morality.

840 "Stage Society's Matinee," ERA, 11 Dec 1909, p. 17.

The Shewing-up of Blanco Posnet contains nothing to warrant the censor's interference. It is no more than "a sermon in crude melo- drama."

841 "Still the Censorhip," ERA, 5 June 1909, p. 19.
The censor appears to be out of touch with popular sentiment in his prohibition of The Shewing-up of Blanco Posnet.

842 T., F. G. "Mr. G. B. Shaw and Forcible Feeding," TIMES, 27 Nov 1909, p. 8.
[A humorous letter poking fun at Shaw and his views on force- feeding prisoners. See also Shaw's letter, TIMES, 25 Nov 1909, p. 4.]

843 Takayasu, Gekko. "Kakumeiteki Kigekika" (A Revolutionary Comic Writer), SHUMI (Tokyo), IV: 1 (Jan 1909), 19-24.
Shaw is less serious as a revolutionary and less sympathetic as a comic writer, but incomparable as a revolutionary comic writer. [A brief survey of the early plays up to Man and Superman. In Japanese.]

844 "The Theatres: Press Cuttings: Gaiety," MANCHESTER CITY NEWS, 2 Oct 1909, p. 7.
Press Cuttings is full of Shaw's "caustic wit and paradoxical humour," and he has something pertinent and witty to say on all sorts of topical matters.

845 V., J. S. "Press Cuttings: Mr. Shaw's Banned Play," STIMES, 11 July 1909, p. 4.
Press Cuttings does not pretend to be a play, but nevertheless satirizes well current events and the personalities surrounding them. The characters are exaggerated but not caricatured.

846 Walbrook, H. M. "The Showing-up of Blanco Posnet," PMG (Dec 1909) [not seen]; rptd in NIGHTS AT THE PLAY (Lond: W. J. Ham-Smith, 1911), pp. 7-11.
[A favorable review of The Shewing-up of Blanco Posnet, expressing incredulity at the censor's prohibition of the play.]

847 "Want Shaw in Parliament," NYT, 9 Feb 1909, p. 4.
A group of socialists are attempting to induce Shaw to stand for a Parliamentary vacancy.

848 "The Week," NATION (NY), LXXXIX (1909), 244-45.
Shaw continues to manufacture paradoxes and this week directs them against Shakespeare and vivisection.

849 White, Matthew, jr. "The Stage: After Dinner with Bernard Shaw," MUNSEY'S MAGAZINE, XLI (Sept 1909), 407.
[An account of Shaw's speech on censorship given at a dinner of the Poets' Club.]

850 Yasunari, Sadao. "Bernard Shaw shomoku" (A Bernard Shaw Bibliography), WASEDA BUNGAKU (Tokyo), No. 47 (Oct 1909), 7-10.
[A list of some 25 Shaviana published in Great Britain and America; annotated. In Japanese.]

1910

---

851 "Admirers Extol Harman as Martyr," NYT, 28 March 1910, p. 4.
Shaw has expressed his admiration for Moses Harman, an American advocate of women's rights.

852 "Art, Music and the Drama," ILN, CXXXVI (5 March 1910), 352.
Misalliance is witty but irrelevant. There is little action and many of Shaw's ideas have been heard before.

853 B. "The Theatre: The Repertory Theatre: II.—Misalliance," SPECTATOR, CIV (26 Feb 1910), 339.
The beginning of Misalliance is boring and contains feeble jokes. The remainder is wittily agile with no pretence to realism.

854 Bab, Julius. BERNARD SHAW (Berlin: S. Fischer, 1910; rvd 1926) [not seen].
[In German.]

855 Beerbohm, Max. "THE MADRAS HOUSE," SAT REV, CIX (1910), 362-63; rptd in AROUND THEATRES, pp. 735-39.
THE MADRAS HOUSE possesses what Misalliance lacks—unity. Shaw also constantly varies his style in order to prevent us from being bored. His serious characters are rendered comic, but clowns cannot be taken seriously.

856 Beerbohm, Max. "Mr. Shaw's 'Debate,'" SAT REV, CIX (1910) 262-64; rptd in AROUND THEATRES, pp. 725-30; rptd in Evans, pp. 200-02.
Misalliance is permeated with unreality. Shaw's characters, no longer unfamiliar and therefore acceptable, parade before the audience in all their ugliness and perfunctoriness. The play is sloppy and unorganized.

857 "Bernard Shaw Explained," NYT, 1 Oct 1910, part II, p. 534.
Shaw's Socialism and Superior Brains is a "lively tract," written with Shaw's "usual skill and vigor."

858 "Big Pension for Every One," NYT, 16 Oct 1910, part III, p. 3.
Shaw has advocated a universal uniform pension of $2,500 a year.

859 Chapman, John Jay. LEARNING AND OTHER ESSAYS (NY: Moffat, Yard, 1910), pp. 149-52.
Because Shaw and G. K. Chesterton are both jesters, it is difficult to take them seriously. In fact, both are crude and somewhat vulgar.

860 "The Charles Dickens Testimonial," TIMES, 1 Nov 1910, p. 12.
Shaw has suggested Dickens should have a monument in London similar to the Walter Scott one in Edinburgh.

861 Chase, Lewis Nathaniel. "Bernard Shaw in France," DIAL, XLVIII (1 April 1910), 229-33; rptd Bordeaux: Imprimerie Nouvelle, 1910.
Shaw is unknown by the French public, and critics hold varying opinions about his social views. Shaw has been influenced by numerous writers, including Nietzsche, Ibsen, Schopenhauer, Darwin, and Ruskin.

862 Chesterton, G. K. "Our Notebook," ILN, CXXXVI (12 March 1910), 372.
Shaw's remarks on eugenics to the Eugenic Education Society have been misrepresented in the press because Shaw does not support the concept of eugenics at all. His ideas on abolishing property and marriage are simply ideas, nothing more.

863 "THE CHOCOLATE SOLDIER," ACADEMY, LXXIX (17 Sept 1910), 278.
It is doubtful whether "Shaw's comedies form a good basis for a parody in comic opera."

864 "THE CHOCOLATE SOLDIER," ERA, 17 Sept 1910, p. 17.
THE CHOCOLATE SOLDIER retains some of Arms and the Man's fantastic humor. "Brilliant shafts of Shaw satire are mingled with more or less neatly-turned rhymes."

865 "Coronation Oath Change is Opposed," NYT, 12 May 1910, p. 4.
Shaw opposes certain aspects of official mourning for a monarch. [See also: " 'G. B. S.' is Right for Once," NYT, 13 May 1910, p. 8.]

866 Deacon, Renée M. BERNARD SHAW AS ARTIST-PHILOSOPHER: AN EXPOSITION OF SHAVIANISM (Lond: A. C. Fifield; NY: John Lane, 1910).
Shaw believes that conflict is essential to drama, as is well revealed in the characters of Judith, Dick, and Anderson in The Devil's Disciple. Shaw also repudiates an absolute point of view about things, which is readily apparent in his characters; these taken as a whole reveal the Shavian mind. The characters regard themselves as instruments of the Life Force; they do what must be done. Shaw is against romance and the romantic view of love, though he upholds love itself. The life force drives people to transcend their own

pleasure. Shaw makes women take the initiative in affairs, but they have a moment of weakness when the men become momentarily strong and assist them.

867 "Debate in One Sitting is Incoherent—Revenge on the Critics?" NYT, 24 Feb 1910, p. 6; rptd in NYTTR 1904-1911, [n. p.].
[Title describes.]

868 Dekobra, Maurice. [Shaw], LA REVUE, 15 March 1910.
Shaw's drama is undramatic; the plays are meant to be read, and are really lectures. [In French.]

869 "Drama: The Week," ATH, No. 4296 (26 Feb 1910), 259-60.
Misalliance is rightly termed a debate; there is no central theme, and it can hardly be said that Shaw's new dramatic, conversational form is developing very well.

870 "Dramatizing Shakespeare," LITERARY DIGEST, XLI (1910), 1155.
The difficulty with putting Shakespeare on the stage in The Dark Lady of the Sonnets is giving him convincing words. Shaw seems to have succeeded.

871 "Duke of York's Theatre," TIMES, 24 Feb 1910, p. 12.
Misalliance comprises a whole catalog of endless talk by people who are "horrors" (if still recognizable).

872 Dukes, Ashley. "Drama," NEW AGE (Lond), ns VI (3 March 1910), 426-27.
Misalliance is foolish, wearisome, and a "lukewarm hash" of Shaw's earlier ideas. The characters are incredible and only too willing to reveal their knowledge of the universe in ten minutes.

873 Dukes, Ashley, "Drama," NEW AGE (Lond), ns VII (30 June 1910), 209-10.
Shaw's recent attacks on critics and the press leave him highly vulnerable to further criticism, especially in light of his own views when he was a critic for SAT REV.

874 Dunton, Edith Kellogg. "By and About Mr. Shaw," DIAL, XLIX (6 Oct 1910), 283-84.
Critics continue to be divided about Shaw. Only Shaw can write his kind of plays and "nobody can match [him] for keen, merciless, compact argument—whirlwind argument, which states its adversary's position with cool, cruel irony, characterizes it with frank, brilliant impertinence, and proves the contrary with a sweep of splendid generalizations supported by an almost impregnable array of detail."

875 Efrov, N. E. "Moskva. Vpechatleniĩa sezona" (Moscow. Impressions of the Season), EZHEGODNIK IMPERATORSKIKH TEATROV (St. Petersburg), I (1910), 118-26.

Caesar and Cleopatra is one of Shaw's best and cleverest plays. His aim throughout is to unmask lies, fight conventions in morality and politics, although for breadth of ideas and originality Man and Superman is superior. Probably the extreme poverty of the English stage nowadays makes Shaw's plays so highly valued. [In Russian.]

876 "Eibundan no taisei" (The Trend of Contemporary English Literature), TAIYO (Tokyo), XVI: 2 (Jan 1910), 182-96.
Shaw is the most conspicuous figure among dramatists. All modern writers are more or less fatalists, but what characterizes him is his national socialistic ideas. It is extraordinary that Britain has produced such a destructive and iconoclastic writer as Shaw. [In Japanese.]

877 " 'G. B. S.' & the 'Dark Lady': Ownership of an Idea," DN, 23 Nov 1910, p. 1.
[Details of the controversy over Frank Harris' and Shaw's representation of Shakespeare in their respective plays, SHAKESPEARE AND HIS LOVE and The Dark Lady of the Sonnets. See also in DN: " 'The Dark Lady,' " 24 Nov 1910, p. 1; E. A. Baughan, "The Dark Lady," 25 Nov 1910, p. 1; Frank Harris, "Mary Fitton," 30 Nov 1910, p. 9.]

878 Godley, Eveline C. "Drama," THE ANNUAL REGISTER 1909 (Lond: Longmans, Green, 1910), part II, pp. 102-06.
[Mention of Shaw's role in the 1909 stage censorship debate.]

879 Grein, J. T. "The Dramatic World," STIMES, 27 Nov 1910, p. 6.
The Dark Lady of the Sonnets is hardly worthy of Shaw's reputation and is in questionable taste.

880 Grein, J. T. "Premieres of the Week," STIMES, 27 Feb 1910, p. 4.
Misalliance would not have been produced but for Shaw being the author. Indeed, he is now living on his past glories—John Bull's Other Island, Man and Superman, and Major Barbara. The characters in Misalliance are mechanical, unconvincing, and inconsistent even within their own terms of reference.

881 Hamilton, Clayton. THE THEORY OF THE THEATRE AND OTHER PRINCIPLES OF DRAMATIC CRITICISM (NY: Holt, 1910), pp. 43, 47, 74, 143, 147, 222-25.
Shaw scorns tradition and his wit helps to attract faddish audiences, though this methodology cannot succeed for long. Man and Superman is not as effective as the works of Schopenhauer and Nietzsche. Shaw's pleasant plays demonstrate the fact that such plays generally "are better suited for service in the theatre than unpleasant plays." His own unpleasant plays have failed to interest people.

882 Harris, Frank. "The Theatre: The Dark Lady of the

Sonnets," ACADEMY, LXXIX (3 Dec 1910), 543-44.
Shaw has clearly borrowed his ideas about the Dark Lady from Harris' earlier writings on Shakespeare. To have such a disciple as Shaw is very complimentary, but only when the disciple adheres to the true doctrine. In this instance Shaw does not do so, and he should have left Shakespeare alone.

883 Hauser, Otto. WELTGESCHICHTE DER LITERATUR (World History of Literature) (Leipzig & Vienna: Bibliographisches Institut, 1910), II, 81.
Shaw pretends to be an anti-romantic writer; he is, however, a devoted romantic. Opposition is his main characteristic. [In German.]

884 Hevesi, Sandor. "Bernard Shaw otthon" (Bernard Shaw at Home), VILAG (Budapest), 11 Sept 1910 [not seen].
[In Hungarian.]

885 "How England Regulates the Drama," CUR LIT, XLVIII (1910), 72-73.
"The immediate cause for the present investigation [of dramatic censorship] has been the suppression of . . . Shaw's remarkable dramas The Shewing-up of Blanco Posnet and Press Cuttings."

886 Howe, P. P. THE REPERTORY THEATRE: A RECORD & A CRITICISM (Lond: Secker, 1910), pp. 16, 29-33, 42, 45, 49, 53-56, 67, 70, 80-82, 91-101, 128, 139, 155-58, 163, 166, 168-69, 174-76, 182, 185, 194, 210, 217-27, 233-34, 236, 240-41.
Shaw is the "symbol of much of the spirit of the revolt" of the new drama; in fact, he is a "whole school in himself, and a bad master." [Essentially an examination of the repertory theatre movement, and of Charles Frohman's repertory season at the Duke of York's Theatre in 1910, with some examination of the role of Shaw's plays within these phenomena. Some attention paid to Misalliance.]

887 "The Husband, the Supertax, and the Suffragists," TIMES, 10 June 1910, p. 7.
[An anthology of correspondence between Shaw and the Special Commissioners of Income Tax on supertax and the assessment of a wife's income.]

888 Kapteyn-Muysken, Geertruida. G. BERNARD SHAW (The Hague: Luctor & Emergo, 1910) [not seen].
[In Dutch.]

889 Katsuya, Kinson. "Shakaihihyoka to shiteno Bernard Shaw o ronzu" (Bernard Shaw as a Critic of Society), GAKUTO (Tokyo), XIV: 3 (March 1910), 1-7; XIV: 4 (April 1910), 3-9.
Shaw never idolizes democracy and socialism and does not believe in progress. However, he is not a pessimist; rather he is an optimist who enjoys laughter rather than weeping. [In Japanese.]

890 Kawashima, Fūkotsu. "Ibsenshigo no gekibungaku" (Dramatic Literature after Ibsen's Death), SHUMI (Tokyo), V: 5 (May 1910), 1-8.
Shaw is the most important dramatist in the western world since Ibsen's death. [In Japanese.]

891 "The Labour Party's Position," TIMES, 7 Jan 1910, p. 4.
Shaw and others have contributed their views on the current strengths of the Labour Party.

892 "London Theatres: The Duke of York's," STAGE, 3 March 1910, pp. 19-20.
Misalliance shows Shaw as a "serio-comic tilter against windmills" as he moves with great rapidity from one topic to another. Certain "allusions to the supposed antagonism between parents and children" can be traced back to Ibsen, while Shaw's impudent and patronizing references to the Bible will be found offensive by the conventional playgoer (whom Shaw despises anyway).

893 "London Theatres: The Haymarket," STAGE, 1 Dec 1910, p. 18.
The Dark Lady of the Sonnets is an incorrigible farce. When Shaw is not laughing openly at Shakespeare, he laughs up his sleeve.

894 "London Theatres: The Lyric," STAGE, 15 Sept 1910, p. 18.
Hardly any of Arms and the Man is to be found in THE CHOCOLATE SOLDIER.

895 "Malleus." "Shaw with Music," SAT REV, CX (1910), 355-56.
THE CHOCOLATE SOLDIER vulgarizes some of the most brilliant and amusing dialogue in English. There is little connection between it and Arms and the Man.

896 M[assingham], H. W. "The Drama: The ELEKTRA as a Play," NATION (Lond), VI (26 March 1910), 999.
Shaw's view of Richard Strauss' ELEKTRA weighs as equally as Ernest Newman's and it is difficult to decide who is right. [For further details, see item 906.]

897 "May Use Lash on Apaches," NYT, 25 Sept 1910, part III, p. 4.
Shaw has come out against the use of whipping as a punishment.

898 Meierhold', V. E. "O postanovke Tseria i Kleopatry na stsene Novogo dramaticheskogo teatra" (The Production of Caesar and Cleopatra at the New Dramatic Theatre), APOLLON (St. Petersburg), No. 4 (1910), 79-80; rptd in V. E. Meierhold', STAT'I, vol I (Moscow: Iskusstvo, 1968), pp. 202-04.
This production of Caesar and Cleopatra has changed Shaw's deeply ironic tone and made it farcical. [In Russian.]

899 "Misalliance: A Debate by G. B. Shaw," DT, 24 Feb 1910, p. 12.
Misalliance is an arbitrarily divided conversation which touches on numerous topics.

900 "Mr. Bernard Shaw on Music," TIMES, 7 Dec 1910, p. 13.
Shaw has lectured the Musical Association on changes in popular taste in music.

901 "Mr. Bernard Shaw on Unemployment," TIMES, 8 Oct 1910, p. 8.
Shaw addressed a meeting on unemployment organized by the Labour Party.

902 "Mr. Shaw on the Poor Law," TIMES, 3 May 1910, p. 12.
Shaw and Sidney Webb have spoken at a meeting on reform of the Poor Laws.

903 "A Modern Media," ERA, 16 July 1910, p. 13.
Press Cuttings was much enjoyed by the audience and was acted "with much spirit."

904 "Murder Easy, Says Shaw," NYT, 21 Aug 1910, part III, p. 2.
In the "silly season" of non-news, Shaw has contributed his views on cremation and other matters.

905 "Musings without Method: The Vestryman of the Theatre," BLACKWOOD'S MAGAZINE, CLXXXVII (April 1910), 585-86.
With Misalliance Shaw thinks he can force anything on the public who should laugh at everything he writes. But the play is nothing more than endless talk which amounts to a "long-drawn travesty of himself."

906 Newman, Ernest. "To the Editor of THE NATION," NATION (Lond), VI (12 March 1910), 915.
Shaw has completely misunderstood Newman's article on Richard Strauss' ELEKTRA [NATION, VI (26 Feb 1910), 843-44], and when Shaw "knows something about the opera," he will be happy to discuss it with him. [For further details of this debate, see NATION (Lond): VI (12 March 1910), 914-15, (19 March 1910), 969, (26 March 1910), 1001-03; VII (2 April 1910), 18-19, (9 April 1910), 54-55; and item 896.]

907 O. "The Theatre," WOLRD, No. 1861 (1 March 1910), 353.
Misalliance is full of talk, and cannot be considered a true play. But its tediousness is balanced by humor and Shaw's torrent of ideas (all old) is leavened by wit.

908 Osanai, Kaoru. "Igirisu niokeru JOHN GABRIEL BORKMAN no Shoen" (The First Performance of JOHN GABRIEL BORKMAN in England), KABUKI (Tokyo), No. 114 (Jan 1910), 26-32; rptd in OSANAI KAORU ENGEKIRON

ZENSHU (The Collected Works of Kaoru Osanai's Dramatic Theory), vol I (Tokyo: Miraisha, 1964), pp. 112-14.
Shaw's review of the first English production of JOHN GABRIEL BORKMAN was very useful when the play was produced for the first time in Japan. [In Japanese.]

909 Platon, I. S. "K postanovke istoricheskoi komedii Bernard Shaw Tsezar i Kleopatra" (On the Production of Bernard Shaw's Historical Comedy Caesar and Cleopatra), EZHEGODNIK IMPERATOR-SKIKH TEATROV (St. Petersburg), No. 1 (1910), 82-89.
The production of Caesar and Cleopatra, with a revised text, has provoked mixed reactions, largely because of the inadequacy of the costumes and settings. [In Russian.]

910 "The Playhouses," ILN, CXXXVII (17 Sept 1910), 410.
THE CHOCOLATE SOLDIER is successful musically, but the libretto scarcely resembles Arms and the Man, which is satirically witty.

911 "Premijera Zanat gospode Warren" (First Night of Mrs. Warren's Profession), OBZOR (Zagreb), LI (1910), 3, 1 [not seen].
[In Croatian.]

912 "Professional Man." "The Public Mourning," TIMES, 13 May 1910, p. 6.
Shaw has not got his facts right with regard to the effects public mourning will have on some people. [See also Shaw's letter, TIMES, 12 May 1910, p. 8.]

913 "The Repertory Theatre," ERA, 26 Feb 1910, p. 17.
Misalliance is a success and elicts much laughter from the audience.

914 Rogers, A[rthur] K[enyon]. "Mr. Bernard Shaw's Philosophy," HIBBERT JOURNAL, VIII (July 1910), 818-37.
Shaw's philosophy is relevant, consistent, and well-considered. Man and Superman demonstrates his creed that reality is life itself, "the great world-force which is blindly energizing in nature" and which results in self-knowledge. Shaw sees things in their "naked reality," and his sense of factual reality is greatly offended by sham and inconsistency. Instinct should guide people, he believes, but the emotions and insincere moralities are to be condemned. Shaw criticizes institutions and thinks individuals should be thoroughly absorbed in their work to the highest professional degree. A defect in Shaw's philosophy is the too prominent role he assigns to instinct. His superman doctrine is also flawed because it is really too idealistic. Shaw's value lies in his "call to clear self-scrutiny and consistency in our social ideals."

915 "The Secret Puritanism of Bernard Shaw," CUR LIT, XLIX (1910), 409-11.

[An overview of some books on Shaw and reviewers' reactions to them.]

916 "Shakespeare Memorial Matinee," ERA, 26 Nov 1910, p. 17.
[On the performance of The Dark Lady of the Sonnets and its plot.]

917 "The Shakespeare Memorial National Theatre: Mr. G. B. Shaw's New Play," TIMES, 25 Nov 1910, p. 13.
The Dark Lady of the Sonnets wittily portrays Shaw's idea that Shakespeare was indebted to everyday, common speech.

918 "Shaw takes a Hand in Waist Strike," NYT, 6 Jan 1910, p. 5.
Shaw has added his commentary on a garment-makers strike in New York. [See also: "Plan to Call Out 3,000 More Strikers," NYT, 7 Jan 1910, p. 6.]

919 "Shaw's Tribute to Rodin," NYT, 19 June 1910, part III, p. 4.
Shaw asserts that any praise of Rodin in superfluous, rather like Adam congratulating God.

920 "The Society of Authors," TIMES, 17 March 1910, p. 3.
Shaw has addressed a meeting of the Society of Authors on the unscrupulous practices of publishers.

921 S[pence], E. F. OUR STAGE AND ITS CRITICS (Lond: Methuen, 1910), pp. 29, 34, 74, 93, 101, 115-116, 253-54, 257-61, 293.
Shaw's work may well outlast all contemporary drama. He is brilliant and wants to startle his audiences. He handles love in an "intensely unsentimental fashion." He also has a strong dislike of amateur theatricals.

922 S[pence], E. F. "The Stage from the Stalls," SKETCH, LXIX (2 March 1910), 246.
Misalliance is a wittily intoxicating play, slightly too long—a topsy-turvy farce.

923 "Spinx." "The Theatre," WORLD, No. 1900 (29 Nov 1910), 820.
The Dark Lady of the Sonnets does not contain very much, but it is still "well clad." It is witty, and Shaw's eloquence is stirring.

924 Street, G. S. "Robertson and Some Others," SAT REV, CX (1910), 75-76.
It is impossible to enjoy both T. W. Robertson and Shaw because the former wrote for children, the latter for adults. However, Misalliance represents a falling off in Shaw's ability. John Bull's Other Island, Major Barbara, and Candida would command attention even if there was nothing but good dialogue in them; Misalliance, by comparison, is dismal.

925 "The Theatre: 'Leaving Aristotle Out,'" TIMES, 20 June 1910, p. 12.

[Extracts from LE JOURNAL DE EDMOND GOT, with references to Shaw's inability to understand critics. See also Shaw's response, TIMES, 23 June 1910, p. 12.]

926 Tree, Viola. "The Censorship of Stage Plays: Another Point of View," NINETEENTH CENTURY, LXVII (1910), 164-72.

The Shewing-up of Blanco Posnet is a sermon and perhaps ought to have failed with the public because it is too religious rather than too blasphemous.

927 Trench, Herbert. "Dramatic Values," SAT REV, CX (1910), 49.

It is good to have Shaw's support for "plays of the higher order," but an endowed theatre is needed for such works to be performed. [See also in SAT REV: Trench, "Dramatic Values and a Suggested Solution," CIX (1910), 815-16; Shaw's letter, CX (1910), 13-14.]

928 Walbrook, H. M. "The Dark Lady of the Sonnets," PMG (1910) [not seen]; rptd in NIGHTS AT THE PLAY (Lond: W. J. Ham-Smith, 1911), pp. 12-15.

The Dark Lady of the Sonnets is original and full of drollery, while some passages soar to heights of eloquent splendor.

929 Walbrook, H. M. "Misalliance," PMG (1910) [not seen]; rptd in NIGHTS AT THE PLAY (Lond: W. J. Ham-Smith, 1911), pp. 1-6.

Misalliance is whimsical, witty, and full of sense; it has as much plot and characterization as most contemporary plays.

930 Watsuji, Tetsuro. "Shaw ni oyoboshitaru Nietzsche no eikyo" (The Influence of Nietzsche on Shaw), TEIKOKU BUNGAKU (Tokyo), XVI: 2 (Feb 1910), 186-90; rptd in WATSUJI TETSURO ZENSHU (Collected Works of Tetsuro Watsuji), vol XX (Tokyo: Iwanami Shoten, 1963), pp. 205-10.

All Shaw's works bear the distinct marks of Nietzschean thought. Mrs. Warren's Profession, for example, shows a woman has the right to pursue happiness regardless of social conventions or criticisms. Such a woman is justified in using appropriate means to gain those results. [In Japanese.]

931 Watsuji, Tetsuro. "Shawgeki kenbutsuki" (Seeing a Shaw Play), TEIKOKU BUNGAKU (Tokyo), XVI: 11 (Nov 1910), 1218-27; XVI: 12 (Dec 1910), 1315-24.

[A favorable review of You Never Can Tell, the first Shaw production in Japan, at the Gaiety Theatre, Yokohama, on 12 Oct 1910. In Japanese.]

932 Winter, William. LIFE AND ART OF RICHARD MANSFIELD WITH SELECTIONS FROM HIS LETTERS. 2 vols

(NY: Moffat, Yard, 1910).

[Numerous passing references to Shaw as a result of Mansfield's portrayal of such roles as Bluntschli and Dick Dugeon.]

933 Yasunari, Sadao.   "Ibsen eiyaku, oyobi kenkyushomoku" (Ibsen's Works Translated into English, and a List of Books on Him), WASEDA BUNGAKU (Tokyo), No. 53 (April 1910), 81-88.

Shaw's The Quintessence of Ibsenism is a book that every student of Ibsen must read. [In Japanese.]

1911

---

934 "The Academic Committee," TIMES, 17 June 1911, p. 12.

Shaw has been elected to the Academic Committee of the Royal Society of Literature.

935 Adcock, A. St. John.   "Bernard Shaw's New Plays," BOOKMAN (Lond), XL (May 1911), 94-95.

The Doctor's Dilemma and Other Plays is entertaining and amusing, although the plays would be more effective if they were independent of the prefaces. The Doctor's Dilemma is farce in the old style; Getting Married is clever but ineffective and superficial; The Shewing-up of Blanco Posnet is full of glorious sentimentality but is untrue.

936 "Arms and the Man at the Criterion," ACADEMY, LXXX (27 May 1911), 663.

Arms and the Man need be seen only once.

937 "Arms and the Man at the Criterion," ERA, 20 May 1911, p. 17.

Arms and the Man is one of Shaw's most popular plays with good dramatic qualitites—good characterization and witty dialogue.

938 "Arms and the Man at the Criterion," ILN, CXXXVIII (27 May 1911), 806, 808.

Arms and the Man is now seen as enjoyable and witty, whereas when it was first produced it exasperated and annoyed.

939 "Art, Music and the Drama," ILN, CXXXIX (7 Oct 1911), 562.

In this revival of Man and Superman the emphasis is on the comedic aspects of the play, and Shaw's philosophy of woman as the eternal hunter is toned down.

940 "At the Play," OBS, 23 April 1911, p. 9.

Fanny's First Play is a genuine play rather than a discussion, and possesses both charm and urgency. Improbabilities of plot are balanced by interesting manipulations.

941 "Attack on Mr. Bernard Shaw," TIMES, 8 June 1911, p. 5.
Professor J. C. Adami of McGill University has called Shaw a "fool for his gibes at Christianity, and decadent for his 'wicked perversion' " in the preface to The Doctor's Dilemma.

942 Bahr, Hermann. [Bernard Shaw], NEUE FREIE PRESSE (Vienna), 19 Jan 1911 [not seen]; trans by John J. Weisert in "Bahr Describes GBS on the Platform," SHAW REVIEW, II: 7 (Jan 1959), 13-15.
[A description of Shaw's performance as an orator.]

943 Bahr, Hermann. "Englisches Gespräch" (English Talk), DIE NEUE RUNDSCHAU, XXII: 1 (1911), 844-49.
Samuel Butler is Shaw's "father" and G. K. Chesterton's "aunt." Shaw writes only about "forbidden" subjects. With the exception of Shaw, all Englishmen are similar. [In German.]

944 Benesić, Julije. "Candida," NARODNE NOVINE (Zagreb), LXXVII (1911), 235 [not seen].
[In Croatian.]

945 "Bernard Shaw and His American Boswell," CUR LIT, LI (Aug 1911), 202-05.
There has been considerable controversy surrounding Archibald Henderson's biography of Shaw [item 985], particularly with Shaw accusing Henderson of inaccurate reporting.

946 "A Bernard Shaw Revival," ERA, 23 Sept 1911, p. 19.
Recently Shaw's work has been disappointing; however, the forthcoming revival of Man and Superman provides an opportunity of analyzing Shaw's methods—his ability to draw on stock material and to inject his own personality into the role of Tanner. Any philosophy in his play is commonplace.

947 Bernstein, Herman. "'Why should I Go to America?' Asks Bernard Shaw," NYT, 14 May 1911, part V, p. 2; rptd in CELEBRITIES OF OUR TIME: INTERVIEWS (1924; rptd Freeport, NY: Books for Libraries, 1968), pp. 100-19.
[A biographical interview, with Shaw's antithetical views of America.]

948 Björkman, Edwin. "À Propos Shaw," FORUM (Lond & NY), XLVI (Nov 1911), 601-07.
[Largely a review of Archibald Henderson's GEORGE BERNARD SHAW (item 985), but interspersed with some subjective commentary by Björkman.]

949 Björkman, Edwin. "The Serious Bernard Shaw," REV OF REVS, XLIII (1911), 425-29; rptd in IS THERE ANYTHING NEW UNDER THE SUN? (NY & Lond: M. Kennerley, 1911), pp. 161-82.

A brief overview of Shaw's life and work reveals three pervasive qualities—"his complete soundness of mind and body, his inflexible sincerity of conviction and purpose, and his remarkable many-sideness."

950 Bosdari, A[lessandro] de. "George Bernard Shaw," NUOVA ANTOLOGIA (Rome), 16 Oct 1911, pp. 549-66.

Italian readers who have never seen or read a play by Shaw (only Candida has been translated as yet) may find a summary of his works to date an aid in deciding whether his work is worth studying. His attraction for readers is mysterious as he overturns all our pre-conceived ideas by his spirit of contradiction, and his air of superiority. [In Italian.]

951 Cabot, Richard C. "The Doctor's Dilemma in Bernard Shaw and in Fact," SURVEY (NY), XXVI (3 June 1911), 381-83.

Shaw's duel thesis in The Doctor's Dilemma is that the medical profession is a conspiracy against public interest and that "the public, in the same blind and staggering fashion, aids and abets the medical profession in the worst of its errors." A doctor's own experience confirms this.

952 Calvert, Mrs. Charles [A. H.]. SIXTY-EIGHT YEARS ON THE STAGE (Lond: Mills & Boon, 1911), pp. 252-60, 262.

[Details of Calvert's recruitment to and acting in Arms and the Man in 1894, its hurried rehearsal, and public reception. Two Shaw letters included.]

953 "Candida: A Personally Conducted Plot," DRAMATIST (Easton, PA), II (April 1911), 164-65.

Candida's two fundamental flaws are that the main conflict lacks realism, and "the weak and sniveling character" of Marchbanks is implausible.

954 Chendi, Ilarie. "Un spirit contemporan. George Bernard Shaw" (George Bernard Shaw. A Contemporary Spirit), CALENDARUL MINERVEI (Bucharest), 1911, pp. 225-38 [not seen].

[In Roumanian.]

955 "Chronicle and Comment: Shaw's Formula," BOOKMAN (NY), XXXIII (Aug 1911), 576-80.

[A summary of Shaw's opinions on French drama as revealed in his preface to THREE PLAYS BY BRIEUX.]

956 Clayton, Walter. "Ten Books of the Month: IV: Three Prefaces and Plays by Bernard Shaw," BOOKMAN (NY), XXXIII (June 1911), 429-30.

Shaw turns the world upside down and laughs at it, although the truths he attempts to point out are, in reality, only half-truths. Also, since he has taught everyone to expect the unexpected from him, he is now forced into rather strained positions.

957 Colvin, Sidney, ed. THE LETTERS OF ROBERT LOUIS STEVENSON (NY: Scribner's, 1911; rptd NY: Greenwood, 1969), vol III, pp. 48-51.
[Letters to William Archer praising Cashel Byron's Profession.]

958 "Criterion Theatre: Arms and the Man," TIMES, 19 May 1911, p. 10.
Arms and the Man still ranks highly among Shaw's lighter works.

959 "Criterion Theatre: Man and Superman," TIMES, 20 Dec 1911, p. 10.
Man and Superman remains a popular play.

960 Dark, Sidney. "Tory Democracy," NEW AGE, (Lond), ns IX (1 June 1911), 114-15.
J. M. Kennedy's assertion [in "Tory Democracy," NEW AGE, ns IX (18 May 1911), 54] that the leading thinkers of the day are either radicals or socialists is wrong. For example, he cites Shaw; but Shaw is "witty, unsatisfactory, a genius at intervals. His one real idea is that woman rules the world by unsentimental commonsense, and that man being wisely passionate is her inferior in what to me are the unessentials."

961 "The Dark Lady of the Sonnets: Bernard Shaw's Soliciting Skit," DRAMATIST (Easton, PA), II (1911), 151-52.
The Dark Lady of the Sonnets is a good example of Shaw's propensity to write "theme for theme sake."

962 "The Doctor's Dilemma: Bernard Shaw's Brilliant Muck-Raking Drama," CUR OP, L (1911), 419-24.
[A favorable review, with extensive extracts.]

963 "Drama," ATH, No. 4355 (15 April 1911), 427-28.
The publication of The Doctor's Dilemma, Getting Married, and The Shewing-up of Blanco Posnet confirms the belief that Shaw's revolutionary ideas are little more than a claim for freedom of thought.

964 "Dramatic Gossip," ATH, No. 4380 (7 Oct 1911), 436.
Man and Superman is a diverting comedy and shows Shaw is becoming popular.

965 Dukes, Ashley. "Drama," NEW AGE (Lond), ns VIII (23 March 1911), 497-98.
In The Doctor's Dilemma, Getting Married, and The Shewing-up of Blanco Posnet Shaw has failed to write a memorable, moving scene. "His diction suffers from elephantiasis" and only his wit saves him from dullness. His puritanism is a failing because it "sets ethics before taste, dessicates illusion, diverts all artistic emotion through the individual to a social end, creates a moral test of pure enjoyment," and prevents Shaw from writing a beautifully intrinsic scene.

966 Dukes, Ashley. "Drama," NEW AGE (Lond), ns VIII (27 April 1911), 616.

Shaw has forestalled all criticism in Fanny's First Play because the critics in the play exhaust every possibility and aspect of Fanny's play. Shaw's work is an immense practical joke.

967 Dukes, Ashley. MODERN DRAMATISTS (Lond: Frank Palmer, 1911), pp. 2, 11, 26-27, 36-37, 57, 65-67, 90, 99, 112, 118-36, 141-42, 150, 224-26, 240-41, 244-45, 247, 265, 274-75.

If Shaw had written only Caesar and Cleopatra, The Devil's Disciple, and The Man of Destiny he would still be "distinctively a modern author." Widowers' Houses made theatrical history and Shaw has proved himself to be a "greater individual force than either Brieux . . . or Hauptmann. . . ." In addition to giving life to the Stage Society, Shaw's works provided the backbone to the Vedrenne-Barker management of the Court Theatre in 1904-07.

Shaw is the most interesting of contemporary dramatists, as well as having the strongest personality and the clearest mind. But he is not as great as Ibsen because he lacks great dramatic craftsmanship, which he covers up with his extensive stage directions (the latter are the proper province of the novel, not the theatre). He is a great crusader (as in Major Barbara) and an intellectual master (as in Man and Superman), but he rarely arouses emotion. The only passion he displays is that of indignation which he makes palatable by his wit.

968 Dunton, Edith Kellogg. "Three Plays for Iconoclasts," DIAL, L (1 April 1911), 257-59; rptd in NATION (NY), XCII (30 March 1911), 325-26.

Shaw is a man of ideas who has "astutely armed himself with a two-edged sword: the Play and the Preface." Of the plays, The Shewing-up of Blanco Posnet is the most striking; "Getting Married is as refreshingly comic as anything Mr. Shaw has written; The Doctor's Dilemma is as deliberately and painstakingly fair-minded."

969 "Equal Wealth for All," TIMES, 1 Dec 1911, p. 7.

Shaw and G. K. Chesterton have debated each other about socialism.

970 "Fanny's First Play," ERA, 22 April 1911, p. 17.

Fanny's First Play, with its caustic witty satire, bears all the marks of Shaw.

971 "Fanny's First Play in Berlin," TIMES, 23 Oct 1911, p. 11.

Fanny's First Play puzzled a well-disposed German audience because it appears to be "gänzlich unmotiviert" [completely unmotivated].

972 Farjeon, Herbert. "The Theatre," WORLD, No. 1921 (25 April 1911), 591.

The parts of Fanny's First Play are greater than the whole, and the piece does not adhere to dramatic rules. Shaw is unable to keep his multitudinous ideas under control.

973 Farjeon, Herbert. "The Theatre," WORLD, No. 1925 (23 May 1911), 761.
Arms and the Man is now a popular play, still a little ahead of its time, and possibly Shaw's best comedy.

974 Farjeon, Herbert. "The Theatre: The G. B. Essence of Shaw," WORLD, No. 1944 (3 Oct 1911), 508.
Man and Superman is a remarkable play in which the "intellectual harlequin, pragmatical philosopher, passionate Puritan, knight-errant breaking innumerable lances with civilisation" all contend with each other. Shaw's philosophy is unconvincing, however, because Tanner is too much a part of Shaw; he should have been made a strong antagonist instead.

975 Friche, V. "Mezhdu tragediei i farsom" (Between Tragedy and Farce), SOVREMENNYI MIR (St. Petersburg), 1911, No. 2, pp. 160-69 [not seen].
[In Russian.]

976 Frohman, Daniel. MEMORIES OF A MANAGER (Garden City, NY: Doubleday, Page, 1911), pp. 29-31.
[Brief details of Frohman's connections with Shaw, including his offer of a guaranteed annual salary if Shaw would write him a play a year. Shaw refused. Also mention of Richard Mansfield's Shavian work.]

977 " 'G. B. S.' as an Economist," NYT, 2 April 1911, part VII, p. 183.
The Commonsense of Municipal Trading is lucid and illuminating, and shows Shaw's clear and frank understanding of the subject.

978 "G. B. Shaw's View of Christ," NYT, 30 May 1911, p. 3.
Shaw has given a lecture in which he declared Christ was a failure.

979 Glover, James M. JIMMY GLOVER HIS BOOK (Lond: Methuen, 1911), pp. 88, 90, 130, 135-37.
[Brief reminiscences of Shaw as a music critic, when his acidity upset Augustus Harris at Covent Garden.]

980 Godley, Eveline C. "Drama," THE ANNUAL REGISTER 1910 (Lond: Longmans, Green, 1911), part II, pp. 101-05.
Misalliance possesses Shaw's "usual brilliant dialogue," but, as a whole, it is "too grotesquely incoherent to be very interesting."

981 Grein, J. T. "The Dramatic World," STIMES, 23 April 1911, p. 6.
Fanny's First Play is a "series of plasticised debates" containing some almost offensive jokes and pusillanimous jibes.

982 Henderson, Archibald. "Bernard Shaw Intime" (Private Bernard Shaw), MERCURE DE FRANCE, XCI (1911), 449-65 [not seen].

GEORGE BERNARD SHAW

[Cited in Hood, p. 244. In French.]

983 Henderson, Archibald. "Bernard Shaw, the Dramatist," DAILY OBSERVER (Charlotte, NC), 5 Feb 1911, p. 3, 12 Feb 1911, p. 9. 19 Feb, 1911, p. 22; rptd as "Bernard Shaw als Dramatiker," DEUTSCHE REVUE, XXXVI (June 1911), 355-68; rptd as "Bernard Shaw: Dramatikern," FINSK TIDSKRIFT, LXIX (June 1911), 176-96 [none seen].

[Cited in Hood, p. 224.]

984 Henderson, Archibald. "Did Bernard Shaw Plagiarize His Shakespearean Play?" NYT, 5 Feb 1911, part V, p. 6.

Shaw's The Dark Lady of the Sonnets is totally different from Frank Harris' SHAKESPEARE AND HIS LOVE. However, the two men are engaged in a long and fiery debate over Harris' charges of plagiarism.

985 Henderson, Archibald. GEORGE BERNARD SHAW: HIS LIFE AND WORKS: A CRITICAL BIOGRAPHY (AUTHORIZED) (Cincinnati: Stewart & Kidd; Lond: Hurst & Blackett, 1911; NY: Boni & Liveright, 1918).

[A high proportion of this work is biographical, written by an enthusiastic admirer, whose critical judgments are similarly tempered. Henderson covers the numerous facets of Shaw's life—early days, as a Fabian, music/art/dramatic critic, etc.—very exhaustively, with frequent interpolations of Shaw's "own" words and views. Three chapters are given over to Shaw as a playwright, with additional chapters on Shaw as a technician, dramatist, artist and philosopher, and as a man. Also provided are: several illustrations, facsimilies of a letter from Shaw to Henderson, the first and last pages of the manuscript of Love Among the Artists; playbills; and a genealogical chart of the Shaw family. This is basic reading, but needs to be used with caution both biographically and critically.]

986 Henderson, Archibald. INTERPRETERS OF LIFE AND THE MODERN SPIRIT (1911; rptd Freeport, NY: Books for Libraries, 1968), pp. 286-330; rptd in EUROPEAN DRAMATISTS (Cincinnati: Stewart and Kidd, 1913; Lond: Richards, 1914; Cincinnati: Stewart & Kidd, 1918; NY: Appleton, 1926), pp. 323-69.

Shaw is a self-advertising showman who loves to astonish people, especially the wise. He is a "strictly constitutional Socialist" who sees issues in intellectual rather than emotional terms. He has a "trenchant and sagacious intellect" which he applies to "individual and social illusions." "If Shaw is a Celtic Molière de nos jours, it is a Molière in whom comedy stems from the individual and tragedy from society. If Shaw is the Irish Ibsen, it is a laughing Ibsen—looking out upon a half-mad world with the riant eyes of a Heine, a Chamfort, or a Sheridan." [Largely biographical and descriptive, rather than analytical.]

118

987 Henderson, Archibald. "Mr. Bernard Shaw and His Biographer," MPOST, 26 May 1911, p. 5.
[A lengthy and detailed repudiation of Shaw's letter (2 May 1911, p. 10), explaining that Shaw saw all of Henderson's biography (item 985) in manuscript, and therefore either explicitly or tacitly approved it.]

988 Henderson, Archibald. "The New Drama in England: H. Granville Barker," FORUM (NY), XLV (June 1911), 707-24.
[An account of recent developments in English drama, with passing references to Shaw as one of the leading exponents.]

989 "The Hitchin Contest," TIMES, 17 Nov 1911, p. 7.
Shaw has had a characteristic discussion with Lord Robert Cecil at a Unionist political meeting.

990 Howorth, Henry H. "Mr. Bernard Shaw's Proposal," TIMES, 13 June 1911, p. 11.
Shaw's letter on the Birkbeck Bank [TIMES, 10 June 1911, p. 10] is full of his "usual ingenious plausibility," but is, in fact, "mischievous." [See also: W. G. Hall, "Birkbeck Bank," TIMES, 14 June 1911, p. 6.]

991 Hueffer [Ford], Ford Madox. MEMORIES AND IMPRESSIONS: A STUDY IN ATMOSPHERES (NY & Lond: Harper, 1911), pp. 134, 141-42.
[Brief, favorable reminiscences.]

992 "The Human Factor in Medicine," NATION (NY), XCII (1911), 286-87.
In The Doctor's Dilemma Shaw, "in sneering at the doctors' mistakes, only presents an interesting combination of anarchistic distaste for authority with the primitive man's fear of witchcraft."

993 "An Inspection of Bernard Shaw," HARPER'S WEEKLY, LV (22 April 1911), 6.
Shaw always challenges the establishment, never closes his eyes to reality, and, provokingly, laughs riotously. These features can be detected in The Doctor's Dilemma and Getting Married.

994 "Irish Actors in a New Bill," SUN (NY), 24 Nov 1911, p. 7.
The Shewing-up of Blanco Posnet is Shaw's worst play: the characters are all Shaw's mouthpieces and the dialogue lacks any coloring.

995 "The Jester with a Purpose," SPECTATOR, CVI (11 March 1911), 360-62.
In the preface to The Doctor's Dilemma Shaw exhibits bad taste, and in that to Getting Married his views are illogical and show a lack of understanding of the institution of marriage. His melodrama, The Shewing-up of Blanco Posnet, however, is "an exceedingly moving story in dramatic form."

996 "Little Theatre," ATH, No. 4356 (22 April 1911), 455-56.
Shaw's attack on critics in Fanny's First Play is in somewhat poor

taste. His attempt to write a conventional play shows no technical progress, although Shaw is able to handle characters whose opinions differ from his own.

997 "The Little Theatre," STAGE, 20 April 1911, p. 18.
If Fanny's First Play is not by Shaw, it certainly ought to be since it bears his characteristic marks. "It has all his satire and his clear vision (which is sometimes confounded with his humour)."

998 "The Little Theatre: Fanny's First Play," DT, 20 April 1911, p. 4.
It takes some time to reach the heart of this skit on Shavian methods, principles and ideas, but ultimately the joke is worth it. There are also flashes of Ibsenism and melodrama, together with long and somewhat tedious discussions.

999 "Little Theatre: Fanny's First Play," TIMES, 20 April 1911, p. 8.
Fanny's First Play lacks coherence, but contains "harmless, good-humoured, middle-aged fun."

1000 "London Theatres: The Criterion," STAGE, 25 May 1911, p. 20.
Shaw's dialogue in Arms and the Man still sparkles, and the whole play still diverts.

1001 "London Theatres: The Criterion," STAGE, 5 Oct 1911, p. 17.
Expediently and fortunately, Don Juan in Hell is cut from this revival of Man and Superman, and certainly Shaw for four-and-a-half hours would prove too much.

1002 "London Variety Stage: The Palace," STAGE, 7 Dec 1911, p. 15.
How He Lied to Her Husband is one of the least Shavian of Shaw's plays, but it is still full of his characteristic satire.

1003 Madrid, Louis. "Brieux and Bernard Shaw: A Note on Two Social Reformers," MASK, IV (July 1911), 13-16.
There is no one in England who equals Shaw as a social reformer; however, Shaw's use of social propaganda explains how little he understands the nature of the theatre, which has nothing in common with social or political reform. Shaw lacks humanity, although he is obviously highly courageous and possesses the "noblest of intentions."

1004 Mair, G. H. ENGLISH LITERATURE: MODERN (NY: Holt; Lond: Williams & Norgate, 1911), pp. 253-45; rptd in Evans, pp. 205-06.
Shaw is the "most remarkable" of the new school of dramatists, although it took time for him to become established. This was because audiences clung to the "stock tradition" and because of

Shaw's weakness in dramatic construction.

1005 "Man and Superman," ERA, 30 Sept 1911, p. 19.
Man and Superman is clearly a witty play and possesses good characterizations. With Tanner, Shaw "never misses an opportunity of
shocking the ordinary person with fixed ideas as to what constitutes
morality."

1006 "Man and Superman: Revival at the Criterion," TIMES, 29
Sept 1911, p. 8.
Man and Superman already begins to date; it is merely "brilliant but
incoherent . . . intellectual patter."

1007 Martin, John. "Books for Social Workers," SURVEY (NY),
XXVI (1911), 562-63.
[A favorable book review of Socialism and Superior Brains and The
Common Sense of Municipal Trading.]

1008 Mencken, H. L. "The New Dramatic Literature," SMART
SET, XXXIII (Aug 1911), 151-58; rptd as "On Playgoers—And on
Hauptmann, Synge, and Shaw," in William H. Nolte, H. L.
MENCKEN'S "SMART SET" CRITICISM (Ithaca, NY: Cornell
UP, 1968), pp. 49-53; rptd in part in Evans, pp. 203-04.
Getting Married is clever, but too smart and tedious. The Shewing-up
of Blanco Posnet is a cheap attempt to shock. The Doctor's Dilemma
is amusing, well-constructed, and Shaw's best play since Man and
Superman.

1009 "Mr. Bernard Shaw's Plea for a National Theatre," TIMES,
28 Feb 1911, p. 10.
[Title describes.]

1010 "Mr. Shaw as Historian," TLS, No. 487 (11 May 1911), 184.
Shaw, in his preface to Brieux's THREE PLAYS, indulges in all kinds
of fantasies regarding French literary history. His attack on the
well-made plays of Scribe and Sardou have led him to believe that a
play must be ill-made to be an artistic success. Hence he has turned
to writing formless conversations.

1011 "Mr. Shaw's Prefaces," TLS, No. 476 (23 Feb 1911), 78.
Shaw's prefaces are more interesting than the actual plays. Of the
prefaces to The Doctor's Dilemma, Getting Married, and The
Shewing-up of Blanco Posnet only the one on marriage is truly
interesting, though it is doubtful everyone will agree with Shaw's
views, brilliant and candid as they are.

1012 Mond, Alfred. "A Reply to Mr. Shaw," TIMES, 25 Oct
1911, p. 7.
Shaw raises some very interesting objections to the Insurance Bill,
but he is motivated more by political considerations than general
principles.

1013 Money, L. G. Chiozza. "The Wickedness of Mr. Shaw," TIMES, 25 Oct 1911, p. 7.
Shaw's argument against the Insurance Bill is full of his usual contradictory, paradoxical illogic.

1014 Montague, C. E. DRAMATIC VALUES (1911; rvd ed NY: Doubleday, Page, 1925), pp. 75-99.
Shaw's plays reach "forward to a theatre rescued from the vested stupidities which go so far to keep our theatre dull." However it is difficult to find any consistent philosophy in Shaw's plays. [Comments on Candida, Arms and the Man, Widowers' Houses, You Never Can Tell, Caesar and Cleopatra, Captain Brassbound's Conversion, and Press Cuttings.]

1015 Muret, Maurice. "Le paradoxe au théâtre. M. George Bernard Shaw" (Paradox in the Theatre. Mr. George Bernard Shaw), JOURNAL DES DEBATS, 5 Aug 1911, p. 1.
Shaw's fame is debatable. With the exception of Candida, his plays are very poor in argument and extremely mediocre in construction. Shaw does not allow love to come into the modern theatre except perhaps to turn it to ridicule. His plays reflect a bitter scepticism and sorry pessimism. Although the plays are brilliantly witty, they are full of obscure allusions and contradictions; they are destined for a small minority of intellectuals. [In French.]

1016 "The New Books," REV OF REVS, XLIII (May 1911), 637.
[Largely an objective description of The Common Sense of Municipal Trading.]

1017 "New Books Reviewed," NORTH AMERICAN REVIEW, CXCIII (1911), 927.
The Doctor's Dilemma, Getting Married, and The Shewing-up of Blanco Posnet is Shaw in typical form. Getting Married is the strongest play, while Blanco Posnet is not so much a play as an excuse to write a preface on censorship.

1018 "The New Drama," TIMES, 10 Nov 1911, p. 4.
A large audience has heard Shaw lecture on Ibsen, himself, and other new dramatists.

1019 "New Plays by Bernard Shaw," NYT, 5 March 1911, part VI, p. 125.
The prefaces to The Doctor's Dilemma, Getting Married, and The Shewing-up of Blanco Posnet demonstrate that the best critic of Shaw is Shaw himself.

1020 [News of the Week], SPECTATOR, CVI (1911), 911.
[Shaw's views on unnecessary washing.]

1021 N[oguchi], Y[onejiro]. "The Artistic Interchange of East and West," GRAPHIC, LXXXIII (18 Feb 1911), 248.

The Shewing-up of Blanco Posnet has been acted as a Japanese adaptation entitled The Horse Thief. In one sense, this is a good thing because if the play were written by a Japanese, the Japan government would not allow it to be acted; Shaw's international reputation prevents such a ban being imposed.

1022 "Notes and News: Bernard Shaw on Education," EDUCATIONAL REVIEW, XLII (Dec 1911), 533-38.

"In his own inimitable manner" Shaw has described and criticized "schools from the patients' point of view."

1023 [Orage, A. R.?]. "Unedited Opinions: On Drama," NEW AGE (Lond), ns IX (18 May 1911), 58.

Shaw is merely a propagandist and belongs in the lecture hall, not the theatre. His plays lack soul, and social problems are not the stuff of which immortality is made.

1024 P[almer], J[ohn]. "Fanny's First Play," SAT REV, CXI (1911), 482-83.

Fanny's First Play is a "jeu d'esprit not high among the works of Shaw." Shaw is a teacher with nothing left to teach; "he can amuse us now with a good conscience."

1025 Pease, Edward R. "Die Fabian Society" (The Fabian Society), ARCHIV FÜR DIE GESCHICHTE DES SOZIALISMUS UND DER ARBEITERBEWEGUNG (Leipzig), I (1911), 333-53.

[Describes Shaw as one of the leaders of opinion in the Fabian Society. In German.]

1026 Peirce, Francis Lamont. "Bernard Shaw: A Prophet Who Laughs," TWENTIETH CENTURY, IV (April 1911), 17-23.

History alone will decide Shaw's reputation. Nevertheless, he is a "luminous thinker," "a clever advertiser," a jester, an egoist, and a social rebel with a "mystic cosmic philosophy."

1027 Pfeiffer, Edouard. LA SOCIETE FABIENNE ET LE MOUVEMENT SOCIALISTE ANGLAIS CONTEMPORAIN (The Fabian Society and the Contemporary English Socialist Movement) (Paris: Giard & Brière, 1911).

[A general history of the Fabian Society, with mention of Shaw's role. In French.]

1028 "The Playhouses," ILN, CXXXVIII (29 April 1911), 630, 632.

Anonymity cannot disguise the fact that Fanny's First Play is by Shaw, which is a "squib" directed at his reviewers. "But he does not break new ground, either intellectually or technically."

1029 Pozza, Giovanni. "Candida di George Bernard Shaw" (George Bernard Shaw's Candida), CORRIERE DELLA SERA (Milan), 3 May 1911; rptd in CRONACHE TEATRALE DI

GIOVANNI POZZA (1886-1913) (The Theatre News of Giovanni Pozza) (Vicena: Neri Pozza, 1971), pp. 588-91.

Candida is full of irony, audacious paradoxes, and contradictions. It is an indefinable comedy, unusual in form, and cannot be classified. [In Italian.]

1030 Randall, Alfred E. "The Last Gasp," NEW AGE (Lond), ns VIII (13 April 1911), 561-62.

In the last ten years, Shaw's grievances have been well aired and now seem quite English. His notions are no longer infused with his interesting, "rancorous Irish wit"; rather Shaw is more like a deadly dull Nonconformist preacher. When he stops writing prefaces he can begin to write plays. [See also the subsequent correspondence in NEW AGE, both defending and attacking Shaw: ns VIII (1911), 573-74, 621-22; ns IX (1911), 20, 22, 46, 69-70, 94, 116, 142, 167, 189.]

1031 Randall, Alfred E. "Shaviana," NEW AGE (Lond), ns VIII (6 April 1911), literary supp, 1-2.

The preface to Getting Married is the work of a showman. Shaw is not a reformer so far as marriage is concerned, nor is he an artist or statesman. And his freaks are merely frauds.

1032 Randall, Alfred E. "Shaw and the Medical Profession," NEW AGE (Lond), ns VIII (30 March 1911), 516-18.

The publication of The Doctor's Dilemma shows that Shaw is a showman rather than a reformer, and close examination of his preface reveals that the horrors he exposes are not particularly horrendous. Shaw's ability is confined to talking and he reached his limit in Man and Superman.

1033 "The Religion of the Future" (Heretics Society pamphlet, 11 July 1911 [not seen]); rptd in THE RELIGIOUS SPEECHES OF BERNARD SHAW, ed by Warren Sylvester Smith (University Park: Pennsylvania State UP, 1963), pp. 29-37.

[The text of Shaw's speech, with commentary on its reception and on Shaw—"gloriously irreverant, transparently sincere, divinely prophetic, and inspiring."]

1034 "The Rights of Dramatists," TIMES, 1 April 1911, p. 6.

Shaw was present at and contributed to a meeting of the dramatists of the Society of Authors.

1035 Russell, Sir Edward. THE THEATRE AND THINGS SAID ABOUT IT (Liverpool: Henry Young, 1911), pp. 9-11, 27, 30.

Shaw's views on Shakespeare are profitable if eccentric. His own plays are full of mordant comment and paradoxical wit. John Bull's Other Island is a tour de force.

1036 Scott, Temple. "Bernard Shaw: The Realizer of Ideals," FORUM (NY), XLV (March 1911), 334-54.

Shaw has been misunderstood, made fashionable, not taken seriously, and believed to be a joker. He makes us laugh at things but not with him because he is absolutely in earnest. He is virtuous because he rebels against existing, bad institutions, and he does not worship idols.

1037 "Shakespeare's 'Dark Lady' in Shavian Drama," CUR LIT, L (Feb 1911), 191-93.
Shaw's The Dark Lady of the Sonnets is one of the most amusing skits he has produced, and the playlet is full of passages of rare eloquence.

1038 "Shaw at the Palace," ERA, 9 Dec 1911, p. 25.
How He Lied to Her Husband is full of wittily turned phrases, and this Shaw piece was well-received by a variety theatre audience.

1039 "Shaw, George Bernard," THE ENCYCLOPAEDIA BRITANNICA, 11th ed (NY: Encyclopaedia Britannica, 1911), vol XXIV, 812-13.
[An objective encylcopaedia entry on the life and works.]

1040 "Shaw Play that London Barred Makes No Ripple Here," NYH, 24 Nov 1911, p. 12.
The wit and satire in The Shewing-up of Blanco Posnet is appreciated in New York, as are the free-thought speeches, but not highly so.

1041 "Shaw vs. Chesterton in a Hot Debate," NYT, 3 Dec 1911, part III, p. 4.
Shaw and G. K. Chesterton have debated socialism; Shaw was fiery and earnest, Chesterton sardonic and scornful.

1042 "The Showing Up of Blanco Posnet," NYT, 24 Nov 1911, p. 13; rptd in NYTTR 1904-1911, [n. p.].
The Shewing-up of Blanco Posnet is not a blasphemous play but a "criminal" one because, for all his wit, humor and thought, Shaw "should still seem to find it necessary to wear the cap and bells."

1043 Slosson, Edwin E. "Various Books of Varying Importance," INDEPENDENT (NY), LXXI (1911), 1073-74.
Shaw believes the only way to be listened to is to irritate people, a theory which he again puts into practise with The Doctor's Dilemma, Getting Married, and The Shewing-up of Blanco Posnet.

1044 "Spelling Reform," TIMES, 30 Jan 1911, p. 4.
Shaw, along with others, spoke to the English Association on the need for spelling reform.

1045 S[pence], E. F. "The Stage from the Stalls," SKETCH, LXXIV (24 May 1911), 204.
In this revival of Arms and the Man the emphasis is less on Shaw and more on the actors, and hence the true spirit of the piece does not emerge.

1046 "The Stage from the Stalls," SKETCH, LXXIV (26 April

1911), 76.

Fanny's First Play is a model Shaw play which presents familiar characters and ideas. Shaw is without equal among dramatists.

1047 "The Stage from the Stalls," SKETCH, LXXV (4 Oct 1911), 402.

[On a revival of Man and Superman being interesting because of the leading actors.]

1048 "The Theatre: Fanny's First Play at the Little Theatre," ACADEMY, LXXX (29 April 1911), 520-21.

Shaw's recent serious efforts have been boring; Fanny's First Play allows the audience to enjoy itself, to shout with laughter at his spontaneously idiotic jokes, his exquisite verbal fireworks, his characteristic philosophy, his acute characterization." However, Shaw should begin the renaissance of the English stage in a mainstream commercial theatre.

1049 "Three Censored Plays," NYT, 4 June 1911, part VI, pp. 341, 346.

Shaw has written a "highly eulogistic" preface to THREE PLAYS BY BRIEUX.

1050 "Three Plays by Shaw," DRAMATIST (Easton, PA), III (Oct 1911), 202-03.

The Doctor's Dilemma, Getting Married, and The Shewing-up of Blanco Posnet all fail as drama; rather they are essays. The only virtue present is wit.

1051 "Used Real Queen's English," NYT, 12 Feb 1911, part III, p. 2.

Shaw has been involved in a debate over the reform of spelling.

1052 "The Variety Theatres," MPOST, 5 Dec 1911, p. 10.

The success of How He Lied to Her Husband depends upon a prior knowledge of Shaw's earlier works.

1053 "The Variety Theatres: The Palace," TIMES, 5 Dec 1911, p. 7.

How He Lied to Her Husband is a delight and "the devil in Mr. Bernard Shaw cannot help mocking at the angel in him."

1054 Walbrook, H. M. "Fanny's First Play," PMG (April 1911) [not seen]; rptd in NIGHTS AT THE PLAY (Lond: W. J. Ham-Smith, 1911), pp. 16-19.

Fanny's First Play is one of Shaw's most amusing plays and is a "brilliant and powerful social commentary."

1055 "Women and an Academy of Letters," TIMES, 24 March 1911, p. 11.

Shaw has expressed his support for the inclusion of women in any future academy of letters.

1912

1056 Albert, John. "Some Plays that are Pleasing New York," LESLIE'S ILLUSTRATED WEEKLY, CXV (14 Nov 1912), 497, 509.
Fanny's First Play is a product of Shaw's audacity and egotism.

1057 Archer, William. PLAY-MAKING: A MANUAL OF CRAFTSMANSHIP (Bost: Small, Maynard, 1912) [also Lond: Chapman & Hall, 1912]; rptd with new intro by John Gassner (NY: Dover [1960]), pp. 31, 54-55, 70-71, 113, 116, 127, 132-36, 138, 192, 203, 235-36, 244, 254, 270-71, 294-95, 309-11, 362, 378, 406.
Shaw's work leads to the strong suspicion that he must write without a scenario, "inventing as he goes along." There are many dangers in his very full stage directions, not least the possibility that characters cease to "express themselves as completely as may be in their own proper medium of dramatic action and dialogue." Shaw has professed (in Getting Married) to have returned to the classical unities; in fact, he has served up a rag-bag of ingredients delivered in a "continuous gush." Act two of The Devil's Disciple provides an example of a dramatist keeping an inartistic secret: it takes Judith a long time to tell her husband what the situation is (Dudgeon being arrested in mistake for Anderson), when she could have told him in a few words. The only reason for this silly play is the development of Judith's character—but that could have been achieved by other means. Shaw is "not, primarily, either a character-drawer or a psychologist, but a dealer in personified ideas. His leading figures are, as a rule, either his mouthpieces or his butts."

1058 "At the Play," OBS, 20 Oct 1912, p. 7.
Overruled is one of the dullest things Shaw has written. Captain Brassbound's Conversion is an honest, straightforward play, with ideas and plot organically bound together in an old sentimental melodramatic form.

1059 "Barrie Triumph; Shaw-Pinero Fiasco," NYT, 15 Oct 1912, p. 9; rptd in NYTTR 1912-1919, [n. p.].
Overruled has failed in London. Shaw's verbal fireworks amount to nothing and the play is unworthy of him.

1060 Baughan, E. A., & L. Godfrey Turner. "Dramatic Critics on Mr. Shaw's 'Roasts,' " LONDON WEEKLY BUDGET, No. 2707 (17 Nov 1912), 3.
Shaw has issued a leaflet to accompany the revival of Captain Brassbound's Conversion. The leaflet attacks critics generally, and Shaw is usually at his best when he is fighting against something.

1061 "Bernard Shaw's Drawn Battle with Paris," CUR LIT, LIII (July 1912), 88-90.

Arms and the Man has met with little success in Paris, while Mrs. Warren's Profession, which has not shocked the French, has fared much better.

1062 Bidou, Henry. [Candida], LE JOURNAL DES DEBATS, 19 February 1912.

The translation of Candida is awkward and incorrect. The play lectures too much and is uninteresting. [In French.]

1063 "Bluntschli not in this War," NYT, 15 Nov 1912, p. 12.

The production in Paris of THE CHOCOLATE SOLDIER is ill-timed. Doubtless Shaw will "tell us that the satire of [Arms and the Man] has reformed Balkan military methods."

1064 Boissard, Maurice. [Mrs. Warren's Profession], LE MERCURE DE FRANCE, 16 March 1912, pp. 412-13.

Shaw is a good, amusing playwright, sometimes a thinker, but far from being Ibsen's equal. Nevertheless, Mrs. Warren's Profession is interesting. [In French.]

1065 Bordeaux, Henry. "Mrs. Warren's Profession," LA REVUE HEBDOMADAIRE, Feb 1912; rptd in LA VIE AU THEATRE: TROISIEME SERIE: 1911-1913 (Paris: Plon-Nourrit, 1913), pp. 142-44.

Mrs. Warren's Profession is inferior to Candida and is a sort of paradoxical imitation of naturalistic literature. Mrs. Warren is a juvenile piece designed to shock the bourgeois. [In French.]

1066 Botez, I. "Bernard Shaw. Man and Superman," in ASPECTE DIN CIVILIZATIA ENGLEZA (Aspects of English Civilization) (Jassy: Viata romaneasca, 1912), pp. 286-301 [not seen].

[In Roumanian.]

1067 Caro, Josef. "G. B. Shaw und Shakespeare" (G. B. Shaw and Shakespeare) in FESTSCHRIFT ZUM 15. NEUPHILOLOGENTAGE (Frankfurt: n. p., 1912), pp. 47-78 [not seen].

[In German.]

1068 "Celebrities Write on Parchment for Future Ages," NYT, 2 June 1912, part V, p. 9; rptd as "Hallucinations!" DAILY EXPRESS (Lond), 13 June 1912, p. 7.

Shaw, along with other notables, has set down his thoughts on playwriting. They are a typically Shavian legacy for posterity.

1069 Cestre, Charles. BERNARD SHAW ET SON OEUVRE (Bernard Shaw and His Work) (Paris: MERCURE DE FRANCE, 1912).

[Includes a survey of Shaw's life and career.] Shaw's theatre of ideas forms a coherent whole, dealing with different themes: a realist's picture of society, the psychology of the romantic hero and of the realistic hero, the use of history, love and conflicts between man and woman, the superman and the life force, naturalistic morals, the relationship between morals and institutions, and religion. Major Barbara is Shaw's major work. Shaw is a philosopher but also an entertainer, making use of parody and burlesque. He is a born rebel, the quintessence of the revolutionary spirit. He is a satirist who wants to change society through individualistic socialism. Shaw uses traditional forms of melodrama, middle-class drama, the history play, vaudeville, comedy of character—but the tone is new, and dramatic structures are overturned by means of irony which takes the spectator by surprise. Major Barbara and Man and Superman are more philosophical comedies which use new techniques. Shaw's theatre is essentially of the intellect and leaves scant room for emotion. His purpose is always serious and the mountebank is also a preacher. [In French.]

1070 "Chronicle and Comment: A Mistake in Identity," BOOKMAN (NY), XXXVI (Dec 1912), 359-60.
[Brief details about Shaw, including his rehearsal methods.]

1071 Clancy, John, et al. "Shaw like Bryan O'Lynn," GAELIC AMERICAN, IX (13 Jan 1912), 5.
Shaw is the "Barnum of literature" who direly needs to "produce a clean bill of sanity."

1072 "Comedy: Fanny's First Play," THEATRE (NY), XVI (Oct 1912), xv, xvii.
Fanny's First Play is an "intellectual treat" for those who like Shaw, who is at his cynical and philosophical best. The play is full of scintillating wit and brilliant satire.

1073 Compton-Rickett, Arthur. A HISTORY OF ENGLISH LITERATURE (Lond: T. C. & E. C. Jack; NY: Dodge [1912]), p. 111.
Shaw and his followers have removed the "conventional sentimentalism and unrealities" of Victorian drama, and made the theatre a social force.

1074 C[ourtney], W[illiam] L[eonard] [?]. "Three New Plays at the Duke of York's Theatre," DT, 15 Oct 1912, p. 11.
In Overruled Shaw "is at his old game of pricking the bubble of our national hypocrisy, proving the absurdity and baselessness of most of our conventional ethics, and trying to persuade us that moral paradoxes are, rightly considered, the most profound of truisms."

1075 "The Criterion: Revival of Man and Superman," WEDNESDAY ERA, 10 April 1912, p. 5.
Man and Superman possesses keen satire and the "Shavian philosophy

is dressed in the most humorous garb."

1076 "Criterion Theatre: <u>Man and Superman</u>," TIMES, 9 April 1912, p. 9.
This revival of <u>Man and Superman</u> proves the play <u>is</u> turning into a popular success.

1077 Davray, Henry. [Shaw], LE MERCURE DE FRANCE, 1 March 1912, p. 201.
Shaw is not an English Molière. He is an innovator who attacks traditional beliefs, paving the way for authors of the future who will be less aggressive and who will produce more substantial works. [In French.]

1078 De Bury, R. [Shaw], LE MERCURE DE FRANCE, 1 March 1912, pp. 169-70.
Shaw's originality is more apparent than real. He is a misanthropist and a misogynist despite his feministic ideas. His is a cold, feelingless theatre with no human sympathy or real humor. For Shaw, realism means vulgarity. [In French.]

1079 De Flers, Robert. [<u>Mrs. Warren's Profession</u>], LE FIGARO, 17 February 1912.
In <u>Mrs. Warren's Profession</u> Shaw emerges as a strange, cynical, realistic dramatist. He does not seem to condemn the main character. [In French.]

1080 DeFor, L. V. [<u>Fanny's First Play</u>], REDBOOK MAGAZINE, XIX (1912), 958.
<u>Fanny's First Play</u> is undeniably clever, but lacks substance. The dialogue is nimble, but the characters are intentionally "thinly veiled types of conventional melodrama."

1081 "Denounces G. Bernard Shaw," NYT, 4 March 1912, p. 7.
The Rev. Henry A. Brann believes Shaw's works are a disgrace, violate moral law, and were written simply for money.

1082 De Pawlowski, G. "<u>La Profession de Madame Warren</u>" (<u>Mrs. Warren's Profession</u>), COMOEDIA, 17 Feb 1912, pp. 1-2.
<u>Mrs. Warren's Profession</u> is an avant-garde play, with a clear vision of the modern world. This naturalistic slice of life becomes a violent criticism of modern society. [In French.]

1083 D'Humières, Robert. [Shaw], LE MERCURE DE FRANCE, 1 April 1912, pp. 449-55.
Shaw's best original idea is his concept of love. He is a Nietzschean and a socialist, and hates sentimentality and false idealism. For Shaw, man is the prey in the love-chase. His attitudes are the reaction of a traditional Celtic temperament to the modern and intellectual environment. This Protestant Irishman is disconcerting for the French, and he is absurdly, suicidally attached to his translator. [In

French.]

1084 "Dinner to Mr. William Poel," TIMES, 2 Dec 1912, p. 8.
Shaw spoke favorably of Poel's earlier production of THE COMEDY
OF ERRORS.

1085 "Divorce Plan Shocks Bishop," NYT, 13 Nov 1912, p. 1.
Shaw believes the moral of proposed divorce legislation is "don't get
married."

1086 "Drama: A Triple Bill and a Shaw Revival," ATH, No. 4434
(19 Oct 1912), 455.
Overruled obscures and confuses Shaw's ideas with his own wit; the
characters are mechanical puppets. If he is not careful, Shaw will
become just another propagandistic bore. Captain Brassbound's Conversion shows Shaw to much better advantage, even though its structures owe much to the old fashioned dramas he scorns so much.

1087 "Dramatic Gossip," ATH, No. 4417 (22 June 1912), 716.
"Its depth and concentration of feeling, its ruthless courage and
sincerity, mark [Mrs. Warren's Profession] as a play of far greater
worth than many of [Shaw's] more recent dramas."

1088 "Duke of York's Theatre: The Triple Bill," TIMES, 15 Oct
1912, p. 8.
There is a tedium of excessive exposition in Overruled; otherwise,
some characters do say some witty things.

1089 "The Duke of York's Triplet: Shaw, Barrie and Pinero,"
ERA, 19 Oct 1912, p. 16.
Overruled lacks plot, characterization, and needs cutting. However,
it is "full of . . . witty, quaint, topsy-turvy ideas."

1090 Dukes, Ashley. "Post-Mortem: A Note on Mr. Bernard
Shaw and the Modern English Theatre," DRAMA (Chicago), VII
(Aug 1912), 78-95.
Shaw's wonderful enthusiasm is "overburdened with Puritanism masked in cleverness, anarchy supported by ignorance, and crudity concealed by wit." Shaw also has a penchant for theorizing the drama
and talking it to death. One of his jokes is to replace the traditional
well-made play with a new dramatic form. Shaw is that most dangerous of leaders—"the untrammelled thinker, without a touch of poetry
in his composition" and without a true sense of the comic spirit. This
can be seen in Major Barbara, Misalliance, Fanny's First Play, The
Doctor's Dilemma, You Never Can Tell, Getting Married, The Man of
Destiny, and Mrs. Warren's Profession.

1091 "The English and Their Censor," CUR LIT, LII (1912), 695-
96.
Shaw, a member of the newer generation of dramatists, mistakes the
stage for the pulpit, and has also suffered from censorship. He

believes that the most dangerous censor is an intelligent one.

1092 "English Dramatists Disgraced," ERA, 25 May 1912, p. 19.
Shaw, by his own means of self-advertising, disgraces all English dramatists with his views in his article on the Titanic disaster. [See also item 1139.]

1093 "Fanny's First Play," AMERICAN PLAYWRIGHT, I (Oct 1912), 321-24.
The problem with Shaw's work is that "he is so intent on satire and so filled with the polemics of his philosophies that he is content . . . to provide an artificial mechanism that finally leaves the impression of insincerity" about the whole of Fanny's First Play.

1094 [Fanny's First Play], MUNSEY'S MAGAZINE, XLVII (1912), 980.
Fanny's First Play is a "very remarkable jumble of satire, melodrama, comedy, and farce."

1095 "Fanny's First Play," NY DRAMATIC MIRROR, LXVIII (18 Sept 1912), 7.
Fanny's First Play is a "unique conceit . . . an indescribable concoction of farce, paradox, satire, nonsense, and fantastic romanticism, ultra modernity offset by medievalism."

1096 "Fanny's First Play," NY DRAMATIC NEWS, LVI (21 Sept 1912), 11-12.
Fanny's First Play is caustic, witty, eccentric, satirical, but a rather too prolonged joke.

1097 [Fanny's First Play], NYT, 22 Sept 1912, part VII, p. 2; rptd in NYTTR 1912-1919, [n. p.].
Fanny's First Play shows that Shaw is a law unto himself in technical terms; the result is highly entertaining.

1098 "Fanny's First Play Screamingly Funny," NYT, 17 Sept 1912, p. 11; rptd in NYTTR 1912-1919, [n. p.].
Fanny's First Play is the most scintillating of contemporary comedies and the talkative element is perfectly acceptable.

1099 "Fanny's First Play Sparkles with Wit of Mr. G. B. Shaw," NYH, 17 Sept 1912, p. 7.
Fanny's First Play, with its typical Shavian jabs at drama critics and the middle-class, should be successful.

1100 "Fanny's Second Play," BOOKMAN (NY), XXXVI (Nov 1912), 284-86.
[A satire on American critics, occasioned by Fanny's First Play.]

1101 Farjeon, Herbert. "The 'Three-Star' Bill," WORLD, No. 1999 (22 Oct 1912), 602-03.
"Overruled is an illuminating little exercise in acrobatic dialectics."

1102 Figgis, Darrell. STUDIES AND APPRECIATIONS (Lond: J. M. Dent, 1912), pp. 240, 250-58.

Shaw's influence on drama has been disastrous because he has removed genuine emotion and substituted "arid intellectualism." Shaw does not create emotion and characters in conflict; rather, he presents puppets who do his bidding. In Ibsen's plays real characters are seen operating within and on real life; in Shaw there is only sardonic philosophy.

1103 Findon, B. W. "Fanny's First Play," PLAY PICTORIAL, XIX: 114 (1912), 49-68.

Fanny's First Play is very amusing with "all the inherent qualities of farce," but written with a high degree of verbal felicity. [With numerous production photographs.]

1104 "G. B. Shaw in New York?" NYT, 4 Sept 1912, p. 1.

[Title describes. See also: "Bernard Shaw in England," NYT, 7 Sept 1912, p. 11.]

1105 Gerrard, Thomas J. "Marriage and George Bernard Shaw," CATHOLIC WORLD, XCIV (Jan 1912), 467-82.

In his preface to Getting Married, Shaw shows his total ignorance of marriage according to the Catholic ideal.

1106 Godley, Eveline [C.] "Drama," THE ANNUAL REGISTER 1911 (Lond: Longmans, Green, 1912), part II, pp. 76-79.

[Details of the successful production of Fanny's First Play.]

1107 Grau, Robert. THE STAGE IN THE TWENTIETH CENTURY (NY: Broadway Publishing, 1912), pp. 17, 75, 220, 294, 338.

[Passing references to Shaw and his associates in this consideration of the American theatre from a business and practical standpoint.]

1108 Grein, J. T. "The Dramatic World," STIMES, 20 Oct 1912, p. 6.

Overruled demonstrates that a careful dramatist can evade the censor, for what appears harmless on the page becomes quite drastic in the theatre. It is witty and "written with a kind of French swiftness."

1109 Hamilton, Clayton. "The Comedy of Atmosphere," BOOKMAN (NY), XXXVI (1912-13), 274-77.

Fanny's First Play is nimbly witty and the most amusing production of the season. Man and Superman is a much greater work and Shaw's most "searchingly philosophical composition."

1110 Hamilton, Clayton. "The Players," EVERYBODY'S, XXVII (1912), 808-13.

Fanny's First Play is the "most meritorious" play of the season, and clearly the product of Shaw. Man and Superman is a brilliant play which discloses Shaw's "habit of substituting an intellectual analysis of emotion for emotion itself."

1111 Hamon, Augustin. THE TECHNIQUE OF BERNARD SHAW'S PLAYS. Trans by Frank Maurice (Lond: C. W. Daniel, 1912).
[See item 1239.]

1112 "He Grumbled through Unconscious," NYT, 18 June 1912, p. 10.
It is a mystery why Shaw has allied himself with anti-vivisectionists, and his own experiences do nothing to advance their cause.

1113 Henderson, Archibald. "Bernard Shaw and English Socialism," DAILY OBSERVER (Charlotte, NC), 25 Feb 1912 [not seen].
[Cited in Hood, p. 224.]

1114 Hevesi, Sándor. "Nem lehessen tudni" (You Never Can Tell), MAGYAR SZÍNPAD (Budapest), 6 Jan 1912 [not seen.]
[In Hungarian.]

1115 "How Shaw Saw Rodin at Work," LIT DIG, XLV (30 Nov 1912), 1015.
[On Shaw's impressions of Rodin creating a bust of Shaw.]

1116 Hyndman, Henry Mayers. FURTHER REMINISCENCES (Lond: Macmillan, 1912), pp. 201-11, 218-39, 264.
Shaw possesses a "great literary faculty" although he does not have the pathos or poetry of Heine. His satiric abilities have exposed many topics, although they have been misconstrued sometimes. One of his failings is the desire to be constantly brilliant; he is a much more sympathetic figure when encountered alone. As a dramatist Shaw is "one of the effective intellectual forces of his time." His first plays (Arms and the Man and Widowers' Houses) are mostly talk and literary epigrams. Much more interesting is the relationship between the plays and Shaw the social essayist and agitator; this can be seen clearly in the prefaces to Major Barbara and Mrs. Warren's Profession.

1117 "Indorses G. B. Shaw's View," NYT, 18 Sept 1912, p. 5.
Mrs. J. Borden Harriman, a political organizer, believes Shaw is correct in his opinion that suffragettes should be allowed to starve themselves to death if they so choose.

1118 "Irish Protestants and Home Rule," TIMES, 7 Dec 1912, p. 8.
At an Irish Home Rule meeting, Shaw proposed a motion calling for an end to "racial and religious feuds in Ireland."

1119 "John Bull's Other Island," ERA, 28 Dec 1912, p. 15.
John Bull's Other Island is one of Shaw's best plays—a convincing,

documentary piece, with an ingenious thesis and delightful humor.

1120 Kaneko, Chikusui. "Ibsen kara Shaw" (From Ibsen to Shaw), TAIYO (Tokyo), XVIII: 1 (Jan 1912), 18-25.
The difference between Ibsen and Shaw reveals the change in times: Shaw's age is more realistic and positivistic than was Ibsen's. The difference becomes clearer in many ways when the two men's works are compared. [In Japanese.]

1121 Kennedy, J. M. ENGLISH LITERATURE 1880-1905 (Lond: Stephen Swift, 1912), pp. 154-205.
By descent Shaw belongs to the unimaginative, non-Catholic, Irish strain. He took up reforming, but not from any position of intellectual strength. Moreover, his work lacks artistic harmony and unity, and is full of inartistic bitterness and restlessness. He posseses no philosophical foundation, although wide reading has given him an open mind. Despite his essays on music and drama, his mind has always been scientific, never imaginative—a fact reinforced by his Fabian essays. Cashel Byron's Profession is Shaw's best novel; nevertheless, it reveals his extreme puritanism. The Quintessence of Ibsenism, with the exception of Man and Superman, is his best work and is full of many acute remarks on many subjects. He does not write drama because he deliberately excludes action; he is really writing tracts, a fact which can be ascribed to his economic turn of mind. His plays are only a series of conversations, or rather arid intellectual discussions. His characters are only Shaw's intellectual children who argue in exactly the same way he does. And while Shaw declaims against current morality, he offers only the same thing in another form. However, he has done much to make English critics familiar with continental European thought.

1122 Kingston, Gertrude. "Lady Cicely Waynflete," LONDON WEEKLY BUDGET, No. 2705 (3 Nov 1912), 5.
Lady Cicely (in Captain Brassbound's Conversion) is an amalgam of numerous female characters and a joy to act. The most interesting scene is the lion-taming process in act two.

1123 "The Kingsway Theatre: Fanny's First Play," TIMES, 2 Jan 1912, p. 9
[A favorable review of Fanny's First Play.]

1124 "Kingsway Theatre: John Bull's Other Island," TIMES, 27 Dec 1912, p. 8.
The theme and wit of John Bull's Other Island is still attractive; the only artistic objection here is Shaw's treatment of Keegan in the final act.

1125 Klauber, Adolph. "Are Actors Too Respectable?" NYT, 7 Jan 1912, part VII, p. 7.
[A brief discussion of Shaw's views on theatre audiences.]

1126 Kobayashi, Suikei. "Shawgeki no kachi" (The Value of Shaw's Plays), JIJI SHINPO (Tokyo), 12 Dec 1912, p. 1, 13 Dec 1912, p. 10.

Although Shaw has a splendid aptitude for expressing his ideas, his dramatic techniques are not admirable since they are only effective momentarily. The so-called Shavian philosophy lacks substance and is not a positive force. [In Japanese.]

1127 Larned, W. T. "Fanny's First Play: An Appreciation in Verse," HARPER'S WEEKLY, LVI (30 Nov 1912), 19.

Fanny's First Play is obviously by Shaw, an admirer of Ibsen and a creator of puppets which are nevertheless enjoyable.

1128 "Let Suffragists Die, Says G. B. Shaw," NYT, 17 Sept 1912, p. 4.

Since there is little else of interest, Shaw's views (on allowing suffragettes to starve themselves to death if they so choose) are occupying the limelight.

1129 "The Little," STAGE, 17 Oct 1912, p. 22.

Captain Brassbound's Conversion is really a farce with "banal incidents." The argumentative side of Shaw is tiresome and long-winded.

1130 "The Little Theatre," ERA, 19 Oct 1912, p. 17.

Captain Brassbound's Conversion is a "capital comedy," with good characterization, plot, and humor. Lady Cicely is an "inimitable invention."

1131 "Little Theatre: Captain Brassbound's Conversion," TIMES, 16 Oct 1912, p. 8.

When Shaw puts new life into old forms, as with Captain Brassbound's Conversion, he succeeds. Lady Cicely and Brassbound have, in act two, what is probably the best scene in all Shaw's work.

1132 "London Theatres: The Duke of York's," STAGE, 17 Oct 1912, p. 21.

Although Overruled reveals Shaw as a "brilliant dialectician" and an ingenious manipulator of conversation and logic, the play is ultimately tedious. The play is all talk and no action.

1133 Lowther, George. "Two Modern Plays," OXFORD AND CAMBRIDGE REVIEW, No. 20 (June 1912), 175–80; rptd in LIVING AGE, CCLXXIV (28 Sept 1912), 781–84.

Candida combines "non-morality of art" with the "force of moral upheaval." By using nonsense and absurdities, Shaw reveals human nature at its most honest. The theme of Candida "is the triumph of human nature over the development of one theory of it." In Arms and the Man chivalry, romanticism, and the heroic ideal are rendered ridiculous. You Never Can Tell shows the breakdown of an artificial culture in favor of honest human nature.

136

1134 Lunn, Hugh. "An Interview with Mr. W. B. Yeats," HEARTH AND HOME (Lond), 28 Nov 1912, p. 229 [not seen]; rptd in E. H. Mikhail, W. B. YEATS: INTERVIEWS AND RECOLLECTIONS, 2 vols (Lond & Basingstoke: Macmillan, 1977), vol I, p. 88.
Shaw is typically Irish, and is "irreverent, headlong, fantastic." He has "the feminine logic, which is fed in Ireland by scholastic philosophy."

1135 Mayer, Hy. "Impressions of the Passing Show," NYT, 22 Sept 1912, part VI, p. 20.
[A cartoon with the caption "Why not a cheer-leader at a Shaw play so the audience may know what to do and when."]

1136 Metcalfe, [J. S.]. [Fanny's First Play], LIFE, LX (26 Sept 1912), 1859.
The audience needs to be fully acquainted with Shaw's idiosyncracies to enjoy Fanny's First Play completely.

1137 Mew, Egan. "Captain Brassbound's Conversion at the Little Theatre," ACADEMY, LXXXIII (26 Oct 1912), 547.
Captain Brassbound's Conversion is a rather tentative, careless, crude and unimportant work, which contains one or two delightful characters.

1138 "Mr. Bernard Shaw on Vivisection," TIMES, 7 June 1912, p. 6.
Shaw has expressed his anti-vivisection views to the fourteenth annual meeting of the British Anti-Vivisection Society.

1139 "Mr. Shaw and the Dramatists," ERA, 1 June 1912, p. 19.
[Extracts from Shaw's statements on the Titanic disaster paralleled with Conan Doyle's criticisms of those statements. See also item 1092. A number of contemporary dramatists wrote to either condemn or agree with Shaw's view.]

1140 Moses, M. J. [Bernard Shaw], METROPOLITAN MAGAZINE, XXXVII (Dec 1912), 31 [not seen].
[Cited in Frederick Faxon, et al, CUMULATED DRAMATIC INDEX 1909-1949, 2 vols (Bost: G. K. Hall, 1965), II, 323.]

1141 Oliver, D. E. THE ENGLISH STAGE: ITS ORIGINS AND MODERN DEVELOPMENTS: A CRITICAL AND HISTORICAL STUDY (Lond: John Ouseley [1912]), pp. ix, xi-xii, 87, 91, 104-06, 110-13, 116, 118, 128, 131-32.
[Random passing comments on Shaw, regarded as a leading contemporary dramatist.]

1142 "Our Greater Dramatists: No. III—Mr. Bernard Shaw," ERA, 13 July 1912, p. 17.
Shaw has been so full of self-advertising that it is difficult to form a

fair estimate of his plays. However, the true note of all his work was struck with <u>Widowers' Houses</u> which reveals him as a reformer rather than as a satirist. That play also demonstrates Shaw's cruel, malignant, bitter tone. Shaw's strengths are a strong imagination for characters and places, and a good witty style.

1143 Palmer, John. "Cold Hash at the Duke of York's," SAT REV, CXIV (1912), 482-83.
<u>Overruled</u> is typical Shaw, and he assumes insolently that everyone has read or seen his previous work. The play is sloppy and careless.

1144 Parker, John, ed. WHO'S WHO IN THE THEATRE (Lond: Pitman; 6 eds 1912-1930).
[Each edition includes a biographical entry on Shaw, as well as other incidental factual information.]

1145 "The Playhouses," ILN, CXLI (19 Oct 1912), 558.
<u>Overruled</u> is a poor example of Shaw's wit and humor, being a labored piece of work. <u>Captain Brassbound's Conversion</u> is one of Shaw's "jolliest" plays.

1146 Pollock, C[hanning]. "<u>Fanny's First Play</u>," GREEN BOOK MAGAZINE, VIII (Dec 1912), 1006.
[Largely recounts the plot.]

1147 "<u>Press Cuttings</u>, Which Postulates that All Great Men are Really Women, Seen for the First Time," NYT, 3 April 1912, p. 8; rptd in NYTTR 1912-1919, [n. p.].
[Title describes. The production was enthusiastically received.]

1148 "PUNCH's Fling at G. B. S.," NYT, 2 June 1912, part III, p. 5.
There is poetic justice in the merciless satire meted out to Shaw in the 22 May 1912 edition of PUNCH.

1149 Ruhl, Arthur. "Some of the New Plays," COLLIER'S NATIONAL WEEKLY, L (5 Oct 1912), 24, 26.
<u>Fanny's First Play</u> reveals Shaw is a more relaxed, mellower puritan than he has been previously. Nevertheless his characteristic satire is still directed at British middle-class ideas and ideals.

1150 Segal, Louis. BERNARD SHAW: A STUDY (Lond: Record Composition Company [1912?]; rptd Folcroft, Pa: Folcroft Library Editions, 1971).
Many elements in Shaw point to his antiromanticism; he is far more interested in intellectualism. Similarly, life is of more interest to him than is art. Romanticists wish to see things whole, while Shaw sees division in everything. In his plays Shaw tackles all the questions of modern life, and his combination of humor and intellect in dealing with them has helped restore respectability to English drama. His intellectuality renders him a natural writer of comedy rather than

tragedy, though he is not a farceur. Widowers' Houses created a stir, an inevitable consequence of its subject matter, and made a "painful impression." The Philanderer reflects the current interest in Ibsenism and is a "fine satire full of irony" which cleverly criticizes society. The grim satire of Mrs. Warren's Profession is comparable to that in Swift's GULLIVER'S TRAVELS, although the ideas are expressed in a thoroughly dramatic and memorable fashion. The criticism and censorship of Mrs. Warren is absurd because Shaw has realistically depicted evils which should be rooted out of society. Arms and the Man was rightly one of Shaw's early successful plays because it is a better play and the satire on common ideas about heroism is effective and reveals Shaw's understanding of militarism. Candida is a "masterpiece of human drama and the prettiest love poem in all works of B. Shaw"; it is the equivalent of Shakespeare's ROMEO AND JULIET. The Man of Destiny, admittedly a trifle, shows Shaw's comprehension of Napoleon and is his first attempt at depicting a historical figure. You Never Can Tell is Shaw at his most brilliant and entertaining; it is "entirely realistic in execution if romantic in conception." The Devil's Disciple is constructed well, some scenes are masterpieces, and the characters rendered artistically. In Caesar and Cleopatra Shaw created the superman who is perfectly natural and does what one would expect in any given set of circumstances. Thus Caesar is a "real masterpiece in human characteristics," while Britannus provides ample satire on the English. The theme of vengeance in Caesar is further developed and amplified in Captain Brassbound's Conversion. Shaw's philosophic genius is at its height in Man and Superman, though the superman motif is an ancient literary one. With John Bull's Other Island Shaw reverts to "worldly criticism," dealing with the situation between Ireland and England, while in Major Barbara he shows that poverty is the root of all evil and that it is a crime to endure poverty. How He Lied to Her Husband is an insignificant piece, though it is "humorous, witty and diverting." The Admirable Bashville fails to rank with Shaw's better works, but The Doctor's Dilemma does. It is "exceptionally well written. The humorous caricatures of different types of physicians and surgeons are remarkably well drawn, and it is as brilliantly clever and whimsical as we are accustomed to in the works of B. Shaw." [With additional chapters summarizing Shaw's artistic traits, his relationship to Ibsen and Nietzsche, his humor, views on marriage, his difficulties with censorship, and biography. This was originally a dissertation, and is poorly written and largely descriptive rather than analytical.]

1151 Sergeenko, P. A., ed. NOVYI SBORNIK PISEM L. N. TOLSTOGO (New Collection of L. N. Tolstoi's Letters) (Moscow, 1912), p. 284-85.
Don Juan's speech in the scene in Hell in Man and Superman is admirable, as is "The Revolutionist's Handbook." Superman will occur when

people are distracted from religion. Shaw's defects are a lack of seriousness and too much satire. [In Russian.]

1152 Shaw, Mary. "My 'Immoral' Play: The Story of the First American Production of Mrs. Warren's Profession," McCLURE'S MAGAZINE, XXXVIII (April 1912), 684-94.
[Title describes.]

1153 "Shaw as Paris Sees Him," NYT, 31 March 1912, part III, p. 3.
The French do not take Shaw seriously and they dislike his "peculiar methods of talking about himself and his work."

1154 "Shaw Attacks Irish Priests," NYT, 25 Feb 1912, part III, p. 4.
Shaw believes the Roman Catholic church cannot tolerate democracy; it would benefit from a good dose of Protestantism.

1155 "Shaw Avoids Socialistic Test," NYT, 10 March 1912, part III, p. 4.
Shaw has declined a manufacturer's offer to see whether he can run a woolen mill on socialistic lines.

1156 "Shaw Comedy Brings Back Mr. Loraine," NYH, 1 Oct 1912, p. 9.
Man and Superman is now less effective and some additions to the script only make the piece more talky.

1157 "The Shaw Extension and Popularisation Company, Unlimited," PUNCH, CXLII (22 May 1912), 398.
[A satiric prospectus for a company "for the acquisition and development of the well-known statesman, playwright, poet, essayist, speaker, vegetarian and hero."]

1158 "Shaw Goes for Critics," NYT, 29 Sept 1912, part III, p. 4.
Shaw has defended Harley Granville-Barker's production of THE TEMPEST and accused critics of being ignorant about stage-craft.

1159 "Shaw May Come, After All," NYT, 20 Sept 1912, p. 11.
A large financial offer may induce Shaw to visit America and lecture. [See also Shaw's denial, "Bernard Shaw Won't Come," NYT, 21 Sept 1912, p. 3.]

1160 "Shaw Mocks Wage Bill," NYT, 4 April 1912, p. 3.
Shaw's satiric speech in London on a wages bill in Parliament provoked considerable mirth.

1161 "Shaw on Women's Rights," NYT, 27 Sept 1912, p. 4.
Shaw made some "characteristic utterances" over the case of a man who refused to pay taxes on his wife's property.

1162 "Shaw Play is given at Suffrage Benefit," SUN (NY), 3 April 1912, p. 11.

Press Cuttings, with its dull wit, would probably never see production without Shaw as the author. It should rest in oblivion.

1163 "Shaw Satire Fills Fanny's First Play," SUN (NY), 17 Sept 1912, p. 11.
Fanny's First Play is a bravura demonstration of Shaw's genius which is here scintillating and sustained.

1164 "Shaw Styles War 'Highest of Sports,' " NYT, 11 Feb 1912, part III, p. 3.
Characteristically, Shaw draws parallels between war and boxing because both have an artificial code of rules.

1165 "Shaw's Shy at the Critics," LIT DIG, XLV (1912), 516-17.
Fanny's First Play will probably be warmly welcomed in New York because Shaw's barbs appear to be directed only at English critics.

1166 "Soldiers and Strikers," TIMES, 4 April 1912, p. 10.
Shaw, in a luminous company, has spoken on the use of the military in strikes.

1167 S[pence], E. F. "The Stage from the Stalls," SKETCH, LXXX (30 Oct 1912), 108-09.
With Overruled it rather appears that Shaw is resting on his laurels. There are some verbal fireworks in the piece, but it is too long and there is clearly some truth in some people's opinion that Shaw is a "back number."

1168 Spender, Harold. "Some Morals of the Titanic," DN, 15 May 1912, p. 6.
Regardless of Shaw's view of what he calls the senseless romantic and heroic demands made during a catastrophe such as the sinking of the Titanic, it is nevertheless true that heroism prevailed and rightly so. [See also in DN: Shaw's article, "The Titanic: Some Unmentioned Morals," 14 May 1912, p. 6, and various correspondence, 16 May 1912, p. 6, 17 May 1912, p. 6, 20 May 1912, p. 6, 22 May 1912, p. 6, 25 May 1912, p. 6.]

1169 "Suffragist's Income-Tax," TIMES, 27 Sept 1912, p. 6.
Shaw was the chief speaker at a meeting of the Women's Tax Resistance League.

1170 Terry, J. E. Harold. "Captain Brassbound's Conversion," OXFORD AND CAMBRIDGE REVIEW, No. 26 (Dec 1912), 132-37.
Captain Brassbound's Conversion is not a great play; Lady Cicely does not charm or convince.

1171 "Things New: At the Theatres," SKETCH, LXXX (23 Oct 1912), 70.
Overruled is not Shaw at his best. Although witty, Shaw is here repetitious and too lengthy. On the other hand, his earlier successful

Captain Brassbound's Conversion still amuses and wears well.

1172 "Tolstoy Rebuked Shaw for Levity," NYT, 7 April 1912, part III, p. 1.
An exchange of correspondence between Shaw and Tolstoy has been published recently. It came to an abrupt end when Shaw joked about good and evil.

1173 "The Tyrannical G. B. S.," ERA, 20 April 1912, p. 13.
[A report of Ashley Dukes's lecture, "Nationality in Playwriting," delivered at the O. P. Club. Dukes thought that Shaw's strongest characteristic was his puritanism and that he was strongly influencing English drama. Shaw is also clearly against musical comedies, such as those presented at the Gaiety Theatre.]

1174 White, M., jr. "The Stage: Pie for the Critics," MUNSEY'S MAGAZINE, XLVIII (Nov 1912), 352-53.
Fanny's First Play is Shaw's tour d'esprit, and in view of the play's content it is diverting to see what the New York critics have to say about its production in that city.

1175 White, M., jr. "The Stage: The Man Who will get Shaw's Next," MUNSEY'S MAGAZINE, XLVIII (Dec 1912), 529.
Robert Loraine is the only person who has managed to induce Shaw to make alterations in Man and Superman (for example, cutting the Inferno scene so that the play could be performed in one evening).

1176 Zueblin, C. "Shavian Socialism: A Book Study," TWENTIETH CENTURY, V (April 1912), 509-14.
[Essentially a book review of Archibald Henderson's book (item 985), but with interpolated commentary.]

1913

1177 "The Abuse of Paradox," NYT, 2 Feb 1913, part VI, p. 50.
Shaw and G. K. Chesterton both abuse paradox because "they often do not mean what they say or say what they mean."

1178 Albini, Ettore. "La professione della signora Warren di George Bernard Shaw" (Mrs. Warren's Profession by George Bernard Shaw), AVANTI! (Rome), 16 Jan 1913; rptd in CRONACHE TEATRALI 1891-1925, (Theatrical Chronicles 1891-1925), ed by G. Bartolucci (Genoa: Teatro Stabile, 1972), pp. 245-50.
Shaw was obliged to defend Mrs. Warren's Profession, but it can defend itself because it contains some of the finest pages of Shaw's moralizing art. Italians were surprised by the play, but its implacable logic was always correct and imposed itself by its dialectical form,

irony, and truth. [In Italian.]

1179 Andrews, Charlton. THE DRAMA TO-DAY (Phila & Lond: Lippincott, 1913), p. 17, 27, 29, 106, 108, 132-42, 148, 150, 177, 196-97, 214, 220-22.

Shaw is an iconoclastic reformer who attacks anything which appears pretentious. However, for every social falsehood he truly exposes, he proffers twenty others wrongly. Often he fails to practice what he preaches, as is evident in his attacks on romanticism which is, in fact, present in his own work. Shaw is more noteworthy as a provocative thinker than as a dramatist.

1180 "Androcles and the Lion," ERA, 3 Sept 1913, p. 14.

Androcles and the Lion is an excellent example of Shaw's method, with its topsy-turvy humor, occasional serious thought and scorn of religious tradition.

1181 [Arahata], Kan[son]. "Iba Takashi ichiza" (Takashi Iba Company), KINDAI SHISO (Tokyo), II: 2 (Nov 1913), 14-15.

There is really nothing important in Arms and the Man. Shaw often boasts about a new philosophy and the superman, but both are absent in this play. It has nothing but poor jokes, cheap quips, mere puns and garrulity. Shaw's iconoclasm is never effective, and he is not a match for that courageous and straightforward Ibsen. [In Japanese.]

1182 Armstrong, Cecil Ferard. SHAKESPEARE TO SHAW: STUDIES IN THE LIFE'S WORK OF SIX DRAMATISTS OF THE ENGLISH STAGE (Lond: Mills & Boon, 1913), pp. 246-323.

If Pinero is ordinary, Shaw is extraordinary. Shaw is an agitator; we are better for having read his work, although we may not like the experience. Widowers' Houses is a good, simple play with a straightforward, well-developed plot; here Shaw is a playwright first and a preacher second. He called The Philanderer a comedy, but that is an elastic term; it is clever, witty and brilliant, but almost boring because it has no sense of drama. Mrs. Warren's Profession, on the other hand, is a complete, consistent dramatic whole of which Aristotle would have approved. Flawless, too, is the construction of Candida which contains delightful characterizations (as does Arms and the Man). With You Never Can Tell Shaw moves into the realm of pure farce; it is full of fun, although the characters cannot be said to be drawn from reality (convincing though they are within the context of the play). The plot of The Devil's Disciple is a familiar one, but Shaw reworks it well and adds good dialogue and characterization. Convincing, too, is the picture Shaw paints in Caesar and Cleopatra and that alone cancels all objections to the play. Captain Brassbound's Conversion is a rich and refreshing work, a flawless comedy; Lady Cecily is not the impossible character some maintain. Man and Superman marks a distinct turning point in Shaw's career.

Previously he was conventional and simply compelled us to listen; with this work, he compels us to think. It is full of much talk which is sometimes difficult to follow, although ultimately it is a non-romantic love play which reaches everyone in the theatre. John Bull's Other Island has no plot; rather it presents contrasts and problems and is purely a study of character and temperament. Similarly plotless is Major Barbara, which also lacks characterization and situation. The play is mere talk which is difficult to follow closely, as is The Doctor's Dilemma. It is original, complicated and interesting, and repays the effort of concentration as Shaw exposes human fallibility. Getting Married is a drama of ideas rather than a conflict of characters; its construction is faultless. The Shewing-up of Blanco Posnet is not a blasphemous work, but deeply religious and sincere.

1183 "At the Play," OBS, 23 Nov 1913, p. 11.
Great Catherine is great fun, but full of all Shaw's old, worn-out ideas.

1184 B. "Great Catherine at the Vaudeville," SPECTATOR, CXI (22 Nov 1913), 867.
Shaw's fooling occasionally "becomes charged with the most serious-minded intentions" as in Androcles and the Lion, and his didacticism sometimes slips into farce as in Great Catherine. However, Shaw's intention in Great Catherine to make the audience laugh succeeds.

1185 Bab, Julius. NEBENROLLEN: EIN DRAMATURGISCHER MIKROKOSMOS (Secondary Parts: A Dramatic Microcosm) (Berlin: Oesterheld, 1913), pp. 121-30.
Nicola in Arms and the Man is, in a sense, the main character and hero of the play. Since he is not able to command, he is willing to serve. A consistent servant, however, seems to be more valuable than an inconsistent master. Nicola, therefore, is an heroic lackey. [In German.]

1186 B[aughan], E. A. "Androcles and the Lion: Shaw's Curious Fable at the St. James's," DN, 2 Sept 1913, p. 7; rptd in Evans, pp. 209-10.
The Lion is so successfully portrayed in Androcles and the Lion that we lose interest in Shaw's later examination of early Christian ideals. The fable is an odd mixture of serious ideas, heavy-handed fooling and witty lines.

1187 Beer, Max. GESCHICHTE DES SOZIALISMUS IN ENGLAND (A History of Socialism in England) (Stuttgart: J. H. W. Dietz, 1913), pp. 434, 436, 462-67.
[On Shaw and the Fabian Society. In German.]

1188 "Bernard Shaw Snubs England and Amuses Germany," NYT, 30 Nov 1913, part V, p. 1.

144

[An extensive account of why Shaw produced Pygmalion first in Germany, together with plot summary and quotations.]

1189 "Bernard Shaw Writes a Fable for Christians," CUR OP, LV (Nov 1913), 330-31.
Androcles and the Lion has shocked, startled and amused London, and Shaw has surpassed himself.

1190 Boyd, Ernest A. "Bernard Shaw and the French Critics," FORUM (NY), L (Aug 1913), 205-16; substantially rptd in APPRECIATIONS AND DEPRECIATIONS: IRISH LITERARY STUDIES (Dublin: Talbot Press; Lond: T. Fisher Unwin, 1917), pp. 122-38.
[A historical account of Shaw productions in France and of the critical reception of those productions.]

1191 C., P. "At the Play: St. James's: Androcles and the Lion," OBS, 7 Sept 1913, p. 5.
Androcles and the Lion is a clever play, but not one on which Shaw has lavished a great deal of art.

1192 [Caesar and Cleopatra], NATION (NY), XCVII (1913), 392.
Caesar and Cleopatra is a very superior extravaganza, although it is "lacking in action, cohesion, credibility, and suspense."

1193 "Caesar and Cleopatra," NY DRAMATIC MIRROR, LXX (22 Oct 1913), 7.
Again, in Caesar and Cleopatra, Shaw's "whimsical mixture of straight drama and satire" has proved successful.

1194 Cannan, Gilbert. "Dramatic Chronicle," POETRY AND DRAMA (Lond), I (1913), 72-75.
[Passing references to Shaw's pioneer work which younger dramatists can build upon and establish a theatre with imagination.]

1195 Cannan, Gilbert. "Dramatic Chronicle," POETRY AND DRAMA (Lond), I (1913), 469-72.
Androcles and the Lion fails to lead one's mind forward; instead, the play leads back to Shaw and his jokes and his "own special and delightful kind of intellectual buffoonery." Shaw's plays (like J. M. Barrie's) do not contain men and women, only puppets.

1196 Carter, Huntly. THE NEW SPIRIT IN DRAMA & ART (NY & Lond: Mitchell Kennerley, 1913), pp. 36-38, 41, 72, 206.
Shaw evolved Ibsen on socialist lines, but he did not have the capacity to understand sexual matters. Nevertheless, he made "amazing conquests" and swayed many followers.

1197 Cather, Willa Sibert. "Plays of Real Life," McCLURE'S MAGAZINE, XL (March 1913), 64-66.
Fanny's First Play is amusing, and sets out to ridicule theatrical,

domestic, and social conventions.

1198 Chapman, John Jay. "Shaw and the Modern Drama," HARPER'S WEEKLY, LVII (19 April 1913), 10; rptd in MEMORIES AND MILESTONES (NY: Moffat, Yard, 1915), pp. 31-41; rptd in part in Evans, pp. 206-08.

Fanny's First Play demonstrates that Shaw is a sincere playwright and we should be grateful for the advances in drama which he has made. "His mind is satisfied when he has apprehended the irreconcilable conflicts in the world of morality. As an artist he is satisfied when he has successfully presented one or some of these conflicts." However, "Shaw's crude and cruel treatment of humanity," which reflects this corrupt age, shows he just wants to be heard and make money.

1199 "Christian Martyrs Burlesqued," LIT DIG, XLVII (27 Sept 1913), 524-25.

In Androcles and the Lion Shaw has "turned the early Christian martyrs into figures of the burlesque stage."

1200 "Christianity and Equality," COMMONWEALTH, 5 Nov 1913 [not seen]; rptd in THE RELIGIOUS SPEECHES OF BERNARD SHAW, ed by Warren Sylvester Smith (University Park: Pennsylvania State UP, 1963), pp. 54-59.

[The text of Shaw's speech, with commentary on the speech and Shaw's delivery of it.]

1201 Courtney, W. L. "Realistic Drama," FORT REV, ns XCIII (1913), 945-61, 1136-53; rptd in OLD SAWS AND MODERN INSTANCES (Lond: Chapman & Hall, 1918).

[A wide-ranging discussion of realism with illustrative references to Shaw.]

1202 Cox, Marion. " 'America has taken the Wrong Direction'— G. B. Shaw," NYT, 17 Aug 1913, part V, p. 8.

[A biographical interview, with Shaw's views on American politics and society, and vivisection.]

1203 "Critics Slash Shaw Play," NYT, 19 Nov 1913, p. 3.

London critics have attacked Great Catherine for its lack of originality, as old-fashioned farce, and for Shaw's usual anti-English gibes.

1204 De Pawlowski, G. "On ne peut jamais dire" (You Never Can Tell), COMOEDIA, 29 Jan 1913, pp. 1-2.

You Never Can Tell is humorous but the general design is less firm than that of other plays. Rather than a work of art, it is merely a lecture full of witty remarks; the fantasy in it is too caricatural. [In French.]

1205 "The Doctor's Dilemma: Revival at the St. James's Theatre," TIMES, 8 Dec 1913, p. 14.

We now enjoy the fascination for physical horror through the medium of the medical profession in The Doctor's Dilemma. It is also pleasing to learn of the fallibility of that profession, especially through Shaw's satiric dialogue and eminent commonsense.

1206 "Don't Applaud, Says Shaw," NYT, 1 Jan 1913, p. 17.
Shaw wants the audience of John Bull's Other Island to sit in total silence and not to applaud or laugh until the end of the play.

1207 "Drama," ATH, No. 4480 (6 Sept 1913), 235-36.
The edge has been taken off Shaw's criticism in the revised version of The Quintessence of Ibsenism, largely because Ibsen has become recognized as a classic. Previously Shaw was tilting against the Establishment; now Ibsen is taken for granted. In places, Shaw's tone is even apologetic.

1208 "Drury Lane Theatre: Caesar and Cleopatra," MPOST, 15 April 1913, p. 11.
Caesar and Cleopatra now has a prologue which pokes good fun at English manners and customs; but the remainder of the play lacks pace. There is no story or character-drawing; the play is more a vehicle for a few flashes of Shaw's wit.

1209 "Drury Lane Theatre: Caesar and Cleopatra," TIMES, 15 April 1913, p. 10.
Shaw may gravely call Caesar and Cleopatra a history, but the historical aspects are only a vehicle which allows his characters to talk and think about the present. The plot is a little confusing, but inconsequential.

1210 Eaton, Walter Prichard. "Fanny's First Play Keen and Stimulating," AMERICAN MAGAZINE, LXXV (Feb 1913), 58.
Fanny's First Play has keen humor, an unusual style, and stimulating ideas. Man and Superman is Shaw's best play because of its narrative interest, "display of Roman candles," and fascinating theme.

1211 "The Economics of Art," TIMES, 21 Oct 1913, p. 12.
Shaw has urged the formation of trade unions in the arts.

1212 Edelman, Isador. "New for Bibliophiles," NATION (NY), XCVII (1913), 259.
Even though there are many dissimilarities, a pattern of influence can be established between Shaw and Congreve.

1213 "English Can't Choose Mates, Says Shaw," NYT, 30 March 1913, part III, p. 4.
Shaw's paradoxical statements on English domestic life will cause him trouble and raise emotions.

1214 "English Plays in Germany," TIMES, 27 Nov 1913, p. 7.
Androcles and the Lion has been produced in Berlin, mystifying the critics who are not favorably disposed to it.

1215 "Fanny's First Play," EDITOR, XXXVII (25 June 1913), 356-57.
Shaw is unique and it is unwise to attempt to copy him. In Fanny's First Play he breaks all the rules of dramaturgy.

1216 "Fanny's First Play: A Shaw Play is a Paradox," DRAMATIST (Easton, Pa), IV (April 1913), 345-46.
Shaw indulges in mental calisthenics, and suffuses Fanny's First Play with wit; but parts of the play are vague and confusing.

1217 "Fanny's First Play: A Typical Shaw Satire," BOOK NEWS (Phila), XXXII (Nov 1913), 178-79.
Fanny's First Play is an inimitably funny play which could have been written only by a genius and an egotist.

1218 Figgis, Darrell. "The Theatre: Mr. Forbes-Robertson's Farewell," ACADEMY, No. 2138 (6 April 1913), 530-31.
Shaw's attempt in Caesar and Cleopatra to deflate the usual heroic conception of Caesar falls flat because the audience laughs at and not with Caesar. Shaw also tries to strip Cleopatra of her traditional associations and thereby gives an untruthful, inhuman portrait. The play has no plot and little construction, and Shaw is witty at the expense of his characters.

1219 "Forbes-Robertson and Bernard Shaw," ERA, 22 March 1913, p. 17.
It is a pity Dramatic Opinions and Essays cannot be republished cheaply, for the volumes clearly demonstrate Shaw's earnest interest in acting.

1220 "Forbes-Robertson's Farewell," ERA, 19 April 1913, p. 14.
Caesar and Cleopatra is one of Shaw's "most entertaining blends of quaint humour, satirical melodrama, and witty farce."

1221 Fowell, Frank, and Frank Palmer. CENSORSHIP IN ENGLAND (1913; rptd NY: Blom, 1969), pp. 193, 197-98, 218, 221-22, 251-54, 267, 349.
[A history of stage censorship, with references to Shaw's difficulties with the censor (for example, Mrs. Warren's Profession and The Shewing-up of Blanco Posnet).]

1222 "Fraud on Mr. Bernard Shaw," TIMES, 12 May 1913, p. 3.
Shaw has been the victim of a scheme to defraud him of 525 pounds.

1223 "French Don't Like Shaw," NYT, 3 Feb 1913, p. 3.
You Never Can Tell has received a negative reception in Paris and the French think Shaw lacks a sense of proportion.

1224 "Future of Hospitals," TIMES, 26 July 1913, p. 7.
Shaw has addressed a section of the British Medical Association on the state of the profession.

1225 G., J. "On ne peut jamais dire" (You Never Can Tell), COMOEDIA, 28 Jan 1913.
The sarcastic verve and bitter humor of You Never Can Tell are both irritating and delightful. [In French.]

1226 "G. B. Shaw's Mother Dead," NYT, 1 March 1913, p. 1.
Shaw inherited his "wit and good-humored, derisive judgment" from his mother.

1227 Galsworthy, John. "The New Spirit in the Drama," LIVING AGE, CCLXXVII (1913), 259-66.
Shaw and other dramatists belong to the new drama which is termed serious. However, Shaw can hardly be called serious even though he is sincere.

1228 Gibbon, J. Morgan. "Mr. Shaw's Play," TIMES, 1 Oct 1913, p. 10.
The Lion is, indeed, the hero of Androcles and the Lion. If this is the best stage representation of Christianity, then the stage ought to give up trying to represent it.

1229 Glover, J[ames] M. JIMMY GLOVER AND HIS FRIENDS (Lond: Chatto & Windus, 1913), pp. 49, 244.
[A brief account of Shaw's revenge for being banned as a critic by Henry Irving.]

1230 Goddard, Harold C. "Correspondence: Bernard Shaw and the Law," NATION (NY), XCVII (1913), 506.
The NATION got it wrong in its editorial [see item 1301]. In fact, Shaw "is the defender of both law and institutions in thundering endlessly into our ears the truth that better laws and better institutions are possible."

1231 Godley, Eveline [C.]. "Drama," THE ANNUAL REGISTER 1912 (Lond: Longmans, Green, 1913), part II, pp. 78-81.
[Brief mention of Shaw in the context of the year's theatrical events.]

1232 "Great Catherine," ERA, 26 Nov 1913, p. 16.
One wonders why Shaw wrote Great Catherine since it can hardly add to his reputation. However, despite his liberties with history, the play amuses.

1233 [Great Catherine], GRAPHIC, LXXXVIII (29 Nov 1913), 1014.
Great Catherine is "simply a variant of an old theme of [Shaw's] — 'Britannicus the Stupid,' framed in a Russian setting."

1234 Grein, J. T. "The Dramatic World," STIMES, 7 Sept 1913, p. 6.
It is possible to see behind Androcles and the Lion Shaw's sardonic

contempt for his listeners. The play is brilliant and full of ideas, but it ultimately leads to mental indigestion.

1235 Grierson, Francis. THE INVINCIBLE ALLIANCE AND OTHER ESSAYS POLITICAL, SOCIAL, AND LITERARY (NY: John Lane; Lond: Bodley Head, 1913), pp. 160-66.
Shaw's approach to topics and propaganda is to be startling and paradoxical, and he will be amusing when he intends to be serious. But he is no fool and is a master cynic. His "weakness lies in the intellectuality of his wit. He can tear down but he cannot construct; he can scatter but he cannot concentrate, and the instruction he affords is rarely in proportion to the amusement."

1236 Grosvenor, Jessie. "Mrs. Pankhurst's Treatment," TIMES, 20 June 1913, p. 10.
Shaw's sympathy for Mrs. Pankhurst [TIMES, 19 June 1913, p. 10] is not shared by everyone, nor is everyone in favor of giving the vote to women. [See also additional correspondence in TIMES: 23 June 1913, p. 5, 25 June 1913, p. 10, 27 June 1913, p. 68, 28 June 1913, p. 6, 30 June 1913, p. 10.]

1237 Guyot, Edouard. LE SOCIALISME ET L'EVOLUTION DE L'ANGLETERRE CONTEMPORAINE (1880-1911) (Socialism and the Evolution of Contemporary England 1880-1911) (Paris: Félix Alcan, 1913), pp. 425-62.
Shaw's socialism will stimulate England, but it is not constructive. [A detailed examination of Shaw's socialist and economic ideas, his notion of evolution, the life force and the superman, with frequent reference to Man and Superman, Mrs. Warren's Profession, and You Never Can Tell. In French.]

1238 Hamilton, Clayton. "Building a Play Backward," BOOKMAN (NY) XXXVIII (1913-14), 610-11.
The last three acts of The Philanderer are anti-climactic after the first.

1239 Hamon, Augustin. LE MOLIERE DU XXe SIECLE: BERNARD SHAW (Paris: Figuière, 1913). Trans by Eden & Cedar Paul as THE TWENTIETH CENTURY MOLIERE: BERNARD SHAW (Lond: Allen & Unwin [1915]; rptd Folcroft, Pa: Folcroft Press, 1972). [This is a series of nine lectures originally given at the Sorbonne in 1911. The third lecture was published separately as THE TECHNIQUE OF BERNARD SHAW'S PLAYS, trans by Frank Maurice (Lond: C. W. Daniel, 1912).]
[Biographical chapters emphasize Shaw's socialism and serious purpose.] Shaw's dramatic work consists essentially of ideas which also embrace the comic and the effects found in Molière. Most notable are the comedy of situation, character and ideas, realism or farce combined with truth, and universalized characters. Woman is the

symbol of the life force, and the superman represents man's development. Shaw's theatre is a school for disrespect and revolt, an unceasing war on society's lying, but the tone of Shaw's laughter is a moralizing one. Shaw alone understood what kind of realism Ibsen brought to the contemporary theatre. Shaw and Molière have the same didactic aim. Their plots are simple with no place for love in them, but everything revolves around the bourgeoisie and contemporary morals. They both attack hypocrisy and romance, emphasizing realism strongly, and both make use of every possible comedic effect from farce on up. Everyday, spoken language predominates in their dialogue, and while their philosophical ideas may differ, both see commonsense and optimism triumphing. Shaw is also reminiscent of Voltaire, Scarron, Rabelais and Beaumarchais. [In French.]

1240 Hamon, Augustin and Henriette Hamon. CONSIDERATIONS SUR L'ART DRAMATIQUE A PROPOS DE LA COMEDIE DE BERNARD SHAW (Considerations on Dramatic Art with Reference to Bernard Shaw's Comedies) (Paris: Figuière, 1913).
Critics are bewildered by Shaw's comedies because they judge them by the standards of the traditional comedy of Scribe. Shaw's comedies conform to classical definitions of the genre. His plays frequently comprise a series of scenes and dialogues while the intellectual action follows a consistent course. Shaw's drama is one long paradox but this is done to make the spectator think. Shaw also uses farce, caricature and other comic devices, but does not study character much. In Shaw's drama there is universal human interest, although, as with Wagner, it will take time before Shaw is recognized fully. [With references to item 1239 and the comparisons there between Shaw and Molière. In French.]

1241 Hartley, C. Gasquoine (pseud of Mrs. Walter M. Gallichan). THE TRUTH ABOUT WOMAN (Lond: Nash; NY: Dodd, Mead, 1913; rptd on microfilm, New Haven: Research Publications, 1977, in HISTORY OF WOMEN, No. 6608), pp. 65-66, 253, 260, 331, 362-63, 395.
Ann, in Man and Superman, embodies a universal female trait; she is aggressive, not passive, and so contradicts the fictions men have generally established about women. [With other passing references to Shaw's views on marriage and prostitution.]

1242 Henderson, Archibald. "Real Conversations with Bernard Shaw," UNIVERSITY OF NORTH CAROLINA MAGAZINE, XLIII (ns XXX) (March 1913), 123-34.
[Biographical; title describes.]

1243 Herford, O. "Celebrities I have not Met," AMERICAN MAGAZINE, LXXV (March 1913), 94.
[A twelve-line poem in which Shaw is compared with Mephistopheles,

Don Quixote, and Diogenes.]

1244 Howe, P. P. "The Dramatic Craftsmanship of Mr. Bernard Shaw," FORT REV, ns XCIV (July 1913), 132-46; rptd in DRAMATIC PORTRAITS (Lond: Secker, 1913), pp. 133-62.

Shaw has adopted the traditional practices of the theatre and playwright in order to expound his particular philosophy. He has provided "intellectual vivacity" but he has not affected the theatre greatly because he has not "profoundly mastered it."

1245 Howe, P. P. "Shaw on Laughter," NYT, 19 Jan 1913, part VI, p. 24.

Shaw is unreasonable in expecting audiences to sit through his plays without laughing or crying.

1246 Jackson, Holbrook. THE EIGHTEEN NINETIES: A REVIEW OF ART AND IDEAS AT THE CLOSE OF THE NINETEENTH CENTURY (Lond: Grant Richards, 1913), pp. 29, 38-39, 50-52, 58, 93, 135, 145, 158, 162, 177, 234-59, 283-84.

Shaw's main contribution has been to ask questions and to criticize institutions and ideas. He has not contributed much to socialism, and he is not really a national influence; his name is known to many but his major appeal is to the middle classes. Nevertheless his ideas are eclectic and few writers "have seen life so realistically as Bernard Shaw."

1247 Kensington, John [Bishop of Kensington]. "Mr. Shaw on Morals," TIMES, 10 Nov 1913, p. 10.

[A letter debate between Shaw and the Bishop of Kensington on the licensing and subsequent alteration of music-hall sketches. See also additional correspondence in TIMES: 8 Nov 1913, p. 8, 11 Nov 1913, p. 5, 12 Nov 1913, p. 5, 13 Nov 1913, p. 10, 14 Nov 1913, p. 5, 15 Nov 1913, p. 11.]

1248 Klauber, Adolph. "Casual Comment on Current Comedies," NYT, 2 Nov 1913, part VII, p. 9.

Although ministers have both attacked and defended Androcles and the Lion, it has been withdrawn primarily because it has failed to attract audiences.

1249 Klauber, Adolph. "The Versatile First-nighter and His Sense of Theatre Values," NYT, 26 Oct 1913, part VII, p. 9; rptd in NYTTR 1912-1919, [n. p.].

It is gratifying to see the success of a thoughtful work such as Caesar and Cleopatra because there is a strong tendency in audiences to respond simply to rather obvious theatrical stimuli.

1250 Lodge, Oliver. "Androcles and the Lion," TIMES, 23 Oct 1913, p. 7.

It is surprising that people have not understood Androcles and the Lion is a "genuinely religious play" and appreciated it more.

1251 "London Theatres: Drury Lane," STAGE, 17 April 1913, p. 22.
This revised version of Caesar and Cleopatra is largely highly enjoyable farce, although there is a serious purpose to Shaw's whimsical perversion of history.

1252 "London Theatres: The Kingsway," STAGE, 2 Jan 1913, p. 24.
John Bull's Other Island, along with Candida and You Never Can Tell, is among Shaw's most popular and attractive work.

1253 "London Theatres: The St. James's," STAGE, 4 Sept 1913, p. 22.
The chief attraction of Androcles and the Lion is the Lion, the "character" who will be most remembered by the average playgoer. It is unlikely that average playgoer will take seriously "Shaw's characteristically ding-dong argumentation about the nature of Christianity."

1254 "London Theatres: The Vaudeville," STAGE, 20 Nov 1913, p. 24.
Great Catherine will be seen by most people as a jeu d'esprit, "a mad burlesque, a screaming farce." However, there is method in Shaw's madness, and he does allow us to see the barbarous side of Catherine's reign.

1255 MacCarthy, Desmond. "Androcles and the Lion," NSTATE, I (1913), 693-94; rptd in THE ENGLISH DRAMATIC CRITICS: AN ANTHOLOGY, 1660-1932, ed by James Agate (Lond: A. Barker, 1932; rptd NY: Hill & Wang, nd), pp. 295-99; rptd in MacCarthy, pp. 102-07.
Androcles and the Lion resembles a medieval miracle play in its mixture of "buffoonery and religion." Shaw is free of "spiritual snobbery" and seeks out human nature wherever it is to be found.

1256 MacCarthy, Desmond. "Drama: Bernard Shaw's 'Julius Caesar,' " NSTATE, I (1913), 82-83; rptd in MacCarthy, pp. 93-97.
Caesar and Cleopatra is a wonderfully imaginative play and reveals Shaw's method of dealing with history. He attempts to rub off the historical patina of Caesar and render him in bright modern colors. The result is Shaw's view of what a great man should be like.

1257 MacCarthy, Desmond. "Drama: Caesar Again," NSTATE, I (1913), 149; rptd in MacCarthy, pp. 97-101.
[MacCarthy's defense of his views in item 1256, concluding "Shaw sees in Julius Caesar only certain qualities because he takes a particular view of greatness."]

1258 "Man in the Stalls." "The Theatres," WORLD, No. 2045 (9 Sept 1913), 396-97.

Androcles and the Lion is a fable and not a burlesque or caricature. It presents Shaw's understanding of religion as he sees it. The play appeals to the intellect rather than the senses, and is a mixture of the witty, humorous and serious.

1259 Massingham, H. W. "Mr. Shaw's Caesar," NATION (Lond), 19 April 1913 [not seen]; rptd in H. W. M.: A SELECTION FROM THE WRITINGS OF H. W. MASSINGHAM (Lond: Cape, 1925), pp. 243-45.

Shaw's Caesar is a "true Fabian hero" who, even in the grand scheme of things, does everything for utilitarian purposes. The play's weakness is that it could be even more imaginative than it is.

1260 Metcalfe, [J. S.]. [Caesar and Cleopatra], LIFE, LXII (6 Nov 1913), 791.

Caesar and Cleopatra is delightfully witty, and Shaw's irreverent toying with history is amusing. If nothing else, the play helps us alter our perspective of the established historical portraits.

1261 "Mr. Bernard Shaw and Morals," SPECTATOR, CXI (1913), 814-15; rptd in LIVING AGE, CCLXXIX (1913), 818-21.

Shaw has entered into a debate with the Bishop of Kensington over the censorship of music-hall sketches. Unfortunately, "the fact is that Mr. Shaw is so inaccurate and careless as an observer that he does not know what is thought even by the simple people who wait in queues outside music-halls, and whose champion he believes himself to be." [See also, Clarence M. Dobell, "Mr. Shaw on Morals," SPECTATOR, CXI (1913), 863.]

1262 "Mr. Bernard Shaw and the Speaker," TIMES, 6 Feb 1913, p. 6.

Shaw has attacked the Speaker of the House of Commons for his attitude towards women's suffrage legislation.

1263 "Mr. Bernard Shaw's The Philanderer a Brilliant Satire Flawlessly Acted," NYH, 29 Dec 1913, p. 8.

It is surprising that, with its timely ideas, The Philanderer has not been produced before in New York.

1264 "Mr. G. B. Shaw at Mme. Tussaud's," TIMES, 24 Dec 1913, p. 11.

A model of Shaw is to be added to the famous Tussaud's waxworks museum.

1265 "Mr. Larkin's Sentence," TIMES, 3 Nov 1913, p. 5.

Shaw has urged Dublin strikers to arm themselves against the police. [See also "The Dublin Deadlock," TIMES, 6 Nov 1913, p. 5.]

1266 "Mr. Shaw and Shakespeare's Birthday," TIMES, 24 April 1913, p. 8.

A humorous letter from Shaw was read out at a meeting of the Urban

Club.

1267 "Mr. Shaw on Ibsen," TLS, No. 608 (4 Sept 1913), 363.
The second edition of The Quintessence of Ibsenism makes the reader
wish it were possible to debate with Shaw directly. Frequently Shaw
moves from a discussion of Ibsen's plays to his own views on the
nature of drama, views difficult to agree with. His assessment of
individual plays is often shrewd.

1268 "Mr. Shaw's New Play at the St. James's: Androcles and
the Lion, " TIMES, 2 Sept 1913, p. 6.
The Lion is the most fortunate character in all Shaw's drama because
he is the only one not to talk. And in the rest of Androcles and the
Lion Shaw shows he can drop his propaganda and give us "simple,
straightforward fun."

1269 "Mr. Shaw's New Play at the St. James's Theatre," DT, 2
Sept 1913, p. 11.
Androcles and the Lion contains some very good pantomime and some
slightly less good wit. Not all the characters are convincing. There
is also some rhetoric on the duty of man.

1270 "Mr. Shaw's New Play: Great Catherine at the
Vaudeville," TIMES, 19 Nov 1913, p. 11.
The insular Englishman, seen previously as Britannus in Caesar and
Cleopatra, reemerges in Great Catherine as Captain Edstaston.
However, the humor of Caesar now wears a little thin in this play.

1271 "Mr. Shaw's New Play: Great Catherine at the Vaudeville
Theatre," DT, 19 Nov 1913, p. 12.
Great Catherine needs the editor's pencil, though doubtless Shaw
himself is pleased with his own wit and ideas. The play is a roaring
farce, full of good and bad jokes, tedious banalities and dull trifling.

1272 "The Modest Shaw Again," NYT, 23 Nov 1912, part VIII, p.
6; rptd in NYTTR 1912-1919, [n. p.] .
Shaw's reputation in Germany has been rehabilitated by the successful production of Pygmalion in Berlin.

1273 "Moral Equivocals," SPECTATOR, CX (1913), 9-10; rptd in
LIVING AGE, CCLXXVI (1913), 633-35.
Shaw is paradoxical and equivocal and will probably not find a permanent place among the English classics. Shaw uses invective and
his own special vocabulary so that "if Mr. Shaw has anything to teach,
his vocabulary effectively prevents him from teaching it."

1274 "Much to Amuse in The Philanderer," NYT, 29 Dec 1913,
p. 7; rptd in NYTTR 1912-1919, [n. p.] .
In The Philanderer Shaw exposes numerous hollow pretenses, though
he often exaggerates and caricatures. The play is amusing, but with
barren stretches.

1275 N., N. "Drama: London Theatres," NATION (NY), XCVII (1913), 316-17.

Androcles and the Lion is a fable and a vehicle for Shaw to offer prophecies to his doting public, although he has his tongue in his cheek. The fooling drags, and once the Shavian glamor is pierced, it is obvious there is no message or substance—just farce.

1276 O., S. "Androcles v. ('Oh! I Say!') Potiphar," ENGLISH REVIEW, XIV (Oct 1913), 465-68.

One of Shaw's "pleasant plays," Androcles and the Lion is obviously allegorical, the lion being the British Lion, Megaera representing the "conventional shrew who doesn't want a vote," Androcles acting the modern husband, and Lavinia the "emancipated woman." Altogether witty and charming.

1277 O'Bolger, Thomas Denis. "George Bernard Shaw's Social Philosophy," Ph.D. dissertation, University of Pennsylvania, 1913 [not seen].

[Cited in Litto, p. 70.]

1278 "Offended by Shaw's Play," NYT, 2 Sept 1913, p. 7; rptd in NYTTR 1912-1919, [n. p.].

Some audience members hissed the London production of Androcles and the Lion because Shaw's satire offended their religious sensibilities. Critics are divided in their opinions.

1279 "Old Shaw Comedy at the Little Theatre," SUN (NY), 29 Dec 1913, p. 9.

The Philanderer is now no more than delightful fooling, although it is evident Shaw had a more serious intent.

1280 Osugi, Sakae. "Chojin no koi—Shawgeki hito to chojin hyoron" (Superman's Love—A Review of Shaw's Man and Superman), KINDAI SHISO (Tokyo), I: 7 (April 1913), 21-25.

It is imperative to enter into Shaw's philosophical world in order to grasp his plays. Characters' personality, feeling and actions are all deeply connected with the author's ideas. Shaw's plays can be classified thus: 1) exposure of social reality (Widowers' Houses, Mrs. Warren's Profession); 2) psychology (Arms and the Man, Caesar and Cleopatra, You Never Can Tell, Man and Superman); 3) ethics (Candida, Captain Brassbound's Conversion, The Devil's Disciple, The Doctor's Dilemma); 4) social philosophy (Getting Married, John Bull's Other Island, Major Barbara, The Shewing-up of Blanco Posnet). The plays of the second group are the best, and the richest of those are those plays which deal with the psychology of love. [In Japanese.]

1281 "Overruled," HEARST'S MAGAZINE, XXIII (May 1913), 680-96.

[An illustrated text of the play.]

1282 Palmer, John. "Caesar and Cleopatra," SAT REV, CXV

(1913), 484-85.

Unfortunately Caesar and Cleopatra reveals all Shaw's moral earnestness and shows a distinct lack of his comic abilities. Shaw's intention is to strip away romanticism and to see things as they really are.

1283 Palmer, John. THE CENSOR AND THE THEATRES (NY: Mitchell Kennerley, 1913), pp. 11, 13, 60-61, 63-64, 92, 94-96, 99, 119, 206, 215, 217, 226-229, 235-38, 257-58, 263-64, 269-70.

[An examination of stage censorship within the context of the 1909 parliamentary select committee on censorship. Passing references to Shaw's plays and his evidence before the committee.]

1284 Palmer, John. "The Doctor's Dilemma," SAT REV, CXVI (1913), 744-45.

The Doctor's Dilemma palls because, for example, the last act is not written as wittily as the first. In addition, this act is repetitious, heavy-handed, and wandering.

1285 Palmer, John. THE FUTURE OF THE THEATRE (Lond: G. Bell, 1913), pp. 7, 15, 34, 39, 80, 90, 97, 101, 103, 106, 116, 120, 123, 129, 132-54, 156, 159, 176, 181-82, 188.

Shaw has never made concessions to the public in order to make himself more popular; nevertheless the Vedrenne-Barker productions at the Court Theatre succeeded because the public discovered a "good thing honestly offered at a fair price." Shaw symbolizes destruction and anarchy, and also represents other dramatists such as Hankin and Galsworthy. Shaw has protested the most and achieved the most; he is the "Socrates of the English dramatic renaissance." He is a puritan (however much he may try to disguise that fact) with a deep-rooted distrust of life. How He Lied to Her Husband is a good example of Shaw's destructive method. Here he assails marital jealousy, a theme handled mechanically on the stage for generations, by destroying all our preconceptions. However, his attacks are often obfuscated by his apparent social propaganda. Shaw's immortal quality is his intellectual buffoonery.

1286 Palmer, John. "Hors D'Oeuvres at the S. James'," SAT REV, CXVI (1913), 293-94.

Although Androcles and the Lion is not Shaw at his best, it will undoubtedly be better than anything else that will be produced during the season.

1287 Palmer, John. "Mr. Shaw's Great Catherine, " SAT REV, CXVI (1913), 648-49.

Great Catherine is an example of "what the professional playwright can do when he does his worst" because Shaw relies solely on theatrical technical devices to carry a play of no substance.

1288 "The Philanderer," NY DRAMATIC MIRROR, LXX (31

Dec 1913), 6.

Although The Philanderer is termed an unpleasant play, it might be better called whimsical.

1289 "The Playhouses," ILN, CXLIII (6 Sept 1913), 350.

Androcles and the Lion is an amusing play, not least for Shaw's creation of the Lion. Shaw reaches his audience's heart through its head and no-one can take offense at his arguments.

1290 "The Playhouses," ILN, CXLIII (22 Nov 1913), 826.

Great Catherine is a characteristically Shavian joke with "breezy" humor. Its one weak point is the arrest scene.

1291 "The Playhouses: Caesar and Cleopatra at Drury Lane,"
    ILN, CXLII (19 April 1913), 502.

Shaw is extending his popularity as this revival of Caesar and Cleopatra (with a new prologue) proves. The play is a mixture of "burlesque history and didacticism, of satire and rhetoric, of stirring situation and comic irreverence."

1292 Porzsolt, K. "Caesar és Cleopatra" (Caesar and
    Cleopatra), PESTI HIRLAP (Budapest), 22 Feb 1913 [not seen].
[In Hungarian.]

1293 "Productions of the Week," ATH, No. 4480 (6 Sept 1913),
    236.

In Androcles and the Lion Shaw has cheapened himself by pandering to his audiences. "If he wishes to retain his position as an educator, he must not descend to mere fooling."

1294 "Pygmalion," NYT, 30 Nov 1913, part V, p. 1.; rptd in
    NYTTR 1912-1919, [n. p.].

Shaw refused to allow the premiere of Pygmalion to take place in London because the critics there always label his work as dull, blasphemous and unpopular.

1295 [Pygmalion], TIMES, 17 Oct 1913, p. 7.

Pygmalion has been excellently received in Vienna. The play was translated with no attempt made at adaptation.

1296 "Realist." "Shavian Accuracy," ERA, 9 July 1913, p. 19.

Shaw is inaccurate in Arms and the Man when he attempts to describe a cavalary charge as it really is. For example, in the Battle of Balaclava, sergeants had difficulty restraining their men from breaking ahead of the line of charge—the opposite of Shaw's contentions.

1297 "Repertory at the St. James's," ERA, 10 Dec 1913, p. 19.

The Doctor's Dilemma is an "excruciatingly clever satirical comedy" and receives a good revival.

1298 "Repertory at the St. James's," STAGE, 11 Dec 1913,
    p. 31.

Although The Doctor's Dilemma is a long, unwieldy, highly individual and irresponsible play, the piece's "audacity, vigour of caricature, grim humour, and revealing touches of drama, all thrown together in a brilliant medley, counteract its formative weakness as a play." Shaw's satire on the medical profession is too transparent to be taken seriously.

1299 Reynolds, Alice Louise. "Bernard Shaw on Art in the Schools," JOURNAL OF EDUCATION, LXXVIII (11 Dec 1913), 598-99.
[Essentially a report of Shaw's lecture "Music and Drama in the Schools."]

1300 Richter, Helene. "Die Quintessenz des Shawismus" (The Quintessence of Shavianism), ENGLISCHE STUDIEN, XLVI (1913), 367-469.
[Examines Shaw as socialist, journalist, antimoralist, and propagandist, with wide reference to the plays, novels, and other works through 1912. In German.]

1301 "The Rule that Proves the Exception," NATION (NY), XCVII (1913), 380.
Shaw is an exponent of a "form of guerrilla warfare against things as they are which consists essentially in rallying the inconsistencies, the contradictions and the logical gaps in our laws and institutions."

1302 "A Russian Criticism of Mr. Bernard Shaw," TIMES, 29 Nov 1913, p. 11.
The London correspondent of VETCHERNIE VREMYA (St. Petersburg) declares Great Catherine to be a "vulgar farce."

1303 S., H. "The Theatres: St. James's Repertory," WORLD, No. 2058 (9 Dec 1913), 1001.
Act four of The Doctor's Dilemma is a breach of good taste and Shaw should have paid heed to the critics about this. The rest of the play combines fine characterization and satire.

1304 Schlumberger, Jean. "On ne peut jamais dire, de Bernard Shaw" (Bernard Shaw's You Never Can Tell), NOUVELLE REVUE FRANÇAISE, 1 March 1913.
You Never Can Tell is most entertaining, with good descriptions of the characters, and reading the plays is more rewarding than seeing them acted. The glorification of youth is one of the less questionable points of contact between Shaw and Molière. [In French.]

1305 Scott, Dixon. "The Reader: Bernard Shaw," BOOKMAN (Lond), XLIV (Sept 1913), 239-53, 255-56, 259; XLV (Oct 1913), 36-42; rptd in rvd form as "The Innocence of Bernard Shaw" in MEN OF LETTERS (Lond: Hodder & Stoughton, 1916), pp. 1-47; rptd in part in Evans, pp. 215-22.

When we realize Shaw is a dupe, his work gains in value because it then becomes less virulent and he becomes more likeable. He has also made the mistake of clinging tenaciously to his opinions (even when he should have changed them), and is constantly attempting to justify himself to himself. Even his philosophy is a concoction which merely satisfies his desire for consistency. However, his sincerity must be recognized as must the fact he has done his best. "Recognize that a passion for purity, gentleness, truth, justice and beauty is the force at the base of all his teaching, and you will find his message one of the most tonic of our time."

1306 Scott-James, R. A. "Bernard Shaw" (1913; unknown source; not seen); rptd in PERSONALITY IN LITERATURE 1913-1931 (Lond: Secker, 1931; NY: Holt, 1932), pp. 34-55.

Shaw is well-known because of his many-sided, influential activities. He rails at things he disagrees with and, in doing so, uses remorseless logic. He is a first-rate business man, but is benevolent. However, after he has attacked certain ideas, he is less than successful in offering reconstructive solutions because his "cut-and-dried Fabian side . . . blinds him to facts of a certain sort." Shaw is "far better as lecturer, debater, pamphleteer, and writer of critical essays than as writer of either romances or plays."

1307 "Sees Christ Recrucified," NYT, 29 Sept 1913, p. 3.

Shaw has emphatically defended Androcles and the Lion against criticisms by the Rev. Morgan Gibbon.

1308 "A Shakespeare Memorial Theatre," TIMES, 16 May 1913, p. 10.

Shaw has spoken in favor of a national theatre which will produce the classics of British drama.

1309 "Shaw an Enigma in Paris," NYT, 23 Feb 1913, part IX, p. 11; rptd in NYTTR 1912-1919, [n. p.].

A French version of You Never Can Tell has the Paris critics at odds with each other and wondering what the piece is about.

1310 "Shaw and Galsworthy Plays in Germany," TIMES, 3 Nov 1913, p. 12.

Pygmalion has been produced "with great success" in Berlin.

1311 "Shaw and the Bishop," NYT, 7 Dec 1913, part VIII, p. 4.

The Bishop of Kensington has attacked the stage, and Shaw has asked him to define what he means by morality.

1312 "Shaw Crowds out Brandes" (1913; unidentified NY newspaper [not seen]); rptd in INDEPENDENT SHAVIAN, VII: 3 (1969), 41-42.

[On a lecture on Nietzsche given by Dr. Georg Brandes, together with Shaw's introductory remarks.]

1313 "Shaw for a Mirthless Playhouse," LIT DIG, XLVI (1913), 231-32.
[Recounts the details of Shaw's protests in England about audience behavior.]

1314 "Shaw has Another Idea," NYT, 18 March 1913, p. 9.
Yet again Shaw has a plan, this time for the preservation of peace in Europe.

1315 "Shaw on 'Marconi Comedy,'" NYT, 13 April 1913, part III, p. 3.
A weekly journal issued by Shaw and Mr. and Mrs. Sidney Webb to advocate collectivism makes for dull reading.

1316 "Shaw Play at Munich," TIMES, 24 Nov 1913, p. 6.
Pygmalion has been produced in Munich and received with "great enthusiasm."

1317 "Shaw Play on Phonetics," NYT, 7 Sept 1913, part III, p. 4.
Pygmalion will be performed in Germany first. It has no sex interest and is literally about phonetics.

1318 "Shaw Raps British Taste," NYT, 15 July 1913, p. 3.
Shaw has attacked the English for refusing to build a national theatre.

1319 "Shaw Says He's a Genius," NYT, 16 March 1913, part IV, p. 5.
Shaw declares he is a genius, makes money as a result, and defines socialism.

1320 "The Shewing-up of Blanco Posnet," TIMES, 15 July 1913, p. 11.
[A favorable review.]

1321 S[pence], E. F. "The Stage from the Stalls," SKETCH, LXXXIII (10 Sept 1913), 298-99.
Androcles and the Lion is a whimsical play in which Shaw makes fun of numerous objects and people in typical fashion, and preaches the value of toleration. The Lion steals the show.

1322 "The Stage from the Stalls," SKETCH, LXXXIV (3 Dec 1913), 264-65.
Shaw's picture of the English officer in Great Catherine is most entertaining, and it does not much matter if he is repeating himself. Catherine emerges as a genuine historical figure, not as a caricature.

1323 "Suffragists Work Ruin in Kew Gardens," NYT, 9 Feb 1913, part III, p. 1.
Shaw's attack on the Speaker of the House of Commons over franchise legislation has been strongly resented.

1324 "Things New: At the Theatres," SKETCH, LXXXII (23

April 1913), 70.

Caesar and Cleopatra is now performed with a new prologue and a restored third act. The former contains some jokes not worthy of Shaw, while the whole play is a bewildering, mixed, melodramatic farce.

1325 "Things New: At the Theatres," SKETCH, LXXXIV (26 Nov 1913), 226.

Although some critics have treated Great Catherine harshly, it is a droll play with Catherine herself emerging as a truly comic character.

1326 Ueda, Bin. "Jo" (Introduction), Hito to Chojin (Man and Superman) trans by Kohyo Hosoda (Tokyo: Keibunkan, 1913), pp. 1-11; rptd in UEDA BIN ZENSHU (Collected Works of Bin Ueda), vol 8 (Tokyo: Kaizosha, 1930), pp. 227-32.

The purport of Man and Superman is to show how the life force moves mankind and causes its evolution. Viewed superficially, this play may give the impression that reality and fantasy are mingled unexpectedly. Because of this, the reader may wonder whether he should take it seriously or not, and draw a rash conclusion that this is a defective work. [In Japanese.]

1327 Villanova d'Ardenghi, Bruno. "L'Idee di G. B. S." (G. B. S.'s Ideas), RIVISTA TEATRALE ITALIANA (Florence), XII: 17 (1913), 1-9, 72-82, 129-43.

Despite Shaw's notoriety as a revolutionary agitator of ideas, he is a genuine playwright. Shaw must also be understood as a critic, philosopher, and sociologist to understand his plays and even the novels. Social reform is predominant in all Shaw's plays, especially Man and Superman. His concept of love is based on the theory that only sexual and sensual attraction exist between man and woman, often masked by sentiment. Love is the axis of life, but marriage is merely a convention, which contributes to delaying the progress of humanity (as in Man and Superman and Candida). Candida is related to Ibsen's THE LADY OF THE SEA and to Nora. Differences of class and temperament between hero and heroine (as in Arms and the Man and Widowers' Houses) prove the existence of what Shaw calls the life force. The source of all errors can be traced back to faulty education (Mrs. Warren's Profession and You Never Can Tell). For Shaw nothing is sacred, including religion and politics (John Bull's Other Island). The latter play also exhibits Shaw's frequent weakness—too much discussion. He also attacks militarism. [In Italian.]

1328 "Whimsical History by English Players," NYT, 21 Oct 1913, p. 9; rptd NYTTR 1912-1919, [n. p.].

Caesar and Cleopatra still contains pugent humor for Shaw is always most enjoyable when he is most extravagant. The play is whimsical with farcical moments.

1329 "Women and Plays," ERA, 15 March 1913, p. 19.
Shaw, Hankin, Galsworthy and others "have let the light of reason into stage-plays." However, the intellectual theatre is now bankrupt, and "the only material success of the advanced school is Fanny's First Play," and that is only a modernized version of an old theme.

1914

1330 Albini, Ettore. "Pigmalione di George Bernard Shaw" (George Bernard Shaw's Pygmalion), AVANTI! (Rome), 24 Nov 1914; rptd in CRONACHE TEATRALI 1891-1925, (Theatrical Chronicles 1891-1925), ed by G. Bartolucci (Genoa: Teatro Stabile, 1972), pp. 285-89.
Shaw's plays are digressions for several characters. What matters in Pygmalion is the irresistible fascination of the concentrated, easy, and brilliant dialogue which illuminates Shaw's ideas. [In Italian.]

1331 "Another Shaw Play," OUTLOOK (NY), CVI (1914), 391.
Although The Philanderer is entertaining, the play's philosophy or morality is baffling.

1332 Archer, William. "Drama: Recent London Productions: The Success of Pygmalion," NATION (NY), XCVIII (1914), 581-82.
Pygmalion is Shaw's "most human" play, containing "some gems of comedy." However, it is rather diffuse and could have been compressed into three acts.

1333 "As Shaw Sees Royalty," NYT, 27 March 1914, p. 1.
Shaw has spoken at a meeting to promote socialist unity.

1334 "Asks Why Censor Didn't Stop Shaw," NYT, 23 Nov 1914, p. 3.
Robert Blatchford thinks Shaw's Common Sense About the War should have been censored. It is a perversion of the truth and another example of Shaw's hunger for notoriety.

1335 "At the Play," OBS, 1 Feb 1914, p. 9.
The Music Cure is Shaw at his most whimsical, and even contains a parody of his own topsy-turvy style.

1336 B. "Shaw's Pygmalion in German," NATION (NY), XCVIII (1914), 373.
A production of Pygmalion in German in New York reveals Shaw has little opportunity in this play for expounding social doctrines.

1337 Barker, Ernest. POLITICAL THOUGHT IN ENGLAND FROM HERBERT SPENCER TO THE PRESENT DAY (NY: Holt;

Lond: Butterworth [1914]), pp. 202-03, 213, 215, 217-18.
Shaw, along with H. G. Wells, has been a rebel as well as a conspicuous figure in the history of socialism.

1338 "Bars Shaw's Adjective," NYT, 4 June 1914, p. 5.
The English theatrical censor allowed Shaw to use "bloody" in
Pygmalion but has proscribed its use in J. B. McCarthy's THE
SUPPLANTERS.

1339 Bennett, Arnold. "Arnold Bennett Answers Shaw," NYT,
18 Nov 1914, p. 3.
Shaw has shown courage in Common Sense About the War and open
discussion is to be welcomed. "Mixed up with the tremendous
common sense, however, is a considerable and unusual percentage of
that perverseness, waywardness, and harlequinading which are apparently an essential element of Mr. Shaw's best work." [See also
Shaw's reply, NYT, 19 Nov 1914, p. 3.]

1340 "Bernard Shaw as a Puritan Answer to the Paganism of
Oscar Wilde," CUR OP, LVI (May 1914), 377.
While both Shaw and Wilde used epigram and paradox, they did so for
differing, counterbalancing purposes. Wilde was pagan, decadent,
perverse; Shaw puritanical, realistic, philosophic.

1341 "Bernard Shaw on the War," NYT, 14 Nov 1914, p. 10.
Shaw's articles on the war (to appear in STIMES) reflect his own
individual view and lack his usual paradoxical, whimsical tone. Many
people will probably agree with his commonsense outlook.

1342 "Bernard Shaw's Bout with the Bishop of Kensington,"
CUR OP, LVI (Feb 1914), 134.
Shaw has locked horns with the Bishop of Kensington over the matter
of censorship of music-hall sketches. Although Shaw's arguments are
brilliant, the cleric's commonsense is superior.

1343 "Bernard Shaw's Boycott of England," CUR OP, LVI (Jan
1914), 30-31.
Shaw has allowed the first performances of Pygmalion to take place
in Vienna and Berlin because his work is always castigated in London,
which ruins his chances for subsequent success on the continent.

1344 "Bernard Shaw's Disturbing Relation to Modern Religion,"
CUR OP, LVI (May 1914), 373.
A recent article by P. Gavan Duffy [item 1361] assures us that
behind Shaw's jester's mask there is a puritan gentleman. It is surely
a sign of the times when Shaw can receive such a tribute from a
Roman Catholic priest.

1345 "Bernard Shaw's Elaborate Squib of Androcles and the
Lion," CUR OP, LVII (1914), 244-48.
[A summary of the mixed critical reviews of Androcles and the Lion,

with extensive extracts of the text.]

1346 "Bernard Shaw's Unqualified Approval of the Cinemato-
graph," CUR OP, LVII (Aug 1914), 105-106.
Shaw sees a great moral purpose in the cinema and it would not be
surprising to find him converting his plays into screenplays.

1347 "Books of the Day: Young Mr. Shaw," OBS, 19 July 1914,
p. 4.
An Unsocial Socialist, although not really a novel, is interesting
because it reveals that Shaw's early work is exactly the same as the
later plays. He uses the same language and themes.

1348 Burton, Richard. LITTLE ESSAYS IN LITERATURE AND
LIFE (NY: Century, 1914), pp. 229-33, 302-06.
Shaw is seen as a purveyor of epigrams and paradoxes, but in fact
there is a unity of teaching and purpose in his plays—particularly his
socialistic passion. In The Shewing-up of Blanco Posnet Shaw is
actually acknowledging the two opposing principles recognized by St.
Augustine—God and the Devil.

1349 "Candida at the Arts Centre," TIMES, 30 Jan 1914, p. 9.
[A favorable review.]

1350 Cannan, Gilbert. "Dramatic Chronicle," POETRY AND
DRAMA (Lond), II (1914), 205-07.
Pygmalion merely barters with its audiences and Shaw is impudent
enough to ask them to be shocked over a single word ["bloody"].

1351 Caro, Josef. "Bernard Shaw und Shakespeare" (Bernard
Shaw and Shakespeare), DIE NEUEREN SPRACHEN, XXII: 7
(Nov 1914), 433-48; XXII: 8 (Dec 1914), 509-25.
Shaw admires Shakespeare's word-music, but attacks his blank verse,
romanticism, pessimism, and feeble nineteenth-century Shake-
spearean productions. Shaw's criticism of Shakespeare is primarily a
criticism of both romanticism and the Elizabethan age. Shaw's
puritan attitude makes his reading of Shakespeare difficult.
[Emphasizes Shaw's criticism of JULIUS CAESAR and ANTONY
AND CLEOPATRA. In German.]

1352 "Censorships Neatly Described," NYT, 1 Dec 1914, p. 12.
In Common Sense About the War Shaw was accurate in his estimate
of censorship.

1353 Chandler, Frank Wadleigh. ASPECTS OF MODERN
DRAMA (1914; rptd [NY]: Macmillan, 1929), pp. 4, 111, 116-
19, 147, 150-51, 172, 216, 278, 295, 302, 307, 312, 336, 344,
346-49, 358, 363, 368, 399-421, 439, 450, 464, 472-73.
Shaw assumes an unmoral attitude in The Doctor's Dilemma when he
has Dubedat declare artistic not ethical laws govern things. In
Candida Shaw reverses usual expectations and provides the sanest

solution to the "eternal triangle" problem. Churchmen receive at least humorous sympathy as is evidenced in Father Keegan (John Bull's Other Island), James Morell (Candida), and Anthony Anderson (The Devil's Disciple). Major Barbara is a bitter, cynical satire in which Shaw reveals the nature of such charities as the Salvation Army, to which he is "notoriously unfair." But "he is stimulating in his criticism of certain tendencies in modern philanthropy, and consistent with his own individualistic philosophy and humility." Similarly in Widowers' Houses Shaw shows personal interests surmount ideas of social justice, and although this piece is sordid and contains contemptible characters, it is rendered effective by its satiric flashes. In Mrs. Warren's Profession Shaw attacks the individual who uses her environment as a pretext for wrong-doing "rather than the conditions of the environment itself." As a satirist Shaw shows wilful exaggeration to demonstrate how things fail to conform to his ideas of how they should be ordered. He exalts reality, instinct, and individualism at the expense of altruism, romance, and sentiment. But even if he does not provide the ultimate truth, "he is none the less brilliant in wit and tonic in thought."

1354 "Chesterton Judge at Dickens Trial," NYT, 8 Jan 1914, p. 1.
Shaw has played the role of foreman of the jury in a mock trial of Edwin Drood held in London. [See also: "The Mystery of a Mystery" (editorial), NYT, 11 Jan 1914, part II, p. 14.]

1355 Colby, F. M. "The Book of the Month," NORTH AMERICAN REVIEW, CC (1914), 147-52.
Shaw is highly talented and, therefore, always does the improbable and unpredictable, as the publication of Misalliance, The Dark Lady of the Sonnets, and Fanny's First Play demonstrates. The prefaces contain many ideas, but these are not always realized and given dramatic form in the plays themselves.

1356 Cunningham, W. "The Guilt of Militarism," NYT, 16 Nov 1914, p. 8.
Shaw fulfilled a valuable service in ridiculing militarism in Arms and the Man, but it is doubtful that his recent solemn pronouncements should be taken seriously.

1357 De Casseres, Benjamin. "Diabolistic Idealists: Shaw, D'Annunzio, Tolstoi," INTERNATIONAL (NY), VIII (April 1914), 129-30.
"Cruel, narrow, puritanical, an anti-individualist and anti-libertarian, Shaw is today the finest type . . . of the diabolical idealists who infect life with their perversive anti-natural doctrines."

1358 Donlin, George Bernard. "Mr. Shaw's New Preface," DIAL, LVII (1914), 74-76.

With Misalliance, The Dark Lady of the Sonnets and Fanny's First Play comes Shaw's preface "Treatise on Parents and Children" which reveals Shaw's characteristic moral focus. Here he indicates his complete disgust with the two chief influences in a child's life—the home and school.

1359 "Drama," ATH, No. 4518 (30 May 1914), 771.
The publication of Misalliance, The Dark Lady of the Sonnets and Fanny's First Play proves the extent to which Shaw's work has become dominated by conversation. And, similarly, the plays themselves have become overpowered by Shaw's prefaces (which often could be placed before any of his plays).

1360 "Drama," NATION (NY), XCVIII (1914), 17-18.
The Philanderer is rather dated, although it is characteristically Shavian. However, it is "devoid of any real dramatic impulse or significance."

1361 Duffy, Rev. P. Gavan. "Shavian Religion," CENTURY MAGAZINE, LXXXVII (April 1914), 908-14.
Despite his irony, wit and use of paradox, Shaw has a serious religious purpose. He has clearly felt religious emotion, otherwise he would not be able to create Major Barbara. He is extravagant and excessive in his desire to show things as they are, particularly Christian theory and practice (rather than Christ's teaching). Ultimately, Shaw is constructive in his awakening of the religious conscience to the "pettiness of shams and deceits," and in his encouragement of self-examination.

1362 "Editorial Notes: Critics and Moles," MASK, VI (April 1914), 369-70.
You Never Can Tell had a mixed critical reception in Naples. The critics complained of the "mental acrobatics" needed to understand the piece and that "Shaw is fettered by his own paradoxes and that the whole effect is alternately irritating and diverting."

1363 Ervine, St. John G. "The Crisis in the Repertory Theatre: I," STAGE, 12 March 1914, p. 34.
If it were not for Shaw's plays, repertory theatres would have perished a long time ago.

1364 F. "Drama: Pygmalion," NATION (NY), XCIX (1914), 504-05.
Pygmalion reflects a certain mellowing in Shaw and is his first play in which the characters are "rightly centered."

1365 "First Nighter." "Pygmalion," NY DRAMATIC MIRROR, LXXI (1 April 1914), 12.
Pygmalion possesses more "universal significance" than most of Shaw's satires, with Doolittle acting as a choric commentator.

1366 "First Nighter." "Pygmalion," NY DRAMATIC MIRROR, LXXII (21 Oct 1914), 8.
Pygmalion is interesting. Doolittle, as Shaw's mouthpiece, comments on English conditions and spouts Shaw's sociological philosophy.

1367 Flagg, James Montgomery. "The Philanderer," HARPER'S WEEKLY, LVIII (17 Jan 1914), 22-23.
The Philanderer is a "delightful ethical farce." It lacks the thorough dramatic substance and consistent theme of Man and Superman, but is witty and gay.

1368 Fox, Paul Hervey. "The Tragedy of 'G. B. S.,'" COLONNADE, VII (March 1914), 207-12.
Shaw is forced to "clothe his ideas in cleverness in order that they may be palatable to a public that does not care to think." His later plays are formless; his plots are so embryonic as to be non-existent. He is more revolutionary than Wilde in his use of paradoxical wit.

1369 Frichet, Oscar. "The Great Bernard and the Manxman: Caricatures of George Bernard Shaw and Hall Caine, Two Revolutionists in the Field of Letters," NATIONAL MAGAZINE, XXXIX (March 1914), 944-46.
Shaw is the most discussed man of letters living and deals daringly with delicate subjects (as in Mrs. Warren's Profession). He disdains other dramatists, has characteristically startling views on poverty and marriage, and hates sham, romance and sentimentality.

1370 "G. B. S. on Bernard Shaw in a Moment of Anonymity," NYT, 1 March 1914, part VII, p. 7.
[See item 168.]

1371 "G. B. S. on 'Mrs. Pat's' Phonetics," NYT, 10 May 1914, part VIII, p. 5.
Shaw has recalled when he had to criticize Mrs. Patrick Campbell's diction some twenty years previously.

1372 "G. B. Shaw Bashful, Declares His Wife," NYT, 29 April 1914, p. 5.
Shaw's wife has described Shaw as bashful and retiring and as being in sympathy with the methods used by the suffragettes.

1373 "G. B. Shaw Justifies Treaty-Breaking," NYT, 20 Dec 1914, part II, p. 2.
Shaw believes it would be suicidal for Germany to respect Belgium's neutrality.

1374 "G. B. Shaw on Militants," NYT, 10 June 1914, p. 4.
Shaw believes the suffragettes "will get the vote after there have been a few hangings."

1375 "G. B. Shaw Petitions President Wilson," NYT, 7 Nov 1914, p. 2.

Shaw wants Wilson to ask the warring countries to leave Belgium.

1376 "G. B. Shaw's Peace Plan," NYT, 1 Jan 1914, p. 3.
Shaw has endorsed Anatole France's idea that England should "fight the aggressor if France and Germany quarrel."

1377 Gee, Joseph. "A British View of Shaw," NYT, 29 Nov 1914, part III, p. 2.
Shaw is highly regarded in England as a dramatist but possesses no talent as a critic of English politics. He is a highly talented self-advertiser.

1378 "German Dramatist Answers G. B. Shaw," NYT, 20 Oct 1914, p. 5.
Herbert Eulenberg has written an open letter to Shaw saying Germany has been forced into its militaristic position. England's "groundless participation" has made Germany's efforts against France and Russia more difficult.

1379 Gilman, Lawrence. "Music and Drama," NORTH AMERICAN REVIEW, CC (1914), 933-34.
Pygmalion may not be Shaw's most dazzling play, but, by comparison, other contemporary works are flat and prosaic.

1380 "A Glimpse in the Theatres," INTERNATIONAL (NY), VIII (April 1914), 132.
Pygmalion does not follow prescribed dramatic rules. Instead, it is reckless, daring, thrilling, and stimulating.

1381 Godley, Eveline [C.]. "Drama," THE ANNUAL REGISTER 1913 (Lond: Longmans, Green, 1914), part II, pp. 71-74.
Androcles and the Lion suffers from "a spirit of farce, inappropriately applied." [With brief references to Great Catherine and The Doctor's Dilemma.]

1382 Goldman, Emma. THE SOCIAL SIGNIFICANCE OF THE MODERN DRAMA (Bost: Richard G. Badger; Toronto: Copp Clark, 1914), pp. 175-95.
Shaw has sincere, serious purposes in his dramas although his intent is often clouded by his humor. His propaganda is often diluted because as an artist he must go to life, and that cannot be molded to set patterns. In Mrs. Warren's Profession and Major Barbara Shaw pulls off "the mask of purity and Christian kindness that we may see their hidden viciousness at work."

1383 [Granville-] Barker, Harley. "Pygmalion in Berlin," HARPER'S WEEKLY, LVIII (11 April 1914), 14-15.
Pygmalion has been successfully produced at the Lessing Theatre in Berlin.

1384 Gregory, Lady [Augusta]. OUR IRISH THEATRE: A

GEORGE BERNARD SHAW

CHAPTER OF AUTOBIOGRAPHY (NY & Lond: Putnam, 1914), pp. 35-37, 93, 140-68, 210-12, 267-79, 299-305.
It is good to have proved Shaw wrong over his idea that there can be no good Irish drama. [With an account of the Dublin production of and controversy surrounding The Shewing-up of Blanco Posnet.]

1385 Grein, J. T. "The Dramatic World," STIMES, 1 Feb 1914, p. 6.
The Music Cure should be accepted simply as a trivial jest and nothing more.

1386 Grein, J. T. "Easter Premieres: Mr. Shaw's Pygmalion at His Majesty's," STIMES, 12 April 1914, p. 11.
Pygmalion is a "play of high jinks." Shaw knows his public and his own powers. The last act needs judicious pruning.

1387 Hackett, Francis. "A Change in Shaw," NEW REP, I (7 Nov 1914), 25.
Shaw has not devoted enough sympathy on Eliza in Pygmalion which is a spurious comedy or an accidental farce. "Shaw has stooped to fabricate a play."

1388 Hamilton, Clayton. "Middle Class Opinion of the Drama," BOOKMAN (NY), XL (1914-15), 413-14.
Pygmalion is not Shaw's best work because it lacks structure; Shaw avoids the "great dramatic situation."

1389 Hamilton, Clayton. STUDIES IN STAGECRAFT (NY: Holt, 1914), pp. 10, 98, 199, 248, 272.
[Passing references to Shaw to illustrate Hamilton's theories of stagecraft.]

1390 Henderson, Archibald. THE CHANGING DRAMA: CONTRIBUTIONS AND TENDENCIES (1914; Cincinnati: Stewart & Kidd, 1919), pp. 4, 7-8, 16, 30-31, 35-36, 38, 46-47, 69-71, 78, 80-81, 84, 90, 102, 105-07, 128, 135-36, 156-59, 168, 170-72, 175-76, 195, 208-209, 214, 217, 219, 221-24, 226, 237, 240-41, 245-47, 253, 256, 258, 266, 278, 298-99.
Shaw has imported into drama the idea that words themselves are actions, and so has given birth to the drama of discussion. He has also made the extensive stage direction an intrinsic part of plays. Mrs. Warren's Profession, an economical, unified play, is weakened by Frank's cynical levity—a result of Shaw's "ineradicable sense of the ridiculous." The driving force behind his dramas is "sociological indignation" and so he has turned the theatre into a factory of thought. He sees the function of drama as the illumination of life in all its aspects. Shaw has brought about other changes such as making his plays readily available in a readable form, although his authorial intrusion in stage directions is a regrettable reversion to the methods of the worn-out novelist.

1391 "Herr Bernard Shaw Makes His Bow in German," CUR OP, LVI (May 1914), 358-59.

Pygmalion has been produced successfully in German in New York, which is a characteristically eccentric introduction to America. However, the translation is deficient, failing to convey Shaw's keen wit.

1392 "Herr G. B. Shaw at the Irving Palace," NYT, 25 March 1914, p. 11; rptd in NYTTR 1912-1919, [n. p.].

Pygmalion, which has yet to be produced in English, has been given in German. The play is characteristically Shavian and was well-received.

1393 Hevesi, Sándor. "Pygmalion," MAGYAR SZÍNPAD (Budapest), 4 Jan 1914 [not seen].
[In Hungarian.]

1394 Hiratsuka, Raicho. "Vivie to sono haha no seikatsu" (Lives of Vivie and Her Mother), SEITO (Tokyo), IV: 1 (Jan 1914), supp 1-10; rptd in HIRATSUKA RAICHO CHOSAKUSHU (Collected Works of Raicho Hiratsuka), vol I (Tokyo: Otsuki Shoten, 1983), pp. 271-78.

Mrs. Warren's Profession shows clearly Shaw as a destroyer of old institutions, morals, religions and customs, and also as a reformer who tries to lead us to a new life by exposing the shortcomings of society and disclosing the truth of modern life. [In Japanese.]

1395 Huneker, James. "James Huneker Reviews a Picturesque London Season," NYT, 21 June 1914, part V, p. 11; rptd in NYTTR 1912-1919, [n. p.].

Shaw enjoys being "low-brow" and at the centre of controversy, regardless of the success or failure of his numerous plays. Perhaps London gets too much Shaw and his continuous showerings of fancy and "not always fatal venom."

1396 Iba, Takashi. "Uma dorobo ni arawareta Shaw no dotokukan" (Shaw's Moral View Expressed in The Shewing-up of Blanco Posnet], KINDAI SHISO (Tokyo), II: 4 (Jan 1914), 6-7.

A modernist spends great effort to exterminate moral sentiments, but he cannot help recognizing the existence of moral passion as the last passion left him. Moral passion cannot be seduced by an power of the human intellect. Shaw expresses this view rather abstractly in The Devil's Disciple and Man and Superman, and it is in The Shewing-up of Blanco Posnet that he makes a desperate condemnation of moral passion. [In Japanese.]

1397 "The Income-Tax and Marriage," TIMES, 25 June 1914, p. 5.
[Shaw's views on income taxes with regard to married couples.]

1398 Jacobs, Joseph. "G. B. Shaw," NYT, 29 Nov 1914, part VI, pp. 536-37.

Misalliance, Fanny's First Play and The Dark Lady of the Sonnets show Shaw acting as devil's advocate and employing his paradoxical methods to assail those things usually considered laudable.

1399 Kaesmann, Evelyn. "London Hears Bernard Shaw's The Music Cure," MUSICAL COURIER (Phila), LXVIII (18 Feb 1914), 40.

The Music Cure is delightful nonsense.

1400 Komiya, Toyotaka. "Shawno buki to hito to" (Shaw's Arms and the Man), SHIN SHOSETSU (Tokyo), XIX: 8 (Aug 1914), 99-108; rptd as "Buki to hito to" (Arms and the Man) in ENGEKI RONSO (Collected Essays on Theatre) (Tokyo: Seibunkaku, 1937), pp. 573-78.

Shaw is talented, brilliant and garrulous, but there is nothing but garrulity in Arms and the Man. Shaw should be despised and not placed on the same level as admirable writers. [In Japanese.]

1401 "Labor Organ Attack Stirs Shaw's Anger," NYT, 27 Nov 1914, p. 4.

The DAILY CITIZEN, an organ of the British Labour Party, has attacked Shaw's Common Sense About the War and Shaw feels he has been betrayed.

1402 "Letters and Art: What's in a Word," LIT DIG, XLVIII (16 May 1914), 1180-81.

The word "bloody" in Pygmalion has shocked the British public; its effect on Americans is hardly likely to be as great.

1403 "London Likes Pygmalion," NYT, 12 April 1914, part III, p. 15; rptd in NYTTR 1912-1919, [n. p.].

[Title describes.]

1404 "London Theatres: His Majesty's: Pygmalion," STAGE, 16 April 1914, p. 22.

Shaw is desperately hard driven to be humorous. Pygmalion has a vulgar theme; Higgins is an improbable character; and Doolittle is used "to vent once more [Shaw's own] narrow prejudices against the middle classes."

1405 McCabe, Joseph. GEORGE BERNARD SHAW: A CRITICAL STUDY (Lond: Kegan Paul, Trench, Trubner, 1914).

Shaw's novels are too labored, written with too little experience, but do reveal some characteristic thought. Shaw was initially an anarchist-socialist, but eventually adopted an anti-anarchist stance on economics and central government. He now believes in absolute equality of income, scorns democracy, thinks revolution is nonsense, and does not think total socialism will occur. Shaw believes in two fundamental realities, matter and the life force; the latter organizes the former. He believes in a superman who cooperates with the will of the life force and this is akin to God in the making; but he is a theist, not a Christian. Shaw is anti-Darwinian, but is informed by outdated biological knowledge.

Shaw's views on marriage are puritanical; he is not in favor of the home or sexual feeling, and is against mere voluptuousness. His answer is a much freer association which does away with the confines and laws of marriage. Shaw favors eugenics, but his arguments about heredity are flawed. He is not specific on the qualities required of breeders nor on how children are to be raised. He ridicules book-learning and believes education should make a more varied appeal to children's minds.

Art for art's sake is mere prostitution to Shaw; he holds that the artist is an embodiment of a special purpose of the life force. Shaw does not write typical plays: he thinks the stage should be an improvement on the pulpit, and disguises his own unpleasant messages with wit, humor and burlesque. He is a realist who is at his weakest when discussing love.

Widowers' Houses is interesting for its amusing dialogue. Mrs. Warren's Profession is based upon an unsound principle: women actually become prostitutes because they want to and not for economic reasons. Arms and the Man was moderately successful as a comedy without a purpose. Candida is Shaw's best play and contains no overt propaganda. However, the play's crisis is artificial and the solution paradoxical. The Man of Destiny is good, but "marred by Shaw's iconoclastic perversity." You Never Can Tell is a spirited comedy, though a little extreme, while The Devil's Disciple is an amusing melodrama which satirizes melodrama. Caesar and Cleopatra and Captain Brassbound's Conversion have no serious purpose, and ironically the serious purpose of Man and Superman has escaped most audiences. Brassbound is loosely constructed, but has good characterization, which cannot be said of Major Barbara which portrays a real world without real people. However, it is extravagantly amusing and has smart dialogue. The Doctor's Dilemma was not successful, not least because of its undramatic first act. Getting Married is a symposium, while Fanny's First Play has good humor and technical excellence.

1406 MacCarthy, Desmond. "Drama: Pygmalion," NSTATE, III (1914), 52; rptd in MacCarthy, pp. 108-11.
Pygmalion is an exhilarating comedy which is full of ideas, possibly too many for Shaw's theme to be clear. It bristles with criticisms of life and is full of "the merriment of intellectual antics."

1407 MacCarthy, Desmond. "Drama: The Doctor's Dilemma," NSTATE, II (1914), 404-05; rptd in MacCarthy, pp. 73-76.
[A laudatory review of a revival of The Doctor's Dilemma.]

1408 MacCarthy, Desmond. "Miscellany: Mr. Shaw on Shakespeare," NSTATE, III (1914), 339; rptd in MacCarthy, pp. 120-23.

Shaw's view of Shakespeare in The Dark Lady of the Sonnets omits an essential human touch and is therefore unacceptable. Shaw believes Shakespeare must be invulnerable and immune to normal feelings.

1409 Macdonald, John F. "English Life and the English Stage," FORT REV, ns XCV (May 1914), 921-32.

Pygmalion ensures that Shaw's name will be known by everyone everywhere. Shaw resembles high-tea: both are unconventional, bewildering, startling and chaotic.

1410 "Man in the Stalls." "The Theatres," WORLD, No. 2066 (3 Feb 1914), 179.

The Music Cure is not worthy of Shaw and is only a second-rate music-hall skit.

1411 "Man in the Stalls." "The Theatres," WORLD, No. 2077 (21 April 1914), 665.

Pygmalion is witty and satiricial, but its success is due equally to the performances. The fuss about "bloody" is unwarranted.

1412 Mantle, Burns. "The Stage: The London Season," MUNSEY'S MAGAZINE, LII (Aug 1914), 528-33.

Shaw plainly intended Pygmalion to be an intellectual farce, but the public will see it more as a romance with some farcical elements.

1413 M[assingham], H. W. "The Drama: Volatile Mr. Shaw," NATION (Lond), XV (18 April 1914), 93-94; rptd in Evans, pp. 226-29.

His Majesty's Theatre is not the place, nor H. B. Tree the actor for Pygmalion which needs to be played quickly and lightly. The point of the play is not clear largely because Shaw a) does not delineate Higgins with sufficient precision; b) fails to maintain a consistent dramatic tone. Doolittle is "almost a masterpiece" of creation but does far too much talking. The structure is daring and brilliant.

1414 Melkus, Dragan. "Junaci" (Arms and the Man), NARODNA OBRANA (Osijek), XIII: 45 (1914), 3 [not seen].
[In Croatian.]

1415 "The Merry Anarch," NATION (NY), XCVIII (1914), 103-04.

So long as one attacks things as they are one can be a revolutionist and have fun. Only the ordinary middle-class citizen worries about patching up society. Shaw is a revolutionist making merry.

1416 Metcalfe, J. S. "Drama," LIFE, LXIV (22 Oct 1914), 720.
Pygmalion lacks Shaw's usual ferocity which is directed not so much at respectability itself but at the restrictions respectability imposes.

1417 Mew, Egan. "The Theatre: Pygmalion at His Majesty's Theatre," ACADEMY, LXXXVI (18 April 1914), 504-05.
Pygmalion is uneven and packed with too many things. The characterization is not fully realized.

1418 [Misalliance, The Dark Lady of the Sonnets and Fanny's First Play], SPRINGFIELD REPUBLICAN, 25 June 1914, p. 5.
[A generally negative book review.]

1419 "Mr. Bernard Shaw on Sex Instruction," TIMES, 20 June 1914, p. 5.
Shaw has contributed his views on sex education at a symposium in London.

1420 "Mr. Bernard Shaw on the War," TIMES, 16 Nov 1914, p. 7.
Shaw has published an article in NYT which is full of his clever acrobatics and which ridicules all England stands for.

1421 "Mr. G. B. Shaw's War Pamphlet," TIMES, 26 Nov 1914, p. 12.
A question has been raised in Parliament about whether Common Sense About the War had been submitted for censorship. It was not. Shaw's work is false, injurious, and detrimental.

1422 "Mr. Shaw on the War," NYT, 15 Nov 1914, part III, p. 2.
In Common Sense About the War Shaw is extremely vitriolic in his indictment of the various participants. However, it is curious that he ridicules England while arguing that England would have been inevitably embroiled in the turmoil.

1423 "Mr. Shaw on the War and Peace," NYT, 22 Nov 1914, part III, p. 2.
The second part of Shaw's Common Sense About the War contains even more sense than the first. His views are "unquestionably enlightening," though his style is almost absurdly whimsical.

1424 "Mr. Shaw's Fun: The Music Cure," DT, 29 Jan 1914, p. 8.
The Music Cure is good honest stuff, a rough-and-tumble of numerous styles, all suffused with Shaw's wit. "The proper parallel is the old comedy of Aristophanes."

1425 "Mr. Shaw's New Play: Pygmalion at His Majesty's: Phonetics and Manners," TIMES, 13 April 1914, pp. 9-10.
Pygmalion begins on a note of exaggeration. Much of the remainder deals with the familiar Shavian concerns about middle-class morality and class divisions, and with Shaw's exposure of the selfish male.

1426 "Mr. Shaw's 'Parent's Assistant,' " SPECTATOR, CXII (1914), 1035-36.
Shaw's "Treatise on Parents and Children" may be self-contradictory at times, but it generally places the public in his debt.

1427 "Mr. Shaw's Play Gets Premiere Here in German," NYH, 25 March 1914, p. 9.

Pygmalion has a "clever, cynical plot."

1428 "Mr. Shaw's Pygmalion," TIMES, 27 March 1914, p. 7.

Pygmalion has been performed in New York in German and pronounced interesting and mildly amusing.

1429 "Mr. Shaw's Scenario," NYT, 14 Dec 1914, p. 10.

Shaw's "inborn dramatic faculty" has served him well in Common Sense About the War. However, he has misused it in his misrepresentations of the British government's motives and conduct.

1430 Moderwell, Hiram Kelly. THE THEATRE OF TO-DAY (1914 [not seen]; NY: Dodd, Mead, 1923), pp. 205, 214-16, 219-20, 222.

Unlike other dramatists, Shaw has tended not to repeat himself. Refreshingly, he takes freedoms with artistic form, his ideas have not stagnated and, without compromising himself, has become a "brilliant commerical success."

1431 Moses, Montrose J. "The World of Drama: Shaw's Latest Fancy," BOOK NEWS MONTHLY (Phila), XXXIII (Dec 1914), 193-94.

After Shaw's previous intellectual gymnastics and acerbic wit, Pygmalion appears romantic and tame. It lacks brilliancy and critical attitudes, but it is a very warm play.

1432 "Mrs. Campbell, Returning to Stage Here, has Best Role in Pygmalion," NYH, 13 Oct 1914, p. 7.

Pygmalion is amusing and contains "rather liberal moral philosophy."

1433 "Mrs. Pankhurst's Appeal," NYT, 2 Dec 1914, p. 3.

In urging men to join the British Army, Mrs. Pankhurst has also attacked Shaw and his ilk. [See also "Hermant Attacks Shaw," NYT, 2 Dec 1914, p. 3.]

1434 "Mrs. Pat Campbell in New Shaw Play," SUN (NY), 13 Oct 1914, p. 9.

Pygmalion is full of wit and humor, and Shaw's characteristic irony and paradox is concentrated in Alfred Doolittle.

1435 "Mrs. Warren's Profession in Dublin," ERA, 25 Nov 1914, p. 13.

A Dublin production of Mrs. Warren's Profession proceeded without the expected intervention. It contains a distasteful subject.

1436 [The Music Cure], ATH, No. 4501 (31 Jan 1914), 172.

The Music Cure is not a magnificent play, but it is definitely Shavian. "It is deficient in form and point."

1437 "The Music-Cure," ERA, 4 Feb 1914, p. 12.

The Music Cure is much more tolerable than Androcles and the Lion and there is "undeniable smartness" in Shaw's piece of satire.

1438 "The Music-Cure: Mr. Shaw's 'Piece of Utter Nonsense,' " TIMES, 29 Jan 1914, p. 8.
Utter nonsense does not suit everyone, but The Music Cure certainly suited its first-night audience.

1439 "The Music-Cure: Production at the Little," STAGE, 29 Jan 1914, p. 26.
"The Music-Cure is made up of the sort of glib and extravagant patter that would go very well to an instrumental turn on the music-hall stage." It is really a pot-bolier that does little for Shaw's reputation.

1440 Nathan, George Jean. "Toujours Shaw," SMART SET, XLIII (June 1914), 145-52.
Shaw has been truly innovative in the theatre, though he is not as great a dramatist as Hauptmann. He has used the theatre as an instrument, rather than allowing the theatre to use him. He has introduced thought and cleverness, and got rid of platitudes. Pygmalion is not top-drawer Shaw, but it does reveal his special talent—"the ability to put the obvious in terms of the scandalous."

1441 Newman, Ernest. "Letters to the Editor: The Sad Case of Bernard Shaw," NATION (Lond), XV (11 July 1914), 563-64.
Yet again Shaw is sadly, tragically wrong in his opinion and misunderstanding of Richard Strauss. Shaw is comically ignorant about Strauss and is also "going off sadly as a controversialist." [For further aspects of this debate see NATION (Lond), XV (1914), 487-88, 525-26, 601, 636, 668-69, 707.]

1442 "The New Plays," THEATRE (NY), XIX (Feb 1914), 58.
The Philanderer proves the Ibsen cult is dead. However, Shaw is never dull, stimulates the mind, but is not overwhelmingly humorous.

1443 "New Plays of the Week," NY DRAMATIC NEWS, LX (17 Oct 1914), 18-19.
Pygmalion is peculiar in parts and unconventional, especially in its glorification of the undeserving poor.

1444 Noguchi, Yone[jiro]. "Bernard Shaw," BOOKMAN (Lond), XLVII (Dec 1914), 75-77; Japanese version rptd in OUSHU BUNDAN INSHOKI (Impressions of the European Literary World) (Tokyo: Hakujitsusha, 1916), pp. 2-15; rptd in KIRI NO LONDON (Fog in London) (Tokyo: Genbunsha, 1923), pp. 96-106. [Biographical.]

1445 Noguchi, Yonejiro. "Shaw wa higeki desu" (Shaw is Tragic), BUNSHO SEKAI (Tokyo), IX: 8 (Aug 1914), 22-28; rptd in OUSHU BUNDAN INSHOKI (Impressions of the European

Literary World) (Tokyo: Hakujitsusha, 1916), pp. 16-27; rptd in KIRI NO LONDON (Fog in London) (Tokyo: Genbunsha, 1923), pp. 106-14.

Shaw's plays are not ridiculous farces nor pantomimes, even though the average audience seems to be enjoying them as such. It is indeed tragic that Shaw is not appreciated properly. Tragic, too, is Shaw not fully using his own brilliant talent, writing instead some foolish farcical pieces. Shaw would be better if he were silent and serious without trying to explain everything. [In Japanese.]

1446 "Notable Men on Board," NYT, 22 May 1914, p. 3.
Alfred Kerr believes Shaw is the "greatest living dramatist for plays dealing with social life."

1447 "Notes of the Week," SAT REV, CXVIII (1914), 186.
[An editorial note deploring Shaw's "The Peril of Potsdam," DN, 11 Aug 1914, p. 4.]

1448 O., S. "Pygmalion (at Home and Abroad)," ENGLISH REVIEW, XVII (May 1914), 276-78.
Pygmalion is "epicene, bloodless, intellectual, and neuter." The hero is an "asexual intellectualist," the heroine lacks animation.

1449 Oswald, Lina. "Recent English Literature," DIE NEUEREN SPRACHEN, XXII: 3 (June 1914), 249-53.
In The Quintessence of Ibsenism Shaw bases his interpretation of Ibsen almost entirely on the social dramas.

1450 Palmer, John. "Life and the Theatre," SAT REV, CXVII (1914), 826-27.
Shaw's characters, such as Anne Whitefield, are not drawn from life, but are rather taken out of books.

1451 Palmer, John. "Mr. Shaw's Romance," SAT REV, CXVII (1914), 499-500.
Pygmalion is a delightful inspiration, but exactly the sort of romance that Shaw used to inveigh against when he was a theatre critic.

1452 Palmer, John. "A Modern Morality," SAT REV, CXVII (1914), 231-32.
Shaw has much to answer for in his uncritical support for Brieux's LES AVARIES, especially since Shaw influences so many people. Is this a deliberate hoax on his part?

1453 Palmer, John. "Pygmalion Again," SAT REV, CXVII (1914), 699-700.
It is a popular superstition that Shaw is a daring person, a superstition fostered by "bloody" in Pygmalion. The reason is that Shaw is really too ethereal and is himself shocked by his own vision of the world.

1454 Pankhurst, Christabel. "Christabel Pankhurst Answers

Bernard Shaw," NYT, 22 Nov 1914, part V, p. 3.
Shaw's Common Sense About the War is "frivolous, inconsistent, destructive, and unprofitable."

1455 Patterson, Ada. "Bernard Shaw as Seen by an American Actress," THEATRE (NY), XIX (May 1914), 234-36.
[Biographical.]

1456 Patterson, Eleanor Cutler. "Mr. Shaw's Views," NYT, 27 Nov 1914, p. 10.
In Common Sense About the War Shaw is writing from the comfort of his safe armchair. Conditions at the war front are entirely different, and Shaw could be condemned by future generations for failing his country in its hour of need.

1457 "The Philanderer," AMERICAN PLAYWRIGHT, III (Feb 1914), 42-47.
Shaw is an "emancipated intellect" who has freed himself from conventionality while obeying dramatic laws.

1458 "The Philanderer," INDEPENDENT (NY), LXXVII (1914), 59.
It is difficult to know why The Philanderer has been revived because much of the play now seems dated. Shaw's satire is also blunted by the passage of time.

1459 "Picture Palaces and Their Influence," TIMES, 30 Jan 1914, p. 4.
Shaw has expressed his approbation of films and hopes to write a scenario some day.

1460 "The Plaint of Bernard Shaw," NYT, 28 Nov 1914, p. 12.
Shaw has a genuine grievance over the Labour Party's attack on Common Sense About the War. However, he does not really understand the working-classes he seeks to champion.

1461 "The Playhouses," ILN, CXLIV (18 April 1914), 624, 627.
Pygmalion is a burlesque romance in which Shaw has "let himself go" in fancy and humanity.

1462 "The Playhouses: The Music Cure at the Little Theatre," ILN, CXLIV (7 Feb 1914), 200.
The Music Cure is a wild burlesque full of high spirits, spontaneous humor and good satire.

1463 "Plays & Players," THEATRE (NY), XX (Dec 1914), 262.
It has taken time for Shaw to establish his reputation in America, but now everything he writes is accepted immediately. Thus with Pygmalion, which is amusing, witty and entertaining; "but it should be curtailed."

1464 "Points Out Flaws in Shaw's Logic," NYT, 20 Nov 1914, p. 2.

R. B. Cunninghame Graham thinks Shaw's logic in <u>Common Sense</u> <u>About the War</u> is faulty and that literary men should stay out of the controversy. Other evidence indicates the war was inevitable anyway.

1465 Pollock, Channing. "<u>The Philanderer</u>," GREEN BOOK MAGAZINE, XI (March 1914), 413-14.

<u>The Philanderer</u> now shows its age. It has dull patches, though there are brilliant bits of Shavianism and intellectual treats.

1466 Pollock, Channing. "Two Dreams and Some Unrealities," GREEN BOOK MAGAZINE, XII (Dec 1914), 1057-58.

<u>Pygmalion</u> is less exciting Shaw. The introduction is tedious, though later there is some humor, irony and philosophy. The play is "quieter," though not less verbose than <u>Caesar and Cleopatra</u> or <u>Man and Superman</u>.

1467 "Praises Shaw's Courage," NYT, 23 Nov 1914, p. 3.

Silas K. Hocking, the novelist, thinks <u>Common Sense About the War</u> displays Shaw's courage and his "excess of cynicism."

1468 Price, William Thompson [?]. "Shaw's Technical Method in <u>The Shewing-Up of Blanco Posnet</u>," AMERICAN PLAY-WRIGHT, III (15 March 1914), 79-84.

<u>The Shewing-up of Blanco Posnet</u> is an admirable technical piece which shows Shaw thinks considerably before he begins to write.

1469 "<u>Pygmalion</u>," ERA, 15 April 1914, p. 15.

<u>Pygmalion</u> fulfils every expectation, although in places it is completely un-Shavian.

1470 "<u>Pygmalion</u> as a Pronouncing Dictionary: Mr. Shaw's Latest Jest," GRAPHIC, LXXXIX (18 April 1914), 684.

<u>Pygmalion</u> is successful, if only for its daring adjective. But Shaw has also portrayed a full-blooded woman in Eliza, while the real comic source is Doolittle. Shaw's attacks on middle-class morality are beginning to pall now because that class is changing very rapidly.

1471 "<u>Pygmalion</u> at His Majesty's," ATH, No. 4512 (18 April 1914), 567.

<u>Pygmalion</u> is modified Shaw and it is easy to ignore any Shavian ideas in it.

1472 "<u>Pygmalion</u> at His Majesty's," OBS, 12 April 1914, pp. 7-8.

Shaw skirts over many potentially interesting questions in <u>Pygmalion</u>, but never deals with any at all fully or in a way which is comprehensible.

1473 "<u>Pygmalion</u> for 3d.: His Majesty's as a Theatre for the People," TIMES, 2 June 1914, p. 11.

A cheap-price matinee of <u>Pygmalion</u> has allowed the "industrial classes" to see the production; Shaw waived his royalties.

1474 "Pygmalion: Mr. Bernard Shaw's Play at His Majesty's Theatre," DT, 13 April 1914, pp. 9-10.

Pygmalion is Shaw's most benign work, full of joy, vigor, and spirit. Occasionally drawn out, it is continuous farce, or "farce discussionary."

1475 "The Quality of Shaw," HARPER'S WEEKLY, LIX (1914), 483.

Pygmalion reveals Shaw's main quality is his wit. People like him not for what he says but because he says it in an "intellectually hilarious way."

1476 "Quite in the Prussian Manner," NYT, 21 Dec 1914, p. 8.

In his recent remarks on the war, Shaw has developed some good, moral analogies, even if they are "wholly worthless and offensive to right reason."

1477 Randolph, Ann. "Shaw Makes Us Laugh Again," NATIONAL MAGAZINE (Bost), XL (May 1914), 186-90.

Fanny's First Play proves Shaw's ability to entertain and to resist being ignored.

1478 Rethy, Joseph Bernard. "A Glimpse into the Theatres," INTERNATIONAL (NY), VIII (Feb 1914), 68.

The Philanderer remains as fresh as ever, and its Ibsen satire is still sharp. It both amuses and startles.

1479 Rich, Stephen G. "George Bernard Shaw," COLONNADE, VII (March 1914), 187-94.

Shaw has used the dramatic form solely as a means of delivering sermons on social topics, sermons which embrace Marx's economic determinism theory. Shaw's views are clear, seldom false, and never stupid.

1480 "Ridder Indorses Shaw," NYT, 18 Nov 1914, p. 3.

Shaw's views in Common Sense About the War have been enthusiastically endorsed by Herman Ridder.

1481 "Rover." "About the Halls," SKETCH, LXXXV (1 April 1914), 414.

The Music Cure is really above the head of the sort of audience which attends the Palace Theatre.

1482 Ruhl, Arthur. "New Plays at a Glance," COLLIER'S NATIONAL WEEKLY, LII (21 Feb 1914), 24.

The Philanderer is most amusing, with the satire deriving from Shaw's comparison of the womanly woman with the manly man.

1483 S., M. "A New Shaw Play in Germany," SPECTATOR, CXII (1914), 16-17.

Pygmalion has been produced in Germany and is popular.

1484 Sakai, Toshihiko. "Gomashio atama" (Gray-white Hair), KINDAI SHISO (Tokyo), II: 5 (Feb 1914), 14-15.
Shaw is an instinctivist who wishes to follow and satisfy all instincts including moral passion. [In Japanese.]

1485 Schelling, Felix E. ENGLISH DRAMA (1914; rptd Delhi: S. Chand, 1963), pp. 218, 313, 331-32.
Shaw has helped make the problem play familiar, and uses good wit and sincerity in his work. However, the current crop of contemporary dramatists (including Shaw) does not contain a "great regenerator of the stage."

1486 "Shaw and Jaures," NYT, 29 Nov 1914, part III, p. 2.
The difference between Shaw and Jean Jaures, both prominent socialists, is that Jaures was sincere while Shaw "is too much interested in himself to take much thought about the reasonableness of what he puts forth."

1487 "Shaw Calls Critics Liars," NYT, 8 Dec 1914, p. 2.
Shaw has accused critics of his Common Sense About the War of falsifying his position with regard to Germany.

1488 "Shaw Can't Praise Russia," NYT, 23 Dec 1914, p. 4.
Shaw believes Britain should make clear that its alliance with Russia is a compromise and not an endorsement of the tyrannous Russian monarchy.

1489 "Shaw Denounces Pro-German Irish," NYT, 2 Dec 1914, p. 3.
Shaw has written a letter urging the Irish to join the side of the French in the war.

1490 "Shaw Drubbing John Bull Again," LIT DIG, XLIX (1914), 1120-21.
Shaw's mission in life is to chastise the English public mercilessly, as is evidenced by his newly published views on the war.

1491 "Shaw Elicits Blame and Praise from TIMES Readers," NYT, 29 Nov 1914, part VII, p. 7.
[Seven letters to the editor in reaction to Common Sense About the War.]

1492 "Shaw 'Inhumanly Cool,' " NYT, 1 Dec 1914, p. 2.
Stockton Axson, President Wilson's brother-in-law, believes Shaw's Common Sense About the War is dispassionate. Shaw forgets that people are ruled by their emotions.

1493 "Shaw is Attacked in House of Commons," NYT, 26 Nov 1914, p. 3.
Shaw and Common Sense About the War have been denounced in the British Parliament. Shaw's statements are false and injurious and should have been censored.

1494 "Shaw Plays in Yiddish," TIMES, 23 March 1914, p. 4.
Shaw's plays are to be performed in Yiddish by Maurice Moscowitch.

1495 "Shaw: Prophet, not Playwright," DRAMATIST (Easton, Pa), V (1914), 417-18.
Shaw is not a dramatist because he ignores every rule of dramaturgy, and because "he is not a human being."

1496 "Shaw Scores Russia," NYT, 2 Sept 1914, p. 8.
Shaw believes England is fighting an insane cause merely for the sake of Russia.

1497 "Shaw Sees America Leader of Tomorrow," NYT, 19 Oct 1914, p. 1.
Shaw has predicted President Wilson will preside at a peace conference after Europe has been ruined by war.

1498 "Shaw Unrepentant in Reply to Critics," NYT, 29 Nov 1914, p. 3.
Shaw has written letters rebutting critics of Common Sense About the War and has not changed his stance.

1499 "Shaw's Adjective Shocks," NYT, 13 April 1914, p. 4.
Shaw has ben criticized for using the word "bloody" in Pygmalion. [See also NYT: 14 April 1914, p. 10, 15 April 1914, pp. 4, 12, 16 April 1914, p. 8.]

1500 "Shaw's Article Raises a Storm," NYT, 22 Nov 1914, p. 3.
Shaw's Common Sense About the War has been vehemently attacked by the British press for its pro-German arguments.

1501 "Shaw's Idea for Neutrals," NYT, 16 Dec 1914, p. 3.
Shaw believes Britain should tell Italians the real reasons why it is fighting Germany.

1502 "Shaw's Latest Play Here in German," SUN (NY), 25 March 1914, p. 5.
The length of Pygmalion is "out of all artistic proportion to its content"; Shaw's humor is not evident in this German version, and the plot is surprisingly transparent.

1503 "Shaw's Pygmalion has Come to Town," NYT, 13 Oct 1914, p. 11; rptd in NYTTR 1912-1919, [n. p.].
Pygmalion is well-received and rightly termed a romance. Shaw tells his story "with brusque diffidence and a wealth of humor."

1504 "Some of Shaw's Errors," LIT DIG, XLIX (1914), 1279.
Shaw's views about the war in his Common Sense About the War have stirred considerable debate. Ford Madox Hueffer [Ford] is just one example of the people ranged against Shaw.

1505 S[pence], E. F. "Pygmalion at His Majesty's Theatre," WESTMINSTER GAZETTE, XLIII (14 April 1914), 3; rptd in

Evans, pp. 223-25.

Various production weaknesses help render <u>Pygmalion</u> unsatisfactory, that and the proliferation rather than unity of ideas. It is credible that Eliza's accent can be altered readily, but it is very different to believe that her intelligence and bearing can improve equally well. But there is an abundance of good, typically Shavian epigram, and Doolittle is a hit.

1506 S[pence], E. F. "The Stage from the Stalls," SKETCH, LXXXVI (22 April 1914), 74-75.

<u>Pygmalion</u> is a very clever play, although Shaw's theory about accents is open to much dispute. The fuss about "bloody" is incomprehensible.

1507 Stahl, Dr. Ernst Leopold. DAS ENGLISCHE THEATER IM 19. JAHRHUNDERT (The English Theatre in the Nineteenth Century) (Munich & Berlin: Oldenbourg, 1914), pp. 40, 137, 168, 201, 210, 223, 233, 236, 238.

[Passing, illustrative references to Shaw. In German.]

1508 Storer, Edward. "Dramatists of To-Day," BRITISH REVIEW, V (Feb 1914), 251-64; rptd in LIVING AGE, CCLXXXI (11 April 1914), 88-95.

Today Shaw's influence on modern English thought appears woefully old-fashioned. His wit is forced, his diatribes unbalanced, and his "prejudices positively parochial." Shaw learned from Wilde that if an artist wishes to influence his age he must be of his age. <u>Arms and the Man</u> criticizes English conventions; <u>Candida</u> is an attempted Ibsen drama. In <u>Widowers' Houses</u>, <u>Major Barbara</u>, and <u>Mrs. Warren's Profession</u> Shaw uses social themes similar to Ibsen's. <u>You Never Can Tell</u> "strikes a happy balance between artificiality and reality, between the iconoclastic mocking spirit of its author and the objective on which it is focussed." Shaw was the first dramatist writing in English to introduce "crowd drama." Society is important in <u>Major Barbara</u>, <u>Man and Superman</u>, <u>The Doctor's Dilemma</u>, and <u>Getting Married</u>. <u>Androcles and the Lion</u> and <u>Great Catherine</u> both contain something of Shaw's old conciseness and force, but with the wit and humor more naive and ingenuous.

1509 "Suggests Curb for Shaw," NYT, 1 Dec 1914, p. 1.

The DAILY EXPRESS (Lond) has pointed out that there are legal sanctions to prohibit such things as <u>Common Sense About the War</u>.

1510 "Surprising News for G. B. Shaw," NYT, 14 Oct 1914, p. 11.

Mrs. Patrick Campbell has told Shaw <u>Pygmalion</u> is a success in New York and that he is a "made man."

1511 Sygietyński, Antoni. "<u>Pigmalion</u>: komedia w 5 aktach Bernarda Shaw" (<u>Pygmalion</u>: Comedy in 5 Acts by Bernard Shaw), DZIEŃ (Warsaw), No. 60 (1914); rptd in O TEATRZE I

DRAMACIE: WYBOR (On Theatre and Drama: Selections) (Cracow: Wydawnictwo literackie, 1971), pp. 503-05.

None of the characters in Pygmalion (except perhaps the housemaid) are real persons but philosophical concepts in the form of caricatures. The entire play is not a comedy from life, but satire forced upon life. [In Polish.]

1512 Terry, J. E. Harold. "Pygmalion," BRITISH REVIEW, VII (July 1914), 145-50.

Pygmalion contains enough material for a ten-minute music-hall sketch, but it is insufficient for a full-length play.

1513 "The Theater," AMERICAN MAGAZINE, LXXVII (June 1914), 104.

Shaw's amiable ridicule of the Ibsen cult in The Philanderer now appears somewhat antiquated.

1514 "The Theatre: The Music-Cure at the Little," ACADEMY, LXXXV (7 Feb 1914), 183.

Superficially The Music Cure is gay and irresponsible, but it possesses deeper sociological observations.

1515 "Things New: At the Theatres," SKETCH, LXXXV (4 Feb 1914), xii.

Nonsense is acceptable if it is clever, but this is not the case with The Music Cure. It is only up to the standard of the music-hall or revue.

1516 Thompson, Alex M. "The Passing Show: Bernard Shaw at His Majesty's," CLARION, No. 1167 (17 April 1914), 3; rptd in Evans, pp. 225-26.

There is no apparent purpose in Pygmalion which, in fact, develops an incident in Smollett's PEREGRINE PICKLE (centering around the use of expletives by a woman). Shaw's handling of the matter is more startling and he succeeds in winning over his audiences by shocking them. The play is also full of good things and wit, but it is really a pot-boiler.

1517 Tilgher, Adriano. "Pigmalione di B. Shaw al Teatro Valle" (Shaw's Pygmalion at the Valle Theatre), LA CONCORDIA (Rome), 11 Dec 1914 [not seen].
[In Italian.]

1518 "To Give 'Serial Plays,' " NYT, 3 April 1914, p. 4.

Shaw has criticized a plan to perform plays serially at the London Coliseum.

1519 "To Mr. Bernard Jaw," PUNCH, CXLVII (25 Nov 1914), 430; rptd in NYT, 20 Dec 1914, part V, p. 10.

In Common Sense About the War Shaw, the "illustrious jester," offers "vitriol" to England and "balsam" to Germany. [In the form of a satiric poem.]

1520 "Topics of the Times," NYT, 23 Nov 1914, p. 10.
Shaw's suggestion that soliders should be given high wages actually
has some merit and is not merely typical of his whimsicality. However, there are some flaws in his argument.

1521 "Transforming Power of Phonetics," LIT DIG, XLIX
(1914), 956-57.
[An appraisal of Pygmalion, largely recounting at third hand the
views of others.]

1522 Troubetzkoy, Pierre. "Shaw Amended," NYT, 24 Dec
1914, p. 8.
Shaw's exposition of neutrality may be tinged with his special humor,
but it is illogical.

1523 Tsubouchi, Shiko. "Eikoku Juichi daishinbun gekihyo bur—
heikaza no Shawgeki ni taishite" (Reviews in Eleven English
Newspapers of a Shaw Play at His Majesty's), ENGEI KURABU
(Tokyo), III: 9 (Sept 1914), 26-38.
[An anthology of reviews of Pygmalion. In Japanese.]

1524 "University Intelligence," TIMES, 19 Jan 1914, p. 13.
Shaw has been invited to lecture on the nature of drama at Oxford
University.

1525 Vengerova, Z. "Bernard Shou" (Bernard Shaw), VIESTNIK
EVROPY (St. Petersburg), XC (June 1914), 200-31.
Shaw's plays atone for the general character of English life, but the
English are proud of those who reject society's principles. Shaw's
plays are a synthesis of the rebellious ideas of the age. While
admiring Tolstoy, Shaw does not follow him; rather he is completing
the work started by Shelley a century ago. Shaw has proceeded from
Marxism to Fabianism, being one of the latter's leading activists. He
has revived the theatre and built up new audiences. Shaw's views on
free love are more troubling to the English than to Russians. Mrs.
Warren's Profession is a rejection of Ibsen's peevishness, while Caesar
and Cleopatra attacks heroism, and Arms and the Man false
romanticism. Man and Superman and Candida are Shaw's most
significant, purely intellectual plays, which also reveal the strong
influence of Schopenhauer and Nietzsche. [In Russian.]

1526 West, Rebecca. "Mr. Shaw's Diverted Genius," NEW REP,
I (5 Dec 1914), 13-14.
Only the purest of contemporary artists can remain aloof from daily
affairs. A recent lecture by Shaw (and the audience's reception of it)
shows why Shaw has become entangled in public affairs.

1527 "Whack at G. B. Shaw," NYT, 28 Nov 1914, p. 2.
Common Sense About the War has been attacked in London as yet

another attempt at self-advertisement by Shaw the jester.

1528 "What's in a Word?" LIT DIG, XLVIII (16 May 1914), 1180-81.
Shaw's use of the word "bloody" in Pygmalion is artistically poor and dramatically illogical.

1529 White, M., jr. "The Stage: Heroines Who Swear," MUNSEY'S MAGAZINE, LIII (Dec 1914), 555-56.
Pygmalion is an admirable object lesson to other playwrights; it is economical and always moves forward, although Shaw normally subordinates action to dialogue.

1530 "Why Shaw Won't Come," NYT, 18 Oct 1914, part VIII, p. 7.
Shaw has given his characteristic reasons for not attending the opening night of Pygmalion in New York.

1915

1531 Araquistain, Luis. "Bernard Shaw ó la crítica funambulesca" (Bernard Shaw or Funambulist Criticism) in POLÉMICA DE LA GUERRA 1914-1915 (Polemics of the War 1914-1915) (Madrid: Renacimiento, 1915), pp. 119-25 [not seen].
[Cited in Rodríguez (MS). In Spanish.]

1532 Araquistain, Luis. "Prólogo: Bernard Shaw y el superhombre" (Prologue: Bernard Shaw and the Superman) in EL SENTIDO COMÚN Y LA GUERRA (Common Sense and the War) (Madrid: Velasco, 1915), [not seen].
[Cited in Rodríguez (MS). In Spanish.].

1533 "Arms and the Man Agreeably Revived," NYT, 4 May 1915, p. 15; rptd in NYTTR 1912-1919, [n. p.].
Arms and the Man remains as fresh as ever, even more so because Shaw's dramatic techniques are now the techniques of the day.

1534 "Arnold Daly and Miss Spong Make Candida a Joy," NYH, 21 May 1915, p. 16.
[Title describes.]

1535 "Arnold Daly Seen in Shaw's Candida," SUN (NY), 21 May 1915, p. 7.
[A favorable review.]

1536 "Barker's Season Happily Launched," NYT, 28 Jan 1915, p. 9; rptd in NYTTR 1912-1919, [n. p.].
Androcles and the Lion is a whimsical, fantastic play unlikely to

arouse much controversy over its subject matter. The Lion, which only a vegetarian could have created, is the most amusing feature of the play.

1537 Barnes, J. H. FORTY YEARS ON THE STAGE: OTHERS (PRINCIPALLY) AND MYSELF (NY: Dutton, 1915), pp. 270-71, 278-79, 282.

[Brief details of this actor's association with Shaw's plays.]

1538 "Bernard Shaw's Common Sense About the War," REV OF REVS, LI (1915), 104-05.

Shaw's views on the war and what must be done are remarkable and controversial.

1539 "Bernard Shaw's Utopian Vision of the Films of the Future," CUR OP, LVIII (June 1915), 411.

Shaw believes the cinema will develop greatly and films will compete seriously with spoken drama.

1540 Beveridge, Albert J. "British War Opinion," COLLIER'S NATIONAL WEEKLY, LV (12 June 1915), 7-8, 28-30.

Because Americans recognize Shaw as one of the "most brilliant intellects of the English-speaking world" they are anxious to learn his views of the war.

1541 Bland, J. O. P. "Self-Appointed Statesman," NINE-TEENTH CENTURY, LXXVII (1915), 560-72; rptd in LIVING AGE, CCLXXXV (8 May 1915), 331-41.

Only in Britain are the makers of fiction permitted to denounce critically the government's policies as Shaw and H. G. Wells have done. The British can close their eyes to this self-appointed role, but they cannot ignore the effect it has on opinion overseas.

1542 Blei, Franz. ÜBER WEDEKIND, STERNHEIM UND DAS THEATER (On Wedekind, Sternheim and the Theatre) (Leipzig: Kurt Wolff, 1915), pp. 100, 122.

Shaw writes either tomfoolery or polemic literature. [In German.]

1543 Borgese, G. A. STUDI DI LETTERATURE MODERNE (Studies in Modern Literature) (Milan: Fratelli Treves, 1915), pp. 178, 196, 198, 201-08.

[On Mrs. Warren's Profession and The Philanderer. In Italian.]

1544 "Britisher Berates Shaw and Wells," NYT, 3 March 1915, p. 3.

Both Shaw and H. G. Wells have been attacked by J. O. P. Bland for their irresponsible opinions which have unduly influenced Americans. [See item 1541.]

1545 "Candida Revived by Arnold Daly," NYT, 21 May 1915, p. 13; rptd in NYTRR 1912-1919, [n. p.].

Candida is Shaw's best play and receives a competent revival. Shaw keeps threatening to prevent Arnold Daly from performing his works.

1546 "A Captain of Revolt," NEW REP, II (20 Feb 1915), 63-64.
Beneath Shaw's veneer as a jester, there lie many admirable qualities which deserve recognition—for example "his lifelong opposition to blind categories and murderous obediences" and his essential humanity.

1547 "Cecil Chesterton Here," NYT, 13 Jan 1915, p. 7.
Cecil Chesterton both agrees and disagrees with some of Shaw's points about Germany's war actions.

1548 "Chesterton Praises Shaw," NYT, 16 Jan 1915, p. 8.
Cecil Chesterton, in a lecture, believes Shaw is sincere and his works will endure. Shaw has also "manufactured an artificial picture of himself which is not true."

1549 Clark, Barrett H.   THE BRITISH AND AMERICAN DRAMA OF TO-DAY: OUTLINES FOR THEIR STUDY (NY: Holt, 1915), pp. vi, 16, 40, 42, 48, 63-90, 93, 117, 170-71, 207, 246.
"All of Shaw's early plays and most of his later ones were protests against the conventions, the lifelessness, the timidity of the day. This he did as a dramatist; as a commentator on life, it is difficult to determine just what he has done." His best plays are Candida, Arms and the Man, Man and Superman, although these are sometimes too talky. [With some biographical detail, a productions list, bibliography of criticism, and study guide notes to Candida, Man and Superman, Getting Married and The Shewing-up of Blanco Posnet.]

1550 "Critics Assail Shaw, Don't Hurt His Piece," NYT, 19 Feb 1915, p. 5.
Critics have attacked the London revival of Fanny's First Play while Shaw has countered with evidence of his general popularity.

1551 "Daly on Shaw," NYT, 11 April 1915, part VII, p. 6.
If Shaw stopped striving to be brilliant he would be great. He would also stop writing conversations if he really loved the theatre.

1552 "Daly Revives Shaw Comedy," NYT, 6 April 1915, p. 11; rptd in NYTTR 1912-1919, [n. p.].
Despite protests from Shaw, Arnold Daly has given a successful revival of You Never Can Tell.

1553 "The Doctor's Dilemma Conventional But Effective," NYH, 27 March 1915, p. 13.
Harley Granville-Barker has staged The Doctor's Dilemma very conventionally. The play itself possesses Shavian wit, but is too long, has too much dialogue, and is entertaining only in places.

1554 Eaton, Walter Prichard. "Good Plays of the Season," COLLIER'S NATIONAL WEEKLY, LIV (2 Jan 1915), 9.

Pygmalion contains satire, romance, "perverse wisdom," and comedy.

1555 Eaton, Walter Prichard. "The Theater: Stage Successes—Foreign vs. American," AMERICAN MAGAZINE, LXXIX (Feb 1915), 42, 84.

Pygmalion is an inspiration of a play and one of the two best plays of the season. As ever, Shaw "has been able to put into plays for the practical theater a wealth of stimulating intellectual ideas, and . . . all his works are instinct with literary style."

1556 F. "The Doctor's Dilemma," NATION (NY), C (1915), 364.

The Doctor's Dilemma is, in essence, a glorified preface, full of Shaw's usual garrulousness.

1557 F. "Granville Barker, Shaw, and Anatole France at Wallack's," NATION (NY), C (1915), 150.

Androcles and the Lion is not entirely typical of Shaw and there is little or no connection in his satire.

1558 F. "Major Barbara at the Playhouse," NATION (NY), CI (1915), 725-26.

Major Barbara is above average Shaw, though much is given over to swift dialogue.

1559 "Fanny's First Play," ERA, 17 Feb 1915, p. 11.

Fanny's First Play remains delightful sense and nonsense. However, the time may be inappropriate for topsy-turvydom which merits only "tolerant amusement."

1560 "Fanny's First Play: Untimely Shaw Revival at the Kingsway," TIMES, 15 Feb 1915, p. 11.

Fanny's First Play these days seems "incongruously trivial."

1561 Fehr, Bernhard. "Zum Fall 'Shaw contra Shakespeare' " (Concerning the Case of "Shaw versus Shakespeare"), DIE NEUREN SPRACHEN, XXII: 10 (Feb-March 1915), 670-72.

Shaw attacks Shakespeare because the "romantic" Elizabethan simply does not fit into Shaw's realistic frame of reference. According to Shaw a poet and dramatist should always be a systematic philosopher. Shakespeare, however, doesn't meet this requirement. [In German.]

1562 "First Nighter." "Arms and the Man," NY DRAMATIC MIRROR, LXXIII (5 May 1915), 8.

Although Arms and the Man is an early play, it still contains characteristics which permeate Shaw's later work.

1563 "First Nighter." "Candida," NY DRAMATIC MIRROR, LXXIII (26 May 1915), 8.

When it was first written Candida was unconventional. Now the public has taken Shaw thoroughly to its heart.

1564 "First Nighter." "The Doctor's Dilemma," NY DRAMATIC

MIRROR, LXXIII (31 March 1915), 8.
Shaw's wit, outrageous treatment of the medical profession, and characterization in The Doctor's Dilemma stimulate interest.

1565 "First Nighter." "Major Barbara," NY DRAMATIC MIRROR, LXXIV (18 Dec 1915), 8.
New York likes Major Barbara better than London does because Shaw criticizes British society more directly. His theory suffers by being worked out in too much detail.

1566 "First Nighter." "You Never Can Tell," NY DRAMATIC MIRROR, LXXIII (14 April 1915), 9.
This revival of You Never Can Tell is successful despite Shaw's threats to Arnold Daly should he produce the piece.

1567 "Friends and Enemies and Mr. Shaw," NYT, 7 April 1915, p. 12.
Shaw has many admirers and critics, but his plays are interesting and cannot be ignored.

1568 "'G. B. S.' Sympathizes Deeply with Grey," NYT, 17 July 1915, p. 2.
Shaw sympathizes with Sir Edward Grey, the British Foreign Secretary, because they both are always getting into trouble for telling the truth.

1569 "Geo. Bernard Shaw on Debt to Belgium," NYT, 28 Jan 1915, p. 4.
Shaw has published an appeal for those suffering in Belgium.

1570 "George Bernard Shaw as a Man of Letters," NYT, 5 Dec 1915, part VI, p. 6.
[A collection of Shaw's correspondence to Louis Calvert on Major Barbara with incidental commentary.]

1571 "German Praise for Shaw," NYT, 23 Jan 1915, p. 3.
The German press thinks Shaw has been misjudged and praises him.

1572 "Germans Quote Shaw," NYT, 9 Aug 1915, p. 3.
The Germans have put up propaganda posters quoting Shaw as saying there was a plot between Sir Edward Grey and the French and Belgian governments to make war on Germany.

1573 "Get Ships, Shaw Tells US," NYT, 7 Dec 1915, p. 4.
Shaw believes America's current pacifism is safe largely because America is strong militarily.

1574 Godley, Eveline [C.]. "Drama," THE ANNUAL REGISTER 1914 (Lond: Longmans, Green, 1915), part II, pp. 69-72.
Pygmalion promised to be the year's novelty, but proved in the event not to be Shaw's best work.

1575 "Grace George in a Shaw Play," NY DRAMATIC NEWS, LXII (18 Dec 1915), 17.

Major Barbara plays as well as it reads and is full of wonderful epigrams.

1576 "Grace George Seen in a Bernard Shaw Play," SUN (NY), 10 Dec 1915, p. 7.

Shaw's philosophy dominates every speech in Major Barbara. Every character talks Shaw, and there is barely any story or characterization.

1577 Hackett, Francis. "The Comedy of War," NEW REP, III (8 May 1915), 18.

Arms and the Man rings true even in these uncertain times because Shaw's feelings are right and because he aimed at revealing the dangers of petty hero-worship.

1578 Hackett, Francis. "Granville Barker in New York," NEW REP, I (30 Jan 1915), 25.

Androcles and the Lion has an engaging story, unrestrained sentiment, and reveals Shaw's lively imagination.

1579 Hackett, Francis. "The Medicine Men," NEW REP, II (10 April 1915), 264.

The Doctor's Dilemma is not as good as most of Shaw's other plays, being possessed of a cynical philosophy and a rather unbelievable plot.

1580 Hamilton, Clayton. "The Long Run in the Theatre," BOOKMAN (NY), XLII (1915-16), 648-50.

Major Barbara is a mixture of merit and defects, and shows Shaw is critical rather than creative, analytical rather than synthetical.

1581 Hamilton, Clayton. "The Non-Commercial Drama," BOOKMAN (NY), XLI (1915), 279-80.

The Doctor's Dilemma is "dramatically interesting" but ultimately not a good play because of the excessive dialogue.

1582 Henderson, Archibald. "Drama in the New Age," SKY-LAND (Charlotte, NC), II (Sept 1915), 389-96 [not seen].
[Cited in Hood, p. 224.]

1583 Henderson, Archibald. "The New Books: Sense and Nonsense About Bernard Shaw," DIAL, LXIX (16 Sept 1915), 210-12.

Some people are still sceptical about Shaw, but the informed know he is a leading thinker and dramatist.

1584 Henríquez Ureña, Pedro. "Libros e ideas: Bernard Shaw" (Books and Ideas: Bernard Shaw), LAS NOVEDADES (NY), No. 1644 (26 Aug 1915), 15 [not seen].
[Cited in Rodríguez (MS). In Spanish.]

1585 "Hits on the Stage: Major Barbara," HARPER'S WEEKLY, LXI (25 Dec 1915), 611.

Shaw always provokes debate over the sincerity of his ideas, but at least he forces people to think. Such is the case with Major Barbara. However, Shaw's qualities as a dramatist are not strong.

1586 Howe, P. P. BERNARD SHAW: A CRITICAL STUDY (Lond: Secker; NY: Dodd, Mead, 1915).

Shaw began with economic theory, allying himself with the Fabians. However, he only substituted a new unreal economics for the un-reality of orthodox economics. He was in love with efficiency and also demanded uniform income for everyone as a means of righting social wrongs. Much of his reasoning is a priori. Essentially, in this period of his life, he was a publicist and political humorist.

Shaw is interested only in art which is concerned with a change of ideas; art should procreate ideas and exclude style. In this he is a puritan, and will destroy anything in the name of good morals and good economics. As a utilitarian, he aims also to irritate because that way people listen; consequently, he has used waggery as a medium. Drama he sees as discussion whose aim is a public change of ideas. Shaw could have been a novelist or a dramatist, but he went into the theatre because it was good enough for his purposes. His novels have no technique—only ideas. Similarly, he believes it is the message of a play, not the play itself, which catches the social conscience. He has an aptitude for quick spirited speech, but is unable to build up, sensitively, dramatic means to achieve dramatic ends. Thus, for example, The Doctor's Dilemma is not tragic because it is about the medical profession and not about Dubedat. The prefaces are much better and more impressive than the plays and render them unnecessary. The prefaces became longer and longer once Shaw got his work into the theatre; hence he has made no technical advances since Arms and the Man. His characters are talkers, mere mouthpieces, although some are sufficiently person-alized.

1587 K., Q. "After the Play," NEW REP, V (18 Dec 1915), 175.

Major Barbara is difficult to understand because it is wordy. There is a profusion of raisonneurs and Shaw tends to over-explain every-thing.

1588 "Kept German Press Quiet," NYT, 5 April 1915, p. 1.

Common Sense About the War has been distributed throughout Italy by German propagandists.

1589 "Killing Men and Letting Babies Die," NYT, 21 Dec 1915, p. 12.

Shaw's remarks on the war are phrased in his characteristic manner and grab attention.

1590 "London Theatres: The Kingsway," STAGE, 18 Feb 1915, p. 22.

Fanny's First Play "seems now, in parts, both tedious in its philosophy and cheap in its humour."

1591 Lord, Daniel A. "Martyrs According to Bernard Shaw," CATHOLIC WORLD, C (Feb 1915), 577-90; also published NY: Paulist Press, 1915.

In Androcles and the Lion Shaw has undercut the devout character of Christian martyrs. In reading this play, one's reaction moves from wrath to astonishment at the incongruities and carelessness of the truth in the play. The same is true of The Man of Destiny and Caesar and Cleopatra. In treating a subject so sacred as Christian martyrs with levity, Shaw has committed a sacrilege against Christianity and is "wrong, utterly, hopelessly wrong" in his approach. "Humor that gives pain is not humor at all," and it is wrong to present Christian martyrs as comedians in a farce. Shaw also fails as a caricaturist because he chooses unimportant characteristics rather than a distinguishing characteristic, and so misses the point of a true caricature. In refusing to take Christian martyrdom and miracles seriously, Shaw also misses absolute truth, and Androcles, Spintho, Lavinia, and Ferrovius are quite contemptible. Thus Androcles is merely a "fable play in every sense of the word."

1592 Lyon, Harris Merton. "The Smooth Shavian: A Greeting to a Visitor," GREEN BOOK MAGAZINE, XIII (March 1915), 388-93.

Shaw should not be taken seriously. His sociology and philosophy in Widowers' Houses, Major Barbara, and Mrs. Warren's Profession fail. Despite his disclaimers, Shaw is a sentimentalist, especially in The Shewing-up of Blanco Posnet, Cashel Byron's Profession, The Man of Destiny, and even Man and Superman. His true calling is in wit and humor, as he displays them in Caesar and Cleopatra, Androcles and the Lion, John Bull's Other Island, Pygmalion, Great Catherine, and Fanny's First Play.

1593 "Man and Superman at the Lyceum," SCOTSMAN, 12 June 1915, p. 9.

Man and Superman has always been popular because of its unconventional subject matter and brilliant dialogue.

1594 "Man and Superman in Full: A Notable Occasion," EDINBURGH EVENING NEWS, 12 June 1915, p. 4.

This is the first time Man and Superman has been produced in its entirety on any stage, and was a daring experiment. "Much of the 'Hell scene' must be regarded either as rank blasphemy or sheer buffoonery, but from neither aspect did it seem to offend any susceptibilities."

1595 Metcalfe, J. S. "Drama: An Early Shaw and Other

Manifestations," LIFE, LXV (8 April 1915), 624.

Shaw reveals again his talent for satirizing British smugness, this time the medical profession in The Doctor's Dilemma. However, this piece is talky and largely undramatic.

1596 Metcalfe, [J. S.]. "Drama: Mostly Mr. Shaw and Major Barbara," LIFE, LXVI (23 Dec 1915), 1242-43.

Shaw might be taken more seriously if, in his own life, he adhered to the ideas he expresses in Major Barbara.

1597 "Miss George in Shaw Play that's on Both Sides of War," NYH, 10 Dec 1915, p. 12.

Major Barbara reveals Shaw's mental dexterity as he attacks virtually everything under the sun—thus he appeals to everyone at sometime or other.

1598 "Mr. Barker Gives Some More Shaw," NYT, 27 March 1915, p. 11; rptd in NYTTR 1912-1919, [n. p.].

The Doctor's Dilemma is too long, desultory, and does not follow accepted and cherished theatrical customs.

1599 "Mr. Daly Welcomed Back to Stage," NYH, 6 April 1915, p. 15.

You Never Can Tell still contains fresh dialogue, even if one or two characters appear somewhat dated.

1600 Moses, Montrose J. "The New York Theatres," BOOK NEWS (Phila), XXXIII (May 1915), 453-54.

The debate on medical ethics in The Doctor's Dilemma raises valid questions that have factual basis. The play's plot gives them a solid fictional context.

1601 "Moskowitz Defines False Patriotism," NYT, 17 March 1915, p. 3.

Dr. Henry Moskowitz believes Shaw is one of the most courageous men alive because of his pronouncements about the war.

1602 "Must Fight to Berlin, Says Bernard Shaw," NYT, 8 Dec 1915, p. 1.

Shaw believes that peace will not occur until the Germans have been defeated all the way to Berlin.

1603 "The New Plays: Park: Arms and the Man," THEATRE (NY), XXI (June 1915), 280-81.

Arms and the Man is now anachronistic which places greater emphasis on the action rather than on Shaw's "verbal brilliance."

1604 "New Plays: The Doctor's Dilemma," NY DRAMATIC NEWS, LXI (3 April 1915), 19.

In The Doctor's Dilemma Shaw's impertinence makes a potentially tragic drama on medical ethics into a thought-provoking comedy.

1605 "Not the Time for Joking," LIT DIG, L (1915), 610.

Perhaps it is an inauspicious time for Shavian humor, as <u>Fanny's First Play</u> proves.

1606 Otaguro, Motoo. "George Bernard Shaw," GENDAI EIKOKU GEKISAKKA (Contemporary British Dramatists) (Tokyo: Rakuyodo), pp. 71-162.

Shaw's dramas are all intellectual and full of wit and irony. In fact it will be his wit that will be most valued a hundred years hence. [In Japanese.]

1607 "Otro artículo de Bernard Shaw" (Another Bernard Shaw Article), LAS NOVEDADES (NY), No. 1621 (18 March 1915), 14 [not seen].

[Cited in Rodríguez (MS). In Spanish.]

1608 Owen, Harold. COMMON SENSE ABOUT THE SHAW (Lond: Allen & Unwin, 1915).

The time has come to denounce Shaw and his methods in <u>Common Sense About the War</u> because Shaw's intellectual honesty and sincerity need to be challenged. His pronouncements about the English position in the war are treasonous and provide ready propaganda for the Germans to use to distort world opinion against England.

1609 Palmer, John. "Mr. Bernard Shaw: An Epitaph," FORT REV, CIII (March 1915), 443-57; rptd as "George Bernard Shaw: Harlequin or Patriot?" CENTURY MAGAZINE, LXXXIX (March 1915), 769-82; rptd as BERNARD SHAW: AN EPITAPH (Lond: Grant Richards, 1915); rptd as GEORGE BERNARD SHAW, HARLEQUIN OR PATRIOT? (NY: Century, 1915); rptd in part in Evans, pp. 230-34.

Shaw will suffer more than any other writer as a consequence of the war because he is more in touch with pre-war life and that has been swept away. His recent public utterances about the war reveal how out of touch he is with the new reality. However, his utterances are not malicious, rather a consequence of having outlived his time.

Seven fallacies about Shaw need to be dispelled because they weigh against him. These fallacies are: 1) that he is very much a public figure; 2) that he is a profoundly original thinker; 3) that he has made extravagant claims for himself as a critic, political thinker, and dramatist; 4) that he is an incorrigible jester; 5) that he is "all-head-and-no heart"; 6) that he is an anarchist; 7) that he is opinionated and lacking in technical ability. The converse of each fallacy is true. Shaw, like any other author, is worth reading not for anything original he might say, but because he has a passionate and personal way of expressing current views. He is inspired by morality rather than aesthetic considerations, as his advocacy of Brieux demonstrates. In <u>Caesar and Cleopatra</u>, for example, he does not create any illusions and deals only in reality; his is a "moral energy and not the energy of the poet." Shaw the puritan has continually attacked the English for their complacency and this has emerged in his pronouncements about the war (in Common Sense About the War). In fact, Shaw is merely restating his earlier views in topical form; however, he is unpopular because times have changed and he hasn't.

1610 Parker, D. C. "Bernard Shaw as Musical Critic," OPERA MAGAZINE, II (June 1915), 14-15.
The Sanity of Art is the work of a pedantic academician. The Perfect Wagnerite is "the Wagnerian gospel very much according to St. Bernard." Shaw's views on Mozart in "The Religion of the Pianoforte" are worth remembering. Musical references also occur in Shaw's plays such as Man and Superman and Fanny's First Play. Arms and the Man provided the plot for THE CHOCOLATE SOLDIER.

1611 "Peace Far Off, Says Bernard Shaw," NYT, 19 Dec 1915, part II, p. 12.
[Title describes.]

1612 "The Playhouses," ILN, CXLVI (20 Feb 1915), 226.
Although Shaw has produced more thoughtful work than Fanny's First Play (and work with better characterization and comedy), this piece is more like a play and less like a discussion than much of what he has done.

1613 Pollock, Channing. "The Doctor's Dilemma," GREEN BOOK MAGAZINE, XIII (June 1915), 1045-48.
The Doctor's Dilemma has little plot or form, but wit in the characterization and dialogue is abundant.

1614 "Powys Belittles G. B. Shaw," NYT, 12 April 1915, p. 6.
J. C. Powys has declared Shaw has "discovered nothing new; that the French had put forth his theories and used his literary style for generations."

1615 "Pygmalion: A Dissection of Dialects," DRAMATIST (Easton, Pa), VI (Jan 1915), 538-40.
Though Pygmalion has more plot and less Shaw than most of his dramas do, Shaw's ego still intrudes far too much and complicates the drama to the point of destroying unity.

1616 "Pygmalion in Venice," TIMES, 16 Nov 1915, p. 8.
An Italian version of Pygmalion has been produced in Venice. The critics liked it but not the audience.

1617 Rehbach, Wilhelm. "George Bernard Shaw als Dramatiker" (George Bernard Shaw as Dramatist), Ph. D. dissertation, University of Erlangen, 1915; published Borna-Leipzig: Druck von R. Noske, 1915) [not seen].
[In German.]

1618 "Revivals and New Plays Seen at the Theatres," THE-

ATRE (NY), XXI (May 1915), 228-29.

Although The Doctor's Dilemma needs editing and its ending is anticlimactic, and although it does not match up to Candida or You Never Can Tell, it is brilliant in wit, exposition of theme, and characterization.

1619 Rubinstein, H. F. "The German Bernard Shaw," FORUM (NY), LIII (March 1915), 375-79.

There are parallels between Hermann Bahr and Shaw. They both possess magnetic personalities, have the ability to laugh at themselves, depict the comic side of tragedy, and their works have some similar themes and characters.

1620 "Says G. Bernard Shaw is being Persecuted," NYT, 5 June 1915, p. 1.

Siegfried Trebitsch says Shaw is being persecuted and his life is in danger because of his friendly stance towards Germany.

1621 Schrader, Marie B. "Madame Critic," NY DRAMATIC MIRROR, LXXIV (18 Dec 1915), 4.

New Yorkers, intolerant as they are, love Shaw's plays, although they mistakenly think Major Barbara is serious rather than comic. All talk and no action, it is nonetheless never dull; such "mental food" is all too rare.

1622 "Second Thoughts on First Nights," NYT, 11 April 1915, part VII, p. 6; rptd in NYTTR 1912-1919, [n. p.].

You Never Can Tell does not date and is, in fact, a better play than Shaw's more recent work which has "grown more and more indifferent and irresponsible dramatically."

1623 "Second Thoughts on First Nights," NYT, 19 Dec 1915, part VI, p. 8; rptd in NYTTR 1912-1919, [n. p.].

[A lengthy discussion of repertory theatre and Major Barbara's role therein. Barbara is an "intellectual adventure," but not a good play.]

1624 "Shaw an Aid to Germans," NYT, 20 Feb 1915, p. 4.

Common Sense About the War is circulating widely in Germany.

1625 "Shaw and Daly in Clash," NYT, 27 March 1915, p. 11.

Shaw is attempting to prevent Arnold Daly from reviving You Never Can Tell in New York. Daly has been responsible for a good deal of Shaw's popularity in America.

1626 "A Shaw Comedy at the Playhouse," NYT, 10 Dec 1915, p. 13; rptd in NYTTR 1912-1919, [n. p.].

Major Barbara is a stimulating, provocative and amusing discussion of an extreme socialistic viewpoint. It belongs in the second rank of Shaw's work because it is loose, ungainly, and discursive.

1627 "Shaw Coming to America," NYT, 13 Jan 1915, p. 1.

Shaw is planning a visit to New York to see his plays produced by

Granville-Barker. [See also: "Shaw Not Coming Here," NYT, 16 Jan 1915, p. 1.]

1628 "Shaw Discovers an Epic," LIT DIG, L (1915), 18-19.
Despite evidence to the contrary, Shaw insists that the "Yellow Book" is really a revelation of England's purposes in the war, rather than of France's.

1629 "Shaw for Forced Service," NYT, 3 Sept 1915, p. 4.
Shaw believes socialists should advocate both civil and military national service.

1630 "Shaw Gibes at Our 'Sedan-Chair Doctrine,' " NYT, 6 March 1915, p. 1.
Shaw has attacked the Monroe Doctrine.

1631 "Shaw Hits at Northcliffe," NYT, 16 June 1915, p. 2.
Shaw has declared that if an Irishman deserves imprisonment for anti-recruiting statements, then so does Lord Northcliffe.

1632 "Shaw in the English Manner Seen Here," SUN (NY), 28 Jan 1915, p. 7.
There is really more interest in Granville-Barker's production methods than there is in Androcles and the Lion which is an "extravagance of fun."

1633 "Shaw Play Viewed Here After 9 Years," SUN (NY), 27 March 1915, p. 7.
The Doctor's Dilemma is old-fashioned Shaw, full of longeurs, dullness and flashes of brilliance.

1634 "The Shaw Plays in New York," OUTLOOK (NY), CX (1915), 404-405.
[A brief overview of the record seven Shaw plays produced in New York.]

1635 "Shaw Urges a League of White Civilization," NYT, 25 Nov 1915, p. 1.
Shaw has suggested there should be a league of western civilization in order to prevent future wars.

1636 "Shaw Urges an Election," NYT, 27 Oct 1915, p. 2.
Shaw believes Britain needs a new government and has attacked those who would censor Lord Northcliffe's press.

1637 "Shaw's Terms of Peace," NYT, 8 May 1915, p. 10.
Shaw has suggested that the Germans be obliged to produce at least one hundred performances of his plays a year for the next twenty-five years if they lose the war.

1638 "Shooting of Fools Shaw's War Mission," NYT, 28 Oct 1915, p. 3.
Shaw has given a lecture focussing on the various illusions surround-

ing the war.

1639 "Six Weeks with the Enemy," TIMES, 19 Feb 1915, p. 7.
Common Sense About the War is being widely circulated by the
Germans as pro-German war propaganda.

1640 "The Spotlight and the Stage: The Doctor's Dilemma,"
INTERNATIONAL (NY), IX (May 1915), 151.
"One of Shaw's most ambitious and deepest plays," The Doctor's
Dilemma "somehow misses fire" on stage. Full of wit and imagination, it reads exceptionally well, but it is "perhaps because so much
intelligence was put into the play that there is no room left for
understanding."

1641 Squire, J. C. [O'Flaherty, V. C.], DIAL, LIX (19 Dec
1915), 550-51.
The Dublin production of O'Flaherty, V. C. may yet be seen in spite
of the sensitive nature of its content.

1642 "Stage Novelty in Two Delightful Plays, Mr. Barker's First
Offerings, " NYH, 28 Jan 1915, p. 13.
The Lion is the star of Androcles and the Lion which shows Shaw in
his "most whimsical vein" and the piece is "jolly good fun."

1643 "Students Hiss Noyes," NYT, 21 May 1915, p. 9.
Alfred Noyes was hissed at the University of Pennsylvania for calling
Shaw unpatriotic and contemptible.

1644 Tall, S. Broughton. "Advice to Shaw: From Novice to
Master," DRAMATIST (Easton, Pa), VI (July 1915), 602-04.
Pygmalion reveals Shaw needs to master his craft; the play should
have less talk and fewer theories together with more action and
unity.

1645 Tatlock, John S. P. "Pygmalion and Peregrine," NATION
(NY), C (1915), 197.
There is a curious similarity between Pygmalion and chapter eighty-
seven of Smollett's PEREGRINE PICKLE.

1646 "$34,000 for Belgian Fund," NYT, 14 Jan 1915, p. 3.
Shaw has donated $260 to the Belgian Relief Fund.

1647 "Through German Eyes," TIMES, 22 April 1915, p. 8.
One of Shaw's letters has been published in a German newspaper and
is full of "his usual witticisms and paradoxes about the war."

1648 Tilgher, Adriano. "Il discepolo del diavolo di B. Shaw all'
Argentino" (Shaw's The Devil's Disciple at the Argentino
Theatre), LA CONCORDIA (Rome), 24 April 1915 [not seen].
[In Italian.]

1649 Tsubouchi, Shoyo. "Kyoka o hyoboseru engeki" (Theatre
Aiming at Enlightenment), KYOKA TO ENGEKI (Enlightenment

and Theatre) (Tokyo: Shobunkan, 1915), pp. 60-254.
Shaw is now the most influential dramatist in the world after Ibsen.
He is one of few contemporary authors who claim openly to write for
the enlightenment and betterment of society. It is important,
however, to remember that an author's intentions and the effect of
his work often differ. Shaw is no exception. Though it might be
romantic mysticism and not a novel idea, his view of man as nature's
vehicle is very interesting. [A detailed exposition of Shaw's life and
works up to Man and Superman, with special emphasis on You Never
Can Tell. In Japanese.]

1650 Upward, Allen. PARADISE FOUND; OR, THE SUPER-
MAN FOUND OUT (Bost & NY: Houghton Mifflin, 1915).
[A comedy set in 2115 in which Shaw is revived in the Shaw
Memorial Hall. Some good humor about the man and his ideas.]

1651 W., S. "Arms and the Man," NATION (NY), C (1915), 545.
Arms and the Man is unmistakably dated and this revival, with all of
Shaw's flippancy, is unsuited to the present mood and what we know
of militarism.

1652 W., S. "You Never Can Tell," NATION (NY), C (1915),
424-25.
You Never Can Tell is probably a fair specimen of Shavian drama and
Shaw attacks numerous topics with equal impartiality. However, the
piece would be no more than fooling were it not for the character of
the waiter.

1653 "Will Stage Shaw's Play," NYT, 18 Nov 1915, p. 3.
O'Flaherty, V. C. will be produced at the Abbey Theatre, Dublin. The
current delay is caused by rehearsal, not censorship, problems.

1916

1654 A[dams], F. P. "Plutarch Lights of History: No. 7:
Bernard Shaw," HARPER'S WEEKLY, LXII (29 April 1916), 457.
A hundred years from now Shaw will be recognized as one of the
greatest men of his age. It should also be recognized that he is both
serious and humorous.

1655 "Banned by the Censor," LIT DIG, LII (8 July 1916), 69-70.
[Gives a summary of O'Flaherty, V. C. because its stage production
has been censored in Dublin and London.]

1656 "Bernard Shaw Asks Us to Give Christianity a Trial," CUR
OP, LXI (Oct 1916), 256-57.
In his preface to Androcles and the Lion Shaw declares he believes in
Christ's message, although, characteristically, he does not believe in

the supernatural appendages of Christianity.

1657 "Bernard Shaw Turned Christian," LIT DIG, LIII (1916), 24. Although in the preface to Androcles and the Lion Shaw declares he is a Christian, critical exegesis demonstrates that his views are a long way from Christianity because he overlooks all metaphysical and theological considerations.

1658 "Bernard Shaw's Getting Married Just Witty Talk," NYH, 7 Nov 1916, p. 6. Getting Married is a boring discussion with "no plot, cohesion and order." It is a dispiriting piece.

1659 "Brilliant Cast in Getting Married," SUN (NY), 7 Nov 1916, p. 4. Getting Married is "brilliantly epigrammatic and at all times clever" and will appeal to those who enjoy intellectual drama.

1660 "Britain Blocks Shaw Tour," NYT, 11 Dec 1916, p. 8. The British government is against Shaw's lecture tour under the auspices of the Drama League of America. It is also censoring his mail. [See also: "Shaw Denies British Bar His Coming Here," NYT, 19 Dec 1916, p. 2, and "Shaw Gives Reasons for not Visiting US," NYT, 3 Jan 1917, p. 9.]

1661 Broun, Heywood. "The Season's Plays," COLLIER'S NATIONAL WEEKLY, LVII (13 May 1916), 23. Major Barbara offers no new social insights, "but it does illumine that splendid piece of theatrical material, the mind of" Shaw.

1662 Burton, Richard. BERNARD SHAW: THE MAN AND THE MASK (NY: Holt, 1916; rptd Havertown, Pa: R. West, 1976). Shaw has adopted the persona of a mountebank in order to procure, not self-advertisement, but a wider audience for his work. [Largely a survey, play-by-play and chronologically, of Shaw's work in a straightforward, plain manner. With additional chapters on Shaw as social thinker, poet and mystic, craftsman, his place in the modern drama, and biography.]

1663 "Captain Brassbound's Conversion," GREEN BOOK MAGAZINE, XV (June 1916), 978-80, 982. Captain Brassbound's Conversion is gentle, whimsical, and platitudinous; it is certainly not scandalous, and the ideas are scarcely original.

1664 "Christianity Upside Down," SPECTATOR, CXVII (1916), 180-82. Although much of what Shaw has to say about Christianity is valuable, he really does not understand the religion. His proposals in the preface to Androcles and the Lion reveal this.

1665 Conolly, F. V. "Bernard Shaw's Solution of Ireland's

Troubles," NYT, 26 Nov 1916, part V, p. 4.
[Title describes this interview of Shaw by Conolly.]

1666 Dell, Floyd. "Shaw and Jesus" (1916 [not seen]); rptd in LOOKING AT LIFE (NY: Knopf, 1924), pp. 69-74.
The force of the preface to Androcles and the Lion is such that everyone will be converted to Christianity and the Church will become redundant.

1667 Dell, Floyd. "Shaw and Religion," SEVEN ARTS, I (1916), 82-88.
Religion is far more important than sex in Shaw's plays. Where sex does exist it "finds its complete, satisfying and ultimate expression in the utterance of well-chosen words."

1668 "Drama," ATH, No. 4606 (June 1916), 303.
Shaw's preface to Androcles and the Lion demonstrates that he needs to be a more utilitarian Christian if he is to be a better Christian. While many of his ideas are lucid, others are provocative and confusing.

1669 Eaton, Walter Prichard. PLAYS AND PLAYERS: LEAVES FROM A CRITIC'S SCRAPBOOK (Cincinnati: Stewart & Kidd, 1916), pp. 188-94, 225, 273, 306, 313, 338, 365, 371, 393.
[Some favorable comments on Androcles and the Lion and other passing references.]

1670 "English Company in New Shaw Play," SUN (NY), 15 Nov 1916, p. 5.
Great Catherine is totally absorbing and a "splendid bit of Shavian humor."

1671 "Entertainments," LIVERPOOL ECHO, 11 April 1916, p. 3.
The Shewing-up of Blanco Posnet, far from being a "crude" melodrama, is a very good and entertaining one. Religious people will be shocked, but this is indeed a moral sermon.

1672 F. "Captain Brassbound's Conversion," NATION (NY), CII (1916), 392
[A review emphasizing the production rather than the play.]

1673 "First Nighter." "Captain Brassbound's Conversion," NY DRAMATIC MIRROR, LXXV (8 April 1916), 8.
Captain Brassbound's Conversion is a very gratifying play which reflects the trend towards the romantic. Lady Cicely's character is developed in novel ways, while Shaw takes care not to distort Brassbound merely for the sake of sentimentality.

1674 Freeman, John. THE MODERNS: ESSAYS IN LITERARY CRITICISM (Lond: Scott, 1916; NY: Crowell, 1917; rptd Freeport, NY; Books for Libraries, 1967), pp. 1-51.
Shaw is a comic playwright who bewilderingly scatters surprises

throughout his dialogue, rather than reserving them for particular moments. "The whole of his characters move in a peculiarly rare atmosphere of inhumanity," while the plays are "mere illustrations of ideas."

1675 " 'G. B. S.' Writes a Novel," LIT DIG, LII (1916), 1328, 1330-32.

Shaw demonstrates that, when challenged, he can write a chapter of a novel in the style of Arnold Bennett, H. G. Wells, or John Galsworthy.

1676 "G. B. Shaw Adopted—," LIT DIG, LIII (1916), 611.

On his sixtieth birthday, Shaw was offered a "spiritual home" in Germany.

1677 "G. B. Shaw Comedy is a Mixed Fare," NYT, 7 Nov 1916, p. 9; rptd in NYTTR 1912-1919, [n. p.] .

Getting Married will appeal more to Shavians rather than to the general public. It is an uneven play "with many moments of sheer intellectual delight and others of tedium when the author insists on repeating again and again."

1678 Gilman, Lawrence. "Drama and Music," NORTH AMERICAN REVIEW, CCIII (1916), 136-38.

Major Barbara has not dated and is particularly suited to the times. It is prophetic and one of the treasures of contemporary comedies.

1679 Gilman, Lawrence. "Drama and Music," NORTH AMERICAN REVIEW, CCIV (1916), 925-28.

In Getting Married Shaw "is betrayed as a shackled poet, a sternly suppressed but frequently eruptive idealist, a naturally romantic soul under duress."

1680 "Giving Shaw with Shaw 3,000 Miles Away," NYT, 12 Nov 1916, part II, p. 7.

[An exchange of correspondence between Shaw and William Faversham on the production of Getting Married.]

1681 "A Glimpse into the Theatres," INTERNATIONAL (NY), X (Jan 1916), 28-29.

Major Barbara, albeit second-rate Shaw, provokes and amuses.

1682 Goddard, Harold. "Plato, Dante and Bernard Shaw," NEW REP, VI (12 Feb 1916), 39-41.

To view Major Barbara prosaically is to miss the point and poetry of the piece. Shaw's loquacity obscures the play's structural ideas which poetically assert the need for religion and philosophy to join forces.

1683 "Grace George in a Shaw Revival," SUN (NY), 30 March 1916, p. 5.

Captain Brassbound's Conversion, like all Shaw's work, lacks true action and depends on its witty and brilliant dialogue. It needs good actors to sustain it.

1684 Hackett, J. D. "Mr. Shaw's Ireland," NYT, 15 April 1916,
p. 2.
Shaw's article "Irish Nonsense About Ireland" is full of the kind of
mistaken opinions to be expected from an "English settler in Ireland."

1685 Harris, Frank. "Bernard Shaw and Jesus the Christ,"
PEARSON'S MAGAZINE, XXXVI (Nov 1916), 428-31.
Shaw's humor obscures from many the fact that he is intensely serious, especially about reform. His communist views influence his
preaching on Christianity in the preface to Androcles and the Lion.
He believes that Christian humanitarianism would have evolved without the existence of Jesus. Shaw has produced "a very fine and fair
criticism of the gospels."

1686 Harris, Frank. "George Bernard Shaw!" PEARSON'S
MAGAZINE, XXXVI (Oct 1916), 339-343.
[Biographical.]

1687 Henderson, Archibald. "Dramatists Critically Studied,"
DRAMA, No. 21 (Feb 1916), 133-38 [not seen].
[Cited in Hood, p. 225.]

1688 "Hits on the Stage: Bernard Shaw," HARPER'S WEEKLY,
LXII (1916), 398.
The tone of Captain Brassbound's Conversion is "disappointingly
genial" to those who like venomous Shaw.

1689 [Hornblow, Arthur]. "Mr. Hornblow Goes to the Play,"
THEATRE (NY), XXIV (Dec 1916), 358, 392.
The narrative of Getting Married is so exciting that the audience
needs coffee to stay awake, although many of the lines are lively.

1690 Hulbert, H. B. "Mr. Shaw's Cynicism," NYT, 26 Oct 1916,
p. 10.
Shaw's views on Anglo-American relations is cynical and not representative of true American feelings.

1691 "Invites Shaw to Lecture," NYT, 17 Nov 1916, p. 8.
The Drama League of America has invited Shaw to visit America and
deliver a series of lectures.

1692 Jowett, John Henry. "Effect of War upon England's
Religious Life," NYT, 17 Dec 1916, part V, p. 6.
[A brief reference to Shaw's belief that Christ could provide an
answer to the world's misery.]

1693 K., Q. "After the Play," NEW REP, VI (8 April 1916), 269.
A revival of Captain Brassbound's Conversion refutes earlier critical
opinion that this piece is not a play. Like many other Shaw plays the
theme of the converted self is very evident.

1694 Kugel', A. R. "Vrachi" (The Doctor's Dilemma), TEATR I ISKUSSTVO (Leningrad), No. 52 (1916); rptd in G. B. Shou, POLNOE SOBRANIE P'ES V SHESTI TOMAKH, III (Leningrad: Iskusstvo, 1979), 636.

Shaw's work is appearing more often in Russia. A recent production of The Doctor's Dilemma shows the play is clever, witty, and well done, although without a real ending. [In Russian.]

1695 Leon, Maurice. "Shaw and German Propaganda," NYT, 16 July 1916, part VII, p. 2.

It is clear Shaw is "the devil's advocate of the German propaganda in the United States."

1696 L[ittell], P[hilip]. "Books and Things," NEW REP, V (22 Jan 1916), 311.

Some new young dramatist needs to come along and demonstrate that Shaw's classification of people by opinion is only one of many possible significant classifications.

1697 Lord, Daniel A. "George Bernard Shaw," CATHOLIC WORLD, CII (March 1916), 768-80, CIII (April 1916), 24-37; also published NY: Paulist Press, 1916.

Shaw has moved from a position of jester to that of philosopher in a very short time. He has also moved from seriousness (as in Widowers' Houses and Mrs. Warren's Profession) to comedy (as in Arms and the Man), and is now "the most serious humorist since Molière" (witness Androcles and the Lion and Pygmalion). Shaw is pre-eminently a satirist, but fails because his satire is "cruel and deadly" and proves him a "hopeless misanthrope." His satire is also mistaken because it attacks Christianity and natural law--subjects "too sacred for satire." His attitude is the result of ignorance and his Irish Protestant upbringing. His religious attitude, therefore, is really "Pantheism, old as the hills, reduced to the last absurdity," since the life-force is impersonal, remote and unfeeling (see Major Barbara and Mrs. Warren). Shaw's characterization of Ireland as a whole is "untrue and unjust" and he does not understand the Irish priest at all. Since his works are founded on untruth, Shaw, as did Tolstoy and Ibsen, will eventually die an artistic death.

1698 MacCarthy, Desmond. "Miscellany: Mr. Shaw on Christianity," NSTATE, VII (1916), 206-08; rptd in MacCarthy, pp. 114-19.

In the preface of Androcles and the Lion Shaw writes like a seer and an ignoramus, and so it is both his worst and most valuable work.

1699 [Mair, Alexander]. "Professor and 'G. B. S.,'" LIVERPOOL ECHO, 10 April 1916, p. 4.

Shaw has a considerable eminence as a playwright, but during the war he has turned his back on the British people and jeered at them in their moment of greatest need. Thus he has increased his reputation with the Germans. It is deplorable, therefore, that The Shewing-up of Blanco Posnet should be staged in Liverpool this week. [Shaw's reply printed in LIVERPOOL ECHO, 14 April 1916, p. 4, as well as other Liverpool newspapers.]

1700 Medley, C. D. "Income and Windfall," TIMES, 30 Dec 1916, p. 4.

Shaw's objections to certain unfair tax provisions which excessively tax windfall income have been met by recent legislation. [Shaw's letter appeared in TIMES, 28 Dec 1916, p. 4. Other correspondence published 1 Jan 1917, p. 4, 2 Jan 1917, p. 13, 4 Jan 1917, p. 9, 6 Jan 1917, p. 9, 8 Jan 1917, p. 9, and 9 Jan 1917, p. 4.]

1701 Mencken, H. L. "The Ulster Polonius," SMART SET, XLIX (Aug 1916), 138-44; rptd in PREJUDICES: FIRST SERIES (NY: Knopf, 1919), pp. 181-90; rptd as "Shaw as Platitudinarian" in William H. Nolte, H. L. MENCKEN'S "SMART SET" CRITICISM (Ithaca, NY: Cornell UP, 1968), pp. 60-63.

Androcles and the Lion sustains Shaw's general formula: "the announcement of the obvious in terms of the scandalous." Shaw is not a heretic "but an orthodox Scotch Presbyterian of the most cocksure and bilious sort."

1702 Metcalfe, J. S. "Drama," LIFE, LXVII (13 April 1916), 706.

Captain Brassbound's Conversion is now a familiar play and belongs to the period of Shaw's writing which was more sugar-coated than his present output.

1703 Metcalfe, [J. S.]. "Drama," LIFE, LXVIII (23 Nov 1916), 904-05.

Regardless of one's opinion of Shaw, his work is always interesting, and such is the case with Getting Married. It is not composed very well, and is full of talk which ranges from the brilliant to the merely verbose.

1704 "Miss George Delightful in Bernard Shaw Play," NYH, 30 March 1916, p. 12.

Captain Brassbound's Conversion is not as "preachy" as some of Shaw's later plays and is "just a good evening's fun." Only Shavians will take him seriously.

1705 "Miss George Gives Some More Shaw," NYT, 30 March 1916, p. 11; rptd in NYTTR 1912-1919, [n. p.].

Captain Brassbound's Conversion has never been as popular as other Shaw plays, although it is a "genially amusing" piece. Its whimsical comedy is reminiscent of J. M. Barrie.

1706 Mr. G. B. Shaw in Typical Prefaces," NYT, 21 May 1916, part VI, p. 217.

The prefaces to Androcles and the Lion, Overruled and Pygmalion are typical, stimulating Shavian fare which delight and amuse even if one disagrees with Shaw's opinion.

1707 Neil, Henry. "An Interview with Shaw," PUBLIC (Chicago), XIX (24 Nov 1916), 1120-21.
[Biographical.]

1708 "New Attractions for New York Playgoers," NY DRAMATIC MIRROR, LXXVI (18 Nov 1916), 7.
If Getting Married were to be judged on the actors' portrayals of Shaw's characters, it would fare better than the drama itself which is repetitive.

1709 "New Attractions for New York Playgoers," NY DRAMATIC MIRROR, LXXVI (25 Nov 1916), 7.
The Inca of Perusalem is talky and tiresome while Great Catherine comprises broady comedy.

1710 "The New Plays," THEATRE (NY), XXIII (Jan 1916), 5, 7, 9.
Shaw is at his best in revealing truths we all know already, and this is true with Major Barbara. This work possesses "definite artistic force" and is peopled with credible, humane characters. It is not so much what Shaw says that commands attention as the way he says it.

1711 "New Plays of the Week," NY DRAMATIC NEWS, LXIII (11 Nov 1916), 11.
Shaw throws some light on the question of marriage in Getting Married, particularly in his notion of people making their own matrimonal contracts. Occasionally the characters seem hopelessly involved, but Shaw resolves everything satisfactorily at the end.

1712 "The New Plays: Playhouse," THEATRE (NY), XXIII (May 1916), 273-74.
Captain Brassbound's Conversion is perfect entertainment, suffused with brilliant dialogue that reveals shrewd truths.

1713 "A New Triple Bill: Novelties at the Birmingham Repertory," ERA, 11 Oct 1916, p. 8.
[Largely an account of the plot of The Inca of Perusalem.]

1714 "O'Flaherty V. C.—Bernard Shaw's Suppressed Play Depicting the Horrors of Heroism," CUR OP, LXI (Aug 1916), 103.
Numerous problems have prevented the production of O'Flaherty, V. C. which is an amusing dialogue in one act.

1715 Parker, H. T. "Shaw's Suppressed Play About the War," NY DRAMATIC MIRROR, LXXVI (22 July 1916), 3.
As yet, O'Flaherty, V. C. remains unperformed, a short play full of the ironies of the human condition, war, and the relationships between England and Ireland as well as between mother and son.

Shaw's characterizations of O'Flaherty and his mother are particularly rich.

1716 Pease, Edward R. THE HISTORY OF THE FABIAN
SOCIETY (Lond: A. C. Fifield, 1916; 3rd rvd ed London: Cass,
1963), pp. 25, 40, 45, 87, 94, 112, 126-27, 134, 159, 173, 223,
258, 265.
[Sundry facts concerning Shaw's association with and participation in
the Fabian Society.]

1717 Pelo, Florence Boylston. "Bernard Shaw—Musician,"
BOOKMAN (NY), XLIII (March 1916), 90-95.
[A brief biographical account of Shaw's musical side.]

1718 "Plays and Players," EVENING EXPRESS (Liverpool), 11
April 1916, p. 3.
The much-debated The Shewing-up of Blanco Posnet has now received
a public performance and "is probably nearer Cashel Byron in conception and treatment than any of Shaw's other plays."

1719 Pollock, Channing. "Sugar and Spice: Major Barbara,"
GREEN BOOK MAGAZINE, XV (Feb 1916), 311-13.
Shaw is the cleverest of people and Major Barbara demonstrates he
has something useful to say about everything. His plays are not
really plays since the characters are mere Shavian mouthpieces and
there is almost no action.

1720 Reid, Louis R. "Shaw and Bahr Compared," NY
DRAMATIC MIRROR, LXXVI (23 Dec 1916), 4.
Arnold Daly and Shaw are at logger-heads and Daly has turned to
producing Hermann Bahr's work. Bahr's plays are like Shaw's but Bahr
"doesn't have to stand on his head to gain a laugh."

1721 "The Repertory Theatre: Three New Plays," BIRMING-
HAM DAILY POST, 9 Oct 1916, p. 8.
Although anonymous, it is easy to guess the authorship of The Inca of
Perusalem, which is an amusing and witty satire.

1722 "Repertory Theatre: Three New Plays in Birmingham,"
BIRMINGHAM DAILY MAIL, 9 Oct 1916, p. 5.
The Inca of Perusalem is an amusing satire. "It opens well, but later
prosiness develops."

1723 Scholes, Percy A. "A Talk with George Bernard Shaw,"
MUSIC STUDENT (Lond), Oct 1916 [not seen]; rptd in INDE-
PENDENT SHAVIAN, XII: 2 (Winter 1973), 23-24.
[Delineates Shaw's views on "British music in general and the
Glastonbury music drama festivals in particular."]

1724 Sedgwick, L. C. R. "A Free Speech Test," NYT, 28 April
1916, p. 10.
A recent case disproves Shaw's assertion that the right of free speech

is alive and well in America.

1725 "The Shavian 'Zoo,' " MPOST, 30 June 1916, p. 2.
Perhaps if Shaw wrote shorter prefaces, or no prefaces at all, he could devote more time to the construction of his plays. The publication of Androcles and the Lion, Overruled, and Pygmalion reveals the dramatist is subjugated to the preacher, talker and reformer in Shaw.

1726 "Shaw Among the Prophets," TLS, No. 750 (1 June 1916), 259.
Shaw's criticism of Christianity in the preface to Androcles and the Lion is faulty because it is merely "pathological" and does not take into account what religion is endeavoring to become. Shaw also misunderstands human nature which is really a mixture of the bestial and the divine, and not what Shaw would have it (rational). But he is right in demonstrating the applicability of Christianity to politics, frightening though that might be to some people.

1727 "Shaw and Dunsany in Grand Street," NYT, 15 Nov 1916, p. 9; rptd in NYTTR 1912-1919, [n. p.].
The Inca of Perusalem is tedious, while Great Catherine is "vastly entertaining."

1728 "Shaw Denounces Shootings," NYT, 11 May 1916, p. 3.
Shaw believes the recent execution of Sinn Feiners was wrong and will make martyrs of those people.

1729 "Shaw Discovers Christianity," INDEPENDENT (NY), LXXXVII (1916), 200-01.
The preface to Androcles and the Lion is excellent and it is clear Shaw is very sympathetic toward Christianity. However, his attacks on St. Paul are "typical of his failure to understand the worth of the organized Christian Church."

1730 "Shaw Dissects Conscription," NYT, 5 Jan 1916, p. 2.
Shaw has presented his views on the various aspects of conscription.

1731 "Shaw on the Munition-Maker," LIT DIG, LII (19 Feb 1916), 438-39.
Major Barbara epitomizes "much of the argument the present war has produced."

1732 "Shaw Play on East Side," NYH, 15 Nov 1916, p. 10.
"There is more active fun in [Great Catherine], more boisterous farce and rough humor, than in any of Mr. Shaw's plays that can be recalled. It really was hilarious."

1733 "Shaw Writes Girl Pacifist," NYT, 7 June 1916, p. 9.
Shaw has written to a thirteen-year-old American girl who had written to him about her pacifist views.

1734 Slosson, Edwin E. "The New Shaw: Recent Phases in the Development of G. B. S.," INDEPENDENT (NY), LXXXVI (1916), 135-38.
Shaw is courageous and kind-hearted, and, although everyone now agrees with his former preachings, he is being ignored by the press.

1735 Smith, C. H. C. "Bouquets for Mr. Shaw," NYT, 19 April 1916, p. 12.
Shaw's "The German Case Against Germany" demonstrates why Shaw should go and live in Germany. England won't miss him.

1736 Stork, Charles Wharton. "The Jumping-Off-Place in Shaw," COLONNADE, XII (Oct 1916), 72-77.
Whether they know it or not, all "intelligent readers of English literature" like Shaw, and those whom he shocks need his idealism most. His "romantic dream" that reason and impulse should be united is exemplified in Caesar and Cleopatra and "The Revolutionist's Handbook." His mysticism comes through in Androcles and the Lion, John Bull's Other Island, and Fanny's First Play. His treatment of Apollodorus in Caesar and Dubedat in The Doctor's Dilemma illustrate his "idealization of the artist." He shares with Emerson reliance on "inspiration rather than logic." The reasons people fail to understand Shaw's idealism are that "he is afraid to be simple lest he should be discovered to be obvious," because he wants people to think for themselves, and because his humor is distracting.

1737 Street, Lawrence. "The Enemies of Shakespeare," THEATRE (NY), XXIII (April 1916), 223-24.
Shaw, with his irreverence in Dramatic Opinions and Essays (and his response to Tolstoy's recent attack on Shakespeare), though not always favorable, has "done more to formulate a true attitude towards Shakespeare than any other critic within recent times."

1738 "Street Watering in London," TIMES, 25 May 1916, p. 3.
Shaw has lectured on the war economy and voiced his opposition to proposals to limit street cleaning.

1739 W., S. "Drama: Getting Married," NATION (NY), CIII (1916), 470.
Getting Married, one of Shaw's poorest plays, is a sermon that belongs in the study, not on the stage.

1740 "Will Act in Shaw Drama," NYT, 12 Nov 1916, part I, p. 19.
Gertrude Kingston is to appear in two Shaw plays.

1741 Woollcott, Alexander. "Second Thoughts on First Nights," NYT, 12 Nov 1916, part II, p. 6.; rptd in NYTTR 1912-1919, [n. p.].
"Getting Married is a witty and somewhat monotonous symposium on the problem of divorce." It is the least satisfying and effective of

Shaw's plays, although it is rivalled in that respect by <u>Misalliance.</u>

1917

1742 Aas, Lars. GEORGE BERNARD SHAW: SOCIALISMENS DIGTER (George Bernard Shaw: Poet of Socialism) (Christiana: n. p., 1917) [not seen].
[In Norwegian.]

1743 Albini, Ettore. "<u>Cesare e Cleopatra</u> di George Bernard Shaw" (George Bernard Shaw's <u>Caesar and Cleopatra</u>), AVANTI! (Rome), 26 April 1917; rptd in <u>CRONACHE TEATRALI</u> 1891- 1925, (Theatrical Chronicles 1891-1925) ed by G. Bartolucci (Genoa: Teatro Stabile, 1972), pp. 301-05.
Shaw's Caesar in <u>Caesar and Cleopatra</u> is restricted in proportion compared to Plutarch's description. Like Shaw's Napoleon, Caesar is an impertinent misogynist, while Shaw makes Cleopatra four years younger than she really was. [In Italian.]

1744 "Assure New Russia of British Regard," NYT, 1 April 1917, part I, p. 3.
Shaw is among several prominent men who have sent messages to the new Russian government assuring it of England's sympathy.

1745 "At the Play," OBS, 28 Jan 1917, p. 5.
Shaw is surely too good a judge of his own work to believe <u>Augustus Does His Bit</u> is a worthwhile play. In it he has relied on one of his obsessions—"the ineptitude and stupidity of the well-born Englishman brought up at a public school."

1746 "At the Play," OBS, 23 Dec 1917, p. 5.
<u>The Inca of Perusalem</u> lacks consistency and direction and "any idea that turns up seems good enough to be put into [the Inca's] mouth. But there is a great deal of shrewdness and truth" in the play.

1747 "Attractions for New York Theatergoers," NY DRAMAT- IC MIRROR, LXXVII (6 Oct 1917), 5.
<u>Misalliance</u> is a thoroughly Shavian piece which treats numerous topics and ideas paradoxically and cynically.

1748 "<u>Augustus Does His Bit</u>: An Exercise in Shavian Wit," TIMES, 23 Jan 1917, p. 11.
Shaw is short on invention and wit in <u>Augustus Does His Bit</u>, repeating as he does his criticisms of soldiering.

1749 "Barrie vs. Shaw in the Realm of Wartime Drama," CUR OP, LXII (June 1917), 405.
Shaw's comic recipe in <u>Augustus Does His Bit</u> fails to entertain.

212

1750 "Berlin Scores Shaw," NYT, 22 Jan 1917, p. 3; rptd in NYTTR 1912-1919, [n. p.].
Critics in Berlin are unanimous in their condemnation of John Bull's Other Island which is "one of Shaw's weakest attempts at playwriting."

1751 "Bernard Shaw Criticized as a Second-Rate Imitator of G. B. S.," CUR OP, LXIII (Nov 1917), 315-16.
The New York production of Misalliance shows that Shaw is little better than a plagiarist, and the worst kind—one who copies himself.

1752 Bolles, William. "Bernard Shaw: A Left Handed Compliment," THEATRE (NY), XXV (April 1917), 200.
Shaw should continue to do all the many things he has done, but he should refrain from riding his socialistic hobby-horse so much.

1753 Boyd, Ernest A. APPRECIATIONS AND DEPRECIATIONS: IRISH LITERARY STUDIES (Dublin: Talbot Press; Lond: T. Fisher Unwin, 1917), pp. 103-38 [pp. 122-38 are substantially a reprint of "Bernard Shaw and the French Critics," item 1190].
The circumstances of his birth made it inevitable that Shaw would be an "intellectual expatriate" and there has been virtually no Irish criticism of Shaw, nor has he influenced Ireland. Shaw should be seen as an Irish Protestant rather than as a puritan because that Protestant imprint was firmly established in childhood and is reflected in the way he handles problems. This emerges most succinctly and characteristically in John Bull's Other Island and its preface. For the same reason, he is able to examine the English disinterestedly and dispassionately. [See also abstract for item 1190.]

1754 "British Leaders Applaud," NYT, 4 April 1917, p. 3.
Shaw is among several prominent British people who have welcomed America's entry into the war.

1755 "Broadhurst: Misalliance," THEATRE (NY), XXVI (Nov 1917), 280.
Although the British disliked him because Shaw "told them too many unpleasant truths about themselves," especially in regard to war, Misalliance is witty, fantastic, and delightful.

1756 Broun, Heywood. "Plays of the Season," COLLIER'S NATIONAL WEEKLY, LVIII (27 Jan 1917), 8.
Getting Married is "the most irritating" play of the season because it does not allow complacency.

1757 "Caesar and Cleopatra," ERA, 30 Nov 1917, p. 19.
Caesar and Cleopatra has two good ingredients essential for successful melodrama—plot and comic relief. However, it probably appeals more to the history student than the average playgoer.

1758 Carus, P. "Bernard Shaw's Prophecy," OPEN COURT,

XXXI (17 Oct 1917), 634-35.

Shaw has recently expressed the view that the English and Germans, although presently at war, will eventually combine because of the similarities in their character and tendencies in politics.

1759 Castro, Antonio. "Prologue," Vencidos (Overruled) (Madrid: Victoria, 1917), pp. i-xviii [not seen].

[Cited in Rodríguez (MD), p. 388. In Spanish.]

1760 Cavacchioli, Enrico. "Le case del vedovo" (Widowers' Houses), IL SECOLO (Milan), 10 Feb 1917; rptd in REVISTA ITALIANA DI DRAMMA (Rome), III: 7 (1978), 123-24.

Widowers' Houses is an absurd, thin comedy in which interesting things are said in a doctrinaire tone enclosed in dialectic. [In Italian.]

1761 Cavacchioli, Enrico. "Il dilemma del dottore di G. B. Shaw" (The Doctor's Dilemma by G. B. Shaw), IL SECOLO (Milan), 16 Feb 1917; rptd in REVISTA ITALIANA DI DRAMMA (Rome), III: 7 (1978), 124-25.

The Doctor's Dilemma is an easy-going comedy, with malicious talk about society and condemnation of morality in the name of morality. Everything is fragmentary and colorless. [In Italian.]

1762 Corbin, John. "Laughing at Society," NYT, 30 Dec 1917, part IV, p. 4; rptd in NYTTR 1912-1919, [n. p.].

How He Lied to Her Husband reveals Shaw "has become the intellectual high priest of pretentious mediocrity." In Getting Married Shaw cuts "circles of satire about his theme and aerially [loops] the loops of paradox; but he [remains] forever outside it."

1763 De Pue, Elva. "Bernard Shaw and His Buried Treasure," SEVEN ARTS, II (1917), 344-55.

Contrary to the impression that Shaw is "cold and devoid of emotion," he is really very susceptible to a variety of feelings. However, he has a strong will-power which controls those feelings.

1764 Dickinson, Thomas H. THE CONTEMPORARY DRAMA OF ENGLAND (Bost: Little, Brown, 1917; rvd 1931), pp. 59, 65-66, 79, 135, 138, 155, 157, 159, 164-65, 167-69, 176-204, 207, 213, 220, 226, 230, 236, 277-79.

Shaw has been misunderstood, and there is much confused thinking with regard to him. He is not a dramatist in the accepted sense, nor is he very popular in the theatre. He is both thinker and pragmatist, but not a philosopher. "Shaw is a tester of values, and therefore more interested in man's experiments and essays toward truth than in any abstract vision of truth." Above all, he is a critic and tests things against his logic. His characters are basically talkers, "vehicles of ideas," and he places them in plays which draw quite markedly on earlier traditions—romances, comedies of manners, and realistic plays. Shaw sells his ideas by means of wit. The end of the first phase of Shaw's work is marked by Captain Brassbound's Conversion, and during this period he was concerned largely to attack any convention he could. After Brassbound Shaw seems to disregard dramatic requirements and is intent simply on writing documents. Man and Superman epitomizes these characteristics, which can be seen again in Getting Married. Nevertheless, there are a considerable number of scenes in various plays which show he could produce moments of pure dramatic magic.

1765 Dickinson, Thomas H. THE INSURGENT THEATRE (NY: B. W. Huebsch, 1917), pp. 23, 143, 228, 231-38, 243.

Initially Shaw, along with Ibsen and Hauptmann, allowed actors to do as they wished, but without any other reward. Indeed, Shaw drew upon the popularity of other less radical dramatists and thereby survived. Shaw still belongs to high-brows, although his plays are becoming trite and he is no longer courageous in his views. [An appendix lists the repertories of non-commerical American theatres in the early years of this century, with numerous references to Shaw.]

1766 Dolléans, Edouard. "L'épreuve de Bernard Shaw" (The Trial of Bernard Shaw), REVUE POLITIQUE ET LITTERAIRE, 24 Nov-1 Dec 1917, pp. 728-31.

Shaw draws comic effects from the contradiction between our idealistic attitudes and actions and their actual, hidden motives. Arms and the Man is a good example of this. Shaw enjoys himself as an indifferent, callous spectator, but one who cannot really understand human emotions. Shaw's characters possess virtuosity, but are not admirable. Even in the more committed plays, the characters, unlike Ibsen's, are dependent on Shaw's thought and will. [In French.]

1767 "First Nights of the Week: Augustus Does His Bit, " ERA, 24 Jan 1917, p. 1.

If this play had not been written by Shaw, it is doubtful whether it would have ever been staged. "It is a jibe, amusing, though a little cheap, at the Foreign and War Offices."

1768 Fischer, Friedrich. "George Bernard Shaw als Dramatiker und sein Verhaltnis zu Henrik Ibsen (George Bernard Shaw as Dramatist and His Relationship to Henrik Ibsen)." Published Ph. D. dissertation, University of Dusseldorf, 1917.

Shaw admires Ibsen as a critic of modern society, as a scorner of popular religion and propriety, as an enemy of so-called ideals. The Quintessence of Ibsenism centres on Ibsen as a critic, not on Ibsen as a poet and playwright. Both Ibsen and Shaw emphasize the moral message of the stage and fight against a theatre of mere entertainment. If Ibsen just describes the problems of mankind, Shaw explains and discusses them. Ibsen is a pessimistic satirist, Shaw a light humorist, a kind of "laughing Ibsen." Ibsen's female characters are more romantic than Shaw's. [In German.]

1769 "G. Bernard Shaw and Misalliance," NYT, 28 Sept 1917, p. 9; rptd in NYTTR 1912-1919, [n. p.].
Misalliance is an "amusing farce" but rather long and discursive. Shaw's wit carries the piece but much of what the play means is obscure.

1770 "Germans in Shaw Comedy," NYT, 22 Nov 1917, p. 11; rptd in NYTTR 1912-1919, [n. p.].
There has been a satisfactory revival of The Doctor's Dilemma in German.

1771 "Getting Married," GREEN BOOK MAGAZINE, XVII (Jan 1917), 5-8.
The prologue to Getting Married is better than the play. The characters have little personality, being vehicles for debate on the theme that divorce should be as simple as marriage.

1772 "Grand Street Beats Broadway," COLLIER'S NATIONAL WEEKLY, LVIII (27 Jan 1917), 38.
Great Catherine acts much better than it reads because it possesses much physical humor, along with its wit, high spirits and geniality. The Inca of Perusalem may also be by Shaw since "it is hard to think of any other author who can be tiresome without being stupid, witty and yet tedious."

1773 Grein, J. T. "The Dramatic World," STIMES, 28 Jan 1917, p. 4.
Augustus Does His Bit is a light satire on various and sundry people during wartime. It is unimportant, but a delightful "firework."

1774 H[ackett], F[rancis]. "After the Play," NEW REP, X (17 Feb 1917), 77; rptd as "Shaw on Marriage," in HORIZONS: A BOOK OF CRITICISM (NY: B. W. Huebsch, 1918), pp. 198-202.
Getting Married consists of Shaw manipulating yet again both his characters and his dialectic.

1775 H[ackett], F[rancis]. "After the Play," NEW REP, XII (6 Oct 1917), 276; rptd as "Time Cannot Wither?" in HORIZONS: A BOOK OF CRITICISM (NY: B. W. Huebsch, 1918), pp. 203-07.
With Misalliance Shaw's tendency to debate has reached new extremes and the play fails to fulfill what is normally expected in drama.

1776 Hamilton, Clayton. "Criticism and Creation in the Drama or, Bernard Shaw and J. M. Barrie," BOOKMAN (NY), XLIV (Feb 1917), 628-32.
Shaw's work has been accepted by the academic, non-theatrical, mind

because his printed works look like literature and are easier to appreciate. Genuinely theatrical dramatists, such as Pinero, H. A. Jones and Barrie, are dismissed because they do not meet these criteria.

1777 Hamilton, Clayton. PROBLEMS OF THE PLAYWRIGHT (NY: Holt, 1917), pp. xi, 110-15, 117, 119-26, 151, 153, 216-17, 231, 246, 275, 302, 305, 309-10, 319.

Lower-class and upper-class opinions prefer Pinero and H. A. Jones to Shaw; but people who know little about drama prefer Shaw. An international jury of dramatists and critics would also rank Shaw's best play third behind the best of Pinero and Jones. Shaw's misfortune has been to "concentrate the admiration of a special public" and one that is "incapable of criticism." In Candida Shaw has given much entertainment, but he ran away from the crucial problem of what Eliza is going to do at the end of Pygmalion. Much of Shaw's success can be attributed to the printed versions of his works which look more like books; Jones and Pinero have not been accepted as dramatic literature because their printed plays still look like plays. Shaw is not a creative artist because he takes apart the elements of life and is incapable of creating characters who can be imagined to live outside the limits of their respective plays.

1778 Hone, J. M. "Mr. Shaw in Ireland," NSTATE, VIII (1917), 568.

After earlier controversy, Shaw, with The Shewing-up of Blanco Posnet, is now an established dramatist in Dublin. In England, he is often regarded as simply a farceur, but in Ireland he is seen as a political commentator. The Inca of Perusalem was received recently in typically Irish fashion—dead silence except for an occasional political cheer. However, the play has moments of fun.

1779 "House of Commons: Mr. Bernard Shaw's Visit to the Front," TIMES, 9 May 1917, p. 10.

A question has been raised in Parliament whether Shaw's visit to the front lines in France was authorized. It was.

1780 "If Germany Wins," TIMES, 10 Aug 1917, p. 7.

Shaw has addressed the Fabian Society Summer School on the war and the proposed peace conference in Stockholm.

1781 "The Inca of Perusalem," SAT REV, CXXIV (1917), 501-02.

The anonimity of The Inca of Perusalem does not fool anyone; it is clearly by Shaw, and Shaw "is the greatest of living stylists in the English theatre."

1782 "Is Bernard Shaw Sincere? The British Satirist Judged by Professional Associates," THEATRE (NY), XXVI (1917), 264, 266.

Various theatrical people are of the opinion that Shaw is, on balance, sincere, although he does take delight in shocking the English.

1783 Leatham, James. THE BLIGHT OF IBSENISM: AN ANAL-YSIS OF THE FIRST OF THE IMMORALISTS (Cottingham: Cottingham Press [1917?]), pp. 58-61.

Shaw, like Shakespeare, does not hint at character; rather, he reveals it in a selective and entertaining manner (as with Burgess in Candida).

1784 "The Letter-Writing Mr. Shaw," NYT, 30 Sept 1917, part III, p. 8.

[A discussion of William Faversham's production of Getting Married, together with a letter from Shaw on Misalliance.]

1785 Littell, Philip. "The Bondage of Shaw," NEW REP, X (21 April 1917), supp 1-3; rptd in BOOKS AND THINGS (NY: Harcourt, Brace & Howe, 1919), pp. 127-39.

Shaw's work is intelligent and does not use "doctored situations." The purpose of his comedies and farces (which are more or less the same) is to destroy the illusion which is part of the structure of society. However, there is hardly any development throughout Shaw's plays: his view and tone has remained consistently the same.

1786 MacCarthy, Desmond. "Drama: The Pioneer Players," NSTATE, X (1917), 307-08.

The Inca of Perusalem shows Shaw is not afraid of anyone, although it may be Shaw is afraid the human race may be "dangerous maniacs at bottom."

1787 MacCarthy, Desmond. "Drama: The Stockpot," NSTATE, VIII (1917), 495-96; rptd in MacCarthy, pp. 129-33.

The Shewing-up of Blanco Posnet is a realist piece which works well in chamber performances. Shaw is good at supplying interesting, minor characters with viewpoints. "The play is a moving and strongly sentimental tract."

1788 MacCarthy, Desmond. "Synge and Shaw," NSTATE, VIII (1917), 399-400; rptd in MacCarthy, pp. 124-28.

Augustus Does His Bit is trivial and unbearably far-fetched; it is all jokes and lacks essential seriousness.

1789 Mais, S. P. B. FROM SHAKESPEARE TO O. HENRY: STUDIES IN LITERATURE (Lond: Richards, 1917), pp. 165-67, 171-72, 174, 177-78.

Shaw lacks "imaginative sympathy" and can write only "definite dialogue" which results in very similar characters. Nevertheless his plays are a "tonic" because "he is actuated by a passion for purity, gentleness, truth, justice and beauty."

1790 "Maxine Elliott's," THEATRE (NY), XXV (March 1917), 150.

Overruled is one act's worth of material left over from Getting Married and is nothing but "dull chatter."

1791 Metcalfe, J. S. "Drama: Mr. Bernard Shaw's Phenomenal Gift of Gab," LIFE, LXX (11 Oct 1917), 590.

Too much talk, too much Shaw, and too much play exhaust the spectators of Misalliance. You can enjoy it if you read it in installments.

1792 Meyer, Annie Nathan. "When is a Play not a Play?" DRAMA (Washington), XXV (Feb 1917), 144-54.

Getting Married is not as satisfactory as many of Shaw's other plays. Other criticism to the contrary, this play is successful as an "illumination of life."

1793 "Mr. Shaw's Misalliance Opens Broadhurst Theatre," NYH, 28 Sept 1917, p. 5.

"Misalliance being characteristically typical of Mr. Shaw, amiable, iconoclastic, and revelling in one gay paradox after another, it of course was mainly conversational."

1794 Moses, Montrose, J. "The Argumentative George Bernard Shaw," BELLMAN, XXIII (20 Oct 1917), 430-32.

Shaw breaks all the dramatic rules, but is a storehouse of ideas. Misalliance is plotless and Shaw gives us "mirth and ideas; farce and rejuvenation."

1795 Moses, Montrose J. "The Drama in New York," BOOK NEWS (Phila), XXXV (Jan 1917), 206.

Although it must have required courage to produce it, Getting Married deserves its current success. One need not read the preface to enjoy the consistent "level of external aptness and surprising jugglery of words."

1796 "New Attractions for New York Playgoers," NY DRAMATIC MIRROR, LXXVII (10 Feb 1917), 6.

Overruled is boring and better read. A clumsy production does not help matters.

1797 "New Shaw Piece at Maxine Elliott," SUN (NY), 3 Feb 1917, p. 4.

Overruled is full of Shaw's usual "sophistry on matrimony" and is not as satisfying, sincere or earnest as Getting Married.

1798 "Noted English Poet Studies America as a Tramp," NYT, 18 March 1917, part VII, p. 9.

[Passing references to Shaw's preface to W. H. Davies' THE AUTO-BIOGRAPHY OF A SUPER-TRAMP.]

1799 "The Omniscient Dramatist," OUTLOOK (NY), CXV (1917), 57.

Recent productions of Shaw's work show he takes many points of view, which some find confusing. However, life itself is multifaceted and Shaw reflects that.

1800 "Pioneer Players," STAGE, 20 Dec 1917, p. 18.
The Inca of Perusalem is pleasant, diverting, and facetious, but of only slight importance. It is an ephemeral piece.

1801 "Pioneer Players: Triple Bill at the Criterion," TIMES, 17 Dec 1917, p. 11.
The Inca of Perusalem is full of talk--a lot of it sound, much of it nonsense. However, it is difficult to tell which is which.

1802 "The Pioneer Plays," ERA, 19 Dec 1917, p. 5.
The verbose introduction to The Inca of Perusalem leaves one in no doubt that the play is by Shaw. Indeed, the play is mostly talk, at times brilliant, amiable, malicious, humorous and trivial, but Shaw succeeds also in a "shrewd Shavian home-thrust at somebody or something."

1803 "Plays Worth While," THEATRE (NY), XXV (Jan 1917), 32-33, 56.
[Largely extracts from Getting Married, with production photographs.]

1804 Pollock, Channing. "Misalliance," GREEN BOOK MAGAZINE, XVIII (Dec 1917), 965-67.
Misalliance is a talky play consisting of leftovers from previous Shaw dramas. The entanglements are "amusing, though not particularly clever."

1805 Ratcliffe, S. K. "The English Intellectuals in War-time," CENTURY MAGAZINE, XCIV (Oct 1917), 826-833.
[Passing reference to Shaw and his negligible activity during the war, in comparison to H. G. Wells, and G. K. Chesterton.]

1806 "Shaw at Armageddon," LIT DIG, LIV (1917), 623-24.
[An account of Shaw in the war zone.]

1807 "Shaw Play Opens New Broadhurst," SUN (NY), 28 Sept 1917, p. 5.
Misalliance belongs to no dramatic genre and is extremely talky. There is familiar material here and "the form is there, but the voice [of Shaw] is not."

1808 "Shaw's Overruled a Harmless Trifle," NYH, 3 Feb 1917, p. 6.
[Title describes.]

1809 "Shaw's Overruled Acted," NYT, 3 Feb 1917, p. 11; rptd in NYTTR 1912-1919, [n. p.].
Overruled is no better than The Inca of Perusalem or How He Lied to Her Husband. Overruled is a "tedious farce."

1810 Slosson, Edwin E. SIX MAJOR PROPHETS (Bost: Little,

Brown, 1917), pp. 1-55.
The war has not changed Shaw's opinions and more people agree with him than ever (even if he is widely disliked). He has eighteenth-century attributes (such as wit and lucidity), but he is also a doctrinaire intellectual. He can be intolerant and too conventional, though his conventions are peculiarly his own. He is also a mystic. [With biographical details and a bibliography.]

1811 "The Stage Society," STAGE, 25 Jan 1917, p. 16.
In Augustus Does His Bit Shaw reveals himself in his "most cynical and scoffing, argumentative and combative vein." The play contains much desultory conversation and flippancy, and is really only an ephemeral piece d'occasion.

1812 "Stage Society: Augustus Does His Bit," DT, 23 Jan 1917, p. 10.
Many people could have written Augustus Does His Bit. Some of the simple jibes are effective enough, but there is much empty fooling and an awkward tedium to the whole piece.

1813 "Useless to Go, Says Shaw," NYT, 11 Aug 1917, p. 3.
Shaw believes it is pointless for British socialists to attend a conference in Stockholm because they will be unable to affect the eventual terms of peace. Those will be decided in traditional fashion.

1814 "War as Seen by Famous Authors," NYT, 2 Dec 1917, part II, p. 8.
Shaw, along with others, has contributed his views on the war to the Library Fund.

1815 "War-Thoughts of Bernard Shaw," LIT DIG, LV (4 Aug 1917), 36.
Initially Shaw's views on the war lost him supporters and attracted detractors. Now the situation is reversed and Shaw has not changed his opinions.

1816 "What the Soldier Thinks of Shaw," LIT DIG, LV (25 Aug 1917), 27.
[An account of some soldiers' reactions is a visit to the war front by Shaw.]

1918

1817 "Adventure of James Huneker as a Literary Steeple-Jack," CUR OP, LXV (Dec 1918), 392-93.
[An account of some of the disagreements between Huneker and Shaw, extrapolated from Huneker's works.]

1818 Alsina, José. "El Humorismo de Bernard Shaw" (Bernard

Shaw's Humor), in MUSEO DRAMÁTICO (Dramatic Museum) (Madrid: Renacimiento, 1918), pp. 179-98 [not seen].
[Cited in Rodríguez (MD), p. 335. [In Spanish.]

1819 Barnard, Alfred. "First Nights of the Week: The Coliseum," ERA, 23 Jan 1918, p. 1.
Annajanska is a slight, but good play with some good dialogue.

1820 Bax, Ernest Belfort. REMINISCENCES AND REFLECTIONS OF A MID AND LATE VICTORIAN (Lond: Allen & Unwin, 1918; rptd NY: Kelley, 1967), pp. 103, 113-117, 165, 262.
[Brief, biographical details of Shaw's political interests, with a short discussion of his use of paradox.]

1821 "Bernard Shaw Again Goes to the Opera," CUR OP, LXV (Sept 1918), 164-65.
Recently Shaw returned, briefly, to his former position as an opera critic. The results reveal he can still write music criticism which can be read and understood.

1822 "Bernard Shaw, Prof. Murray, and Lord Burnham Expect America will be Potent for a Sane and Lasting Peace," NYT, 1 Jan 1918, p. 3.
[Title describes.]

1823 Bolshevism Burlesqued," GRAPHIC, XCVII (26 Jan 1918), 122.
Annajanska must be by Shaw because the author satirizes Russia in the same way as Shaw satirized Home Rule in John Bull's Other Island.

1824 Clark, Barrett H. EUROPEAN THEORIES OF THE DRAMA: AN ANTHOLOGY OF DRAMATIC THEORY AND CRITICISM FROM ARTISTOTLE TO THE PRESENT DAY, IN A SERIES OF SELECTED TEXTS, WITH COMMENTARIES, BIOGRAPHIES, AND BIBLIOGRAPHIES (Cincinnati: Stewart & Kidd, 1918 [not seen]; NY & Lond: D. Appleton, 1925), pp. 420, 471-75, 478.
After early literary hack work, Shaw came under the influence of the Fabians, and also became an influential critic who attacked current notions about drama. "To him the theater is merely a means and not an end." [With a brief bibliography of Shaw's criticism and plays, and excerpts from his dramatic theories.]

1825 "Coalition Victory Predicted," TIMES, 15 Nov 1918, p. 8.
Shaw has spoken on various aspects of coalition government.

1826 "Comedy: Mrs. Warren's Profession," THEATRE (NY), XXVII (April 1918), 218.
Mrs. Warren's Profession "seems almost mid-Victorian by comparison

with latter-day stage presentations."

1827 "G. B. Shaw, Labor Candidate," NYT, 4 Dec 1918, p. 3.
Shaw's name has unexpectedly appeared as a Labour Party candidate for East Middlesborough.

1828 Grein, J. T. "The Dramatic World," STIMES, 27 Jan 1918, p. 4.
Annajanska is completely unworthy of Shaw and possesses infantile humor and a puerile plot.

1829 "London Variety Stage: The London Coliseum," STAGE, 24 Jan 1918, p. 10.
Annajanska is "milk and water Shavianism." It is both clever and un-exciting, with some brilliant lines; the humor, however, is not always successful.

1830 Maude, Aylmer. LEO TOLSTOY (NY: Dodd, Mead, 1918), pp. 292-93.
[Tolstoy's brief views on Shaw, especially Shaw's desire to be surprisingly original; with a letter from Shaw to Tolstoy.]

1831 Metcalfe, J. S. "Drama: And the Children's Teeth are Set on Edge," LIFE, LXXI (28 March 1918), 518.
Mrs. Warren's Profession's "slimy undercurrent" renders it an unpleasant, though probably harmless, play.

1832 Michaud, Régis. MYSTIQUES ET RÉALISTES ANGLO-SAXONS, D'EMERSON À B. SHAW (Anglo-Saxon Mystics and Realists, from Emerson to B. Shaw) (Paris: Armand Colin, 1918), pp. 255-94.
Shaw is both artist and revolutionary. He condemns sentimental illusion and attacks haughty, imperialistic Victorian England. Though puritanical, Shaw defends real artists, technicians and masters. He also defends Ibsen and, like him, attacks hypocrisy, idealism, and romance. Shaw depicts women who try to find men who will help them make nature fulfill its goal; the life force is all powerful. Shaw also portrays the superman who is the philosopher-athlete who will change society. The plays are lively, paradoxical, full of surprising comic characters, and rich in the conflict of ideas. The war has not changed Shaw who continues to rail against patriotism and chauvinism. [In French.]

1833 "Minute Visits in the Wings," NYT, 24 March 1918, part IV, p. 11.
Mary Shaw defends Shaw from various criticisms by theatrical people. Too often those people misinterpret the humorous letters Shaw frequently sends them.

1834 "Mrs. Warren's Profession," NY DRAMATIC MIRROR, LXXVIII (23 March 1918), 7.

The revival of Mrs. Warren's Profession without the accompanying "tumult and agitation" of ten years ago allows the audience to enjoy Shaw's sermonizing and honesty in this fine play.

1835 "Mrs. Warren's Profession," NYT, 12 March 1918, p. 11.
Members of the New York Police Department attended the revival of Mrs. Warren's Profession.

1836 "No Paper for Literature," TIMES, 4 May 1918, p. 8.
Shaw has complained about the shortage of paper and the hardships it is causing authors.

1837 Phelps, William Lyon. THE TWENTIETH CENTURY THEATRE: OBSERVATIONS ON THE CONTEMPORARY ENGLISH AND AMERICAN STAGE (NY: Macmillan, 1918), pp. 5, 7, 10-11, 18, 62, 90, 122-24, 126.
Shaw's plays seem almost like footnotes to his prefaces. [With details of Shaw's relationship with Louis Calvert as revealed through letters.]

1838 "The Playhouses," ILN, CLII (2 Feb 1918), 152.
The heroine of Annajanska is typically Shavian, but the wit and humor are commonplace.

1839 "A Revolution Playlet," TIMES, 22 Jan 1918, p. 9.
In Annajanska Shaw portrays another in his long line of shrews, but on this occasion he has not bestowed much intellect on her. Shaw has really limited himself to a few commonplaces about revolution.

1840 Shapiro, Nathaniel S. "G. B. S. in Hackneyed Moments," THEATRE (NY), XXVII (May 1918), 300.
In Mrs. Warren's Profession, Man and Superman, The Inca of Perusalem, Caesar and Cleopatra, Misalliance, Getting Married, and Great Catherine, it is evident Shaw uses conventional, hackneyed comic methods successfully.

1841 "Shaw Makes Sport of 'War Aims' Slump," NYT, 12 Jan 1918, p. 2.
Shaw has, again, rendered an assessment of the war and is critical of many aspects.

1842 "Skimpole, Herbert" [pseud of Julius Herman]. BERNARD SHAW: THE MAN AND HIS WORK (Lond: Allen & Unwin, 1918).
Shaw is England's greatest laughing philosopher, who is torn between intellect and instinct. He feels most strongly about those things which the ordinary man feels least strongly about. His novels reveal his inability to appreciate the "poetry of everyday life, the romance of the daily round." The novels are really a scientific series with the objective of discovering the best type of man. The Quintessence of Ibsenism is Shaw's best critical work, although he is guilty of

manipulating the tone of Ibsen's plays to suit his own theories. The theatre was bound to appeal to Shaw because he is an essentially theatrical person who loves to put himself before the public. Additionally, his internal struggle (of egoism and socialism, intellect and instinct, reason and action) requires the objective realization which the plays can permit. [With brief, largely descriptive comments of the plays. Overall, a superficial, juvenile adoration of Shaw.]

1843 Test, Sam. "A Trade Union Army," NYT, 28 Nov 1918, p. 12.
In Common Sense About the War Shaw has exceeded the jester's privileges he usually reserves to himself. Moreover, Shaw's proposals to unionize armies are clearly impractical.

1844 Williams, Harold. MODERN ENGLISH WRITERS: BEING A STUDY OF IMAGINATIVE LITERATURE 1890-1914 (1918 [not seen]; 3rd rvd ed Lond: Sidgwick & Jackson, 1925), pp. 257-67.
Shaw, an optimist, is influenced by Ibsen and writes plays with a moral purpose. [With an overview of the life and works; Candida is the greatest success.]

1919

1845 Amico, Silvio d'. "Shaw e i 'grotteschi' " (Shaw and the "Grotesques"), L'IDEA NAZIONALE (Rome), 5 Feb 1919.
Were Shaw not a Fabian by temperament, he would be a Bolshevik in politics and art. He methodically inverts all the traditional theatrical situations and all the technical procedures of Scribe. "Grotesque" playwrights, such as Pirandello, are not essentially preachers who use their comedies to defend or overthrow social or political theses. The cerebration of Pirandello has nothing in common with that of Shaw's exquisite frigidity and verbal play. [In Italian.]

1846 Archer, William. "Wanted, a New G. B. S.," NATION (Lond), 2 Nov 1919, 266-67.
Shaw has really been a "slave to some kink in his brain" and has not been the positive force he could have been. However, it is not too late for him to change his ways and offer wise, sane and helpful counsel. [References to Heartbreak House.]

1847 "Arms and the Man," TIMES, 12 Dec 1919, p. 12.
Even after the war Shaw's views on warfare in Arms and the Man can still be appreciated, as too can his anti-romantic view of heroic love. The play is carefully constructed.

1848 "Bernard Shaw Baiting English in New Playlet," NYH, 13 March 1919, part II, p. 9.

Augustus Does His Bit becomes montonous after a while because Shaw's baiting of the War Office is a one-sided affair.

1849 "Books of the Week: The Return of Mr. Shaw," TIMES, 2 Oct 1919, p. 11.

During the war Shaw remained very much in the background. Of his new books Heartbreak House is the most interesting, but it does not represent a new departure. Shaw continues to criticize English society in his "settled tradition."

1850 "Candida cu N. Bălțățeanu" (Candida with N. Baltateanu), RAMPA (Bucharest), 17 Sept 1919 [not seen].
[In Roumanian.]

1851 Chesterton, G. K. "Shaw versus Chesterton: II: Mr. Shaw and the Danger of Living," LIVING AGE, CCCII (1919), 81-84.
[Originally published in NEW WITNESS; not seen].

Shaw is really "so steeped in the English Victorian prejudice" that he is unable to recognize what needs to be done to restore post-war Europe.

1852 Corbin, John. "Bernard Shaw as a War Casualty," NYT, 7 Dec 1919, part VIII, p. 716.

The published version of Heartbreak House reveals that Shaw's ideas and techniques are basically burned out.

1853 Corbin, John. "Shaw Champs His Bit," NYT, 13 March 1919, p. 9; rptd in NYTTR 1912-1919, [n. p.].

Augustus Does His Bit "lacks the atmospheric milieu, the salient character and the dramatic movement of its predecessors, and Augustus shrinks in proportion."

1854 Cumberland, Gerald. SET DOWN IN MALICE: A BOOK OF REMINISCENCES (NY: Brentano's, 1919), pp. 11-21, 44, 94, 133, 156, 174, 208, 210, 269.
[Largely an account of a visit with Shaw.]

1855 Cunliffe, J. W. ENGLISH LITERATURE DURING THE LAST HALF CENTURY (NY: Macmillan, 1919), pp. 119-50.

Shaw has changed dramatic standards, although his plots are careless, his characters freqently burlesques of themselves. There are many sides to his philosophy, but he is never merely negative (just as he is never merely a jester). He will probably be most admired for his wit, humor, "intellectual keeness and brilliance of epigram."

1856 Dell, Floyd. "Love Among the Shavians," (1919 [not seen]); rptd in LOOKING AT LIFE (NY: Knopf, 1924), pp. 169-77.

Shaw's heroes are exemplars of the neurotic fear of romantic love.

Shaw needs to portray them as accepting themselves for what they are and have them admit their essential romantic follies.

1857 "Drama: Arms and the Man," ATH, No. 4678 (26 Dec 1919), 1407.
Arms and the Man has now assumed the status of a classic drama.

1858 Ellis, S. M. GEORGE MEREDITH: HIS LIFE AND FRIENDS IN RELATION TO HIS WORK (Lond: Grant Richards, 1919), pp. 247-48.
[Details of Meredith's rejection of Immaturity, with a letter from Shaw.]

1859 Enăşescu, A. "Bernard Shaw: Candida," LUCEĂFARUL (Bucharest), XIV: 11 (1 Jan 1919), 241-42 [not seen].
[In Roumanian.]

1860 Ervine, St. John. "Mr. Shaw Does His Bitterest," OBS [not seen]; rptd in LIVING AGE, CCCIII (1919), 493-95.
Much in Heartbreak House and Other Plays is familiar Shaw. Especially characteristic is "the impish intrusion of Mr. Shaw himself on the stage with the barest pretense that he is a character in the play." Heartbreak is really a parable and the "most bitter and wildly comic piece he has yet composed."

1861 Fagure, Emil D. "Teatrul Naţional, Candida" (Candida at the National Theatre), ADEVĂRUL (Bucharest), 10 Sept 1919 [not seen].
[In Roumanian.]

1862 "First Nights of the Week: Arms and the Man," ERA, 17 Dec 1919, p. 13.
Arms and the Man is every whit as stimulating as it was when first produced twenty-five years ago. Shaw deliberately sets out to show the "seamy side" of warfare, but the recent war has reminded people of other aspects.

1863 Franc, Miriam Alice. IBSEN IN ENGLAND (Bost: Four Seas, 1919; rptd Folcroft, Pa: Folcroft Press, 1970), pp. 28-29, 31, 34-35, 37, 40-42, 52, 54-55, 83-84, 93, 97, 100-01, 104-05, 109, 117, 127, 137, 140, 144-45, 148, 158, 160.
Shaw, a vivacious, brilliant and paradoxical critic, supported Ibsen in England. However, Shaw often exaggerated and was himself "a preacher lacking all poetry." This backfired on Shaw particularly when he placed Ibsen above Shakespeare in The Quintessence of Ibsenism.

1864 Galsworthy, John. ANOTHER SHEAF (Lond: Heinemann, 1919), pp. 88-109.
[Passing, antithetical references to Shaw in a survey of the contemporary state of drama.]

1865 H[ackett], Francis. "Half Way House," NEW REP, XX (12 Nov 1919), 327-28.

The preface to Heartbreak House is charming, though less fruitful on second reading. The play has stale ideas and tiresome mechanics. O'Flaherty, V. C. is amusing and is "the simplest and the best thing in the book."

1866 Halperin, Josef. BERNARD SHAWS WINKE FÜR DIE FRIEDENSKONFERENZ (Bernard Shaw's Suggestion for the Peace Conference) (Zurich: 1919) [not seen].

[Cited in Dan H. Laurence, BERNARD SHAW: A BIBLIOGRAPHY (Oxford: Clarendon Press, 1983), p. 901. In German.]

1867 Harris, Frank. CONTEMPORARY PORTRAITS: SECOND SERIES (NY: Frank Harris, 1919), pp. 1-44.

Shaw humorously attacks the faults of the establishment and is very effective and full of critical energy. He is comparable to Molière in his wit and range of thought. His criticism for SAT REV was simple, direct, lucid and sincere. Shaw's best plays are The Devil's Disciple, Caesar and Cleopatra, and Candida. Mrs. Warren's Profession had the fault of defending conventions, while on other occasions he has been too preoccupied with "the play of mind." For example, Caesar is thin and bloodless in comparison to Shakespeare's ANTONY AND CLEOPATRA, although the former is very interesting intellectually.

1868 "Heartbreak House--Shaw's Symbolical Play of a Ship," CUR OP, LXVII (Oct 1919), 228-32.

The names of Shaw's characters in Heartbreak House are reminiscent of those of Thomas Love Peacock, and he appears to have drawn on the techniques of Charlie Chaplin and Mack Sennett comedies, although Shaw indicates his debt to Chekhov. Heartbreak "reveals a more religious, visionary, prophetic Shaw."

1869 Herrmann-NeiBe, Max. "Berliner Theater" (Berlin Theatres), DIE NEUE SCHAUBÜHNE, I: 11 (1 Nov 1919), 353-56.

Shaw's attack against the military and so-called heroes in Arms and the Man is not radical enough. [In German.]

1870 "House of Commons: Mr. Bernard Shaw," TIMES, 21 March 1919, p. 16.

[A parliamentary question on whether any official steps were being taken to deal with Shaw's misleading statements on British responsibility for the war.]

1871 "Impavidum Ferient Ruinae," NATION (NY), CIX (1919), 659.

Heartbreak House is soft in tone, "extraordinarily symbolistic in fable and structure" and has a touch of weariness. It may not "ultimately rank with Shaw's best work; it is worthy of all that is most memorable in his mind and art."

1872 "Irish Tailors Fall Foul of G. B. Shaw," NYT, 24 Nov 1919, p. 15.
Irish tailors have written to the manager of the Abbey Theatre, Dublin, asking him to remove Androcles from Androcles and the Lion because the character ridicules their profession.

1873 Lall, Chaman. "Shaw, the Show, and the Shawn or What's Wrong with the Theatre?" COTERIE, No. 3 (1919), 74-78.
Shaw's genius has overshadowed the contemporary theatre. "Shaw broke in the walls dividing tragedy and comedy, introduced a hundred tricks for forcing attention, above all told the truth."

1874 "The Laugh Sardonic," SPECTATOR, CXXIII (1919), 543-44.
Heartbreak House demonstrates Shaw is losing contact with primary reality. A performance of Heartbreak might render it intelligible, but reading it is simply "a trial of endurance between author and reader."

1875 "League of Nations or Another War," TIMES, 3 Jan 1919, p. 8.
Shaw has spoken at a demonstration in support of a League of Nations. The alternative to the latter is another war.

1876 [List of New Books], ATH, No. 4640 (4 April 1919), 151.
In Peace Conference Hints Shaw is fearless and clearsighted, although his logic is inhuman (which makes him a modern day Swift). At times he appears to be unduly fair to the Germans.

1877 "London Theatres: The Duke of York's," STAGE, 18 Dec 1919, p. 18.
There might have been some doubts about a revival of Arms and the Man had it been produced closer to the war.

1878 Lynd, Robert. "Mr. Shaw as Pamphleteer," NSTATE, XIII (1919), 281-82.
Among prose plays in English, few are so witty and "even in character-drawing" as Man and Superman and John Bull's Other Island. Likewise, few prose pamphlets rank with Common Sense About the War or Peace Conference Hints, or the vitally important FABIAN ESSAYS. Shaw's pamphlet style is jovial, personal, and often "ludicrously misunderstood."

1879 Lynd, Robert. OLD AND NEW MASTERS (Lond: T. Fisher Unwin, 1919), pp. 142-48.
Shaw has the unfailing ability to irritate people. He has made himself a public figure, though some would say he is a poseur. He is an artist who observes others closely and reveals the truth about matters.

1880 Metcalfe, J. S. "Drama: Prosperity and Stagnation," LIFE, LXXIII (27 March 1919), 504.

Augustus Does His Bit is of no importance.

1881 Metcalfe, J. S. "Drama: Shaking the Temple's Pillars," LIFE, LXXIII (6 March 1919), 372.

George M. Cohan has at least as much right as Shaw does to claim to be greater than Shakespeare.

1882 "Mr. Bernard Shaw's Heartbreak House," SAT REV, CXXVIII (1919), 382-83.

Heartbreak House is a variant of THE CHERRY ORCHARD except that Chekhov is a comedian, Shaw a prophet. However, whereas Chekhov creates real people, Shaw fails to convince us of the reality of his characters. Moreover, Shaw "the psychological melodramatist, springs his intellectual and emotional crises upon us with as little imaginative preparation as the ordinary melodramatist."

1883 "Mr. Shaw and the Peace," NATION (Lond) [1919; not seen]; rptd in LIVING AGE, CCCI (1919), 477-80.

Peace Conference Hints is "the best bit of wit and wisdom on [the war] yet published," although critics of Shaw's position will do their best to deny this fact.

1884 "Mr. Smillie on Slums," TIMES, 5 May 1919, p. 10.

[On Shaw's support for the cooperative societies movement.]

1885 "Mr. Wells's Straight Talk to Objectors," TIMES, 1 Dec 1919, p. 16.

[Includes Shaw's message to a conscientious objectors' organization.]

1886 M[urry], J[ohn] M[iddleton]. "Reviews: The Vision of Mr. Bernard Shaw," ATH, No. 4668 (17 Oct 1919), 1028-29; rptd in Evans, pp. 243-46.

Heartbreak House is like a "portentous" American film, though it is difficult to recognize Shaw's picture of pre-war Europe. It seems Shaw has attempted to force the Russian formula (found in Chekhov's THE CHERRY ORCHARD) on to English society.

1887 Neumann, Alfred. "Münchner Theater" (Munich Theatres), DIE NEUE SCHAUBÜHNE, I: 2 (15 Feb 1919), 59-62.

The Man of Destiny is a play full of "pleasing hero worship." [In German.]

1888 "Notes on New Books," DIAL, LXVII (1919), 448-49.

Heartbreak House reveals the Shaw of 1919 is "a little jaded and conventional" when compared with the Shaw of Major Barbara.

1889 "On the London Stage," NYT, 13 July 1919, part IV, p. 2.

Shaw has given a characteristic address on the predicament of the contemporary theatre.

1890 Pérez de Ayala, Ramón. "La dramaturgia de Bernard Shaw" (Bernard Shaw's Dramaturgy), LAS MÁSCARAS (Madrid), II (1919), 309-15 [not seen].
[Cited in Rodríguez (MD), p. 336. In Spanish.]

1891 Pérez de Ayala, Ramón. "El Don Juan de Bernard Shaw" (Bernard Shaw's Don Juan), LAS MÁSCARAS (Madrid), II (1919), 284-309 [not seen].
[Cited in Rodríguez (MD), p. 338. In Spanish.]

1892 "The Playhouses," ILN, CLV (20 Dec 1919), 1048.
Arms and the Man now has more point than it has ever done, causes much laughter, and does not offend.

1893 Rebreanu, Livio. "Teatrul Naţional: Candida" (Candida at the National Theatre), SBURĂTORUL (Bucharest), II: 22 (1919), 519 [not seen].
[In Roumanian.]

1894 "Reviews: The Philanderers," NATION (Lond), XXV (27 Sept 1919), 770; rptd in Evans, pp. 235-38.
The return of intellectual life to England is signalled by Heartbreak House which embodies Shaw's indictment of warfare and examines the society which allowed England to be drawn into war. Shaw depicts "intellectual decadence," a lack of courage, and sentimental self-indulgence.

1895 Roberts, R. Ellis. "The Last of the Victorians," BOOKMAN (Lond), LVII (Nov 1919), 76, 78.
Heartbreak House and Other Plays "reeks with Victorianism," and only Heartbreak itself deserves serious consideration. It is reminiscent of Strindberg, rather than Chekhov, and is a "sheer allegory."

1896 S., J. "Drama: In the Sick Room," ATH, No. 4647 (23 May 1919), 374.
Not everyone would agree with Shaw's analysis of the current state of the theatre, nor with his prescription for remedying the situation (ie. national endowment).

1897 "Shaw on Jails," SURVEY, XLII (1919), 540-41.
[A brief account of Shaw's opinions of jails with passing commentary.]

1898 "Shaw Sketch Good But a Trifle Late," SUN (NY), 13 March 1919, p. 9.
Augustus Does His Bit is hardly an apposite piece now the war is over and Shaw is correct in calling it a trifle.

1899 Tilgher, Adriano. "La Colonnella di G. B. Shaw al Valle" (Major Barbara by G. B. Shaw at the Valle Theatre), IL TEMPO (Rome), 25 Oct 1919 [not seen].

[In Italian.]

1900 Tilgher, Adriano. "La prima commedia di Fanny di G. B. Shaw" (Fanny's First Play by G. B. Shaw), IL TEMPO (Rome), 26 Nov 1919 [not seen].

[In Italian.]

1901 Turner, W. J. "Drama," LOND MERCURY, I (1919-20), 111-14.

In attempting to rejuvenate the drama, people must realize it is a "much bigger thing than Mr. Shaw, Ibsen, Chekhov, or anyone else." Man and Superman is not the work of a first-rate dramatist such as Shakespeare or Sophocles.

1902 Turner, W. J. "Drama," LOND MERCURY, I (1919-20), 240-43.

Shaw is the "great spiritual survival of the nineteenth century" who has a passion for playwriting and who wishes to organize the universe. However, there is now no interest in discussing social problems on stage and Man and Superman is "more absolutely dead than Tennyson's BECKET."

1903 Turner, W. J. "Dramatic Literature," LOND MERCURY, I (1919-20), 114-15.

Shaw's recent decline in popularity can be ascribed to his predictable consistency. However, he has always retained his intellectual integrity. Heartbreak House has all the old brilliancy, the characters (though exaggerated) have more imaginative reality than many Shavian figures. Moreover, the dialogue is concentrated, intense and savage, and Shaw's moral passion is gloomier and not marred by his earlier adolescent, inconsequential flippancy.

1904 [Walkley, A. B.?]. "The English Marivaux, TLS, No. 924 (2 Oct 1919), 529; rptd in Evans, pp. 239-42.

The publication of Heartbreak House and Great Catherine is to be welcomed because it is like putting the clock back and meeting old ideas and characters. There are also good reasons for calling Shaw the English Marivaux—his artificial emotion, dialogue, brainy women.

1905 W[alkley], A. B. "Plays Around Players: Methods of Dramatic Fiction," TIMES, 1 Oct 1919, p. 11

Shaw, in the preface to Great Catherine, admits he has occasionally written a play with a particular actor or actress in mind. However, he does not explain why this might be a good practice at times.

1920

1906 Amico, Silvio d'. "La tecnica teatrale de Bernardo Shaw"

(Bernard Shaw's Theatrical Technique), IL TEATRO DEI FANTOCCI (The Marionette Theatre) (Firenze: Vallecchi, 1920) [not seen].
[In Italian.]

1907 "At the Play," OBS, 15 Feb 1920, p. 10.
Pygmalion is Shaw's funniest play; he "keeps to the point, and he keeps to the characters, and he talks sense which he believes to be true."

1908 Bakshy, Alexander. "Correspondence: Theatricality," ATH, 9 Jan 1920, p. 36.
Productions of Arms and the Man need to use highly theatrical means to express Shaw's realism.

1909 Beer, M. DER BRITISCHE SOZIALISMUS DER GEGENWART (Contemporary British Socialism) (Stuttgart: J. H. W. Dietz, 1920), pp. 6-7.
[On Shaw and the Fabian Society. In German.]

1910 Benchley, R. C. "Drama: Something Good," LIFE, LXXVI (9 Dec 1920), 1100.
Heartbreak House contains delightful characters and witty dialogue.

1911 "Bernard Shaw Admits Being a Classic and Assails 'Illiterate' Detractors," CUR OP, LXIX (Nov 1920), 658-60.
Shaw is accused of putting a good deal of Shakespeare into his plays and he has responded in characteristic fashion.

1912 "The By-Elections," TIMES, 27 March 1920, p. 11.
Shaw has sent a message of support to the Labour Party candidate for the Northampton seat.

1913 "Candida Revived," TIMES, 2 March 1920, p. 14.
We have all come to accept Shaw's moral values in Candida, whereas previously Shaw was condemned for his disregard of such values. However, Candida herself is hardly worth fighting over.

1914 Cannan, Gilbert. "The English Theatre During and After the War," THEATRE ARTS MAGAZINE (NY), IV (1920), 21-24.
Shaw's work was not produced much, if at all, during the war. Additionally, his views on the war provoked much hostility (which ultimately led to the collapse of the repertory system that relied greatly on Shaw's fashionable popularity).

1915 Černik, A. "Poznámky o uměni" (Notes on Art), ROVNOST (Brno), No. 266 (1920), 8-9.
[On Fanny's First Play at the National Theatre, Prague. In Czech.]

1916 Duffin, Henry Charles. THE QUINTESSENCE OF BERNARD SHAW (Lond: Allen & Unwin, 1920; rvd 1939).
Shaw sets out to evaluate morals and attitudes to see what intrinsic

value they have. He sees that standards and values change, and hence morality can be only relative, not absolute. Lady Cicely Waynflete (Captain Brassbound's Conversion), for example, does not talk of duty, rather she does as she pleases. In particular, Shaw attacks puritanism and desires true liberty. His conception of women is close to that of the Greeks, and he presents them on a lower plane than men. Candida (Candida) is the only supreme woman; the remainder are generally less worthy and pleasant than the men. The lietmotif of the theme of woman is her maternal aspect. Love is portrayed completely devoid of romance because Shaw thinks man is the creation of woman solely so that woman can ensure procreation. Woman is not the romantic object man makes her. Shaw rarely depicts a happy marriage because he believes the institution is an irrational one and that incompatibility is an intrinsic feature of marriage. Shaw attacks poverty, believing that the pursuit of money is the "most promising feature that the world exhibits to-day." People cannot live a worthy, noble life in poverty; therefore, it must be abolished absolutely. Similarly, women should be free to live their lives without having to resort to marriage or prostitution. Shaw ignores God, whom he has replaced by the life force. This is not straightforward evolution, for Shaw is contemptuous of the purposeless quality of Darwinism. The life force presses on with a compelling sense of its own end, and Man is its final creation. Such is Shaw's religion. He is also a social democrat, although his work often presents contrary evidence to a belief in democracy. Some of the machinery of democracy, Shaw demonstrates, can be simply used by a strong man. Assent to democracy, moreover, cannot be absolute because democracy depends on the variable quality of people. Ultimately Shaw's philosophy is pragmatic.

1917 Eliot, T. S. "The Possibility of a Poetic Drama," THE SACRED WOOD (1920; rptd Lond: Methuen, 1969), pp. 67-68.
Because Shaw's plays illustrate a social theory, they cannot fulfill the requirements of true drama.

1918 Ervine, St. John. "Some Impressions of My Elders Bernard Shaw and J. M. Synge," NORTH AMERICAN REVIEW, CCXI (1920), 669-81; rptd in SOME IMPRESSIONS OF MY ELDERS (NY: Macmillan, 1922), pp. 189-239.
People often enjoy Shaw's wit and ignore what he says. Nonetheless, we think about his ideas. Because he gave himself so completely to his mind, Shaw was "incapable, apparently, of understanding the beauty and fascination of mere irrelevancy" and natural beauty. But his wit saved him by keeping him in continuous contact with normal men.

1919 F., J. "Seven Plays: Heartbreak House, " BOOKMAN (NY), LII (1920-21), 565-66.
Heartbreak House is satiric, stinging, "intensely amusing and human,"

and inexplicable.

1920 Firkins, O. W. "Drama: Bernard Shaw in Heartbreak House at the Garrick Theatre," WEEKLY REVIEW (NY), III (1 Dec 1920), 540-41.
The thesis of Heartbreak House evokes no sympathy. Only the character of the burglar arouses any interest.

1921 Firkins, O. W. "Drama: Shaw's O'Flaherty V. C.—Other One-Act Plays," WEEKLY REVIEW (NY), III (4 Aug 1920), 114-16.
O'Flaherty, V. C., though a "facile, cheap, and undramatic" satire on recruiting, succeeds and produces many laughs from Shaw fans.

1922 "First Nights of the Week," ERA, 18 Feb 1920, p. 12.
Pygmalion enjoys a welcome revival, but it no longer has its original shock value.

1923 Fischer, Walther. BERNARD SHAW IN SEINEN DRAMATISCHEN WERKEN (Bernard Shaw in His Dramatic Works) (Würzburg: J. Franks, 1920) [not seen].
[In German.]

1924 Francés, José. "Catalina Bárcena en Pigmalion" (Catalina Barcena in Pygmalion), LA ESFERA (Spain), No. 362 (11 Dec 1920) [not seen].
[Cited in Rodríguez (MS). [In Spanish.]

1925 Franić-Požežanin, I. "G. B. S. i Racine" (G. B. S. and Racine), KAZALIŠNI LIST (Zagreb), I (1920-21), 3-4 [not seen].
[In Croatian.]

1926 "G. B. Shaw Protests," NYT, 7 Jan 1920, p. 21.
Shaw has protested that an article of his on Ireland was criticized only when it appeared in America.

1927 Gad, Lily. BERNARD SHAW, PROFET OG GØGLER (Bernard Shaw: Prophet and Mountebank) (Copenhagen: S. Hasselbal¢h [1920]) [not seen].
[In Danish.]

1928 "German Stage of To-day," TIMES, 25 May 1920, p. 8.
Among ever-increasing post-war costs, the German theatre is having a hard time of it. But Shaw is proving to be a major attraction with Pygmalion, Great Catherine, and Candida all being successful. However, it is Mrs. Warren's Profession which has aroused the greatest interest.

1929 Gillet, L. "Six Comédies de Bernard Shaw" (Six Comedies by Bernard Shaw), REVUE DES DEUX MONDES, 1 Feb 1920, pp. 675-86.
Shaw's humor in Heartbreak House, Great Catherine, and Playlets of

the War scandalizes people and makes them think. Heartbreak is a comedy of love, with nothing Russian in it; it is about rich, cultured pre-war England. [In French.]

1930 Grimmich, J. "Shawova premiera v Redutë" (A Shaw First-Night at the Reduta Theatre), ROVNOST (Brno), I (1920), 5-6.
[On a production of Fanny's First Play. In Czech.]

1931 H[ackett], F[rancis]. "The Carpentier Fight: Bennett vs. Shaw," NEW REP, XXI (14 Jan 1920), 198-200.
Shaw's and Arnold Bennett's reactions to the Carpentier-Beckett fight were rather different.

1932 Hamilton, Clayton. SEEN ON THE STAGE (NY: Holt, 1920), pp. 57-62.
Shaw is the author of such well-made plays as Arms and the Man, Candida, You Never Can Tell, and Man and Superman. But at the height of his career he became lazy and decided the public would accept anything he might churn out. Getting Married and Misalliance are formless.

1933 [Heartbreak House], SPRINGFIELD REPUBLIC, 11 Jan 1920, p. 13a.
Shaw's contempt in Heartbreak House is as intense as Swift's. The preface is "the freshest and most forceful thing in the book."

1934 "Heartbreak House: First Production in Vienna," OBS, 21 Nov 1920, p. 15.
Despite a clever translation and good staging, Heartbreak House is only partially successful. There is too much discussion in the play and not enough drama.

1935 "Heartbreak House has Shaw Humor at its Brightest," NY CLIPPER, LXVIII (17 Nov 1920), 32.
With almost no plot, this is hardly even a play, but the talk about the fate of the leisure class and about marriage is "wonderful to hear."

1936 "Heartbreak House Revisited," NYT, 21 Nov 1920, part VI, p. 1; rptd in NYTTR 1920-1926, [n. p.].
"For all the sportive antics in which this extravaganze indulges, Heartbreak House is as lofty and austere a play as Shaw has written." It is "genuinely religious," but the second act seems intolerably long.

1937 Henderson, Archibald. "The Drama of the Future," SOUTHERN REVIEW (Ashville, NC), I (1920), 15-19 [not seen].
[Cited in Hood, p. 225.]

1938 Herrmann-NeiBe, Max. "Berliner Theater" (Berlin Theatres), DIE NEUE SCHAUBÜHNE, II: 1 (Jan 1920), 37-40.
[A favorable review of Pygmalion. In German.]

1939 Herrmann-NeiBe, Max. "Berliner Theater" (Berlin Theatres), DIE NEUE SCHAUBÜHNE, II: 6 (June 1920), 150-61.
Mrs. Warren's Profession is reformatory rather than revolutionary. It throws a cruel flashlight on the "proprieties" of capitalistic society. [In German.]

1940 Herrmann-NeiBe, Max. "Berliner Theater" (Berlin Theatres), DIE NEUE SCHAUBÜHNE, II: 7 (July 1920), 191-93.
This production of Great Catherine reduces the work to coarse fun. Shaw's humor is more restricted than Wilde's. [In German.]

1941 Hind, C. Lewis. AUTHORS AND I (NY & Lond: John Lane, 1920), pp. 256-61.
A volume of Shaw plays is always a momentous event and "the modern stage would be [barren] without Ibsen and Shaw!"

1942 "Irish Cheer Its Sallies," NYT, 22 June 1920, p. 9; rptd in NYTTR 1920-1926, [n. p.].
O'Flaherty, V. C. is a "sparkling" piece and it is no wonder that it was banned from production in England during the war.

1943 Ishida, Kenji. KAIZOKINO BUNGAKUSHA BERNARD SHAW (Bernard Shaw, A Man of Letters in the Age of Reorganization) (Kyoto: Kobundo, 1920).
There are two types of literary men. One accepts the morality and religion of his age just as they are, and beautifies and poetizes them with an unsurpassed skill. The other rejects and tries to transform them. Tennyson, for example, belongs to the former, and Shaw to the latter type. Shaw's name should not be overlooked as a thinker who has reconstructed modern society. [In Japanese.]

1944 Jameson, Storm. MODERN DRAMA IN EUROPE (NY: Harcourt, Brace & Howe, 1920), pp. xix, xxii, 111-12, 125-26, 129, 131, 137-47.
Shaw was influenced by Ibsen, but he did not possess Ibsen's talent for characterization. Shaw's plays remain in the world of thought rather than becoming real life; the drama of ideas is interesting but one-sided. "Moreover, Mr. Shaw attacks not conceptions of life, but conditions; not faiths, but systems."

1945 Johnston, Sir Harry. MRS. WARREN'S DAUGHTER: A STORY OF THE WOMAN'S MOVEMENT (NY: Macmillan, 1920); rptd on microfilm, New Haven, CT: Research Publications (History of Women, No. 7477), 1976.
[A fictional continuation of Mrs. Warren's Profession.]

1946 Kasack, Hermann. "Münchner Theater" (Munich Theatres), DIE NEUE SCHAUBÜHNE, II: 8 (Aug 1920), 241-45.
[Passing references to Androcles and the Lion and The Doctor's Dilemma. In German.]

1947 Kuhe, Ernest. "Drama," THE ANNUAL REGISTER 1919 (Lond: Longmans, Green, 1920), part II, pp. 57-60.

Although Arms and the Man was revived in 1919, the year was not-able for the absence of any new works by Shaw or Pinero.

1948 Lewisohn, Ludwig. "Critics and Creators of the Theatre," BOOKMAN (NY), L (Feb 1920), 589.

Heartbreak House is more symbolic than Shaw's other work; he is also "as searching and as profound and as vital . . . yet softer and mellower and more imaginative."

1949 Lewisohn, Ludwig. "Drama: The Homeless Muse," NATION (NY), CXI (1920), 622-23.

Heartbreak House is "brave and beautiful" and of "universal validity"; however, on stage, it is "thin, silvery, and aloof," "fragile," and "frayed."

1950 "London Theatres: The Aldwych," STAGE, 12 Feb 1920, p. 20.

Pygmalion's original success was secured largely through curiosity and notoriety, but the play no longer shocks.

1951 M., D. L. "Drama: Nietzsche and Shaw," ATH, No. 4731 (31 Dec 1920), 899.

O'Flaherty, V. C. is Shaw's wisest, least perverse work, full of "golden sense."

1952 M., D. L. "Drama: You Never Can Tell," ATH, No. 4727 (3 Dec 1920), 770.

You Never Can Tell is one of Shaw's sweeter plays, and only needs a tolerable production for it to succeed.

1953 Martin, John J. "The New Plays on Broadway," NY DRAMATIC MIRROR, 26 June 1920, p. 1289.

O'Flaherty, V. C. is "formless" and "venomous" and, though ostensibly a tirade against England, is really a subtle picture of Ireland.

1954 "The Meticulous Shaw," NYT, 14 Nov 1920, part VI, p. 1.

[Correspondence between Shaw and Lee Simonson, scenic director for the New York production of Heartbreak House.]

1955 "Mr. Bernard Shaw and the Film," TIMES, 27 March 1920, p. 13.

Shaw "has refused an offer of a million dollars for the film rights of all his plays."

1956 "Mr. Bernard Shaw's New Plays," TIMES, 28 May 1920, p. 10.

Shaw has spoken at Croyden about his latest play, Back to Methuselah.

1957 "Mr. Shaw's Newest Woman," NYT, 19 Dec 1920, part III,

p. 21.

Shaw has detected a change in women, who have ceased aping men and are now asserting their femininity.

1958 Moulan, Frank. "The Humor of Gilbert and Shaw," THEATRE (NY), XXXI (1920), 158-60.

Shaw's humor aids his satire and intellectual pugilism and challenges the world. Gilbert "sees life with a twinkle."

1959 "Municipal Music," TIMES, 6 May 1920, p. 14.

Shaw has spoken to the British Music Society on public subsidies for music.

1960 "O'Flaherty, V. C.: Mr. Shaw's Other Ireland Play," TIMES, 21 Dec 1920, p. 8.

O'Flaherty, V. C. contains some good humor at the expense of both the English and Irish. O'Flaherty's views about the war are distinctly Shavian.

1961 "Pigmalión" (Pygmalion), LA PLUMA (Spain), No. 6 (Nov 1920), 329-30 [not seen].

[Cited in Rodríguez (MS). In Spanish.]

1962 "Play by Mr. Bernard Shaw," TIMES, 2 Nov 1920, p. 10.

[An announcement of the forthcoming production of Heartbreak House in Vienna.]

1963 "Pygmalion at the Aldwych," ILN, CLVI (21 Feb 1920), 302.

Pygmalion's original popularity depended on a swear word. This revival demonstrates the piece is much more of a true drama than some of Shaw's other work.

1964 "Pygmalion: Revival at the Aldwych," TIMES, 11 Feb 1920, p. 14.

Pygmalion remains a notable play and still pleases and surprises as it did when it was first produced.

1965 Reid, Louis R. "The New Plays on Broadway," NY DRAMATIC MIRROR, 20 Nov 1920, p. 947.

Heartbreak House is "verbose, chaotic, artificial," but it "impresses through the sparkle of its dialogue" and is "better to listen to than most dramatists at their best."

1966 Rodríguez Acasuso, Luis. "Algunas consideraciones sobre Bernard Shaw" (Some Reflections on Bernard Shaw), DEL TEATRO AL LIBRO (On the Theatre and Books) (Buenos Aires: Cooperativa Editorial Limitada, 1920), pp. 151-58 [not seen].

[Cited in Rodríguez (MD), p. 337. In Spanish.]

1967 Rothenstein, William. TWENTY-FOUR PORTRAITS: WITH CRITICAL APPRECIATIONS BY VARIOUS HANDS (NY:

Harcourt, Brace, 1920), [n. p.] .

Shaw is now taken for granted, as are all great writers. Only bad work from him would be surprising, and he has paraded us with "the modernity of his tastes."

1968 Ruyssen, Henri. "Revue du théâtre anglais" (Review of the English Theatre), LA REVUE GERMANIQUE, 1920, pp. 284-319.

Heartbreak House is perhaps the most brilliant fantasy Shaw has ever written, and is both paradoxical and true, amusing and useless. Great Catherine is an excellent farce. O'Flaherty, V. C. is a play with a recruiting purpose. The Inca of Perusalem is a satire of the Kaiser and the governments of Europe. Augustus Does His Bit satirizes the silliness in many military and civilian offices. Annajanska is a symbolic comedy. [In French.]

1969 "Shaw Called a 'Colossal Joke' as a Prize-fight Reporter," LIT DIG, LXV (17 April 1920), 146-48.

Shaw's attempt to report a professional boxing match reveals he "knows as much about the noble art of self-defense as a Patagonian knows about a thé dansant."

1970 "Shaw Play that England Barred is Acted Here," SUN & NYH, 22 June 1920, p. 9.

O'Flaherty, V. C. is one of Shaw's "little sarcasms" in his usual form of a Socratic dialogue.

1971 "Shaw vs. the Theatre Guild," NYT, 19 Dec 1920, part VI, p. 1.

The Theatre Guild, with its production of Heartbreak House, has discovered that Shaw is very autocratic.

1972 Spong, Hilda. "Working with Pinero, Barrie and Shaw," THEATRE (NY), XXXII (July-Aug 1920), 32, 34.

Shaw's female characters make one wonder if he understands women at all. "His sympathies with human nature are only remotely related, because his real sympathy is with his own intellectual opinion."

1973 "The Stage Society," STAGE, 23 Dec 1920, p. 17.

O'Flaherty, V. C. is rendered boring by Shaw's continuous persiflage.

1974 Swinnerton, Frank. "The Drama: Pygmalion," NATION (Lond), XXVI (20 March 1920), 857-58.

Pygmalion in revival remains amusing nonsense and is far from being Shaw's best play because it possesses no fundamental criticism of life.

1975 "The Theatre: Shaw's Heartbreak House," SUN (NY), 11 Nov 1920, p. 16.

Heartbreak House is a "conversational debauch. But the dialogue is meaty, often amusing and thoroughly Shavian."

1976 "They must have a Cause," NYT, 7 Sept 1920, p. 14.
Shaw has drawn some good and useful distinctions on the reasons for
and morality of hunger-strikers.

1977 Tilgher, Adriano. "Cesare e Cleopatra di G. B. Shaw al
Valle" (Shaw's Caesar and Cleopatra at the Valle Theatre), IL
TEMPO (Rome), 9 April 1920 [not seen].
[In Italian.]

1978 "Tragedy and Comedy," SAT REV, CXXX (1920), 517-18.
O'Flaherty, V. C. is full of "brimming comicality and deadly political
surgery" directed at both the English and Irish. In addition it
possesses truly dramatic situations and some fine characterization.

1979 Vedia y Mitre, Mariano de. "Nota preliminar"
(Preliminary Note), EL HÉROE Y SUS HAZAÑAS (Heroes and
Their Exploits) (Buenos Aires: Cooperativa Editorial Limitada,
1920), pp. 5-19 [not seen].
[Cited in Rodríguez (MS). On Arms and the Man. In Spanish.]

1980 Williamson, Claude C. H. WRITERS OF THREE
CENTURIES 1789-1914 (Lond: Grant Richards, 1920), pp. 381-
90.
Shaw is a "violent and didactic man" whose prefaces are the dullest
work of any genius. However, he is "brilliant in art, tense in thought,
and a master of the drama of satire." Man and Superman is one of
the best plays, satirizing contemporary philosophy in brilliant dialogue. If Shaw had stuck to writing comedies, he might have ranked
with Sheridan.

1981 Willoughby, D. ABOUT IT & ABOUT (Lond: T. Fisher
Unwin; NY: Dutton [1920]), pp. 127, 153-60, 209-10, 216.
Shaw is a meteor, but his "dangerous" reputation is undeserved. His
life force and superman theories now verge on the tiresome, though
originally they were seen as a tough subject. He has, however,
improved his era, ground his revolutionary axe over and over again
(though he prefers government to revolution). "His manner is
frivolous, because he is nearly an Englishman, but he sometimes
means what he says because he is almost an Irishman."

1982 Woollcott, Alexander. "The Play," NYT, 11 Nov 1920, p.
11; rptd in NYTTR 1920-1926, [n. p.].
"Heartbreak House, despite the doldrums of tedium into which its
second act flounders toward the end, is quite the larkiest and most
amusing one that Shaw has written in many a year, and in its graver
moments the more familiar mood of Shavian exasperation gives way
to accents akin to Cassandra's."

1983 "You Never Can Tell," TIMES, 23 Nov 1920, p. 10.
You Never Can Tell revives quite well, although some of the ideas
about women's suffrage hardly merit curiosity value. In places the

language seems stilted.

1921

1984 A. "G. B. S.," BOOKMAN (Lond), LX (Aug 1921), 210-11.
Shaw is an institution and so people's rections to his work have
become stereotypical. Back to Methuselah is no exception, although
the preface is an excrescence and Shaw could have made his point
without expounding scientifically on creative evolution.

1985 "After 12 Years," TIMES, 21 July 1921, p. 8.
The revival of The Shewing-up of Blanco Posnet proves that when
Shaw's plays "are written they are so original that they are looked on
with suspicion. When they cease to be looked on with suspicion they
are no longer original."

1986 Agate, James. "Heartbreak Shaw," SAT REV, CXXXII
(1921), 504-05; rptd in ALARUMS AND EXCURSIONS (Lond:
Grant Richards, 1922; rptd Freeport, NY: Books for Libraries,
1967), pp. 187-92.
Critics of Heartbreak House fail to appreciate what Shaw is attempting. In his relentless pursuit of truth (based on genuine scientific
natural history) he disregards all the conventional dramatic rules;
and, indeed, we shouldn't expect anything else from him. As entertainment, the play is dull and incoherent.

1987 Anders, Margarete. "Die Historischen Komoedien von
George Bernard Shaw" (The Historical Comedies of George
Bernard Shaw), Ph.D. dissertation, University of Heidelberg,
1921.
[Cited in Lawrence F. McNamee, DISSERTATIONS IN ENGLISH
AND AMERICAN LITERATURE: THESES ACCEPTED BY AMERI-
CAN, BRITISH AND GERMAN UNIVERSITIES, 1865-1964 (NY &
Lond: Bowker, 1968), p. 533. In German.]

1988 Andréadès, A. "La dernière pièce de Bernard Shaw"
(Bernard Shaw's Latest Play), LE FIGARO, 12 Dec 1921.
Heartbreak House is a collection of aphorisms, often right, more
often cruel, always original on almost all topical questions: family
life, politics, sexual relationships. [In French.]

1989 [Arms and the Man], NYT, 6 March 1921, part VI, p. 1;
rptd in NYTTR 1920-1926, [n. p.].
A Berlin production of Arms and the Man was interrupted by Bulgarians who found the piece an affront to their country.

1990 [Back to Methuselah], SPRINGFIELD REPUBLICAN, 25
Sept 1921, p. 9a.

Shaw's mysticism and spirituality are the most appealing features of Back to Methuselah.

1991 "Back to Methuselah—Bernard Shaw's New Gospel," CUR OP, LXXI (July 1921), 71-73.
Back to Methuselah "is all a gigantic intellectual efflorescence." Parts of it are like "solemn scripture" while others are a cross between A MIDSUMMER NIGHT'S DREAM and GULLIVER'S TRAVELS.

1992 Begbie, Harold. "The Scandal of Mr. Bernard Shaw," LABOUR CHRONICLE [not seen]; rptd in LIVING AGE, CCCXI (1921), 467-69.
Shaw's recent statements about England being committed to a conflict with America is mischievous, monstrous, absurd and disastrous. Perhaps Shaw has had a temporary lapse of sanity.

1993 Bell, Clive. "The Creed of an Aesthete," NEW REP, XXIX (1921-22), 241-42; rptd in THE FACES OF FIVE DECADES: SELECTIONS FROM FIFTY YEARS OF THE "NEW REPUBLIC" 1914-1964 (NY: Simon & Schuster, 1964), pp. 74-77.
Shaw is a didactic rather than an aesthete and he cannot believe other people are different from himself unless they are culpably stupid. This is demonstrated by Back to Methuselah where Shaw argues that because life is a purposeless accident everything must be worthless. [See also Shaw's reply: NEW REP, XXIX, 361-62.]

1994 Benchley, Robert C. "Drama," LIFE, LXXVIII (29 Dec 1921), 18.
[An unfavorable review of THE CHOCOLATE SOLDIER.]

1995 "Bernard Shaw Bewilders the Critics," CUR OP, LXX (Feb 1921), 207-09.
The New York production of Heartbreak House has given occasion for the critics to be divided in their opinions of Shaw.

1996 "Bernard Shaw 'Gets Religion,'" LIVING AGE, CCCX (1921), 554-57.
The critical concensus about the publication of Back to Methuselah is favorable and some critics find that Shaw's abilities have mellowed and ripened with the years.

1997 "Bernard Shaw: Prigodom premijere Candide u Narodnom pozorištu" (Bernard Shaw: On the Occasion of the First Night of Candida at the National Theatre), ŽIVOT (Split), XXIII (1921), 572 [not seen].
[In Croatian.]

1998 Brawley, Benjamin. A SHORT HISTORY OF THE ENGLISH DRAMA (NY: Harcourt, Brace, 1921), pp. 224-26, 230, 236.
Shaw's personality takes precedence over his brilliant work which is

generally a means to an end (rather than being truly theatrical).

1999 "British Case Raises Mixed Jury Debate," NYT, 29 Jan 1921, p. 2.
Shaw argues that both the male and female members of a jury trying a divorce case should have been treated equally.

2000 Brunelli Bonetti, Bruno. LE IDEE DI BERNARDO SHAW (Bernard Shaw's Ideas) (Firenze: La Nave [1921?]) [not seen].
[In Italian.]

2001 "Carpentier Shaw's Choice," NYT, 30 June 1921, p. 13.
Shaw believes George Carpentier will beat Jack Dempsey at boxing.
[See also: "'Is that So?' Says Jack," NYT, 1 July 1921, p. 10.]

2002 Carroll, Sydney W. "The Dramatic World," STIMES, 23 Oct 1921, p. 4.
Heartbreak House is Shaw's Homeric nod, for there is no reason why we should be condemned to sit through this four-hour-long political tract.

2003 Carroll, Sydney W. "The Dramatic World: The Sunday Theatre: A Reply to Mr. Shaw," STIMES, 30 Jan 1921, p. 6.
Shaw's views on keeping theatres closed on Sundays are muddle-headed.

2004 Castellón, José. "Las ideas socialistas y filosóficas de Bernard Shaw" (Bernard Shaw's Socialist and Philosophical Ideas), LA ESFERA (Spain), No. 376 (19 March 1921) [not seen].
[Cited in Rodríguez (MS). In Spanish.]

2005 Chesterton, G. K. THE USES OF DIVERSITY (NY: Dodd, Mead, 1921), pp. 241-47.
Shaw is a large, dogmatic, likable egoist.

2006 "CHOCOLATE SOLDIER Anew," NYT, 13 Dec 1921, p. 24; rptd in NYTTR 1920-1926, [n. p.].
Little has been done to the libretto of THE CHOCOLATE SOLDIER which was never very strong despite the original force of Arms and the Man.

2007 "CHOCOLATE SOLDIER is Finely Revived at the Century," NY CLIPPER, LXIX (21 Dec 1921), 12.
[A favorable review of THE CHOCOLATE SOLIDER.]

2008 "THE CHOCOLATE SOLDIER Revived Successfully at Century Theatre," SUN (NY), 13 Dec 1921, p. 14.
THE CHOCOLATE SOLDIER has the advantage of the best operetta libretto because it is based on Arms and the Man.

2009 Claretie, Leo. "Le Héros et le Soldat" (Arms and the Man), LA REVUE MONDIALE, CXLII: 9 (1 May 1921), 91.

Arms and the Man is full of gaiety and humor. [In French.]

2010 "Court Theatre: Heartbreak House," DT, 19 Oct 1921, p. 7.
It takes Shaw a long time to arrive at any conclusions in Heartbreak House, and his loquacity seems to get worse as he gets older. The characters are Shavian puppets and are as inconsistent as Shaw's needs dictate. At least his wit is as good as ever.

2011 "Cubism in Thought," TLS, No. 1016 (7 July 1921), 433.
In Back to Methuselah Shaw mistakes thought about religion for religion itself. This failure comes from trying "to make an abstract life out of his disgust of actual things and the common place he finds in them."

2012 Dilnot, Frank. "Master Minds at Short Range," OUTLOOK (NY), CCXXVIII (1921), 290.
[A brief interview with Shaw.]

2013 "The Drama: The Gospel of Andrew Undershaft," NATION & ATH (Lond), XXIX (23 April 1921), 142, 144.
Major Barbara is Shaw's most thoughtful and poetic work, and one in which he displays his greatest ability to create characters. Some of the discussions are overly lengthy, but the play as a whole is remarkably vital.

2014 Eliot, T. S. "London Letter: Mr. Bernard Shaw," DIAL, LXXI (Oct 1921), 453–55.
While Hardy is a Victorian, Shaw is an Edwardian with a free and easy mind which lacks an interest in continuous reasoning. Because Shaw has not been appreciated sufficiently he has been satisfied with producing the epigram rather than demonstrating his true, underlying seriousness.

2015 Engel, Fritz. BERNARD SHAW UND SEINE BERSTEN BÜHNENWERKE (Bernard Shaw and His Best Stage Works) (Berlin & Leipzig: Franz Schneider, 1921).
[A 55-page pamphlet providing a critically orthodox overview of Shaw's major works. In German.]

2016 Ervine, St. John. "At the Play: Mr. Shaw in Despair," OBS, 23 Oct 1921, p. 11.
Heartbreak House is a clever play with some Chekhovian influence. "Chekhov saw Russia through human beings, whereas Mr. Shaw sees England through Mr. Shaw's opinions." This and all Shaw's plays are religious.

2017 "Everyman at the Queen's," ERA, 27 July 1921, p. 11.
[A favorable review of The Dark Lady of the Sonnets and The Shewing-up of Blanco Posnet.]

2018 "The Everyman: The Showing-up of Blanco Posner" [sic],
ERA, 23 March 1921, p. 12.
[A favorable review of The Shewing-up of Blanco Posnet, How He
Lied to Her Husband, and The Dark Lady of the Sonnets.]

2019 "Fireworks," OUTLOOK (NY), CXXVII (1921), 131.
Heartbreak House is a good, if talky play (although that is probably
why it attracts audiences). It hardly rocks the foundations of society.

2020 "First Nights of the Week: Shavian Wit and Whimsicality," ERA, 26 Oct 1921, p. 9.
Heartbreak House has no plot and very little action, but there is a
great measure of thought which moves with "Shavian wit and whimsicality and topsiturviness."

2021 Frank, Glenn. "The Tide of Affairs: Weeding the Garden
of Eden," CENTURY (NY), CII (1921), 631-35.
Shaw's theory of creative evolution in Back to Methuselah is his
"mature confession of faith" and a "stimulating intellectual adventure." Shaw's plays possess five characteristics: "a clash of
conceptions," "friction of developing wills," simultaneous action and
exposition, collective rather than individual characters, and original
endings.

2022 "Garrick: Heartbreak House," THEATRE (NY), XXXIII
(Jan 1921), 31-32.
Heartbreak House is "delightfully bizarre, extravagantly fantastic,
perfectly impossible, but withal, splendidly entertaining."

2023 "George Bernard Shaw Wants to Know 'Whose Baby is
Ruth,'" NYT, 29 Oct 1921, p. 1.
Shaw is ignorant about Babe Ruth.

2024 "Great Catherine: An Illusion Destroyed," TIMES, 19 Feb
1921, p. 8.
Great Catherine amuses no longer; the Englishman appears improbable and the Empress is mechanical. "The other marionettes are even
less interesting."

2025 Grein, J. T. "The Eloquence of G. B. S.," ILN, 5 Feb 1921
[not seen]; rptd in THE WORLD OF THE THEATRE:
IMPRESSIONS AND MEMOIRS, MARCH 1920-1921 (Lond:
Heinemann, 1921), pp. 147-48.
Shaw's commonsense and eloquence have destroyed any arguments in
favor of theatrical performances seven days a week.

2026 Hackett, Francis. "On to Eternity!" NEW REP, XXVII
(1921), 85-86.
The publication of Back to Methuselah reinforces the notion that
"Shaw is still unbearably brilliant."

2027 Hall, Edwin H. "Mr. Shaw Again," WEEKLY REVIEW

(NY), V (9 July 1921), 35.

In spite of the fact that Shaw attempts to redeem the human race, he seems to revel in its foibles.

2028 "Heartbreak House," DRAMATIST (Easton, Pa), XII (Jan 1921), 1041-42.

The "rudderless dreadnaught of dramatic rhetoric" in Heartbreak House attracts audiences by flattery; "it assumes to soar above the multitude and graciously invites it to make the ascent to an altitude beyond its zone."

2029 "Heartbreak House," TIMES, 19 Oct 1921, p. 8.

In Heartbreak House Shaw expatiates on his favorite topics, affords some amusement, and forgets what drama is about.

2030 Henderson, Archibald. "Bernard Shaw Redivivus," NYT, 12 June 1921, part III, pp. 4-5, 31.

Back to Methuselah, Shaw's Bible of evolution, places Shaw alongside other leading visionaries.

2031 "Interviewing Bernard Shaw and Sacha Guitry," LIVING AGE, CCCXI (1921), 555-56.

In a recent interview Shaw was willing to talk about almost any subject apart from his own work.

2032 "Invincible Pessimists," NYT, 12 Dec 1921, p. 14.

Recent events, such as the Washington conference, have rendered Shaw's pessimistic prognostications rather foolish.

2033 "John Bull's Other Island," ERA, 14 Sept 1921, p. 5.

John Bull's Other Island may have literary value, but it is a defective stage piece. It lacks action and there are several long, tedious passages.

2034 "John Bull's Other Island," TIMES, 10 Sept 1921, p. 6.

John Bull's Other Island may be stimulating, but it is too long and somewhat out of date.

2035 Jones, Henry Arthur. "Enemies of England: G. B. Shaw Dissected," SUNDAY CHRONICLE (Manchester), 4 Dec 1921, pp. 3, 5.

Shaw did much to foment discord between England and America in the war; in fact, he was the best propaganda machine the Germans possessed. Shaw has also failed [in his review of Jones' MY DEAR WELLS in SUNDAY CHRONICLE, 20 Nov 1921, p. 2] to answer Jones' contention that Shaw was intent on destroying the British Empire and that private enterprise should be safeguarded from wholesale socialism.

2036 Jones, Henry Arthur. "Jones Tackles G. B. Shaw," NYT, 12 Sept 1921, p. 2.

Shaw is a "criminal anarch" for predicting war between Britain and

America. [See also Shaw's reply: NYT, 20 Sept 1921, p. 3, and Jones' refusal to serve on a committee with Shaw, 21 Sept 1921, p. 19.]

2037 Jones, Henry Arthur. "Mr. Bernard Shaw as Mischief-Maker," MPOST, 13 Sept 1921, p. 4.

Shaw, with insane malevolence, has suggested that Lloyd George has committed himself to a war between England and America. This is untrue and a "foul and crazy assertion." [See also in MPOST: Shaw's reply, 20 Sept 1921, p. 4, and further letters from Jones, 21 Sept 1921, p. 6, and " C. E. S.," 22 Sept 1921, p. 6.]

2038 Jones, Henry Arthur. MY DEAR WELLS: A MANUAL FOR THE HATERS OF ENGLAND (Lond: Eveleigh Nash & Grayson, 1921), pp. xv, 255-86; rptd in part as "Jones Turns Guns on Shaw," NYT, 23 Oct 1921, part VII, pp. 2,7.

It behoves Shaw, as a fomenter of anti-English propaganda in the war and strikes after the war, to strenghten and assist H. G. Wells' socialistic and anarchial views.

2039 Kellner, Leon. DIE ENGLISCHE LITERATUR DER NEUESTEN ZEIT VON DICKENS BIS SHAW (Recent English Literature from Dickens to Shaw) (Leipzig: Bernhard Tauchnitz, 1921), pp. 26, 29, 37, 102, 127, 381-97.

[A biographical and critical overview. In German.]

2040 Lee, Vernon. "Back to Butler: A Metabiological Commentary on G. B. S.," NSTATE, XVII (1921), 674-76.

Back to Methuselah is really "Back to Butler," whose "anthropocentric, ego-centric analogies" Shaw takes over. However, it is Shaw's own "dramatising-moralising preferences," called purposive evolution, which he opposes to Darwinian fatalism. Both Butler and Shaw are attracted by the "drama of human wisdom and folly."

2041 Leubuscher, Charlotte. SOZIALISMUS UND SOZIALISIERUNG IN ENGLAND (Socialism and Socialization in England) (Jena: Gustav Fischer, 1921), pp. 21-22, 25.

[On Shaw and cooperative production. In German.]

2042 Lewisohn, Ludwig. "Books: Shaw Among the Mystics," NATION (NY), CXII (1921), 850.

Back to Methuselah is less brilliant and eloquent than Shaw's earlier work, though it possesses all his former energy. He has not discerned the true nature of his Ancients: "he means them to inspire awe; they arouse pity and disgust like the Struldbrugs of Swift."

2043 Lewisohn, Ludwig. THE MODERN DRAMA: AN ESSAY IN INTERPRETATION (NY: B. W. Huebsch, 1921), pp. 46, 70-71, 76, 121, 147, 149, 182, 184, 191-202, 211, 218.

Shaw has produced greater comedy than Wilde, although he is appalled at the muddleheadedness of people. He is no mere jester, but a naturalist who seeks the truth, primarily about poverty, war, and love. The central theme of Man and Superman and Getting Married is freedom and flexibility in the relationships between men and women, although subjugation to the life force is clearly not for everyone. His plays are structured after the pattern of his development of thought, and his dialogue is "bare, sinewy, rapid." Shaw's characters are not independent creations but a reflection of the dramatist's own mind.

2044 Littlewood, S. R. "Shaw as a Classic," REV OF REVS, LXIII (May 1921), 403.
Shaw's innovation of the discussion play has proved "a technical 'blind alley.' " However, some of his individual characters possess great appeal and are appreciated by younger generations of playgoers.

2045 "London Theatres: The Court: Heartbreak House," STAGE, 20 Oct 1921, p. 16.
The characters in Heartbreak House, an extremely lengthy play, are only caricatures. There is no plot, merely an interaction of characters and the ideas for which they stand.

2046 "London Theatres: The Court: John Bull's Other Island," STAGE, 15 Sept 1921, p. 16.
The Irish problem is always present and Shaw's views remain topical. The play is lengthy, rambling, and devoid of any dramatic and theatrical interest.

2047 "London Theatres: The Everyman: Major Barbara Revived," STAGE, 21 April 1921, p. 14.
[Largely a discussion of the production.]

2048 Lynd, Robert. "Shaw Begins a New Bible," DN, 23 June 1921, p. 6.
The publication of Back to Methuselah shows that Shaw, as usual, is a prophet who startles and amazes. Some people, however, will not be enthusiastic at some of his suggestions, although time will tell whether he has written his best or worst work.

2049 M., D. L. "The Drama: Heartbreak House," NATION & ATH (Lond), XXX (29 Oct 1921), 185-86.
Heartbreak House presents us with "a misreading of English society and national character," which might be expected from an Irish genius. It is also difficult to associate with any one character who might represent Shaw's views.

2050 M., D. L. "The Drama: John Bull's Other Island," NATION & ATH (Lond), XXIX (24 Sept 1921), 898, 900.
It is irrelevant to discuss whether Shaw's picture of Ireland as depicted in John Bull's Other Island is accurate in contemporary terms; rather, what we have is the vision of a genius which is worthy of intrinsic study.

2051 M., D. L. "The Drama: Shaw—Schopenhauer," NATION &
ATH (Lond), XXIX (28 May 1921), 336, 338.
The sex-theory in Man and Superman should probably be credited to
Schopenhauer, but Shaw is clearly responsible for the penetrating
subtleties which emerge in the play itself.

2052 MacCarthy, Desmond. "Drama: The Shaw Season,"
NSTATE, XVI (1921), 616; rptd in MacCarthy, pp. 40-43.
You Never Can Tell is fresh and inventive, with clear-cut character
portrayals. The dialogue brims with Shavian insights.

2053 MacCarthy, Desmond. "Everyman Theatre Company,"
NSTATE, XVII (1921), 471.
Shaw presents a convincing picture of Shakespeare in The Dark Lady
of the Sonnets. The Shewing-up of Blanco Posnet "is a passionate,
moving and forcible play, and technically an example of brilliant
velocity."

2054 MacCarthy, Desmond. "Miscellany: Back to Methuselah,"
NSTATE, XVII (1921), 384-85; rptd in MacCarthy, pp. 134-39;
rptd in Evans, pp. 265-69.
In Back to Methuselah Shaw has written "an impressive preface
insisting on the paramount importance of religion" in human life, "but
he has produced five plays in which there is hardly a gleam of religious emotion." Shaw's religion has very limited appeal.

2055 MacCarthy, Desmond. "Miscellany: Heartbreak House,"
NSTATE, XVIII (1921), 103-04; rptd in MacCarthy, pp. 143-49;
rptd in Evans, pp. 257-58.
Heartbreak House is "the subtlest and queerest" of Shaw's plays and,
perhaps, the best written, but its artistic defects and incongruities go
far to offset the profundity of its social vision. The root of the
problem is Shaw's indifference to dramatic art.

2056 MacGowan, Kenneth. THE THEATRE OF TOMORROW
(NY: Boni & Liveright, 1921), pp. 110, 182, 226, 230, 234, 265-
66.
Shaw broke whatever dramatic rules he chose, although up to 1910
the European theatre remained essentially realistic. Spiritual values
manage to permeate Getting Married even though Shaw is an avowed
propagandist-philosopher.

2057 "Major Barbara," TIMES, 19 April 1921, p. 8.
Major Barbara deserves more frequent revival and the dialogue remains remarkably contemporary.

2058 "Major Barbara: Successful Revival at the Everyman,"
ERA, 20 April 1921, p. 5.
Act two of Major Barbara equals anything Shaw has written, although parts of acts one and three are somewhat dull (particularly
the opening exposition).

2059 M[assingham], H. W. "The Drama: Mr. Shaw's Morality Play," NATION & ATH (Lond), XXVIII (1921), 879; rptd in H. W. M.: A SELECTION FROM THE WRITINGS OF H. W. MASSINGHAM (Lond: Cape, 1925), pp. 243-45.
The Shewing-up of Blanco Posnet is exactly the kind of play which feeds and develops the apparently growing taste for serious drama, which deals with man and his condition.

2060 M[assingham], H. W. "Reviews: Back to Methuselah," NATION & ATH (Lond), XXIX (1921), 509-10; rptd as "Shaw and Swift" in MODERN ENGLISH ESSAYS: VOLUME FOUR (Lond & Toronto: Dent, 1922), pp. 103-10; rptd in H. W. M.: A SELECTION FROM THE WRITINGS OF H. W. MASSINGHAM (Lond: Cape, 1925), pp. 159-64.
Shaw should really have written religious plays earlier and should have been a creative rather than a critical artist. Now he has done so, although the style and artistry of the individual parts of Back to Methuselah are uneven.

2061 Meltzer, Charles Henry. "G. B. S.—High Priest of Misanthropy," THEATRE (NY), XXXIII (1921), 238, 240.
Shaw is deconstructive in every possible way and the Shaw fad is beginning to die out.

2062 Meltzer, Charles Henry. "Heartbreak House and Other Plays," ARTS & DECORATION," XIV (Jan 1921), 213, 240.
Heartbreak House is dull and formless, and its characters are symbols or abstractions who talk and act like no normal humans. Shaw always thrusts his overweening self into his plots and characters, and ruins the proper course of his drama by loquacity and disgressions.

2063 Miller, Dickinson S. "Beauty and Use," NEW REP, XXVIII (1921), 255, 257.
Shaw is confused when he asserts that the function of criticism is to hold forth moral truths.

2064 Miller, Dickinson S. "The Strange Case of Mr. Chesterton and Mr. Shaw," NEW REP, XXVIII (1921), 10-13.
Although Shaw and G. K. Chesterton have much to offer to the world, their ideas are now "sadly dimmed and dimished." The problem is that neither man knows how to manage his ideas.

2065 Millett, Fred B. CONTEMPORARY BRITISH LITERA-TURE, rvd John M. Manly & Edith Rickert (NY: Harcourt, Brace, 1921 [not seen]; 3rd rvd ed 1935), pp. 56-59, 455-64.
Shaw is a "daring practitioner of the social drama" who attacks contemporary thought and is indebted to Ibsen and Brieux. However, he has been destructive rather than constructive. His early drama-turgy is conventional, but he became bolder with experience and in his later work minimizes plot and comic relief in favor of discussing

ideas. [With a bibliography of criticism.]

2066 "New Books Reviewed," NORTH AMERICAN REVIEW, CCXIV (1921), 715-16.
Back to Methuselah confirms Shaw is a terrifying prophet who does not spare his contemporaries. However, Shaw's satire at times breaks down into pessimsim, and his Ancients are almost as distressing as Swift's Struldbrugs.

2067 "New Irish Plea by Shaw," NYT, 6 Sept 1921, p. 2.
Shaw believes Ireland fears that an alliance with Britain would mean fighting America at some point.

2068 [News of the Week], SPECTATOR, CXXVII (1921), 318.
Shaw has written a silly article on Lloyd George heading for war with America. Shaw should be more responsible.

2069 Norwood, Gilbert. EURIPIDES AND SHAW (Lond: Methuen, 1921; rptd Toronto: University of Toronto Press, 1951), pp. 1-48, 52, 58, 60, 71, 74, 79-81, 95-107, 155, 159, 173-74, 186, 193.
The common characteristics of Euripides and Shaw are: 1) challenging accepted beliefs and assumptions, particularly by turning inside out typical heroes; 2) the theme of revenge, especially people obtaining redress for themselves when prevented by law from pursuing normal compensation; 3) socialist and feminist ideas; 4) strong critical treatment by contemporaries. One of Shaw's consistent dramatic methods is to take a traditional romantic situation and develop it in his own anti-romantic fashion. He stresses the importance of instinct, is a constructive thinker and a master of epigrammatic wit.

2070 O., S. "Back to Methuselah," ENGLISH REVIEW, XXXIII (Aug 1921), 136-40.
Responding to the natural reflex of the puritan race to found a new religion, Shaw has at last succumbed in Back to Methuselah.

2071 O., S. "Heartbreak House and—an Actress," ENGLISH REVIEW, XXXIII (Nov 1921), 426-28.
Heartbreak House is difficult but unquestionably gripping. Instead of action, plot, mystery, sentiment, or possessive climax, we are given antithesis, interlude, extraneosity, and anticlimax.

2072 Pearson, Ruth R. "Bernard Shaw, Rebel or Imperialist?" NEW REP, XXVIII (1921), 192.
Shaw's views in Back to Methuselah and his views elsewhere on Ireland leave one wondering whether he is a rebel or an imperialist.

2073 Pelikan, F. "Shawova Filosofie Manzelstvi" (Shaw's Philosophy of Matrimony), RUCH FILOSOFICKY, 1921, pp. 21ff [not seen].
[Cited in Amalric, p. 476. In Czech.]

2074 Phelps, William Lyon. ESSAYS ON MODERN DRAMA-
TISTS (NY: Macmillan, 1921), pp. 67-98.
Shaw has enjoyed the task of lecturing humanity and trying to set the
world right. He has led a life of reason and produced some of the
greatest plays in the history of the theatre. He has been influenced
by Schopenhauer, Nietzsche, Ibsen, Samuel Butler and Rousseau.

2075 "The Playhouses," ILN, CLIX (24 Sept 1921), 420.
John Bull's Other Island, although once appealing, now seems an
anachronistic and lengthy play.

2076 "The Playhouses: Mr. Shaw's Heartbreak House at the
Court," ILN, CLIX (29 Oct 1921), 586.
Heartbreak House is peopled by lunatics who talk at great length and
who demonstrate Shaw's formula of breaking all the rules. This has
been seen before in Man and Superman, but here it is pushed one step
further and all restraint is abandoned.

2077 Pollard, Alfred W. "Shakespeare: A Standard Text," TLS,
No. 1001 (24 March 1921), 196.
Shaw should prove his assertions [TLS, 17 March 1921, p. 178] about
the way in which Shakespeare's plays were transmitted from manu-
cript to print. [See also in TLS: 31 March 1921, p. 211, 7 April 1921,
p. 228, 14 April 1921, p. 244, 21 April 1921, p. 259.]

2078 Prazakova, Klara. "Shawova Dramata o Irské Otazce"
(Shaw's Dramas on the Irish Question), JEVISTÉ, II (1921), 587ff
[not seen].
[Cited in Amalric, p. 476. In Czech.]

2079 "Prigodom premijere Candide u Narodnom pozoristu" (On
the Occasion of the First Night of Candida at the National
Theatre), ZHIVOT (Sarajevo), III (1921), 527 [not seen].
[In Croatian.]

2080 "The Radical Snail," NYT, 22 Nov 1921, p. 18.
Shaw may be a self-styled radical, but his recent views on armaments
show he is being outdistanced by progress.

2081 Rageot, G. "De Shakespeare à M. Bernard Shaw" (From
Shakespeare to Bernard Shaw), REVUE POLITIQUE ET
LITTERAIRE, LIX (4 June 1921), 366-68.
Arms and the Man is a charming, lively play about how conventional
and artificial a certain idea of heroism was. True bravery begins
with fear, at least in civilized man. [In French.]

2082 "Ridicules G. B. Shaw's Fling at Conference," NYT, 20
Nov 1921, part I, p. 2.
Shaw has been ridiculed by Robert Blatchford for his prophecy that
the Washington conference will be a failure.

2083 R[oyde]-S[mith], N[aomi] G. "Heartbreak House,"

WESTMINSTER GAZETTE, LVIII (19 Oct 1921), 6; rptd in Evans, pp. 248-50.

Heartbreak House is long and (since it has been published already) lacking in expectancy. Nor is there any connection in style or theme with Chekhov. There are echoes of earlier plays (particularly Man and Superman, Major Barbara, The Philanderer, and You Never Can Tell), but nothing new; even the topical references are already dated.

2084 Salt, Henry S. SEVENTY YEARS AMONG SAVAGES (Lond: Allen & Unwin, 1921), pp. 61, 75, 80-83, 88, 93, 95, 98, 109, 113, 151, 166, 174, 210.

[Numerous biographical references.]

2085 "Says Bernard Shaw lacks Aestheticism," NYT, 23 Oct 1921, part II, p. 12.

[The partial text of a letter from George Moore to Frank Harris.] "Shaw is without any aestheticism whatsoever, and, being without any synthesis, he cannot pursue a train of thought for more than a few lines, and has then to contrive his escape in joke."

2086 "Says Lloyd George Declared War on US," NYT, 23 June 1921, p. 5.

Shaw believes Lloyd George's speech at the Imperial Conference contains a declaration of war against America.

2087 Schneider, Louis. "Les Premières à Paris: Le Héros et le Soldat" (Premieres in Paris: Arms and the Man), LA SUISSE, 7 April 1921.

Arms and the Man expresses absolute and deliberate nihilism, but Shaw scoffs at heroism and passion with good humor and gaiety. The plot is thin but mercilessly true and cruelly funny. [In French.]

2088 Seldes, Gilbert. "Struldbrugs and Superman," DIAL, LXXI (1921), 227-231.

In Back to Methuselah Shaw urges us to a "new aspiration and a new Will." He is essentially a mystic and religious. There are also definite correlations between the Struldbrugs of Swift's GULLIVER'S TRAVELS and Shaw's Ancients.

2089 "Shaw Ridicules $10,000 offer for His Name on American Film," NYT, 26 May 1921, p. 1.

[Title describes. See also NYT, 27 May 1921, p. 19.]

2090 "Shaw Says Avon Bard would like Chaplin," NYT, 13 May 1921, p. 3.

In supporting a scheme to show films at Stratford, Shaw has averred that Shakespeare would have delighted in Charlie Chaplin.

2091 "Shaw Wants Man to Live 1,000 Years," NYT, 23 June 1921, p. 8.

Back to Methuselah is about to be published and enshrines Shaw's new religion of creative evolution. It is not his complete "Bible" but the beginnings of one.

2092 "Shaw's Political Pessimism," LIT DIG, LXXI (19 Nov 1921), 27-28.
[A second-hand account of the debate between Shaw and H. A. Jones about England's relationship with America.]

2093 Slosson, Preston. "The Conversion of Bernard Shaw," INDEPENDENT (NY), CVI (23 July 1921), 24-25.
In Back to Methuselah Shaw "has found his pulpit and his creed," although his apparent conversion to religion should come as no surprise to readers of Man and Superman and Androcles and the Lion. Shaw came to religion by way of biology and realized he might as well call his "life force" God. The central idea of Methuselah "is that will power, as it may be developed in future ages, can prolong human life indefinitely."

2094 Squire, J. C. "Books of the Day: A Metabiological Pentateuch," OBS, 26 June 1921, p. 4; rptd in BOOKS REVIEWED (Lond: Hodder & Stoughton, 1922) pp. 122-28; rptd in Evans, pp. 260-64.
The preface to Back to Methesulah is less witty and thought-provoking than many of Shaw's others. However, the play shows no diminution in his powers, except perhaps his congenital predisposition to garrulity.

2095 "Sunday Opening of Theatres," TIMES, 25 Jan 1921, p. 8.
Shaw opposed the idea of Sunday theatrical performances at a meeting of the British Drama League.

2096 Sutton, E. Graham. "In the Russian Manner," BOOKMAN (Lond), LXI (1921-22), 169-70.
The Shaw of Heartbreak House compares more than favorably with Chekhov and Tolstoy.

2097 Swinnerton, Frank. "The Drama: O'Flaherty, V. C.," NATION (Lond), XXVIII (1921), 479-80.
Shaw's purpose in O'Flaherty, V. C. is to "insult stupidity" and to make people as clear-sighted as he is. Shaw is opposed to lies and cant and wants to put an end to "muddled emotionalism." The play is amusing, racy and witty.

2098 "Tarn." "Mr. Shaw's New Book," SPECTATOR, CXXVII (1921), 18-19.
"The thing that marks out Back to Methuselah from among most of Mr. Shaw's works as being in many ways his most mature and most serious book, is the fact that its object is for once not purely negative."

2099 "Tarn." "The Theatre: Everyman Theatre, Hampstead—

The Shaw Season," SPECTATOR, CXXVI (1921), 682-83.
[Favorable reviews of Major Barbara and Candida.]

2100 "Tarn." "The Theatre: Heartbreak House at the Court Theatre," SPECTATOR, CXXVII (1921), 559-60.
Heartbreak House is a very impressive play because in it Shaw has "cast aside his specious clarity," although it is easy to understand why others are puzzled, bored or exasperated by it.

2101 "Theatre Arts Bookshelf," THEATRE ARTS MONTHLY, V (1921), 249-50.
Back to Methuselah is on a par with Goethe's FAUST and Wagner's PARSIFAL, and is the most complete expression of Shaw's philosophy. Methuselah is extraordinary in conception and is "alternately humorous, bizarre and exalted."

2102 Turner, W. J. "Chronicles: Drama," LOND MERCURY, IV (1921), 88-90.
The production of The Shewing-up of Blanco Posnet, The Dark Lady of the Sonnets, How He Lied to Her Husband and The Doctor's Dilemma shows there is always an audience for Shaw. Posnet, though unfamiliar, is interesting and clearly never merited the censorship it suffered originally. Dark Lady is better than Lied while Dilemma "has frequent moments of Mr. Shaw at his best."

2103 Turner, W. J. "Drama," LOND MERCURY, V (1921-22), 199-201.
Heartbreak House is more consistently comic than any other of Shaw's works and his "light-hearted and light-minded volubility [has] become much deeper in tone with age." Shaw's characters lack any inner life because he deals in externals only and in "intellectual consciousness." Neither is what makes complex beings.

2104 "The Utopia of G. B. S.," SAT REV, CXXXII (1921), 43-44.
Back to Methuselah, Shaw's picture of Utopia, describes not only an improvement in human nature but shows how that change is to be effected. The work insists on spiritual values which results in a strong religious sense.

2105 Walkley, A. B. "The Drama with a Mission," FORUM (Phila), LXVI (1921), 489-94.
Shaw is, with other dramatists, moralistic, didactic and propagandistic.

2106 Weiss, Aureliu. "George Bernard Shaw," VIATA ROMÂNEASCĂ (Bucharest), XII: 6 (1921), 362-78 [not seen].
[In Roumanian.]

2107 "What Next--As Shaw Sees It," MENTOR, IX (April 1921), 29-30.
[Largely an account of Shaw's prophecies for Ireland.]

2108 Willard, Oswald Garrison. "A Net for Mr. Shaw," NYT, 21 Aug 1921, part II, p. 2.
[An invitation to Shaw to visit America, with Shaw's refusal. See also NYT, 1 Sept 1921, p. 16—Shaw's refusal to visit Chicago.]

2109 Williams, Ernest E. "G. B. S. and the Censor," DN, 9 July 1921, p. 4.
Shaw probably voted against a resolution to abolish theatrical censorship because it was tied to an amendment which sought to strengthen current laws against impropriety in public entertainments. [See also DN, 1 July 1921, p. 3, 6 July 1921, p. 4.]

2110 Woollcott, Alexander. "Life is too Short," BOOKMAN (NY), LIII (1921), 550-52.
Back to Methuselah is honest, austere, and dizzying to read, and will be extremely difficult to stage.

1922

2111 Agate, James. "Two Dramatists," SAT REV, CXXXIII (1922), 167-8; rptd in AT HALF-PAST EIGHT: ESSAYS OF THE THEATRE 1921-1922 (Lond: Cape, 1923), pp. 75-79.
Shaw's characters embody their author's thoughts and the plays contain tough ideas. [With comparisons to Galsworthy's methodology.]

2112 Anderson, Alex. "A Complete Edition of Tolstoy," TLS, No. 1060 (11 May 1922), 308.
Shaw is right in calling for a complete edition of Tolstoy's works, but clear guidelines need to be established. [Shaw's letter appeared in TLS, 4 May 1922, p. 292.]

2113 Andrews, Kenneth. "Broadway, Our Literary Signpost," BOOKMAN (NY), LX (1922), 279-81.
Back to Methuselah is undramatic and a "mass of incohate verbiage."

2114 Andrews, Kenneth. "Broadway, Our Literary Signpost," BOOKMAN (NY), LV (1922), 388-89.
[A favorable review of Candida.]

2115 "Androklo i lav (uoci premijere)" (Androcles and the Lion [On the Eve of the First Night]), KAZALISNI LIST (Osijek), I: 12 (1922), 25-26; I: 14 (1922), 7-8 [not seen].
[In Croatian.]

2116 "Back to Methuselah," NYT, 7 March 1922, p. 11; rptd in NYTTR 1920-1926, [n. p.].
In Back to Methuselah Shaw covers an overabundance of topics, and the play is not without its tedious moments.

2117 Benchley, Robert C. "Drama: The Twenty-One Day Shaw-Cycle Race," LIFE, LXXIX (16 March 1922), 18.
The first installment of Back to Methuselah forecasts boredom (as in the Garden of Eden scene) and humor (as in the Lloyd George-Asquith sequence).

2118 "Bernard Chaw [sic]: Androkle i lav" (Bernard Shaw: Androcles and the Lion), KAZALISNI LIST (Zagreb), XII (1922), 5-6; XIV (1922), 7-8 [not seen].
[In Croatian.]

2119 "Bernard Shaw in the Orient," LIVING AGE, CCCXV (1922), 787-88.
Robert Nichols reports that Arms and the Man was played very well in Tokyo. However, the Chinese fail to share the enthusiasm of the Japanese, finding Shaw's plays "too muchee talkee."

2120 "Bernard Shaw to Doctors," NYT, 17 Sept 1922, part II, p. 10.
Shaw has added to his role as the "general adviser to the universe" by lecturing doctors on "the advantages of being unregistered." He treated the topic in his "usual paradoxical vein."

2121 Birrell, Francis. "The Problem of the Problem Play," NSTATE, XIX (1922), 609.
The first act of Widowers' Houses "is a marvelous achievement for a beginner." But its weakness is that it propounds a really good problem without providing the sort of denouement essential in the theatre.

2122 Bjorkman, Edwin. "Evolution a la Shaw," SUN (NY), 22 March 1922, p. 18.
In Back to Methuselah Shaw is attempting to demonstrate that evolution should be consciously directed by man.

2123 "Books and Authors," NYT, 21 May 1922, part III, p. 20.
Shaw and more than 90 signatories have commended the forthcoming complete English edition of Tolstoy's works.

2124 Călin, Alex. "Pygmalion," RAMPA (Bucharest), 13 May 1922 [not seen].
[In Roumanian.]

2125 Campbell, Mrs. Patrick. MY LIFE AND SOME LETTERS (Lond: Hutchinson [1922]), pp. 142-43, 146, 159-60, 212, 220, 248-70, 292-95, 334, 336-38.
Shaw is both charming and enraging, and his apparent lack of consideration for people is a result of his brilliant impudence. [With numerous letters and bridging commentary.]

2126 "Candida, Shaw's Clever Play, Has Good Revival," NY CLIPPER, LXX (29 March 1922), 20.

Candida is Shaw's finest play and undoubtedly surpasses any comedy in English written in the last hundred years.

2127 Chubb, Percival. "Bernard Shaw's Religion and Its Latest Phase in Back to Methuselah," STANDARD (NY), IX (July 1922), 1-7.

Shaw's philosophy in Back to Methuselah is nothing new and can be found in Thomas Hill Green's ideas, for example. Shaw fails to provide prophecy in his message; evolution is all very well, but what will follow? Nevertheless, Methuselah is a great first step.

2128 Claretie, Leo. [Arms and the Man], LA REVUE MONDIALE, CXLVIII, 1 June 1922.

Arms and the Man is an amusing comedy and a success. [In French.]

2129 Claretie, Leo. [The Doctor's Dilemma], LA REVUE MONDIALE, CXLVIII (1 June 1922), 335-36.

The Doctor's Dilemma is a vigorous comedy. [In French.]

2130 Constance, Jennie M. "Some Tendencies of the English Speaking Drama," POET LORE, XXXIII (1922), 385-94.

[Passing reference to Shaw in the context indicated by the title.]

2131 Crawford, Jack. "Broadway Goes Back to Shaw," DRAMA (Chicago), XII (April 1922), 233.

If Heartbreak House was a convincing demonstration that Shaw's dialogue acts surprisingly well, Back to Methuselah clinches the argument. Shaw's appeal in Methuselah is often emotional as well as intellectual.

2132 Dubech, Lucien. "L'Anarchie de M. Bernard Shaw" (Bernard Shaw's Anarchy), LA REVUE UNIVERSELLE, 1 June 1922, pp. 667-72.

Shaw's anarchy comprises humor, illogicality and childishness, and is intended to scandalize a puritan country. Mrs. Warren's Profession is not without merit, although Shaw philosophizes and attacks all social values. The Doctor's Dilemma is incoherent and absurd. [In French.]

2133 Ervine, St. John. "The Realistic Test in Drama," YALE REVIEW, ns XI (1922), 285-303.

[Passing mention of Shaw in determining what dramatic realism is.]

2134 "The Eternal Need," SPECTATOR, CXXVIII (1922), 549-51.

Shaw believes the life force exists, but he shows some misunderstanding of the Anglican religion. The true religion of Christ needs to be practiced nowadays.

2135 "The Everyman Theatre: Widowers' Houses Revived," ERA, 6 Sept 1922, p. 9.

Widowers' Houses is obviously a very early play because it is so completely Shavian. Amusing, serious-minded, it exposes slum-landlordism with deadly accuracy.

2136 "Fanny's First Play," TIMES, 7 Feb 1922, p. 8.
Fanny's First Play has almost assumed the stature of a stage classic.

2137 "Fanny's First Play at Everyman's" ILN, CLX (18 Feb 1922), 240.
Fanny's First Play now seems old-fashioned in places, and this is the price Shaw must pay for using the theatre for journalistic purposes.

2138 "First Installment of Shaw Play Seen at the Garrick," NY CLIPPER, LXX (22 March 1922), 20.
However reverent and well-cast this production might be, Back to Methuselah "is just about as suited to the stage as Webster's Dictionary."

2139 Grant, Percy Stickney. ESSAYS (1922; rptd Freeport, NY: Books for Libraries, 1968), pp. 9-32.
Shaw is serious and can write good plays—indeed they throb with life. His fame will not be limited by his choice of contemporary topics or blemishes in his craftsmanship. He stands a chance of becoming immortal.

2140 "Greenwich Village: Candida," THEATRE (NY), XXXV (June 1922), 374, 379.
Candida is the "masterpiece of the Shavian collection."

2141 G[riffith], H[ubert]. "Widowers' Houses," OBS, 10 Sept 1922, p. 9.
Widowers' Houses now seems a flimsy and unconvincing play, and its only interest is in comparison with Shaw's later work.

2142 Hallenam, C. T. "How to Meet Bernard Shaw," NYT, 19 Feb 1922, part VII, p. 2.
It is easier to meet the Prince of Wales than Shaw. You need an appointment and something exceptionally interesting to say.

2143 Henderson, Archibald. "Mr. Shaw Takes Up Prison Reform," NYT, 29 Oct 1922, part III, p. 4.
Shaw's preface to HISTORY OF ENGLISH PRISONS UNDER LOCAL GOVERNMENT by Sidney and Beatrice Webb is "extraordinarily shrewd and caustic."

2144 [Hornblow, Arthur], "Mr. Hornblow Goes to the Play," THEATRE (NY), XXXV (May 1922), 305-06.
Back to Methuselah is mostly witty but interminable, and the value of producing it is questionable.

2145 "How Shaw Bags the Universe," LIT DIG, LXXIII (1 April 1922), 30-31.
The New York production of Back to Methuselah has proved to be a

test of the audience's endurance.

2146 Huneker, Josephine, ed. LETTERS OF JAMES GIBBONS HUNEKER (NY: Scribner's, 1922; Lond: T. Werner Laurie [1922/23]), pp. 14, 18, 23-24, 55, 93, 131-32, 140, 156, 164, 168, 172, 211, 242, 261, 263, 286, 295.
[Non-consecutive passing references.]

2147 "Interim." "Pygmalion de Bernard Shaw" (Bernard Shaw's Pygmalion), FLACARA LITERARA (Bucharest), VII: 20 (1922), 321 [not seen].
[In Roumanian.]

2148 "The Irish Madness," NYT, 22 Aug 1922, p. 16.
Shaw's conciliatory efforts over the Irish civil war appear to be in vain.

2149 Jameson, Storm. "Among the New Books," YALE REVIEW, ns XI (1922), 429-30.
Back to Methuselah demonstrates Shaw's position as "an intellectual giant among dramatists" because he has "drawn power from the centre of his being, from his fundamental and intuitive knowledge of truth."

2150 Kerr, Alfred. "Remeeting Shaw: A German's Impression," LIVING AGE, CCCXIV (1922), 579-81 [originally in BERLINER TAGEBLATT, 16 July 1922; not seen].
[Biographical interview.]

2151 "Last Play is Farther than Theater Guild can Reach," SUN (NY), 14 March 1922, p. 16.
The final moments of Back to Methuselah are undramatic. It is also clear this vision of the future is the product of an old man.

2152 Lewisohn, Ludwig. THE DRAMA AND THE STAGE (NY: Harcourt, Brace, 1922; rptd NY & Lond: Johnson Reprint Corporation, 1968), pp. 158-67.
Shaw knows what the world is like and has never lived in any ivory tower. Heartbreak House is an important and symbolistic play in which Shaw breaks down poeple's protective illusions about such matters as the last war. Nevertheless he is also a great comic playwright whose best plays "quiver with dramatic life." In Back to Methuselah Shaw surprisingly constructs a mysticism based upon what is apparently scientific reasoning. However, his achievement falls short of his earlier work and is not as eloquent. The very qualities of life that sustain Man generally Shaw believes to be negligible.

2153 Lewisohn, Ludwig. "Drama: Shaw and the Theater," NATION (NY), CXIV (1922), 323.
With Back to Methuselah Shaw has put God, Man and the universe back into the theatre which is the theatre's ancient, heroic purpose.

2154 "London Theatres: The Everyman," STAGE, 9 Feb 1922, p. 14.

Fanny's First Play is now somewhat dated but the "torrential spate of dialogue" still amuses.

2155 "London Theatres: The Everyman," STAGE, 9 March 1922, p. 14.

Arms and the Man is well-known and a trenchant attack on warfare.

2156 "London Theatres: The Everyman," STAGE, 20 April 1922, p. 14.

Misalliance is a "characteristically long and many-faceted piece of Shavian discussion," although it can never be called a play.

2157 "London Theatres: The Everyman," STAGE, 25 May 1922, p. 14.

You Never Can Tell "shows Shaw in his happiest vein as a detached laughing philosopher stepping aside in order to deal with human nature and its follies."

2158 "London Theatres: The Everyman," STAGE, 7 Sept 1922, p. 16.

The current topicality of poor housing conditions has probably made this revival of Widowers' Houses more appropriate than it might otherwise have been.

2159 Lunaček, Vladimir. "Cezar i Kleopatra" (Caesar and Cleopatra), OBZOR (Zagreb), LXIII: 172 (1922), 1 [not seen]. [In Croatian.]

2160 M., D. L. "The Drama: A Masterpiece Revived," NATION & ATH (Lond), XXXI (1922), 775-76.

There is a good case to be made that Widowers' Houses is Shaw's best play. It is lean and tense, with no superfluity of dialogue and with relentless action. Relentless, too, is Shaw's attack on things which need reforming.

2161 M., D. L. "The Drama: Fanny's First Play," NATION & ATH (Lond), XXX (1922), 736.

Fanny's First Play is one of Shaw's most finished plays and resembles a ballet of lively ideas. Shaw's cynicism is healthy if a little over-bearing.

2162 MacCarthy, Desmond. "Drama: One Old and Three New Plays," NSTATE, XIX (1922), 13-15; rptd in MacCarthy, pp. 155-59.

Getting Married is all brilliant talk, and although there is no development, there is mild emotional tension created by successive situations. Shaw's "gift for . . . smiting directness of speech, tells magnificently."

2163 MacGowan, Kenneth. "Broadway at the Spring,"

THEATRE ARTS MAGAZINE, VI (1922), 179-82.
[An unfavorable review of Back to Methuselah.]

2164 Mantle, Burns, ed. THE BEST PLAYS OF 1921-22 AND THE YEAR BOOK OF THE DRAMA IN AMERICA (Bost: Small, Maynard, 1922), pp. 476-77, 516-18, 530-31.
[Production details of THE CHOCOLATE SOLDIER, Mrs. Warren's Profession, Back to Methuselah, and Candida.]

2165 Miles, Carlton. "Jaunts Into Brightest England," THEATRE (NY), XXXVI (Oct 1922), 213, 258.
[Biographical.]

2166 "Misalliance," TIMES, 19 April 1922, p. 10.
There are more likeable characters in Misalliance than Shaw's other plays, and his satire is good-humored.

2167 "Misalliance: Interesting Revival at the Everyman," ERA, 19 April 1922, p. 5.
Misalliance is the wittiest of Shaw's later plays. It is a disquisition on marriage, with poignant points, but no nearer a solution than was Getting Married.

2168 "Mr. Shaw and Mr. Wiggam Disagree," CENTURY MAGAZINE (NY), CIV (Aug 1922), 552-62; rptd in Albert Edward Wiggam, THE NEW DECALOGUE OF SCIENCE (Lond & Toronto: n. p. [1924]), pp. 265—87.
[An exchange of correspondence between Shaw and Wiggam on neo-Darwinism and natural selection. Wiggam, inter alia, claims Back to Methuselah reveals Shaw's woeful lack of knowledge about evolution.]

2169 "Molière the Master," TIMES, 19 Jan 1922, p. 8.
Shaw spoke at a meeting of the British Academy where a lecture on Molière was given.

2170 "More Facts about Bernard Shaw," ARTS AND DECORATION, XVIII (Dec 1922), 79.
Shaw is the best contemporary writer of English prose and "the most original and profound of literary critics."

2171 "Mrs. Pat Campbell's Life and Letters from Famous Men," NYT, 19 Nov 1922, part III, p. 4.
[Passing reference to Shaw in a review of Campbell's MY LIFE AND SOME LETTERS.]

2172 "'Much Too Clever,' Says Shaw, 'In a World of Fools,'" NYT, 16 May 1922, p. 1.
[Shaw's humorous reply to the suggestion he should be chairman of the international commission on Russia's debt.]

2173 Murry, John Middleton. "Pencillings," TIMES, 30 June

1922, p. 16; rptd in PENCILLINGS: LITTLE ESSAYS IN LITER-
ATURE (Lond: Collins, 1923), pp. 90-108.
Shaw is an excellent critic of Shakespeare; his judgments force one to
think.

2174 Murry, J[ohn] Middleton. THE PROBLEM OF STYLE
(Lond: Oxford UP, 1922), p. 67.
Shaw and Samuel Butler are "two modern and closely allied masters
of plain prose."

2175 Nadëjde, Iosif. "Pygmalion de Bernard Shaw" (Bernard
Shaw's Pygmalion), ADEVĂRUL (Bucharest), 13 May 1922 [not
seen].
[In Roumanian.]

2176 "News of the Week," SPECTATOR, CXXIX (1922), 257-58.
[A partially critical account of Shaw's views on Irish freedom
fighters.]

2177 "O'London, John." "London Book Talk," NYT, 11 June
1922, part III, p. 20.
Shaw agrees with Dean Inge that fiction should not be used for "diag-
nosing pathological cases." He also believes the Victorian age indulged in too much prudery.

2178 Ould, Hermon. "The Contemporary Theatre," ENGLISH
REVIEW, XXXIX (1922), 39-42, 345-47, 548-50; XXXV (1922),
144-46, 232-35.
[Passing references to Shaw's works in a review of the theatrical
season.]

2179 Parker, Robert Allerton. "The Shaw Endurance Test,"
INDEPENDENT (Bost), CVIII (25 March 1922), 310; rptd in
ARTS & DECORATION, XVI (April 1922), 426-27.
Back to Methuselah is an endurance test which is tiresome and bor-
ing. Shaw's theme is impressive, but the play fails because Shaw does
not adhere to traditional dramatic structures and devices.

2180 Pearson, Hesketh. MODERN MEN AND MUMMERS (NY:
Harcourt, Brace, 1922), pp. 7-32.
"We moderns are the products of Bernard Shaw" who has had an
"ennobling influence on the spirit of his age." Shaw is not very good
on the topic of sex, but is much better on religion and statecraft, and
on two or three occasions has produced works which deal with the
fundamental aspects of life. He reigns supreme as a prophet-artist,
notably in Three Plays for Puritans. [With some biographical detail
and some commentary from Shaw.]

2181 Playgoer. "The Shaw Cycle is Two Down with One to Go,"
SUN (NY), 7 March 1922, p. 14.
Part III of Back to Methuselah is "Shaw at his best and wittiest.

264

Because of its long stretches of dialogue unrelieved by action . . . 'The Tragedy of an Elderly Gentleman' is Shaw at his worst with first one character and then another struggling in a sea of words."

2182 Playgoer. "The Shaw Cycle Makes a Good Start at Garrick," SUN (NY), 28 Feb 1922, p. 12.

Back to Methuselah is "a highly stimulating excursion into speculative philosophy" and, as creative evolution is popular nowadays, Shaw allies himself with the majority for once.

2183 "The Playhouses: Getting Married at Everyman's," ILN, CLX (8 April 1922), 532.

Getting Married is characteristically Shavian with the addition of an overall scheme.

2184 Prazakova, Klara. "Armada Spasy Na jevisti-Shawova hra Major Barbara" (The Salvation Army on the Stage—Shaw's Major Barbara) JEVISTÉ, III (1922), 125ff [not seen].
[Cited in Amalric, p. 476. In Czech.]

2185 Prazakova, Klara. "Posledi-Shawovo dilo-satira a mysterium" (Shaw's Latest Work—A Satire and Mystery Play), JEVISTÉ, III (1922), 440-44 [not seen].
[Cited in Amalric, p. 476. In Czech.]

2186 Prazakova, Klara. "Posledni Shawovo dilo: biologicka pentalogie" (Shaw's Latest Work: A Biological Pentateuch), JEVISTÉ, III (1922), 375-79 [not seen].
[Cited in Amalric, p. 477. In Czech.]

2187 Prazakova, Klara. "Posledni Shawovo dilo v sluzbach nabozenstvi dv-acatého Sloteti" (Shaw's Latest Work in the Service of Twentieth-Century Religion) JEVISTÉ, III (1922), 281ff [not seen].
[Cited in Amalric p. 476. In Czech.]

2188 Ruyssen, Henri. "Le Théâtre anglais" (The English Theatre), LA REVUE GERMANIQUE, 1922, pp. 287-302.

Back to Methuselah is not a play but a philosophical treatise—the gospel of a new religion, creative evolution. The long preface is the most interesting part of this work. [In French.]

2189 S., E. G. "Fanny First Play: At the Everyman," BOOKMAN (Lond), LXI (March 1922), 288.

Fanny's First Play is full of "rich comedy, despite the fact that its humour 'dates' more than that of any Shavian play."

2190 Scheidweiler, Paula. "Mannheimer Theater" (Mannheim Theatre), DIE NEUE SCHAUBÜHNE, IV: 2 (Feb 1922), 44-47.

The Doctor's Dilemma is the most brilliant of recent comedies. [In German.]

2191 "Second Version of Shaw Play Seen at the Garrick," and "Back to Methuselah Last Installment Runs to Year 31,920," NY CLIPPER, LXX (5 April 1922), 20.
Part III of Back to Methuselah is uninteresting and unpleasant; Part IV contains burlesque which lightens the play. Part V, though talky, holds up quite well and is not overly long.

2192 "Shakespeare's Plays," TIMES, 8 Dec 1922, p. 10.
Shaw participated in a meeting about the proposed Shakespeare National Theatre.

2193 "Shaw as Exhibit 'A.,' " NYT, 22 March 1922, p. 6.
Shaw has rebutted Sir Arthur Quiller-Couch's statements on alcohol.

2194 "Shaw Finds Irish Dispute 'Too Silly,' " NYT, 21 Aug 1922, p. 13.
After a visit to Dublin Shaw believes the Irish political leaders do not know what they are doing.

2195 "Shaw, George Bernard," THE NEW INTERNATIONAL ENCYCLOPAEDIA, 2nd ed (NY: Dodd, Mead, 1922), vol XX, 796-97.
[An encyclopedia entry surveying the life and works.]

2196 "Shaw Might Consider a Political Job for £4,000 a Year and Handsome Pension," NYT, 24 Feb 1922, p. 1.
Shaw has declined an offer to be the Parliamentary candidate for West Edinburgh.

2197 "Shaw's Candida," SUN (NY), 23 March 1922, p. 16.
Candida is Shaw's most easily acted piece and lends itself to a variety of interpretations.

2198 Shipp, Horace. "The Contemporary Theatre," ENGLISH REVIEW, XXXIV (1922), 145-48, 439-41.
[Passing references to Shaw in a review of the theatrical season.]

2199 Svrček, Jaroslav. "Německa činohra" (German Film of Candida), ROVNOST (Brno), No. 167 (1922), 6 [not seen].
[In Czech.]

2200 "3 Evenings to Play Single Shaw Drama," NYT, 23 Jan 1922, p. 8.
The presentation of Back to Methuselah over three evenings will be a unique experiment in New York. [See also "Word from Mr. Shaw," NYT, 5 Feb 1922, part VI, p. 1 on Shaw's reaction to changes requested for this production.]

2201 "Tolstoy's Works," TIMES, 29 April 1922, p. 17.
[The text of a letter by Shaw and others on the need for a complete English edition of Tolstoy's works, with additional comments by Thomas Hardy.]

2202 "Topics of the Day: The Prisoner," SPECTATOR, CXXIX (1922), 165-67.

Shaw's preface to Mr. & Mrs. Sidney Webb's HISTORY OF ENGLISH PRISONS UNDER LOCAL GOVERNMENT is full of witty polemics. His argument may not be faultless, but Shaw makes some useful points about delinquency.

2203 Turner, W. J. "Chronicles: Drama," LOND MERCURY, VI (1922), 88-90.

Getting Married is a crude morality play full of amusing and brilliant dialogue. The characters are not fully rounded, although they are "modelled with extraordinary skill." Shaw shows no understanding of passionate love.

2204 "Widower's Houses [sic]," TIMES, 5 Sept 1922, p. 8.

Widowers' Houses succeeds most when Shaw is at his most satirical.

2205 Woollcott, Alexander. "The Play," NYT, 28 Feb 1922, p. 17; rptd in NYTTR 1920-1926, [n. p.].

Back to Methuselah is a political fantasy which contains some beautiful and searching things and is worth staging.

2206 Woollcott, Alexander. "The Play," NYT, 23 March 1922, p. 11; rptd in NYTTR 1920-1926, [n. p.].

Candida is Shaw's best play, probably the "finest comedy written for the English theatre in the last hundred years." It will be read and performed long after Back to Methuselah is forgotten.

2207 Woollcott, Alexander. "The Play: No Matter," NYT, 14 March 1922, p. 11; rptd in NYTTR 1920-1926, [n. p.].

There are magnificent speeches in Back to Methuselah, but Shaw's straining prophecies paralyze the imagination and are devoid of humor.

2208 Woollcott, Alexander. "Second Thoughts on First Nights," NYT, 30 April 1922, part VII, p. 1.

[Largely Shaw's letter to George C. Tyler on the American production of Pygmalion.]

2209 "Worse than Shakespeare," NYT, 18 June 1922, part II, p. 4.

[An unfocussed editorial on Shaw's criticism of J. M. Barrie.]

2210 "Wratislavius." "Teatrul Naţional, Erou si soldat de Bernard Shaw" (Bernard Shaw's Arms and the Man at the National Theatre), OPINIA (Jassy), 23 Sept 1922 [not seen].

[In Roumanian.]

2211 Young, Stark. "Back to Creation," NEW REP, XXX (1922), 80-81.

Back to Methuselah is "the same Shaw, with his argument, his infectious animation of words, his way of being now in earnest and now posing a little; the same Shavian social comedy, delightful, insistent, witty, insolent, eloquent, overlong, tiresome before it is over, but better after all than anything else of its kind."

1923

2212 Archer, William. THE OLD DRAMA AND THE NEW: AN ESSAY IN RE-VALUATION (Bost: Small, Maynard, 1923), pp. 35, 48-49, 113-14, 126-27, 279, 283, 307, 310, 338, 340-57, 363-64, 369, 383.
Shaw may be the most brilliant intellect in the theatre, but he is not a born dramatist because he lacks the "power of projection . . . . He cannot throw his characters outside himself." His characters are no more than ingenious and amusing puppets. To be a good dramatist he needs to practice much more self-discipline and not to sacrifice the logic of character and situation just to gain a momentary effect. That is not to say Shaw does not have his brilliant side, but with the possible exception of Candida, none of his plays is consistently good all the way through.

2213 Arns, Karl. "Fremde Literatur" (Foreign Literature), DIE SCHÖNE LITERATUR, XXIV: 8 (15 April 1923), 150-52.
Fanny's First Play and Heartbreak House reveal that the main features of Shaw's plays are satire, parody, and exaggeration. His dramatic composition is not always satisfactory. The preface to Heartbreak seems more important than the play. [In German.]

2214 "Back to Methuselah! A Meta-biological Pentateuch," ERA, 17 Oct 1923, p. 8.
Back to Methuselah "is certainly the most remarkable contribution to dramatic literature of the century. It is a curious conglomeration of beautiful poetry and Shavian wit."

2215 "Back to Methuselah: Production in Birmingham," STAGE, 18 Oct 1923, p. 17.
The topicality of Part II of Back To Methuselah will prove a defect in the long run simply because succeeding generations will not understand the political allusions.

2216 Bakshy, Alexander. THE THEATRE UNBOUND (Lond: Cecil Palmer, 1923), pp. 108-15.
Shaw's later plays failed to fulfill the promise of the earlier because the raisonneur is too dominant. Shaw is at his most successful when he presents life (rather than discussing or representing it).

2217 Baughan, E. A. "Back to Methuselah," FORT REV, ns CXIV (Nov 1923), 827-34.
Back to Methuselah has its lapses, but it reveals Shaw's intense

genius. The play is moving, full of wit, humor and "sympathy for human suffering. In no other play has he so opened to us the doors and windows of his mind."

2218 B[enchley], R[obert] C. "Drama: Three Little Rascals," LIFE, LXXXI (8 Feb 1923), 18.
The really terrible first act of Jitta's Atonement suffers from predictability, but the play becomes more amusing as it goes along.

2219 "A 'Bernard Shaw Festival,'" TIMES, 8 Sept 1923, p. 6.
[An announcement of the forthcoming production of Shaw plays at the Birmingham Repertory Theatre.]

2220 "Bernard Shaw on Statesmen," NYT, 2 Sept 1923, part VII, p. 8.
Shaw has some strong opinions of how politicians should be selected, but some of his proposed methods are flawed.

2221 "Bernard Shaw on Vegetarians," NYT, 9 Dec 1923, part IV, p. 10.
[A report of Shaw's remarks to the Vegetarian Society of London University.]

2222 "Bertha Kalich in New Role," NYT, 18 Jan 1923, p. 16; rptd in NYTTR 1920-1926, [n. p.].
Shaw is the adapter of Jitta's Atonement and his hand can be seen only here and there. It is really the work of the original author, Siegfried Trebitsch.

2223 Birrell, Francis. "The Drama: Mr. Shaw's Pot-Boiler," NATION & ATH (Lond), XXXIII (1923), 500.
Perhaps Shaw wrote Fanny's First Play so quickly that he did not have time to spoil it, for it is certainly one of his best achievements and certainly not the pot-boiler he called it.

2224 Brandenburg, Hans. "Shaw, Bernard, Cashel Byrons Beruf" (Bernard Shaw's Cashel Byron's Profession), DIE SCHÖNE LITERATUR, XXIV: 6 (15 March 1923), 113.
In Cashel Byron's Profession boxing is presented as a view of life. Shaw's well-written play frequently resembles a sketch or film. [In German.]

2225 Brock, H. I. "Saint Joan and Bernard Shaw," NYT, 30 Dec 1923, part IV, pp. 3, 8.
Shaw is an "inexorable image breaker" and has suffused St. Joan's character with commonsense, although she is "no less miraculous" for that. A letter to Emanuel Reicher on his attempts to cut the script of Heartbreak House shows Shaw's attitude to such ideas.

2226 "Candida," TIMES, 10 June 1923, p. 12.
It may be the eccentricity of the characters in Candida which prevents the play from dating.

2227 "Charity Pays More for a Shaw Play," NYT, 25 Nov 1923, part II, p. 4.

In response to a request for special financial dispensations in producing his plays, Shaw explains at length why amateurs pay higher royalties than professionals.

2228 Claretie, Leo. "Pygmalion," LA REVUE MONDIALE, CLVI (1 Nov 1923), 95-96.

Pygmalion is a rather disconcerting fantasy, a Rousseauist attack on worldly society. The play teems with mad improbabilities and lacks feeling. [In French.]

2229 Corbin, John. [The Devil's Disciple], NYT, 6 May 1923, part VII, p. 1; rptd in NYTTR 1920-26, [n. p.].

The Devil's Disciple is only superficially melodramatic and does not contain any novel philosophy. Shaw is a "farce comedian" who wants to enforce his ideas.

2230 Corbin, John. "The Play," NYT, 29 Dec 1923, p. 8; rptd in NYTTR 1920-1926, [n. p.].

Saint Joan is an impressive play because of the way in which Shaw reveals the genesis of martyrdom. However, it is full of all the well-known Shavian tricks and ideas.

2231 Cumberland, Gerald. WRITTEN IN FRIENDSHIP: A BOOK OF REMINISCENCES (Lond: Grant Richards, 1923 [not seen]; NY: Brentano's, 1924), pp. 24-25, 32, 59, 82, 91, 102, 142-44, 146-47, 246.

[Largely biographical snippets.] "All Shaw's books might be included in a 'How To' series."

2232 Desmond, Shaw. "Dunsany, Yeats, and Shaw: Trinity of Magic," BOOKMAN (NY), LVIII (Nov 1923), 260-66.

Shaw is a "flippant satyr" who is able to conjure with words, and loves to "enshroud himself in the mystery of paradox." The real Shaw appears in Keegan in John Bull's Other Island.

2233 "The Devil's Disciple," THEATRE (NY), XXXVIII (July 1923), 17, 20.

Even though Shaw's basic insincerity and shallowness flaw The Devil's Disciple, the "pyrotechnics and scintillating wit of the dialogue" keep the audience's interest.

2234 "Devil's Disciple: Shaw Revival at the Garrick," NY CLIPPER, LXXI (25 April 1923), 14.

Although The Devil's Disciple is an early play, giving only hints of the wit and satire to come, it is an effective melodrama.

2235 Dukes, Ashley. THE YOUNGEST DRAMA: STUDIES OF FIFTY DRAMATISTS (Lond: Ernest Benn, 1923), pp. 3, 11, 17, 44-47, 67; p. 44 rptd in Evans, pp. 273-74.

Shaw is the sincerest modern dramatist and he has also remained consistently advanced in his views (which have covered numerous topics). His moral passion has spoken out against hypocrisy, prostitution, slavery, poverty, and disorder. Wrongheaded people have thought Shaw was "trivial because he was witty, and shallow because he was paradoxical." However, they were simply victims of his intellectual pyrotechnics which reveal the reverse of everything. He has created unromantic heroes, such as Bluntschli in Arms and the Man, who challenge the received opinion of the past, present and future.

2236 "Early Shaw," NYT, 24 April 1923, p. 24; rptd in NYTTR 1920-1926, [n. p.].
The Devil's Disciple reveals Shaw was both too determined to be original and "too solicitous to provide 'good theatre.'" Thus it is a mixture of melodrama and philosophic paradox.

2237 "Everyman Theatre," TIMES, 3 April 1923, p. 8.
The externals of The Doctor's Dilemma may have dated, but essentially the play remains a thought-provoking work.

2238 Farjeon, Herbert. "Shaw and Supershaw," SAT REV, CXXXVI (1923), 436-37.
In Back to Methuselah Shaw creates his notion of the superman in his own image, although Shaw's reversal of the order of nature is not to be believed.

2239 Fawcett, James Waldo. "One Hundred Critics Gauge Walt Whitman's Fame," NYT, 10 June 1923, part III, pp. 6, 14.
[Title describes. Shaw's estimate is placed first.]

2240 Fehr, Bernhard. DIE ENGLISCHE LITERATUR DES 19. UND 20. JAHRHUNDERTS (English Literature of the 19th and 20th Centuries) (Berlin: Akademische Verlagsgesellschaft Athenaion, 1923), pp. 300, 303-04, 313, 323, 338, 389, 391, 476-77, 485-97, 500, 508.
[Passing references to Shaw, and a chapter on his personality, his "Ibsenism," his view of Shakespeare, his idea of the life force, and his attitude towards religion. In German.]

2241 Gillet, L. "En écoutant Vive Mathusalem" (On Hearing Back to Methuselah), REVUE DES DEUX MONDES, XVIII (1 Dec 1923), 674-85.
Back to Methuselah reveals Shaw's conception of humanity and his new vision of evolution. It is an interminable, cold play. Throughout, there is much humor and mockery of contemporary affairs. [In French.]

2242 Gillison, J. A. "Mr. Shaw on Jenner," NATION & ATH, XXXII (1923), 718.
Shaw [in "Jenner," NATION & ATH, 3 Feb 1923, pp. 678-80] demon-

strates his ability to write, but clearly does not know what he is writing about. His article lacks substance and evidence to substantiate his views. [See also subsequent correspondence, pp. 749-50, 783-84, and 819-21.]

2243 Grein, J. T. "The World of the Theatre: Shaw in Flemish," ILN, CLXII (27 Jan 1923), 134; rptd in THE NEW WORLD OF THE THEATRE 1923-1924 (Lond: Martin Hopkinson, 1924), pp. 22-24.

A revival of The Philanderer in Antwerp reveals this is a wonderful comedy if it can be produced properly. What it needs most is lively, swift acting to counteract what can be viewed as Shaw's verbosity and love of side-issues.

2244 Guedalla, Philip. "Under the Knife: XIII: Mr. Bernard Shaw," ILN, CLXIII (20 Oct 1923), 692; rptd in MEN OF LETTERS (Lond: Hodder & Stoughton [1927]), pp. 87-98.

Even at an early age Shaw has always been an elder statesman ready to lecture his fellow countrymen, often invoking the names of great men in his support. In contrast to contemporaneous dramatists, Shaw presents us with fantastic puppets (instead of characters) who inhabit a kind of grotesque fairyland. He always breaks the so-called rules of drama, largely because he is a dealer in words.

2245 Guiterman, Arthur. "Bernard Shaw's History," NYT, 6 May 1923, part II, p. 6.

The Devil's Disciple reveals Shaw's "queer notions of American history and geography." [See also "Geographer Shaw," NYT, 11 June 1923, p. 12. and "Shaw's American History," NYT, 13 June 23, p. 18.]

2246 Hammond, Josephine. "The Quillurgence of Shaw," PERSONALIST, IV (1923), 149-65, 253-60; V (1924), 33-46.

Shaw lets his pen run away with him, as Back to Methuselah demonstrates. However, he is intensely earnest, wants to lead people into an acceptance of his new commandments, and wants to be seen as a prophet-philosopher. In Mrs. Warren's Profession we have dramatized sociology which led to second-rate imitations. Shaw should have spent more time perfecting his dramatic art. His Dramatic Opinions and Essays is much better because it was written before his decline into garrulity. The latter notwithstanding, we are left with a few fine plays.

2247 "Hergesheimer Hustled by the Literary Giants," NYT, 8 April 1923, part IV, p. 3.

For a variety of reasons, Shaw does not believe the cinema threatens the written word.

2248 Hevesi, Sandor. SHAW BREVARIUM: AZ ÍRÓ, AZ EMBER ÉS A MŰVEK (Shaw Brevarium: The Author, The Man, and The Works) (Budapest: Rózsavolgyi, 1923).

[Analyzes the most prominent English, French and German critical writings on Shaw, and provides extracts from Shaw's prose and plays, emphasizing his socialist outlook. In Hungarian.]

2249 "Jitta's Atonement with Bertha Kalich at the Comedy," NY CLIPPER, LXX (24 Jan 1923), 14.
The first act of Jitta's Atonement is dramatically convincing.

2250 Jones, Henry Arthur. "Bernard Shaw as a Thinker," ENGLISH REVIEW, XXXVI (1923), 532-36; XXXVII (1923), 65-74, 227-31, 644-48; XXXVIII (1924), 345-50.
Shaw is wrong in thinking that the diverse nations can be changed suddenly and molded into an homogenous civilization of his devising. He has also failed to realize the various factors which prevent most people from being assured of a comfortable position in life. He blames moral and spiritual factors when, in fact, everything has a material cause. Furthermore, it is illogical to believe that the stupidity of the leisured and educated is responsible for the situation.

2251 "Kahn Sees Advance in American Music," NYT, 7 Nov 1923, p. 29.
Mary Lawton, after interviewing Shaw, reports he believes there will be a universal prohibition of hard liquor.

2252 Knudsen, Hans. "Shaw, Bernard, Fannys erstes Stück" (Bernard Shaw: Fanny's First Play), DIE SCHONE LITERATUR, XXIV: 21-22 (15 Nov 1923), 417.
Fanny's First Play is not as brilliant as Shaw's later plays, but like his better works it is full of witticisms and paradoxical statements. [In German.]

2253 [Kuhe, Ernest]. "Drama," THE ANNUAL REGISTER 1922 (Lond: Longmans, Green, 1923), part II, pp. 75-79.
In the past season Shaw has been represented on the London stage only by revivals.

2254 Lewisohn, Ludwig. "Drama: Three Plays," NATION (NY), CXVI (1923), 578.
[A favorable review of The Devil's Disciple.]

2255 "Libraries and Adult Education," TIMES, 20 Sept 1923, p. 7.
[A report of a conference where a paper on Shaw was given. Shaw "was not an original thinker. He co-ordinated the views of a great many writers, but his Socrates was undoubtedly (Samuel) Butler."]

2256 Littell, Robert. "Nine in a Taxi," NEW REP, XXXIV (1923) 299-300; rptd in READ AMERICA FIRST (1926; rptd Freeport, NY: Books for Libraries, 1968), pp. 172-82.
The Devil's Disciple provokes admiration and condemnation, although the exact response varies according to one's own outlook and temper-

ament.

2257 "London Theatres: The Everyman," STAGE, 1 Feb 1923, p. 18.

"The Shavian gibes and barbs [in The Philanderer] seem less pungent and pointed" than when the play was first produced.

2258 "London Theatres: The Everyman," STAGE, 5 April 1923, p. 18.

[A favorable review of The Doctor's Dilemma.]

2259 MacLachlan, H. D. C. "Studies in Sin: Sinning at Long Range," CHRISTIAN CENTURY, XL (22 March 1923), 361-65.

Even though Widowers' Houses has a romantic element, it focusses on abuse of the poor. Christians should take a role in reorganizing society to achieve equality and justice.

2260 Mais, S. P. B. SOME MODERN AUTHORS (NY: Dodd, Mead, 1923), pp. 311-17.

Shaw's reputation is variable, but he is a phenomenon in that he is a "Puritan without hypocrisy." His greatest strength is that he is an ascetic farceur. The best, enduring plays are Man and Superman and Candida.

2261 Mantle, Burns, ed. THE BEST PLAYS OF 1922-23 AND THE YEAR BOOK OF THE DRAMA IN AMERICA (Bost: Small, Maynard, 1923), pp. 17, 561-62.

The Devil's Disciple pleased its audience and enjoyed a good run.

2262 Marbury, Elisabeth. MY CRYSTAL BALL: REMINIS-CENCES (NY: Boni & Liveright, 1923), pp. 106-09.

[Genial reminiscences by an early Shaw agent.]

2263 Marcel, Gabriel. "Pygmalion de Bernard Shaw" (Bernard Shaw's Pygmalion), LA NOUVELLE REVUE FRANCAISE, No. 122 (1 Nov 1923), 618-19.

Pygmalion is one of Shaw's best works, full of tender fantasy and critical intelligence. Shaw's French translators take liberties with the original text. [In French.]

2264 Margolin, N. S. "Iz tsikla neosushchvlennyx postanovok: Dom, gde razbiraiut serdtsa" (From a Cycle of Unrealized Pro-ductions: Heartbreak House), EKHO (Moscow), No. 7 (15 Feb 1923), 15-16.

[Meyerhold prevented Eisenstein's first planned production of Heart-break House. In Russian.]

2265 Miall, Agnes M. "Glimpses of the Great," NYT, 7 Jan 1923, part IV, p. 1.

[Brief details of an interview with Shaw.]

2266 "Mr. Shaw's Pygmalion in French: Puzzled Actors and

Critics," TIMES, 1 Oct 1923, p. 11.
Shaw's blend of thesis play and social comedy in Pygmalion confused everyone concerned with this Paris production.

2267 "Mr. Shaw's Saint Joan," TIMES, 29 Dec 1923, p. 8.
Saint Joan is to be produced in New York. A private performance has already been "enthusiastically received."

2268 "Mr. Shaw's Tribute to Sheridan," TIMES, 27 Oct 1923, p. 12.
Shaw has unveiled a memorial to Sheridan at Bath, and given a speech on Sheridan.

2269 Morgan, Charles. "The Coming Race: Letter to George Bernard Shaw," REV OF REVS, LXXVIII (Dec 1923), 438-42.
Back to Methuselah raises many points about creative evolution, but Shaw has failed to cover several ramifications of his theories.

2270 Nevison, Henry W. CHANGES AND CHANCES (Lond: Nisbet, 1923), pp. 191-92.
[An anecdote about Shaw reviewing Wagner for the DAILY CHRONICLE.]

2271 "News in Brief," TIMES, 5 Sept 1923, p. 7.
Shaw is to unveil a memorial to Sheridan in Bath.

2272 [News of the Week], SPECTATOR, CXXX (1923), 1071.
Shaw and G. K. Chesterton have debated the meaning of R. U. R.

2273 Nicolaysen, Lorenz. BERNARD SHAW: EINE PHILOSOPHISCHE STUDIE (Bernard Shaw: A Philosophical Study) (Munich: Rösl, 1923).
[This strange pamphlet, loaded with philosophical jargon, is only tangentially related to Shaw, despite its title. In German.]

2274 Nicolaysen, Lorenz. "Untersuchungen ueber Bernard Shaw" (An Examination About Bernard Shaw), Ph. D. dissertation, University of Hamburg, 1923.
[In German.]

2275 "Offers Shaw Irish Remedy," NYT, 16 March 1923, p. 6.
Shaw believes that all Irish Free Staters should be provided with arms and be ready to kill rioters. [See also: "His Plan Proves Successful," NYT, 3 May 1923, p. 18.]

2276 Pearson, Hesketh. "G. B. S. v. G. K. C.," ADELPHI, I (1923-24), 298-306; rptd in LIVING AGE, CCCXIX (1923), 35-39; rptd as "Shaw--Chesterton: Two Masters of Wit and Paradox Break a Lance over the Absorption of Alcohol," in Louis Leopold Biancolli, ed, BOOK OF GREAT CONVERSATIONS (NY: Simon & Schuster, 1948), pp. 498-506.
[A "transcription" of a conversation between Shaw and Chesterton,

"the two greatest word jugglers of the century."]

2277 Playgoer. "Kalich Comes to Comedy in Jitta's Atonement," SUN (NY), 18 Jan 1923, p. 14.
Jitta's Atonement would benefit from more of Shaw's own humor, although the dialogue and characterization improve as Shaw takes a firmer grip on this adaptation.

2278 "Politička satira Bernara Šo-a: karikaturi Lojda Džordža i Askvita na bini" (Political Satire of Bernard Shaw: Caricatures of Lloyd George and Asquith on the Stage), VREME (Belgrade), III (1923), 696 [not seen].
[On Back to Methuselah. In Serbian.]

2279 "Premieres of the Week: The Philanderer," ERA, 1 Feb 1923, p. 12.
The Philanderer has not dated. "It is one of those philosophical farces at which Shaw shines."

2280 "Provincial Productions: Back to Methuselah," STAGE, 11 Oct 1923, p. 17.
Part I of Back to Methuselah is the most impressive, and the dialogue (at times) rises to poetic heights even though it is written in prose.

2281 Rathbun, Stephen. "Theater Guild Presents Saint Joan, the New Shaw Play, at Garrick Theater," SUN & GLOBE (NY), 29 Dec 1923, p. 4.
Saint Joan is very interesting, although lacking a thoroughly Shavian touch. Shaw's treatment of Joan is far less mordant than Voltaire's.

2282 "Repertory," STAGE, 18 Oct 1923, p. 14.
The provincial repertory system has helped make possible the staging of Back to Methuselah in Birmingham.

2283 R[hodes], R. C[rompton]. "Back to Methuselah," BIRMINGHAM POST, 11 Oct 1923, p. 8.
In Part II of Back to Methuselah Shaw has not entirely succeeded in conveying pettiness without being petty. His effort to express his notion of Man's collective will to survive is obscured in jargon. Shaw's satire is biting but too prolonged.

2284 R[hodes], R. C[rompton]. "Back to Methuselah," BIRMINGHAM POST, 12 Oct 1923, p. 8.
Although Part III of Back to Methuselah is set 250 years ahead, Shaw shows things have changed little. But his view is clouded somewhat by the less than favorable production conditions.

2285 R[hodes], R. C[rompton]. "Back to Methuselah: The Last Phase," BIRMINGHAM POST, 13 Oct 1923, p. 10; rptd in Evans, pp. 270-71.
Part V of Back to Methuselah ends with a speech which "surpasses in beauty and profundity any words of John Milton." Indeed, all Shaw's

276

speculations here are brilliant, sometimes beyond immediate comprehension. He ultimately emerges as being at his greatest, whether one accepts him as theologian, philosopher, or dramatist.

2286 R[hodes], R. [Crompton]. "The New Shaw Play," BIRMINGHAM POST, 10 Oct 1923, p. 6.
In Part I of Back to Methuselah Shaw's thesis (on Man's will to secure the survival of the species) is stated with admirable simplicity. Shaw's conception is essentially audacious.

2287 Rice, Virginia. "On Not Interviewing Shaw," BOOKMAN (NY), LVI (Feb 1923), 722-24.
[An account of a meeting/non-interview with Shaw.]

2288 "Riot at Shaw Comedy," NYT, 10 Feb 1923, p. 10.
Serbian students halted the performance of Arms and the Man at a Czech theatre because Shaw's play ridiculed Balkan soldiers.

2289 Ryder, H. Osborne. "Back to Methuselah: A Drama of Personalism," METHODIST REVIEW, CVI (Jan 1923), 70-77.
Back to Methuselah is a dramatic presentation of the philosophy of personalism which holds that reality is personal rather than impersonal. Creative evolution is closely related to personalism.

2290 Schneider, Louis. "Les premières à Paris: Pygmalion" (First Nights in Paris: Pygmalion), LA SUISSE, 4 Oct 1923.
The adapters of Pygmalion have given the play a Parisian setting which is out of keeping with the piece's essentially English character. The result is that everything is rather obscure, but not unpleasant. [In French.]

2291 Shanks, Edward. "The Drama: Faith and Unfaith," OUTLOOK (Lond), LII (8 Sept 1923), 194.
Shaw demands that tradition be proved right before he will accept it, while G. K. Chesterton holds exactly the opposite viewpoint.

2292 "Shaw and the Guild Again," NYT, 6 May 1923, part VII, p. 1.
There has been an exchange of correspondence between Shaw and the Theatre Guild, New York, over the casting of Dick Dudgeon in The Devil's Disciple. Shaw insisted on final approval.

2293 "Shaw Scolds the Writing Craft," ARTS AND DECORATION, XVIII (March 1923), 87.
Shaw's comments about the Shakespeare Memorial theatre reveal yet again that he will always take "the opposite side of any popular idea or ideal." He is the buffoon who loves controversy for its own sake.

2294 "Sheridan and Shaw," NYT, 25 Nov 1923, part II, p. 6.
Shaw has unveiled a tablet to Sheridan in Bath and provided some comments on him. Of course, Shaw could not be expected to approve Sheridan's high comedies.

2295 "Topics of the Times," NYT, 7 March 1923, p. 14.
Shaw's proposal for restoring peace in Ireland has some merit, but it is rather belated.

2296 Wilde, Percival. THE CRAFTSMANSHIP OF THE ONE-ACT PLAY (Bost: Little, Brown, 1923), pp. 12, 38, 40, 56, 91, 125, 164, 217, 235, 272, 301, 345, 359.
[Frequent citation of Shaw and his work in this "how to" handbook.]

2297 Wilson, Edmund. "The Theatre," DIAL, LXXV (1923), 100.
The Devil's Disciple is not very interesting Shaw, and this revival is not very good.

2298 Wood, Herbert G. "G. Bernard Shaw and Religion," CONTEMPORARY REVIEW, CXXIII (1923), 623-28; rptd in LIVING ISSUES IN RELIGIOUS THOUGHT: FROM GEORGE FOX TO BERTRAND RUSSELL (Lond: Allen & Unwin, 1924; rptd Freeport, NY: Books for Libraries, 1966), pp. 122-32.
Although Shaw's views on religion suffer somewhat from his flippant style, he offers practical ideas for a religious revival. However, his reading of the Bible is often selective and biased so that he can support his own views on subjects such as marriage.

2299 Woollcott, Alexander. [Saint Joan], NYH, 29 Dec 1923, p. 3 [not seen]; rptd in Evans, pp. 275-77.
Despite defects, Saint Joan contains greatness, and the epilogue is particuarly important.

2300 Wright, Ralph. "Only Twelve Years," NSTATE, XXI (1923), 419.
Fanny's First Play is dated with jokes and moments of seriousness which have lost their meaning today. It is very funny, but "seems at times intolerably intolerant" and provincial.

2301 "You Never Can Tell," TIMES, 5 June 1923, p. 16.
Emphasis on the seaside setting in You Never Can Tell gives this production a "new and unexpected flavor."

2302 Young, Stark. "At the Neighborhood," NEW REP, XXXVI (1923), 257.
The Shewing-up of Blanco Posnet is "the wildest farce, now tiresome, now compelling, a melodramatic riot, insistent preachment, penny dreadful and Wild West Morality in one."

2303 Young, Stark. "Saint Joan," NEW REP, XXXVII (1923-24), 205-06.
Post-performance reflection on Saint Joan renders the play better than it really is. Its greatness lies in the potential it suggests and promises rather than in what Shaw actually achieves on stage.

1924

2304 Adcock, St. John. "G. B. S. at Home," BOOKMAN (Lond), LXVII (Dec 1924), 150-53.
[An interview, with substantial quotations attributed to Shaw.]

2305 Agate, James. "The Dramatic World," STIMES, 24 Feb 1924, p. 4.
Back to Methuselah "remains one of the faultiest productions which has ever issued from a great mind, and its performance, for those who deem the theatre to be a place of theatrical entertainment, is a mystery and a mistake."

2306 Agate, James. "The Dramatic World," STIMES, 30 March 1924, p. 6 and 29 June 1924, p. 6; rptd in THE CONTEMPORARY THEATRE, 1924 (Lond: Chapman & Hall, 1925), pp. 67-78; rptd in RED LETTER NIGHTS (Lond: Cape, 1944), pp. 211-18; rptd in JAMES AGATE: AN ANTHOLOGY (NY: Hill & Wang, 1961), p. 65-70; rptd in Evans, pp. 288-90; rptd in DRAMA CRITICISM: DEVELOPMENTS SINCE IBSEN: A CASEBOOK, ed by Arnold P. Hinchliffe (Lond: Macmillan, 1979), pp. 156-162.
Shaw's preface to Saint Joan is full of sanity, erudition and flippancy, and Shaw tries to prove his portrait of St. Joan is the right one while everyone else's is wrong. However, Shaw tends to overdo matters, and one can have too much of a good thing. The play itself is interesting, if uneven—the epilogue, for instance, is really unnecessary after all that has gone before.

2307 Andréadès, A. "La Sainte Jeanne de Bernard Shaw" (Bernard Shaw's St. Joan), REVUE POLITIQUE ET LITTERAIRE, LXII (20 Dec 1924), 854-57.
The idea of Shaw treating the subject of Joan of Arc was something to be feared, but in the end the fear proved baseless. For Shaw, Joan is a saint and the portrait he traces of her and her persecutors is an exact one historically. The first tableau is lively and picturesque; the succeeding ones are verbose. The epilogue, a typical Shavian phantasmagoria, shows that the earth is not yet ready to welcome its saints. [In French.]

2308 Araquistain, Luis. "El laborismo inglés. Los intelectuales" (The English Labour Party: The Intellectuals), REPERTORIO AMERICANO (Costa Rica), VIII: 7 (5 May 1924), 115-16 [not seen].
[Cited in Rodríguez (MS). In Spanish.]

2309 Archer, William. "The Psychology of G. B. S.," BOOKMAN (Lond), LXVII (Dec 1924), 139-41; rptd in LIVING AGE, CCCXXIV (1925), 206-09; rptd in Evans, pp. 300-04.

Shaw's failing is that he always attempts to make the world conform to his own preconceived notions. "Voltaire, with no more genius or eloquence than Shaw's, revolutionised the world; Shaw, a professed revolutionist, will revolutionise nothing."

2310 "Arms and the Man in Berlin," TIMES, 9 Oct 1924, p. 13.
[A report of cuts made in the Berlin production of Arms and the Man at the request of the Bulgarian minister, with a letter by Shaw.]

2311 Armstrong, Martin. "Methuselah and Mr. Shaw," SPECTATOR, CXXXII (1924), 320-21.
Although in his preface to Back to Methuselah Shaw promised plays without the "distractions and embellishments" of earlier works, he begins to fulfill that promise only in the fourth play of the cycle. The first and last plays are "the most impressive" Shaw has produced.

2312 Arns, Karl. "G. K. Chesterton," DER GRAL, XVIII: 4 (Jan 1924), 210-11.
Shaw is a heartless writer without poetry; he is full of irony and "expression." [In German.]

2313 "Back to Methuselah: A Sombre Week of Shaw," ERA, 27 Feb 1923, p. 8.
Back to Methuselah fails as a whole and in its parts. The play is too long and tedious, and nothing dramatic happens. Its thought is too shadowy and vague to make a real contribution, and it can be doubted whether it means anything at all.

2314 Baeza, Ricardo. "Bernard Shaw y Hauptmann" (Bernard Shaw and Hauptmann), REVISTA DE OCCIDENTE (Spain), III (Jan-March 1924), 111-14 [not seen].
[Cited in Rodríguez (MS). In Spanish.]

2315 Beer, M. DAS ENGLAND DER GEGENWART (Contemporary England) (Berlin: Verlag für Sozialwissenschaft, 1924), pp. 9, 59, 88.
[On Shaw as a member of the Fabian Society. In German.]

2316 Benchley, Robert C. "Drama: Extra Heavy Cream," LIFE, LXXXIII (24 Jan 1924), 18.
Saint Joan is "lucid," "crystal-clear," and "magnificent" in places, but it needs cutting.

2317 "Bernard Shaw and the Bulgarian," LIVING AGE, CCCXXIII (1924), 354.
A recent Berlin production of Arms and the Man led to diplomatic representations by the Bulgarian minister and Shaw's text was cut. Shaw protested in the BERLINER TAGEBLATT [letter reproduced].

2318 "Bernard Shaw Assails American Critics," CUR OP, LXXVI (June 1924), 815.
Saint Joan has not been appreciated by the critics and Shaw has

characteristically launched into a diatribe on their abilities.

2319 "Bernard Shaw Season at Paris Theatre," TIMES, 23 July 1924, p. 12.
The Macdona company is to present ten Shaw plays in repertory in Paris.

2320 Bernstein, Herman. CELEBRITIES OF OUR TIME: INTERVIEWS (NY: Lawren [1924]; rptd Freeport, NY: Books for Libraries, 1968), pp. 110-19.
[An interview; biographical.]

2321 Birrell, Francis. "The Drama: Mr. Shaw's Latest Surprise," NATION & ATH, XXXV (1924), 15-16.
Saint Joan reveals Shaw's ability to surprise us—a rare gift. He has written a chronicle play which is relatively free from comment and is close to his sources. The major fault is the play's length, and the epilogue in particular could be dispensed with.

2322 Birrell, Francis. "The Drama: Mr. Shaw's Testament," NATION & ATH, XXXIV (1924), 763-64.
In Back to Methuselah Shaw has sacrificed dramatic quality for the sake of expounding his philosophy. There is no order to the work and Shaw frequently demonstrates his contempt for his audiences. But there is some good writing and some amusing scenes.

2323 Birrell, Francis. "The Drama: The Disadvantages of Being Clever," NATION & ATH, XXXV (1924), 509-10.
The original, clever preaching in Getting Married has now fallen from fashion and it no longer appears brilliant and bold. Moreover, discussion of the institution of marriage has become boring.

2324 Boyd, Ernest [A.]. PORTRAITS: REAL AND IMAGINARY (NY: Doran, 1924), pp. 189-92; rptd in MODERN WRITERS AT WORK, ed by Josephine K. Piercy (NY: Macmillan, 1930), pp. 191-94.
Shaw's criticism of the English holds little interest for the Irish, while his knowledge and analysis of Irish literature is very limited.

2325 Brown, Ivor. "The Methuselad," SAT REV, CXXXVII (1924), 203.
The critic's task is not to judge Shaw's thesis in Back to Methuselah, but rather to evaluate whether he has rendered it dramatically effective. On this score the play fails; for example, the characterization is superficial and unworthy of Shaw. However, he does produce some fine prose passages which embody his philosophy.

2326 Brown, Ivor. "Saint Joan and Saint Henrik," SAT REV, CXXXVII (1924), 349-50.
Saint Joan is a good play because the central character appeals to Shaw as an "alone-standing woman, the realist at war with romantic

shams." He has also not intellectualized her, but rendered her instinctive; she acts and is unromantic.

2327 "Bulgarians Protest Shaw Play in Berlin," NYT, 25 Sept 1924, p. 25.
The Bulgarian legation in Berlin has requested that Arms and the Man not be performed there because it ridicules Bulgaria. [See also: "Shaw Chides Bulgars Offended by His Play," NYT, 7 Oct 1924, p. 8.]

2328 Bulloch, J. M. "Methuselah as a Five-Night Play," GRAPHIC, CIX (1924), 248.
Shaw uses Back to Methuselah to illustrate his thesis that evolution follows, not Darwin's principles, but a first cause and man's will ("the very basis of socialism").

2329 Bulloch, J. M. "The Re-Beatifying of Joan of Arc," GRAPHIC, CIX (1924), 482.
In taking history literally and in observing more conventions of the drama than he does usually, Shaw has created a "very great play" in Saint Joan. The slang and the epilogue flaw the drama, but characterization and the sense he generates of "spiritual force" are exceptionally fine.

2330 "But It wouldn't be Cricket," NYT, 30 Oct 1924, p. 18.
"No one will be deceived by Bernard Shaw's alleged preference for baseball over cricket."

2331 Canby, Henry Seidel. "Saint George and Joan," SATURDAY REVIEW OF LITERATURE (NY), I (2 Aug 1924), 4.
Shaw wrote Saint Joan because he identifies himself intimately with Joan and the play is Shaw's "apologia pro vita mea." The play is also very modern and packed with psychology.

2332 Caro, J. "Bernard Shaw: Saint Joan," ENGLISCHE STUDIEN, LVIII (1924), 434-39.
[Book review. In German.]

2333 "Catching Up with Shaw," NATION (NY), CXIX (1924), 407-08.
The future will prove that Shaw first gave currency to ideas that will eventually become platitudinous.

2334 "Censor Delays Shaw Play," NYT, 18 Oct 1924, p. 18.
The production of Saint Joan in Vienna has been delayed by the censor.

2335 "Churchill Divides Unionist Leaders," NYT, 16 March 1924, part I, p. 5.
Shaw finds virtues in several parliamentary candidates (including Winston Churchill), but will support the socialist candidate (Fenner Brockway).

2336 Corbin, John. [Saint Joan], NYT, 6 Jan 1924, part VII, p. 1; rptd in NYTTR 1920-1926, [n. p.].
Saint Joan's "most pertinent ideas are of infinitely less moment than the finely sympathetic and powerfully dramatic portrait of Joan which they obscure and all but submerge." Shaw's earlier plays provide prototypes for Joan.

2337 "Court Theatre," TIMES, 19 Feb 1924, p. 10.
With Back to Methuselah Shaw has become a classic.

2338 Crawford, Jack. "Broadway is Inspired," DRAMA (Chicago), XIV (Feb 1924), 178, 96.
Saint Joan is a work of genius that "may not again be equalled in this age." It is a play of extraordinary emotional intensity and marvellous intellectual force. Shaw's concern is with inspiration and the failure of the inspired person in a world where all is politics and expediency.

2339 "The Cremation Society," TIMES, 29 April 1924, p. 9.
Shaw has become a member of the Cremation Society.

2340 "Crites" [T. S. Eliot]. "A Commentary: St. Joan," CRITERION, III (1924), 4-5; rptd in Evans, pp. 293-94.
Saint Joan reveals Shaw's mind clearly, though Man and Superman is probably more of a masterpiece. Shaw manipulates ideas brilliantly, but those ideas stem from Victorian thinkers. His Joan is a sacrilege because he "has turned her into a great middle-class reformer."

2341 D'Arcy, M. C. "Bernard Shaw's St. Joan," MONTH, CXLIV (Aug 1924), 97-105.
Shaw's "cheap and incompetent criticism of Christ and Christianity" in Androcles and the Lion made many people fearful when Shaw turned to Saint Joan as a subject. Surprisingly, Saint Joan reveals Shaw's sympathy for the saint, but Shaw "has still much to learn about the essence of Catholicism" and he should not have made Joan a Protestant.

2342 "The Devil's Disciple at the Everyman," ERA, 8 Oct 1924, p. 12.
The Devil's Disciple has all the elements to make it popular and is every bit as good as the Adelphi melodramas Shaw copied. It is "as satisfying intellectually as it is exciting dramatically."

2343 Duffin, Henry Charles. "Bernard Shaw and a Critic," CORNHILL, LVI (Jan 1924), 31-40.
[Largely Shaw's response to Duffin's book about him (item 1916).]

2344 E. "Saints and Martyrs," INDEPENDENT (NY), CXIII (1924), 106.
Most will agree with Shaw that he has reestablished medieval values in Saint Joan. This is the most intelligent and plausible story about Joan, and the play is "sympathetic, witty, satirical, ironic" and very

interesting.

2345 "England Lifts Ban on Play by Shaw," NYT, 7 Sept 1924, part I, p. 24.
After twenty-two years Mrs. Warren's Profession has been granted a license by the Lord Chamberlain.

2346 Ervine, St. John. THE ORGANISED THEATRE: A PLEA IN CIVICS (NY: Macmillan, 1924), pp. 13, 22-23, 34, 40, 45, 81, 83, 98, 116-18, 145-46, 164-65, 190, 200.
[Ervine's view of the theatre, illustrated with reference to numerous figures including Shaw.]

2347 "Everyman Theatre," TIMES, 25 Sept 1924, p. 8.
The Devil's Disciple is a relic of Shaw's past, from which he divorced himself by writing Heartbreak House.

2348 "Everyman Theatre," TIMES, 28 Oct 1924, p. 10.
The good humor of Misalliance sets it apart from Shaw's other work.

2349 F., H. de W. "Shaw at His Best," INDEPENDENT (NY), CXII (1924), 55.
Apart from the epilogue, Shaw is at his finest in Saint Joan because he keeps "his irresponsibility in check and give[s] rein to his wit." Within the structure of a simple plot, he balances Modernism and Fundamentalism, as well as the Church's intellectual and humanitarian aspects, and altogether he illustrates "a critical turning-point in religion and politics."

2350 F., J. "The Editor Recommends—The Rights of Women and Saints," BOOKMAN (NY), LIX (1924), 729-30.
Saint Joan is exhilarating and it is obvious the Maid is Shaw's ideal.

2351 Farrar, John. "To See or Not to See," BOOKMAN (NY), LIX (1924), 60-61.
[A favorable review of a production of Saint Joan.]

2352 Foster, Jeanne. [A Super-Flapper], TRANSATLANTIC REVIEW, I (March 1924), 73-74 [not seen]; rptd in Weintraub, pp. 29-30.
Saint Joan is "tedious and loquacious" and Joan is a "pert hoyden."

2353 Freeman, Donald. [Saint Joan], NYT, 9 Nov 1924, part VIII, p. 2; rptd in NYTTR 1920-1926, [n. p.].
Max Reinhardt has given Saint Joan a superlative production in Berlin and transformed it into a "mighty spectacle." This supercedes the competent productions in London and New York.

2354 "G. B. S., Lyrist," LIVING AGE, CCCXXI (1924), 1017.
Even though it is an extravagant notion and not very good, Shaw has written a lyric [printed].

2355 "G. B. Shaw Condemns 'Parrot Talk' English," NYT, 14

June 1924, p. 11.
Shaw is among those campaigning against slovenly speech and believes native speakers should enunciate so that foreigners can understand. [See also: "Bernard Shaw Chides 'Slovenly' Articulation," NYT, 6 July 1924, part VIII, p. 2.]

2356 Gémier, Firmin. "Bernard Shaw à l'Odéon" (Bernard Shaw at the Odeon), PARIS-SOIR, 23 Jan 1924.
Here at last is an intelligent production of Arms and the Man, full of wit and humor. Shaw is an Irishman and a socialist; he is a genius but also popular. [In French.]

2357 "Getting Married Revived at the Everyman," ERA, 16 July 1924, p. 6.
Although the divorce laws have been changed since Getting Married was first produced, it is still full of good sense. There are some parts which are tedious, and the jokes are not quite as funny as they were. Nevertheless this disquisitory play is a lot better than most other plays.

2358 Gillet, Louis. "Une Nouvelle Jeanne d'Arc anglaise" (A New English Joan of Arc), REVUE DES DEUX MONDES, XXII (1 Aug 1924), 687-97.
In Saint Joan Shaw treats his subject seriously and follows the true course of history. Shaw is only interested in heroes, in Supermen, in the problem of inspiration and the tragedy of genius. Joan is possessed of splendid good sense and great strength of imagination. Shaw sees in Joan the saint of the future, the image of the equality of the sexes, the woman who has cast out servitude and the poison of love. [In French.]

2359 Gillis, J. M. "George Bernard Shaw," CATHOLIC WORLD, CXVIII (Jan 1924), 525-33; rptd in FALSE PROPHETS (1925 [not seen] ; NY: Macmillan, 1934), pp. 1-19.
Opinions vary on whether Shaw is a great thinker or merely a charlatan. However, his ability to write brilliant dialogue is certain. Shaw's "method is that of a mountebank, or a jester," in which pose he has "hypnotized" England, and "bamboozled" America. With this pose goes a habit of "melodramatic exaggeration" by which he attacks virtually all established social, religious and moral attitudes. Shaw is completely pessimistic and considers the human race totally depraved. He is a "hopeless misanthrope, a satirist without a heart, a pessimist, an immoralist, and an atheist," and, as such, his "importance is enormously overestimated."

2360 Golding, Henry J. "Bernard Shaw and His St. Joan," STANDARD (NY), XI (Nov 1924), 83-87.
As no other dramatist can, Shaw in Saint Joan has painted an enormous canvas and compresses much extremely well. Joan's background is successfully depicted, but her inner life is not. Shaw's

characters "exist in virtue of the thought they express rather than in virtue of the feeling they communicate." They are points of view, not centres of emotion.

2361 Graham, James. "Shaw on Saint Joan," NYT, 13 April 1924, part VIII, p. 2; rptd in Weintraub, pp. 15-22.
The production of Saint Joan has caused controversy in Paris and Shaw has contributed his own letter to the debate. His "violent diatribe" will have litte effect because the French are more interested in their own opinions.

2362 Grein, J. T. THE NEW WORLD OF THE THEATRE 1923-1924 (Lond: Martin Hopkinson, 1924), pp. 2, 8, 22-25, 27, 35, 57, 82, 128, 215, 220.
[Reprints item 2243 with other passing references.]

2363 Grein, J. T. "The World of the Theatre: About Shaw's Back to Methuselah," ILN, CLXIV (8 March 1924), 416.
Back to Methuselah is a magnificent jest in which Shaw attempts to deal with the whole of creation. For Shaw life is a tragi-comic problem, not the least part of which is the audiences which flock to see his work. Whether his is a great mind or not, Shaw can certainly not be ignored by anyone.

2364 Griffith, Hubert. "The Week's Theatres," OBS, 24 Feb 1924, p. 9.
The length of Back to Methuselah has been overcriticized for the play is really quite tolerable. Shaw builds his arguments with lucidity and irresistible logic to the extent that actionless (i.e. discussion) drama reaches its apotheosis. Shaw's philosophical stance is, as usual, exaggerated for the sake of effect, and it boils down to a simple message on the need for change.

2365 Griffith, Hubert. "The Week's Theatres," OBS, 30 March 1924, p. 11.
Saint Joan is disappointing because Shaw does not concentrate sufficiently on Joan and allows himself to be distracted by other interests. Shaw evades the task of giving us an "insight into the unknowable," and instead paints the portrait of the Joan we all know.

2366 Guedalla, Philip. A GALLERY (Lond: Constable, 1924), pp. 73-81.
Shaw is an "inverted Peter Pan" who has always been old enough to lecture his countrymen on a myriad of topics. He has invested his plays with "fantastic puppets" who are the vehicles for his "inimitable" monologues. He has never adhered to the rules of traditional drama, but it is to be hoped his example is not followed by others.

2367 Hamilton, Clayton. CONVERSATIONS ON CONTEMPORARY DRAMA (NY: Macmillan, 1924), pp. 42-67.
Shaw's work is so consistent that it is easy to predict what he will say

on any given subject, and such is the case with Saint Joan, a poor play. It is tedious, garrulous and unmoving because Shaw writes a treatise on Joan instead of embodying her. The play is successful in the theatre because it is a fashionable piece; audiences are actually bored by it but are afraid to say so. Nevertheless, Shaw has produced good work, notably Candida which is a great play and was the turning point of Shaw's career. His later successes were the result of the special audience attracted to his work, particularly to his propagandistic ideas. The earlier plays show sound construction; only when he became fashionable did Shaw disdain the fundamentals of dramaturgy.

2368 Harker, Joseph. STUDIO AND STAGE (Lond: Nisbet, 1924), pp. 185-90, 244-45.
Shaw knows the "theatre inside-out and upside-down." [With a letter from Shaw and Harker's comments on his scenery for Caesar and Cleopatra.]

2369 "He Tells 'Em to Look Near Home," NYT, 17 June 1924, p. 18.
Shaw has jeered at the English for expressing concern over steer-roping while being unconcerned about fox-hunting. However, the former is new to England; the latter is justified by tradition.

2370 Hegemann, Werner. FRIDERICUS ODER DAS KÖNIGSOPFER (Fridericus or the Sacrifice of the King) (1924; rvd Hellerau: Jakob Hegner, 1926), pp. 18, 29, 45-47.
[Passing reference to Shaw and male chastity, and Shaw and Nietzsche's idea of the superman. In German.]

2371 [Helburn, Theresa]. "Visiting the G. B. Shaws," NYT, 21 Sept 1924, part VII, p. 2.
[Title describes. Biographical.]

2372 Henderson, Archibald. "Bernard Shaw Talks of His Saint Joan," LITERARY DIGEST AND INTERNATIONAL BOOK REVIEW, II (1924), 286-87, 289.
[Title describes.]

2373 Henderson, Archibald. "Das Grosse und das Kleine Welttheater: Ein Gesprach mit G. B. Shaw Aufgezeichnet von Henderson aus Amerika" (Big and Small International Theatre: A Conversation with G. B. Shaw Sketched by Henderson of America), PREUSSISCHE JAHRBÜCHER, CXCVI (May 1924), 115-32 [not seen].
[Cited by Hood, p. 225. In German.]

2374 Henderson, Archibald. "The Drama, the Theatre, and the Films," FORT REV, CXXII (Sept 1924), 289-302; rptd in HARPER'S MONTHLY MAGAZINE, CXLIX (Sept 1924), 425-35; rptd as "Das Drama, das Theater, der Film," DIE NEUE

RUNDSCHAU, XXXV (Nov 1924), 1115-29.
[A conversation between Shaw and Henderson on the topic indicated by the title.]

2375 Henderson, Archibald. "Literature and Science," FORT REV, CXXII (Oct 1924), 504-23; rptd as "Ulysees and Einstein: A Dialogue between Bernard Shaw and Archibald Henderson," FORUM (NY), LXXII (Oct 1924), 453-62; rptd as "Literatur und Wissenschaft," DIE NEUE RUNDSCHAU, XXXVI (Jan 1925), 28-48.
[A conversation between Shaw and Henderson on a wide variety of topics.]

2376 Henderson, Archibald. "Things in General: A Dialogue between Bernard Shaw and Archibald Henderson," FORT REV, CXXI (May & June 1924), 619-27, 764-76; rptd HARPER'S MONTHLY MAGAZINE, CXLVIII (May 1924), 705-18.
[Title describes.]

2377 "History on the Stage," OUTLOOK (Lond), LIII (19 April 1924), 262.
In Saint Joan Shaw mixes fact and fiction as he pleases, which he is entitled to do.

2378 Holms, J. F. "The Devil's Disciple," NSTATE, XXIII (1924), 735.
As with many fashionable plays, The Devil's Disciple does not wear well after twenty-five years. One wonders how it could ever have appeared novel or daring as its "inverted sentimentality" makes for dreary listening. However, there are several good farcical scenes and witty dialogue.

2379 [Hornblow, Arthur]. "Mr. Hornblow Goes to the Play," THEATRE MAGAZINE (NY), XXXIX (March 1924), 15-16.
Although satire still occurs, we see "a more kindly, humane Shaw" in Saint Joan. Shaw takes a few liberties with history, but the play is "the best play from the constructive and dramatic viewpoint Shaw has yet written."

2380 Horwill, Herbert W. "What Shaw has up His Sleeve," NYT, 2 Nov 1924, part III, p. 10.
[Brief comments on Shaw as a lecturer.]

2381 "How Shaw Rehearses," NYT, 23 March 1924, part VIII, p. 2.
[An account of Shaw's rehearsal methods for Back to Methuselah.]

2382 Ilijić, Stjepan. "Djavolov učenik prvi put u zagrebačkom kazalistu" (The Devil's Disciple for the First Time at the Zagreb Theatre), HRVATSKI LIST (Osijek), V: 247 (1924), 6-7 [not seen].

[In Croatian.]

2383 "J'accuse: The Dramatists v. Civilization," ENGLISH REVIEW, XXXVIII (April 1924), 599-602.
Shaw, in Back to Methuselah, and Galsworthy, in THE FOREST, suit the real purpose of British theatre by dealing with important contemporary issues. Shaw treats "the cosmic evolution of human life and the salvation of the human race," Galsworthy "the whole matter of competitive society."

2384 "Joan of Arc Recreated by Shaw," LIT DIG, LXXX (19 Jan 1924), 26-27.
A survey of New York critics' reactions to Saint Joan produces mixed opinions. The play is seen as either one of the finest or as yet another example of Shaw's "interminable rag-chewing."

2385 Jourdain, Eleanor F. THE DRAMA IN EUROPE IN THEORY AND PRACTICE (NY: Henry Holt, 1924), p. 134.
Shaw's plays arouse no intensity of feeling and comprise an awkward mixture of romantic and critical elements. "His works will live mainly as a clever picture of a passing phase of society."

2386 Kellock, Harold. "A Saint Militant," FREEMAN (NY), VIII (16 Jan 1924), 447-49.
In the twenty-five years since Shaw began to write, critical reaction to him has changed from derision, disfavor, and offended sensibilities to great enthusiasm whenever a new play appears. The latest, Saint Joan, has all the typical Shavian touches plus an uncustomary tenderness.

2387 [Kraus, Karl?]. "Ein Spassvogel" (A Jester), DIE FACKEL, XXVI: 668 (Dec 1924), 139-42.
[A gloss on Shaw's bon mots and witticisms.] Shaw's worst joke is Siegfried Trebitsch, his German translator. [In German.]

2388 Law, Richard Bonar. "Mr. Shaw, God, and Saint Joan," OUTLOOK (Lond), LIII (14 June 1924), 410.
With Saint Joan, a very great play, Shaw has finally become serious and found his philosophy.

2389 Lewisohn, Ludwig. "Drama: The Great Legend," NATION (NY), CXVIII (1924), 96-97.
Saint Joan is an "obviously first-rate work by a first-rate thinker and artist." Shaw has yet again embodied the "great and central legend by which mankind lives"—namely, the person who perceives and sees through "sham and cant and all spiritual unreality" and who suffers as a result.

2390 THE LIBRARY OF JOHN QUINN, 5 parts (NY: Anderson Galleries, 1924), part 4, pp. 859-67, items 8672-769; rptd as COMPLETE CATALOGUE OF THE LIBRARY OF JOHN QUINN

SOLD BY AUCTION IN FIVE PARTS, 2 vols (NY: Lemma, 1969), pp. 859–67, items 8672–769.
[A biographical introduction, with a listing of the Shaw items for sale. Of bibliographical importance.]

2391 Linares, Antonio G. de. "La Santa Juana de Bernard Shaw" (Bernard Shaw's Saint Joan), LA ESFERA (Spain), No. 538 (26 April 1924) [not seen].
[Cited in Rodriguez (MS). In Spanish.]

2392 Logasa, Hannah, and Winifred Ver Nooy. AN INDEX TO ONE-ACT PLAYS (Bost: Faxon, 1924), pp. 29, 39, 42, 67, 101, 106, 140, 144, 153, 168, 251.
[Primary bibliography.]

2393 "London Theatres: The Court," STAGE, 21 Feb 1924, p. 16.
Back to Methuselah is a brilliant and thoughtful play, and of the first part "mention should be made of the noble, exalted, and for once in a way mystical note to which the formerly almost incorrigible farceur attains."

2394 "London Theatres: The Court," STAGE, 28 Feb 1924, p. 18.
"The unwonted vein of mysticism in Bernard Shaw is displayed again in this last Part of a grandiose, if not absolutely grand, work [Back to Methuselah], the striking merits of which, as well as its undeniable longeurs and long stretches of dullness, call for faithful record, and not cheap facetiousness worse than that of the author of his lighter mood."

2395 "London Theatres: The Everyman," STAGE, 17 July 1924, p. 14.
There is an undoubted boom in Shaw, but it is ridiculous to say his plays are masterpieces and better than Shakespeare. Getting Married is a typical bit of "Shavian impudence" masquerading as philosophy.

2396 "London Theatres: The Everyman," STAGE, 2 Oct 1924, p. 18.
The Devil's Disciple is a very fine construction and possesses trenchant philosophy, wit and satire, although some of the characterization obviously embodies Shaw himself.

2397 "London Theatres: The Everyman," STAGE, 30 Oct 1924, p. 18.
Misalliance is interminably verbose and a characteristically Shavian piece of impudence. It is "almost unpleasantly frank."

2398 "London Theatres: The New," STAGE, 3 April 1924, p. 18.
Saint Joan is "boldly planned and executed" and is invested with noble thought and purpose.

2399 Lynd, Robert. "G. B. S. as G. O. M.," BOOKMAN (Lond), LXVII (Dec 1924), 141-43; rptd in Evans, pp. 304-06.
Shaw no longer surprises and shocks and has become a famous, accepted author. He "is a writer of comic imagination and serious intellect, and of the two . . . his imagination is the gift of the more serious importance to mankind."

2400 MacCarthy, Desmond. "Drama: A Note on Misalliance," NSTATE, XXIV (1924), 139; rptd in MacCarthy, pp. 160-61.
Misalliance is not one of Shaw's masterpieces, but it brilliantly displays his power of making discussion into first-class theatrical entertainment and of "blending the utterly fantastic with piercing insight into fact."

2401 MacCarthy, Desmond. "Drama: Back to Mr. Shaw," NSTATE, XXIV (1924), 15; rptd in MacCarthy, pp. 139-42.
Back to Methuselah is "a tremendous effort of the imagination on the part of a man who in some directions has obviously deep insight, to express the meaning of life. It cannot be boring to anyone who . . . has tried to think." Its philosophy is evolutionary pantheism, "with pronounced Manichean sympathies," which are especially apparent in the Ancients.

2402 MacCarthy, Desmond. "Drama: St. Joan," NSTATE, XXIII (1924), 13-14; rptd in MacCarthy, pp. 166-70; rptd in Weintraub, pp. 34-38.
Saint Joan is about personal religious inspiration battling against organized religion. The weakness of the play is that its "atmosphere is neutralised by [Shaw's] peculiar dramatic method of making each character speak with a self-conscious awareness of the orientation of his own point of view, which is utterly foreign to the times."

2403 MacCarthy, Desmond. "Miscellany: St. Joan," NSTATE, XXII (1924), 758-59; rptd in MacCarthy, pp. 162-65; rptd in Weintraub, pp. 31-34.
Saint Joan is primarily a religious play rather than a historical one. Shaw's purpose is to breathe twentieth-century religious ideas into this historical fable, and he has made Joan their mouthpiece. The central theme "is the struggle of religious inspiration against the world, down the ages."

2404 M[acCarthy], D[esmond]. "Mr. Shaw's Last Preface," NSTATE, XXIII (1924), 444, 446.
Although Saint Joan does not gain anything from being read, it remains eminently actable. Shaw, in the preface, writes as though he is alone and isolated in the world, yet no dramatist is more written about and prestigious.

2405 Mantle, Burns, ed. THE BEST PLAYS OF 1923-24 AND THE YEAR BOOK OF THE DRAMA IN AMERICA (Bost: Small,

Maynard, 1924), pp. 6, 378-79.
Saint Joan is "unlifelike" but its historical discussion is interesting.
[With cast details and an outline of the plot.]

2406 Mariátegui, J. M. "Volviendo a Matusalén por Bernard Shaw" (Back to Methuselah by Bernard Shaw), VARIEDADES (Peru), No. 948 (May 1924) [not seen].
[Cited in Rodríguez (MS). In Spanish.]

2407 Miller, Nellie Burget. THE LIVING DRAMA: HISTORICAL DEVELOPMENT AND MODERN MOVEMENTS VISUALIZED: A DRAMA OF THE DRAMA (NY & Lond: Century, 1924), pp. 283, 297-304.
Shaw is not a dramatist in the usual sense because he is concerned more with ideas than with technique. His characters are types and Shaw is more interested in expounding his notions rather than in developing characters. Nevertheless he has vigorously assailed social institutions and injustices, and he has satirized the emotions which underline civilization.

2408 "'Mr. Shaw,'" OUTLOOK (Lond), LIII (29 March 1924), 214.
Only Shaw is entitled to the appellation "Mr. Shaw" and it is confusing to have a politician with the same name.

2409 "Mr. Shaw's Back to Methuselah Cycle," ILN, CLXIV (1 March 1924), 386.
Back to Methuselah contains austere thought which can also be lyrically expressed. Its great arguments are often punctuated by cheap, tasteless satire, and Shaw is given to haranguing his audiences.

2410 "Mr. Shaw's Novels," TLS, No. 1192 (20 Nov 1924), 758.
Shaw's novels are still worth reading for their sense of humor, although a sense of probability is somewhat lacking. His prose is brisk and athletic, and he produces dramatic scenes and dialogue (even if he seems bored by pure narration).

2411 Morgan, A. E. TENDENCIES OF MODERN ENGLISH DRAMA (NY: Scribner's, 1924), pp. 42-92.
Shaw built upon and expanded the trail-blazing work of Pinero and H. A. Jones in the development of English drama. He attacked the practises and ideals of Victorian drama, particularly by developing his own heroines. Similarly, his heroes are different. A close examination of his plays reveals he is a social iconoclast, though his works are seldom political. Shaw's philosophy may not be complete or perfect, but it is a genuine contribution to human thought.

2412 "Moscow Ridiculous, G. B. Shaw Declares," NYT, 8 Dec 1924, p. 1.
Shaw has urged the Russian government to get rid of the Third International if it wishes to be taken seriously in Europe and obtain the

cooperation of English socialists.

2413 Moult, Thomas. "Bernard Shaw's New Masterpiece," BOOKMAN (Lond), LXVI (1924), 261-62.
Saint Joan is a noble play, full of historical truth, and shows Shaw has had his share of hero-worshipping.

2414 "Mrs. Warren Reaches the English Stage," LIVING AGE, CCCXXIII (1924), 353-54.
[Details of the imminent London production of Mrs. Warren's Profession, with a comment by Shaw.]

2415 "Mrs. Warren's Profession: Production in Paris," DT, 10 Sept 1924, p. 6.
Mrs. Warren's Profession aroused considerable curiosity, but it is difficult to say whether anyone was really shocked. Much of the subject matter is now out of date, and the serious tone often turns into vaudeville as the characters endeavor to be witty.

2416 Nathan, George Jean. "The Theatre," AMERICAN MERCURY, I (1924), 241-43.
Saint Joan is another step in the decline of Shaw's genius because he tries to prove he really has a heart.

2417 "New Theatre: Saint Joan," DT, 27 March 1924, p. 12.
There has been no memorable version of Saint Joan until now, even though Shaw himself still suffuses the play. Shaw's view of history may not be everyone's, but he exposes clearly the ironies of the varying motives and circumstances which surrounded Joan's two trials. Joan is a beautiful creation based solely on faith and simplicity.

2418 "An Open Letter," FREEMAN, VIII (27 Feb 1924), 582-83.
[An invitation to Shaw to visit America, with answers to his objections to certain American institutions.]

2419 "The Philanderer: Revival at the Everyman," ERA, 31 Dec 1924, p. 14.
Much of The Philanderer seems old-fashioned now and it contains many dreary, uninteresting passages.

2420 Phillips, R. Le Clerc. "With Great Men Behind the Scenes," NYT, 14 Sept 1924, part IV, p. 4.
Shaw was invited to contribute an article on communism in Russia for a two-volume history of the twentieth century to be published by the Encyclopedia Britannica. He declined because of his ignorance of the subject and because of the lack of financial reward.

2421 Pirandello, Luigi. "Pirandello Distills Shaw," NYT, 13 Jan 1924, part IV, pp. 1, 14; rptd in Weintraub, pp. 23-28; rptd in Evans, pp. 279-84.
The audience's muted reaction to Saint Joan is puzzling for Shaw now

appears to believe "less in himself, and more in what he is doing." Shaw reveals a new depth of tolerance, pity and poetry, and he thoroughly respects artistic considerations.

2422 Pope, T. Michael. "The Drama: The Solitude of the Saint," OUTLOOK (Lond), LIII (5 April 1924), 235.
[A favorable review of Saint Joan.]

2423 "Premieres of the Week: Back to Methuselah," ERA, 20 Feb 1924, p. 6.
Part one of Back to Methuselah is moving and beautiful. Shaw is a prophet and is recognized in his own country.

2424 "Premieres of the Week: Saint Joan," ERA, 2 April 1924, p. 6.
At last Saint Joan has been made into flesh and blood, and stripped of romance and sentimentality. The achievement is due both to Shaw and to Sybil Thorndike as Joan. The trial scene is a very necessary focus for the story, and the epilogue is not the anti-climax others have suggested.

2425 "Prime Minister on Indian Talent," TIMES, 8 Feb 1924, p. 9.
Shaw has attended a lecture at the India Office in London.

2426 "Pure, Simon" [pseud of Frank Swinnerton]. "The Londoner: Mr. Shaw and Pure English," BOOKMAN (NY), LIX (Aug 1924), 701-02.
Shaw is right in stressing the importance of correct pronunciation and articulation.

2427 Rascoe, Burton. "Shaw, the Maid, and American Folk Drama," ARTS & DECORATION, XX (Feb 1924), 17, 79.
The attitudes which most people have about Shaw have been conditioned solely by their sympathy with or antipathy for the social ideas Shaw espouses. Although the effectiveness of Saint Joan would be improved if the talking were cut down, the play is nonetheless a highly intelligent and moving entertainment. The play may be didactic, but Shaw remains the dramatic genius of this period.

2428 Reade, Arthur E. E. "Idealism versus History," LABOUR MONTHLY, VI (June 1924), 369-75; rptd in LIVING AGE, CCCXXII (1924), 175-78.
Saint Joan is "one of the finest historical plays ever written" even if it may not be Shaw's greatest work. Shaw has surpassed himself in stagecraft and the whole possesses a "Homeric simplicity."

2429 Roberts, R. Ellis. "Saint Joan," BOOKMAN (Lond), LXVI (1924), 139-40.
Saint Joan disappoints because Shaw lacks any historical sense and fails to convey the "spirit of the time."

2430 Robinson, Lennox. "At the Play: Mr. Bernard Shaw," OBS, 30 March 1924, p. 11.

Shaw's reputation is so high that he can do nothing to destroy it. With Saint Joan we feel as though we are at a feast given by a great master, and we can be only grateful that he has given us this piece. However, it is not his best play, although its beauty and poetry make it far from being his worst.

2431 Rylands, George. "The Drama: Time's Revenges," NATION & ATH, XXXV (1924), 692.

Shaw, like Swinburne, makes people wake up, although both "are the idols of the schoolboy of yesterday." The Man of Destiny, however, "is as fresh as ever" and will survive much better than most of Shaw's work.

2432 "Saint Joan," TLS, No. 1172 (3 July 1924), 417.

Saint Joan is unlike anything Shaw has written because he has been moved by his subject. Technically the play is a surprise because Shaw has wedded his ideas and action, and has given the whole an artistic life.

2433 "Saint Joan: A New Play by Bernard Shaw," WOMAN CITIZEN, ns VIII (9 Feb 1924), 13.

Saint Joan "is one of the outstanding successes of the season" and Winifred Lenihan was born for the role of Joan.

2434 "Saint Joan and Saint Bernard," WORLD TODAY, XLIV (June 1924), 5-6.

New plays like Saint Joan augur well for British drama. Although some passages are irritating, others possess great beauty.

2435 "Saint Joan: The Play of the Season," WOMAN'S HOME COMPANION, LI (May 1924), 124.

[Photographs of the Theatre Guild production, New York.]

2436 Seldes, Gilbert. "The Theatre," DIAL, LXXVI (Feb 1924), 206.

Although in Saint Joan "the interest is in our modern relation to both the martyr and to the assassins," neither the text nor the production of the play is successful.

2437 Shanks, Edward. BERNARD SHAW (Lond: Nisbet; NY: Henry Holt, 1924).

Little need be said of Shaw's novels in which inexperience is much in evidence. They are stiff, arid works, but do reveal unexpected opinions and a trenchant style. As a critic, Shaw was concerned with criticism of the standards of conduct depicted in the plays he saw. He thought that moral standards change and that, consequently, the theatre should reflect that change. He was always concerned with effecting improvements.

As a playwright, Shaw wanted to express intelligent ideas which are well written and well acted. He has a nearly perfect gift of dramatic exposition; whatever materials he works with, he achieves the maximum effect. However, he has introduced no exceptional technical innovations and generally follows much after Ibsen's mode. There is a wide variety of topics in his plays, although he has moved steadily in the direction of philosophy. He has chafed against the restrictions of realism in his desire to "rejoice in the vast potentialities" of human nature. His characters are "ready-made and we know no more of them than they tell us themselves"; they have no independent reality and are static abstractions from humanity. In essence, Shaw's characters are merely the background for his ideas. Shaw also has a strong comic spirit which is not always under control, and he has a weakness for cheap jokes. He writes natural, vigorous, vivid dialogue.

The prefaces reveal the argumentative Shaw who is always ready to give a lecture, and he cannot resist the impulse to write them. They have become something of a joke; however, although they are sometimes muddleheaded, it is still possible to enjoy them.

Shaw's philosophy or advice is to do something which is good. We should not dream or be idle. His plays are a glorification of real life without sham. Shaw is really deeply religious and his life force is God, although he desperately avoids calling it God. This puts off some readers because they think his ideas are all scientifically based.

2438 Shanks, Edward. "The Drama: Back to Methuselah," OUTLOOK (Lond), LIII (1 March 1924), 143.
Shaw attempts to express comprehensively and seriously his philosophy in Back to Methuselah, but the attempt is faulty and unsuccessful.

2439 Shanks, Edward. "The Drama: 'In the Snare,' " OUTLOOK (Lond), LIV (12 July 1924), 33.
In Arms and the Man Shaw substituted "a new type of melodramatic hero for the wooden old heroes that have so long held the stage."

2440 "Shaw and Chesterton Argue over Breakfast," NYT, 10 Feb 1924, part II, p. 7.
Shaw believes breakfast should consist of fruit imported from America; Chesterton espouses bacon and eggs.

2441 "Shaw Berates All Who Feed on Flesh," NYT, 24 Oct 1924, p. 11.
Shaw has participated in a discussion on the benefits of vegetarianism for people's dispositions.

2442 "Shaw Enters the Lists for Joan of Arc," NYT, 20 July 1924, part III, p. 5.
The preface to Saint Joan contains much sound research, and Shaw's

logic is consistently maintained and reasonable. "He defends and magnifies the maid."

2443 "Shaw Makes Debut on Radio to 4,000,000," NYT, 21 Nov 1924, p. 2.

Shaw thoroughly enjoyed himself when he read O'Flaherty, V. C. on British radio. [For the unfavorable critical reception see: "All Theatrical Productions Not Adapted for Radio," NYT, 21 Dec 1924, part VIII, p. 16.]

2444 "Shaw Play a Vienna Hit," NYT, 26 Oct 1924, p. 30; rptd in NYTTR 1920-1926, [n. p.].

Saint Joan is successful in Vienna, although the play's meaning goes over the audience's head.

2445 "Shaw Plus," OUTLOOK (NY), CXXXVI (1924), 338-39.

Apart from the epilogue, Saint Joan is "Shaw plus a dramatic forcefulness which he has seldom attained."

2446 "Shaw Raps Boston Critics," NYT, 11 April 1924, p. 23.

Shaw has commented caustically on those who want to ban his books from schools in Needham, Mass.

2447 "Shaw Sees Death of League," NYT, 27 Nov 1924, p. 2.

Shaw believes the attitude of the British government towards the Egypt crisis will destroy the League of Nations.

2448 "Shaw Sees Peace in Danger," NYT, 1 Nov 1924, p. 6.

Shaw believes the peace of Europe will be endangered if either Lords Grey or Curzon becomes foreign minister for Britain.

2449 Sheridan, Charles James. "Creatures of Circumstance: III: Mr. George Bernard Shaw," OUTLOOK (Lond), LIII (28 June 1924), 448-49.

Shaw's "unspoiled arrogance" has proved invaluable in advertising his gifts, but has "limited his scope as an artist." Shaw's political teachings are paradoxical and therefore stultified. "In essentials Shaw's philosophy is Toryism."

2450 Shipp, Horace. "History in the Theatre," ENGLISH REVIEW, XXXVIII (1924), 742-45.

Shaw's Saint Joan, a masterpiece, affords an excellent illustration of any dramatist's difficulty in deciding on the use of historical fact. Shaw makes Joan a magnificent figure and applies his historical belief that "humanity moves slowly forward because desire creates will, and will creates Society in its image."

2451 Shuford, Augusta. "English Undefiled," NYT, 27 July 1924, part IV, p. 2.

Shaw's views on spoken English are all very well and good, but he fails to answer the question of what exactly is standard English.

2452 Smith, Daniel L. [Letter to the Editor], NEEDHAM CHRONICLE (Mass), March [?] 1924 [not seen].
[Smith was shocked that his daughter was required to read Shaw's plays in her high-school English class. A full account of this controversy, including a letter by Shaw, is given by R. F. Bosworth, "G. B. S. 'Apologizes'!" SHAW REVIEW, XXIII (1980), 17-20.]

2453 "Socialismo y geniocracia" (Socialism and "Geniocracy"), LA ANTORCHA (Mexico), I: 1 (4 Oct 1924), 2 [not seen].
[Cited in Rodríguez (MS). In Spanish.]

2454 Spicer-Simson, Theodore. MEN OF LETTERS OF THE BRITISH ISLES (NY: W. E. Rudge, 1924), pp. 114-16.
Shaw is a "resolute radical" who has attacked the absurdity of numerous facets of life and who wants us to think when we watch his plays.

2455 Squire, J. C. "Chronicles: Drama," LOND MERCURY, X (1924), 89-91.
Saint Joan is a chronicle play, but to Shaw's mind the life and exploits of Joan are only a preliminary to something far more interesting: her trial and the arguments about her trial. The play has some minor flaws, but in the trial scene Shaw "has never done anything better . . . nothing so fine."

2456 Squire, J. C. "Drama," LOND MERCURY, IX (1924), 541-43.
Back to Methuselah makes for interesting reading, but is undramatic when performed. Shaw, who has straight-jacketed his poetic nature, is a confirmed joker even when he attempts to be serious. His industry, however, is admirable.

2457 Stage, Robin. "Saint Joan: A Play Review," METROPOLITAN (NY), LIX (May 1924), 42.
Saint Joan is one of Shaw's most thought-provoking dramas and is quite different from his other works. "It is a great play."

2458 "Stage Pronunciation," NYT, 14 April 1924, p. 16.
Shaw will defend even the pronunciation of the words of his plays, although there is much evidence to support variant pronunciation.

2459 Strachey, J. St. Loe. "A Book of the Moment: St. Joan and Mr. Shaw," SPECTATOR, CXXXIII (1924), 18-19.
In Saint Joan Shaw is at his best, and the preface equals the play in value. His arguments for the church are balanced, but they reveal its essential weakness. Joan lives out her faith into martyrdom for the sake of the "Evolutionary Appetite." In fact, the Church of England evidently fulfills Shaw's requirements for reform of the Roman Church.

2460 Strunsky, Simeon. "About Books, More or Less: Mr. Shaw

has a Heart," NYT, 10 Aug 1924, part III, p. 4.
Saint Joan and its preface reveal many aspects of Shaw's essential
humanity. However, as his remarks in 1916 about Roger Casement
demonstrate, he lacks the final touch of humanity, "the capacity for
reverence."

2461 Sutton, Graham. "The Quintessence of Shavianism,"
BOOKMAN (Lond), LXV (March 1924), 287-89.
Back to Methuselah is constructive, optimistic, and insists on responsibility. Despite its apparent faults, the play argues for creative
evolution as a positive faith which will help man to progress.

2462 Sutton, Graham. "Shaw and the Younger Generation,"
BOOKMAN (Lond), LXVII (Dec 1924), 145-50.
It took the younger generation a time to find out Shaw, for his works
were never found in school. In addition, the anti-Shaw faction, which
regards him as merely a buffoon, has hindered general acceptance of
Shaw's achievement. But his moral passion, which stresses each
individual's personal responsibility, cannot be denied.

2463 "Svîataîa Ioanna" (Saint Joan), ZHIZN' ISKUSSTVA
(Moscow), No. 51 (16 Dec 1924), 15 [not seen].
[On the production at the Leningrad Academy Drama Theatre. In
Russian.]

2464 Tairov, A. Ia. "Iz stenograma disputa o sovremennom
teatrom" (Report of Dispute on Contemporary Theatre), 15 Nov
1924 [source unknown]; rptd in A. Ia. Trabskii, et al, RUSSKII
SOVETSKII TEATR 1921-1926 (SOVIET RUSSIAN THEATRE
1921-1926) (Leningrad: Iskusstvo, 1975), pp. 253-54.
Saint Joan was produced in Moscow because it was the only play by
which the present-day direction of the theatre could be represented.
The part of Joan is very difficult, and the play is entirely
contemporary showing that all revolutionary movements occur at the
moment of social collapse and come from below. [In Russian.]

2465 "Tarn." "Saint Joan at the New Theatre," SPECTATOR,
CXXXII (1924), 538-39.
In Saint Joan, Shaw has written the best of our modern chronicle
plays. He succeeds in making real this story of a peasant girl and her
incredible exploits. To each of the extraordinary happenings of the
story he has found a clue. Everything seems inevitable without
seeming predetermined.

2466 "Tarn." "The Theatre: Two Plays," SPECTATOR, CXXXII
(1924), 283-84.
Part one of Back to Methuselah was "momentous, fatal and moving,
and at the same time full of beauty and fresh charm"; the second
part, however, "consists largely of brilliant and witty but sometimes
trivial satire which, though amusing in itself, is often irritating and

even tedious in effect, because it obstructs and obscures the main issue so finely raised in the first play."

2467 "Teatrul National, Candida" (Candida at the National Theatre), PATRIA (Cluj), 18 Dec 1924 [not seen].
[In Roumanian.]

2468 Tittle, Walter. "Mr. Bernard Shaw Talks About St. Joan," OUTLOOK (NY), CXXXVII (1924), 311-13; rptd in BOOKMAN (Lond), LXVII (Dec 1924), 143-44; rptd in Weintraub, pp. 8-14.
[A short account of Shaw's concept of Joan and how it differs from other writers'.]

2469 Tittle, Walter. "Portraits in Pencil and Pen," CENTURY (NY), CVIII (1924), 785-89.
[A biographical interview while Shaw sat for a portrait.]

2470 Trebitsch, Siegfried. "A Visit to Bernard Shaw," LIVING AGE, CCCXX (1924), 221-24.
[Biographical. Originally in VOSSISCHE ZEITUNG (Berlin), 28 Nov 1924; not seen.]

2471 V[an] D[oren], C[arl]. "Books and Affairs: Fools of God and Doctors of the Church," CENTURY (NY), CVIII (Sept 1924), 718-20.
Saint Joan is another version of Shaw's favorite character who is steady in will and unyielding. Shaw also portrays dramatically two opposing forces (of conservation and creation) and shows how inevitable and unavoidable was their collision. To this he adds his dose of broad comedy which clinches his argument. Anyone who thinks the epilogue is anticlimactic has simply missed the point of the play's overall structure in which Joan's death is merely an episode.

2472 Vernon, Frank. THE TWENTIETH-CENTURY THEATRE (Lond: Harrap, 1924), pp. 19-21, 30-31, 35, 37-41, 43-48, 50, 59, 65-67, 91, 98-101, 108-09.
Shaw was a decisive influence on drama in the 1890s although as a dramatist he was still on the sidelines. When he finally emerged, Shaw appealed more aurally than visually, but his propaganda appears more in his prefaces than in the plays themselves. Whatever liberties Shaw takes with dramatic forms succeed because he is first and foremost a great dramatist.

2473 W[alkley], A. B. "Entertainments: Superbity," TIMES, 9 July 1924, p. 12.
The preface to Saint Joan demonstrates Shaw's use of "remorseless logic" to drive us to his conclusions about things.

2474 [Walkley, A. B.]. "New Theatre: Mr. Shaw's Latest Play," TIMES, 27 March 1924, p. 12; rptd in Evans, pp. 285-87.
In Saint Joan Shaw held himself in check until the epilogue, which is

an "artistic error" because of its incongruities. Nevertheless, the play is one of Shaw's "finest achievements."

2475 [Walkley, A. B.]. "Saint Joan: Sancta Simplicitas," TIMES, 26 March 1924, p. 12.
It is to be hoped Shaw will not meddle with history in Saint Joan.

2476 "Waterloo Bridge," TIMES, 1 April 1924, p. 7.
Shaw has expressed his views on the proposed development of Charing Cross and Waterloo Bridge.

2477 West, Rebecca, "Interpreters of Their Age," SATURDAY REVIEW OF LITERATURE, I (1924), 41-42; rptd in Evans, pp. 297-99.
Hardy is a greater person than Shaw, as any literate mind can determine.

2478 Wilson, Edmund. "Bernard Shaw Since the War," NEW REP, XXXIX (27 Aug 1924), 380-81; rptd in Weintraub, pp. 39-44.
Before World War I there was no problem Shaw felt he could not solve, but now he reveals a longer term view of things and a "deeper feeling for human nature." This is evident in Saint Joan which, though still social criticism, is "longer-sighted and less hopeful than has been his wont."

2479 Wolfe, Humbert. "The Theatre: The Man of Destiny," SPECTATOR, CXXXII (1924), 995-96.
The Man of Destiny is, in effect, Shaw's first step on his way to Saint Joan. The action flows from the characters which explode some conventional beliefs but are also "consistent and alive."

2480 Woolf, Leonard. "The World of Books: Mr. Shaw's Saint Joan," NATION & ATH, XXXV (1924), 511.
Saint Joan is certainly a great play and demonstrates Shaw's sustained ability, wisdom and mental agility. He does not grow old; rather, his strength as a dramatist increases (despite claims to the contrary that his work is mere wit, brilliance and argumentation). The young owe more to Shaw than to anyone else living; like Erasmus, he is a "really civilized man." The play is intellectual and universal.

2481 Woollcott, Alexander. "Richard Bird as Marchbanks," SUN (NY), 13 Dec 1924, p. 7.
Candida certainly does not deserve to gather dust as it is the finest English language play since THE TEMPEST.

2482 Wyatt, Euphemia Van Rensselaer. "Bernard Shaw and His Saint Joan," CATHOLIC WORLD, CXIX (May 1924), 196-205.
Shaw's thesis is Saint Joan "is to prove that in the end the laugh is on the Church, and that the halo of sanctitude has been meted out to one who was really a Protestant!" To further offend conservative

Britishers, Shaw hails Joan as a Nationalist as well. The play is marked by inaccuracy and is not Shaw's masterpiece.

2483 Young, Stark. [Candida], NYT, 21 Dec 1924, part VII, p. 1; rptd in NYTTR 1920-1926, [n. p.].
[A discussion of Marchbanks and Richard Bird's performance of the role.]

2484 Young, Stark. "The Play," NYT, 13 Dec 1924, p. 12; rptd in NYTTR 1920-1926, [n. p.].
Candida is already a classic of its generation, although Shaw often insists on his point too much.

2485 "Zanat gospóde Warren" (Mrs. Warren's Profession), KAZALISNI LIST (Zagreb), II (1924), 12 [not seen].
[In Croatian.]

1925

2486 "The Acting in Candida," LIT DIG, LXXXIV (7 Feb 1925), 28-29.
A survey of critics' reactions to a New York revival of Candida shows there is now more emphasis placed on the acting than on the play itself.

2487 Agate, James. "The Dramatic World," STIMES, 3 May 1925, p. 6, and 4 Oct 1925, p. 6; rptd in THE CONTEMPORARY THEATRE, 1925 (Lond: Chapman & Hall, 1926), pp. 224-34.
Caesar in Caesar and Cleopatra is Shaw's "hero because he is Shavian. His ideas are unclouded by idealism or any kind of romantic nonsense." However, Shaw's portrayal of him makes the man too perfect. Since economic conditions have improved, the interest in Mrs. Warren's Profession lies more in the "spiritual state of the slave-driver" than anything else. Mrs. Warren herself presents a thin argument about trafficking in sin. However, she is a well-rounded character, while the rest are only abstractions.

2488 [Androcles and the Lion], NYT, 29 Nov 1925, part VIII, p. 1; rptd in NYTTR 1920-1926, [n. p.].
Shaw's plays, including Androcles and the Lion, are now a standard part of the American repertory and there is nothing better on the stage.

2489 [Arms and the Man], NYT, 4 Oct 1925, part IX, p. 1; rptd in NYTTR 1920-1926, [n. p.].
Arms and the Man is a "rattling good comedy" which has withstood the test of time far better than Pinero's THE SECOND MRS. TANQUERAY. Shaw's views on militarism no longer shock, however,

because people are now in accord with Shaw's mood.

2490 B., W. H. "Shaw Season: Mrs. Warren's Profession Ably Acted," BIRMINGHAM GAZETTE, 28 July 1925, p. 4.
Mrs. Warren's Profession is the most moral play ever produced, and it is puzzling why it was ever banned. "The play amounts to a scathing exposure of the society that tolerates Mrs. Warren's profession and fattens on it."

2491 Bab, Julius. SHAKESPEARE: WESEN UND WERKE (Shakespeare: Nature and Works) (Stuttgart, Berlin & Leipzig: Union Deutsche Verlagsgesellschaft, 1925), pp. 17-18, 206, 227-28.
[Passing comments on Shaw's assessment of Shakespeare. In German.]

2492 Balmforth, Ramsden. THE ETHICAL AND RELIGIOUS VALUE OF THE DRAMA (Lond: Allen & Unwin, 1925 [not seen] ; NY: Adelphi, 1926), pp. 152-96, 245.
Shaw's criticism of the New Testament in the preface to Androcles and the Lion is stimulating and provocative. The play itself is pure comedy infused with biting irony and satire, so much so that Shaw will soon be regarded as the Aristophanes of this age. In Androcles Shaw addresses the question by what means war can be eradicated and his method is far more effective than hundreds of sermons. Man and Superman represents, perhaps, a change of emphasis in Shaw's mind, "from the hope and ideal of economic and political education to that of biology and creative evolution." As a stage play it is impossible, although powerful, honest, courageous and truthful. In Saint Joan Shaw does not stick to absolute historical truth, which is an unrealistic goal anyway. But it is a great play which argues we should tolerate as much heretical thought as possible since all evolution in thought and ideas has seemed at first heretical.

2493 Beaunier, André. [Saint Joan], L'ECHO DE PARIS, 29 April 1925, p. 4 [not seen].
[Cited in Weintraub, p. 215. In French.]

2494 Benchley, Robert [C]. "Drama: Housewarming," LIFE, LXXXV (30 April 1925), 20.
It is easier to commend the fine cast and production of Caesar and Cleopatra than to write on Shaw, as "at no time does a reviewer look so silly as when he is praising Shaw—unless it is when he is knocking him."

2495 Benchley, Robert [C]. "Drama: Vienna Letter," LIFE, LXXXVI (20 Aug 1925), 18.
The Russian production in Vienna of Saint Joan outShaws Shaw in its parody and burlesque.

2496 "Bernard Shaw Reviews His War Record: A Dialogue

between Bernard Shaw and Archibald Henderson," CENTURY (NY), CIX (Jan 1925), 290-304; rptd as "The Great War and the Aftermath," FORT REV, CXXIII (Jan-Feb 1925), 1-12, 145-52; rptd as "Der Kreig und seine Nachwehen," FRANKFURTER ZEITUNG, 1-2, 5, 7, 11 Jan 1925.
[Title describes.]

2497 Berton, Claude. "Sainte Jeanne: Les Visages de la Comédie Parodiques" (Saint Joan: Aspects of Parodic Comedy), NOUVELLES LITTERAIRES, 16 May 1925, p. 7 [not seen].
[Cited in Weintraub, p. 209. In French.]

2498 Bidou, Henri. "Sainte Jeanne" (Saint Joan), LE JOURNAL DES DEBATS, 4 May 1925, p. 3.
Saint Joan is a great success and in keeping with Shaw's thought. It presents a picture of the times and of the social forces which intervene in history. [In French.]

2499 Billy, André. "Sainte Jeanne" (Saint Joan), LE MERCURE DE FRANCE, CLXXX (June 1925), 485-89.
In Saint Joan Shaw shows Joan as a heroine who foreshadows all modern philosophies: liberty of thought, monarchic state control, nationalism, and militarism. Enlivened by Shaw's humor, the play's greatest merits are artistic and psychological. [In French.]

2500 Bone, Muirhead. "Letters to the Editor: English Sculpture," TIMES, 18 June 1925, p. 12.
Shaw's view, that Jacob Epstein's panel is "puny [and] inadequate" [TIMES, 17 June 1925, p. 17], is wrong. However, his support of Epstein himself is welcome.

2501 Bonner, G[eorge] H. "The Present State of the Drama," NINETEENTH CENTURY AND AFTER, XCVII (1925), 746-55.
The problem with Saint Joan is that Shaw leaves us at a loose end and fails to fulfill the expectations he himself has generated in the play.

2502 Borges, Jorge Luis. [Saint Joan], SAGITARIO (Argentina), No. 4 (Nov-Dec 1925), 79-80 [not seen].
[Cited in Rodríguez (MS). In Spanish.]

2503 Braybrooke, Patrick. THE GENIUS OF BERNARD SHAW (Phila: Lippincott, n. d. [1925]).
Widowers' Houses is a cynical, but hopeful play, showing that strict ethics are insufficient in coping with worldly problems. "The Philanderer is a reproach to the Maker of the Universe who appears to be either an arbitrary force or a supreme construction of useless situations." Mrs. Warren's Profession is "a very telling study of an absolutely detestable woman," but there is no reason why audiences should not see this kind of play. In all three unpleasant plays Shaw hints that man needs to change before the insoluble becomes soluble. This is a "distinct foreshadowing of the Super-Man idea."

Arms and the Man is a brilliant play on a subject Shaw knows nothing about; however, the dialogue is exceptional. Candida is a "dialectic concerning love, not as a personal emotion so much as an intellectual experiment carried out by a person who treats it as a sort of ideal rather detached from a particular individual." The Man of Destiny is peopled solely by Shavian mouthpieces and marks a change in Shaw's program. You Never Can Tell is highly conventional and therefore lacking in interest.

Shaw's strongest, but not best, play is The Devil's Disciple which "deals a most effective blow at organised religion." "Caesar and Cleopatra bombards the absurd contention that savage people can be improved by mere rational suggestion." Marriage as the ideal consummation of love is attacked in Captain Brassbound's Conversion, though Shaw does not advocate free love. This group of plays shows how man's institutions fail him and that happiness cannot be achieved through them. Hope is offered in the potential of the life force which needs a superman to utilize it.

Much attention has been lavished on The Doctor's Dilemma and Getting Married because the subjects of medicine and marriage are central concerns. Shaw's arguments on medicine are uneven, but eminently sensible on marriage. Both works are pessimistic, with man struggling hopelessly in the dark, from which Shaw will lead us.

The life force can be termed Shaw's religion and finds strong but inexact expression in Man and Superman. If the life force is Shaw's God it is clear, in Androcles and the Lion, that Christ cannot be God because Shaw's excellent discussion of Jesus renders him personal, which the life force cannot be. Ferrovius' sincerity and Christian charity, which reflect the "curious stability of man," find further expression in Eliza Doolittle in Pygmalion: we know she will remain a flower-girl at heart.

Shaw the Irishman is also Shaw the politician, and this emerges in John Bull's Other Island and Major Barbara. He "sees Ireland exactly as it is, exactly as it will be so long as the English government refuses to treat that country in a reasonable manner and let it well alone." The crux of Major Barbara is the paradox of the Salvation Army using Undershaft's money to save men's souls when that money is derived from work aimed at destroying their bodies.

Shaw's war plays are mere satire, and not worthy of his genius. Heartbreak House, however, usefully reflects how World War I affected both Europe and the theatre. Saint Joan is a marvellous, though sometimes sentimental, play whose preface warrants more attention than it has received.

Generally, Shaw's characters are "remarkably true to actual life" because he draws characters whose essence is very familiar to him.

305

Shaw's claim to fame will be decided by posterity, but no history of the great men of the twentieth century will be able to ignore him.

2504 Brisson, Pierre. "Le Théâtre" (The Theatre), LES ANNALES DES POLITIQUES ET LITTERAIRES, LXXXIV (10 May 1925), 495.

Because Shaw is so ready to satirize, few people expected him to write a play about Joan of Arc (Saint Joan) without his customary irreverences. Depicting the maid with a reverence and sensitivity of which many thought him incapable, Shaw traces to its tragic end the struggle against feudal aristocracy and ecclesiastical hierarchy into which Joan had unwittingly thrust herself. [In French.]

2505 "British Condemn Charges," NYT, 10 July 1925, p. 6.

Shaw, along with other prominent men, has condemned the trial of John Thomas Scopes (in Dayton, Tennessee) for teaching evolution.

2506 Brock, H. I. "Bernard Shaw Welcomes a Stranger," NYT, 25 Jan 1925, part IV, p. 3.

An interview with Shaw reveals he is "not his satanic majesty, but a benignant old gentleman."

2507 Brock, H. I. "The Guild Holds a Housewarming," NYT, 5 April 1925, pp. 7, 22.

The Theatre Guild, New York, has opened a new theatre and will present Caesar and Cleopatra in a new version.

2508 Bromfield, Louis. [Arms and the Man], NATION (NY), LXII (1925–26), 321.

[A favorable review of Arms and the Man.]

2509 [Brown, Ivor]. "The Theatre: Super-Man and Sub-Woman," SAT REV, CXL (1925), 433–34.

Caesar and Cleopatra is obviously an early play, and Shaw has "restated much of its contents more cogently" in his later work. As a weapon against romantic drama it has become redundant because cynical plays are now in vogue.

2510 Buckland, J. H. "Saint Joan," HISTORY, IX (Jan 1925), 273–87.

The history teacher can learn much from Saint Joan on how history can be taught and about the picture of medieval problems Shaw presents.

2511 Butler, Mary. "An Admirer of Candida," NYT, 12 April 1925, part VIII, p. 2.

Candida is a thoroughly admirable play and does not insist on any particular moral.

2512 "Caesar and Cleopatra: Brilliant Revival at the Kingsway," ERA, 25 April 1925, p. 4.

Caesar and Cleopatra is the most dramatic of Shaw's plays, with good speeches and fine characterization. It has all the force of a brand new play.

2513 "Caesar Shaw," NYT, 19 April 1925, part IX, p. 1; rptd in NYTTR 1920-1926, [n. p.].

In Caesar and Cleopatra Shaw carries further the idea in Byron's DON JUAN and attempts to show Caesar's "natural greatness."

2514 Callender, Harold. "Anxious Critics Despair of New Age," NYT, 25 Jan 1925, part IV, p. 13.

Shaw is numbered among several modern writers who have given us pessimistic prophecies.

2515 "Candida," THEATRE MAGAZINE (NY), XL (Feb 1925), 64.

The superb performance of Katherine Cornell and others make this revival of Candida an example of "what the theatre might become, under ideal circumstances."

2516 "Candida Here Again," NYT, 10 Nov 1925, p. 23; rptd in NYTTR 1920-1926, [n. p.].

Candida has found a permanent place in the American repertory "as a more human comedy of manners than seemed inherent in Bernard Shaw's fin de siecle dialectics."

2517 Canfield, Mary Cass. "Caesar and Cleopatra," NEW REP, XLII (1925), 262-63; rptd in GROTESQUES AND OTHER REFLECTIONS (NY & Lond: Harper, 1927), pp. 172-81.

Caesar and Cleopatra is a thoroughly theatrical entertainment because Shaw here piles on the melodramatic effects. But the piece also has excellent characterization, can be very poetic in the midst of farce and is constantly full of "typical Shavian shocks and surprises."

2518 Carter, Huntly. THE NEW SPIRIT IN THE EUROPEAN THEATRE 1914-1924: A COMPARATIVE STUDY OF THE CHANGES EFFECTED BY THE WAR AND REVOLUTION (NY: Doran [1925]), pp. 45-46, 54, 57-58, 190, 253, 261, 271.

Shaw found the theatre a better place for his Fabian propaganda than any lecture hall. However, on the subject of sex he is very misinformed; in Mrs. Warren's Profession he is "more concerned with uttering his unscientific opinion than in telling the scientific truth." The play was laughed at in Paris because audiences could not understand Shaw's fuss over a "problem" which is an accepted aspect of daily life.

2519 "The Censorship of the Drama," SPECTATOR, CXXXV (1925), 261-62.

[Brief details of Shaw's opposition to theatrical censorship, in response to a questionnaire sent to him and other leading theatrical figures.]

2520 "The Censorship of the Drama," SPECTATOR, CXXXV (1925), 405-06.
Shaw's letter [item 2519] confirms the belief in an optional theatrical censorship.

2521 "Cesar şi Cleopatra" (Caesar and Cleopatra), RAMPA (Bucharest), 6 Sept 1925 [not seen].
[In Roumanian.]

2522 "The Chelsea Palace: A Shaw Season," STAGE, 5 Feb 1925, pp. 18-19.
It would seem Shaw is becoming popular and there are close to capacity audiences for this season at what used to be a variety theatre. No fewer than fourteen plays are to be presented.

2523 Clark, Barrett H. A STUDY OF THE MODERN DRAMA: A HANDBOOK FOR THE STUDY AND APPRECIATION OF THE BEST PLAYS, EUROPEAN, ENGLISH, AND AMERICAN, OF THE LAST HALF CENTURY (1925; NY & Lond: Appleton, 1928), pp. 19, 39, 82, 147-48, 197-98, 221, 225, 227, 236-38, 242, 246, 250-63, 265, 270, 272, 281-83, 309, 313-14, 348, 352, 379, 403.
Shaw has made a many-faceted contribution to the drama. His plays are brilliant satires on contemporary prejudices. The philosophical aspects of his work have gained greater currency than his artistic aspects, perhaps because he has favored the thesis play. When the artist in Shaw overshadows the moralist he gives a good play.

2524 Collis, J. S. SHAW (Lond: Cape; NY: Knopf, 1925).
Shaw has been unsuccessful in Ireland because the Irish are insular and jealous of his international success. It is a mistake to think Shaw has changed in recent years; he is now actually more revolutionary—rather it is his audiences which have changed.

"The Revolutionist's Handbook" is muddleheaded right from its inappropriate title. All Shaw's ideas occur embryonically in the novels and early works (The Quintessence of Ibsenism, The Perfect Wagnerite), and Shaw later "produced reasons for his various articles of faith." In fact, Shaw was "born a mystic." "All his plays are one long cycle in which he again and again proclaims his faith that every man is a Man of Destiny, a Servant of the Life Force, and a Temple of the Holy Ghost." Thus the message of his plays is that people should listen to the promptings of the spirit within, the life force.

Shaw is not consistent (e.g. Back to Methuselah), but offers rather "steady constructive criticism." People wrongly imagine Shaw to be solely destructive, when in fact he always proposes alternatives to the things he attacks (e.g. marriage in Getting Married). Nevertheless, his work appears topsyturvy, especially if he is seen as a moralist rather than as the natural historian he is. Shaw is

alwaysserious about children and education (e.g. the preface to
Misalliance). His wit needs to be viewed in perspective: it did him
good service but is generally overrated. Shaw's prose, especially in
its mystical moments, is poetic, and Shaw is able to hold audiences of
all types (though never through flights of rhetorical oratory). Shaw's
dramatic technique hinges on effective dialogue above all else, which
accounts for the popularity of Getting Married which is indeed all
talk. The characters, far from being unrealistic and mere
embodiments of Shaw, are very real and devoid of the romanticism
people expect in the theatre. [Rather generalized remarks, with
numerous references to the plays, and a detailed consideration of
Heartbreak House.]

2525 "Conference Opens on Birth Control," NYT, 26 March
1925, p. 18.
Shaw advocates birth control because it reflects the voluntary,
rational, controlled abilities of man. [See also: "Scientists Plead for
Birth Control Idea," NYT, 29 March 1925, part IX, p. 6.]

2526 "Correct English a Myth, Says Shaw," NYT, 17 June 1925,
p. 27.
Shaw has addressed an international conference of philologists on the
difference between British and American English. [See also: "Shaw
Starts Trouble," NYT, 18 June 1927, p. 6.]

2527 "Cronică dramatică. Discipolul diavolului" (Dramatic
Chronicle. The Devil's Disciple), RAMPA (Bucharest), 7 Oct
1925 [not seen].
[In Roumanian.]

2528 Cullen, J. F. "Shaw and America," NYT, 4 Jan 1925, part
VIII, p. 19.
Shaw has never visited America and it would be interesting to know
why.

2529 Darlington, W. A. LITERATURE IN THE THEATRE AND
OTHER ESSAYS (Lond: Chapman & Hall, 1925), pp. 151-56.
The topical political satire in Back to Methuselah is not very good,
and appears rather mean. In much of parts one through three Shaw is
simply spinning his wheels and the material is spread thinly. But with
part four the theme moves on again and Shaw reveals he is a man of
wide vision and can indeed handle a large theme without making himself appear petty.

2530 Debech, Lucien. "Sainte Jeanne" (Saint Joan), L'ACTION
FRANCAISE, 3 May 1925, p. 2 [not seen].
[A theatre review. Cited in Weintraub, p. 216. In French.]

2531 Debech, Lucien. "Sainte Jeanne" (Saint Joan), REVUE
UNIVERSELLE, XXI (1 June 1925), 655 [not seen].
[Cited in Weintraub, p. 212. In French.]

2532 De Flers, Robert. [Saint Joan], LE FIGARO, 11 May 1925, p. 2 [not seen]; rptd in Evans, pp. 295-96.
Saint Joan is "the most elevated and most tender work" about this woman; it is an "immortal" tragedy which will endure.

2533 "Denounces Shaw as England's Foe," NYT, 20 Oct 1925, p. 9.
H. A. Jones attacks Shaw for his anti-British attitudes in his forthcoming MR. MAYOR OF SHAKESPEARE'S TOWN. [See also: "Shaw Smiles at Jones," NYT, 21 Oct 1925, p. 22, and "Poodle and Saint Bernard," NYT, 25 Oct 1925, part VIII, p. 14.]

2534 Díez Canedo, Enrique. "Juana de Arco, actualidad literaria" (Joan of Arc: Literary Actuality), EL SOL, 9 June 1925; rptd in CONVERSACIONES LITERARIAS: TERCERA SERIE: 1924-1930 (Mexico: J. Mortiz, 1964), pp. 96-100 [not seen].
[Cited in Rodríguez (MD), p. 339. In Spanish.]

2535 Dobree, Bonamy. HISTRIOPHONE: A DIALOGUE ON DRAMATIC DICTION (Lond: Hogarth P, 1925), p. 37.
Of successful contemporary dramatists "only Shaw appears to regard stage speech as something with a nature of its own, but his theatre prose overmuch resembles that of his prefaces."

2536 Drury, Francis K. W. VIEWPOINTS IN MODERN DRAMA: AN ARRANGEMENT OF PLAYS ACCORDING TO THEIR ESSENTIAL INTEREST (Chicago: American Library Association, 1925), pp. 16, 40, 45, 51, 57, 64, 76-77.
[A descriptive catalogue of plays arranged by content.]

2537 Dyde, S. W. "Shakespeare in the Eyes of Bernard Shaw," QUEEN'S QUARTERLY, XXXII (Jan 1925), 276-84.
Shaw's preface to Saint Joan rightly criticizes Shakespeare's conception of Joan. However, Shaw broadens his attack to include other conceptions of medieval life, and here he has not considered fully the evidence of Shakespeare's work.

2538 Ebel, Walter. "Das Geschlechterproblem bei Bernard Shaw" (The Sex Question by Bernard Shaw), Ph. D. dissertation, University of Königsberg, 1925 [not seen].
[In German.]

2539 Eicker, H. D. "Tragische Gehalt von Shaws St. Joan" (The Tragic Quality of Shaw's Saint Joan), NEUEREN SPRACHEN, XXXIII (1925), 195-200 [not seen].
[Cited in Amalric, p. 478. In German.]

2540 "England and America: Contrasts: A Conversation between Bernard Shaw and Archibald Henderson," BOOKMAN (NY), LX (Jan 1925), 578-83.

[Title describes.]

2541 E[rvine], St. J[ohn]. "The Week's Theatres," OBS, 4 Oct 1925, p. 11.

Mrs. Warren's Profession shows Shaw was infintely better than Sardou in writing a well-made play and marks his zenith in reform and propaganda. Since this play he has let his artistic temper have more sway.

2542 Eulenberg, Herbert. GEGEN SHAW: EINE STREITSCHRIFT: MIT EINER SHAW-PARODIE DES VERFASSERS (Against Shaw: A Pamphlet: With a Parody of Shaw by the Author) (Dresden: Carl Reissner, 1925).

Shaw is not a poet but a clown, a chameleontic opportunist obeying the dictates of the public, a destroyer of romanticism, and a fighter against passion. He is an arrogant critic of Shakespeare, a shameless playwright debunking all heroes (Caesar, Napoleon), a singer of mediocrity and cowardice, and an author who derides the sublime. His characters are mere preachers on the stage. Saint Joan is an offence against history. [In German.]

2543 "The Everyman: The Philanderer," STAGE, 1 Jan 1925, p. 13.

This revival of The Philanderer, a "once topical skit," is worthwhile more for the acting than anything else.

2544 Fagure, Emil D. "Teatrul Naţional. Cesar şi Cleopatra" (National Theatre. Caesar and Cleopatra), LUPTA (Bucharest), 6 Sept 1925 [not seen].

[In Roumanian.]

2545 Fernández Almagro, Melchor. "La Santa Juana de Bernard Shaw" (Bernard Shaw's Saint Joan), REVISTA DE OCCIDENTE, IX (1925), 129-33 [not seen].

[Cited in Rodríguez (MD), p. 339. In Spanish.]

2546 Fineman, Frances [Saint Joan], NYT, 11 Jan 1925, part VII, p. 2; rptd in NYTTR 1920-1926, [n. p.].

A Moscow production of Saint Joan has suffered from cuts by the director and the censor, and Joan has been completely remodelled.

2547 Forbes-Robertson, Sir Johnston. A PLAYER UNDER THREE REIGNS (Lond: T. Fisher Unwin, 1925), pp. 55, 124, 198-99, 243-46.

The role of Caesar in Caesar and Cleopatra was created with Forbes-Robertson in mind, and the play was well received in North America. London audiences did not appreciate Shaw's human and humane Caesar.

2548 Fox, A. W. "St. Joan," MANCHESTER QUARTERLY, II (1925), 179-98 [not seen].

[Cited in Amalric, p. 478.]

2549 Fréjaville, Gustave. [Saint Joan], LE JOURNAL DES
DEBATS, 30 April 1925, p. 5.
Saint Joan is a clear, vivid vision, full of intelligence and poetry. [In
French.]

2550 "From Alpha to Omega," NATION & ATH, XXXVII (1925),
135.
Caesar and Cleopatra may not be Shaw's best play, but it is very good
because of its wit and lively characters.

2551 " 'G. B. S.' Cigar," NYT, 22 Nov 1925, part IV, p. 18.
Shaw is so popular in Germany his portrait appears on a new brand of
cigars.

2552 "G. B. Shaw Assails Medical Council," NYT, 23 Oct 1925,
p. 6.
Shaw has attacked the composition and policies of the British General
Medical Council.

2553 Gabriel, Gilbert W. "Beginneth the Shaw Cycle," SUN
(NY), 15 Sept 1925, p. 26.
Arms and the Man "is opera bouffe in all its design and Offenbach in
all its essence."

2554 Gabriel, Gilbert W. "The Guild Does Its Double Duty,"
SUN (NY), 24 Nov 1925, p. 26.
The Man of Destiny is a bravura piece which reads as "shrewdly and
gayly" as any of Shaw's work. Androcles and the Lion is a "celebrated
harlequinade of faiths and fatuities."

2555 Gardner, Emily. "Miss Wood and Miss Cornell," NYT, 10
May 1925, part VIII, p. 2.
Peggy Wood's portrayal of Candida in Candida displays "clear and
beautiful comprehension."

2556 "Go On Communists' Bail," NYT, 5 Nov 1925, p. 12.
Shaw is one of several people to stand bail surety for twelve
communisits arrested for sedition in London. [See also: "G. B. Shaw
Ridicules Moscow Communists," NYT, 4 Dec 1925, p. 5, and "Topics
of the Times: Worse for Being in the Right," NYT, 5 Dec 1925,
p. 18.]

2557 Gould, Gerald. "Mr. Shaw and Mr. Bryan," SAT REV, CXL
(1925), 65; rptd in THE RETURN TO THE CABBAGE AND
OTHER ESSAYS AND SKETCHES (Lond: Methuen, 1926), pp.
122-26.
Shaw should admit that his ideas about creative evolution are really
based on faith. He is wrong to claim his ideas are founded in science.

2558 "The Guild and Mr. Shaw," NYT, 20 Sept 1925, part VIII,

p. 2.

[An anthology of correspondence between Shaw and the Theatre Guild of New York on the production of his plays.]

2559 H., C. "Epitaph on a Writer of Plays," OUTLOOK (Lond), LV (21 March 1925), 200.

[Humorous verse on Shaw.]

2560 H., G. F. "The World of the Theatre: On Farce—Caesar and Cleopatra," ILN, 2 May 1925, p. 876.

Shaw is a "born farceur" in the tradition of Molière and Cervantes. Caesar and Cleopatra is full of wit, wisdom, irony, paradox and characterization.

2561 Hamilton, F. H. "Mr. Bernard Shaw's Definitions," SPECTATOR, CXXXV (1925), 695.

Shaw's definitions of capitalism, socialism and communism are hopelessly incomprehensible.

2562 Hamon, H., and M. Hamon. "Chronique Dramatique" (Dramatic Chronicle), JOURNAL DES DEBATS, XXXII (8 May 1925), 792-93.

The success of Shaw's Saint Joan arises from his ability to bring the sentiments of his audience into accord with his own. Joan arrests the movement of this world and makes her burning inevitable. Shaw sees Joan as representing the two great forces which transformed the medieval world into the modern; free-thought in the spiritual order wherein the faithful communicate with God directly and without recourse to the ecclesiastical hierarchy, and nationalization wherein the subject is directly connected to the king without recourse to the feudal hierarchy. [In French.]

2563 Hamon, M., and H. Hamon. "Comment Ecrire une Pièce Populaire" (How to Write a Popular Play), ANNALES POLITIQUES ET LITTERAIRES (Paris), LXXXIV (3 May 1925), 469-70 [not seen].

[In French.]

2564 Harris, Frank. "George Bernard Shaw," LA NOUVELLE REVUE FRANCAISE, No. 142 (1 July 1925), 36-73 [not seen].

[In French.]

2565 Henderson, Archibald. "George Bernard Shaw—Intime," REVIEWER (Richmond, Va & Chapel Hill, NC), V: 1 (Jan 1925), 42-50 [not seen].

[Cited in Hood, p. 226.]

2566 Henderson, Archibald. "Literatura y Erotismo: Lo que dice Bernard Shaw (Coloquio con A. Henderson)" (Literature and Eroticism: What Bernard Shaw Says [Conversation with A. Henderson]), REVISTA DE OCCIDENTE, VII (March 1925), 302-

32 [not seen].
[Cited in Hood, pp. 226-27. In Spanish.]

2567 Henderson, Archibald. TABLE-TALK OF G. B. S.: CONVERSATIONS ON THINGS IN GENERAL BETWEEN GEORGE BERNARD SHAW AND HIS BIOGRAPHER (NY & Lond: Harper, 1925); excerpt rptd in James Hurt, ed, FOCUS ON FILM AND THEATRE (Englewood Cliffs, NJ: Prentice-Hall, 1974), pp. 149-53.
[Title describes. Biography.]

2568 Henderson, Archibald. "The Universal Shaw," NYT, 13 Sept 1925, part VIII, p. 2; rptd as "Bernard Shaw's World Conquest," THEATRE GUILD BULLETIN, II (Nov 1927), 7, 16-17.
[A general account of Shaw's rise from obscurity to world-wide prominence.]

2569 Heugel, Jacques. "Sainte Jeanne" (Saint Joan), LE MENESTREL, 8 May 1925.
Saint Joan possesses a tragic powerfulness and demonstrates Shaw's understanding of history and thought. Shaw is a poet. [In French.]

2570 Huizinga, Johan. [Bernard Shaw's Saint], DE GIDS, LXXXIX (1925), part II, 110-20, 220-32, 419-31 [not seen]; rptd in MEN AND IDEAS, trans James S. Holmes and Hans von Marle (Lond: Eyre & Spottiswoode, 1960), pp. 207-39; rptd in Weintraub, pp. 54-85.
In writing Saint Joan Shaw has comprehended the important Hegelian principle of the truly tragic conflict between right and right. Shaw is not concerned with the past but with the lesson Joan's case can teach today. He has shunned the romantic, the heroic, the truly tragic, and poetic sublimity. [In Dutch.]

2571 Jackson, Holbrook. "Robert Bridges, George Moore, Bernard Shaw and Printing," FLEURON: A JOURNAL OF TYPOGRAPHY, IV (1925), 43-53.
Shaw is among those writers who are most interested in the revival of printing as an art. He has controlled his books from the time of their writing through the printing process. The typography of his books has not varied since the printing of Plays Pleasant and Unpleasant.

2572 "Jitta's Atonement," TIMES, 27 Jan 1925, p. 12.
Shaw has changed the tone of the original play on which Jitta's Atonement is based, and we should be grateful for the literary gymnastics he has introduced. However, Jitta is probably a travesty of the original.

2573 "Jitta's Atonement at the Grand, Putney Bridge," ERA, 28 Jan 1925, p. 5.
Jitta's Atonement is clearly a joint effort between Siegfried

Trebitsch and Shaw. The former wrote a grim Ibsenesque piece, and Shaw has touched up its deadly seriousness and added some humor.

2574 Jones, Henry Arthur. "Mr. Jones and Mr. Shaw," EVENING STANDARD (Lond), 6 Nov 1925, p. 3.
There has been a delay in the publication of H. A. Jones' MR. MAYOR OF SHAKESPEARE'S TOWN in which Shaw is attacked. [See also: "Mr. Henry Arthur Jones and Mr. George Bernard Shaw," EVENING STANDARD, 19 Nov 1925, p. 5.]

2575 Jones, Henry Arthur. MR. MAYOR OF SHAKESPEARE'S TOWN (privately printed, 1925) [not seen].
[The book is a protest against Shaw being allowed to propose a toast to Shakespeare's memory in Stratford-upon-Avon.]

2576 Jones, Henry Arthur. WHAT IS CAPITAL? (Lond: Eveleigh Nash & Grayson, 1925).
Shaw is wrong in demanding the abolition of capitalistic laws and in his advocacy of communist laws.

2577 Jung, Werner. LA "JEANNE D'ARC" DE BERNARD SHAW (Bernard Shaw's Joan of Arc) (Brussels: La Renaissance de l'Occident, 1925) [not seen].
[In French.]

2578 Kaneko, Takanosuke. "Bernard Shaw, genjitsushugi ni tsuite" (Bernard Shaw, on His Realism), KYUSHU NIPPO (Fukuoka, Japan), 21 Sept 1925, p. 6; rvd as "Bernard Shaw no genjitsushugi" (Bernard Shaw's Realism), KEIZAI ORAI (Tokyo), IV: 7 (July 1927), 215-24.
Shaw's realistic view of Fabianism is strongly reflected in his plays. Arms and the Man, for example, shows that an heroic dreamer cannot get anything from reality, and that a realist wins the final triumph. [In Japanese.]

2579 "Keeping Up with Bernard Shaw," LIVING AGE, CCCXXIV (1925), 345-46.
Shaw appreciates, secures and deserves more publicity than anyone else, as a glance at his recent activities reveals. A highlight was his reading of O'Flaherty, V. C. on English radio.

2580 Kikuchi, Kan, and Shuji Yamamoto. "Bernard Shaw," EIKOKU AIRURANDO KINDAIGEKI SEIZUI (The Quintessence of Modern Drama in England and Ireland) (Tokyo: Shinchosha, 1925), pp. 63-81.
Shaw claims to be a social reformer. To him playwriting is nothing but one of the tools for propagating his ideas. Opinions will differ as to whether or not such an attitude would be appropriate as a dramatist, but fortunately he is a born dramatist. [In Japanese.]

2581 "King Edward's Hospital Fund," TIMES, 11 June 1925,

p. 11.

Hilaire Belloc and Shaw have debated about what the future will bring (for charitable purposes).

2582 "Kingsway Theatre," TIMES, 22 April 1925, p. 12.
[A review of a revival of Caesar and Cleopatra, concentrating on the acting.]

2583 "Knudsen, Hans. "Bühnen. Berliner Uraufführungen" (Theatre. Berlin First Nights), DIE SCHÖNE LITERATUR, XXVI: 11 (Nov 1925), 522-23.
Back to Methuselah is not a play but a witty debate, a mere illustration to an extensive preface. [In German.]

2584 Kooistra, J. "St. Joan," ENGLISH STUDIES, VII (Feb 1925), 11-18.
[A book review of Saint Joan which considers Shaw's creativity, historical accuracy, characterization, humor, dramatic effects, and the epilogue.]

2585 Krutch, Joseph Wood. "Drama: A Religious Farce," NATION (NY), CXXI (1925), 688-89.
Androcles and the Lion is one of Shaw's happiest efforts in which he "rises far above mere satire and . . . mingles mysticism with buffoonery." The play is a "religious farce" which reveals Shaw's passionate faith.

2586 Krutch, Joseph Wood. "Drama: Better than Shakespeare?" NATION (NY), CXX (1925), 500.
Caesar and Cleopatra possesses "superior intellectual force" to Shakespeare's ANTONY AND CLEOPATRA, and Shaw has created a great man rather than a great lover. Shakespeare "sets me dreaming" while Shaw stirs the passions.

2587 Krutch, Joseph Wood. "Drama: These Charming People," NATION (NY), CXXI (1925), 364.
Arms and the Man is not Shaw's best play because as an early work it uses merely conventional situations "touched off with the Shavian philosophy."

2588 [Kuhe, Ernest]. "Drama," THE ANNUAL REGISTER 1924 (Lond: Longmans, Green, 1925), part II, pp. 63-66.
Even though Shaw's interpretation of Joan in Saint Joan may be questionable, there is no doubt the piece is a tour de force and one of the highlights of the theatrical year. On the other hand, Back to Methuselah, because of its "prodigious length," can never capture the public.

2589 L., M. B. "The Sanity of Genius Excites Us Again," NYT, 30 Aug 1925, part IV, p. 17.
[Some reference to Shaw's opinion of Max Nordau in a general dis-

cussion of sanity and its psychological aspects.]

2590 "Lacon" [Edmund Henry Lacon Watson]. LECTURES TO LIVING AUTHORS (1925; rptd Freeport, NY: Books for Libraries, 1968), pp. 19-28.
Shaw's plays read better than they perform, which is perhaps as well since the Shaw boom is probably over for good. His success was achieved by being an intellectual bully. Most of his writing "is a personal explanation."

2591 Leisegang, H. "B. Shaws heilige Johanna" (B. Shaw's Saint Joan), NEUE JAHRBÜCHER FÜR WISSENSCHAFT UND JUGENDBILDUNG, I (1925), 635-48 [not seen].
[Cited in Amalric, p. 478. In German.]

2592 Liebermann, F. "Shaws Bildnis der Jungfrau von Orléans" (Shaw's Portrait of the Maid of Orleans), HISTORISCHE ZEITSCHRIFTE (Munich), CXXXIII: 1 (1925), 20-40 [not seen].
[Cited in Amalric, p. 478. In German.]

2593 Little, E. Graham. "Doctors and the Public," TIMES, 26 Oct 1925, p. 15.
In discussing the case of Dr. F. W. Axham, Shaw [TIMES, 23 Oct 1925, p. 10] has forgotten that the General Medical Council does have legal jurisdiction. [See also other letters on the subject in TIMES: 28 Oct, p. 15; 29 Oct, p. 15; 30 Oct, p. 13; 31 Oct, p. 13; 2 Nov, p. 15; and 12 Nov, p. 10.]

2594 Littlefield, Walter. "Shaw's Sarcasm Stirs Retort," NYT, 13 Dec 1925, part IX, p. 11.
Shaw and Henry Bernstein have been trading literary blows ever since Saint Joan was produced in Paris.

2595 "London Theatres: The Kingsway: Caesar and Cleopatra," STAGE, 23 April 1925, p. 18.
[A review of the mounting, acting, and history of Caesar and Cleopatra.]

2596 "London Theatres: The Regent: Mrs. Warren's Profession," STAGE, 1 Oct 1925, p. 18.
The economic times have changed so much since Mrs. Warren's Profession was written that it has lost much of its former point.

2597 "London Theatres: The Regent: Saint Joan Revived," STAGE, 22 Jan 1925, p. 18.
Saint Joan is a "ridiculously over-praised" play and Shaw "has lately, with preposterous lack of balance and hysterical gush, been styled the foremost dramatist of the world." Shaw does have many fine qualities, but his "excessive volubility and tiresome assertion of his personality" spoil his work.

2598 "Lord Rectors and Their Critics," NYT, 14 Oct 1925,

p. 24.
Shaw has lent his support to G. K. Chesterton in the upcoming election of the Rector of Glasgow University.

2599 Ludlam, Helen. "Peggy Wood as Candida," NYT, 12 April 1925, part VIII, p. 2.
Peggy Wood's beautiful performance as Candida in Candida deserves far wider recognition.

2600 Lunacharskii, A. "Popuchiki v Evrope: po povodu pis'ma Bernarda Shou v IZVESTIĬAKH" (Fellow-Travellers in Europe: On the Occasion of Shaw's Letter in IZVESTIĬA), IZVESTIĬA (Moscow), 9-11 Jan 1925, 18 Jan 1925, 20 Jan 1925 [not seen].
[In Russian.]

2601 MacCarthy, Desmond. "Drama: Does Shaw Date?" NSTATE, XXIV (1925), 362; rptd in MacCarthy, pp. 80-83.
All writers who have been deeply involved in the life of their times date. But Shaw's plays also have an enduring quality—the quality of genuine originality and integrity in their point of view—that outlasts topicality. This is true of The Philanderer.

2602 "Man and Superman in Full," TIMES, 24 Oct 1925, p. 12.
Audiences now appear tolerant of Man and Superman and its serious dialogue; indeed, Shaw's wit is now more intrusive than helpful.

2603 Mantle, Burns, ed. THE BEST PLAYS OF 1924-25 AND THE YEAR BOOK OF THE DRAMA IN AMERICA (Bost: Small, Maynard, 1925), pp. vii, 3-4, 22, 504-05, 570-71.
The production of Candida was an outstanding success and "established a record for consecutive performances that had previously not been equalled in the thirty years of the play's life." Caesar and Cleopatra also had a good production.

2604 Marcel, Gabriel. "Sainte Jeanne" (Saint Joan), L'EUROPE NOUVELLE, 9 May 1925, p. 620.
Saint Joan depended upon Georges and Ludmilla Pitoëff for its production. [In French.]

2605 Mariátegui, José. "Bernard Shaw y Juana de Arco" (Bernard Shaw and Joan of Arc), VARIEDADES (Peru), No. 919 (10 Oct 1925), 2314-15 [not seen].
[Cited in Rodríguez (MS). In Spanish.]

2606 Markov, P. A. "Teatral'naĭa zhizn' v Moskve: nachalo sezona 1924-25 g." (Moscow Theatrical Life: Start of 1924-25 Season), PECHAT' I REVOLUTSIIA (Moscow), I (1925); rptd in O TEATRE, vol. III (Moscow: Iskusstvo, 1976), pp. 207-10.
Saint Joan in its Moscow production is a failure. Shaw's paradox was to blend historical reality and the historical Joan. [In Russian.]

2607 Mauriac, François. "Sainte Jeanne par Bernard Shaw au

Théâtre des Arts" (Saint Joan by Bernard Shaw at the Arts Theatre), LA NOUVELLE REVUE FRANCAISE, XXIV (1 June 1925), 1048-51.
Shaw gives us the illusion that he is the only sensible man and that the rest of the world is talking nonsense. He is much inferior to Charles Peguy on Joan. Shaw praises Joan for being a heretic and disguises her as a Protestant, but he knows nothing of the admirable pliability of the Roman Catholic Church in these matters. [In French.]

2608 "Mr. Bernard Shaw Prevails: The Censor's Surrender," MPOST, 29 Sept 1925, p. 13.
Mrs. Warren's Profession is no longer a daring play, and it is a wonder it has been banned for so long. However, it still possesses dramatic force and is one of Shaw's best plays (even if he does tend to digress too much on economics).

2609 "Mr. Shaw's Plays in Paris," TIMES, 12 Jan 1925, p. 15.
The Macdona Players' repertory of Shaw plays has been received favorably in Paris.

2610 "Mr. Shaw's St. Joan at Venice," TIMES, 19 Oct 1925, p. 11.
Saint Joan has been given an "enthusiastic" reception in Venice.

2611 "Mr. Shaw's Translation of Austrian Play," TIMES, 6 Jan 1925, p. 10.
Shaw has translated Siegfried Trebitsch's FRAU GITTAS SÜHNE with the title Jitta's Atonement. It is to be presented in Fulham.

2612 Moeller, Philip. "Speeded Up," NYT, 29 April 1925, p. 20.
The opening performance of the revival of Caesar and Cleopatra was too slow, but the production has now been speeded up to normal pace.

2613 "Mrs. Warren's Profession," TIMES, 29 Sept 1925, p. 12.
The first public London performance of Mrs. Warren's Profession was received with "perfect equanimity," even though its theme is not a topic for polite conversation.

2614 "Mrs. Warren's Profession at the Regent," ERA, 3 Oct 1925, p. 8.
Shaw has said what he had to say in Mrs. Warren's Profession much more bittingly in the plays he has written since the play was banned. The problem of prostitution is still with us, but the economic circumstances have changed in the last thirty years. The play is interesting mainly as a historic document.

2615 "Mrs. Warren's Profession: G. B. Shaw's Banned Play on Tour," ERA, 1 Aug 1925, p. 6.
Serious playgoers will wonder why Mrs. Warren's Profession was ever banned. Shaw, doubtless, has exaggerated his facts to give force to

his sermon, but he does make us wonder at the economic system which gives rise to the necessity for prostitution.

2616 "N. Y. U. Students Like Shaw," NYT, 17 May 1925, part I, p. 2.

For the third time, New York University students have selected Shaw as their favorite dramatist.

2617 Nadějde, Iosif. "Cesar și Cleopatra" (Caesar and Cleopatra) ADEVĂRUL (Bucharest), 6 Sept 1925 [not seen].
[In Roumanian.]

2618 Nadějde, Iosif. "Discipolul diavolului" (The Devil's Disciple) ADEVĂRUL (Bucharest), 7 Oct 1925 [not seen].
[In Roumanian.]

2619 Nathan, George Jean. "The Theatre," AMERICAN MERCURY, IV (1925), 244-45.

In Candida Shaw translates the "hokum of the popular theatre" into the best example of "intelligent sentimental writing."

2620 Nathan, George Jean. "The Theatre," AMERICAN MERCURY, V (1925), 244-45.

Caesar and Cleopatra is such a good, rich play it can be staged almost anywhere.

2621 Nevinson, Henry W. MORE CHANGES MORE CHANCES (Lond: Nisbet, 1925), pp. 121, 225, 297, 321.
[Biographical references.]

2622 "New Shaw Play Reported," NYT, 11 May 1925, p. 17.
Shaw has written a new play entitled "The Trial of Jesus." [See also: "Masefield is Author of Play About Christ," NYT, 12 May 1925, p. 3.]

2623 Nicoll, Allardyce. BRITISH DRAMA: AN HISTORICAL SURVEY FROM THE BEGINNINGS TO THE PRESENT TIME (Lond: Harrap, 1925), pp. 350-51, 353-54, 361, 363-64, 366, 369-70, 382, 388, 435-44, 449, 451.

Shaw is the chief dramatist of the age and is vital and fresh. The key words to his work are intellectuality and rebellion, for he dislikes the sentimental and the romantic; he believes we should be ruled by reason. He is a great destroyer of evil and has satirized ruthlessly many facets of society with penetrating vision. He has brought new methods of fusing fantasy and reality, although there is some danger in his innovative prefaces and stage directions (especially when those devices are mimicked by lesser playwrights).

2624 Oldfather, W. A. "Mr. Shaw and the APOLOGY of Socrates," CLASSICAL JOURNAL, XXI (1925-26), 286-90.

Shaw's version of Socrates' defense (when on trial for his life) is novel, startling and wrong. Hence his analogy between Socrates and Joan in the preface to Saint Joan "limps badly."

2625 "Omicron." "From Alpha to Omega," NATION & ATH, XXXVII (1925), 324.
Saint Joan is very successful in Paris and has provoked much discussion.

2626 "Omicron." "From Alpha to Omega," NATION & ATH, XXXVIII (1925), 17.
Mrs. Warren's Profession reveals Shaw's qualities of wit, dialogue, and situation; however, his characters are empty.

2627 "100 Nights for Saint Joan," NYT, 28 Feb 1925, p. 4.
Saint Joan has been performed 100 times in Berlin and shows Berlin audiences are interested in serious drama.

2628 Palmer, John. "A Modern Morality," SAT REV, CXL (1925), 531-32.
Saint Joan "despite its permanent intellectual appeal, belongs quite obviously to the generation of logicians and realists of which Mr. Shaw was the most brilliant example. Mr. Shaw's treatment of Joan is of 1895."

2629 Palmer, John. "The Productions of Georges Pitoëff," FORT REV, CXVIII (1925), 202-16.
[A survey of Pitoëff's career and his productions of Androcles and the Lion, Candida, and Saint Joan.]

2630 Pennell, Joseph. "Pennell Paints the Early Shaw," NYT, 1 Nov 1925, part IV, pp. 1, 22.
[Biographical sketch.]

2631 "Philosophy of Fashion," NYT, 15 March 1925, p. 6.
Ironically, Shaw loves to dress up but finds he is unable to complete with others.

2632 Piéchaud, Martial. "Sainte Jeanne" (Saint Joan), REVUE HEBDOMADAIRE, 13 June 1925, p. 226 [not seen].
[Cited in Weintraub, p. 208. In French.]

2633 "The Play," NYT, 15 Sept 1925, p. 28; rptd in NYTTR 1920-1926, [n. p.].
Arms and the Man remains a vital play, but this revival fails to adequately catch all its Shavian quality.

2634 Playfair, Nigel. THE STORY OF THE LYRIC THEATRE HAMMERSMITH (Lond: Chatto & Windus, 1925), pp. 120, 137.
Shaw reading one of his own plays on the radio was excellent entertainment.

2635 "The Playhouses: Caesar and Cleopatra According to Shaw," ILN, 9 May 1925, p. 934.
Shaw's conception of the two leading characters in Caesar and Cleopatra is rather crude, but much of the rest of the play and its

technique is rich.

2636 Praz, Mario. "Santa Giovanna di GBS" (GBS's Saint Joan), LA FIERA LETTERARIA, 20 Dec 1925 [not seen]; rptd in CRONACHE LETTERARIE ANGLOSASSONI (Anglo-Saxon Literary Chronicle) (Rome: Edizioni di Storia e Letteratura, 1950), vol I, pp. 160-64.

Rather than a chronicle play, Saint Joan is a garland of imaginary conversations; instead of characters, Shaw builds up conversations. Characters crop up in the stage directions, molded by a few notions of rudimental psychology. Shaw's essentially antimelodramatic point of view ends up by being antidramatic: his characters have no individuality. [In Italian.]

2637 "Provincial Productions: Mrs. Warren's Profession," STAGE, 30 July 1925, p. 15.

[A favorable review of Mrs. Warren's Profession.]

2638 Rageot, G[aston]. "Sainte Jeanne" (Saint Joan), REVUE POLITIQUE ET LITTERAIRE, LXIII (6 June 1925), 385-87.

Saint Joan is the noblest and most intelligent homage paid to the glory of the saint. The object of Shaw's satire is English society and morals. Joan is seen as the enemy of the English. Shaw attacks everything conventional, while sincerely speaking the truth. He explains Joan's attitude as the result only of the action of human forces such as reason and commonsense. [In French.]

2639 Ravennes, Jean. "Sainte Jeanne" (Saint Joan), LA REVUE FRANCAISE, 5 June 1925, pp. 639-40.

Saint Joan is a moment of hypocrisy. Shaw makes Joan a saint of the Anglican religion and a forerunner of Luther. [In French.]

2640 "Regent Theatre," TIMES, 15 Jan 1925, p. 12.

Repeated viewing of Saint Joan allows one to overlook its weaknesses and concentrate on its strengths.

2641 "Regent Theatre: Mrs. Warren's Profession," DT, 29 Sept 1925, p. 12.

It is indicative of the progress and health of the theatre that we can wonder why Mrs. Warren's Profession was ever censored. It is unfortunate, too, because the play, which was ahead of its time, must inevitably appear somewhat dated now.

2642 R[hodes], R. C. "Birmingham Amusements: Prince of Wales Theatre: Mrs. Warren's Profession," BIRMINGHAM POST, 28 July 1925, p. 14.

Shaw handles his theme boldly and adroitly, and Mrs. Warren's Profession is witty. "Whether the moral of the piece is of any importance to society is a matter for argument."

2643 "Rialto Gossip," NYT, 1 March 1925, part VII, p. 1.

Shaw's royalties for Candida, a thirty-year-old play, are extremely favorable and lucrative.

2644 Rich, John. "A Tip to Playgoers," NYT, 26 April 1925, part VIII, p. 2.

Caesar and Cleopatra is much more intelligible if one has read Arthur Weigall's THE LIFE AND TIMES OF CLEOPATRA first.

2645 Rivoire, André. "Sainte Jeanne" (Saint Joan), LE TEMPS, 4 May 1925, p. 3. [not seen].

[Touches on the brilliance of the French translation. Cited in Weintraub, p. 207. In French.]

2646 Rockow, Lewis. CONTEMPORARY POLITICAL THOUGHT IN ENGLAND (Lond: Parsons; NY: Macmillan [1925]), pp. 85, 93, 103-05, 123, 127, 184, 258, 260, 266-75, 284.

Shaw came to socialism as an "aesthetic reaction" to existing unpleasant conditions (such as poverty) as can be seen in his contributions to FABIAN ESSAYS. His plays show he is an avowed political dramatist, and his doctrine emerges clearly in Widowers' Houses, Mrs. Warren's Profession, and Man and Superman. In the first two works he attacks capitalism and poverty, offering solutions to both ills as well as other problems. Shaw's didacticism is never concealed, but he is never merely negative; his doctrine of eugenics in Superman propounds a positive philosophy for the future—a combination of socialism and eugenics. Shaw's general criticism of life has enriched the age.

2647 Ropes, Arthur R. "History as Shaw is Wrote," CONTEMPORARY REVIEW, CXXVII (1925), 341-50.

An examination of Arms and the Man, The Man of Destiny, Heartbreak House, and Saint Joan reveals Shaw's weak grasp of history and of the means of transforming it for the stage.

2648 Royde-Smith, N[aomi] G. "The Drama," OUTLOOK (Lond), LV (25 April 1925), 281.

Caesar and Cleopatra in revival reveals it "has not worn nearly so well as Mr. Shaw's early comedies of manners."

2649 Royde-Smith, N[aomi] G. "The Drama: Comedy—Shavian and Otherwise," OUTLOOK (Lond), LVI (31 Oct 1925), 292.

Man and Superman shows that when "allowed to argue in great streams of his unmatched crystalline prose, Shaw holds and delights the mind even when he annoys the intelligence and ignores the experience of other men."

2650 Ruegg, A. "B. Shaw auf dem Wege nach Damaskus" (B. Shaw on the Road to Damascus), SCHWEIZER RUNDSCHAU,

XXV (1925), 158-67, 326-28, 464-73 [not seen].
[Cited in Amalric, p. 478. In German.]

2651 Runchey, Geraldine. "Three Plays," CANADIAN MAGAZINE, LXIV (April 1925), 74-75.
Candida's technique, characterization, and emotional beat are flawless. Shaw's people are human, the production interesting, and the players excellent.

2652 "Saint Joan at the Regent," ERA, 21 Jan 1925, p. 1.
Saint Joan is the finest thing Shaw has ever done. There may be minor faults, but these pale before "the spiritual significance of this supreme work of art."

2653 "Saint Joan in Paris," LIVING AGE, CCCXXVI (1925), 73-74.
The Paris production of Saint Joan generated mixed reactions, despite very favorable circumstances. Perhaps the French did not enjoy seeing Shaw use one of their great national figures used merely as a vehicle for Shaw's ideas.

2654 Salomé, Réné. "Sainte Jeanne" (Saint Joan), ETUDES, CLXXXV (5 Oct 1925), 79 [not seen]
[Review, cited in Weintraub, p. 216. In French.]

2655 Seldes, Gilbert. "The Theatre," DIAL, LXXVIII (1925), 525.
Caesar and Cleopatra is "one of Shaw's noble plays," full of intellectuality; the new prologue is superfluous.

2656 "Shakespeare Birthday Observed in England," NYT, 24 April 1925, p. 10.
Shaw proposed the toast at a luncheon held in Stratford-upon-Avon to mark Shakespeare's birthday. Characteristically, Shaw prefaced his remarks with "Shakespeare and I." [See also: "Shakespeare and I," NYT, 27 April 1925, p. 16.]

2657 "Shakespeare's Birthday," TIMES, 24 April 1925, p. 10.
Shaw attended the Shakespeare celebrations at Stratford-upon-Avon and spoke about London audiences.

2658 Shanks, Edward. "The Drama: St. Joan Again," OUTLOOK (Lond), LV (24 Jan 1925), 57.
Saint Joan in revival wears well and is Shaw's and the time's greatest play.

2659 "Shaw and Belloc Debate 'What is Coming,'" NYT, 28 June 1925, part IX, p. 1.
While Shaw has definite ideas on what the future holds and believes social evolution is necessary, Belloc believes the future is inscrutable. [See also letters to the editor under the title "Shaw and Religion," NYT, 12 July 1925, part VIII, p. 12.]

2660 "Shaw and Snowden in 'Communist Tilt,' " NYT, 13 June 1925, p. 4.

Shaw believes Philip Snowden's use of the word "communist" to describe British agitators is incorrect.

2661 "Shaw Assails British Medical Council: Says Some Doctors Can Hardly Tie Shoelaces," NYT, 3 Sept 1925, p. 27.

[Title describes.]

2662 "Shaw Backs Epstein in Art Controversy," NYT, 17 June 1925, p. 3.

Shaw thinks Jacob Epstein's sculpture as a memorial to W. H. Hudson is a worthy piece of work, if rather too small. [See also: Kathleen Woodward, "An Epstein Work Again Stirs London," NYT, 19 July 1925, part IV, p. 10.]

2663 "Shaw Calls Ideas of Bryan 'Infantilism'; Without Evolution, He Says, There is No Hope," NYT, 10 June 1925, p. 1.

Shaw believes William Jennings Bryan's advocacy of fundamentalism is infantile.

2664 "Shaw Claims the Credit," NYT, 13 Nov 1925, p. 6.

Shaw has claimed credit for the Locarno Treaty.

2665 "Shaw Dances the Tango," NYT, 13 Feb 1925, p. 21.

[Title describes.]

2666 "Shaw Expresses Doubt of Writing More Plays," NYT, 2 March 1925, p. 15.

Shaw feels he should "leave the writing . . . of plays to younger men." [See also: "May Write More Plays," NYT, 3 March 1925, p. 21.]

2667 "Shaw is Sarcastic on Macdonald Dinner," NYT, 14 May 1925, p. 14.

Shaw has declined an invitation from T. P. O'Connor to a dinner in honor of Ramsey Macdonald.

2668 "Shaw Joins the Saints," NYT, 4 July 1925, p. 10.

A portrait of Shaw in stained-glass is to be dedicated in the Ethical Church of London.

2669 "Shaw Preparing Book for Women," NYT, 4 Sept 1925, p. 24.

Shaw's forthcoming The Intelligent Woman's Guide to Socialism and Capitalism is bound to be successful because everything he writes is read widely.

2670 "Shaw Says He's Mad and Everybody Else," NYT, 22 June 1925, p. 17.

In appealing for funds for a "nerve school" Shaw has admitted that he was once a nervous wreck and that most people are unfit to live with.

2671 "Shaw Sees 4-Hour Work Day and Equal Pay in Ideal State," NYT, 27 Nov 1925, p. 19.
[Title describes. See also: "Shaw Foresees a Four-Hour Working Day," NYT, 20 Dec 1925, part VIII, p. 3.]

2672 "Shaw Versus Roosevelt on Birth Control," WORLD TODAY, XLVI (Sept 1925), 845-50.
[An exchange of letters between Shaw and Theodore Roosevelt reflecting their differing opinions on birth control.]

2673 "Shaw Warns Theatres to Lookout for Radio," NYT, 21 March 1925, p. 4.
[Title describes. See also: "Shaw Warns of Radio," NYT, 4 April 1925, p. 20.]

2674 " 'Shaw, You Know Nothing About Art,' Said Pennell," LIT DIG, LXXXVII (28 Nov 1925), 40, 42.
[A second-hand account of Joseph Pennell's sketch of earlier days when he knew Shaw.]

2675 "Shaw's Defeat in Paris," LIT DIG, LXXXVI (4 July 1925), 31.
In Paris Saint Joan has been judged to be both boring and irreverent.

2676 Souday, Paul. "Shaw's Joan Appears in Paris," NYT, 14 June 1925, part III, p. 20.
Shaw's Saint Joan has been received extremely well in Paris, although his ideas on Joan are not entirely original. Shaw is a much better dramatic talent than Pirandello.

2677 "Soviet Stops Shaw's Play for His Slap at Zinovieff, NYT, 6 Jan 1925, p. 1.
The run of Saint Joan in Moscow has been terminated for political reasons and a production in Petrograd has been cancelled. Official news releases obfuscate the real reasons for this development. [See also: "Soviet Fooled London on Shaw: Didn't Stop His Play St. Joan," NYT, 7 Feb 1925, p. 17.]

2678 Spencer, Sidney. THE MESSAGE OF SHAW'S "SAINT JOAN" (Edinburgh: Committee of St. Mark's Unitarian Church, 1925) [not seen].

2679 Speth, William. "Sainte Jeanne," (Saint Joan), LA REVUE MONDIALE, CLXV (15 May 1925), 197-98.
Shaw has found the secret of making historical plays amusing. Saint Joan is a masterpiece which sets us thinking and entertains us. [In French.]

2680 "A Static Revolutionist," NYT, 6 Feb 1925, p. 16.
Despite what others say, the time has come to evaluate what Shaw really is (rather than to accept his own self-appraisal). He has achieved much, but many of his plays are bombastic, "disproportion-

ed, distorted, lopsided."

2681 Strachey, J. St. Loe. "Lines on Seeing One of Mr. Shaw's Comic Tragedies," LIT DIG, LXXXV (30 May 1925), 32.
[A poem on Shaw's "piercing and devastating honesty."]

2682 Svrček, Jaroslav. "Svata Janá (Saint Joan), ROVNOST (Brno), No. 294 (1925), [n.p.; not seen].
[In Czech.]

2683 "Theatre Guild to Give Cycle of Shaw Plays," NYT, 17 Jan 1925, p. 12.
[Details of plans to give an extensive repertory of plays over two years.]

2684 Tittle, Walter. "Mr. Shaw Sits for His Portrait," OUTLOOK (NY), CXXXIX (1925), 302-03.
[An interview, concentrating on Shaw's verbal gems.]

2685 Tittle, Walter. "Mr. Shaw Talks of Art, Labor, and Neckties," OUTLOOK (NY), CXXXIX (1925), 342-45.
[Title describes.]

2686 "To Give More Shaw Plays," NYT, 12 Oct 1925, p. 21.
The Washington Square Players have been granted permission to perform three Shaw plays, which add to their growing Shavian repertoire.

2687 Torretta, Laura. "L'Originalità di Bernhard Shaw" (The Originality of Bernard Shaw), NUOVA ANTOLOGIA (Rome), CCXLIII, series 6 (1 Sept 1925), 42-53.
Shaw, probably seduced by Nietzsche, distinguishes between virtue and goodness, a paradox from which he draws great effects. This concept is the key to interpreting his heroes and heroines. [In Italian.]

2688 Tucker, Anne C. "Will Miss Wood Please Bow?" NYT, 26 April 1925, part VIII, p. 2.
Peggy Wood's performance of Candida in Candida is that of an "extraordinarily gifted artist."

2689 "Two of Mr. Shaw's Little Jokes," NYT, 24 Nov 1925, p. 28; rptd in NYTTR 1920-1926, [n.p.].
[On successful revivals of The Man of Destiny and Androcles and the Lion.]

2690 "University News: St. Andrews," TIMES, 16 Oct 1925, p. 9.
Shaw, along with Galsworthy, has been nominated for the rectorship of St. Andrews University.

2691 Van Doren, Carl. "Mark Twain and Bernard Shaw," CENTURY (NY), CIX (March 1925), 705-10.
Shaw and Twain are both geniuses, although there are differences in

their candor, culture, intellectual temper, and philosophy. Shaw values pure ideas and Twain does not. Twain's treatment of Saint Joan is black and white and set in history; in Saint Joan Shaw takes Joan out of history and sets her among his contemporaries. For Shaw, the opposition is not between good and evil but between initiative and inertia. Shaw makes dramas out of the Lamarckian hypothesis, while Twain makes epics out of a Darwinian orientation which denies the agency of free will. Both men love horse-play, are sardonic, and can also shift to moving eloquence and tenderness.

2692 Van Doren, Carl, and Mark van Doren. AMERICAN AND BRITISH LITERATURE SINCE 1890 (NY & Lond: Century, 1925), pp. 89, 124, 156, 185, 193, 212, 214, 216, 220-34, 237-38, 242-43, 251-58, 261, 263, 273, 329-30.

Shaw's work possesses as much wit as Wilde's and has a sense of social responsibility which questions every basic assumption. Shaw's comedy is "properly destructive" because it bristles with ideas, and it champions intellectual and spiritual force. "His plays are a succession of attempts to show will triumphant over weakness, intelligent hope triumphant over blind pessimism, and reason triumphant over sensual habit." Shaw's masterpiece is Man and Superman because it is Shaw's best expression of his distinctly modern ideas in brilliant form. Back to Methuselah is almost equally important and "belongs without a question with the finest literature of the first quarter of the twentieth century." [With brief discussion of nearly all the plays.]

2693 Van Kan, J. "Bernard Shaw's Saint Joan: An Historical Point of View," FORT REV, CXXIV (July 1925), 36-46.

Saint Joan is the first serious attempt to give a dramatic rendering of Joan based upon a truly historical foundation, and deserves a historical criticism. The play is also a work of art. Shaw's portrayal of Joan does not always take sufficient account of the facts; elsewhere, Shaw distorts the medieval setting.

2694 Walkley, A. B. STILL MORE PREJUDICE (Lond: Heinemann, 1925), pp. 118-22.

Shaw is a very reasonable, potent man because he does not parade his prejudices before us, but rather drives his arguments on through relentless logic. This is now evident in Saint Joan, although Shaw is a little less than kind in his acknowledgments to Anatole France's life of Saint Joan which he consulted.

2695 "Want Shaw as St. Andrews Rector," NYT, 16 Oct 1925, p. 18.

Shaw and Galsworthy have been nominated for the rectorship of St. Andrews University.

2696 Wells, Geoffrey H. A BIBLIOGRAPHY OF THE BOOKS AND PAMPHLETS OF SHAW, WITH OCCASIONAL NOTES BY

G. B. SHAW (Lond: Bookman's Journal, 1925).
[Title describes. Originally issued as supplements to BOOKMAN'S JOURNAL XI (March 1925), & XII (April 1925). Additional notes and additions were printed in July and Sept 1925. A revised edition (Lond: Bookman's Journal, 1929) contains revisions published in BOOKMAN'S JOURNAL, 3rd series, XVI: 7-8 and XVII: 9.]

2697 "WGBS Making Arrangements to Broadcast Shaw's Play," NYT, 19 April 1925, part X, p. 15.
Randolph Somerville, the director of the New York University Players, believes Shaw's plays will adapt well to radio.

2698 Whitehead, George. BERNARD SHAW EXPLAINED: A CRITICAL EXPOSITION OF THE SHAVIAN RELIGION (Lond: Watts, 1925; rptd Folcroft, Pa: Folcroft, 1972).
In a sense Shaw is a Christian, Pantheist, Theosophist, atheist, follower of Nietzsche; in another sense he is exactly the opposite. Because he is a dramatist, and not a philosopher, he is inconsistent in thought and expression. In the plays he embraces numerous philosophies, from Nietzsche to Bunyan, from Christ to Ibsen, and his own life has been similarly versatile and encompassing. His failings as a writer are "perversity, exaggeration, inconsistency, and ineradicable juvenility." Shaw opposes sloppy thinking and sentiment, and "is the sworn foe of complacency" of any kind. "He is the advance guard of the coming Superman, and, take him all in all, is one of the most remarkable products the Life Force has so far evolved."

2699 Williams-Ellis, A. "Mr. Shaw and Immortality," SPECTATOR, CXXXIV (1925), 278-79.
The great interest in Shaw these days is whether future generations will hold our attitudes on Shaw. Some plays seems almost entirely poetic (Androcles and the Lion, Caesar and Cleopatra, Saint Joan, and Heartbreak House). Technically, some seem as lineal descendants of Ben Jonson.

2700 Williams-Ellis, A. "The Theatre: Play, Player, or Producer?" SPECTATOR, CXXXIV (1925), 10.
Of the season's plays, only The Philanderer sparkles. Although it is dated, it is still "gay and lively with its irony and its wit and its brisk clashes of temperament."

2701 Woollcott, Alexander. "Shaw's Caesar and Cleopatra," SUN (NY), 14 April 1925, p. 22.
Caesar and Cleopatra is an "endlessly delightful comedy."

2702 Young, Stark. "As to Peggy Wood," NYT, 5 April 1925, part IX, p. 1.
[A discussion of Wood's performance of Candida in Candida.]

2703 Young, Stark. "Caesar Shaw," NYT, 19 April 1925, part IX, p. 1; rptd in IMMORTAL SHADOWS (NY & Lond: Scribner's,

1948), pp. 57-60; rptd in NYTTR 1920-1926, [n.p.].
There are affinities between Byron's Don Juan and Shaw's Caesar in
Caesar and Cleopatra. With Caesar Shaw strives to portray "natural
greatness" which is to say Caesar takes "the course that perfects and
maintains his own nature." The rest of the characters desire things
which will ultimately ruin them.

2704 Young, Stark. [Candida], NYT, 26 April 1925, part VIII,
p. 1; rptd in NYTTR 1920-1926, [n. p.].
How great a role is can be assessed by the number of interpretations
it can sustain. Candida in Candida is just the sort of character to
bear multiple embodiments.

2705 Young, Stark. "The Play," NYT, 14 April 1925, p. 27; rptd
in NYTTR 1920-1926, [n. p.].
Time has taken the edge off Shaw's work and it can now be evaluated
more clearly. Caesar and Cleopatra "is, from the standpoint of
imagination and theatrical and intellectual contrivance and invention,
the greatest of his works."

2706 Young, Stark. "The Prompt Book," NYT, 5 April 1925,
part IX, p. 1; rptd in NYTTR 1920-1926, [n. p.].
Candida is not realistic; rather it is "poetic satire under a biting,
realistic mask."

1926

2707 A., E. S. "The Maid Storms the Lyceum," SPECTATOR,
CXXXVI (1926), 632.
Saint Joan is Shaw's "noblest achievement" and will endure for ever.

2708 Aas, Lars. BERNARD SHAW OG HANS VERKER
(Bernard Shaw and His Work) (Oslo: Gyldendal, 1926) [not
seen].
[For a less than favorable review of this book, see BOOKMAN
(Lond), LXXII (1927), 184. In Norwegian.]

2709 Agate, James. THE COMMON TOUCH (Lond: Chapman &
Hall, 1926), pp. 221-26.
Throughout his career Shaw has challenged most basic assumptions by
standing them on their heads and by forcing us to think in fresh ways.
[References to Candida.]

2710 Agate, James. "Mr. Bernard Shaw's Shockers" [talk given
on BBC radio, 19 July 1926]; pub in MY THEATRE TALKS
(Lond: Barker, 1933), pp. 55-61.
"Hand in hand with [Shaw's] frenzy for intellectual honesty has
always gone a curious passion for saying the shocking thing in the

shocking way."

2711 Agate, James. A SHORT VIEW OF THE ENGLISH STAGE 1900-1926 (Lond: Herbert Jenkins, 1926), pp. 24-25, 35-36, 59-63, 68-72, 77-79.

Saint Joan was successful because Shaw wrote it and because he has managed to gain the public eye for so long. His arguments about the financing of plays may be correct, but he will not be able to change the play-going public's habits in order to achieve financial success. In the 1890s Shaw's work was not popular because he was known to be an intellectual. However, he figured largely in the renaissance of English drama which came about in the Vedrenne-Barker management of the Court Theatre, and he is now the "giant of the period."

2712 Agnew, Ewan. "The Theatre: A Mixed Bag," SPECTATOR, CXXXVII (1926), 515.

Subsequent historical events have rendered true everything Shaw wrote in Arms and the Man.

2713 "Agrees with Shaw in Religious Views," NYT, 4 Oct 1926, p. 18.

Dr. Harry Neumann agrees with Shaw that the quality of one's life is more important than traditional religious beliefs.

2714 Akita, Ujaku. "Saint Joan o mite Shaw ga suki ni natta" (I Became Fond of Shaw When I Saw Saint Joan), TEATORU (Tokyo), I: 2 (April 1926), 105-08.

Shaw's intentions in Saint Joan are to describe Joan as an example of reversed values between truth and public sentiment, as a symbol of the new nationalism, and as an object of iconoclastic and historical investigation. [In Japanese.]

2715 Amico, Silvio d'. "Santa Giovanni di Shaw" (Shaw's Saint Joan), LA TRIBUNA (Rome), 6 Feb 1926; rptd in Silvio d'Amico, CRONACHE DEL TEATRO (Theatrical Chronicles), ed by E. F. Palmieri II (Bari: Laterza, 1964), 521-26.

Shaw, in Saint Joan, takes a central position over Joan. He finds her condemnation just, as a heretic and nationalist. Saint Joan is neither a play nor a chronicle, but a polemic; it is somewhat less brilliant than usual, but is more logical and could have been more so if Shaw had not gratuitously altered the historical dates. [In Italian.]

2716 "Arms and the Man," DRAMATIST (Easton, Pa), XVII (Jan 1926), 1291-92.

Like all Shaw's plays, Arms and the Man lacks emotion, concreteness, and technique. It possesses intellectual excellence, and needs acting well.

2717 "Arms and the Man Revived at the Everyman," ERA, 22 Sept 1926, p. 1.

World War I finished any romantic notions connected with war, and the remarkable thing is that Shaw said it all over thirty years ago in Arms and the Man, which remains fresh and entertaining.

2718 Atkinson, J. Brooks. "The Play," NYT, 16 Nov 1926, p. 24; rptd in NYTTR 1920-1926, [n. p.].

"The truth seems to be that Pygmalion, never the most brilliant play by this brilliant dramatist, has lost some of its lustre in the momentous years since it was written."

2719 Atkinson, J. Brooks. [Pygmalion], NYT, 21 Nov 1926, part VIII, p. 1; rptd in NYTTR 1920-1926, [n. p.]

Shaw should still be a revolutionary, but this revival of Pygmalion reminds us of how blandly and benevolently Shaw is now accepted. He is in danger of becoming the grand old man of European literature.

2720 B., R. "G. B. S.—70," LIT DIG, XC (28 August 1926), 28.

[A sentimental poem on Shaw's seventieth birthday.]

2721 Barnard, Eunice Fuller. "G. B. S.: The Father of the Flapper," NEW REP, XLVII (1926), 272-73.

Even though many people have never seen a Shaw play, Shaw's influence remains profound for he has created the manners of the times. The prototype of the flapper is to be found very early in his works. [See also: R. Clyde White, "Correspondence: Who is the Flapper's Father?" NEW REP, XLVII (1926), 339.]

2722 Barretto, Larry. "The New Yorker," BOOKMAN (NY), LXIV (1926-27), 731.

[A favorable review of Pygmalion.]

2723 Belfrage, Cedric. "Shaw Postcards Cherished," NYT, 8 Aug 1926, part VII, p. 8.

Shaw has used postcards to great effect in his efforts as a self-publicist.

2724 Bennett, Charles A. "Life through Fiction: II: Major Barbara," BOOKMAN (NY), LXIII (March 1926), 32-36.

Shaw's doctrine of collective guilt in Major Barbara is correct "when it points out that complete freedom and an absolutely clear conscience" are unattainable. However, it is wrong in urging us to sacrifice whatever personal freedom or rectitude we can grasp.

2725 "Bernard Shaw as a Modern Molière," LIT DIG, XCI (23 Oct 1926), 28.

Shaw belongs in Molière's tradition, and Plays Pleasant and Unpleasant will come to be recognized as the most important contribution to European comedy since TARTUFFE and LE MISANTHROPE.

2726 Bettany, F. G. STEWART HEADLAM: A BIOGRAPHY (Lond: John Murray, 1926), pp. v, 54, 87-89, 104-05, 125-28, 135, 139-41, 221, 232.

[Numerous biographical details in connection with Shaw's relationship with Headlam, a prominent clergyman.]

2727 Bidou, H. "Bernard Shaw," JOURNAL DES DEBATS, No. 315 (13 Nov 1926), 1.

Shaw is the chief journalist of our times. All that is unexpected, paradoxical, and flashy in the columnist's art, he uses to adorn his theatre. He has a quick wit, is clear-sighted, and is almost always right. [In French.]

2728 Bidou, H. "Le Disciple du Diable" (The Devil's Disciple), JOURNAL DES DEBATS, No. 101 (12 April 1926), 3.

The Devil's Disciple is one of the least satisfactory of Shaw's plays, with unexpected characterization. Shaw is very witty, deliberately seeks scandal, and is provokingly satirical. However, when his buffoonery is on the point of disgusting us, he suddenly proffers a true, profoundly moving remark, and we are won over again. [In French.]

2729 Birrell, Francis. "The Drama: Literature—and Otherwise," NATION & ATH, XXXIX (1926), 764.

Arms and the Man remains one of Shaw's "happiest" works with its flawless technique and convincing characterization.

2730 "Bits and Bats," SPECTATOR, CXXXVII (1926), 862.

Translations and Tomfooleries really comprises Shaw's "desksweepings," although they are more acceptable than most authors' major works.

2731 "Blanco Posnet at the Coliseum," TIMES, 16 Oct 1926, p. 10.

[An announcement of a forthcoming production of The Shewing-up of Blanco Posnet, together with a brief stage history. See also: "Sir J. Martin-Harvey at the Coliseum," TIMES, 19 Oct 1926, p. 13.]

2732 Blankenagel, John C. "Shaw's Saint Joan and Schiller's JUNGFRAU VON ORLEANS," JOURNAL OF ENGLISH AND GERMANIC PHILOLOGY, XXV (1926), 379-92; rptd in Edward C. Wagenknecht, JOAN OF ARC: AN ANTHOLOGY OF HISTORY AND LITERATURE (NY: Creative Age, 1948), pp. 279-92.

Shaw's and Schiller's portraits of Saint Joan differ quite markedly and each reflects its own age. Schiller gives "free rein to his poetic imagination," while Shaw is much more rationalisitc. The success of each portrait is a matter of personal taste.

2733 Boyd, Ernest. "Readers and Writers," INDEPENDENT (NY), CXVII (1926), 274.

Shaw turned from writing novels to writing plays because he perceived the theatre was a more effective place for his socialistic propaganda. Actually his plays were staged because they were commerically viable. Ultimately, he will be left isolated, clinging to his dogma unnoticed.

2734 Boyd, Ernest. "Readers and Writers," INDEPENDENT (NY), CXVII (1926), 505.

Although there are common bases to the ideas of Shaw and H. L. Mencken, their relative attitudes towards socialism are completely divergent.

2735 Boyd, Thomas. "My Favorite Fiction Character," BOOKMAN (NY), LXIII (March 1926), 58-59.

[Boyd's favorite characters are Ann Whitefield in Man and Superman, and D'Artagnan in THE THREE MUSKETEERS.]

2736 Brandenburg, Hans. "Zur Bilanz der jüngsten literarischen Vergangenheit. Von 1900 bis 1925" (An Account of the Recent Literary Past. From 1900 to 1925), DIE SCHÖNE LITERATUR, XXVII: 7 (July 1926), 294-99.

A typical play by Shaw reads like a chapter from Nietzsche, like a brilliant feuilleton. Shaw presents his ideas in the form of a play to ensure greater effect. [In German.]

2737 Brecht, Bertolt. "Ovation für Shaw" (Ovation for Shaw), BERLINER BÖRSEN-COURIER, 25 July 1926 [not seen]; rptd as "Three Cheers for Shaw," BRECHT ON THEATRE: THE DEVELOPMENT OF AN AESTHETIC, ed by John Willett (NY: Hill & Wang, 1964), pp. 10-13.

Shaw sees it as his duty to always act with "decency, logic and humour" in every situation or confrontation, even when doing so will create opposition. This is Shaw's means of terrorizing people. His plays appeal to one's reason and he creates his dramatic worlds from opinions. "The opinions of his characters constitute their fates. Shaw creates a play by inventing a series of complications which give his characters a chance to develop their opinions as fully as possible and to oppose them to our own." Shaw delights in shattering stereo-typical associations. It is also clear he likes to write and his enjoyment is infectious. [In German.]

2738 Brown, Ivor. "Citizen Shaw," SAT REV, CXLII (1926), 91-92.

Shaw has become accepted as a master in his own time and has done much good for Britain. He is seen everywhere expending his energies on multifarious topics.

2739 Brown, Ivor. "The Theatre: Some Moral Matters," SAT REV, CXLI (1926), 295-96.

The production of Mrs. Warren's Profession provokes all the old arguments about theatrical censorship. The real question so far as this play is concerned is not whether it is harmful but whether it can do anything good and be useful. In fact, it is a clumsy, melodramatic piece, with some flashes of brilliance.

2740 Bry, E. Chr. "Shaw," HOCHLAND (Munich), XXIII (1926), 408-25, 574-85 [not seen.]
[Cited in Amalric, p. 479. In German.]

2741 Calverton, V. F. SEX EXPRESSION IN LITERATURE (NY: Boni & Liveright, 1926), pp. 18, 255, 261, 289-92.
[References to Mrs. Warren's Profession and The Shewing-up of Blanco Posnet as expressions of "contemporary sex release in literature."]

2742 Camba, Julio. "Bernard Shaw y el premio Nóbel" (Bernard Shaw and the Nobel Prize), EL SOL (Spain), 23 Nov 1926, p. 1 [not seen].
[Cited in Rodríguez (MS). In Spanish.]

2743 Camba, Julio. "El donjuanismo y los superhombres" (Donjuanism and Supermen), EL SOL, No. 14 (1926), 3-4 [not seen].
[Cited in Rodríguez (MD), p. 338. In Spanish.]

2744 Cammaerts, Emile. "Molière and Bernard Shaw," NINETEENTH CENTURY, C (Sept 1926), 413-21; rptd in Evans, pp. 307-09.
Plays Pleasant and Unpleasant reveals Shaw has made the most signif-icant contribution to European comedy since Molière. Both men write plays which are essentially character studies.

2745 Carb, David. "Seen on the Stage," VOGUE, LXVII (15 Jan 1926), 87, 130.
The Man of Destiny is Shaw's "tour de force of badinage." Androcles and the Lion needs to be cut, but it is still "one of the gayest and most incisive of Shavian works."

2746 Castro, Cristóbal de. "Otro fenómeno literario: Joyce, Bernard Shaw, escandalizado" (Another Literary Phenomenon: Joyce, Bernard Shaw, Scandalized), LA ESFERA (Spain), No. 629 (23 Jan 1926), 2-3. [not seen].
[Cited in Rodríguez (MS). In Spanish.]

2747 Chesterton, G. K. "Chesterton Surveys Shaw at 70," NYT, 25 July 1926, part IV, pp. 1, 21.
[A survey of Shaw as a man who has sought the truth and an assessment of whether he has found it.]

2748 Chubb, Edwin Watts. "The Conceit of Bernard Shaw," STORIES OF AUTHORS (NY: Macmillan, 1926), p. 414-20.
[A brief uncritical discussion of whether or not Shaw was conceited.]

2749 Clark, Barrett H. "Contemporary English Dramatists, I," ENGLISH JOURNAL, XV (1926), 490-99.
Shaw belongs to the front rank of contemporary dramatists. How-

ever, Shaw's Chekhovian attempt (Heartbreak House) was beyond his abilities. Back to Methuselah is fascinating in places, but generally wearying. Saint Joan is more attractive, though Shaw should have focussed on her character and been less garrulous. Like Barrie and Galsworthy, Shaw's best work belongs to the pre-World War I period.

2750 "Contra Shaw," LIVING AGE, CCCXXVIII (1926), 211-12.
Shaw may now be the most popular European comic dramatist, and so it is difficult to believe he was once esoteric. However, a book by Herbert Eulenberg raises objections against Shaw, none of them new.

2751 C[raig], E[dward] G[ordon]. "The Colossus: G. B. S.," MASK, XII (1926), 21-23.
Shaw should really stop talking about subjects he is not an authority on and stick to what he knows. [See subsequent correspondence between Shaw and Craig, pp. 81-82, 116-17.]

2752 "Dem Siebzigjährigen Bernard Shaw" (To Celebrate the Seventieth Birthday of Bernard Shaw), DIE LITERARISCHE WELT, II: 30 (23 July 1926), 1.
[Birthday congratulations from various celebrities. In German.]

2753 "Disputes Shaw's View of Inquisition." CHRISTIAN CENTURY, XLIII (4 Feb 1926), 153.
In Saint Joan Shaw has not attempted to discover historical fact; rather, he has searched out material for a sermon on the crimes of his contemporaries.

2754 "Dr. Wise Denounces Erskine's Novels," NYT, 13 Dec 1926, p. 24.
Saint Joan is Shaw's greatest work and reveals he is not a pagan.

2755 "The Doctor's Dilemma at the Kingsway," ERA, 24 Nov 1926, p. 9.
The Doctor's Dilemma is an amusing play which satirizes well the medical profession, not least through the sparking dialogue.

2756 Douglas, W. R. "G. B. S., dramaturgo y comerciante" (G. B. S., Dramatist and Merchant), LA PRENSA (Argentina), 3 Oct 1926; rptd in HUMANIDADES (Argentina), XV (1927), 365 [not seen].
[Cited in Rodríguez (MS). In Spanish.]

2757 Edwards, G. B. "Shaw," ADELPHI, IV (1926), 17-32.
Shaw is an artist-philosopher of life whose "art is both self-consciously sociological and unself-consciously autobiographical." He created five heroes: Marchbanks, the hero as poet; Caesar, the hero as conqueror; Undershaft, the hero and mystic; Joan, the hero as saint; and Don Juan, the hero as philosopher. The latter, however, also reveals Shaw's weaknesses and his betrayal of love, courage and life.

2758 Eliot, T. S. "Books of the Quarter," CRITERION, IV (April 1926), 389-90; rptd in Weintraub, pp. 92-93.
Shaw's prestige is in decline as J. M. Robertson's MR. SHAW AND "THE MAID" demonstrates. The latter work is valuable, and shows Shaw's inability to devote himself wholeheartedly to any cause.

2759 Eulenberg, Herbert. "Eulenberg kontra Shaw" (Eulenberg Versus Shaw), DIE LITERARISCHE WELT, II: 4 (22 Jan 1926), 6.
[A brief sketch written in defense of Eulenberg's 1925 pamphlet, item 2542. In German.]

2760 "Everyman Theatre," TIMES, 17 Sept 1926, p. 10.
Arms and the Man is now the amusing sermon of a prophet whose prophecies have been fulfilled and accepted.

2761 Fagure, Emil D. "Ioana d'Arc" (Saint Joan), LUPTA (Bucharest), 5 Feb 1926 [not seen].
[In Roumanian.]

2762 Fagure, Emil D. "Medicul in dilemă" (The Doctor's Dilemma), LUPTA (Bucharest), 17 Dec 1926 [not seen].
[In Roumanian.]

2763 Falcon, Cesar. "Bernard Shaw, Premio Nobel" (Bernard Shaw: Nobel Prize), EL SOL (Spain), 22 Nov 1926, p. 1 [not seen].
[Cited in Rodríguez (MS). In Spanish.]

2764 "The Fortunes of Saint Joan," LIVING AGE, CCCXXIX (1926), 335-36.
Evidence of the popularity of Saint Joan is its revival in England, Berlin, and Paris, and in its translation and production in Madrid and Belgrade (as the fifth Shaw play to be translated into Serbian).

2765 "French to Film Shaw Book," NYT, 1 Dec 1926, p. 29.
A French film company is seeking the film rights to Cashel Byron's Profession.

2766 Fuchs, James, ed. THE SOCIALISM OF SHAW (NY: Vanguard, 1926).
Shaw's prolixity has gained him international fame, though his plays have had only a "weak-to-middling hold upon the stage." His plays are "the spoken operetta of social criticism" and Fabianism has provided the inspiration of all his literary work. [With biographical and an anthology of some of Shaw's socialist pieces.]

2767 Fujii, Akio. "George Bernard Shaw," EIKOKU NO GENDAIGEKI (Contemporary British Drama), (Tokyo: Kenkyusha, 1926), pp. 82-110.
[A general introduction to Shaw's life and works up to Saint Joan. In Japanese.]

2768 "Future of the Labour Party," TIMES, 27 July 1926, p. 14.
[The celebration of Shaw's seventieth birthday as the guest of the Parliamentary Labour Party.]

2769 "G. B. S. at Seventy," REV OF REVS, LXXIV (1926), 312-13.
[A report of Shaw's speech (at a dinner honoring him) which was banned by the government from being broadcast on radio.]

2770 "G. B. S. versus H. M. G.," INDEPENDENT (NY), CXVII (1926), 143.
The British government has demonstrated its stupidity in preventing Shaw from broadcasting his seventieth birthday anniversary speech on radio.

2771 " 'G. B. S.' Wins the Nobel Prize in Literature," WORLD REVIEW (Chicago), III (6 Dec 1926), 167.
[Title describes.]

2772 "G. B. Shaw Denounces Our 'Anarchical' Films," NYT, 25 June 1926, p. 3.
Shaw has condemned American films "with their anarchical doctrines of heroes who [are] permitted to break all law and order."

2773 "G. B. Shaw Turns Financier," NYT, 3 April 1926, p. 14.
Shaw has lent an English council 150,000 pounds for housing purposes.

2774 Gabriel, Gilbert W. "Guild Revives Pygmalion," SUN (NY), 16 Nov 1926, p. 28.
Pygmalion is full of "humor and wisdom, cutting nonsense, bright paradox and unshadowed truth, terseness, playful rightness."

2775 Gardiner, A. G. PORTRAITS AND PORTENTS (NY & Lond: Harper, 1926), pp. 253-60. [American title: CERTAIN PEOPLE OF IMPORTANCE.]
Shaw has become so eminent that his role of prophet is in great danger. He may also be extravagant and have limitations, but "he is the brightest spirit in the world to-day."

2776 "George Bernard Shaw," WORLD REVIEW (Mt. Morris, IL), II (14 June 1926), 261.
High school students "who have a good sense of humor" and "who want truthful ideas about the world we live in" will enjoy Shaw's plays, particularly Arms and the Man, Candida, The Man of Destiny, The Philanderer, and Androcles and the Lion. Some of the plays are "thrillers," for example The Devil's Disciple and Saint Joan. Back to Methuselah has far-reaching thought in it. Don't be tempted to skip the prefaces.

2777 "Germany Greets Shaw," LIVING AGE, CCCXXX (1926), 599-600.
[Details of Germans celebrating Shaw's seventieth birthday.]

2778 Grein, J. T. "Notes About Bernard Shaw," ILN, CLXIX (7 Aug 1926), 236.

Despite his "bantering and blustering" speech at age seventy, Shaw's "loftiness of mind is equalled by the goodness of his heart," although his goodness is seldom made public.

2779 Grein, J. T. "The World of the Theatre: 'G. B. S.'s' First Play Revived," ILN, CLXIX (14 Aug 1926), 290.

[An account of the history of the first production of Widowers' Houses and its subsequent performances.]

2780 Grein, J. T. "The World of the Theatre: The Macdona Players in The Doctor's Dilemma," ILN, CLXIX (11 Dec 1926), 1164.

If Shaw had written only the first act of the The Doctor's Dilemma he would be a master of drama. The play is also a "human document" which "rings true."

2781 Groos, René. "B. Shaw," MERCURE DE FRANCE, CXCII (15 Dec 1926), 513-26; rptd in ESQUISSES (St. Felicien en Vivarais & Paris: Pigeonnier, 1928), pp. 37-59.

Shaw is a fashionable personality, a "universal Molière," a dramatic genius, and a clever man who marshals his popularity. He is not an artist, but a journalist and a polemicist who does not admire literature. Burlesque and paradox are his favorite weapons as he paints a topsy-turvy world unable to resist the temptation of facile, childish effects. His characters are living paradoxes: virtuous rascals, illiterate philosophers, respectable madams. Nevertheless there are truly beautiful things in Saint Joan. Shaw detests romance and senti-mentality. He is a puritan at heart. The weakness of his comedies is that they all deal with the part played by women. [In French.]

2782 Hamon, A. "Le Disciple du Diable" (The Devil's Disciple), LA REVUE MONDIALE, 1 April 1926, pp. 258-62.

The main themes of The Devil's Disciple are religion and hypocrisy, parent-child relationships, and antimilitarism. The characters are drawn with great mastery; the play is simultaneously comic and tragic, a comedy of ideas and characters. [In French.]

2783 Harris, Frank. "Bernard Shaw," DIE NEUE RUNDSCHAU, XXXVII (1926), 7 [not seen].

[Cited in Amalric, p. 479. In German.]

2784 Hayes, J. J. "Sophocles and Yeats Win Dublin," NYT, 26 Dec 1926, part VII, p. 4; rptd in NYTTR 1920-1926, [n. p.].

The Shewing-up of Blanco Posnet falls rather flat in comparison with its companion presentation, Yeats' translation of OEDIPUS REX.

2785 Henderson, Archibald. "George Bernard Shaw Self-Revealed," FORT REV, CXXV (April-May 1926), 433-42, 610-

18.
[In this conversation Shaw defines the difference between old-fashioned and modern drama.]

2786 "High Court of Justice," TIMES, 23 Oct 1926, p. 5.
[A brief report on a law case over film rights to THE CHOCOLATE SOLDIER. See also: "Chancery Division," TIMES, 23 Feb 1927, p. 5; "High Court of Justice," TIMES, 19 March 1927, p. 4., 22 March 1927, p. 5.]

2787 "Hits at Medical Council," NYT, 21 Jan 1926, p. 3.
Shaw, yet again, has attacked the practices of the British General Medical Council.

2788 Horwill, Herbert W. "London Literary News," NYT, 12 Sept 1926, part III, p. 10.
[Brief biographical details.]

2789 The Importance of Being a Socialist," NATION (NY), CXXIII (1926), 209.
Shaw's socialism is largely irrelevant. The important thing is that he saw life and developed his artistic point of view.

2790 "Jaunts and Jollities," SAT REV, CXLII (1926), 555.
[A favorable review of Translations and Tomfooleries.]

2791 Jennings,   Richard.   "The   Theatre,"   SPECTATOR, CXXXVII (1926), 792.
[A favorable review of The Shewing-up of Blanco Posnet.]

2792 Jennings,   Richard.   "The   Theatre,"   SPECTATOR, CXXXVII (1926), 956.
This revival of The Doctor's Dilemma lacks plausibility because the play has inherent weaknesses, is dated, and because of casting problems.

2793 Kaye, Joseph. "The Superman at Seventy!" THEATRE MAGAZINE (NY), XLIV (Sept 1926), 17, 56.
Shaw has not changed much over the years and "piles up a comfortable fortune on a diet of wit and vegetables."

2794 Kikuchi, Kan. "Jibunni eikyoshita gaikoku sakka" (Foreign Writers Who have Influenced Me), TEATORU (Tokyo), I: 3 (May 1926), 82-84.
Shaw is the foreign writer whom I have read most. [In Japanese.]

2795 "Kingsway Theatre," TIMES, 18 Nov 1926, p. 12.
The Doctor's Dilemma is a conflicting mixture of scenes which will endure and scenes which are already dated.

2796 Kitamura, Kihachi. "Shaw no gikyoku to gendai" (Shaw's Play and the Present Age), ENGEKI SHINCHO (Tokyo), I: 2 (May 1926), 15-19; rptd in ATARASHIKI ENGEKIE (Towards a

New Drama) (Tokyo: Genshisha, 1926), pp. 136-47.
What underlies Saint Joan is Shaw's criticism and satire on present-day society. It is not a comedy, but the tragedy of Joan who was killed and who was blameless. [In Japanese.]

2797 Knudsen, Hans. "Bühnen: Berliner Uraufführungen" (Theatre: Berlin First Nights), DIE SCHÖNE LITERATUR, XXVII: 1 (Jan 1926), 41-42.
Back to Methuselah is not very suitable for the stage. [In German.]

2798 [Kraus, Karl?]. "Eine bemerkenswerte Mahnung" (A Noteworthy Warning), DIE FACKEL, XXVIII: 743 (Dec 1926), 102-103.
Siegfried Trebitsch's translations of Shaw are terrible failures. [In German.]

2799 Krleza, M. "Sedamdeset godina George Bernarda Shawa" (Seventieth Birthday of George Bernard Shaw), JUTRARNI LIST (Zagreb), XV (1926), 18-19 [not seen].
[In Croatian.]

2800 Krog, Helge. "Bernard Shaw" [source unknown; 1926?]; rptd in MENINGER OM BØKER OG FORFATTERE (Opinions About Books and Writers) (Oslo: H. Aschehoug, 1929), pp. 185-94 [not seen].
[In Norwegian.]

2801 Krog, Helge. "Bernard Shaw: Jeanne d'Arc" (Bernard Shaw: Saint Joan) [source unknown; 1926]; rptd in MENINGER OM BØKER OG FORFATTERE (Opinions About Books and Writers) (Oslo: H. Aschehoug, 1929), pp. 195-201 [not seen]; rptd in RENT UT SAGT (Plainly Spoken) (Oslo: H. Aschehoug, 1954), pp. 174-81.
Saint Joan dispells the skepticism of the rationalists and the sentimentality of the romanticists about Joan. Those who feel that because of the intellectual and realistic emphasis in his writing Shaw is not a poet have a very narrow definition of the word poet. [In Norwegian.]

2802 Krutch, Joseph Wood. "Drama: Nodding Homer," NATION (NY), CXXIII (1926), 566-67.
Pygmalion does not display fully Shaw's talents. "He wished to write a comedy which should analyze the meaning of manners, but was betrayed into a farce which is often no more than superficial extravaganza."

2803 [Kuhe, Ernest]. "Drama," THE ANNUAL REGISTER 1925 (Lond: Longmans, Green, 1926), part II, pp. 68-72.
1925 was notable for a vogue in revivals of Shaw's work, particularly Mrs. Warren's Profession.

2804 "Lasky Offer of $75,000 Tempts G. B. Shaw," NYT, 18 Nov 1926, p. 26.

Shaw has been tempted by an offer of $75,000 for the screen rights of Cashel Byron's Profession, starring Gene Tunney. Shaw would prefer Jack Dempsey as the villain. [See also: "G. B. Shaw Answers Tunney's Criticism," NYT, 22 Nov 1926, p. 6; "Tunney Disclaims Criticism of Shaw," NYT, 23 Nov 1926, p. 24; "In the Matter of Gene Versus Bernard," NYT, 24 Nov 1926, p. 22; "Shaw Flattered by Report Tunney will Pay Him a Visit," NYT, 4 Dec 1926, p. 1.]

2805 Lewis, Wyndham. THE ART OF BEING RULED (NY & Lond: Harper, 1926), pp. 55-58.

The "kindliness" seen in Saint Joan smacks of "moral charlatanism." Shaw understands Joan's situation but "desecrates it with his weak-minded, chilly worldliness." The same can be said of Back to Methuselah.

2806 "London Puts Shaw in Scrooge Class," NYT, 23 Dec 1926, p. 11.

In London Shaw is being called Scrooge because he believes Christmas is an "unbearable nuisance." [See also: "Not Scroogeized; Only Standardized," NYT, 27 Dec 1926, p. 14; "Chides Shaw on Christmas," NYT, 6 Jan 1927, p. 8.]

2807 "London Theatres: The Everyman," STAGE, 29 July 1926, p. 16.

The satire of Widowers' Houses is as keen as ever, and we should not forget Shaw had practical experience of what he was writing about.

2808 "London Theatres: The Kingsway," STAGE, 25 Nov 1926, p. 18.

The Doctor's Dilemma has been revived successfully.

2809 "London Theatres: The Lyceum: Saint Joan," STAGE, 1 April 1926, p. 18.

Although the public has taken Saint Joan and Sybil Thorndyke to its heart, it should be noted the piece is marred by long-windedness, unnecessary indulgence in slang, and the tiresome epilogue.

2810 "London Theatres: The Strand: Mrs. Warren's Profession," STAGE, 4 March 1926, p. 18.

The fuss that there were new lines in Mrs. Warren's Profession seems to be unjustified, for if there were any they are unnoticeable. However, audiences continue to devour Shaw's "strong meat."

2811 "Lord Oxford on a Free Press," TIMES, 19 March 1926, p. 11.

T. P. O'Connor saved Shaw's job as a journalist by making him a music critic.

2812 Loraine, Robert. "What G. B. S. Thought When He was

Drowning," COSMOPOLITAN, LXXXI (July 1926), 23.
[Title describes.]

2813 Mantle, Burns, ed. THE BEST PLAYS OF 1925-26 AND THE YEAR BOOK OF THE DRAMA IN AMERICA (NY: Dodd, Mead, 1926), pp. 442, 493-94, 499-500.
[Production details and plot outlines of Arms and the Man, Candida, Androcles and the Lion, and The Man of Destiny.]

2814 Mariátegui, José Carlos. "Bernard Shaw," VARIEDADES (Chile), No. 698 (18 Sept 1926); rptd in CENTAURO (Chile), No. 4 (May 1950), 12; rptd in EL ALMA MATINAL Y OTRAS ESTACIONES DEL HOMBRE DE HOY (The Morning Soul and Other Conditions of Men of Today) (Lima: Amauta, 1959), III, 139-46 [not seen].
[Cited in Rodríguez (MS). In Spanish.]

2815 Martínez Ruiz, José. "La transición teatral" (Theatrical Transition), LA PRENSA (Argentina), 1 Aug 1926 [not seen].
[Cited in Rodríguez (MS). In Spanish.]

2816 Mellersh, H. E. L. "Shaw, Wells, and Creative Evolution," FORT REV, CXXV (Feb 1926), 178-88.
The quarrel between the "crude materialism" of the Social Darwinists and the "ill-tempered conservatism" of the established church provides the background for Shaw's Back to Methuselah and Wells' OUTLINE OF HISTORY. Shaw has hope for the future through the creed of creative evolution as shown by Androcles and the Lion, Back to Methuselah, and Saint Joan.

2817 Michael, Friedrich. "Theaterspielplan und deutsches Drama" (Theatre Repertory and German Drama), DIE SCHÖNE LITERATUR, XXVII: 8 (Aug 1926), 337-43.
Shaw belongs with the most popular playwrights on the German stage.
[In German.]

2818 "Mr. G. B. Shaw Awarded Nobel Prize," TIMES, 12 Nov 1926, p. 14.
[Title describes. See also Shaw's proposal for the prize money: "Mr. Shaw and the Nobel Prize," TIMES, 19 Nov 1926, p. 14.]

2819 "Mr. Shaw and His Bothersome Money," LIT DIG, XCI (4 Dec 1926), 29.
Shaw has a cavalier attitude towards money. He spurns the Nobel Prize money but is very hard-nosed in negotiating the film rights for one of his early novels.

2820 "Mr. Shaw at Play," TLS, No. 1292 (4 Nov 1926), 765.
Translations and Tomfooleries is a useful anthology of Shaw's shorter pieces but some will "find their enjoyment of these extravagances damped by the immoderate love of horseplay and that Mr. Shaw in-

343

dulges in his irresponsible moments."

2821 "Mr. Shaw Frankly Dons the Cap and Bells," NYT, 31 Oct 1926, part III, pp. 2, 19.
Shaw's Translations and Tomfooleries reflects Shaw the buffoon, although he can be serious as well. "For him the world's not a stage but the big top with the three rings," but "his only regret" is he can't perform in all three rings simultaneously.

2822 "Mr. Shaw's Birthday," SPECTATOR, CXXXVII (1926), 171.
[A humorous editorial on Shaw's seventieth birthday.]

2823 "Mr. Shaw's Trifles," TIMES, 2 Nov 1926, p. 20.
Translations and Tomfooleries contains several plays which range from the inconsequential to the interesting.

2824 Morgan, Charles. "Molière and Shaw, NYT, 5 Dec 1926, part VIII, p. 1.
The very qualities which now make Shaw famous will probably damage his future reputation. He also deserves the Nobel Prize, but should not have received it before Thomas Hardy.

2825 "Mrs. Warren's Profession at the Strand," ERA, 10 March 1926, p. 1.
Mrs. Warren's Profession must have dated somewhat, despite Shaw's protestations to the contrary, for it is produced in costumes of the 1890s. Shaw is not at his best: the characterization is poor, with Shaw giving us the externals rather than fully fleshed out people.

2826 Muckermann, F. "Zeitmasse Literaturfragen: B. Shaw" (Time and Literary Questions: B. Shaw), STIMMEN UND ZEIT, LVII (1926), 139-46 [not seen].
[Cited in Amalric, p. 479. In German.]

2827 Muir, Edwin. "Translations and Tomfooleries," NATION & ATH, XL (1926), 341.
There is little of the Shaw we know in this collection of plays, Translations and Tomfooleries. This is because what makes Shaw a good dramatist is not imagination or an ability to create characters, but "moral enthusiasm and suppleness of mind. When he is not exercising these he is merely a shadow of himself."

2828 Muret, M[aurice]. "La 'Fausse Gloire' de M. Bernard Shaw" (The False Glory of Bernard Shaw), JOURNAL DES DEBATS, No. 272 (1 Oct 1926), 3; rptd as "That Man Shaw: A Disgrace to the Theatre," LIVING AGE, CCCXXXI (1926), 434-37.
Shaw is a pseudo-great man, a sham apostle and reformer. He is the poet of mediocrity and baseness. His intolerable prefaces explain his conception of the world; that is a socialist, Fabian conception which

shows Shaw is a cautious revolutionary who knows how to please the petty bourgeois and small-minded lower-middle-class. He enjoys the license granted to buffoons. [In French.]

2829 Nadějde, Iosif. "Medicul in dilemă" (The Doctor's Dilemma), ADEVĂRUL (Bucharest), 18 Dec 1926 [not seen]. [In Roumanian.]

2830 "The New Books: Drama," SATURDAY REVIEW OF LITERATURE (NY), III (1926), 396.
Translations and Tomfooleries has the occasional Shavian touch, but the publication of this volume is really a "rather melancholy occasion."

2831 Noll, Anna. "G. B. S.s historische Dramen" (G. B. S.'s Historical Dramas), Ph. D. dissertation, University of Vienna, 1926 [not seen].
[Cited in Amalric, p. 479. In German.]

2832 Noroom, Carl H. "Shaw is Urged to Consider Consumer-Ownership Plan," NYT, 26 Dec 1926, part VIII, p. 8.
Shaw should consider a plan whereby the people of the world become stock-holders of its resources.

2833 NOVÉ ČESKÉ DIVADLO 1918-1926 (The New Czech Theatre 1918-1926) (Prague: Aventium, 1926).
[Provides details of Shaw productions in Prague during 1918-26. In Czech.]

2834 Noyes, E. S. "A Note on PEREGRINE PICKLE and Pygmalion," MODERN LANGUAGE NOTES, XLI (1926), 327-30.
There are numerous and obvious parallels between PEREGRINE PICKLE and Pygmalion. However, Shaw denies categorically that he has ever read Smollett's work.

2835 [Ogden, C. K.]. "Bernard Shaw Defends Socialism," FORUM (NY), LXXVI (Nov 1926), 651-60; rptd in REV OF REVS, LXXIV (1926), 659.
[Shaw's response to eleven questions about socialism with some interspersed commentary on socialism generally by Ogden.]

2836 "Omicron." "Plays and Pictures," NATION & ATH, XL (1926), 301.
Like many of Shaw's plays, The Doctor's Dilemma pleases with its intellectuality and craftsmanship. However, Shaw's ultimate handling of the play is worrisome and disappointing.

2837 "Other New Books," THEATRE ARTS MONTHLY, X (1926), 874.
Translations and Tomfooleries is merely foolish and represents a desk-sweeping exercise on Shaw's part.

2838 [Pearson, Hesketh.] THE WHISPERING GALLERY: BEING LEAVES FROM A DIPLOMAT'S DIARY (Lond: Lane, 1926), pp. 61-62, 92, 116-22, 236-27.
[Genial personal reminiscences.]

2839 Peper, Elisabeth. "George Bernard Shaws Beziehungen zu Samuel Butler dem Jüngeren.'" (George Bernard Shaw's Relationship to Samuel Butler the Younger), ANGLIA, L (1926), 295-316.
[An examination of connections in ideas and techniques between Shaw and Butler, with particular reference to Major Barbara, Misalliance, Back to Methuselah, EREWHON and THE WAY OF ALL FLESH. In German.]

2840 Percy, Esmé. "The Humanity of Shaw," HUMANIST, Dec 1926 [not seen].
[Cited in C. L. & V. M. Broad, DICTIONARY TO THE PLAYS AND NOVELS OF BERNARD SHAW, p. 130.]

2841 "The Playhouses: Mrs. Warren's Profession at the Strand," ILN, CLXVIII (13 March 1926), 480.
Mrs. Warren's Profession is interesting as something of a curiosity and as a piece which originally shocked conventionality. However, it is "deplorably inhuman."

2842 "Political Notes," TIMES, 22 July 1926, p. 14.
The question has been raised as to why permission to broadcast speeches at Shaw's seventieth birthday celebrations has been denied.
[See also: "Mr. Bernard Shaw's Speech," TIMES, 28 July 1926, p. 8.]

2843 Pribilla, M. S. J. "Die Jungfrau von Orleans eine protestantische Heilige-Theolog zu-B. Shaw" (The Maid of Orleans a Protestant Saintly Theologian to B. Shaw), STIMMEN UND ZEIT, LVII (1926), 241-59 [not seen].
[Cited in Amalric, p. 479. In German.]

2844 "Pure, Simon" [Frank Swinnerton]. "The Londoner: A Septuagenarian G. B. S.," BOOKMAN (NY), LXIV (Oct 1926), 177-79; rptd in A LONDON BOOKMAN (Lond: Secker, 1928), pp. 260-63.
Although Shaw's seventieth birthday has been ignored by the British government, he is nevertheless a great man and venerated.

2845 "Pure, Simon" [Frank Swinnerton]. "The Londoner: Mr. Shaw and Broadcasting," BOOKMAN (NY), LXIV (1926-27), 330-31.
[An editorial on Shaw being banned from making a radio broadcast.]

2846 "Put Out of Shaw's Home," NYT, 1 July 1926, p. 4.
An American has made determined and unsuccessful efforts to see Shaw. Also, Shaw has declined to support the cause of lowering the

voting age for women from thirty to twenty-one.

2847 "Pygmalion," L'INDEPENDENT BELGE, 6 Oct 1926.
The characters in Pygmalion are too artificial, but the dialogue gives great intellectual pleasure. [In French.]

2848 "Pygmalion: From Stone to Flesh," DRAMATIST (Easton, Pa), XVII (1926), 1319-20.
Pygmalion demonstrates Shaw had promise twenty years ago, but he is now "mere pose and impudence."

2849 Ray, Violet. "The Theatre," CRITERION, IV (1926), 350-54.
The Shewing-up of Blanco Posnet and Androcles and the Lion have become classics, and, as a play for children, Androcles is "one of the best."

2850 Robertson, J. M. MR. SHAW AND "THE MAID" (Lond: Cobden-Sanderson, [1926]); pp. 91-100 rptd in Weintraub, pp. 86-91.
[A "demonstration" that "the reader who would know the truth about the age of (Saint Joan) . . . will do well to dismiss Mr. Shaw's assurance that Saint Joan tells him all he needs to know."]

2851 Royde-Smith, N[aomi] G. "The Drama: Plays: Unpleasant," OUTLOOK (Lond), LVIII (7 Aug 1926), 127.
Widowers' Houses is not a very good play, but it remains "unstaled by time" and is interesting because it is suffused with Shaw's youthful indignation.

2852 S., H. S. "On Mr. Bernard Shaw's 70th Birthday," TIMES, 26 July 1926, p. 16.
[An inconsequential celebratory poem.]

2853 "Saint Joan," TIMES, 25 March 1926, p. 14.
Saint Joan is probably Shaw's best play and bears repeated viewing.

2854 "Saint Joan at the Lyceum," ERA, 31 March 1926, p. 8.
Saint Joan is the most popular play of the time and audiences greet it with enormous enthusiasm.

2855 Sander, Gustav H. SHAWS "SAINT JOAN" IM UNTERRICHT DER OBERPRIMA (Shaw's Saint Joan in Sixthform Instruction) (Frankfurt, 1926) [not seen].
[In German.]

2856 "Santa Juana de Shaw en La Plata" (Shaw's Saint Joan in La Plata), MARTIN FIERRO (Argentina), No. 35 (5 Nov 1926), 132 [not seen].
[Cited in Rodríguez (MS). In Spanish.]

2857 Sarolea, Charles. "Has Mr. Shaw Understood Joan of Arc?" ENGLISH REVIEW, XLIII (Aug 1926), 175-82; rptd in

Weintraub, pp. 94-101.
In Saint Joan, Shaw distorts his heroine's personality and misrepresents her mission. He is extraordinarily ignorant of the medieval atmosphere and conditions surrounding her life.

2858 "Says He Refused Scenario by Shaw," NYT, 11 Oct 1926, p. 11.
D. W. Griffith reports that in 1917 he turned down Shaw's offer to write a film scenario. [See also: "Shaw Can't Recall Scenario Rejection," NYT, 12 Oct 1926, p. 31.]

2859 "Shaw Admits Learning the Tango at Madeira, But has neither Time nor Youth for it Now," NYT, 28 Jan 1926, p. 6.
[Title describes.]

2860 "Shaw Adopts Code Signature to Foil Pests; Bemoans the Penalties of Being a Celebrity," NYT, 10 Jan 1926, part II, p. 1.
[Title describes. See also: Claire Price, "Bernard Shaw Shrinks from His Wide Renown, NYT, 2 May 1926, part IX, p. 10.]

2861 "Shaw and Bourchier Challenge Censor," NYT, 28 Feb 1926, part I, p. 29.
Shaw and Arthur Bourchier are to produce Mrs. Warren's Profession with some additional lines not approved by the censor.

2862 "Shaw and Germany Again," LIVING AGE, CCCXXXI (1926), 83-84.
Shaw's adulation of Germany over England is based on faulty premises.

2863 "Shaw and Hall Caine Characters in Play," NYT, 26 Nov 1926, p. 2.
Shaw does not object to being impersonated in HIS WILD OAT. [See also: "Shaw to the Life in Play WILD OAT," NYT, 28 Nov 1926, part I, p. 30; "Shaw and Caine on Stage," NYT, 1 Dec 1926, p. 24; Claire Price, "Shaw Shows How to Impersonate Shaw," NYT, 26 Dec 1926, part IV, p. 10.]

2864 "Shaw and the Nobel Prize," OUTLOOK (NY), CXLIV (1926), 425-26.
Shaw is being perfectly honest in declaring monetary awards are injurious to literature. He has declined the money attached to the Nobel Prize.

2865 "Shaw and Wells Assailed by Briton," NYT, 28 March 1926, part I, p. 12.
Captain Gilbert Frankau has attacked Shaw for his socialist writings. [See also: "G. B. Shaw Belittles Frankau's Criticism," NYT, 30 March 1926, p. 16.]

2866 "Shaw as a Music Critic," NYT, 12 Dec 1926, part VIII, p. 12.

[Biography.]

2867 "Shaw Avoids Cremators," NYT, 21 Oct 1926, p. 18.
Shaw has declined an invitation to attend a convention of cremators.

2868 "Shaw Bids Us Send No Money to Erin," NYT, 3 Oct 1926, part II, p. 19.
Shaw believes Americans should not send money to Ireland but instead force the Irish to care for themselves.

2869 "Shaw Defends the Films," NYT, 26 Feb 1926, p. 6.
Shaw has protested that because he regards films as a vulgar form of entertainment, "he is better occupied in writing plays."

2870 "Shaw Explains Film Ban," NYT, 13 Feb 1926, p. 17.
Shaw has rejected offers for the film rights to his plays because they would then have no value in the theatre.

2871 "Shaw Favors Women on Censorship Staff," NYT, 12 June 1926, p. 4.
Shaw supports the proposal that a woman should also assist the Lord Chamberlain in the censorship of plays.

2872 "Shaw for Rebuilding Stratford Theatre," NYT, 2 April 1926, p. 23.
[Title describes.]

2873 "Shaw Gives Place to Inge," NYT, 18 Dec 1926, p. 6.
Shaw regards Dean Inge as the greatest writer living in England.

2874 "Shaw has Name Reduced," NYT, 7 Nov 1926, p. 20.
Shaw's name has been displayed so prominently at a London music-hall that he has asked it be reduced in size.

2875 "Shaw Highly Honored," OUTLOOK (NY), CXLIV (1926), 392.
Shaw has been awarded the Nobel Prize, though it is clearly for his accumulative rather than singular achievement.

2876 "Shaw Hits Seventy," LIVING AGE, CCCXXX (1926), 550-52.
England's artistic stupidity has caused Shaw pain, especially when his work has been better appreciated in America and Germany. However, a dinner given in his honor by politicians who wanted to hear him speak on politics demonstrates why Shaw remains in England.

2877 "Shaw is Mystified by His Nobel Prize," NYT, 12 Nov 1926, p. 8.
Shaw has suggested he has won the Nobel Prize because he wrote nothing in 1925. [See also: "Approve Award to Shaw," NYT, 13 Nov 1926, p. 4; "There Seems a Change in Mr. Shaw," NYT, 13 Nov 1926, p. 16; "Shaw Takes Honor, But Not Nobel Cash," NYT, 19 Nov 1926,

p. 1; "Mr. Shaw and the Prize," NYT, 20 Nov 1926, p. 16; "Shaw Prize Ruling to be Made Today," NYT, 20 Nov 1926, p. 16; "Shaw will 'Hold' Nobel Prize Money," NYT, 21 Nov 1926, p. 8; "Shaw's Refusal of Prize Money may be 'Transient,' He Says," NYT, 25 Nov 1926, p. 27.]

2878 "Shaw Jests on Funeral," NYT, 6 July 1926, p. 23.
Shaw has declined to attend a historical pageant, declaring the only one he expects to attend will be his own funeral.

2879 "Shaw Links Applause to Brawls in Church," NYT, 7 Feb 1926, p. 4.
Shaw believes applause is inappropriate for a serious play.

2880 "Shaw, Master of the Unconventional Play," WORLD REVIEW (Chicago), III (6 Dec 1926), 167.
[A brief survey of Shaw's career demonstrating that the plays are numerous, varied, and carry the stamp of his "inimitable and arresting genius."]

2881 "Shaw Once Skeptic as to Plays Here," NYT, 24 Dec 1926, p. 18.
Correspondence published this day reveals Shaw was sceptical about the early productions of his plays in America.

2882 "Shaw Pleads Brain Fag," NYT, 7 Oct 1926, p. 44.
Shaw has declined an invitation to write a vaudeville skit.

2883 "Shaw Refuses to Let Labor Use Play Free," NYT, 13 June 1926, part I, p. 13.
Shaw has refused to allow a free performance of The Shewing-up of Blanco Posnet as part of a labor demonstration.

2884 "Shaw Rejects Woman Plea," NYT, 19 June 1926, p. 12.
Shaw has declined the invitation of the Actresses' Franchise League to support the cause of women.

2885 "Shaw Says He is Ignorant of Joan," NYT, 19 Sept 1926, part X, p. 10.
Although he wrote Saint Joan, Shaw has asserted he does not understand Joan herself.

2886 "Shaw Silent on Birthday," NYT, 25 July 1926, part I, p. 7.
Shaw has no comment on the various arrangements to celebrate his seventieth birthday. [See also: "Shaw's Birthday Sees Controversy," NYT, 26 July 1926, p. 4; "Shaw Feted at 70, Jousts in Old Style with All His Enemies," NYT, 27 July 1926, pp. 1-2; "Shaw at Seventy," NYT, 27 July 1926, p. 16; "Hard Days for Great Men," 28 July 1926, p. 16; "Shaw Thanks Germany for Recognizing Him While 'Dangerous and Disreputable' in Britain," NYT, 1 Aug 1926, pat II, p. 1; "Bernard Shaw Lectures on an Errant World," NYT, 15 Aug 1926, part VIII, p. 3; "Karel Capek Puts Shaw in His Gallery of Celebrities," NYT, 15 August 1926, part VIII, p. 3.

2887 "Shaw Upheld in Suit Here Over Film Rights," NYT, 16 Sept 1926, p. 20.
Shaw's contention, that an American court does not have jurisdiction over him and his attitude towards a film version of THE CHOCOLATE SOLDIER, has been upheld.

2888 "Shaw Wants $2,500,000," NYT, 17 Nov 1926, p. 7.
Shaw asserts the British censor owes him $2,500,000 for holding up the production of his plays over the years.

2889 "Shaw Wields Pen as an Economist," NYT, 17 Aug 1926, p. 4.
Shaw has attacked the British government for "halving [the] value of war loan stock by inflation." [See also: "Wells Upholds Shaw on British Loan Stock," NYT, 19 Aug 1926, p. 19; "Genius and Finance," NYT, 20 Aug 1926, p. 16.]

2890 Sirlin, Lázaro. "La sexuología en las comedias de Jorge Bernard Shaw" (Sexology in George Bernard Shaw's Comedies), SAGITARIO (Argentina), No. 7 (Oct-Nov 1926), 50-58 [not seen].
[Cited in Rodríguez (MS). In Spanish.]

2891 Skinner, R. Dana. "Mid-Season," INDEPENDENT (NY), CXVI (1926), 48.
In Androcles and the Lion Shaw reveals his fundamental weakness-- his "compelling necessity . . . to defend himself by ridicule from those deeper truths and mysteries of life to which his instinct leads him and against which his hard old rationalism rebels." That is, he attacks everything to which he is actually instinctively attracted.

2892 "A Slavonian Saint Joan: Shaw and Shakespeare in the Croatian Language," GRAPHIC, CXIV (1926), 417.
[Production photographs and details of the successful production of Saint Joan in Zagreb.]

2893 Steinbrinck, O. "Einige Bemerkungen über G. B. Shaw— Dr. Bücher" (Some Observations About G. B. Shaw and Dr. Bücher), BUECHERWELT: ZEITSCHRIFT FÜR BIBLIOTHEKS- UND BÜCHERWESEN (BORROMÄUSVEREIN) (Bonn), XXIII (1926), 57-61 [not seen].
[Cited in Amalric, p. 479. In German.]

2894 "Strand Theatre," TIMES, 4 March 1926, p. 12.
The characterization in Mrs. Warren's Profession has both a certain roughness and vigor.

2895 Stuckey, Laurence. "Man and Superman," DRAMA (Chicago), XVI (March 1926), 205-06.
[An account of Shaw proposing the toast to Shakespeare at the annual Shakespeare Festival, Stratford-upon-Avon.]

2896 Svrček, Jaroslav. "Pohostinska hra" (A Guest Performance), ROVNOST (Brno), No. 28 (1926), [n. p.; not seen].
[On Saint Joan. In Czech.]

2897 Svrček, Jaroslav. "Slavnostní večer 70-tych narozenin Bernarda Shaw'a" (Evening Celebration of Bernard Shaw's 70th Birthday), ROVNOST (Brno), No. 256 (Sept 1926), 6 [not seen].
[On Back to Methuselah. In Czech.]

2898 Tetauer, Frank. "Shawův filosoficky kriticism" (Shaw's Philosophical Criticism), TVORBA, 1926, pp. 189-94, 213-16. [not seen].
[Cited in Amalric, p. 479. In Czech.]

2899 Tilgher, Adriano. "La grande Caterina di Shaw al Quirino" (Shaw's Great Catherine at the Quirino Theatre), IL MONDO (Rome), 23 June 1926 [not seen].
[In Italian.]

2900 "Translations and Tomfooleries," LIVING AGE, CCCXXXI (1926), 376.
The first two acts of Jitta's Atonement leave a bad taste in the mouth. Shaw's bag of dramatic tricks elsewhere in this volume is tiresome, but no other playwright can entertain like Shaw.

2901 Trebitsch, Siegfried. "Bernard Shaws Ruhm" (Bernard Shaw's Reputation), DIE LITERARISCHE WELT, II: 30 (23 July 1926), 1-2.
[On Shaw's reputation in Germany. In German.]

2902 Trebitsch, Siegfried. "Der deutsche Aufstieg B. Shaws" (B. Shaw's German Ascent), WELTBÜHNE, XXII (1926), 29 [not seen].
[Cited in Amalric, p. 479. In German.]

2903 Vidakovic, A. "Pozorisno: Sveta Jovanka od Bernarda Soa" (Theatrical Letter: Saint Joan by Bernard Shaw), LETOPIS MATITSE SRPSKE (Novi Sad), CCCVIII (April-May 1926), 92-94.
Saint Joan is probably Shaw's greatest play: it is bold, original and Joan is not romanticized. Shaw has always been a cynic, and the epilogue is full of bitter truths. [In Serbian.]

2904 "Vienna Correspondence," SPECTATOR, No. 5138 (1926), 1108-09.
The Reinhardt Theatre in Vienna has a preference for a repertory of English plays, particularly by Shaw and Galsworthy. Shaw is also well liked in Germany, but "decidedly unpopular in Hungary."

2905 "Viereck Says Kaiser is Happy in Exile," NYT, 24 Aug 1926, p. 9.
George Sylvester Viereck, the poet, has had three interviews with Shaw whom he found vastly witty and talkative.

2906 W. "Das Wöchentliche Shaw-Bulletin" (The Weekly Shaw-Bulletin), DIE LITERARISCHE WELT, II: 21-22 (21 May 1926), 11.

Shaw has at last finished The Intelligent Woman's Guide to Socialism and Capitalism and has sent it to the printer. [In German.]

2907 Walbrook, H. M. A PLAYGOER'S WANDERINGS (Lond: Leonard Parsons, 1926), pp. 14-15, 23, 28-29, 30-31, 42, 59.

Shaw's plays come close to being a playgoer's ideal, though they are perhaps already dated.

2908 W[alkley], A. B. "Entertainments: Wirelessed Shaw," TIMES, 20 Jan 1926, p. 10.

Passion, Poison and Petrifaction was not an artistic success on the radio, probably because Shaw has never, in his works, supplied "pure aesthetic pleasure."

2909 Walkley, A. B. "George Bernard Shaw: An Explanation of the 'Celebrity' of the Noted Playwright and Publicist," VANITY FAIR (NY), XXVI (April 1926), 62, 114.

Shaw came along when the "old romantic theatre was dying of inanition," and, instead of giving people art for art's sake, gave them something to think about.

2910 Wertheimer, Egon. "George Bernard Shaw: Seine Gestalt in Englischen Zeitungsausschnitten" (George Bernard Shaw: His Character in English Newspaper Excerpts), DIE LITERARISCHE WELT, II: 33 (13 Aug 1926), 4.

[Excerpts from numerous British newspaper articles written to celebrate Shaw's seventieth birthday. In German.]

2911 "Where Shaw Stands," LIT DIG, XC (14 Aug 1926), 28-29.

Now Shaw is seventy there is a general trend to try to provide some estimation of the man. On the whole, the conclusion appears to be that he certainly cannot be ignored, his literary abilities stand above those of most other writers, but he is not one of the twelve immortals.

2912 "Why Bernard Shaw Never Washes His Face," LIT DIG, XCI (2 Oct 1926), 38, 40, 45.

[An account of Shaw's various personal habits and abstinences.]

2913 "Widowers' Houses Revived at the Everyman," ERA, 4 Aug 1926, p. 8.

Widowers' Houses has stood the test of time better than, say, Mrs. Warren's Profession, if only because the characterization is less exaggerated.

2914 Wittfogel, K. A. "That Man Shaw: The Clown of the Bourgeoisie," LIVING AGE, CCCXXXI (1926), 437-39.

Shaw is not a revolutionary Marxist and wants social reform only so long as it occurs after his death. However, he has been a "persistent destroyer of . . . bourgeois ideals." Since he writes comedies he can say much that is unconventional: "Shaw is the Shakespearian fool of the last period of bourgeois culture, but, as Lenin said, Shaw is one thing for the bourgeoisie and something quite different for the revolution."

2915 Yeats, W. B. AUTOBIOGRAPHIES: REVERIES OVER CHILDHOOD AND YOUTH AND THE TREMBLING OF THE VEIL (Lond: Macmillan, 1926), pp. 173, 344-49, 362-63, 401.
Arms and the Man begins as "crude melodrama" and becomes "excellent farce." Although it is "inorganic" it possesses the energy of a sewing machine. [Yeats and Shaw also met occasionally at meetings of the Socialist League.]

2916 Young Stark. "Gozzi and Shaw," NEW REP, XLIX (1926-27), 41-42.
A revival of Pygmalion tends to reinforce the impression that time renders Shaw's plays more humane and lasting. However, "the play is . . . intellectual farce, with everything pushed to an extravagance in persons, themes and events."

2917 "Zangwill Praises Shaw," NYT, 22 Feb 1926, p. 2.
Israel Zangwill has lauded Shaw for his faith in Jewish translators and agents.

1927

2918 Abbott, Lawrence F. "Shavian Flights of Fancy," OUTLOOK (NY), CXLVI (1927), 278-79.
The public's demand for sensational news in the newspapers can always be satiated by accounts of Shaw's latest pronouncements.

2919 "Academy Rejects Portrait of Shaw," NYT, 27 April 1927, p. 4.
John Collier's portrait of Shaw has been rejected by the Royal Academy in London.

2920 "Action for Damages by Mr. Bernard Shaw," TIMES, 4 Feb 1927, p. 13.
Shaw has begun an action in New York to prevent the publication of some of his letters.

2921 "Adelphi or Whitehall Court: 'The Modesty of G. B. S.,' " MASK, XIII (1927), 131-32.
When Shaw is being interviewed by a journalist he reveals that he is truly inimitable.

2922 "Advice from Writers," NYT, 5 March 1927, p. 14.

[An editorial on Shaw's advice to an aspiring writer.]

2923 Agate, James. PLAYGOING: BEING ONE OF A SERIES OF ESSAYS EDITED BY J. B. PRIESTLEY AND ENTITLED THESE DIVERSIONS (Lond: Jarrolds, 1927), pp. 77-78.
Back to Methuselah is Shaw's most "unseeable masterpiece." Shaw is long-winded and has no sense of the theatre.

2924 Atkinson, J. Brooks. "G. B. S.," NYT, 4 Dec 1927, part X, p. 1; rptd in NYTTR 1927-1929, [n. p.].
Shaw is fortunate in his interpreters in America. He may never have had an original idea, but he himself is original. "One of the most refreshing of Mr. Shaw's qualities is his insistence upon seeing things simply."

2925 Atkinson, J. Brooks. "The Play," NYT, 22 Nov 1927, p. 33; rptd in NYTTR 1927-1929, [n. p.].
The Doctor's Dilemma "is long, garrulous, inconclusive and over-reaching. But the jokes hammered into the text every so often still stimulate the risibilities."

2926 B., F. R. "A Night at the Theatre," OUTLOOK (NY), CXLVII (1927), 532, 534.
In The Doctor's Dilemma, as in all Shaw's plays, the characters never change during the course of the drama. Shaw is possessed of keen wit, showmanship and "expert theatrical brains."

2927 Bauer, G. "Le Théâtre: La Grande Catherine de M. Bernard Shaw" (The Theatre: Bernard Shaw's Great Catherine), LES ANNALES POLITIQUES ET LITTERAIRES, LXXXVIII (20 March 1927), 295.
The spirit of provocation is the basis of Shaw's talent: it missed the mark in The Man of Destiny but succeeded with Mrs. Warren's Profession and Saint Joan. Great Catherine is more of an interlude than a play of major importance; it is trivial, but with some pleasant and neat psychological nuances. [In French.]

2928 "Begins Use of Shaw's Nobel Prize," NYT, 9 Nov 1927, p. 18.
The Anglo-Swedish Nobel Prize committee, using Shaw's Nobel Prize money, is to publish new translations of Strindberg and Lagerloff.

2929 Bellinger, Martha Fletcher. A SHORT HISTORY OF THE DRAMA (NY: Henry Holt, 1927), pp. 339-41.
Shaw is the most conspicuous social reformer on the English stage. He is fluent, witty, courageous, and a passionate moralist. Many of his long plays are pure argument and the best characters he has created are projections of himself. He no longer shocks in 1927.

2930 Benchley, Robert [C.]. "Drama: Second-Hand Heresy," LIFE, XC (15 Dec 1927), 21.

Although The Doctor's Dilemma is far from being Shaw's best play, it is better than most of Shakespeare.

2931 Benninghoff, L. "Geburt des historischen Dramas?" (The Birth of Historical Drama?), DER KREIS ZEITSCHRIFT FÜR KÜNSTLERISCHE KULTUR, IV (March 1927), 129-35 [not seen].

[Cited in Amalric, p. 479. In German.]

2932 B[ishop], G. W. "Shaw and Strindberg," ERA, 23 Nov 1927, p. 5.

The Glimpse of Reality is an interesting trifle, but far from Shaw at his best. In fact, his ideas here were much better expressed in The Shewing-up of Blanco Posnet.

2933 Brisson, Pierre. "Saint Jeanne" (Saint Joan), LE TEMPS, 27 June 1927, p. 3 [not seen].

[Cited in Weintraub, p. 216. In French.]

2934 Brock, H. I. "An Old Tolstoy Letter Rebukes Shaw's Levity," NYT, 25 Sept 1927, part VIII, p. 10.

[A discussion of Leo Tolstoy's rejection of Shaw's superman "in favor of salvation by simple religious faith."]

2935 Carb, David. "Seen on the Stage," VOGUE, LXIX (15 Jan 1927), 82-83.

This revival of Pygmalion shows how dated most of Shaw's plays become. Except for Candida, they record earlier customs and social problems that seem odd or faded now.

2936 Cardozo, J. L. "St. Joan Once More," ENGLISH STUDIES, IX (1927), 177-84.

Shaw could delete some parts of Saint Joan and alter the tone somewhat. Nevertheless "it is a play of power and beauty."

2937 "Chesterton Tilts with Lady Rhondda," NYT, 28 Jan 1927, p. 6.

Shaw was chairman of a debate in London on "The Menace of the Leisured Woman." [See also: "Women of Leisure in Doubt on Debate," NYT, 30 Jan 1927, part II, p. 1; "'G. B. S.' Sums Up the Debaters," NYT, 13 Feb 1927, pp. 3, 8.]

2938 Clutton-Brock, A. ESSAYS ON LITERATURE & LIFE (1927; rptd Freeport, NY: Books for Libraries, 1968), pp. 182-89.

Back to Methuselah reveals "the natural man thinking about the nature of the universe," although Shaw mistakes thinking about religion for religion itself. The play comes to a barren climax because Shaw fails to present something worth desiring, and religion always offers some desirable, achievable objective.

2939 Cohn, Erna. ELTERN UND KINDER BEI BERNARD SHAW (Parents and Children in Bernard Shaw's Works), Ph. D. dissertation, University of Leipzig, 1927; rptd Leipzig: Druck von Helm & Torton, 1927.

Shaw hates compulsory family affection as a sentimental romantic notion. He fights against all sense of property and economic dependence within families and wants children to rebel against their parents' authority. He attacks a child's blind respect for his or her parents and condemns the so-called "will-breaking principle." According to Shaw children should obey nothing but their sense of what is right. Children are the experiment of the life force and parents should not try to prevent this experiment. [In German.]

2940 "Collector Here Gets Proofs of Shaw Plays," NYT, 4 Sept 1927, part I, p. 16.

[Brief details of Shaw's corrections to five plays.]

2941 "Crowd Hoots G. B. Shaw," NYT, 2 Oct 1927, p. 8.

A radio broadcast debate between Shaw and Chesterton was disrupted by people shut out of the hall where the actual debate was being held.

2942 Cunliffe, John W. MODERN ENGLISH PLAYWRIGHTS: A SHORT HISTORY OF THE ENGLISH DRAMA FROM 1825 (NY & Lond; Harper, 1927), pp. 7-8, 16, 28, 31, 54-83, 92, 98, 122, 143, 199, 209-10, 252.

Shaw is undoubtedly the "central figure in the revival of the modern drama." Widowers' Houses has little plot and unsympathetic characters though there are flashes of wit. Mrs. Warren's Profession presents Shaw at his most propagandistic, and after that play his work takes on more artistry. However, Shaw's concessions to matters purely theatrical are reflected in Arms and the Man." Candida marked the "real beginning of the Shaw vogue." Heartbreak House was hardly written to placate English public opinion. The beginning of the 1920s saw a real change in the public's opinion of Shaw and he has become widely accepted. Shaw found Saint Joan appealing because she possessed the commonsense to penetrate accepted beliefs and offered foresight and standards of justice.

2943 Dickinson, Thomas H. AN OUTLINE OF CONTEMPO-RARY DRAMA (Bost: Houghton Mifflin, 1927), pp. 194-207.

Shaw has attacked falsity and imposture, has ridiculed wrong-headed morality, and dispelled cant. His work also offers much that is positive in its seriousness and cosmic view of things. Shaw has a deep regard for humanity as a whole.

2944 "Dr. Adler Answers Shaw on Fascism," NYT, 6 Nov 1927, part III, p. 7.

Frederick Adler, head of the Socialist and Labor International organization, has taken Shaw to task for his views on Mussolini and fascism.

2945 "Don't Aid Ireland, Says Shaw; 'She is an Incorrigible Beggar,' " NYT, 1 Dec 1927, p. 1.
[Title describes. See also: "Kind Words from Bernard Shaw," NYT, 4 Dec 1927, part III, p. 4; "Shaw Says England Beats Erin Begging," NYT, 5 Dec 1927, p. 29; "Calls Shaw Phrasemonger," NYT, 8 Dec 1927, p. 31.]

2946 Dowling, A. "Bernard Shaw y Santa Juana" (Bernard Shaw and Saint Joan), LA NACIÓN (Argentina), 30 Oct 1927 [not seen] .
[Cited in Rodríguez (MS). In Spanish.]

2947 Drinkwater, John. THE ART OF THEATRE-GOING (Bost & NY: Houghton Mifflin, 1927), pp. 11-13, 41, 45, 53, 60, 81-83, 90-92, 94-95, 112, 186, 203.
Shaw's dramatic criticism conveyed a sense of the original acting. His plays broke the technical traditions best embodied in Pinero's works. While Shaw has not eschewed popular success, he has sought primarily to advance his own social vision on the stage. Indeed, Shaw would have written plays regardless of their reception because drama was the best form of expression for his ideas.

2948 Dukes, Ashley. DRAMA (NY: Henry Holt; Lond: Williams & Norgate, 1927), pp. 96-97.
Shaw injected vigor into the theatre, although he tended to be more Ibsenite than Ibsen. His positive quality, apart from his irrepressible wit, is his passionate indignation.

2949 Ebel, Walter. "Das geschlechtsproblem bei Bernard Shaw" (The Problem of Mankind in Bernard Shaw's Works), ZEITSCHRIFT FÜR FRANKZOSISCHEN UND ENGLISCHEN UNTERRICHT, XXVI (1927), 20-33, 186-99 [not seen] .
[Cited in Amalric, p. 479. In German.]

2950 "Elects English Authors," NYT, 23 Sept 1927, p. 15.
Shaw was among a number of English authors elected to the Dramatists' Guild.

2951 Erskine, John. "The Secret of Sane Living," DELINEATOR (NY), CXI (Oct 1927), 38, 113-114; rptd in THE DELIGHT OF GREAT BOOKS (Indianapolis: Bobbs-Merrill, 1928), pp. 277-94.
Shaw's genius as a sage, a wit, a great dramatist, a critic of life, and a prophet of the modern world can be best observed in a masterpiece like Candida. The play's greatness lies in its dramatic but simple plot and in its characters. As with all great plays, the effect of Candida "is to make us wiser about human nature in general, especially about ourselves."

2952 "Even Shaw is Censored," NYT, 2 Nov 1927, p. 26.
Shaw's praise of Mussolini and Fascism is really only possible in

England. He would be censored in Italy itself.

2953 Farjeon, Herbert. "The London Stage," GRAPHIC, CXVIII (17 Dec 1927), 528.
This revival of Getting Married proves that Shaw's plays will survive as classics because they portray aspects of the time in which they were written, but even more because they are such wonderful comedy.

2954 Firkins, Ina Ten Eyck. INDEX TO PLAYS 1800-1926 (NY: Wilson, 1927), pp. 168-69.
[Primary bibliography.]

2955 Fricken, Roy Henri. "Stage Censorship—Past, Present and Future," THEATRE MAGAZINE (NY), XLV (June 1927), 20, 62, 64.
[Title describes; references to Mrs. Warren's Profession.]

2956 "G. B. S. as Mussolini's Champion," LIT DIG, XCV (26 Nov 1927), 14-15.
[An account of the reactions to Shaw's defense of fascism and Mussolini.]

2957 "G. B. Shaw Condemns Sex Appeal in Movies," NYT, 19 Nov 1927, p. 5.
Shaw believes films should contain more interest and less sex-appeal. [See also: "Shaw Chides the Movie Producer," NYT, 4 Dec 1927, part XI, p. 2.]

2958 "G. B. Shaw is Sure Tunney Won Fight," NYT, 9 Oct 1927, p. 3.
Shaw has seen a film of the Gene Tunney-Jack Dempsey fight and supports Tunney.

2959 Gabriel, Gilbert W. "George Bernard Shaw: An Exciting Minority of One," MENTOR (Springfield, Ohio), XV (May 1927), 1-7.
[A genial mixture of potted biography and bland criticism.]

2960 Gabriel, Gilbert [W.]. "Last Night's First Night," SUN (NY), 22 Nov 1927, p. 18.
Even though The Doctor's Dilemma is far from being Shaw's best work, it does possess "pungency and wit." Its faults are its "Molièresque maunderings."

2961 Genn, Beatrice S. "Back to Methuselah—An Appreciation," ENGLISH JOURNAL, XVI (1927), 143-45.
The structure of Back to Methuselah reveals "Shaw's creative imagination at its best" and the play's message "strikes a wholesome note."

2962 [George Bernard Shaw], TIMES, 11 Oct 1927, p. 17.
Shaw attended the cremation of Mrs. H. G. Wells.

2963 "Getting Married: Shaw's Conversation at the Little Theatre," ERA, 7 Dec 1927, p. 17.
[A review concentrating on the acting.]

2964 Havaux, Arturo. "Los socialistas y Bernard Shaw" (The Socialists and Bernard Shaw), ACCIÓN SOCIALISTA (Argentina), V: 11 (10 Dec 1927), 326-28 [not seen].
[Cited in Rodríguez (MS). In Spanish.]

2965 Henderson, Archibald. "Bernard Shaw and America (My Friend Bernard Shaw: III)," AMERICAN (NY), 23 Jan 1927, march of events.
[Biography.]

2966 Henderson, Archibald. "Bernard Shaw and Prizes (My Friend Bernard Shaw: II)," AMERICAN (NY), 9 Jan 1927, march of events, p. 3.
[Biography.]

2967 Henderson, Archibald. "Bernard Shaw and the World War (My Friend Bernard Shaw: IV)," SUNDAY CHRONICLE (Manchester), 23 Jan 1927 [not seen].
[Cited in Hood, p. 227.]

2968 Henderson, Archibald. "Bernard Shaw on the Problem of Children (My Friend Bernard Shaw: VII)," AMERICAN (NY), 13 Feb 1927, march of events, p. 3.
[Title describes.]

2969 Henderson, Archibald. "Bernard Shaw on Women (My Friend Bernard Shaw: VI)," SUNDAY CHRONICLE (Manchester), 6 Feb 1927 [not seen].
[Cited in Hood, p. 228.]

2970 Henderson, Archibald. "Bernard Shaw, The Man (My Friend Bernard Shaw: I)," AMERICAN (NY), 2 Jan 1927, march of events, p. 1.
[Biographical.]

2971 Henderson, Archibald. "The Genius of Bernard Shaw (My Friend Bernard Shaw: V)," SUNDAY OBSERVER (Charlotte, NC), 20 Feb 1927, part III, p. 7 [not seen].
[Cited in Hood, p. 227.]

2972 Henderson, Archibald. "George Bernard Shaw: Legend and Man," REV OF REVS, LXXV (1927), 49-58.
[An overview of Shaw's life and the legend Shaw himself created.]

2973 Henderson, Archibald. "God as Visualized by Bernard Shaw (My Friend Bernard Shaw: IX)," SUNDAY CHRONICLE (Manchester), 13 March 1927 [not seen].
[Cited in Hood, p. 228].

2974 Henderson, Archibald. "The Real Bernard Shaw," VIRGINIA QUARTERLY REVIEW, III (1927), 177-89.
[A brief biographical outline with passing critical references.]

2975 Henderson, Archibald. "Shaw as a Prize Winner," BRETANO'S BOOK CHAT, VI: 6 (May–June 1927), 25-27.
[Title describes.]

2976 Henderson, Archibald. "Shaw's Vision of the Future (My Friend Bernard Shaw: VIII)," AMERICAN (NY), 20 Feb 1927, march of events, p. 4.
[Title describes.]

2977 Hobson, J. A. "Must We Scrap Democracy?" NATION & ATH, XLII (1927), 344-46.
Shaw's "tirade against democracy" is really a "bundle of half-truths . . . . He must be well aware that a Mussolini would make short shrift of such a disturber of the intellectual peace as Bernard Shaw in Fascist England."

2978 "Introducing 'G. B. S.,' " REV OF REVS, LXXV (1927), 48.
[A brief biography and bibliography.]

2979 Isaacs, Edith J. R., ed. THEATRE: ESSAYS ON THE ARTS OF THE THEATRE (Bost: Little, Brown, 1927), pp. 20, 63, 97-98, 280-81.
Shaw has influenced contemporary actors deeply, as have Ibsen and Hauptmann. He is also notable for guarding the integrity of his text.

2980 J., L. "Shaw in Spanish," SUN (NY), 12 May 1927, p. 22.
Although Pygmalion is a curious choice to perform in Spanish, the result is creditable.

2981 Jennings, Richard. "The Theatre," SPECTATOR, CXXXIX (1927), 250.
Shaw's Overruled is even more oppressive than Strindberg's THE FATHER.

2982 Kane, W. T. "George Bernard Shaw," MONTH, Aug 1927, pp. 115-26.
Shaw's "great gifts" are squandered because, even "though he fancies himself the supreme rationalist because he can make his logical processes correct, he is the supreme intolerant because he assumes, without question and upon prejudiced sentiment, the premises for his logic."

2983 "Kingsway Theatre," TIMES, 20 Jan 1927, p. 10.
Pygmalion is now "rather an exhibition of marvellously talking and walking figures than an affair of human interest."

2984 "Kingsway Theatre," TIMES, 11 Feb 1927, p. 12.
Shaw's dialectic in Man and Superman has lost none of its fire, power

or wit.

2985 Kodiček, Josef, and M. Rutte. NOVÉ ČESKÉ DIVADLO 1927 (The New Czech Theatre 1927) (Prague: Aventinum, 1927), pp. 123-24.
[Both Candida and The Doctor's Dilemma were produced in Prague in 1927. In Czech.]

2986 Krutch, Joseph Wood. "Drama: Papa Shaw," NATION (NY), CXXV (1927), 690.
Despite every admiration for Shaw, The Doctor's Dilemma is not a very good play because it lacks pace and surprise.

2987 Lalou, René. PANORAMA DE LA LITTERATURE ANGLAISE CONTEMPORAINE (The Panorama of Contemporary English Literature) (Paris: Kra, 1927), pp. 8, 95, 98, 138, 161-73, 193, 207, 230.
Shaw is a star of the contemporary English theatre and a descendant of Samuel Butler and Laurence Sterne. Shaw is a literary acrobat and a prophet who expounds the philosophy of progress. [In French.]

2988 Legouis, Emile, and Louis Cazamian. A HISTORY OF ENGLISH LITERATURE: VOLUME TWO: MODERN TIMES (1660-1914) (NY: Macmillan 1927), pp. 398, 409, 416, 454, 461, 464-68, 470-71, 486-87, 497.
Shaw's major characteristic is a "fearless intellectual criticism," the principles of which resemble those of Samuel Butler. Shaw's wit animates his ideas, and although his social ideas are derivative they are presented courageously. Indeed, he believes that "since all social evils are caused by the lack of intellectual courage, the cure in every case must be sought in the logic of courageous thought."

2989 Lewis, F. R. "G. B. S.: An Appreciation," STAGE, 30 Dec 1927, p. 20.
Shaw is an artist-philosopher who attempts to show the conflict between man's will and his environment. Discussion is at the core of Shaw's work, which ranges over many of the dramatic genres. His characterizations are as numerous as his themes, while he frequently flouts the conventional rules of technique.

2990 " 'Limit Ships' Size,' Jellicoe Advises," NYT, 2 May 1927, p. 4.
British soliders in China contrast markedly with Shaw's picture in Man and Superman.

2991 "Little Theatre," TIMES, 6 Dec 1927, p. 14.
Getting Married is an irritating but fascinating discussion—a "theatrical contrivance."

2992 "Little Theatre," TIMES, 27 Dec 1927, p. 5.
You Never Can Tell covers a myriad of topics which are unified "by

the wit and satirical lightness and the dexterity which are peculiar to the early Shavian drama."

2993 "London Theatres: The Kingsway: <u>Man and Superman</u>," STAGE, 17 Feb 1927, p. 18.
The current revival stresses the satirical and comic side of <u>Man and Superman</u>, a play which is always worth producing.

2994 "London Theatres: The Kingsway: <u>Pygmalion</u> Revived," STAGE, 27 Jan 1927, p. 18.
<u>Pygmalion</u> makes a welcome revival, and although it is impossible to think and laugh simultaneously, there are deeper things beneath the superficial foolery.

2995 Ludwig, Emil. "Are There Great Men Today?" NYT, 28 Aug 1927, part IV, pp. 1-2.
[Shaw is listed as a great man.]

2996 MacCarthy, Desmond. "Drama: The Gaiety of Bernard Shaw," NSTATE, XXIX (1927), 569-70; rptd in MacCarthy, pp. 176-80.
Shaw's distinguishing characteristic as a writer is "a little fountain of irrational gaiety" which is the key to understanding his plays. <u>Overruled</u> adheres to this principle.

2997 Maerz, A. "Simplified Spelling Plans Arouse an Earnest Protest," NYT, 23 Jan 1927, part VII, p. 14.
Shaw should not have been appointed to the B. B. C.'s advisory committee on pronunciation because he will only make people the butt of his fooling.

2998 "<u>Man and Superman</u> at the Kingsway," ERA, 16 Feb 1927, p. 1.
<u>Man and Superman</u> is the best comedy in London, and whatever the critical or intellectual debate about this piece, the average playgoer will find much to divert him. Notable is Shaw's wit, his graceful and balanced writing and his attack on shams and hypocrisies.

2999 Maude, Cyril. BEHIND THE SCENES WITH CYRIL MAUDE (Lond: John Murray, 1927), pp. 152, 161, 163-74 [Also entitled LEST I FORGET].
Contains a letter from Shaw and the text of <u>The Interlude at the Playhouse</u>.

3000 Minnigerode, F. L. "Shaw Chides the Nations," NYT, 5 June 1927, part IV, p. 10.
[An interview with Shaw on the topic of disarmament.]

3001 "Mr. Bernard Shaw and Fascism," TIMES, 13 Oct 1927, p. 14.
Shaw has written to a Turin newspaper and defended fascism.

3002 "Mr. G. B. Shaw and the Cinema," TIMES, 19 Oct 1927, p. 12.
Shaw spoke widely about films at the London Pavilion Theatre.

3003 [Morgan, Charles?] "The Drama in Captivity," TLS, No. 1330 (28 July 1927), 509-10.
[A review article of several books, but which indicates Shaw's use of newly gained theatrical freedoms to express his ideas. Shaw is also seen as being largely untheatrical but as having "a sense of a new and different theatre."]

3004 Morgan, Charles. [Getting Married], NYT, 25 Dec 1927, part VIII, p. 1; rptd in NYTTR 1927-1929, [n. p.].
What lives in this London revival of Getting Married is Shaw's "solid argument" written at white heat.

3005 "Mussolini Critics Draw Shaw's Fire," NYT, 14 Oct 1927, p. 5.
Shaw supports Mussolini and believes he is doing for Italy what Napoleon did for France.

3006 Nakagawa, Ryoichi. "Bernard Shaw kenkyu" (A Study of Bernard Shaw), TSUKIJI SHOGEKIJO (Tokyo), IV: 1 (Jan 1927), 17-19; IV: 3 (March 1927), 22-30; IV: 4 (April 1927), 7-14; IV: 6 (June 1927), 10-15; IV: 9 (Dec 1927), 26-32.
[A review of Shaw's life, Pygmalion and Back to Methuselah. In Japanese.]

3007 "Obras de Bernard Shaw, traducidas por J. B." (Bernard Shaw's Works, Translated by J. B.), NOSOTROS (Argentina), No. 212 (Jan 1927), 128-29 [not seen].
[Cited in Rodríguez (MS). In Spanish.]

3008 "Offered Shaw ⨼5,000 to Come Here to Dine," NYT, 21 May 1927, p. 25.
Shaw has admitted that he was once offered 5,000 pounds by an American hostess for the quickest of social visits to America.

3009 O'Dell, George E. "The Secret in the Poet's Heart," STANDARD (NY), XIII (Feb 1927), 186-87.
Shaw is most constructive when he demonstrates that man should possess a moral purpose and follow it disinterestedly and with "self-control, sacrifice, equanimity." This concept is well illustrated by Marchbanks, Caesar, and Brassbound.

3010 "Omicron." [Getting Married], NATION & ATH, XLII (1927), 452.
Getting Married demonstrates it is possible to write a purely intellectual play.

3011 Page, Will A. BEHIND THE CURTAINS OF THE BROADWAY BEAUTY TRUST (NY: Edward A. Miller, 1927), pp. 209-27.

[Page decided to mount a repertory season of ten Shaw plays in 1902. The ensuing correspondence between Page and Shaw reveals several aspects of Shaw's character. Text of four letters from Shaw.]

3012 "'Penal' Schooldays of G. B. S.,'" LIT DIG, XCV (24 Dec 1927), 21-22.

[An account of Shaw's responses to a questionnaire on his schooldays.]

3013 Peper, Elisabeth. "George Bernard Shaw Beziehungen zu Samuel Butler dem Jüngeren" (George Bernard Shaw's Relationship to Samuel Butler the Younger), Ph. D. dissertation, University of Königsberg, 1927 [not seen].

[In German.]

3014 "A Pioneer of Shaw," NYT, 15 Jan 1927, p. 14.

Shaw should be grateful to the late Arnold Daly for pioneering his plays in America.

3015 "The Problems of English," TIMES, 17 June 1927, p. 11.

Shaw has spoken on dialects at an international conference on English.

3016 "Pure, Simon" [Frank Swinnerton]. "The Londoner: Mr. Shaw, Mr. Hardy, and the Nobel Prize," BOOKMAN (NY), LXIV (Feb 1927), 720-21.

Shaw does not need the Nobel Prize because he is already famous and affluent, and in any case the prize is not awarded on literary merit. Thomas Hardy would have been a worthier recipient, although his literary merit is now outmoded.

3017 "Pygmalion Revived at the Kingsway," ERA, 2 Feb 1927, p. 9.

Pygmalion may not be Shaw's best play, but it is still entertaining and provocative. He handles the opening scene economically, while the second act is marked by its wit and wisdom.

3018 "The Rival Satirists," NYT, 27 Sept 1927, p. 26.

Dean Inge's latest pronouncements almost oblige Shaw to say something even more startling. Both men are good at obtaining publicity.

3019 Rodríguez Lafora, Gonzalo. DON JUAN: LOS MILAGROS Y OTROS ENSAYOS (Don Juan: Miracles and Other Essays) (Madrid: Biblioteca Nueva, 1927) [not seen].

[On Man and Superman. Cited in Rodríguez (MS). In Spanish.]

3020 Rodríguez-Larreta, A. "El mensaje de Bernard Shaw" (Bernard Shaw's Message), LA NACIÓN (Argentina), No. 115 (11 Sept 1927), 1-3 [not seen].

[Cited in Rodríguez (MS). In Spanish.]

3021 "Royal Academy and Mr. John Collier," TIMES, 27 April 1927, p. 11.

A portrait of Shaw by John Collier is not to be hung in the Royal Academy's summer exhibition.

3022 Sadoveanu, Ion Marin. "Medicul in dilemă" (The Doctor's Dilemma), GÎNDIREA (Bucharest), VII (1927), 33-34 [not seen]. [In Roumanian.]

3023 Saito, Takeshi. SHICHO O CHUSHINTOSERU EIBUNGAKUSHI (A Historical Survey of English Literature with Special Reference to the Spirit of the Times) (Tokyo: Kenkyusha, 1927), pp. 430-33.

Shaw writes plays to propagate his own ideas of life, and the plays always look like illustrations of long prefaces. It is difficult for the reader to enter into the world of literature by reading Shaw's works, although they are certainly brilliant and to some extent successful. [In Japanese.]

3024 Sanders, William Stephen. EARLY SOCIALIST DAYS (Lond: Hogarth, 1927), pp. 19, 26, 41-48, 56, 58.

[Details of Shaw's association with the Fabian Society.]

3025 Sayler, Oliver M. "The Play of the Week," SATURDAY REVIEW OF LITERATURE (NY), IV (3 Dec 1927), 372.

The Doctor's Dilemma "more patently than most of his other plays, reveals Bernard Shaw as the greatest living prophylactic agent for the salutary inoculation of the body politic and social."

3026 "Shaw Backs Heckscher," NYT, 24 Oct 1927, p. 26.

Shaw has lent his support to a plan to replace slum tenements in New York City.

3027 "Shaw Champions Cause of an Old Postman Who Stole Ten Shillings and Lost Pension," NYT, 21 Dec 1927, p. 1.

[Title describes.]

3028 "Shaw Commends Rotary," NYT, 14 April 1927, p. 8.

Shaw has commended Rotary International and emphasized that service is what counts.

3029 "Shaw Denies Caviare Dish," NYT, 24 April 1927, part II, p. 6.

Shaw asserts he is still a faithful vegetarian.

3030 "Shaw Doubts Red Success," NYT, 8 Nov 1927, p. 3.

Shaw believes the Russian communist government is an interesting experiment but does not believe it will succeed.

3031 "Shaw Gives Germany Naval Prestige in War," NYT, 16 Sept 1927, p. 24.

Shaw believes Germany possessed superior naval power at the Battle of Jutland.

3032 "Shaw has Poverty Ban," NYT, 20 Nov 1927, part I, p. 26.
Shaw advocates killing anyone earning more or less than one thousand pounds.

3033 "Shaw Hopes Ford has Taught a Lesson," NYT, 17 July 1927, p. 15.
Shaw believes that anti-Semitism "has been put to shame."

3034 "Shaw Impersonated," LIVING AGE, CCCXXXII (1927), 174-75.
Shaw has been impersonated in a play entitled HIS WILD OAT and he assisted the actor playing the role.

3035 "Shaw Lauds Lawrence, Conqueror of Arabia," NYT, 4 Feb 1927, p. 10.
[Title describes.]

3036 "Shaw Moves Home from Adelphi Flat," NYT, 12 June 1927, part II, p. 4.
[Title describes. See also: "Bernard Shaw Moves," NYT, 29 July 1927, p. 19.]

3037 "Shaw Mute on Marriage," NYT, 24 Jan 1927, p. 4.
Shaw has declined to contribute to a forthcoming book on marriage.
[See also: "Hatred the Well of Truth," NYT, 25 Jan 1927, p. 20.]

3038 "Shaw Not Ready for Abbey," NYT, 5 Nov 1927, p. 6.
Shaw does not believe Westminster Abbey should be enlarged.

3039 "Shaw Rails at Girl Here," NYT, 2 March 1927, p. 12.
Shaw has called Mariam Stephenson an "ingenious young liar" after she sent her "Philosophy of Shaw" paper to him.

3040 "Shaw Recalled as a Studious Boy," NYT, 1 May 1927, part IX, p. 4.
[Title describes.]

3041 "Shaw Retaliates Upon Biographers," NYT, 25 March 1927, p. 21.
Shaw Desmond has been rebuked by Shaw for inaccurate biography.

3042 "Shaw Revisits Place of 'Slavery' as Clerk; Veteran of His 40-Year Absence Snubs Him," NYT, 12 Sept 1927, p. 11.
[Title describes.]

3043 "Shaw Says Britain was Ready for War," NYT, 24 Jan 1927, p. 5.
[Shaw's views on World War I. See also: "Germany should have Known," NYT, 29 Jan 1927, p. 14.]

3044 "Shaw Says He Needs the Prayers of All," NYT, 4 May 1927, p. 25.

Shaw will not be changing his religious views.

3045 "Shaw Scores Doctors on Osteopathy Stand," NYT, 12 Feb 1927, p. 4.
[Title describes.]

3046 "Shaw Sees Conflict within Royal Family," NYT, 6 May 1927, p. 25.
Shaw has detected a difference in the British royal family over blood sports.

3047 "Shaw Tells British to Seek a Dictator," NYT, 24 Nov 1927, p. 14.
[Title describes.]

3048 "Shaw Threatens Suit Over Letters," NYT, 21 Jan 1927, p. 13.
Shaw has threatened to sue Will A. Page for publishing his letters in BEHIND THE CURTAINS OF THE BROADWAY BEAUTY TRUST. [See also: "Shaw will Sue on Letters," NYT, 22 Jan 1927, p. 7; "Shaw Sues Page for Using Letters," NYT, 4 Feb 1927, p. 21; "Files Reply in Shaw Suit," NYT, 25 Feb 1927, p. 9; "Page Says Shaw Suit is Publicity Stunt," NYT, 23 March 1927, p. 7; "Shaw Wins, Halting Sale of Page Book," NYT 7 April 1927, p. 5.]

3049 "Shaw und Mussolini" (Shaw and Mussolini), DER DEUTSCHE VOLKSWIRT, II: 4 (28 Oct 1927), 106.
In a letter to Friedrich Adler, Shaw has declared himself an admirer of Mussolini and Fascism. [See also: "Mr. Shaw and Mr. Mussolini," LIVING AGE, CCCXXXIII (1927), 965-73; "Mr. Shaw and Mussolini," NATION & ATH, XLII (1927), 106-107, 148, 215-16, 273. Additional correspondence by Shaw and others is found in BERNARD SHAW & FASCISM (Lond: Favil [1927]).]

3050 "Shaw Wins Round in Film Dispute," NYT, 19 March 1927, p. 5.
[Details of a legal suit over Arms and the Man and THE CHOCO-LATE SOLDIER. See also: "Shaw Wins Suit on CHOCOLATE SOLDIER Film; Judge Hits at 'California Backwoodsman,'" NYT, 22 March 1927, p. 29.]

3051 "Shaw Yields to Children," NYT, 31 Jan 1927, p. 5.
Shaw rarely refuses a request from a child for an autograph.

3052 "Shaw's Latest Vicissitude," LIVING AGE, CCCXXXII (1927), 1119.
Shaw's wit has been revealed yet again as the Royal Academy has declined a portrait of him and accepted instead one of Aldous Huxley.

3053 "Spaniards Act Shaw's Pygmalion," NYT, 12 May 1927, p. 25; rptd in NYTTR 1927-1929, [n. p.].
The problem of Spaniards coping with the Cockney accent in

Pygmalion is resolved by the omission of that feature.

3054 Spearing, James O. [Caesar and Cleopatra], NYT, 6 Nov 1927, part IX, p. 2; rptd in NYTTR 1927-1929, [n. p.]
[An extensive review of a Princeton University revival of Caesar and Cleopatra.]

3055 Stier, Theodore. WITH PAVLOVA ROUND THE WORLD (Lond: Hurst & Blackett [1927]), chapters XVI-XVII [not seen]; rptd in SHAW REVIEW, X (1967), 18-33.
[A series of anecdotes about Shaw and actors involved in Shaw's plays performed at the Court Theatre during the Vedrenne-Barker management. Stier was musical director of the theatre.]

3056 "Studio and Street," NYT, 24 July 1927, part VII, p. 3.
Shaw has supervised a screen test of Sybil Thorndike for a possible film of Saint Joan.

3057 "Sturgis Blast Stirs Shaw," NYT, 19 Nov 1927, p. 14.
Shaw has defended his stage directions in Saint Joan against the comments of actor David Sturgis.

3058 Svrček, Jaroslav. "Messaliance" (Misalliance), ROVNOST (Brno), No. 302 (Nov 1927), 4 [not seen].
[In Czech.]

3059 Svrček, Jaroslav. "Neměcka činohra" (German Film: The Doctor's Dilemma), ROVNOST (Brno), No. 330 (Dec 1927), 6 [not seen].
[In Czech.]

3060 Svrček, Jaroslav. "Pygmalion," ROVNOST (Brno), No. 92 (31 March 1927) [not seen].
[In Czech.]

3061 "The Tate Gallery," TIMES, 1 Dec 1927, p. 9.
Shaw spoke at the unveiling of mural paintings by Rex Whistler.

3062 "Telegrams in Brief," TIMES, 5 Jan 1927, p. 9.
Saint Joan has been performed in French in Brussels to an enthusiastic reception.

3063 "To Translate Strindberg," NYT, 15 Feb. 1927, p. 27.
Shaw wants the Anglo-Swedish Literary Foundation (operated with funds from his Nobel Prize) to make a translation of Strindberg's works its first task.

3064 "Visitor." "Concerning Mr. Bernard Shaw: His New Home, His Clavicord, His Gramophone and Himself," NATIONAL GRAPHIC (Lond), CXVIII (15 Oct 1927), ii.
[Title describes. Biographical.]

3065 Wells, H. G. "Mr. Wells Appraises Mr. Shaw," NYT, 13

Nov 1927, part V, pp. 1-2, 16.

Despite his appearance, his use of language, his rag-bag assortment of ideas, Shaw has contributed nothing to the world. Curiously, in the future, Shaw will be more difficult to forget than Pavlov and his scientific experiments. [See also: "Never Called Pavlov Scoundrel, Says Shaw," NYT, 13 Nov 1927, part II, p. 2; Carl C. Peterson, "Mr. Wells Stands Accused of Knocking over a Dummy," NYT, 20 Nov 1927, part III, p. 5.]

3066 Wells, H. G. "What is the Good of Shaw," SUNDAY EXPRESS (Lond), 13 Nov 1927, pp. 12, 7.

Shaw writes well, has created a striking persona and has produced some lively theatre. "It seems almost ungracious to raise the question whether he has ever had anything but himself to express." He is full of rhetoric, but ultimately vacuous.

3067 Wilson, P. W. "Shaw Makes Mankind His Heir," NYT, 24 April 1927, part IV, pp. 1, 18.

[Biographical interview.]

3068 Woolf, S. J. "Mr. Shaw Sits for His Portrait," NYT, 7 Aug 1927, part IV, pp. 1-2.

[Biographical interview.]

3069 "Wratislavius." "Teatrul Naţional. Medicul in dilemă" (National Theatre. The Doctor's Dilemma), OPINIA (Jassy), 25 Nov 1927 [not seen].

[In Roumanian.]

3070 Young, Stark. "Fantastic Comedies," NEW REP, LIII (1927-28), 96-97.

Shaw will do almost anything to drive home his argument, as The Doctor's Dilemma proves by being an act too long. He sacrifices art for argument, although at bottom he is sincere and honest.

3071 Young, Stark. THE THEATER (NY: Doran, 1927), pp. 61, 66-67, 73, 75, 128, 161-62.

Shaw "often writes what is at bottom brilliant cerebal farce," though his work is often regarded as untheatrical. Superficially he employs realism, but his work is actually "fantastic, fervid and poetical."

1928

3072 Abascal, Luis. "Candida de Bernard Shaw" (Bernard Shaw's Candida), CRITERIO, No. 29 (20 Sept 1928), 378-80 [not seen].

[Cited in Rodríguez (MD), p. 338. In Spanish.]

3073 Abascal, Luis. "Candida, de George Bernard Shaw. El

himno nacional, de F. A. de Zavalía" (George Bernard Shaw's Candida: F. A. de Zavalia's National Hymn), CRITERIO, No. 28 (13 Sept 1928), 347-48 [not seen].
[Cited in Rodríguez (MD), p. 338. In Spanish.]

3074 Abascal, Luis. " 'Zinzen' ('Intereses') de Bernard Shaw, en el Odéon" (Bernard Shaw's Dramatic Interests, at the Odeon), CRITERIO, No. 7 (19 April 1928), 218 [not seen].
[Cited in Rodríguez (MS); on Widowers' Houses. In Spanish.]

3075 Abel, H. G. "Mill and Socialism," NATION & ATH, XLIV (1928-29), 613-14.
[Disputes Shaw's view that J. S. Mill became an avowed socialist.]

3076 Achard, Paul. "Bernard Shaw est-il un mauvais Anglais?" (Is Bernard Shaw a Bad Englishman?), PARIS-MIDI, 13 Feb 1928.
In Heartbreak House Shaw is sarcastic about everything that is English, but a great writer serves his country in his own way, and the critical spirit is one of the factors of the European mind.   [In French.]

3077 Adcock, St. John.   GLORY THAT WAS GRUB STREET: IMPRESSIONS OF CONTEMPORARY AUTHORS (Lond: Sampson Low, Marston [1928]), pp. 1-12.
Shaw is probably widely disliked because he attacks orthodoxies. He has been mistaken for a jester and called much worse, but he has delivered sugar-coated hard truths and got people to swallow them.

3078 " 'AE' Talked to Shaw Without Knowing It," NYT, 7 Feb 1928, p. 12.
George Russell, in a lecture, recounted meeting Shaw in Dublin without realizing who he was.

3079 "American Debut of G. B. S.," LIT DIG, XCVIII (28 July 1928), 21.
Shaw has visited America and appeared on Movietone news.

3080 "Anglo-Swedish Literary Foundation," TIMES, 17 Sept 1928, p. 17.
[Details of the first annual report of the Anglo-Swedish Literary Foundation, established by Shaw's Nobel Prize money to promote Anglo-Swedish literary relations.]

3081 "Another Landmark of Old London to Go," NYT, 17 June 1928, part III, p. 6.
Shaw objects strenuously to the destruction of Charing Cross and its bridge for traffic improvements.

3082 Araquistain, Luis. "Bernard Shaw y el fascismo" (Bernard Shaw and Fascism), REPERTORIO AMERICANO (Costa Rica), XVI: 23 (14 Jan 1928), 29-30 [not seen].
[Cited in Rodríguez (MS). In Spanish.]

3083 Araquistain, Luis. "El esteta ante la Historia" (The Aesthetician Compared with History), REPERTORIO AMERICANO (Costa Rica), XVI: 14 (14 April 1928), 217 [not seen].
[Cited in Rodríguez (MS). In Spanish.]

3084 Araquistain, Luis. "El histrionismo literario" (The Literary Theatrical Profession), REPERTORIO AMERICANO (Costa Rico), XVI: 3 (21 Jan 1928), 39 [not seen].
[Cited in Rodríguez (MS). In Spanish.]

3085 "Armistice Stirs British Emotions," NYT, 11 Nov 1928, p. 28.
Shaw has protested against the British observance of Armistice Day.

3086 "Arts Theatre: A Quadruple Bill," STAGE, 2 Feb 1928, p. 24.
If Shaw's name were not attached to it, it is doubtful whether The Fascinating Foundling would have been produced.

3087 "Arts Theatre Club," TIMES, 30 June 1928, p. 10.
The Fascinating Foundling is a "quite irresponsible jeu d'esprit."

3088 "Arts Theatre: Quadruple Bill," DT, 30 Jan 1928, p. 6.
The Fascinating Foundling is a "little squib . . . its texture is too brilliant for its flimsy framework."

3089 Atkinson, J. Brooks. [Major Barbara], NYT, 2 Dec 1928, part X, p. 1; rptd in NYTTR 1927-1929, [n. p.].
In Major Barbara Shaw "argues his thesis with an opportunistic and positive wit, though not with his usual humor."

3090 B.-W., J. "Back to Methuselah," NSTATE, XXX (1928), 761-62.
In Back to Methuselah Shaw's doctrine of evolution, being entirely rational, leaves out consideration of "the essence of creation," by which means "something quite new and different is produced." There is nothing new here.

3091 Bab, Julius. DAS THEATER DER GEGENWART. GESCHICHTE DER DRAMATISCHEN BÜHNE SEIT 1870 (The Contemporary Theatre: A History of the Dramatic Stage Since 1870) (Leipzig: J. J. Weber, 1928), pp. 43, 97-98, 101-05, 108, 126, 129-30, 194, 205-07, 210.
[Deals with Shaw's plays as performed on the contemporary stage. In German.]

3092 "Back to Methuselah Revived at the Court," ERA, 7 March 1928, p. 4.
This slightly revised version of Back to Methuselah is successful.

3093 Balmforth, Ramsden. THE PROBLEM-PLAY AND ITS

INFLUENCE ON MODERN THOUGHT AND LIFE (NY: Henry Holt, 1928), pp. 12, 34-37, 41-42, 62, 94-108.

In <u>Major Barbara</u> Shaw is both constructive and destructive because he shows how ineffective cheap and easy philanthropy is and how Mammon can be made to serve righteous purposes by an intelligent mind. There are scenes of "scalding" satire and also places where Shaw virtually shouts directly at us. He is, at bottom, a truly religious person because he attempts to convey a conception of a supreme spirit (the life force) which, when understood, can give men a more abundant life. The careful reader will note how frequently Shaw uses the language of Jesus, Saint Paul, and John Bunyan, which is a reflection of how Shaw's life force and the Christian concepts are linked. <u>The Shewing-up of Blanco Posnet</u> illustrates how Shaw's spirit deals with the apparently unredeemable.

3094 Beal, Wallis. "Shaw's Unbaked Bricks," NYT, 15 July 1928, parts II & III, p. 5.
Shaw's ill-conceived remarks, this time about bricks, show he is wearing out.

3095 Benchley, Robert [C.]. "The Theatre," LIFE, XCII (14 Dec 1928), 13.
<u>Major Barbara</u> is the sort of play to keep audiences awake, even though its message is rather obvious at times.

3096 Benson, E. F. "George Bernard Shaw," SPECTATOR, CXLI (1928), 127.
[A ten-line epitaph terming Shaw a communist and vegetarian, and commenting sarcastically on his socio-economic views.]

3097 "Bernard and Anatole," NYT, 15 March 1928, p. 24.
The fact that Shaw is a socialist should not interfere with efforts to obtain the Order of Merit for him.

3098 "Bernard Shaw Calls on Menjou in London," NYT, 20 May 1928, part I, p. 13.
[Title describes. See also: "Mr. Shaw and Mr. Menjou," NYT, 3 June 1928, part VIII, p. 8 (an account of their conversation); "Menjou and Bride Back from Paris," NYT, 6 June 1928, p. 27.]

3099 "Bernard Shaw—el socialismo y la mujer" (Bernard Shaw—Socialism and Woman), EL MERCURIO (Peru), 6 Sept 1928, p. 13 [not seen].
[Cited in Rodríguez (MS). In Spanish.]

3100 "Bernard Shaw habla sobre la educación" (Bernard Shaw Talks About Education), LA NUEVA ERA (Chile), II: 9 (Dec 1928), [n. p.; not seen].
[Cited in Rodríguez (MS). In Spanish.]

3101 "Bernard Shaw todavía" (Bernard Shaw Still), EL

MERCURIO (Peru), 7 Oct 1928, p. 11 [not seen].
[Cited in Rodríguez (MS). In Spanish.]

3102 Bidou, H[enry]. "La Maison des Coeurs Brisés" (Heartbreak House), JOURNAL DES DEBATS, XXXV, part I (27 Jan 1928), 164-66 [not seen].
[A review of Heartbreak House. In French.]

3103 Blei, Franz. "Bernard Shaw: Wegweiser für die intelligente Frau zum Sozialismus und Kapitalismus" (Bernard Shaw: The Intelligent Woman's Guide to Socialism and Capitalism), DIE LITERARISHCE WELT, IV: 45 (9 Nov 1928), 10.
Shaw is a very reasonable guide in The Intelligent Woman's Guide to Socialism and Capitalism; he definitely favors civil war. [In German.]

3104 Boissy, Gabriel. "Mlle Falconetti chante et Bernard Shaw s'égare" (Miss Falconetti Sings and Bernard Shaw Goes Astray), COMOEDIA, 31 Dec 1928.
The Inca of Perusalem is a pretentious and absurd sketch, full of vacuous remarks. [In French.]

3105 "Books of the Week: Mr. Shaw's Utopia," TIMES, 5 June 1928, p. 8.
The Intelligent Woman's Guide to Socialism and Capitalism has marks of greatness, although the work is paradoxical, sprawling, and lacks a sense of humility on Shaw's part.

3106 Boyd, Ernest. "Readers and Writers," INDEPENDENT (NY), CXX (1928), 604.
The Intelligent Woman's Guide to Socialism and Capitalism is frequently a brilliant application of Fabian socialism to present-day conditions. "His logic is perfect and his industry excessive."

3107 Breuer, Robert. "Theater in Berlin" (Berlin Theatres), DIE VOLKSBÜHNE, III: 7 (Oct 1928), 30-32.
Shaw is a very superficial moralist, but he may be more successful than his Victorian predecessor, Dickens. [In German.]

3108 Broun, Heywood, and Margaret Leech. ANTHONY COMSTOCK: ROUNDSMAN OF THE LORD (Lond: Wishart, 1928), pp. 20-21, 46, 246-54.
[An account of Comstock's part, as a reformer of morality, in the furor over the New York production of Mrs. Warren's Profession.]

3109 Brown, John Mason. "The Laughter of the Gods," THEATRE ARTS MONTHLY (NY), XII (1928), 94-96.
Although The Doctor's Dilemma is verbose in places, it contains scenes which arrest the heart and the mind.

3110 "Bumptiousness versus G. B. Shaw," LIVING AGE,

CCCXXXV (1928-29), 369.
Shaw declining an invitation to speak to a group in Glasgow has prompted remarks about his lack of courtesy.

3111 Burley, T. L. G. PLAYHOUSES AND PLAYERS OF EAST ANGLIA (Norwich: Jarrold, 1928), p. 100.
Shaw himself, as well as his plays, has been in the Maddermarket Theatre, Norwich.

3112 Burns, C. Delisle. "Book Reviews," INTERNATIONAL JOURNAL OF ETHICS, XXXIX (Oct 1928), 109-11.
The Intelligent Woman's Guide to Socialism and Capitalism is really about the morals and ethics of economic justice and is "refreshingly candid and courageous." There are some questions Shaw does not answer, and perhaps the book is too long and expensive.

3113 Bury, J. B. "Shavian Economics," SAT REV, CXLV (1928), 701-02.
The Intelligent Woman's Guide to Socialism and Capitalism is a remarkably accurate vision of the future in which Shaw sees economic equality taking place. Shaw's political theories, as expounded in parts, is the least satisfactory part of the book.

3114 Busse, A. "Bernard Shaws Sozialismus" (Bernard Shaw's Socialism), WÜRTTEMBERGER ZEITUNG (Stuttgart), XXII: 171 (24 July 1928), 2-3.
The Intelligent Woman's Guide to Socialism and Capitalism is a witty and humorous book, but it presents no convincing theory of socialism. [In German.]

3115 Butcher, Fanny. "Shaw Pens Master Book on Socialism; Tenets Made Clear," CHICAGO DAILY TRIBUNE, 2 June 1928, p. 13.
[An extremely favorable review of The Intelligent Woman's Guide to Socialism and Capitalism.]

3116 Carb, David. "Seen on the Stage," VOGUE, LXXI (15 Jan 1928), 120.
On the whole, The Doctor's Dilemma "is fearfully long-winded, it hammers in every point, overstates every idea, repeats type characteristics interminably."

3117 Caro, Josef. "Bernard Shaw," FESTSCHRIFT ZUM 75 JÄHRIGEN BESTEHEN DER REALSCHULE MIT LYZEUM DER ISR. [AELITISCHE] RELIGIONSGESELLSCHAFT (Festschrift for the 75th Anniversary of the Modern High School for Girls of the Israeli Religious Society) (Frankfurt: [n. p.], 1928), pp. 68-78 [not seen].
[In German.]

3118 Carr, Philip. [Heartbreak House], NYT, 12 Feb 1928,

part VIII, p. 1; rptd in NYTTR 1927-1929, [n. p.].
Heartbreak House has been revived, not very successfully, in Paris.

3119 Chesterton, G. K. "Shakespeare and Shaw," SHAKESPEARE REVIEW, I (May 1928), 10-13.
Shakespeare, who could be gay and frivolous when he chose, had the advantage of writing in an era which had inherited the best of ancient culture. Shaw, only superficially frivolous, writes earnestly for exactly the opposite reason.

3120 Chislett, William, jr. MODERNS AND NEAR-MODERNS (1928; rptd Freeport, NY: Books for Libraries, 1967), pp. 129-45.
Shaw's wit and humor are admirable, but his ideas are not attractive. "There is something incomplete about him . . . . He doesn't praise God or Nature or Woman. God is too dependent on Man, Nature hardly figures at all, and woman is a primitive and a hoyden."

3121 Clark, Evans. "Bernard Shaw Sums Himself Up," NYT, 10 June 1928, part IV, pp. 1, 22.
The Intelligent Woman's Guide to Socialism and Capitalism is a monumental sermon in which Shaw tries to save souls by economic means.

3122 "Court Theatre," TIMES, 6 March 1928, p. 14.
Back to Methuselah is something of an endurance test which repays the effort required to watch it.

3123 D'Arcy, Rev. M. C. "Bernard Shaw's Intelligent Woman's Guide: Some Opinions," CRITERION, VIII (1928), 195-201.
Shaw's views in The Intelligent Woman's Guide to Socialism and Capitalism will commend themselves only to a minority of socialists because Shaw belongs to the passing "rationalist school of thought and not [to] the more recent and modernist."

3124 De Casseres, Benjamin. "Bernard Shaw: All Spray, No Fountain," THEATRE MAGAZINE (NY), XLVIII (Sept 1928), 18, 64.
Shaw is a "preacher of socialism in his plays and books [but] is a hard-boiled capitalist at heart."

3125 "Dr. Krass Rejects 'Turning of Cheek,'" NYT, 17 Dec 1928, p. 28.
A rabbi has employed Major Barbara in a sermon and believes some traits of Undershaft and Barbara need to be combined.

3126 Duffin, Henry Charles. "Shaw: The Later Plays," CORNHILL MAGAZINE, LXV (Dec 1928), 672-80.
Heartbreak House, Back to Methuselah, and Saint Joan constitute a religious trilogy. Heartbreak depicts " a religionless society, a world without form and void," while Methuselah presents a metaphysical

faith in a metaphysical life force. Joan's "theme is the compelling force of a religious idea" but the play is outmoded.

3127 Dukes, Ashley. "A Doll's House and the Open Door," THEATRE ARTS MONTHLY (NY), XII (1928), 21-38.
[Mostly on Janet Áchurch and Charles Carrington, but with passing references to Shaw, and two letters by Shaw.]

3128 "Emil Ludwig Here for Lecture Tour," NYT, 11 Jan 1928, p. 3.
Shaw is one of the greatest men in Europe, "far greater as an educator than a playwright."

3129 "Entertainments: Mr. Shaw and the French," TIMES, 21 Feb 1928, p. 14.
The French do not warm to Heartbreak House because they find its characters bloodless. However, the real problem is that Shaw's rhetoric does not accord with French notions of life.

3130 "Entertainments: The Theatres: Mr. Shaw's Plays in Canada," TIMES, 23 Aug 1928, p. 10.
The rights to perform Shaw's plays in Canada have been granted to Maurice Colbourne.

3131 Ervine, St. John. HOW TO WRITE A PLAY (Lond: Allen & Unwin, 1928), pp. 39, 44, 76, 86-87, 94, 99-100, 113.
Shaw made an elementary dramatic mistake in repeating the word "bloody" in Pygmalion, although intellectually it was justified. Candida, Widowers' Houses, Heartbreak House, Back to Methuselah, and Saint Joan prove the point that dramatists begin writing short plays and then become garrulous. Shaw frequently changes direction in the middle of his speeches, but he is careful to put formal speeches into his characters' mouths sometimes. He "has an astounding capacity for making words work, but he is sometimes capricious and insists on holding them down."

3132 Ervine, St. John. "Mr. Shaw and the Traveller," SPECTATOR, CXLI (1928), 983-84.
The utopia presented in The Intelligent Woman's Guide to Socialism and Capitalism in which one's life is to be laid in neat and undeviating lines causes wonder about the individual who wanders about the world.

3133 Ervine, St. John. "The Shavian Belief," YALE REVIEW, ns XVIII (1928-29), 290-301.
The Intelligent Woman's Guide to Socialism and Capitalism is a virtuoso performance which definitively sets out Shaw's gospel. Anything else he may write on socialism must of necessity be either commentary or repetition.

3134 "The Essex Murder Trial," TIMES, 10 May 1928, p. 8.

[A Parliamentary question on Shaw's allegation that murder trial evidence had been tampered with.]

3135 Farjeon, Herbert. "The London Stage," GRAPHIC, CXIX (17 March 1928), 451.
Shaw's arguments in Back to Methuselah imply that he believes that since our wisdom increases as we grow older, a world of older people will progress rapidly.

3136 Farjeon, Herbert. "The London Stage," GRAPHIC, CXIX (31 March 1928), 534.
Part five of Back to Methuselah contains some curiosities, such as the theory that one day people will be "hatched out of eggs," but Shaw's "final prospect" is very much like that outlined in Christian theology, which has always been revolutionary.

3137 "For American Readers," TIMES, 2 June 1928, p. 11.
The American edition of The Intelligent Woman's Guide to Socialism and Capitalism contains a special foreword for Americans.

3138 "G. B. S. as Woman's Guide," LIT DIG, XCVIII (7 July 1928), 18-19.
The Intelligent Woman's Guide to Socialism and Capitalism puts the seal of Shaw being the equivalent to Voltaire or Ibsen in their day. His ideas are familiar, but his scheme is consistent and connected.

3139 "G. B. Shaw Expounds His Socialism Idea," NYT, 1 June 1928, p. 7.
Shaw's views on socialism in The Intelligent Woman's Guide to Socialism and Capitalism are clear and "may prove embarrassingly lucid for the British Labor Party."   [See also: "Bernard and Karl," NYT, 2 June 1928, p. 16.]

3140 "Garland Extols Hardy," NYT, 23 Jan 1928, p. 17.
Hamlin Garland, in a lecture, said of Shaw: "he talks really worse than he is."

3141 "Gets Shaw on Phonograph," NYT, 18 April 1928, p. 18.
Shaw has made a recording of "Spoken English and Broken English."

3142 Grossmann, K. "Zu Bernard Shaw Vermächtnis" (Bernard Shaw's Legacy), NEUER SCHWEIZER RUNDSCHAU, XXI (1928), 776-83 [not seen].
[Cited in Amalric, p. 480. In German.]

3143 Guerra, Guido. "Bernard Shaw, bañista y misántropo" (Bernard Shaw, Mineral Water Drinker and Misanthropist), LA NACIÓN (Chile), 14 Oct 1928 [not seen].
[Cited in Rodríguez (MS). In Spanish.]

3144 Hamon, A[ugustin], and H[enriette] Hamon. L'auteur de Sainte Jeanne" (The Author of Saint Joan), L'ILLUSTRATION

(Paris), No. 392 (28 July 1928), 1-41 [not seen].
[In French.]

3145 Hanemann, Henry William. "Oh, Shaw," MOTION PICTURE CLASSIC (NY), XXVIII (Nov 1928), 48-49, 83.
Though Shaw says he is busy, he admits to enjoying being in the movies, and may take over the industry. He asserts that he will play the parts of Garbo, Clara Bow, Adolphe Menjou, and others whom he admires because the future of the cinema depends upon his beard.

3146 Hannam-Clark, Theodore. DRAMA IN GLOUCESTER-SHIRE (THE COTSWOLD COUNTY): SOME ACCOUNT OF ITS DEVELOPMENT FROM THE EARLIEST TIMES TILL TO-DAY (Gloucester: Minchin & Gibbs; Lond: Simpkin Marshall, 1928), pp. 128, 139, 157.
[Brief details of Shaw productions in Gloucestershire.]

3147 Haugaard, Aase. "Bernard Shaw at Geneva," LIVING AGE, CCCXXXV (1928-29), 268-69.
[An account of Shaw's responses to students' questions on a range of topics.]

3148 Henderson, Archibald. "Bernard Shaw's Socialism," INSTITUTE MAGAZINE (Columbia University Institute of Arts and Sciences), I: 1 (Oct 1928), 22 [not seen].
[Cited in Hood, p. 228.]

3149 Henríquez Ureña, Pedro. "Notas sobre literatura inglesa" (Notes About English Literature), HUMANIDADES (Argentina), XVIII (1928), 103-22 [not seen].
[Cited in Rodríguez (MS). In Spanish.]

3150 Hirst, Francis W. "Mr. Bernard Shaw's Theory of Socialism and Capitalism," CONTEMPORARY REVIEW, CXXXIV (Nov 1928), 568-75.
In The Intelligent Woman's Guide to Socialism and Capitalism Shaw believes wealth should be divided and maintained equally among all the classes.

3151 Hollis, Christopher. "Some Notes on Mr. Shaw's St. Joan," DUBLIN REVIEW, CLXXXII (April 1928), 177-88; rptd Lond: Catholic Truth Society, 1932.
In depiciting the characters in Saint Joan, Shaw has played fast and loose with historical fact. Part of Shaw's failure in this play is his disbelief in miracles.

3152 "Home Secretary and Mr. Baldwin," TIMES, 10 Sept 1928, p. 14.
Sir William Joynson-Hicks believes The Intelligent Woman's Guide to Socialism and Capitalism is far-fetched.

3153 Horsnell, Horace. "The Drama: Back to Methuselah,"

OUTLOOK (Lond), LXI (17 March 1928), 345.

Back to Methuselah is a biological thesis which amuses but is unlikely to make converts. The play is loquacious but Shaw is a "first-rate topical satirist."

3154 Horwill, Herbert W. "Mr. Shaw is not in a Great Hurry," NYT, 15 Jan 1928, part IV, p. 16.

Shaw, despite his evangelism, has not been in a hurry to finish The Intelligent Woman's Guide to Socialism and Capitalism.

3155 "The Intelligent Woman's Guide to Socialism and Capitalism," LIVING AGE, CCCXXXIV (1928), 1113.

Shaw's thinking in The Intelligent Woman's Guide to Socialism and Capitalism is woolly at times, and his merit now is "not that he himself produces much original thought, but that he starts the minds of his readers working."

3156 Irzykowski, Karol. "G. B. Shaw: Człowiek i nadczłowiek" (G. B. Shaw: Man and Superman), ROBOTNIK (Warsaw), No. 57 (1928), 3; rptd in RECENZJE TEATRALNE: WYBÓR (Theatrical Reviews: A Selection) (Warsaw: Państwowy Instytut Wydawniczy, 1965), pp. 228-32.

Shaw differs from Strindberg in Man and Superman in that he is "good-natured," and has created the most original couple of lovers since MUCH ADO ABOUT NOTHING. Shaw can create characters, but prefers to argue and discuss. This is didactic poetry at its best. [In Polish.]

3157 Jan, Edward von. "Das literarische Bild der Jeanne d'Arc" (The Literary Image of Joan of Arc), BEIHEFTE ZUR ZEITSCHRIFT FÜR ROMANISCHE PHILOLOGIE, LXXVI (1928), 46-52, 172-80 [not seen].

[Cited in Amalric, p. 480. In German.]

3158 Kemmis, E. [Guía para la mujer inteligente] (The Intelligent Woman's Guide to Socialism and Capitalism), ACCION SOCIALISTA (Argentina), VI: 6 (22 Sept 1928), 187, 192 [not seen].

[Cited in Rodríguez (MS). In Spanish.]

3159 Kornmann, R. "Begegnung mit Shaw" (Interview with Shaw), ANNALEN, II (1928), 351-56 [not seen].

[Cited in Amalric, p. 480. In German.]

3160 Kostomlatsky, S. "Shaw and Moral-Passions," THE YEAR-BOOK OF THE ANGLO-AMERICAN CLUB UNION OF CZESKOLSLOVAKIA (Prague: n. p., 1928), pp. 42-46 [not seen].

[In Czech.]

3161 Krutch, Joseph Wood. "Drama: G. B. S. and the Test of

Time," NATION (NY), CXXVII (1928), 666-67.

Major Barbara withstands the test of time and seems more explicit and substantial than, say, The Doctor's Dilemma. However, Shaw has a tendency to lose grasp of his "simple propositions for the kind of rapt ecstacy which sometimes seizes him."

3162 Laski, Harold J. "Bernard Shaw's Intelligent Woman's Guide: Some Opinions," CRITERION, VIII (1928), 191-94.

The Intelligent Woman's Guide to Socialism and Capitalism forces the reader to examine his own beliefs. Shaw is incisive in his argument against the existing order, but less successful in advocating equal incomes. He is unsuccessful in his method of achieving a transition between the old and the new orders.

3163 Laski, Harold J. "Mr. Shaw as a Socialist," SATURDAY REVIEW OF LITERATURE (NY), IV (1928), 981, 984.

We should be grateful that in The Intelligent Woman's Guide to Socialism and Capitalism Shaw has set out coherently his considered view of socialist theory. The work is "an arresting revelation of [Shaw's] own mind . . . the work of a great humanist."

3164 Lasserre, Jean. "L'Inca de Perusalem" (The Inca of Perusalem), L'AMI DU PEUPLE DU SOIR, 31 Dec 1928.

The Inca of Perusalem contains a few commonplace ideas on peace, and should not have been performed. [In French.]

3165 "Letters by G. B. Shaw Sold," NYT, 11 Oct 1928, p. 17.

Shaw has threatened to sue if any letters written by him (and sold to third parties) are published. [See also: "Shaw Gives Advice and Issues Warning," NYT, 28 Oct 1928, part III, p. 6; "To Publish Shaw Letters," NYT, 16 Nov 1928, p. 7; "350 Shaw Letters to be Published," NYT, 26 Dec 1928, p. 3.]

3166 Levy, Rudolf. "G. B. Shaws 'Wegweiser'" (G. B. Shaw's "Guide"), JÜDISCHE RUNDSCHAU, 27 Nov 1928, supp, [n. p.].

In The Intelligent Woman's Guide to Socialism and Capitalism Shaw appeals to the conscience of mankind. A mastery of both language and social science is characteristic of Shaw. Shaw's guide is a matter of great interest to the Jewish reader. [In German.]

3167 "London Theatres: Mrs. Warren's Profession," STAGE, 9 Feb 1928, p. 18.

The subject matter of Mrs. Warren's Profession is now a commonplace in ordinary conversation and so does not shock as it did originally.

3168 "London Theatres: The Court," STAGE, 8 March 1928, p. 18.

The first parts of this revival of Back to Methuselah are attracting crowded audiences. Much of the play is enthralling.

3169 "London Theatres: The Court," STAGE, 15 March 1928, p. 18.
The third and fourth parts of Back to Methuselah are both thrilling and tedious.

3170 "London Theatres: The Court," STAGE, 22 March 1928, p. 18.
Shaw devotees continue to flock to Back to Methuselah "in spite of certain arid patches in the plains and jungles of Shaw's oratory and philosophic discussion."

3171 Lunacharskii, A. "Predislovie" (Foreword), ANATOLE FRANCE: POL'NOE SOBRANI SOCHINENII (Anatole France: Collected Works), XIV (1928), 7-13 [not seen].
[On Shaw, Schiller, and France's view of Saint Joan. In Russian.]

3172 Lynd, Sylvia. "Mr. Shaw's Guide," BOOKMAN (Lond), LXXIV (1928), 147-48.
[A descriptive book review of The Intelligent Woman's Guide to Socialism and Capitalism.]

3173 M., G. "Magdeburger Theater" (Magdeburg Theatres), DIE VOLKSBÜHNE, III: 8 (Nov 1928), 32-33.
The Doctor's Dilemma is topical but chatty. [In German.]

3174 MacCormac, John. "Bernard Shaw on Films," NYT, 27 May 1928, part VIII, p. 5.
Shaw is very interested in films as a new art form, and has quite a lot of experience in the field. [See also: "Are They Art?" NYT, 12 June 1928, p. 26.]

3175 Mac Donagh, Emiliano. "El debate sobre la propiedad entre Bernard Shaw y Chesterton" (The Debate About Property Between Bernard Shaw and Chesterton), CRITERIO, No. 40 (6 Dec 1928), 304-06 [not seen].
[Cited in Rodríguez (MS). In Spanish.]

3176 Macy, John. "Shaw Tells the World," NATION (NY), CXXVI (1928), 695-96.
The Intelligent Woman's Guide to Socialism and Capitalism is the finest example of exposition on its subject, and is a beautiful essay.

3177 Mantle, Burns, ed. THE BEST PLAYS OF 1926-27 AND THE YEAR BOOK OF THE DRAMA IN AMERICA (NY: Dodd, Mead, 1928), pp. 11, 29, 31, 426.
Pygmalion was a popular success, and Caesar and Cleopatra was chosen best play of the year by the Community Arts Association of Santa Barbara, California.

3178 Mantle, Burns, ed. THE BEST PLAYS OF 1927-28 AND THE YEAR BOOK OF THE DRAMA IN AMERICA (NY: Dodd, Mead, 1928), pp. 16-17, 455-56.

[Production details and a plot outline of The Doctor's Dilemma.]

3179 Marcus, Hans. "Besuche bei Londoner Dichtern" (Visits with London Writers), ARCHIV, CLII (June 1928), 202-09 [not seen].
[Cited in Amalric, p. 480. In German.]

3180 Mason, Michael. "Mr. Shaw, Shakespeare, and the Secondary Schoolboy," NINETEENTH CENTURY (Lond), CIII (1928), 525-36.
Saint Joan has been set as an examination text by the University of London, which invites comparison between Shaw and Shakespeare. The ultimate question this raises is "not why Shakespeare's poetic drama claims our adoration, but why Mr. Shaw has never given us a lyric play equal in the power of beauty, as in the beauty of power, to his prose epic, St. Joan."

3181 [Maxwell, Perriton]. "The Editor Goes to the Play," THEATRE MAGAZINE (NY), XLVII (Feb 1928), 38, 40.
There is much "dry, superficial verbiage" in The Doctor's Dilemma, but Dubedat's death scene lifts the play to tremendous heights.

3182 "Meaning Just What?" NYT, 10 June 1928, part III, p. 4.
There is little meaningful to be deduced from the fact that Shaw's The Intelligent Woman's Guide to Socialism and Capitalism is popular with Book-of-the-Month subscribers.

3183 Mierow, Herbert Edward. "A Modern Euripides," SEWANEE REVIEW, XXXVI (1928), 24-26.
Saint Joan is very similar in both spirit and technique to Euripides' work and can be criticized for having Euripides' dramaturgical weaknesses. However, the weaknesses are more apparent than real.

3184 "Minister Rebukes Shaw for 'Insolence,'" NYT, 3 Nov 1928, p. 12.
Shaw's flippant refusal to deliver a lecture to Glasgow Trinity Literary Society has resulted in the president of the society rebuking Shaw. [See also: "Blames 'Maconachie' for Rebuke to Shaw," NYT, 4 Nov 1928, part I, 14.]

3185 Mogilevskiĭ, A. I., et al. TEATRY MOSKY 1917-1927 (Theatres of Moscow 1917-1927) (Moscow: Akademiía khudozhestvennykh nauk, 1928), pp. 161-95.
[Details of Shaw productions in Moscow during 1917-27. In Russian.]

3186 Mumford, Lewis. "Bernard Shaw's Case for Equality," NEW REP, LV (1928), 177-78.
The Intelligent Woman's Guide to Socialism and Capitalism is the "last great Fabian tract," although it offers us nothing new from Shaw by way of ideas. He reiterates his earlier proposals and formulas which date back to the 1880s.

3187 Nathan, George Jean. "The Theatre: Shaw as a Lover,"
AMERICAN MERCURY, XIII (Feb 1928), 246-48.
Like many Shaw plays, The Doctor's Dilemma ages badly. Shaw's
work will survive as a curiosity of early twentieth-century intellectual drama and for the excellent love scenes it contains.

3188 Nevinson, Henry W. LAST CHANGES LAST CHANCES
(Lond: Nisbet, 1928), pp. 96-97, 106, 160-61, 174, 267-68, 274,
343.
[Miscellaneous biographical references.]

3189 "New Book by Shaw to be Published Soon," NYT, 24 May
1928, p. 14.
The Intelligent Woman's Guide to Socialism and Capitalism, Shaw's
"last will and testament to humanity," will be published very shortly.
[See also: "Shaw Discovers Intelligence in American Women," NYT,
25 May 1928, p. 24.]

3190 "New Shakespeare Theatre," TIMES, 6 Jan 1928, p. 8.
Shaw supports the design selected for the new Memorial Theatre at
Stratford-upon-Avon.

3191 Nicoll, Allardyce. READINGS FROM BRITISH DRAMA
(NY: Crowell [1928]), pp. 311, 337, 414-17.
Shaw is one of the leading dramatists of the modern classical school;
his chief motive is ridiculing romanticism.

3192 Niebuhr, Reinhold. "Socialism Simplified," CHRISTIAN
CENTURY, XLV (1928), 952.
In The Intelligent Woman's Guide to Socialism and Capitalism, Shaw
reveals he is a "melioristic socialist" and his theories ought to be a
tonic to Americans. "If the book were only not so large and so
expensive it might become a real textbook for the masses."

3193 P[ease], M. S. "Shorter Notices," EUGENICS REVIEW
(Lond), XX (1928-29), 287-88.
The Intelligent Woman's Guide to Socialism and Capitalism is
essentially a massive restatement of an article Shaw published in
1894. Shaw says nothing new on eugenics, but it is good he gives
"prominence to the eugenic argument in the advocacy of his policy,
instead of ignoring altogether the biological aspect of man."

3194 Phelps, William Lyon. "As I Like It," SCRIBNER'S
MAGAZINE, LXXXIV (1928), 744-45.
Shaw is the happiest person and still pursues numerous interests with
buoyant interest.

3195 "Picks 3 Dramatists as Greatest Today," NYT, 10 Dec
1928, p. 24.
Archibald Henderson lists Shaw with Pirandello and O'Neill as the
greatest contemporary dramatists.

3196 Pickthorn, Kenneth. "Bernard Shaw's Intelligent Woman's Guide: Some Opinions," CRITERION, VIII (1928), 205-14.
Shaw's "intellectual breadth and rectitude" in The Intelligent Woman's Guide to Socialism and Capitalism commands admiration, but other facets of the book—his facetiousness, inaccuracies of fact, argumentative method, faulty logic—leave much to be desired. Ultimately, the futurist society he advocates would be full of undesirable characteristics.

3197 "Pola Negri to See Shaw," NYT, 29 Nov 1928, p. 32.
Pola Negri hopes to persuade Shaw to sell her the film rights to one of his plays. [See also: "Pola Negri to Screen Shaw's Cleopatra," NYT, 1 Dec 1928, p. 14.]

3198 Preistley, J. B. "The Interview," SAT REV, CXLV (1928), 763-64.
[A humorous and satiric "vision" of life in a socialist state as advocated by Shaw.]

3199 Rageot, Gaston. "Un Ennemi des Anglais" (An Enemy of the English), REVUE POLITIQUE ET LITTERAIRE (Paris), LXVI (18 Feb 1928), 121-23; rptd as "Heartbreak House in Paris," LIVING AGE, CCCXXXIV (1928), 733-35.
In Heartbreak House Shaw is a passionate satirist of English customs. In order to surprise his audience he deals in the unreal, in fantasy, so that all his characters and situations are stripped of traditional trappings. [In French.]

3200 Ratcliffe, S. K. "Mr. Shaw's Dogma," NSTATE, XXXI (1928), 292-93.
The Intelligent Woman's Guide to Socialism and Capitalism is the accumulation of Shaw's social and economic theories which he has been expounding for fifty years in his inimitable way. The weakness of his economic theory is that he neglects to consider the production of the wealth he would distribute equally and is indifferent to "organic social growth." And he "would be the first to damn the mechanised State of his own devising."

3201 Rathbun, Stephen. "Major Barbara," SUN (NY), 20 Nov 1928, p. 20.
Major Barbara remains fresh, is one of Shaw's most characteristic plays, and the conversation could be written only by him.

3202 "Raymond, E. T." [pseud of Edward R. Thompson]. PORTRAITS OF THE NEW CENTURY (THE FIRST TEN YEARS) (Garden City, NY: Doubleday, Doran, 1928), pp. 47-53.
Shaw's early work might be considered bold, but it was certainly not as good as Saint Joan or Back to Methuselah. He is now banal and dated, and his thought is perishable (though not his wit). He has influenced contemporaries but he does not belong in the small group

of writers "who have changed the course of history."

3203 Reboux, Paul. "L'Inca de Perusalem" (The Inca of Perusalem), PARIS-SOIR, 31 Dec 1928.
The Inca of Perusalem is endless chit-chat. [In French.]

3204 "Refused at First, Shaw Tells How He Finally Met Strindberg," NYT, 25 March 1928, part III, p. 8.
[Title describes. See also: "Shaw and Strindberg," NYT, 13 April 1928, p. 24.]

3205 "Revival of Shaw Play Well Done by Guild," NYT, 20 Nov 1928, p. 28; rptd in NYTTR 1927-1929, [n. p.].
Major Barbara stands up well in revival, especially since Shaw's views are now more pertinent. However, this dramatic debate is reduced to overly long monologues in the final act.

3206 Rey, Etienne. "La Maison des Coeurs Brisés" (Heartbreak House), COMOEDIA, 18 Jan 1928, pp. 1-2.
Shaw is a scoffer, an erratic ideologist, whose mind is fantastic and changeable. Heartbreak House is a sequence of ironical conversations, an original philosophical entertainment which is well worth seeing. [In French.]

3207 Robbins, Frances Lamont. "Speaking of Books," OUTLOOK (NY), CXLIX (1928), 396.
The Intelligent Woman's Guide to Socialism and Capitalism is a sincere book, but Shaw's interests and views now seem dated.

3208 Robertson, D. H. "Reviews: Mr. Shaw's Economics," NATION & ATH, XLIII (1928), 300.
The Intelligent Woman's Guide to Socialism and Capitalism is arranged haphazardly, has a loose texture, and a deafening rhetoric. However, the ideas are not very complex, for what Shaw presents paradoxically has now become rather commonplace.

3209 Rosenbach, E. "Shaw (St. Joan) und Hebbel" (Shaw [Saint Joan] and Hebbel), ARCHIV, CLIII (June 1928), 232-35 [not seen].
[Cited in Amalric, p. 480. In German.]

3210 Rosenberg, Kate. "How Mrs. Shaw has Aided G. B. S.," NYT, 30 Dec 1928, part IX, p. 2.
[Title describes.]

3211 Rowse, A. L. "Bernard Shaw's Intelligent Woman's Guide: Some Opinions," CRITERION, VIII (1928), 201-05.
The Intelligent Woman's Guide to Socialism and Capitalism may be among Shaw's most important works because "as a social critic he has had no equal in his own lifetime." His artistic work will be "outpassed by a good half-dozen writers of our time."

3212 Roxane. "Guía de la mujer inteligente por Bernard Shaw" (The Intelligent Woman's Guide by Bernard Shaw), EL MERCURIO (Peru), 30 Sept 1928, p. 13 [not seen].
[Cited in Rodríguez (MS). In Spanish.]

3213 Rubinstein, H. F. THE ENGLISH DRAMA (Lond: Ernest Benn, 1928), pp. 70-79.
Shaw has made a great contribution to the spiritual side of drama and has never compromised his integrity. He has refused to provide mere entertainment, and his lapses (e. g. Pygmalion) have been counterbalanced by such pieces as Heartbreak House.

3214 Saenger, Samuel. "Bernard Shaws Bekenntnisbuch" (Bernard Shaw's Book of Confessions), NEUE RUNDSCHAU, XXXIX: 2 (1928), 590-94.
Like all great satirists and humorists, Shaw can be considered as a moralist. He is also widely read. In The Intelligent Woman's Guide to Socialism and Capitalism the techniques of capitalism and economic imperialism are extremely well explained. Shaw has no illusions about progress. [In German.]

3215 Saenger, Samuel. "Londoner Eindrücke" (London Impressions), NEUE RUNDSCHAU, XXXIX: 1 (1928), 660-65.
Shaw's plays are days of judgment on the stage. His amusing way of presenting things cannot be taken seriously. [In German.]

3216 Schröer, A. "Shaviana," ENGLISCHE STUDIEN (Leipzig), LXII: 3 (1928), 383-94.
[Notes on The Emperor and the Little Girl, Shaw's use of punctuation, and the model for Henry Higgins in Pygmalion. In German.]

3217 "Shavian Economics," SAT REV, CXLV (1928), 701-02.
In The Intelligent Woman's Guide to Socialism and Capitalism Shaw's argument is similar to that of social evolution and will "probably prove a remarkably accurate vision of the future." Shaw's political theories are less satisfactory than his economic one but the book "might be said to be Mr. Shaw's gentlest prose telling of deepest thought."

3218 "Shaw Adds Jokes on Immortality," NYT, 6 June 1928, p. 27.
Shaw's recent views on immortality are another example of his excellent clowning. [See also: "Shaw Puts Future on Personal Basis," NYT, 8 July 1928, part III, p. 1.]

3219 "Shaw Alters Lines in Play Because of Asquith's Death," NYT, 26 Feb 1928, part I, p. 1.
Because of the recent death of Asquith, Shaw has altered some lines in Back to Methuselah for an upcoming revival.

3220 "Shaw and Wells Rap Seizure of Sex Novel," NYT, 6 Oct

1928, p. 6.
Shaw and H. G. Wells have protested the seizure of Miss Radclyffe Hall's THE WELL OF LONELINESS.

3221 "Shaw Answers Sydenham," NYT, 28 Jan 1928, p. 4.
Shaw has declined, forcibly, to be on a committee to resolve the authorship of Shakespeares' plays.   [See also: "As to Shakespeare," NYT, 25 March 1928, part III, p. 5.]

3222 "Shaw Approves DAWN," NYT, 19 Feb 1928, part II, p. 2.
Shaw believes that DAWN, a film depiciting the life of Edith Cavell,should be shown. [See also: "Selwyn Won't Drop Cavell Film Plan," NYT, 7 March 1928, p. 29.]

3223 "Shaw as a Prophet Reorganizes World," NYT, 23 Nov 1928, p. 3.
Shaw has speculated the world will be reorganized in the future—curiously along lines coincident with his own views.   [See also: "Shaw Peers Deeply into the Future," NYT, 9 Dec 1928, part XI, p. 5.]

3224 "Shaw Assails a Bishop," NYT, 26 Feb 1928, part I, p. 3.
Shaw has attacked an Irish bishop for his advocacy of corporal punishment for children.

3225 "Shaw Breaks the Law," NYT, 9 June 1928, p. 3.
Shaw consistently breaks the speed limit for cars.

3226 "Shaw Defends Czechs in Minority Dispute," NYT, 9 Dec 1928, part III, p. 3.
Shaw believes Hungarians living in Czechoslovakia are being treated fairly.

3227 "Shaw Denies Warrior Play," NYT, 20 Dec 1928, p. 25.
Shaw has denied he is writing a play about the unknown warrior.

3228 "Shaw Fears Ellis Island," NYT, 4 Jan 1928, p. 10.
Yet again, Shaw has resisted invitations to visit America.

3229 "Shaw First Edition Sold Here for $660," NYT, 15 March 1928, p. 13.
[On the sale of a first edition of Cashel Byron's Profession. See also: "Shaw Returned the $1 as Fee for Autograph," NYT, 16 March 1928, p. 4.]

3230 "Shaw for Ever," OUTLOOK (NY), CXLIX (1928), 289-90.
[A humorous account of Shaw hypothesizing on the effects of his becoming immortal.]

3231 "Shaw for Talking Movies," NYT, 20 July 1928, p. 21.
Jed Harris, a theatrical producer, reports Shaw is very enthusiastic about talking movies.

3232 "Shaw Gay at Crown Offer," NYT, 24 Oct 1928, p. 7.
Shaw is highly amused at the offer of the American "throne" by a group of American "royalists."

3233 "Shaw Says Ibsen Exposed Shaw Woman," NYT, 20 March 1928, p. 6.
Shaw has lectured on Ibsen for the British Drama League.

3234 "Shaw Takes a Dig at Curious Americans," NYT, 23 May 1928, p. 3.
Shaw's most recent gibe is to wonder why an American has not rented his former apartment.

3235 "Shaw to Appear in Film," NYT, 29 May 1928, p. 9.
Shaw will appear in Movietone films and present a series of lectures. [See also: Mordaunt Hall, "G. Bernard Shaw Acts in Movietone," NYT, 26 June 1928, p. 29; Mordaunt Hall, "G. B. S.'s Talking Shadow," NYT, 1 July 1928, part VIII, p. 3.]

3236 "Shaw Turns Wrath Against Dean Inge," NYT, 14 Jan 1928, p. 5.
Inge criticized Saint Joan for being an apology for the inquisition, and Shaw has retaliated by calling Inge a monster.

3237 "Shaw would have Wed Clara Butt, He Says," NYT, 17 April 1928, p. 15.
[Title describes.]

3238 "Sister Socialist." "The Intelligent Woman and G. B. S.," SPECTATOR, CXL (1928), 837-38.
Shaw, in The Intelligent Woman's Guide to Socialism and Capitalism, has an acute, intricate, generous mind. However, the book raises numerous questions and it seems Shaw is "too much a rationalist."

3239 "Sixty Years of Social Thought," TLS, No. 1375 (7 June 1928), 417-18.
Shaw's The Intelligent Woman's Guide to Socialism and Capitalism is placed in useful perspective by Walter Bagehot's THE ENGLISH CONSTITUTION and F. J. C. Hearnshaw's A SURVEY OF SOCIALISM—all three books having been published fortuitously at the same time.

3240 Somerville, Peter F. "Mr. Bernard Shaw and Socialism," SPECTATOR, CXL (1928), 870.
Shaw, as an unknown, would have been poorly treated had there been socialist governments. He misunderstands the nature of such entities, which are essentially suppressive.

3241 "Sometimes Too Much is Known," NYT, 17 July 1928, p. 20.
An anecdote about a female buyer of The Intelligent Woman's Guide

to Socialism and Capitalism reveals the danger of attempting to appeal to intelligent people.

3242 Speth, William. "La Maison des Coeurs Brisés" (Heartbreak House), LA REVUE MONDIALE, CLXXXI: 4 (15 Feb 1928), 419-21.

Heartbreak House is a desultory, rambling conversation. Shaw juggles with ideas and the main characters are sometimes amusing but mean nothing to the audience. [In French.]

3243 Svrcek, Jaroslav. "Caesar a Kleopatra" (Caesar and Cleopatra), ROVNOST (Brno), No. 70 (March 1928) [not seen]. [In Czech.]

3244 "The Tailteann Festival," TIMES, 13 Aug 1928, p. 9.
Shaw has declined an award for Saint Joan.

3245 "Les Tenues Pittoresques de Bernard Shaw à l'Heure du Bain" (Bernard Shaw's Picturesque Dress at Bath-time), L'ILLUSTRATION (Paris), LXXXVI, part II (1 Sept 1928), 231 [not seen.]
[In French.]

3246 Tetauer, Frank. "Filosofie Shawových her a předmluv" (Philosophy of Shaw's Plays and Prefaces), PRÁCE Z VĚDECKÝCH ÚSTAVŮ (Prague), XXXI (1928), 71-179.

The life and works of Shaw, though having international and revolutionary significance, are typically English and essentially traditional. Shaw sought to preach a new religion which must be made popular and a matter of necessity to all, in spiritual as well as material life. All his main writings are therefore contributions to the modern practice of this new religion, with the philosophy of creative evolution as the axis of this activity. The plays are dramatic representations of the conflicts resulting from the contacts of men who have missions with the rest of mankind, including the common people, capitalists and aristocrats. Hence Shaw's interest in Caesar, Napoleon, Lenin and others. Being himself an incarnation of the life force, Shaw based his creations on his own experience: hence the spiritual affinity of all his heroes. The prefaces are attempts to codify the material out of which he dramatized his ideas. [In Czech.]

3247 "Tolstoy Told Shaw He Jested Too Much," NYT, 28 Feb 1928, p. 5.
In a letter to Shaw about Man and Superman, Tolstoy told Shaw he wanted to surprise his readers too much and this distracted from the essence of the play. [See also: "The Leopard's Spots," NYT, 29 Feb 1928, p. 24.]

3248 Torres Bodet, Jaime. "Conversaciones imaginarias: Shaw" (Imaginary Conversations: Shaw), CONTEMPORÁNEOS: NOTAS DE CRÍTICA (Contemporary Critical Notes) (Mexico: n. p.,

1928), pp. 131-40 [not seen].
[Cited in Rodríguez (MS). In Spanish.]

3249 "Trade a Nuisance, Shaw Tells Audience," NYT, 26 Nov 1928, p. 25.
[Title describes.]

3250 Trebitsch, Siegfried. "Questions That Shaw could not Resist," NYT, 18 Nov 1928, part V, p. 3.
[Interview.]

3251 "Tunney to Meet Shaw Sept. 15; Dramatist Cuts Vacation," NYT, 27 Aug 1928, p. 1.
[Title describes.]

3252 "Urges Clergy Copy Wells and Shaw," NYT, 4 Oct 1928, p. 10.
An English clergyman has urged the younger generation to turn to H. G. Wells and Shaw for ideas about moral and religious problems, rather than the church.

3253 Vančura, Zdenek. "Filosofie vývoje u H. G. Wellse a G. B. Shaw" (Philosophy of Evolution in the Works of H. G. Wells and G. B. Shaw), PRÁCE Z VĚDECKÝCH ÚSTAVŮ (Prague), XXXI (1928), 12-24.
From the beginning, Shaw's work contained all the elements from which he later developed his own philosophy of evolution. In The Perfect Wagnerite he works out an allegory of ethical evolution, demonstrating that all organic beings are the product of a life force which tends to incarnate itself in increasingly highly developed, conscious beings, and man outgrows his ideals. Archaism in the sphere of thought is a necessary condition of mental evolution, but it cannot be universally practised as long as the greatest part of the population lives in economic dependence. In Man and Superman Shaw brings biology into his scheme: if a man is enslaved by a woman, he cannot perform his true function. [In Czech.]

3254 Ward, A. C. TWENTIETH-CENTURY LITERATURE 1901-1925 (1928 [not seen]); rptd as TWENTIETH-CENTURY LITERATURE 1901-1940 (Lond: Methuen, 1940), pp. 5-7, 16, 85, 87-100, 115-118, 126, 132, 202-03, 241-42.
[An overview of Shaw's life and works.] Whatever may be Shaw's standing as a dramatist, it could have been greater because he subordinated his artistic ability to his moral purpose. His plays are "a continuous record of the long struggle between artist and moralist. Whenever he found himself as a artist, as a master of prose, he was possessed by the dread of being merely an artist, a dilettante."

3255 Washio, S. "Shaw: A Japanese Criticism," TRANS-PACIFIC (Tokyo), XVI (28 July 1928), 5.
Shaw is a conventional English idealist as far as socialism is

concerned. The Intelligent Woman's Guide to Socialism and Capitalism shows the influence of the humanitarian idealism that has been the product of English imaginative literature.

3256 Weaver, John V. A. "Poetry in Bernard Shaw," BOOKMAN (NY), LXVII (Aug 1928), 657-61.

It is possible to rearrange the line-lengths of Shaw's prose to reveal what is, in effect, authentic poetry. [Examples given.]

3257 Webb, Arthur. "Dublin Finds Talk in Literary Prizes," NYT, 29 July 1928, part II, p. 9.

Shaw has won a literary prize connected with the Tailteann Games, even though he may not appear to collect it. [See also: "Irish Award Arts Prizes," NYT, 12 August 1928, part I, p. 9.]

3258 West, Rebecca. "Contesting Mr. Shaw's Will: An Analysis of G. B. S.'s Final Word on Women and Socialism," BOOKMAN (NY), LXVII (July 1928), 513-20.

Women should read The Intelligent Woman's Guide to Socialism and Capitalism, but they should not be expected to take it seriously because "as a guide to peace upon earth" Shaw has done much better in his plays. Quite often Shaw is factually wrong and follows received opinion.

3259 West, Rebecca. THE STRANGE NECESSITY: ESSAYS AND REVIEWS (Lond: Cape, 1928), pp. 199-204, 206.

Shaw's achievement was to popularize intellectuality, which he did by means of his skilful craftsmanship in writing plays which forced people to swallow his dialectic. He was able to convince us that his dialogue is realistic when in fact it is akin to grand opera in the large sweep of its "orchestrations." Only his historical plays possess realistic dialogue.

3260 Whipple, Leon. "Letters & Life: Thunder on Both Hands," SURVEY, LX (1928), 483-84.

The Intelligent Woman's Guide to Socialism and Capitalism, which may be dismissed by the young as inconsequential, is "extraordinarily clear and readable." However, there are flaws and inconsistencies because Shaw's system is "too complete and too rational."

3261 Wild, Friedrich. DIE ENGLISCHE LITERATUR DER GEGENWART SEIT 1870: DRAMA UND ROMAN (Contemporary English Literature Since 1870: Drama and the Novel) (Wiesbaden: Dioskuren, 1928) [not seen].

[In German.]

3262 Wilson, Edmund. "Movietone and Musical Show," NEW REP, LV (1928), 226-27.

The Movietone film of Shaw is very impressive, with his innocence being particularly striking.

3263 Woodbridge, Benjamin Mather. "Bernard Shaw's Spiritual Forbear, Alexandre Dumas fils," HARVARD GRADUATES MAGAZINE, XXXVI (1928), 533-38 [not seen].

3264 "World Peace Moves Attacked by Shaw," NYT, 5 April 1928, p. 7.
Shaw believes that current patriotic fervor is unconducive to peace talks.

3265 "Would Lift Marriage Bars," NYT, 11 Feb 1928, p. 19.
Shaw has expressed his support for the removal of all genetic restrictions on marriage.

3266 Yáñez Silva, N. "Charlas de teatro: La crítica francesa y la Santa Juana de Bernard Shaw" (Theatre Gossip: French Criticism and Bernard Shaw's Saint Joan), DIARIO ILUSTRADO (Chile), 24 Sept 1924 [not seen].
[Cited in Rodríguez (MS). In Spanish.]

3267 Zachrisson, Robert Eugen. MODERN ENGELSK VÄRLDSASKÅDNING I LITTERATURENS SPEGEL (Modern English Ideology Reflected in Literature) (Uppsala & Stockholm: Almqvist & Wiksells [1928]) [not seen].
[Essays on Shaw, Hardy, Kipling, Galsworthy and Wells. In Swedish.]

1929

3268 Abascal, Luis. "Cándida de Shaw" (Shaw's Candida), CRITERIO, No. 70 (July 1929), 313-34 [not seen].
[Cited in Rodríguez (MD), p. 338. In Spanish.]

3269 Abascal, Luis. "El teatro: César y Cleopatra de G. Bernard Shaw" (The Theatre: Caesar and Cleopatra by G. Bernard Shaw), CRITERIO, No. 48 (31 Jan 1929), 154 [not seen].
[Cited in Rodríguez (MS). In Spanish.]

3270 "Actor Coached by G. B. S.," NYT, 5 May 1929, part IX, p. 5.
[An account of Shaw coaching Shayle Gardner for Saint Joan.]

3271 Alcalá-Galiano, Alvaro. "Bernard Shaw: Superhombre intelectual" (Bernard Shaw: Intellectual Superman), LA NACIÓN (Argentina), 6 Oct 1929, 13 Oct 1929; rptd in REPERTORIO AMERICANO (Costa Rica), XIX: 19 (16 Nov 1929), 297-98, XIX: 23 (14 Dec 1929), 360-62 [not seen].
[Cited by Rodríguez (MS). In Spanish.]

3272 Allen, Percy. "Shaw's Dramatic Genius Directed at Smug

Complacency of Wrongs," CHRISTIAN SCIENCE MONITOR, 30 July 1929, p. 7.

Shaw's "satire of social conventions has shocked, amused and inspired a generation of playgoers and brought him international fame."

3273 "Als Shaw anfing, berühmt zu werden" (When Shaw Began to Become Famous), WELTSTIMMEN (Stuttgart), III (Aug 1929), supp, [n. p.].

[Title describes. Anecdotal. In German.]

3274 "American Girl Upsets Shaw's 'Apple Cart,' " NYT, 19 Aug 1929, p. 22.

Edna Peters, a "typical American girl," has upset Shaw by calling him a typical Englishman.

3275 "The Apple Cart," PLAY PICTORIAL, LV: 331 ([1929]), 57-76.

The Apple Cart, though billed as an extravaganza, might be better labeled a comedy of manners, carefully exaggerated.

3276 "The Apple Cart," TIMES, 18 Dec 1929, p. 12.

[A synopis of Shaw's answer to German critics of The Apple Cart.]

3277 "The Apple Cart at the Queen's," ERA, 25 Sept 1929, p. 6.

The Apple Cart is an excellent, entertaining amusement whose humor "ranges from the extremely subtle to the broadly funny." It is a reflective play with "moments of wonderful grandeur."

3278 "The Apple Cart in Berlin," TIMES, 22 Oct 1929, p. 15.

The Berlin production of The Apple Cart has delighted audiences and confused critics.

3279 "The Apple Cart Staged in Warsaw," CHRISTIAN SCIENCE MONITOR, 2 July 1929, p. 10.

It was an honor to have The Apple Cart staged in Poland before it was produced in the English-speaking world. The political satire was quickly understood, although the first act was unduly long. The dialogue is brilliant and witty, the translation good.

3280 Arens, Franz. "Bernhard Shaw als Instruktor der intelligenten Frau" (Bernard Shaw as an Instructor of the Intelligent Woman), DAS DEUTSCHE BUCH (Leipzig), IX (1929), 19-20.

In The Intelligent Woman's Guide to Socialism and Capitalism Shaw, a master of dialogue and antithesis, does not give a systematic account of economic systems. He is not an orthodox Marxist, but nevertheless a fierce fighter against capitalism. [In German.]

3281 Arns, Karl. "Das moderne Engländertum in der englischen Literatur der Kriegs- und Nachkriegszeit" (The Modern Englishman in the English Literature of the War and the Post-War Age), HANDBUCH DER ENGLANDKUNDE. ZWEITER

TEIL (Handbook to England. Part Two), ed by Paul Hartig and Wilhelm Schellberg (Frankfurt: Moritz Diesterweg, 1929), pp. 321-57.
[Places Shaw in the context of modern cultural and social tendencies, with an emphasis on The Intelligent Woman's Guide to Socialism and Capitalism and Heartbreak House. Shaw, Wells and Galsworthy are seen as members of the old generation in comparison with the revolutionary ideas of younger writers. In German.]

3282 Aronstein, Philipp. "Englische Dramatik" (English Drama), HANDBUCH DER ENGLANDKUNDE. ZWEITER TEIL (Handbook to England. Part Two), ed by Paul Hartig and Wilhelm Schellberg (Frankfurt: Moritz Diesterweg, 1929), pp. 146-97.
Shaw is the most powerful literary personality since the Elizabethan era. A characteristic feature of Shaw's plays is the variety of settings and problems. [In German.]

3283 "Artist Loses Work That Shaw Signed," NYT, 13 Dec 1929, p. 36.
Sava Botzaris has lost an autographed portrait of Shaw which the latter signed to help the artist financially.

3284 "Bar Shaw Play in Dresden," NYT, 14 Dec 1929, p. 5.
The Apple Cart has been banned in Dresden.

3285 Becker, May Lamberton. "A Letter from London," SATURDAY REVIEW OF LITERATURE (NY), VI (1929), 110.
The production of The Apple Cart resembled an act of public worship rather than a theatrical event. The second act is really an interpolation, and without it the play would be unflawed.

3286 Belfoe, A. M. A. "Le Théâtre a Londres: La Voiture de Pommes, par Bernard Shaw" (The London Theatre: Bernard Shaw's The Apple Cart), LE FIGARO, 28 Oct 1929.
The title of The Apple Cart gives a good idea of the form of the play. It is really an illustrated pamphlet and not Shaw's best play. [In French.]

3287 Belgion, Montgomery. OUR PRESENT PHILOSOPHY OF LIFE (Lond: Faber, 1929), pp. 24-26, 28-29, 31, 49-122, 199, 281, 284, 286, 292, 301-02.
Shaw is "chiefly the apostle of the Superman and the advocate of Equality of Income," and sees the supremacy of "the will" as essential. He depicts characters who do what they like and who embody the notion that we have a duty not to be poor.

3288 Berg, G. "Englische Zeitschriften" (English Periodicals), DIE NEUE BÜCHERSCHAU, VII (1929), 622.
The discussions about socialistic utopias, instigated by H. G. Wells and Shaw, have come to an end. At last Shaw is considered a serious

writer in Britain. [In German.]

3289 Bernard, Jean-Jacques. "César et Cléopatre" (Caesar and Cleopatra), L'EUROPE NOUVELLE, 5 Jan 1929, p. 10 [not seen].
[Cited in Weintraub, p. 211. In French.]

3290 "Bernard Shaw cumplió ayer 73 años" (Bernard Shaw Reached 73 Yesterday), ZIG-ZAG (Chile), No. 1275, 27 July 1929 [not seen].
[Cited in Rodríguez (MS). In Spanish.]

3291 "Bernard Shaw's England," GRAPHIC, CXXV (21 Sept 1929), 503.
[Photographs of the London production of The Apple Cart.]

3292 B[ishop], G. W. "The Apple Cart: Opening of the Malvern Festival," ERA, 21 Aug 1928, pp. 1, 6.
In The Apple Cart Shaw paints a pessimistic future for Labour politics, but in King Magnus he gives us one of his "greatest creations." There are many unforgettable scenes and the play needs to be seen repeatedly.

3293 B[ishop], G. W. "London Productions: Major Barbara," ERA, 13 March 1929, p. 8.
Major Barbara is not dated because the problems it deals with are still present in society. The second act is the equal of anything in modern drama, and the final act is profound. The opening scene is perhaps "a trifle attenuated."

3294 Bishop, G. W. "A Walk and a Talk with Mr. Shaw," OBS, 8 Sept 1929, pp. 15-16.
An interview with Shaw reveals the political significance of The Apple Cart: there is no governing class, rather the real governors are members of all classes. Shaw also discusses the future of the cinema and his possible involvement in it.

3295 Bland, Alan. "Shaw Retains 'Common Touch' While Writing," CHRISTIAN SCIENCE MONITOR, 30 July 1929, p. 7.
Shaw's "stage directions help actors to interpret his plays."

3296 Bond, C. J. "Eugenics and Bernard Shaw," EUGENICS REVIEW (Lond), XXI (July 1929), 159-61 [not seen].

3297 Bornhausen, Karl. "Das religiöse Leben in England" (Religious Life in England), HANDBUCH DER ENGLAND-KUNDE. ZWEITER TEIL (Handbook to England. Part Two), ed by Paul Hartig and Wilhelm Schellberg (Frankfurt: Moritz Diesterweg, 1929), pp. 237-75.
[Includes an analysis of Saint Joan.] Saint Joan represents the English way of religion; Joan is a female Cromwell. [In German.]

3298 Bosdari, Alessandro de. "G. B. Shaw," STUDI DI LETTERATURE STRANIERE (Studies in Foreign Literature) (Bologna: [n. p.] , 1929); not seen] .
[In Italian.]

3299 Bottomley, Gordon. "The Shaw Festival at Malvern," LOND MERCURY, XX (1929), 622-23.
The Malvern Festival is unique for it celebrates the achievements of a living writer. To hear in sequence Caesar and Cleopatra, The Apple Cart, Heartbreak House, and Back to Methuselah was to "gain new respect for Mr. Shaw's constructive thought and creative energy." All the plays remind us of the "vocal quality" of Shaw.

3300 "Break-up of Empire Proposed by Maxton," NYT, 5 Aug 1929, p. 7.
Shaw has attended a summer school organized by the British Labour Party. [See also: "Shaw Denies Labor is Popular Party," NYT, 6 Aug 1929, p. 6; "Shaw Defines Socialism as Work for Everybody," NYT, 25 Aug 1929, part IX, p. 4.]

3301 Broad, C. Lewis, and Violet M. Broad. DICTIONARY TO THE PLAYS AND NOVELS OF BERNARD SHAW WITH BIBLIOGRAPHY OF HIS WORKS AND OF THE LITERATURE CONCERNING HIM WITH A RECORD OF THE PRINCIPAL SHAVIAN PLAY PRODUCTIONS (Lond: A. & C. Black, 1929; rptd St. Clair Shores, MI: Scholarly P, 1972).
[Title describes.]

3302 B[rown], I[vor]. "Mr. Shaw's New Play: The Apple Cart," MANCHESTER GUARDIAN, 20 Aug 1929, pp. 11-12; rptd in Evans, pp. 313-16.
Shaw takes on the role of devil's advocate in The Apple Cart with regard to the nature of democracy; he here depicts it at its most clownish. Curiously and unusually, Shaw offers nothing constructive to balance his mischievousness.

3303 Brown, Ivor. "The Theatre: Army Orders," SAT REV, CXLVII (1929), 317-18.
Major Barbara survives very well and remains an "urgent" piece of drama which mixes comedy with character perfectly. The second act is one of Shaw's best, which only bad acting could ever ruin.

3304 Brown, Ivor. "The Theatre: John Bull's Other Scold," SAT REV, CXLVIII (1929), 240-41.
Although The Apple Cart is not a great play, it is provocative and mischievous. Shaw has broken all the dramatic rules, and given his own species of play.

3305 Brown, Ivor. "The Theatre: Mr. Shaw's Sour Apples," SAT REV, CXLVIII (1929), 212-13.
The Apple Cart is no more than a flimsy political cartoon which is

grotesque and reveals Shaw is out of touch with reality. The characters are no more than dummies and Shaw's dialectic is very weak.

3306 Burton, Elizabeth Eaton. "G. B. S. Abroad and at Home: The Apple Cart is Produced in Warsaw," DRAMA (NY), XX (Oct 1929), 6-7.
The Polish premiere of The Apple Cart demonstrates that Shaw's political paradoxes have universal appeal. Only the character of King Magnus is developed; the rest are unfinished sketches.

3307 Callender, Harold. "The Fabians Conquer Britain," NYT, 8 Dec 1929, part V, pp. 1-2, 15.
[A discussion of Fabianism with references to Shaw.]

3308 Calvo, Luis. "El teatro en Madrid: La temporada 1928-1929" (The Theatre in Madrid: The 1928-1929 Season), LA NACIÓN (Argentina), 25 Aug 1929 [not seen].
[Cited in Rodríguez (MS). In Spanish.]

3309 "Carados." "The Apple Cart: George Bernard Shaw as an Anti-Revolutionist, "SUNDAY REFEREE (Lond), 25 Aug 1929, p. 5.
The Apple Cart is a debate comprised of speeches of abnormal lengths, which still interested many in the audience. It bristles with

sparkling Shavian wit.

3310 Carpenter, Bruce. THE WAY OF THE DRAMA: A STUDY OF DRAMATIC FORMS AND MOODS (NY: Prentice-Hall, 1929), pp. 16, 40, 73, 104-05, 130, 211-12.
Shaw derived part of his "acidity" from Ibsen. He has a "broader if not deeper intellect" than Wilde, and "his character is stronger." He is not the best of dramatists because he gives us ideas rather than actable plays. He was a "great stimulus to Jones and Pinero."

3311 Carr, Philip. [Caesar and Cleopatra], NYT, 6 Jan 1929, part VIII, p. 4; rptd in NYTTR 1927-1929, [n. p.].
The reception of the revival of Caesar and Cleopatra in Paris reveals that the French are beginning to tire of Shaw.

3312 "Chamberlain Talk Wins British Praise," NYT, 28 Jan 1929, p. 2.
Shaw has been attacked in British newspapers for his views on pacifism and the relationship of Britain to America.

3313 Cheney, Sheldon. THE THEATRE: THREE THOUSAND YEARS OF DRAMA, ACTING AND STAGECRAFT (Lond & NY: Longmans, 1929), pp. 380, 434, 451-52, 458-61, 463-64.
Shaw infused realistic drama with its greatest potentiality and made it an intellectual entity. His characters behave naturally, but his plays do not possess warm, sensuous theatricality.

3314 Chesterton, G. K. "Three English Prophets and the War," NYT, 3 March 1929, part V, pp. 3, 21.

Shaw, along with Kipling and Wells, made predictions for the twentieth century which never came true. [See also: "Bernard Shaw Replies to Chesterton," NYT, 10 March 1929, part V, p. 22.]

3315 Churchill, Winston. "George Bernard Shaw," PALL MALL, August 1929, p. 16 [not seen]; rptd in GREAT CONTEMPORARIES (NY: Putnam, 1937), pp. 35-44; extract rptd in Evans, pp. 311-12.

The characteristics of Shavian drama are now world-renowned and Shaw stands second only to Shakespeare. Shaw was startlng, broke dramatic traditions regarding structure, and replaced characterization with debate. Even twenty years after its premiere Major Barbara contains no suggestion it is out of date.

3316 Colum, Padraic. "The Theatre," DIAL, LXXXVI (1929), 169-70.

This revival of Major Barbara is not very good because it lacks the grandeur Shaw put into the play. The production is in too low a key.

3317 "A Comedy Built on Futility," IRISH TIMES (Dublin), 26 Aug 1929, p. 4.

Heartbreak House is really a great play and not the superficial comedy it might appear. It belongs in the tradition of Chekhov, Gorky and Ibsen in its study of futility.

3318 "Court Theatre," TIMES, 24 Dec 1929, p. 10.

Arms and the Man is now perceived as comedic rather than farcical and all Shaw's earlier prophecies have been remarkably accurate.

3319 D., M. "The Apple Cart in London," DT, 18 Sept 1929, p. 8.

The Apple Cart is now described as a "political extravaganza in two acts and an interlude" (rather than as a comedy in three acts). This better suits the play, for act two is extraneous to the main action, even though it provides a tour de force for the actress playing Orinthia.

3320 D'Angelo, Evelyn. "George Bernard Shaw's Theory of Stage Representation," QUARTERLY JOURNAL OF SPEECH, XV (1929), 330-49.

It is possible to determine Shaw's theory of play production by culling his numerous works. The key words in his theory are "natural" and "real"—he believes an audience should see "real things happening to real people."

3321 D[arlington], W. A. "Mr. G. B. Shaw's New Play," DT, 20 Aug 1929, p. 6.

The Apple Cart is not one of Shaw's best plays, but it is very interesting in its demonstration that it is the men who administer a system who are important, not the system itself.

3322 "Degree for Shaw Urged," NYT, 7 Feb 1929, p. 30.
There is a proposal for the National University of Ireland to award Shaw a degree. [See also: "Irish Refuse to Give a Degree to Shaw," NYT, 13 March 1929, p. 4.]

3323 "Discussing Prices with Shaw," LIT DIG, CIII (26 Oct 1929), 22.
C. R. W. Nevinson has indicated he will willingly sell his paintings cheaply if Shaw will drastically reduce the price of theatre seats for his plays.

3324 "Dresden and The Apple Cart," TIMES, 14 Dec 1929, p. 9.
The acting minister of education has halted rehearsals of The Apple Cart in Dresden because the play might offend socialists.

3325 Dukes, Ashley. "And So to Malvern," THEATRE ARTS MONTHLY (NY), XIII (Oct 1929), 729-33.
"The Apple Cart is no more than the bait of novelty to draw us to Malvern and its Festival."

3326 Düsel, F. "Der Kaiser von Amerika" (The Apple Cart), WESTERMANNS MONATSHEFTE (Berlin), CXLVII (Dec 1929), 417-19 [not seen].
[In German.]

3327 "Dutch Art Proves Rich London Feast," NYT, 4 Jan 1929, p. 5.
Shaw was one of the earliest visitors to an exhibition of Dutch art at Burlington House, London.

3328 Enchenique Gandarillas, J. M. "La última comedia de Bernard Shaw" (Bernard Shaw's Latest Comedy), DIARIO ILUSTRADO (Chile), 3 Oct 1929 [not seen].
[On The Apple Cart. Cited in Rodríguez (MS). In Spanish.]

3329 "Entertainments: Mr. Shaw's New Play," TIMES, 15 June 1929, p. 12.
The Apple Cart has been produced in Warsaw. [See also TIMES, 20 June 1929, p. 20 for a photograph of a scene from the Warsaw production.]

3330 "Entertainments: Mr. Shaw's New Play," TIMES, 20 Aug 1929, p. 10.
After Shaw's negative stance during the war, his pro-British views in The Apple Cart are rather remarkable.

3331 Ervine, St. John. "At the Play," OBS, 25 Aug 1929, p. 11; rptd in Evans, pp. 322-23.
The Apple Cart is a "superb medley of pantomime and morality play." It is akin to a revue and does not conform to orthodox dramaturgical

notions. Some people have failed to perceive Shaw's "fantastic wisdom and brilliant discourse" which is remarkable at his age.

3332 Ervine, St. John. "Shaw, George Bernard," THE ENCYCLOPAEDIA BRITANNICA, 14th ed (Lond, NY, Chicago, Toronto: Encyclopedia Britannica, 1929), XX, 469-71.
[A survey of Shaw's life, works, ideas, etc.]

3333 Evans, B. Ifor. "An Open Letter to G. B. S.," SPECTATOR, CXLIII (1929), 271-72.
In his earlier days Shaw was obliged to resort to various tactics in order to get a hearing. Now, however, Shaw has been raised on a pedestal so high that the real man has been lost from view. Shaw has been deified. He should write an autobiography to set the record straight.

3334 Farjeon, Herbert. "The London Stage," GRAPHIC, CXXIII (16 March 1929), 406.
The first act of Major Barbara is poor Shaw, the second brilliant, and the third a vehicle for what he has to say on materialism as a religion.

3335 Farjeon, Herbert. "The London Stage," GRAPHIC, CXXV (31 Aug 1929), 369.
If The Apple Cart were a play by a new dramatist, it would excite admiration, but much of the satire repeats that in past Shaw plays, and some of the comedy is unworthy of Shaw.

3336 Farjeon, Herbert. "Mr. G. B. Shaw Upsets The Apple Cart," DC, 20 Aug 1929, p. 7.
The Apple Cart will be less popular than Saint Joan because it has no human interest. It has passages of penetrating wit "punctuated by jokes of the music-hall breed."

3337 Fischer, O. "Poznamka K'Majoru Barbare. G. B. Shaw" (A Note on Major Barbara by G. B. Shaw), PANORAMA, VII (1929), 218-20 [not seen].
[Cited in Amalric, p. 481. In Czech.]

3338 "Future of the Theatre," TIMES, 31 Aug 1929, p. 8.
[Largely a report of Shaw's speech on the theatre at a supper in Malvern.]

3339 G., F. "Bernard Shaw und die junge Dichtergeneration" (Bernard Shaw and the Generation of Young Authors), DIE VOLKSBÜHNE, III: 11 (Feb 1929), 44-45.
Shaw is the most important living playwright. His dreams are living reflections but contain too much conversation. His ironic criticism becomes a positive life force. To a certain extent, Brecht, Bronnen, Bruckner and Hasenclever belong to the Shaw school. [In German.]

3340 García, Lautaro. "Bernard Shaw y la radio" (Bernard Shaw and the Radio), EL DIARIO ILUSTRADO (Chile), 5 Jan 1929 [not seen].
[Cited in Rodríguez (MS). In Spanish.]

3341 Groom, Bernard. A LITERARY HISTORY OF ENGLAND (Lond & NY: Longmans, Green, 1929), pp. 357, 361-63.
Shaw is first a critic, then a dramatist; his work may be entertaining, but ideas are of paramount importance. He belongs to the "order of social and political critics."

3342 Gruber, Franz. "Kölner Schauspielhaus" (Cologne Theatre), DIE VOLKSBÜHNE, III: 10 (Jan 1929), 28-29.
The Doctor's Dilemma is witty and efficient, but the dialogue is too chatty. [In German.]

3343 H., R. "Mr. Shaw's New Play," MPOST, 20 Aug 1929, pp. 9, 11.
Shaw's hold on the theatrical and critical world is such that it rushes everywhere and anywhere to see his plays. The Apple Cart is a keen, critical political satire, with long disquisitions that reveal Shaw as a master of the art of the soliloquy.

3344 Haas, Margarete. "Bernard Shaws unromantische Auffassung der Frau" (Bernard Shaw's Unromantic Conception of Woman), NEUEREN SPRACHEN, XXXVII (1929), 45-49 [not seen].
[Cited in Amalric, p. 481. In German.]

3345 Hall, Mordaunt. "The Screen," NYT, 7 Sept 1929, p. 15.
[Brief details of Shaw and his talk for Movietone news.]

3346 Hearnshaw, F. J. C. A SURVEY OF SOCIALISM: ANALYTICAL, HISTORICAL, AND CRITICAL (Lond: Macmillan, 1929), pp. 74-75, 83, 227, 294, 296, 299, 359, 361, 363, 376.
Shaw's socialistic views could be regarded as "irresponsible levity" except that they are repeated seriously by others. He has confused the public as to what socialism means.

3347 Henderson, Archibald. "Bernard Shaw on Women and Children," GOLDEN BOOK MAGAZINE, IX (Feb 1929), 75-77.
Shaw uses the mask of a "cosmic comedian" to hide his real self. Saint Joan is "the noblest and the greatest play in the English language since the time of Shakespeare." Shaw supports female suffrage and thinks children need better education.

3348 Henderson, Archibald. "Bernard Shaw the Man," GOLDEN BOOK MAGAZINE, IX (Jan 1929), 40-42.
[An anecdotal account of how Henderson became Shaw's biographer.]

3349 Henderson, Archibald. "Bernard Shaw's Vision of the

Future," GOLDEN BOOK MAGAZINE, IX (March 1929), 91-93.
[Title describes.]

3350 Henderson, Archibald. "Is Shaw a Dramatist? G. B. S. Answers His Critics in Authentic Utterances Selected by His Biographer," FORUM (NY), LXXXII (Nov 1929), 257-61; issued in variant form as IS BERNARD SHAW A DRAMATIST? (NY & Lond: Mitchell Kennerley, 1929).
[Shaw answers the charges that he is a lecturer, not a dramatist; that he deliberately upset all the dramaturgical rules; that he has no talent for playwriting; that his plays lack structure and that his characters are not human beings; that several of his plays are merely theatrical entertainment; that his plays violate Aristotle's rules; and that the plays have no emotional situation.]

3351 Herbert, A. P. "In Defence of the Speed Limit: A Reply to Mr. Shaw," OBS, 22 Dec 1929, pp. 11-12.
Shaw is tolerable so long as he sticks to imaginary, creative topics; but he is tiresome when he holds forth on really important matters such as speed limits. [See Shaw's views, OBS, 15 Dec 1929, pp. 17-18, and further correspondence in OBS, 29 Dec 1929, pp. 3, 15, and 5 Jan 1930, p. 9.]

3352 Holmes, Maurice. SOME BIBLIOGRAPHICAL NOTES ON THE NOVELS OF GEORGE BERNARD SHAW: WITH SOME COMMENTS BY BERNARD SHAW (Lond: Dulau [1929]).
[A factual and bibliographical account of the novels and the history of their publication.]

3353 Hopkins, Roy. "Where 'G. B. S.' Obtains a Bit of Fresh Air," NATIONAL MAGAZINE (Bost), LVII (March 1929), 259, 281.
[A description of Ayot St. Lawrence and Shaw's home there in genial, gossipy manner.]

3354 Huneker, James [Gibbons]. ESSAYS. Selected by H. L. Mencken (NY: Scribner's, 1929), pp. 1-27.
The prefaces to the plays are the quintessence of Shaw and will be remembered long after the plays are forgotten. Serious or not, Shaw is a delightful and entertaining writer, who tells the truth at all costs.

3355 "I. L. P. Summer School," TIMES, 5 Aug 1929, p. 12.
[Details of Shaw's participation in the Independent Labour Party's summer school. See also: "Some Socialist Fallacies," TIMES, 6 Aug 1929, p. 7.]

3356 "La iglesia y el humorista Bernard Shaw" (The Church and the Humorist Bernard Shaw), NUEVA REVISTA PERUANA, I: 2 (Oct 1929), 301-12 [not seen].
[Cited in Rodríguez (MD), p. 336. In Spanish.]

3357 "Ingenious Advertising," NYT, 15 March 1929, p. 24.
Shaw's refusal to participate in an advertising campaign by Harrods store has been used ingeniously by Harrods. [See Harrods' advertisement, "Bernard Shaw and Harrods," NYT, 15 March 1929, p. 15.]

3358 Jarnes, B. "Los autores y las obras. Carta de Madrid" (Writers and Works: Madrid Letter), LA NACIÓN (Argentina), 17 March 1929 [not seen].
[Cited in Rodríguez (MS). In Spanish.]

3359 Jennings, Richard. "The Theatre: Major Barbara," SPECTATOR, CXLII (1929), 417.
After twenty-five years, Major Barbara has dated very little because the abuses it describes still exist. The "admirable" second act is still fresh; the only dated characters are Undershaft and Cholly Lomax.

3360 Jessup, Mary E. "G. B. S. Abroad and at Home: The Apple Cart is Produced at Malvern," DRAMA (NY), XX (Oct 1929), 6, 8.
In the overall context of the Malvern Festival and the repertoire of Shavian plays, The Apple Cart disappoints. The characterizations and dialogue are good, but the construction is deficient (particularly the second act which breaks the overall continuity of the play).

3361 Kellen, Tony. "Die Jungfrau von Orleans in der Weltliteratur" (Saint Joan in World Literature), WELTSTIMMEN (Stuttgart), III (1929), 218-25.
Shaw's Saint Joan has no real belief in God; she just has enormous reasoning power. [In German.]

3362 K[ellen], T[ony]. "Ein Mann, der Shaw nicht verehrt" (The Man Who Doesn't Admire Shaw), WELTSTIMMEN (Stuttgart), III (Jan 1929), supp, [n. p.].
[An anecdote about a stage-hand who wanted more pay because he had been forced to listen to Shaw's plays. In German.]

3363 Klabund [Alfred Henschke]. LITERATURGESCHICHTE. DIE DEUTSCHE UND DIE FREMDE DICHTUNG VON DEN ANFÄNGEN BIS ZUR GEGENWART (Literary History. German and Foreign Literatures from the Beginnings to the Present Time) (Wein: Phaidon, 1929), pp. 306-07.
Shaw is Britain's conscience. [With a brief survey of Shaw's life and works. In German.]

3364 Knudsen, H[ans]. "Der Kaiser von Amerika" (The Apple Cart), PREUSSISCHE JAHRBUCHER (Berlin), CCXVIII (Dec 1929), 403-04 [not seen].
[A review of The Apple Cart. In German.]

3365 L., J. W. "Malvern Festival," MALVERN GAZETTE, 23 Aug 1929, pp. 3-4, 8-9.
[Extensive factual coverage of the opening of the festival.] The

satire in The Apple Cart is generalized rather than particularized. Shaw is still brilliant, but has mellowed while retaining his lofty ideals. Back to Methuselah is the pièce de résistance of the festival, even though it contains more discussion and less action than any of the other plays.

3366 L., J. W. "Malvern Festival: The Second Week," MALVERN GAZETTE, 30 Aug 1929, p. 9.
Heartbreak House stands high in Shaw's repertoire for pure fun; its serious aspects can be heeded or ignored as one chooses. Caesar and Cleopatra is perhaps the most difficult of the plays being produced at the festival, but it is successfully carried off.

3367 Le Mesurier, Mrs. [Lilian]. THE SOCIALIST WOMAN'S GUIDE TO INTELLIGENCE: A REPLY TO MR. SHAW (Lond: Benn, 1929).
The Intelligent Woman's Guide to Socialism and Capitalism is a very provocative book and is full of "flaws, fallacies and inconsistencies . . . . It is amazing that even an ordinarily clever man, much less one with a super-brain like Mr. Shaw's, should have perpetrated seriously some of the remarks he has allowed himself to make. It is a still greater strain on credulity to suppose that he really believed them all himself. Yet in the main I cling to my belief in Mr. Shaw's sincerity."

3368 "Letters from Shaw to be Sold in London," NYT, 15 Oct 1929, p. 8.
[Title describes.]

3369 "London Theatres: The Queen's," STAGE, 19 Sept 1929, p. 16.
Shaw has produced better work than The Apple Cart in which he seems to be content to simply wear his professional jester's cap.

3370 "London Theatres: Wyndham's," STAGE, March 1929, p. 16.
[A successful revival of Major Barbara.]

3371 Lucas, F. L. "Literary Trifling," NATION & ATH, XLVI (1929), 249-51.
[A humorous "conversation" between Shaw and Dr. Johnson.]

3372 M., A. E. "How Shaw Fares at Malvern," IRISH TIMES (Dublin), 23 Aug 1929, p. 4.
The festival is very successful. It is ironic that the enfant terrible of the 1890s now seems to desire conformity, even in such matters as dress at the theatre. Nevertheless there is much keen Shavian wit and satire in parts of Back to Methuselah, which the audience enjoyed thoroughly.

3373 M., A. E. "Shaw Festival at Malvern," IRISH TIMES (Dublin), 22 Aug 1929, p. 4.

Back to Methuselah is certainly the biggest, though not greatest, contemporary play. Shaw now seems to appeal to middle-aged women, and perhaps the festival is his swan song.

3374 M., P. J. "Getting Married: The Opera House Macdona Season," MANCHESTER GUARDIAN, 19 Aug 1929, p. 11.
Getting Married is "more like a Platonic dialogue than any other Shaw play" and its dramatic properties lie in its conflict of ideas (rather than of characters).

3375 MacCarthy, Desmond. "Miscellany: The Apple Cart and Mr. Belloc's Apples," NSTATE, XXXIII (1929), 739-40; rptd in MacCarthy, pp. 181-87; rptd as "Mr. Belloc's Apples," SATURDAY REVIEW OF LITERATURE (NY), VI (1930), 705-06.
The Apple Cart may be all talk, but it is arranged theatrically, and the central idea (that democracy is a fraud) is essentially true.

3376 Mac Donagh, Emiliano. "Comentario" (Commentary), CRITERIO, No. 57 (4 April 1929), 426-27 [not seen].
[Cited in Rodríguez (MS). In Spanish.]

3377 Macdonald, Edward J. "Shaw's New Play," COMMONWEAL, X (18 Sept 1929), 497-98.
The Apple Cart possesses no action, although it is a dexterous and witty play. Unfortunately, Shaw offers nothing to replace the object of his destructive satiric attacks, and the play would have been better written by Chesterton.

3378 McK., My. "Shaw's Saint Joan in Tokyo," TRANS-PACIFIC (Tokyo), XVII (14 Nov 1929), 6.
[An unsuccessful revival of Saint Joan.]

3379 "Maior Barbara de Bernard Shaw" (Bernard Shaw's Major Barbara), LUPTA (Bucharest), 13 Nov 1929 [not seen].
[In Roumanian.]

3380 "The Malvern Festival," ERA, 21 Aug 1929, p. 6.
The opening performance of The Apple Cart was a unique event in British theatre history.

3381 "Malvern Festival," IRISH TIMES (Dublin), 24 Aug 1929, p. 4.
The total effect of Back to Methuselah is rather bewildering and reveals that Shaw the comic makes a greater impression than Shaw the philosopher.

3382 "Malvern Festival," TIMES, 19 Aug 1929, p. 10.
Sir Edward Elgar has opened the Bernard Shaw exhibition at Malvern Public Library.

3383 "Malvern Festival: Methuselah Revisited," TIMES, 24 Aug 1929, p. 8.

Back to Methuselah has considerable faults, not least its length, "harshness, angularity, incoherence," and Shaw's weakness for a quip just when his philosophy is beginning to carry the piece along.

3384 "Malvern Festival: Two Earlier Plays of Mr. Shaw," TIMES, 26 Aug 1929, p. 10.
The strains of the Shavian repertory at Malvern show somewhat in the performances of Caesar and Cleopatra and Heartbreak House.

3385 "Malvern to See Shaw's New Play The Apple Cart," CHRISTIAN SCIENCE MONITOR, 30 July 1929, p. 7.
There is world-wide interest in the season of Shaw's plays at Malvern.

3386 Mantle, Burns, ed. THE BEST PLAYS OF 1928-29 AND THE YEAR BOOK OF THE DRAMA IN AMERICA (NY: Dodd, Mead, 1929), pp. 8, 20, 22, 24, 418-19.
[Passing mention of Shaw productions in America outside New York, and New York production details of Major Barbara.]

3387 Marshall, Ernest. "Britons Put Trust in Envoys at Hague," NYT, 25 Aug 1929, part III, p. 8.
[A brief report of Shaw at the Malvern Festival and the plays to be produced.]

3388 Masbach, Ilse. "Berliner Bericht" (Berlin Account), DER GRAL, XXIV: 3 (Dec 1929), 257-61.
[A review of The Apple Cart. In German.]

3389 Merel, J. "Guía de la mujer inteligente para el conocimiento de socialismo y capitalismo por Jorge Bernard Shaw (George Bernard Shaw's The Intelligent Woman's Guide to Socialism and Capitalism), RENOVACIÓN (Argentina), Nos. 75-76 (March-April 1929), [not seen].
[Cited in Rodríguez (MS). In Spanish.]

3390 Miethke, Kurt. "Anekdoten" (Anecdotes), WELTSTIMMEN (Stuttgart), III (Oct 1929), supp, [n. p.].
[An anecdote of Shaw as a vegetarian. In German.]

3391 Miloslavić, J. "Izjave Bernarda Šo o polititsi, umetnosti i nashoj zemlji" (Bernard Shaw's Statements on Politics, Science, and Our Country), POLITIKA (Belgrade), 23 May 1929 [not seen].
[In Serbian.]

3392 Minnigerode, Fitzhugh L. "The Play That Shaw May Never Write," NYT, 20 Oct 1929, part V, pp. 3, 20.
Shaw has outlined the plot of a play about the Unknown Soldier, but has not developed the piece beyond that.

3393 "Misli Georg Bernar Shaw-a o drami i pozorištu, Dubrovniku i Jugoslaviji" (Thoughts of George Bernard Shaw on

Drama and the Theatre, Dubrovnik and Yugoslavia), DUBROVAČKA TRIBUNA (Dubrovnik), I (1929), 1-2, 15 [not seen].
[In Croatian.]

3394 "Mr. Bernard Shaw at Plymouth," TIMES, 17 Oct 1929, p. 13.
Shaw spoke on education when he opened a university hostel in Plymouth.

3395 "Mr. Shaw Looks at A. D. 1962," DAILY MAIL (Lond), 20 Aug 1929, p. 9.
The Apple Cart is full of talk, but "even the most commonplace and ordinary ideas are wrapped up in new ways."

3396 "Mr. Shaw Looks at Lombard Street," SPECTATOR, CXLIII (1929), 240-41.
By its first performance, The Apple Cart is already out of date politically.

3397 "Mr. Shaw on the Nineties," TIMES, 12 Oct 1929, p. 13.
Shaw attended a luncheon of the Critics' Circle and criticized critics.

3398 "Mr. Shaw Retorts," DAILY EXPRESS (Lond), 21 Aug 1929, p. 1.
Shaw is angry with Hannen Swaffer's review of The Apple Cart, although he seems amused that he has "educated his public beyond himself."

3399 "Mr. Shaw Sets Up His Apple Cart in Poland," LIT DIG, CI (8 June 1929), 25.
[Details of the forthcoming first production of The Apple Cart in Warsaw which Shaw thought appropriate because the play's political message was more apposite to Poland than anywhere else.]

3400 "Mr. Shaw's New Play," IRISH TIMES (Dublin), 20 Aug 1929, p. 4.
Shavians and Fabians are not very orthodox people, and The Apple Cart is not Shaw's best work. It is verbose and the satire verges on mere caricature.

3401 Miyajima, Shinzaburo. "Gendai eibungaku no keiko" (The Tendency of Contemporary English Literature), GENDAI EIKOKU BUNGEI INSHOKI (Impressions of Contemporary English Literature) (Tokyo: Sanseido, 1929), pp. 1-69.
[A general survey of contemporary English literature with a detailed exposition of Saint Joan as one of the representative works of the 1920s. In Japanese.]

3402 Monner-Sans, J. M. "Algo acerca del teatro de hoy" (Something About the Theatre of Today), LA NACIÓN (Argentina), 22 Dec 1929 [not seen].

[On Candida. Cited in Rodríguez (MS). In Spanish.]

3403 Morgan, Charles. "Mr. Shaw Once More," NYT, 15 Sept 1929, part IX, p. 2.
Saint Joan really made Shaw a popular dramatist, but he will be remembered by posterity for what he reveals about the opinions and manners of his age and for "certain memorable fragments." You Never Can Tell will be his only play to survive as a totality.

3404 Morgan, Charles. "More About Mr. Shaw's Play," NYT, 8 Sept 1929, part IX, p. 1; rptd in NYTTR 1927-1929, [n. p.].
The second act of The Apple Cart is a failure, for it is intended as light relief but Shaw's humor does not come off. However, acts one and three, with their criticism of democracy, have appeal.

3405 Morgan, Charles. "Shaw's New Play Praises England," NYT, 20 Aug 1929, p. 30; rptd in NYTTR 1927-1929, [n. p.].
The Apple Cart possesses Shaw's usual "good nonsense" but does not show Shaw's full dramatic range.

3406 Morris, Gwladys Evan. TALES FROM BERNARD SHAW (NY: Frederick A. Stokes, 1929).
[Shaw's plays turned into tales "told in the jungle" (quite literally). The plays thus transmogrified are Major Barbara, Candida, Man and Superman, Arms and the Man, Mrs. Warren's Profession, The Doctor's Dilemma, Captain Brassbound's Conversion, The Devil's Disciple, Fanny's First Play.]

3407 Moses, Montrose J. "An Evening with Shaw," REV OF REVS, LXXIX (Jan 1929), 152, 154.
Major Barbara retains its vitality although it lacks plot and is argumentative.

3408 Motter, T. H. Vail. THE SCHOOL DRAMA IN ENGLAND (Lond, NY, Toronto: Longmans, Green, 1929), pp. 82, 179, 200.
[A study of drama in schools with passing reference to performance of Shaw's work.]

3409 Muckermann, Friedrich. "Eine Rundfunkansprache über Bernard Shaw" (A Radio Program on Bernard Shaw), DER GRAL, XXIII: 6 (March 1929), 433-37.
Saint Joan shows Shaw's ability to tolerate opinions different from his own. [In German.]

3410 Nadějde, Iosif. "Om si supraom La Teatrul Naţional" (Man and Superman at the National Theatre), ADEVĂRUL (Bucharest), 10 May 1929 [not seen].
[In Roumanian.]

3411 Nadějde, Iosif. "Profesiunea D-nei Warren" (Mrs. Warren's Profession), ADEVĂRUL (Bucharest), 26 Oct 1929 [not seen].
[In Roumanian.]

3412 Nathan, George Jean. "Clinical Notes," AMERICAN MERCURY, XVII (July 1929), 370-73.

Shaw's work reveals that, for Shaw, sex is "at once unpleasant, deplorable and disgusting." His rhetoric may occasionally camauflage this antipathy but that has only a temporary effect.

3413 [National University of Ireland], TIMES, 13 March 1929, p. 18.

A proposal that the National University of Ireland confer a special academic honor on Shaw has been defeated.

3414 Nevinson, H. W. "Upsets the 'Apple Cart,'" NEW LEADER (Lond), XVI (23 Aug 1929), 9; rptd in Evans, pp. 317-20.

Shaw's achievement to date is enormous. He has the "finest critical mind in Europe" and has ruthlessly exposed the foibles and follies of England. It is all the more remarkable that such a conservative town as Malvern should hold a festival in Shaw's honor. However, The Apple Cart is "badly constructed in its dramatic form and pernicious in its moral."

3415 "The New Shaw Play: First Production in Poland," OBS, 28 April 1929, p. 19.

[Advance details of the production of The Apple Cart in Warsaw.]

3416 "New Work by Shaw is of Ellen Terry," NYT, 15 Dec 1929, part I, p. 28.

[Biographical.]

3417 "New Yorker Gets Shaw Manuscript," NYT, 20 Sept 1929, p. 13.

Gabriel Wells has acquired the holograph manuscript of Widower's Houses.

3418 Norgate, Matthew. "The Drama: Mr. Shaw's Jam Sandwich," NATION & ATH, XLV (1929), 680-81.

The Apple Cart is an undisguised sermon on democracy. But as a tract the piece is not very illuminating or brilliant, and it lacks form.

3419 O'Connor, T. P. MEMOIRS OF AN OLD PARLIAMEN-TARIAN. 2 vols (Lond: Benn, 1929), II, 256, 265-69.

[Biographical.]

3420 "$1,500 'Shaw' Work Not His, Says G. B. S.," NYT, 24 March 1929, part I, p. 3.

Shaw has issued a warning to collectors regarding Shaviana offered for sale. [See also: "Marking Up Books," NYT, 25 March 1929, p. 24; Thomas Hatton, "The Shaw Annotations," NYT, 29 April 1929, p. 22; Philip Moeller, "The Shaw Annotations," NYT, 12 May 1929, part III, p. 5.]

3421 "Un Paradoxe de Bernard Shaw" (A Paradox of Bernard

Shaw), JOURNAL DES DEBATS, XXXVI, part 2 (1 Nov 1929), 718 [not seen].
[In French.]

3422 Perrins, Meredith D. "The Malvern Hills," TIMES, 9 Oct 1929, p. 15.
Shaw is to be commended for drawing attention to the destruction of the Malvern Hills (TIMES, 8 Oct 1929, p. 17). [See also: TIMES, 11 Oct 1929, p. 10.]

3423 Pickering, J. Russell. "Letters to the Editor: Musical Copyright," TIMES, 4 Dec 1929, p. 10.
Shaw's letter [TIMES, 2 Dec 1929, p. 13] reveals he does not understand what the Musical Copyright Bill is all about.

3424 Pippett, R. S. "Mr. Shaw's Mystery Play," DAILY HERALD (Lond), 20 Aug 1929, p. 4.
The faithful Shaw followers will doubtless be somewhat puzzled by The Apple Cart because it is difficult to see what he advocates. It is a conversational marathon which is stimulating and exciting, but pointless.

3425 "Playboy." "The Play's the Thing," DAILY HERALD (Lond), 22 Aug 1929, p. 9.
No doubt the preface to The Apple Cart will reveal Shaw's intentions; however, it is the most interesting political play since Saint Joan. The effects Shaw uses are various both in kind and quality.

3426 Ponce, Aníbal. "Santa Juana en el teatro de los Pitoëf" (Saint Joan in the Pitoëff's Theatre), REVISTA DE FILOSOFIA (Argentina), XXX (Jan-June 1929), 155-59 [not seen].
[Cited in Rodríguez (MS). In Spanish.]

3427 Powell, Dilys. "Ideas and the Play," STIMES, 25 Aug 1929, p. 4.
When Shaw began as a dramatist, the drama lacked ideas; now, in The Apple Cart, ideas have got the upper hand completely. And, for once, the preface to the published play will be better than the play itself. The problem lies in the glorious, long speeches which unfortunately impede seriously what little action there is in this "political satire, flavoured with farce and served with romance."

3428 "Prince Induces Carnera to Wear Shirt in Ring; Shaw Hissed for Fancied Snub of Britisher," NYT, 29 Nov 1929, p. 10.
Shaw has been hissed at a boxing match because the crowd thought he was snubbing the Prince of Wales.

3429 "Provincial Productions: The Apple Cart," STAGE, 22 Aug 1929, p. 21.
The Apple Cart is a "brilliant political satire, full of characteristically and sparklingly witty dialogue, irony, and sallies" against

various institutions. "It seems a queer instance of the whirligig of time bringing in its revenges that G. B. S., the quondam Fabian, should now appear almost in the guise of a Fascist."

3430 "Radio Ban on Shaw is Lifted for 'Point of View' Broadcast," NYT, 24 Aug 1929, p. 11.
[Title describes.]

3431 R[hodes], R. C. "The Shaw Festival at Malvern," BIRMINGHAM POST, 20 Aug 1929, p. 14.
The Apple Cart displays "incomparable vivacity" and Shaw's "fine faculty for putting his ideas into the mouths of persons who have the illusion of reality." The play and its political thought needs a careful hearing since not all its complexity can be absorbed at one hearing.

3432 R[hodes], R. C. "The Shaw Festival at Malvern," BIRMINGHAM POST, 21 Aug 1929, p. 12.
Shaw's powers are far from failing: he is the "greatest man in the theatre to-day, because his interests are still unbounded." Back to Methuselah is a moving and beautiful work, and it is difficult to see how some people can term it dull and tedious. It belongs with Saint Joan and Heartbreak House as being among Shaw's highest achievements.

3433 R[hodes], R. C. "The Shaw Festival at Malvern," BIRMINGHAM POST, 24 Aug 1929, p. 16.
Heartbreak House is Shaw's finest play and one in which "the contrast of ideas is more important than the conflict of physical action." Every line is suffused with wit, humor, unexpectedness and humanity. It is not a tedious allegory of World War I, but a fine social comedy.

3434 R[hodes], R. C. "The Shaw Festival at Malvern," BIRMINGHAM POST, 26 Aug 1929, p. 10.
Caesar and Cleopatra, in comparison to the other plays at the festival, is obviously an earlier piece, but it is nonetheless enjoyable for that. Shaw has placed in Caesar's mouth some of the most pregnant and dramatic words in English dramatic literature since Shakespeare.

3435 "Rhodes Scholars Feted," NYT, 10 July 1929, p. 7.
Shaw has attended a garden party in honor of Rhodes Scholars.

3436 Rhys, Ernest. "Shaw the Talker," NY WORLD, 10 Feb 1929 [not seen].

3437 Rider, Dan. ADVENTURES WITH BERNARD SHAW (Lond: Morley & Mitchell Kennerley, jr. [1929]).
[Genial biographical reminiscences. Rider apparently also assisted Archibald Henderson in his work on Shaw.]

3438 Rivas-Cherif, C. "Teatro de arte y arte del teatro. Acotaciones a Cándida" (Theatre of Art and the Art of the Theatre: Directions to Candida), LA NACIÓN (Argentina), 14

July 1929 [not seen].
[Cited in Rodríguez (MS). In Spanish.]

3439 Rothstein, Th. BEITRÄGE ZUR GESCHICHTE DER ARBEITERBEWEGUNG IN ENGLAND (Contributions to the History of the Labor Movement in England) (Wien & Berlin: Verlag für Literatur und Politik, 1929), pp. 363-64, 448.
[A brief introduction to Shaw and the Fabian Society. In German.]

3440 Sadoveanu, Ion Marin. "Om şi supraom" (Man and Superman). GÎNDEREA (Bucharest), IX: 5 (1929), 204-05 [not seen].
[In Roumanian.]

3441 Sadoveanu, Ion Marin. "Profesiunea D-nei Warren" (Mrs. Warren's Profession), GÎNDEREA (Bucharest), IX: 11 (1929), 367 [not seen].
[In Roumanian.]

3442 "The Sale Room," TIMES, 26 March 1929, p. 5.
First editions of several of Shaw's plays have been sold. [See also: "The Sale Room," TIMES, 30 March 1929, p. 17.]

3443 "The Sale Room," TIMES, 8 June 1929, p. 11.
Several of Shaw's manuscripts have been sold at auction at Sotheby's.

3444 "The Sale Room," TIMES, 14 Nov 1929, p. 11.
Sotheby's has auctioned some of Shaw's letters to J. E. Vedrenne.

3445 Sanín Cano, Baldomero. "Bernard Shaw, o el sentido común" (Bernard Shaw, or Common Sense), LA NACIÓN (Argentina), 17 March 1929, rptd in REPERTORIO AMERICANO (Costa Rica), XVIII: 13 (6 April 1929), 193-97 [not seen].
[Cited in Rodríguez (MS). In Spanish.]

3446 Schmidt, Conrad. "Shaws Sozialismus" (Shaw's Socialism), SOZIALISTISCHE MONATSHEFTE, LXVIII (21 Jan 1929), 69-70.
Shaw's point of view in The Intelligent Woman's Guide to Socialism and Capitalism recalls abstract utilitarian reasoning of the Enlightment. The guide is contemplative rather than aggressive. [In German.]

3447 Sée, Henri. "Le socialism et le capitalisme expliqués par Bernard Shaw" (Socialism and Capitalism Explained by Bernard Shaw), LA GRANDE REVUE, Aug 1929, pp. 295-305.
The Intelligent Woman's Guide to Socialism and Capitalism reveals Shaw is not a prisoner of any particular dogma. While his definition of capitalism is hardly felicitous, Shaw appears moderate and not in favor of violent revolution. Socialism will be beneficial to all. [In French.]

3448 Selden, Charles A. "Shaw Tells Critics They're Never Good," NYT, 12 Oct 1929, p. 7.
[A report of Shaw's attendance and address at the annual luncheon of the Critics' Circle, London.]

3449 "Shaw Advises Razing Oxford, Cambridge," NYT, 16 Oct 1929, p. 4.
Shaw has advocated the destruction of Oxford and Cambridge universities and the building of local, decentralized universities.

3450 "Shaw, Bernard: Cashel Byrons Beruf" (Bernard Shaw's Cashel Byron's Profession), DER GRAL, XXIV: 3 (Dec 1929), 285.
Cashel Byron's Profession is Shaw's best novel, although the plot is rather trivial. An edition of Shaw's works could well do without his novels. [In German.]

3451 "Shaw Book Brings $2,850," NYT, 27 Feb 1929, p. 16.
A first edition of The Quintessence of Ibsenism has been sold for $2,850, along with other Shaw items.

3452 "Shaw Defends Law Checking Car Speed," NYT, 16 Dec 1929, p. 8.
[Title describes.]

3453 "Shaw Denies Basing Role on Pilsudski," NYT, 1 Oct 1929, p. 12.
Shaw has denied that King Magnus in The Apple Cart is based on Polish Marshal Pilsudski.

3454 "Shaw Feels 'Tempted' To Have Head Cut Off," NYT, 17 March 1929, p. 5.
[A report of Shaw's characteristic response to the news of an invention to keep severed head alive.]

3455 "The Shaw Festival," MALVERN NEWS, 24 Aug 1929, p. 5.
[An extensive, factual report of various aspects of the Malvern Festival, including non-critical reviews of The Apple Cart and Back to Methuselah.]

3456 "The Shaw Festival: Production of The Apple Cart," WORCESTER DAILY TIMES, 20 Aug 1929, p. 2.
Shaw is a law to himself so far as dramaturgy goes, but he infuses a marvellous vitality into The Apple Cart. The second act is somewhat curious because it could be omitted without spoiling the play. It is an astonishing mixture of many elements, but it never fails to entertain.

3457 "Shaw Finds Talkies Opening New Field," NYT, 19 May 1929, p. 26.
[Title describes. See also: "The Theatrical Lottery," NYT, 20 May 1929, p. 24.]

3458 "Shaw Gets Laughs as Expert on Sex," NYT, 14 Sept 1929, p. 2.
Shaw has addressed the World League for Sex Reform and made several proposals.

3459 "Shaw Gibes at Titles in Address on Radio," NYT, 15 Oct 1929, p. 8.
Shaw has given an address on democracy on British radio. [See also: "Shaw Turns His Microscope on Democracy," NYT, 8 Nov 1929, part X, p. 3; H. L. Shatford, "Mr. Shaw's Writings," NYT, 10 Nov 1929, part III, p. 5.]

3460 "Shaw Hoist on His Own Petard," LIT DIG, CII (21 Sept 1929), 27-28.
Shaw has discovered it is dangerous to be nonchalantly witty. In response to some adverse dramatic criticism to The Apple Cart at Malvern, he said parliamentary correspondents should have covered the event. As it happens, one such did and came to the same conclusion as the drama critics.

3461 "Shaw Holds British Must Reform Rule," NYT, 22 Nov 1929, p. 8.
Shaw believes that the form of British democracy must be changed. [See also: "The Dictatorship Complex," NYT, 24 Nov 1929, part III, p. 4; "As Shaw Would Change Politics and Culture," NYT, 16 Dec 1929, part XI, p. 8.]

3462 "Shaw in Berlin," GRAPHIC, CXXVI (16 Nov 1929), 339-40.
[Photographs of the Reinhardt production of Der Kaiser von Amerika (The Apple Cart) and of the London production.]

3463 "Shaw in the Garden," NYT, 19 Jan 1929, p. 16.
Shaw's famous report of the Beckett-Carpentier boxing match helped to establish the career of the late "Tex" Rickard.

3464 " 'Shaw' is Shaw's Guest," NYT, 6 March 1929, p. 10.
T. E. Lawrence was Shaw's guest at a performance of Major Barbara in London.

3465 "Shaw Letter Brings $240," NYT, 14 Nov 1929, p. 5.
Several Shaw manuscripts have been sold.

3466 "Shaw Off to Tunney Isle," NYT, 16 April 1929, p. 6.
Shaw is to vacation on the island of Brioni. [See also: "Shaw and Tunney Boon Companions," NYT, 25 April 1929, p. 30; "Shaw Silent on Tunneys," NYT, 29 May 1929, p. 7.]

3467 "Shaw Play Festival at Malvern," IRISH TIMES (Dublin), 21 Aug 1929, p. 6.
"How far Shaw's fame has carried him from the hated and feared revolutionary of twenty years ago may be gathered when he is feted

here in the quiet respectability of Shakespeare's England." It would have been better had the festival been in Dublin, which is a "city of youth" which needs the influence of such a Dublin man.

3468 "Shaw Rejects Irish Plea," NYT, 2 Aug 1929, p. 4.
Shaw has refused to contribute to the restoration of Sir Walter Raleigh's church in Ireland.

3469 "Shaw Says Invitation is 35 Years Too Late," NYT, 14 April 1929, p. 28.
Shaw has been invited to be an independent candidate in the upcoming election and has declined.

3470 "Shaw Sees Americans Becoming Red Indians," NYT, 26 Oct 1929, p. 9.
[A report of Shaw's comments on Americans.]

3471 "Shaw Sees Apple Cart," NYT, 18 Sept 1929, p. 35.
Shaw attended inconspicuously the London premiere of The Apple Cart which he has now altered very slightly. [See also: "MacDonald Warns Mrs. Shaw not to Alienate General Dawes," NYT, 19 Sept 1929, p. 1.]

3472 "Shaw Sees Liberalism Still Active in Britain," NYT, 30 Sept 1929, p. 13.
[Title describes.]

3473 "Shaw Seriously Ill; Wife Calls in Doctor," NYT, 28 Feb 1929, p. 29.
[Title describes. See also: "G. B. Shaw Interviews Himself on His Illness," NYT, 1 March 1929, p. 14.]

3474 "Shaw Sets Conditions Talkies Must Meet," NYT, 8 Sept 1929, part I, p. 3.
Shaw will allow his plays to be made into films when producers and actors have learned the technique.

3475 "Shaw's Ideas on Talkers," NYT, 27 Oct 1929, part IX, p. 8.
[A report of Shaw's views on films and actors.]

3476 "Shift Scene of Shaw Play," NYT, 10 April 1929, p. 7.
The locale of Arms and the Man has been changed from Bulgaria to Albania in the current production in Prague.

3477 Shipp, Horace. "The Consistency of Bernard Shaw," ENGLISH REVIEW, XLIX (1929), 508-10.
The Apple Cart shows us that once again Shaw is a deadly serious person and almost uncannily consistent. Here we find him "at his old game of examining institutions and the place of the superman in making and being made by them."

3478 Shipp, Horace. "The Gospel According to the Drama-

tists," ENGLISH REVIEW, XLVIII (1929), 483-84.
Shaw's <u>Major Barbara</u> discusses thoroughly the problem that "goodness is everywhere weak, and self-seeking powerful."

3479 "Short Radio Waves," NYT, 13 Oct 1929, part X, p. 19.
Shaw has refused to write a play for radio.

3480 Slonimski, Antoni. "New Shaw Play Hits 'Political Humbug,' " NYT, 15 June 1929, p. 6; rptd in NYTTR 1927-1929, [n. p.].
[An account of the Warsaw production of <u>The Apple Cart</u>.]

3481 "Soare Z. Soare despre <u>Maior Barbara</u>" (Soare Z. Soare in <u>Major Barbara</u>), RAMPA (Bucharest), 10 Nov 1929 [not seen].
[In Roumanian.]

3482 Spaini, A. "El mundo y Bernard Shaw" (The World and Bernard Shaw), CARÁTULA (Argentina), No. 138 (25 Oct 1929) [not seen].
[Cited in Rodríguez (MS). In Spanish.]

3483 Stephensen, P. R. "The Whirled Around: Reflections upon Methuselah, Ichthyphallos, Wheels and Dionysos," LONDON APHRODITE, No. 5 (April 1929), 338-41.
Shaw has vulgarized very badly Nietzsche's superman by overemphasizing his intellectual aspects and denying him "blood." Shaw, who has never had an original thought in his life, has also not taken account of Freud's research because his mind had become ossified by the time Freud's work was known.

3484 Sulek, Alisa. "Bernard Šo o nama i o sebe" (Bernard Shaw on Us and Himself), VREME (Belgrade), IX: 2694 (1929), 7 [not seen].
[In Serbian.]

3485 Swaffer, Hannen. " 'G. B. S.' With Nothing New to Say," DAILY EXPRESS (Lond), 20 Aug 1929, pp. 1-2.
<u>The Apple Cart</u> shows Shaw is years behind the times: he "is no longer a prophet, but a rather pathetic figure." His ideas belong to a silly boy, while England itself is moving onwards to a new destiny.

3486 Szapiro, Jerzy. "Warsaw Prepares for Shaw's New Play," NYT, 19 May 1929, part IX, p. 2.
[A report on the imminent production of <u>The Apple Cart</u> in Warsaw.]

3487 "Talk of Honor for Shaw," NYT, 27 Feb 1929, p. 15.
There is, again, speculation that Shaw's name may appear on the annual Honors List. [See also: "Kipling and Shaw Mentioned," NYT, 1 March 1929, p. 9.]

3488 " 'Tay Pay' Reviews Rise of Irish Party," NYT, 5 July 1929, p. 18.

T. P. O'Connor recounts how he avoided firing Shaw from the STAR (Lond), by making him a music critic.

3489 Tetauer, Frank. SHAW: IDEOLOGIE A DRAMATIKA (Shaw's Ideas and Dramatic Art) (Prague: [n. p.], 1929) [not seen].
[In Czech.]

3490 "Theatre Guild to Give Shaw's Latest Play," NYT, 1 March 1929, p. 22.
The Theatre Guild, New York, which has given American premieres of several of Shaw's plays, is to present The Apple Cart.

3491 Thorndike, Ashley H. ENGLISH COMEDY (NY: Macmillan, 1929), pp. 8, 303, 391, 435, 513, 537, 540, 560-61, 563-64, 566, 570, 574-79, 580-82, 586, 591, 593-94.
Shaw was an important influence in the 1890s, although his early plays derive from Ibsen. However, Shaw's personality is strongly impressed on each work and so he is far from being merely derivative. He is, like Ben Jonson, outspoken and voluminous in his ridicule of follies, although in a play such as The Philanderer he can be discursive and strident. For Shaw talk means action; he builds on and advances old traditional forms of comedy, as in Candida. The main contribution of his work is not its "individuality and novelty but rather its service in bringing drama again into unity with the main literary tradition."

3492 Thorndike, Russell. SYBIL THORNDIKE (Lond: Thornton Butterworth, 1929), pp. 203-04, 206, 268, 290-94, 307-09.
[An account of Shaw's relationship with Sybil Thorndike, particularly when she played Saint Joan.]

3493 Timuş, V. "Maior Barbara" (Major Barbara), RAMPA (Bucharest), 14 Nov 1929 [not seen].
[In Roumanian.]

3494 "Twilight of the Shavian God," LIT DIG, CII (20 July 1929), 19-20.
The Polish premiere of The Apple Cart is a disappointment because it is, at times, devastatingly dull. It can only be regarded as a minor Shavian work.

3495 "Una aventura de Bernard Shaw" (Bernard Shaw's Adventure), EL MERCURIO (Peru), 31 March 1929, p. 15 [not seen].
[Cited in Rodríguez (MS). In Spanish.]

3496 Vancura, Zdněk. "Rozpor ve filosofii Bernada Shawa" (A Discrepancy in Bernard Shaw's Philosophy), CASOPIS PRO MODERNI FILOSOFII (Prague), XVI (1929), 273-76 [not seen].
[Cited in Amalric, p. 481. In Czech.]

3497 Vatteone, A. C. "El teatro de Bernard Shaw" (Bernard Shaw's Theatre), LA NACIÓN (Argentina), 16 July 1929, pp. 11-12; 23 July 1929, p. 12 [not seen].
[Cited in Rodríguez (MS). In Spanish.]

3498 W., J. B. "Major Barbara," NSTATE, XXXII (1929), 730-31.
The weaknesses of Major Barbara are the lack of conflict within characters and Shaw's failure to put his own ideas to the test.

3499 Wagenknecht, Edward. A GUIDE TO BERNARD SHAW (NY & Lond: Appleton, 1929).
Shaw's work is "based so definitely on his theory of art and of life"; hence, an expository, rather than a critical, guide to his life, theories, social gospel and religion is called for.

3500 Wells, Gabriel. "Mr. Shaw's Dislike of the Term Gentleman Evokes a Rough and Ready Definition," NYT, 27 Oct 1929, part III, p. 5.
[Title describes.]

3501 "Wells Buys Shaw MS.," NYT, 14 June 1929, p. 26.
Gabriel Wells has bought the manuscript of Widowers' Houses. [See also, on Wells' purchase of the manuscript of You Never Call Tell: "$6,000 Paid in London for Shaw Manuscript," NYT, 24 July 1929, p. 7.]

3502 Wiegler, Paul. "Merkmale der heutigen Auslandsliteratur" (Characteristics of Contemporary Foreign Literature), WELTSTIMMEN (Stuttgart), III (Feb 1929), supp, [n. p.].
Shaw, Wells, and Galsworthy are the grand old men of the literary "left." Shaw attacks the moral standards of the puritans. [In German.]

3503 "Wratislavius." "Profesiunea D-nei Warren de Shaw" (Mrs. Warren's Profession by Shaw), OPINIA (Jassy), 13 Dec 1929 [not seen].
[In Roumanian.]

3504 "Wyndham's Theatre," TIMES, 6 March 1929, p. 14.
Major Barbara remains alive because it is "concerned far less with the prejudices of society than with the confusion of the soul."

1930

3505 Amico, Silvio d'. "L'Imperatore d'America di Shaw al Valle" (The Emperor of America [The Apple Cart] at the Valle Theatre), LA TRIBUNA (Rome), 25 April 1930; rptd in his CRONACHE DEL TEATRO (Theatrical Chronicles), ed by E. F.

Palmieri (Bari: Laterza, 1964), vol. II, 74-78.
The Apple Cart shows Shaw at his maturity—energetic, Nietzschean, socialistic, anti-democratic. His technique is vertiginous and the exasperating dialogue derives from centuries of English humor. Shaw's comedies are based, not on plot or intrigue, but on idea. [In Italian.]

3506 Anderson Imbert, Enrique. "Más sobre Bernard Shaw" (More About Bernard Shaw), LA NACIÓN (Argentina), 23 Aug 1930, pp. 14, 27 [not seen].
[Cited in Rodríguez (MS). In Spanish.]

3507 "Another Shavian Quip," LIVING AGE, CCCXXXIX (1930-31), 207-08.
Shaw has drawn a parallel between early Christianity and modern socialism.

3508 "The Apple Cart in Berlin," TIMES, 4 Feb 1930, p. 12.
A special performance of The Apple Cart was given in Berlin for members of the Reichstag who enjoyed the piece.

3509 "The Apple Cart in Milan," TIMES, 3 Feb 1930, p. 10.
The Apple Cart has received an unenthusiastic response in Milan because English life is little understood or appreciated in Italy.

3510 Araquistain, Luis. LA BATALLA TEATRAL (The Theatrical Battle) (Madrid: Mundo Latino, 1930), pp. 183-90.
[On Saint Joan. In Spanish.]

3511 "Arms and the Man: Revived at the Court," ERA, 1 Jan 1930, p. 12.
World War I has proved Shaw right in his opinions about war, and so Arms and the Man remains far from being dated. It also refutes the notion that there is no action in Shaw's plays.

3512 "Arts Theatre," TIMES, 1 May 1930, p. 14.
Jitta's Atonement becomes hilarious when Shaw finally get to grips with and changes his romantic original.

3513 "Arts Theatre: Jitta's Atonement," STAGE, 8 May 1930, p. 13.
Jitta's Atonement alters a "typical Continential drama" into a series of long conversations which pad out "a story so frail that it appears to be mainly the tedious linking up of a couple of ideas."

3514 Atkinson, J. Brooks. "Shaw's 'Applecart' Pokes Fun at Us," NYT, 25 Feb 1930, p. 30; rptd in NYTTR 1930, [n. p.]
The Apple Cart "is as bad a play as only Bernard Shaw would think of writing in the ripeness of his years. But if we must listen to unending conversation in the theatre . . . let Mr. Shaw write it."

3515 Attenborough, Charles L. "Film Censorship," TIMES, 19

Feb 1930, p. 15.
Shaw [TIMES, 17 Feb 1930, p. 15] does not seem to be aware that the censorship of films may be appealed.

3516 Barton, Ralph. "Theatre," LIFE, XCV (14 March 1930), 18.
The Apple Cart sandwiches one act of "sheer horseplay" between two dull acts. Politicians satirize themselves sufficiently on their own; Shaw succeeds only in boring.

3517 [Beach, Stewart]. "Israel Re-created," THEATRE MAGAZINE (NY), LI (April 1930), 14-15, 45.
The Apple Cart arouses only a "mildly curious interest" and is one of Shaw's lesser works.

3518 "Beautifying G. B. S.," LIT DIG, CVI (30 Aug 1930), 17.
Shaw goes to a beauty parlor for his tonsorial requirements.

3519 Bellamy, Francis R. "The Theatre," OUTLOOK AND INDEPENDENT (NY), CLIV (1930), 429.
The Apple Cart is a "brilliant mixture of pure burlesque with intellectual coruscations."

3520 B[ishop], G. W. "Arms and the Man as a Talkie," OBS, 5 Oct 1930, p. 11.
Shaw has granted the movie rights of Arms and the Man to Basil Dean.

3521 Bishop, G. W. "Mr. Shaw Replies to Mr. Craig," OBS, 26 Oct 1930, p. 19.
[Shaw's response to Craig's hostile remarks about Shaw in his HENRY IRVING, item 3542. See also: "Mr. Craig and Irving," OBS, 26 Oct 1930, p. 20; "Letters to the Editor" (by Craig, Laurence Irving and Joe Grahame), OBS, 2 Nov 1930, p. 10; "Letters to the Editor" (by Compton Mackenzie), OBS, 9 Nov 1930, p. 10.]

3522 Bloch, Jean-Richard. DESTIN DU THEATRE (The Destiny of the Theatre) (Paris: Gallimard, 1930), pp. 85-86.
Saint Joan is a model of what historical drama might be. [In French.]

3523 Brandl, L. "Entstehungsgeschichtliches zu Bernard Shaws Pygmalion" (The Origin and History of Bernard Shaw's Pygmalion), GERMANISCH ROMANISCHE MONATSSCHRIFT, XVIII (1930), 443-57 [not seen].
[Cited in Amalric, p. 481. In German.]

3524 Braybrooke, Patrick. THE SUBTLETY OF GEORGE BERNARD SHAW (Lond: Cecil Palmer, 1930).
Widowers' Houses and The Philanderer demonstrate Shaw's early aim of using the theatre as a mode of attack. Arms and the Man is a good play, but lacks the sustained brilliance of Candida, Shaw's best work. In the latter he exposes the "deadly unworldliness" of the cleric,

while he shows his understanding of Candida who cares nothing for the conceited, somewhat poetic Marchbanks. Shaw's "wartime genius" is demonstrated in Augustus Does His Bit and O'Flaherty, V. C.; in the former, he writes on what English patriotism really amounts to, and in the latter on the Irish "violent denunciation of patriotism." The Devil's Disciple oscillates between politics and theology, and could be mistaken for a religious play. It is "a play for Puritans in the sense that it is a play for those who object to the austerity, not to say ungeniality, of the Puritans." The Doctor's Dilemma reveals all Shaw's attitudes to the medical profession and though it is verbally brilliant it is "less brilliant in thought." In Man and Superman Shaw takes considerable license with traditional dramaturgy and has really written a philosophical tract full of brilliant Shavian dialogue. Its main themes are those of the life force and of the unscrupulous pursuit of man by woman in the "fulfilment of her own power of creation." Major Barbara shows the disturbing influence of the Salvation Army on England, although Shaw does defend it and rather makes audiences admire it. Saint Joan is somewhat unShavian, with Shaw sympathetic towards Joan, seeing her "almost as a feminine counterpart of himself, smashing up her dull contemporaries by showing them the way they ought to go." [Each play above is examined in some detail. With additional, more generalized chapters on Shaw and marriage, Shaw and Christianity, and Shaw and children.]

3525 "Britain Prohibits White Slave Film," NYT, 17 Feb 1930, p. 5.
Shaw has protested the censorship of THE NIGHT PATROL, a film about white slavery. [See also: "Shaw on Film Censors," NYT, 9 March 1930, part IX, p. 8.]

3526 "Briton Finds Mencken 'As Genial As Shaw,' " NYT, 26 Jan 1930, p. 3.
[H. L. Mencken and Shaw briefly compared.]

3527 "Broadcast English," TIMES, 20 Aug 1930, p. 7.
[Details of a report on spoken English published by the B. B. C. Shaw was chairman of the Advisory Committee responsible for the report.]

3528 Brock, H. I. "Shaw the Youthful Pictured by Shaw," NYT, 7 Sept 1930, part V, pp. 4-5, 14.
The preface to Immaturity provides Shavian autobiographical insights.

3529 Brophy, John. "The Greatest of Our Contemporaries," SAT REV, CL (1930), 588.
Shaw is somewhat wide of the mark in dubbing Einstein the "greatest of our contemporaries." Certainly, the person who has had most influence in the twentieth century so far is Shaw himself.

3530 Brown, Ivor. "The Spirit of the Age in Drama," FORT REV, ns CXXVIII (1930), 596-605.
Shaw's contribution to modern drama has been to introduce "unruly brilliance" in the construction of his plays. This anarchy is good "when it liberates a Shaw," but is unsuccessful with lesser lights who should stick to the well-made play formula.

3531 Brown, Ivor. "The Theatre: Better than Shakespeare?" SAT REV, CXLIX (1930), 264.
The production of The Dark Lady of the Sonnets and Androcles and the Lion at the Old Vic is a sign that Shaw has been canonized, at least at that theatre which holds Shakespeare sacred.

3532 "Calls Bernard Shaw Outstanding Puritan," NYT, 10 Feb 1930, p. 26.
J. H. Holmes believes Shaw is the "prophet of radicals" and a puritan.

3533 "Can't Print Shaw Letters," NYT, 8 April 1930, p. 13.
Shaw has refused to allow the publication of his letters to Ellen Terry. [See also: "George Bernard Shaw to Ellen Terry," NYT, 13 April 1930, part III, p. 7.]

3534 Carb, David. "Seen on the Stage," VOGUE, LXXV (12 April 1930), 132.
The Apple Cart fails to fulfill the promise of stimulating ideas: a conflict between constitutional monarchy and democracy bogs itself down in long monologues, and only the cleverness of the urbane dictator, Magnus, saves his throne.

3535 Chesterton, G. K. "Keeping Up with Mr. Shaw," LIVING AGE, CCCXXXVIII (1930), 616-19.
The Apple Cart is probably the best play Shaw has written and demonstrates he is far more up-to-date than critics realize.

3536 "Chesterton Here, Lampoons Shaw," NYT, 21 Nov 1930, p. 26.
Chesterton calls Shaw a puritan, "pouring righteous indignation into the wrong things." [See also: "A Chiel has been Taking Notes," NYT, 22 Nov 1930, p. 16.]

3537 Clemens, C. "A Visit to Bernard Shaw," OVERLAND MONTHLY AND OUT WEST MAGAZINE, ns LXXXVIII (Sept 1930), 273, 285, 288.
[Title describes. Biographical.]

3538 Colbourne, Maurice. THE REAL BERNARD SHAW (Toronto: Dent, 1930; rptd Lond: Dent, 1939; NY: Dodd, Mead, 1940; rptd and enlarged Lond: Dent; NY: Philosophical Library, 1949) [also trans as LE VERITABLE G. B. SHAW by Albert Bailly (Brussells: La Sixaine, 1947).]
Clues to Shaw's personality are more plentiful in his prefaces than in

the plays, because in the latter Shaw gives every character "in turn 100 percent support" and for the dramatic moment "is that character." As the merchant of his own publicity, Shaw is not guilty of conceit; rather, he wisely takes advantage of the English sense of innate superiority that suffers foreign criticism because it will not be taken seriously. Shaw, whose knowledge is visionary, remains consistent to his original philosophy, only deepening it by "examining it from one angle after another." Many dismiss the seriousness of Shaw's vision because he chooses wit rather than solemnity of manner.

3539 Cookman, A. V. [Saint Joan], NYT, 29 June 1930, part VIII, p. 1; rptd in NYTTR 1930, [n. p.].
[Details of a London revival of Saint Joan by Georges Pitoëff and company who have modified the original somewhat.]

3540 Cornwallis-West, G. EDWARDIAN HEY-DAYS OR A LITTLE ABOUT A LOT OF THINGS (Lond & NY: Putnam, 1930), pp. 265-66, 271-72, 307-13.
Mrs. Patrick Campbell created a stir in Pygmalion by uttering the word "bloody" on stage. Shaw gave Cornwallis-West useful advice about the latter's play, THE MOUSETRAP. [With an anecdote about Shaw and lengthy excerpts of Shaw's letters to Cornwallis-West.]

3541 "Court Theatre," TIMES, 18 March 1930, p. 14.
Misalliance is full of too much talk, although it has many ideas and much wit.

3542 Craig, Edward Gordon. HENRY IRVING (Lond: Dent, 1930), pp. 6, 23, 26, 71, 85, 89, 105, 147-59, 168, 195, 197-98, 241-43.
Shaw's plays probably are not really liked, but they do manage respectable runs and they do play; such was also the case with Scribe. Irving did not perform in any of Shaw's plays because they are full of gab and overloaded with stage directions which limit an actor's interpretative abilities. Also, many of Shaw's stage directions set down in print what he had already seen Irving do on stage, as a detailed examination of The Man of Destiny reveals.

3543 Cutler, B. D., and Villa Stiles. MODERN BRITISH AUTHORS: THEIR FIRST EDITIONS (NY: Greenberg, 1930), pp. 125-31.
[Brief bibliographical descriptions of first editions of Shaw's works through 1929.]

3544 D[arlington], W. A. "Bernard Shaw 'Translates,'" DT, 1 May 1930, p. 8.
Act one of Jitta's Atonement is very much Siegfried Trebitsch's, but after that Shaw's notion of translation is quite different from most people's. A sense of irony creeps in act two, and by the third act

Shaw is fully in his own "characteristically anti-romantic vein."

3545 De Casseres, Benjamin. MENCKEN AND SHAW: THE ANATOMY OF AMERICA'S VOLTAIRE AND ENGLAND'S OTHER JOHN BULL (NY: Silas Newton, 1930).
Mencken is a "rare type of American intellectual honesty and prejudiced sincerity"; by contrast, Shaw all the more appears "a commonplace type of American hypocrisy and publicity shark." His social propaganda and asceticism have no foundation in nature, psychology or common sense. Take away from Shaw "the self-ravished Narcissan and the redeemer illusion—and there remains a clever and versatile ladies' smoking-room wisecracker—nothing more."

3546 "The Devil's Disciple at the Savoy," ERA, 10 Sept 1930, p. 1.
The Devil's Disciple proves it is difficult to outgrow Shaw and the piece is better than when it was first performed.

3547 "Einstein Praises Shaw," NYT, 28 Oct 1930, p. 12.
Albert Einstein believes Shaw's humor has helped people to "think freely about life and its problems."

3548 "An Elusive Refuser," NYT, 27 July 1930, part IX, p. 2.
There are many things Shaw has refused, including a peerage and visiting America.

3549 "Entertainments," TIMES, 20 March 1930, p. 14.
The next Malvern Festival will include seven plays by Shaw.

3550 "Entertainments: The Film World," TIMES, 13 Aug 1930, p. 8.
Shaw has contracted for the film version of How He Lied to Her Husband.

3551 "Entertainments: The Theatres: Canada and Mr. Shaw's Plays," TIMES, 14 Aug 1930, p. 8.
[Details of Maurice Colbourne's tour of Canada with a Shavian repertory.]

3552 Fairchild, Henry Pratt. "Mrs. Holt Arranging Shaw Dinner," NYT, 18 Jan 1930, p. 16.
There is to be a Town Hall Club dinner as a tribute to Shaw. [See also: "Shaw Testimonial Leaves Him Cold," NYT, 20 Jan 1930, p. 14.]

3553 Farjeon, Herbert. "The London Stage," GRAPHIC, CXXVIII (1930), 654.
The setting of Saint Joan by Georges Pitoëff was superb, but the performance of Joan by Ludmilla Pitoëff, though beautiful, lacked the credibility of that of Sybil Thorndike.

3554 "Fear of Complexes Seen as Causing Sin," NYT, 20 Aug 1930, p. 9.
Shaw has urged allowing condemned prisoners to conveniently commit suicide.

3555 Feick, Irmgard. "Shaw, Bernard, Wegweiser für die intelligente Frau zum Sozialismus und Kapitalismus" (Bernard Shaw: The Intelligent Woman's Guide to Socialism and Capitalism), JAHRBÜCHER FÜR NATIONALÖKONOMIE UND STATISTIK, LXXVII (1930), 288-90.
Shaw's The Intelligent Woman's Guide to Socialism and Capitalism is a work of art of strong moral principles and warm-hearted kindness. The mechanisms of economy and society are well explained. Shaw is an advocate of state socialism. [In German.]

3556 Fielding, W. J. "The Play of the Month," SKETCH BOOK MAGAZINE (NY), VII (April 1930), 33.
In The Apple Cart, Shaw "the redoubtable Sage now applies his eloquent slap-stick to democracy." The play is a "flow of glorious nonsense."

3557 "French Season at the Globe: Sainte Jeanne," ERA, 18 June 1930, p. 6.
This French adaptation of Saint Joan brings a realization of the play's greatness and of the differing approaches which can be used. This production is spiritual, mystical and formal; it has quiet, devotional strength.

3558 "A Friendly Argument with Mr. Shaw," NYT, 24 Aug 1930, part VIII, p. 2.
Theresa Helburn, executive director of the Theatre Guild, New York, takes exception to Shaw's remark that the theatre is dead.

3559 Fyfe, Hamilton. SIR ARTHUR PINERO'S PLAYS AND PLAYERS (NY: Macmillan, 1930), pp. 36, 60, 70, 95, 113, 149, 172, 193, 201, 262, 282.
Shaw's farces are witty, rather than humorous, and the characters in them are really Shaw in numerous guises.

3560 "G. B. Shaw Letters to Go at Auction," NYT, 27 April 1930, part II, p. 4.
Included in the sale of Shaviana are some letters to Frank Harris.

3561 "G. B. Shaw Museum Urged," NYT, 20 Sept 1930, p. 2.
Shaw admirers are urging the Dublin city authorities to acquire his birthplace and convert it into a Shaw museum.

3562 Garland, Hamlin. "Roadside Meetings of a Literary Nomad," BOOKMAN (NY), LXXI (June 1930), 308-10; rptd in ROADSIDE MEETINGS (NY: Macmillan, 1931), pp. 428-42.
[An account of meeting with Shaw.]

3563 "Globe Theatre," TIMES, 11 June 1930, p. 12.
Saint Joan has been given in French in London in an interpretation which sees it as an "essentially religious work of dramatic art."

3564 Griffith, Hubert. "The London Stage," GRAPHIC, CXXIX (1930), 427.
The revival of The Devil's Disciple has fine first and second acts; the third needs a larger stage. Although most think of Shaw as a "supreme intellectual," his best effects as a playwright are got when he is a mystic and romantic."

3565 Guiterman, Arthur. "Impudent Interviews," in Malcolm S. MacLean and Elisabeth K. Holmes, comps, MEN AND BOOKS (NY: Richard R. Smith, 1930), pp. 397-99.
[Biographical.]

3566 Hackett, Francis. "The Post-Victorians," BOOKMAN (NY), LXXI (March 1930), 20-26.
Shaw was a radical and certainly an eminent post-Victorian, although he too is beginning to merge with the past. Unfortunately, Shaw has not meant business; like other Irish writers he "has allowed his vivid social sense to compel him to create a mask, an artificial, superficial personality, so that the writing man and the real man have never tragically merged."

3567 Harris, Frank. OSCAR WILDE: HIS LIFE AND CONFESSIONS (Garden City, NY: Garden City Publishing, 1930), pp. 137, 330, 383, 387-404, 434, 448, 458.
When asked about Shaw and his work, Wilde admitted that he is "a man of real ability but with a bleak mind." While Shaw possesses wit, he has "no passion, no feeling."

3568 Hasegawa, Nyozekan. "Anchi feminisuto toshiteno Bernard Shaw" (Bernard Shaw as an Anti-feminist), KAIZO (Tokyo), XII: 9 (Sept 1930), 2-17; XII: 10 (Oct 1930), 173.
Shaw is an eager supporter of feminist movements, but as a dramatist he is an unbending anti-feminist, not because his plays do not revolve around sexualism, but because they do not make up a history with women as central figures. [In Japanese.]

3569 Henderson, Archibald. CONTEMPORARY IMMORTALS (1930; rptd Freeport, NY: Books for Libraries, 1968), pp. 83-96.
[A generalized overview of Shaw's life and work which sees him as "the world's greatest living writer."]

3570 "High Cost of Compromise," CHRISTIAN CENTURY (Chicago), XLVII (1930), 1585-86.
Shaw has called on the British Labour Party to return to its principles, even though that would bring about defeat in the next general election.

3571 Hopkins, R. Thurston. "My First Book," BOOKMAN (Lond), LXXIX (1930), 184.

[Details of Shaw's childhood reading. Biographical.]

3572 Hutchens, John. [The Apple Cart], THEATRE ARTS MAGAZINE (NY), XIV (1930), 370, 373.

The Apple Cart is a mellow and discursive, undramatic debate on monarchy and democracy.

3573 Ishida, Kenji. "Hikari wa Tohoyori" (Light from the East), EIGO SEINEN (Tokyo), LXIII: 4 (May 1930), 110; rptd in KIRISUTOKYOTEKI BUNGAKUKAN (The Christian View of Literature) (Tokyo: Kenkyusha, 1932), pp. 380-84.

Irving Babbit and Shaw both urge the importance of self-control and renunciation. Shaw preaches self-control as a preparatory arrangement for doing great works in this world. [In Japanese.]

3574 Jennings, Richard. "Mr. Shaw on Democracy," SPECTATOR, CXLV (1930), 945-46.

Shaw's long-awaited preface to The Apple Cart elucidates the play, explaining his criticisms of democracy and revealing Magnus as no better than his advisors.

3575 Jennings, Richard. "The Theatre," SPECTATOR, CXLV (1930), 407.

In The Devil's Disciple Shaw appears to parody himself, creating a lesser satire than his later The Apple Cart.

3576 Jones, Doris Arthur. THE LIFE AND LETTERS OF HENRY ARTHUR JONES (Lond: Gollancz, 1930), pp. 112, 139-40, 151-52, 155, 170, 175-76, 179, 181, 183-85, 198-99, 203-04, 211-12, 220, 222, 250, 307, 310-32, 348-50, 394, 404. [Published NY: Macmillan, 1930 as TAKING THE CURTAIN CALL: THE LIFE AND LETTERS OF HENRY ARTHUR JONES.]

[Many biographical details of the relationship between Shaw and Jones, particularly their tempestuous disagreements during World War I. Numerous letters also reproduced.]

3577 Krutch, Joseph Wood. "Drama: The Impenitent Shaw," NATION (NY), CXXX (1930), 338, 340.

Although some would argue The Apple Cart is an argumentative and actionless play, Shaw's suppleness and dexterity is delightful. However, the play's defect is one common to Shaw's work: his "enraptured eloquence" is not sufficient to supply the link between reason and vision. For that Shaw needed to be a poet.

3578 [Kuhe, Ernest]. "Drama," THE ANNUAL REGISTER 1929 (Lond: Longmans, Green, 1930), part II, pp. 47-50.

After R. C. Sherriff's JOURNEY'S END, Shaw's The Apple Cart was probably the most significant theatrical event of 1929, although opinion was strongly divided on the play's merits.

3579 Laski, Harold. "Four Literary Portraits: Bernard Shaw," LIVING AGE, CCCXXXIX (1930-31), 289-92.
Shaw is a great man who has realized people enjoy being preached at about their sin. He is perceptive, has prevented us from being complacent, and enjoys fighting (although as an end in itself). He is a great humanist, an autocrat who must be in control, and has been magnificently consistent.

3580 Lavrin, Janko. STUIDES IN EUROPEAN LITERATURE (NY: Richard R. Smith, 1930), pp. 80-98.
When Ibsen and Shaw are compared it is easy to see "all the difference between a romantic-aristocratic father and his realistic-democratic descendant." Shaw is an emancipated nonconformist concerned with contemporary problems, although he may now have lost popularity with the younger generation.

3581 Lawrence, D. H. A PROPOS OF LADY CHATTERLEY'S LOVER (Lond: Mandrake, 1930), pp. 25-26, 28-32.
Shaw knows little about sex; indeed, he is flippant, vulgar and cocksure on the subject.

3582 Lockridge, Richard. "The Apple Cart," SUN (NY), 25 Feb 1930, p. 30.
The Apple Cart is not Shaw's best work. It is a sensible play from a man who used to turn the world upside down. Shaw's cleverness is apparent here and there, but the piece lacks his old fire and sparkle.

3583 "London Theatres: The Court: Misalliance Revived," STAGE, 20 March 1930, p. 16.
Misalliance is not dated and Shaw lovers will delight in seeing the play with the full text (parts of which were cut in the original performance).

3584 "London Theatres: The Globe: Sainte Jeanne," STAGE, 12 June 1930, p. 14.
This French production of Saint Joan shows clearly that the fine plot of the saint needed cloaking only with suitable language, which Shaw has done.

3585 "London Theatres: The Old Vic: Shakespeare and Shaw," STAGE, 27 Feb 1930, p. 18.
[A discussion of the production aspects of Androcles and the Lion and The Dark Lady of the Sonnets.]

3586 "London Theatres: The Savoy," STAGE, 4 Sept 1930, p. 14.
This revival of The Devil's Disciple serves primarily as a vehicle for John Martin-Harvey as Dudgeon.

3587 "Lord Darling Upholds Flogging Prisoners," NYT, 5 Feb 1930, p. 9.

Shaw has expressed his opposition to flogging.

3588 Macauley, Thurston. "Drama's Colossus Admits He is That," NYT, 9 Feb 1930, part III, p. 1.
Shaw is the most famous dramatist of the age, a title readily admitted by all including Shaw himself.

3589 MacCarthy, Desmond. "Sainte Jeanne" (Saint Joan), NSTATE, XXXV (1930), 332-34; rptd in MacCarthy, pp. 170-75.
The production in French of Saint Joan reveals it is "one of the very few fine religious plays in existence" and that it is "also intensely dramatic."

3590 "Magazine Planning Suit Against Shaw," NYT, 4 Feb 1930, p. 17.
PLAIN TALK is threatening to sue Shaw because he objects to the publication of his letters by the magazine.

3591 "Malvern Dramatic Festival," TIMES, 1 Sept 1930, p. 8.
Shaw has been entertained by the Malvern Urban District Council and has spoken of the need to protect the Malvern Hills.

3592 Mantle, Burns, ed. THE BEST PLAYS OF 1929-30 AND THE YEAR BOOK OF THE DRAMA IN AMERICA (NY: Dodd, Mead, 1930), pp. 4, 15, 18, 27, 31-32, 482-83, 500.
The Apple Cart is "a distinguished job of writing . . . but a somewhat involved and overlong discussion of English politics."

3593 Maude, Alymer. THE LIFE OF TOLSTOY (Lond: Oxford UP, 1930), vol. II, pp. 108, 376, 389, 391, 450, 460-64; rptd in part in Evans, pp. 184-85.
Tolstoy thought Shaw was original, but it was a pity that Shaw allowed his desire to be surprising to be so dominating. This feature is readily apparent in Man and Superman and The Shewing-up of Blanco Posnet. [An exchange of letters between Shaw and Tolstoy is also printed.]

3594 "Misalliance at the Court," ERA, 19 March 1930, p. 4.
Misalliance is a formidable play broken down into a series of easily digested scenes. The piece tends to pall when there are a lot ot characters on stage, but goes better in the duologues.

3595 "Mr. Bernard Shaw and the Old Vic," TIMES, 21 Feb 1930, p. 12.
[Largely a letter from Shaw on his own appearance at the Old Vic theatre fifty years previously.]

3596 "Mr. Shaw and Mr. Craig to the Wars," NYT, 30 Nov 1930, part IX, p. 2.
Shaw and Gordon Craig have been conducting a debate about each other in the columns of the OBS.

3597 "Mr. Shaw on Art," OBS, 16 Nov 1930, p. 13.
[An account of Shaw's address to the Art Workers' Guild on 14 Nov 1930.]

3598 Morgan, Charles. [The Devil's Disciple], NYT, 21 Sept 1930, part IX, p. 2; rptd in NYTTR 1930, [n. p.].
The Devil's Disciple can be seen as a stirring melodrama or as a forerunner of the later Shaw. It remains a delightful and amusing piece.

3599 Mortimer, Raymond. "The Drama: Stars from France," NATION & ATH, XLVII (1930), 376.
[A favorable review of Saint Joan.]

3600 Moses, Montrose J. "The Court Jester's Apple Cart," REV OF REVS, LXXXI (April 1930), 144-45.
The Apple Cart is a discourse, not a play, composed of the "mere sweepings" of Shaw's mind.

3601 Mount, T. E. "Shaw's Statement Regarded as Embarrassing to Lewis," NYT, 28 Dec 1930, part III, p. 2.
Shaw's statement [NYT, 19 Dec 1930, p. 1] on Sinclair Lewis' Nobel Prize acceptance speech reveals Shaw "as a joker of doubtful taste."

3602 "The Old Vic," TIMES, 25 Feb 1930, p. 12.
Androcles and the Lion is a "brilliant patchwork precariously stitched together by a thread of idea."

3603 "Players' Theatre," TIMES, 8 July 1930, p. 12.
The Fascinating Foundling is enjoyable and amuses even after Shaw's satirical jabs have passed.

3604 Playfair, Nigel. HAMMERSMITH HOY: A BOOK OF MINOR REVELATIONS (Lond: Faber, 1930), pp. 170-72, 175.
[Brief details of Playfair's involvement with the Stage Society and the production of You Never Can Tell and Candida.]

3605 "Plays By Shaw to Go On the Air," NYT, 19 Jan 1930, part VIII, p. 17.
Cecil Lewis will introduce Shaw's plays which are to be radio broadcast in America.

3606 Popoff, Georg. "Luncheon with Shaw," LIVING AGE, CCCXXXIX (1930-31), 149-56.
[Title describes.]

3607 "Professor Einstein in London," TIMES, 29 Oct 1930, p. 12.
Shaw proposed the toast to Albert Einstein at a dinner held in his honor.

3608 Rhondda, Lady. "Shaw's Women: Artist-Philosophers and Their Dangers," TIME AND TIDE, XI (1930), 300-01.
Women have never had the role of artist-philosophers. Shaw's women are possible and even attractive creations upon which real women

might well begin to model themselves.

3609 Rhondda, Lady. "Shaw's Women: If St. Joan had not been a Saint. . . ?" TIME AND TIDE, XI (1930), 468-70.
In Saint Joan, Shaw's achievement is remarkable. Alone of all men writing today he reveals himself to be "a man whose concern with people of either sex lies in the fact that they are human beings."

3610 Rhondda, Lady. "Shaw's Women: The Conduit-Pipe Theory," TIME AND TIDE, XI (1930), 395-96.
Woman's place, as defined by Shaw, is not to be a human being but a conduit-pipe for human beings. Shaw's view of women is particularly dangerous because he puts a halo around his "conduit-pipes" and gives over to women the whole responsibility for the coming generation.

3611 Rhondda, Lady. "Shaw's Women: The Shavian Eve," TIME AND TIDE, XI (1930), 436-38.
Back to Methuselah, written some twenty years later than Man and Superman, shows that Shaw's views on Everywoman have not altered greatly.

3612 Rhondda, Lady. "Shaw's Women: The Shavian Everywoman," TIME AND TIDE, XI (1930), 331-34.
Shaw has come closer than any man who has written during the last thirty or forty years to drawing flesh-and-blood women with real reactions and real individualities; but usually they are unfinished sketches with big bits of them left blank. His women give the feeling of being effectively painted trees with no real roots.

3613 Rhondda, Lady. "Shaw's Women: Why Ann is a Cad," TIME AND TIDE, XI (1930), 364-66.
Although Shaw drew in the heroine of Man and Superman a perfectly good surface portrait, he never discovered what really produced her. He missed the obvious fact that Ann's superficial failings and her whole attitude to life were the product not of nature but of her environment.

3614 Roberts, R. Ellis. "The Inhibitions of Bernard Shaw," BOOKMAN (Lond), LXXIX (Oct 1930), 4-7.
Reading Shaw's collected works confirms Chesterton's earlier estimate that Shaw is a puritan (in the best sense of the word).

3615 Russell, Frances Theresa. "Complicated Bernard Shaw," UNIVERSITY OF CALIFORNIA CHRONICLE, XXXII (1930), 468-90.
Shaw is a romanticist just as much as he is a cynic, pessimist or propagandist. He frequently uses artists as the medium for his romanticism. He is also a realist and satirist, providing a heightening compliment to his romanticism.

3616 Salt, Henry S. COMPANY I HAVE KEPT (Lond: Allen &

Unwin, 1930), pp. 47, 66, 81, 96-97, 122, 134, 162, 173, 190, 205.
[Numerous biographical references, in particular to Shaw as a Fabian/socialist.]

3617 "Savoy Theatre," TIMES, 3 Sept 1930, p. 10.
The Devil's Disciple contains many of the features of melodrama, but they cannot disguise the fact that Shaw had a very serious theme when he wrote this play in his "unregenerate youth."

3618 Scott-James, R. A. "G. B. S. on Democracy," SAT REV, CL (1930), 797.
We should be grateful for The Apple Cart and its preface because Shaw has given his ideas a new setting and the public constantly needs to be educated about political systems. However, Shaw refrains from delineating his ideal system.

3619 "A Shavian Preface," TLS, No. 1506 (11 Dec 1930), 1061.
Shaw's preface to The Apple Cart is rather bland. Shaw founders "on the rock of collectivist dogma" which is his "only secure foothold amid the waves of his intellectual restlessness." The play itself is witty and stimulating.

3620 "Shaw Admires Will Rogers's Admiration, But Rogers has No Chance to Express It," NYT, 25 Jan 1930, p. 3.
[Details of Rogers' visit with Shaw. See also: "Will Rogers Back; Seasick in Gales," NYT, 7 Feb 1930, p. 22.]

3621 "Shaw at the Old Vic," ERA, 26 Feb 1930, p. 4.
The Dark Lady of the Sonnets is "witty, audacious and full of charm." Androcles and the Lion remains as captivating as ever with its "charming morality . . . naivety and wise humour."

3622 "Shaw Attacks Labor," NYT, 28 Nov 1930, p. 2.
Shaw is now a disillusioned socialist, more nearly resembling a Tory.
[See also: "Shaw Criticizes MacDonald," NYT, 29 Nov 1930, p. 16.]

3623 "Shaw Calls Einstein 'Universe Creator,'" NYT, 29 Oct 1930, p. 12.
[Title describes. See also: "Shaw Introduces Einstein," NYT, 30 Oct 1930, p. 26.]

3624 "Shaw Finally Allows Play to be a Talkie; 'Poor Old Theatre Is Done For,' He Remarks," NYT, 8 Aug 1930, p. 1.
Shaw has signed a film contract for How He Lied to Her Husband.
[See also: "Back from Hollywood," NYT, 13 Aug 1930, p. 18.]

3625 "Shaw Helps Direct Talkie," NYT, 28 Oct 1930, p. 12.
Shaw has assisted in the direction of the film of How He Lied to Her Husband.]

3626 "Shaw in New Preface Calls Father Drunkard; Says Ostracism Made Son Crude in Manner," NYT, 2 Aug 1930, p. 6.

[Title describes. See also: "Shaw Strikes Back at Reproach from Pulpit; Says Preacher Misquoted Him on His Father," NYT, 4 Aug 1930, p. 8.]

3627 "Shaw, in Screen Talk, Jokes About His Age," NYT, 25 Oct 1930, p. 20.

[Title describes.]

3628 "Shaw is Britain's 'Best Brains' by Vote of SPECTATOR Readers," NYT, 27 June 1930, p. 11.

[Title describes.]

3629 "Shaw Lauds Besier for Browning Play," NYT, 21 Aug 1930, p. 13.

Shaw has praised Rudolf Besier's THE BARRETTS OF WIMPOLE STREET, produced at the Malvern Festival.

3630 "Shaw Makes Plea for State Theatre," NYT, 1 Feb 1930, p. 14.

Shaw has lent his support for a national theatre in England.

3631 "Shaw Play Heard on Radio," NYT, 22 Jan 1930, p. 27.

How He Lied to Her Husband has been broadcast on American Radio.

3632 "Shaw Praises War Book," NYT, 23 Nov 1930, part III, p. 3.

Shaw has praised J. M. Kenworthy's NEW WARS; NEW WEAPONS.

3633 "Shaw Project Defeated," NYT, 3 Dec 1930, p. 2.

Shaw's proposal to disband the Stage Society has been soundly defeated.

3634 "Shaw Refused to Accept Title; Wants to Keep His Own Name," NYT, 30 Sept 1930, p. 1.

[Title describes. See also: "When Peerages Handicap Fame," NYT, 3 Oct 1930, p. 26.]

3635 "Shaw Says New Russian Films Should Make Hollywood Blush," NYT, 6 Dec 1930, p. 12.

[Title describes.]

3636 "Shaw Sells Rights to Film His Plays," NYT, 28 May 1930, p. 31.

[Title describes. See also: "Denies Shaw Gave Rights," NYT, 29 May 1930, p. 26.]

3637 "Shaw Tells Labor How to Win Defeat," NYT, 4 Aug 1930, p. 8.

Shaw believes the Labour Party needs to introduce drastic reforms in order to overcome voter disillusionment.

3638 "Shaw-Terry Letters to be Published Soon," NYT, 30 Nov 1930, part I, p. 18.

[Title describes. See also: "Letters Show Shaw Adored Miss Terry,"

NYT, 5 Dec 1930, p. 1.]

3639 "Shaw to Write on Doctors," NYT, 5 Oct 1930, part III, p. 8.
Shaw is reportedly collecting material for a book on the medical profession.

3640 "Shaw Turns Banter on Morrow and Reed," NYT, 2 Feb 1930, part I, p. 23.
Shaw has directed his witty banter at several subjects, including the London naval conference between Britain and America.

3641 "Shaw's 'Benignant Deviltry,' " LIT DIG, CIV (15 March 1930), 23-24.
The Apple Cart has met with some success in New York, although it is greatly aided by the production it is given. It is the best of all the bad plays produced so far this season.

3642 "Shaw's Devil's Disciple," LIT DIG, CVI (27 Sept 1930), 16.
[Background details about the forthcoming revival of The Devil's Disciple.]

3643 "Shaw's First Novel to be Published Soon," NYT, 1 Aug 1930, p. 40.
Immaturity is to be published as part of a collected set of Shaw's work.

3644 "Shaw's 'Makers of Universes': Achievements of the Eight," NYT, 2 Nov 1930, part IX, p. 4.
Shaw has made a challenging speech on eight men who have discovered the universe for us.

3645 Shelley, Henry C. "Henry Arthur Jones," BOOKMAN (Lond), LXXVIII (June 1930), 194, 196.
Shaw was a life-long friend of H. A. Jones and held him and his work in high esteem.

3646 Shipp, Horace. "The Stage as Rostrum," ENGLISH REVIEW, L (1930), 510-11.
Whether we like or agree with Shaw, we must recognize he almost monopolizes the theatre of intelligence in London today. Shaw's success with every class of audience is based on the fact that "his plays are full of ideas carried forward by the most amazing mental shock tactics; and his sense of humour makes the work far funnier than any sitting-on-bandboxes farce."

3647 Shipp, Horace. "With Bernard Shaw at Malvern," BOOKMAN (Lond), LXXIX (Oct 1930), 7-10.
[An account of productions at the Malvern Festival, which reaffirm the three outstanding qualities of Shaw's work—his consistency, sincerity, and constructiveness.]

3648 Skinner, Richard Dana. "The Play and Screen: Shaw's Apple Cart," COMMONWEAL (NY), XI (1930), 535.

The Apple Cart, despite some amusing passages, lacks dramatic substance. The problem lies in the fact that Shaw is "the apostle of a transient idea," unlike Belloc or Chesterton who fight "for principles rather than mere ideas, for passionate beliefs rather than theories."

3649 "South African Soil," TIMES, 6 Sept 1930, p. 15.

Shaw was present at a talk on South African agriculture and was persuaded to say a few words afterwards.

3650 "Soviet and the 'Coming War,'" TIMES, 26 June 1930, p. 15.

Shaw's views on a potential war against Russia, along with those of other leading figures, have been published by IZVESTIA.

3651 "Speed Limits and Death," NYT, 4 Jan 1930, p. 18.

It is difficult not to agree with those who protest Shaw's proposal to do away with speed limits for vehicles.

3652 "The Stage Society," TIMES, 3 Dec 1930, p. 12.

Shaw has expressed his lack of support for the Stage Society, although a motion to dissolve the Society was defeated.

3653 Stewart, Herbert L. "The Puritanism of George Bernard Shaw," ROYAL SOCIETY OF CANADA PROCEEDINGS AND TRANSACTIONS, 3rd series, XXIV, section 2 (1930), 89-100.

The case for Shaw being a puritan inheres in three qualities that he has in common with Puritanism: a certain austerity, a certain obstinacy, and a certain ruthlessness. To liken Shaw to the Puritans is not to doubt that he has been an immensely valuable social stimulant. His puritanic qualities "had a needful part to play, and it is the same qualities—served by his unique talent—that have made Shaw the most effective scourge of our timid acquiescences and our mental sloth." [Wide reference to the plays.]

3654 "Summer Schools," TIMES, 4 Aug 1930, p. 12.

Shaw has spoken for a reform bill at the summer school of the Independent Labour Party.

3655 Sunne, Richard. "Books in General," NSTATE, XXXVI (1930), 304.

The Apple Cart and its preface can only be understood if one remembers that Shaw has been relentlessly driven to help the millions of people who suffer deprivations in many, if not most, areas of life. The younger generation should not be blasé about Shaw and his achievements.

3656 Sutton, Graham. "The Stranger in Our Gates," BOOKMAN (Lond), LXXVIII (1930), 252.

[A favorable review of a revival of Saint Joan.]

3657 "Teatrul Ventura. <u>Nu si stie</u>" (Ventura Theatre. <u>You Never Can Tell</u>), ADEVĂRUL (Bucharest?), 11 Sept 1930 [not seen].
[In Roumanian.]

3658 Terry, Altha Elizabeth. JEANNE D'ARC IN PERIODICAL LITERATURE, 1894-1929, WITH SPECIAL REFERENCE TO BERNARD SHAW'S "SAINT JOAN"; A BIBLIOGRAPHY (NY: [Publications of the Institute of French Studies Inc, 1930]).
[Title describes.]

3659 "The Theatres: Shakespeare Memorial Scheme," TIMES, 9 Jan 1930, p. 8.
[Shaw's views on a national theatre and details of Charles Macdona's Shavian repertory at the Court Theatre.]

3660 Timuş, V. "Cronică dramatică. Teatrul Maria Ventura. <u>Nu se şite</u>" (Dramatic Chronicle. Maria Ventura Theatre. <u>You Never Can Tell</u>), RAMPA (Bucharest), 10 Sept 1930 [not seen].
[In Roumanian.]

3661 "To Print Early Shaw Tale," NYT, 7 March 1930, p. 4.
Shaw's fifty-year old novel, <u>Immaturity</u>, is to be published for the first time.

3662 "Too Hot for Shaw to Talk," NYT, 30 Aug 1930, p. 6.
Since it was too hot for Shaw to give a lecture, he gave a swimming display instead.

3663 Trask, C. Hooper. [<u>The Apple Cart</u>], NYT, 9 March 1930, part IX, p. 4; rptd in NYTTR 1930, [n. p.].
Max Reinhardt's Berlin production of <u>The Apple Cart</u> reinforces the impression that Shaw has been assimilated by the English and that he is a less vital force.

3664 Tully, Jim. "The Wittiest Man in the World," VANITY FAIR, XXXIV (June 1930), 64, 94.
[An interview. Shaw is an attractive and philanthropic man.]

3665 "Über demokratie und parlamentarismus" (About Democracy and Parliamentarianism), NEUE RUNDSCHAU (Berlin), XLI, part 2 (Oct 1930), 443-68 [not seen].
[In German.]

3666 "Una 'desgracia' de Bernard Shaw" (Bernard Shaw's "Misfortune"), ABC (Spain), 17 July 1930, p. 14 [not seen].
[Cited in Rodríguez (MS). In Spanish.]

3667 Viereck, George Sylvester. GLIMPSES OF THE GREAT (NY: Macaulay, 1930), pp. 8-22.
[An interview.]

3668 W., E. Vr. "The Drama: II. Plays of Some Importance: The Apple Cart," CATHOLIC WORLD (NY), CXXXI (April 1930), 78-79.

The Apple Cart should be shorter and the preface longer. The first act is lengthy and dull, the idea is clever, the vehicle "a little appealing and pathetic."

3669 Wainger, Bertrand M. "Henry Sweet—Shaw's Pygmalion," STUDIES IN PHILOLOGY, XXVII (1930), 558-72.

Henry Sweet, a figure too significant in English scholarship to be buried in the preface to Pygmalion, warrants his own biography.

3670 Wakefield, Gilbert. "The Theatre: A Devil with No Disciples," SAT REV, CL (1930), 313.

The revival of The Devil's Disciple reinforces the fact that Shaw has no disciples among practising dramatists, although he has undoubtedly influenced them.

3671 Wakefield, Gilbert. "The Theatre: 1910 and—1890?" SAT REV, CXLIX (1930), 354-55.

Misalliance is mostly talk of an academic, impersonal nature, although it is lively and amusing.

3672 Ward, A. C. THE NINETEEN-TWENTIES: LITERATURE AND IDEAS IN THE POST-WAR DECADE (Lond: Methuen, 1930 [not seen]; 3rd ed rptd Folcroft, Pa: Folcroft, 1975), pp. 8, 18-30, 33, 69-70, 124.

Back to Methuselah is the work of a tired genius and needs compressing greatly. However, Shaw's ideas here have at least pointed the direction his generation should follow. Saint Joan is so good dramatically that "its metaphysical purpose can be conveniently overlooked." The Intelligent Woman's Guide to Socialism and Capitalism is limited by its size, but is a "masterpiece of clear English prose." The Apple Cart reveals Shaw can still respond to the times and its problems and that he is still a "healthy and stimulating irritant to the body politic of Western civilization."

3673 "Where All is Sunshine," NYT, 23 Nov 1930, part IX, p. 1; rptd in NYTTR 1930, [n. p.].

The Apple Cart has received a successful production in Los Angeles.

3674 Wisehart, M. K. "Humbug, Hate and Whither are We Drifting?" MENTOR (Springfield, OH), XVIII (March 1930), 16-19, 68.

[Largely an interview with Shaw.]

3675 "Works on Shaw Biography," NYT, 2 Nov 1930, p. 4.

Frank Harris is preparing a Shaw biography.

3676 Young, Stark. "The Neighborhood and the Guild," NEW REP, LXII (1930), 99-100.

<u>The Apple Cart</u> is not overwhelmingly interesting, though it does contain intelligent talk, ideas, and Shaw's usual tricks and turns. His manner is milder than before.

Index

AUTHORS

Included here are authors of articles and books on Shaw, editors and compilers of works in which criticism on Shaw appears. Numbers after each name refer to the item(s) in the bibliography where the name occurs.

441

Attenborough, Charles L.:
3515
Austin, L. E.: 155
B.: 853, 1184, 1336
B., F. R.: 2926
B., G. W.: 2
B., R.: 2720
B., W. H.: 2490
B.-W., J.: 3090
Bab, Julius: 724, 854, 1185,
2491, 3091
Baeza, Ricardo: 2314
Bahr, Hermann: 942, 943
Bailly, Albert: 3538
Bakshy, Alexander: 1908,
2216
Balfour, Edith: 381
Balmforth, Ramsden: 2492,
3093
Barker, Ernest: 1337
Barker, J. Ellis: 637
Barlow, George: 2
Barnard, Alfred: 1819
Barnard, Eunice Fuller:
2721
Barnes, J. H.: 1537
Barnicoat, Constance A.:
382
Barretto, Larry: 2722
Bartolucci, G.: 1178, 1743
Barton, Ralph: 3516
Bauer, G.: 2927
Baughan, E. A.: 187, 255,
490, 877, 1060, 1186, 2217
Baumann, Arthur A.: 491
Bax, E. Belfort: 87, 88, 1820
Beach, Stewart: 3517
Beal, Wallis: 3094
Beaunier, André: 2493
Becker, May Lamberton:
3285
Beer, Max: 1187, 1909, 2315
Beerbohm, Max: 47, 55, 56,
57, 73, 89, 90, 110, 111,
133, 156, 157, 158, 188,
189, 256, 257, 258, 259,
260, 383, 384, 385, 492

493, 494, 495, 638, 639,
855, 856
Beers, Henry A.: 261
Begbie, Harold: 1992
Belfoe, A. M. A.: 3286
Belfrage, Cedric: 2723
Belgion, Montgomery: 3287
Bell, Clive: 1993
Bellamy, Francis R.: 3519
Bellinger, Martha Fletcher:
2929
Benavente, Jacinto: 725
Benchley, Robert C.: 1910,
1994, 2117, 2218, 2316,
2494, 2495, 2930, 3095
Benesič, Julije: 944
Bennett, Arnold: 112, 1339
Bennett, Charles A.: 2724
Benninghoff, L.: 2931
Benson, E. F.: 3096
Berg, G.: 3288
Bernard, Jean-Jacques: 3289
Bernstein, Eduard: 266
Bernstein, Herman: 947,
2320
Berton, Claude: 2497
Besant, Annie: 643
Beswick, Harry: 387
Bettany, F. G.: 160, 2726
Beveridge, Albert J.: 1540
Biancolli, Louis Leopold:
2276
Bidou, Henry: 644, 1062, 2498,
2727, 2728, 3102
Billy, André: 2499
Birmingham, George A.: 729
Birrell, Francis: 2121, 2223,
2321, 2322, 2323, 2729
Bishop, G. W.: 2932, 3292,
3293, 3294, 3520, 3521
Björkman, Edwin: 948, 949,
2122
Bland, Alan: 3295
Bland, Hubert: 91
Bland, J. O. P.: 1541
Blankenagel, John C.: 2732
Blathwayt, Raymond: 59

442

1672
F., H. de W.: 2349
F., J.: 1919, 2350
Fagan, James Bernard: 748
Fagure, Emil D.: 1861, 2544,
   2761, 2762
Fair, Philip O. S.: 2
Fairchild, Henry Pratt: 3552
Falcon, César: 2763
Farjeon, Herbert: 972, 973,
   974, 1101, 2238, 2953, 3135,
   3136, 3334, 3335, 3336, 3553
Farr, Florence: 526
Farrar, John: 2351
Farrer, Reginald: 213
Fawcett, James Waldo: 2239
Fehr, Bernhard: 1561, 2240
Feick, Irmgard: 3555
"Femina": 527
Fernández Almagro, Melchor:
   2545
Fielding, W. J.: 3556
Figgis, Darrell: 1102, 1218
Filon, Augustin: 44, 292
Findon, B. W.: 1103
Fineman, Frances: 2546
Firkins, Ina Ten Eyck: 2954
Firkins, O. W.: 1920, 1921
"First Nighter": 1365, 1366,
   1562, 1563, 1564, 1565,
   1566, 1673
Fischer, Friedrich: 1768
Fischer, O.: 3337
Fischer, Walther: 1923
Fitzgerald, C. C. Penrose:
   214
Fitzgerald, Percy: 416
Flagg, James Montgomery:
   1367
Florence, Jean: 664, 749
Forbes, Avary H.: 380
Forbes-Robertson, Sir Johnston:
   2547
Ford, James L.: 293
Foster, Jeanne: 2352
Fowell, Frank: 1221
Fowke, V. De S.: 665

Fox, A. W.: 2548
Fox, Paul Hervey: 1368
Franc, Miriam Alice: 1863
France, Wilmer Cave: 294
Francés, José: 1924
Franić-Požežanin, I.: 1925
Frank, Glenn: 2021
Freeman, Donald: 2353
Freeman, John: 1674
Fréjaville, Gustave: 2549
Friche, V.: 975
Frichet, Oscar: 1369
Fricken, Roy Henri: 2955
Frohman, Charles: 750
Frohman, Daniel: 976
Fuchs, James: 2766
Fujii, Akio: 2767
Fyfe, H. Hamilton: 418, 419,
   420, 528, 529, 530, 666,
   751, 752, 3559
G., F.: 3339
G., J.: 1225
Gabriel, Gilbert W.: 2553,
   2554, 2774, 2959, 2960
Gad, Lily: 1927
Galsworthy, John: 1227,
   1864
García, Lautaro: 3340
Gardiner, A. G.: 2775
Gardner, Emily: 2555
Garland, Hamlin: 3562
Garnett, Edward: 753, 754
Gassner, John: 1057
Gawsworth, John: 212
Geddie, J. Liddell: 123
Gee, Joseph: 1377
Gémier, Firmin: 2356
Genn, Beatrice S.: 2961
Gerrard, Thomas J.: 1105
Gibbon, J. Morgan: 1228
Gillet, Louis: 1929, 2241,
   2358
Gillis, J. M.: 2359
Gillison, J. A.: 2242
Gilman, Lawrence: 533, 1379,
   1678, 1679
Glover, James M.: 979, 1229

219, 220, 221, 222, 223,
302, 544, 678, 679, 680,
765, 766, 982, 983, 984,
985, 986, 987, 988, 1113,
1242, 1390, 1582, 1583, 1687,
1937, 2030, 2143, 2372, 2373,
2374, 2375, 2376, 2565, 2566,
2567, 2568, 2785, 2965, 2966,
2967, 2968, 2969, 2970, 2971,
2972, 2973, 2974, 2975, 2976,
3148, 3347, 3348, 3349, 3350,
3569
Henríquez Ureña, Pedro: 1584,
3149
Henschke, Alfred: 3363
Henslowe, Leonard: 545, 546
Herbert, A. P.: 3351
Herford, O.: 1243
Herman, Julius: 1842
Herrmann-NeiBe, Max: 1869,
1938, 1939, 1940
Heugel, Jacques: 2569
Hevesi, Sandor: 884, 1114,
1393, 2248
Hinchliffe, Arnold P.: 2306
Hind, C. Lewis: 1941
Hirata, Tokuboku: 681
Hiratsuka, Raicho: 1394
Hirst, Francis W.: 3150
Hobson, J. A.: 2977
Hoffsten, Ernest Godfrey:
224
Hollis, Christopher: 3151
Holmes, James S.: 2570
Holmes, Maurice: 3352
Holms, J. F.: 2378
Hone, J. M.: 1778
Hopkins, R. Thurston: 3571
Hopkins, Roy: 3353
Hornblow, Arthur: 1689,
2144, 2379
Horsnell, Horace: 3153
Horwill, Herbert W.: 2380,
2788, 3154
Howe, P. P.: 886, 1244, 1245,
1586
Howells, W. D.: 303

Howorth, Henry H.: 990
Hueffer, Ford Madox: 991
Huizinga, Johan: 2570
Hulbert, H. B.: 1690
Huneker, James: 117, 225,
304, 305, 432, 1395, 3354
Huneker, Josephine: 2146
Hunt, Bampton: 433
Hurt, James: 2567
Hutchens, John: 3572
Hyndman, H. M.: 6, 1116
"I.": 434, 548
Iba, Takashi: 1396
Ilijić, Stjepan: 2382
"Inquirer": 118
"Interim": 2147
Irving, Laurence: 3521
Irzykowski, Karol: 3156
Isaacs, Edith J. R.: 2979
Ishida, Kenji: 1943, 3573
J., L.: 2980
Jackson, Holbrook: 550, 683,
1246, 2571
Jacobs, Joseph: 1398
Jameson, Storm: 1944, 2149
Jan, Edward von: 3157
Jarnes, B.: 3358
Jennings, Richard: 2791,
2792, 2981, 3359, 3574,
3575
Jessup, Mary E.: 3360
Johnston, Sir Harry: 1945
Jones, Doris Arthur: 3576
Jones, E.: 127
Jones, Henry Arthur: 227,
2035, 2036, 2037, 2038,
2250, 2574, 2575, 2576
Jourdain, Eleanor F.: 2385
Jowett, John Henry: 1692
Joyce, James: 774
Judson, Leonard: 438
Jung, Werner: 2577
K., H. A.: 94
K., Q.: 1587, 1693
Kaesmann, Evelyn: 1399
Kane, W. T.: 2982
Kaneko, Chikusui: 1120

Lunaček, Vladimir: 2159
Lunacharskii, A.: 2600, 3171
Lunn, Hugh: 1134
Lynd, Robert: 1878, 1879,
2048, 2399
Lynd, Sylvia: 3172
Lyon, Harris Merton: 1592
M., A. E.: 3372, 3373
M., C. E.: 558, 782
M., D. L.: 1951, 1952, 2049,
2050, 2051, 2160, 2161
M., G.: 3173
M., P. J.: 3374
M., T.: 2
M., W.: 4
McAdam, Robert L.: 2
Macauley, Thurston: 3588
McCabe, Joseph: 1405
MacCarthy, Desmond: 449,
559, 1255, 1256, 1257, 1406,
1407, 1408, 1698, 1786, 1787,
1788, 2052, 2053, 2054, 2055,
2162, 2400, 2401, 2402, 2403,
2404, 2601, 2996, 3375,
3589
MacCormac, John: 3174
Mac Donagh, Emiliano: 3175,
3376
Macdonald, Edward J.: 3377
Macdonald, John F.: 1409
MacGowan, Kenneth: 2056,
2163
McK., My: 3378
Mackenzie, Alexander: 2
MacLachlan, H. D. C.: 2259
Macy, John: 3176
Madrid, Louis: 1003
Maerz, A.: 2997
Mair, Alexander: 1699
Mair, G. H.: 1004
Mais, S. P. B.: 1789, 2260
"Malleus": 895
Mallock, W. H.: 35, 783
"Man in the Stalls": 1258,
1410, 1411
Manager, THE TIMES Book
Club: 561

Manly, John M.: 2065
Mantle, Burns: 1412, 2164,
2261, 2405, 2603, 2813,
3177, 3178, 3386, 3592
Marbury, Elisabeth: 2262
Marcel, Gabriel: 2263, 2604
Marcus, Hans: 3179
Margolin, N. S.: 2264
Mariátegui, J. M.: 2406
Mariátegui, José: 2605, 2814
Markov, P. A.: 2606
Marquand, Elsie: 577
Marshall, Ernest: 3387
Martin, John: 1007
Martin, John J.: 1953
Martínez Ruiz, José: 2815
Masbach, Ilse: 3388
Mason, Ellsworth: 774
Mason, Michael: 3180
Massingham, H. W.: 15, 896,
1259, 1413, 2059, 2060
Masterman, C. F. G.: 326
Mathew, William: 2
Maude, Aylmer: 784, 1830,
3593
Maude, Cyril: 168, 2999
Maude, Ralph: 168
Mauriac, François: 2607
Maurice, Frank: 1239
Maxwell, Perriton: 3181
Mayer, Hy: 1135
Medley, C. D.: 1700
Meierhold', V. E.: 898
Melkus, Dragan: 1414
Mellersh, H. E. L.: 2816
Meltzer, Charles Henry:
2061, 2062
Mencken, Henry L.: 327,
687, 1008, 1701
Mendez, Britz: 328
Merel, J.: 3389
Metcalfe, J. S.: 785, 1136,
1260, 1416, 1595, 1596,
1702, 1703, 1791, 1831,
1880, 1881
Mew, Egan: 1137, 1417
Meyer, Annie Nathan: 1792

Oliver, D. E.: 1141
"O'London, John": 2177
"Omicron": 2625, 2626, 2836, 3010
Orage, A. R.: 1023
Osani, Kaoru: 697, 801, 802, 803, 908
Osugi, Sakae: 1280
Oswald, Lina: 1449
Otaguro, Motoo: 1606
Ould, Hermon: 2178
Owen, Harold: 1608
"Oxford": 2
Page, Will A.: 3011
Palmer, Frank: 1221
Palmer, John: 1024, 1143, 1282, 1283, 1284, 1285, 1286, 1287, 1450, 1451, 1452, 1453, 1609, 2628, 2629
Palmieri, E. F.: 2715, 3505
Pankhurst, Christabel: 1454
Parker, D. C.: 1610
Parker, H. T.: 1715
Parker, John: 1144
Parker, Robert Allerton: 2179
Patrick, David: 123
Patterson, Ada: 1455
Patterson, Eleanor Cutler: 1456
Payne, George Henry: 583
Payne, William Morton: 79
Pearson, Hesketh: 2180, 2276, 2838
Pearson, Ruth R.: 2072
Pease, Edward R.: 1025, 1716
Pease, M. S.: 3193
Peirce, Francis Lamont: 1026
Pelikan, F.: 2073
Pelo, Florence Boylston: 1717
"Pendennis": 584
Pennell, Joseph: 2630
Peper, Elisabeth: 2839, 3013
Percy, Esmé: 2840

Pérez de Ayala, Ramón: 1890, 1891
Perrins, Meredith D.: 3422
Perry, Jennette Barbour: 124
Peterson, Carl C.: 3065
Pfeiffer, Edouard: 1027
Phelps, William Lyon: 1837, 2074, 3194
Phillips, R. Le Clerc: 2420
Pickering, J. Russell: 3423
Pickthorn, Kenneth: 3196
Piéchaud, Martial: 2632
Piercy, Josephine K.: 2324
Pierson, Edgar: 172
Pippett, R. S.: 3424
Pirandello, Luigi: 2421
Platon, I. S.: 909
"Playboy": 3425
Playfair, Nigel: 2634, 3604
"Playgoer": 2181, 2182, 2277
Poland, Harry B.: 807
Pollard, Alfred W.: 2077
Pollock, Channing: 1146, 1465, 1466, 1613, 1719, 1804
Ponce, Aníbal: 3426
Pope, T. Michael: 2422
Popoff, Georg: 3606
Porzsolt, K.: 1292
Postlewait, Thomas: 9
Powell, Dilys: 3427
Power, J. Danvers: 125
Pozza, Giovanni: 1029
Praz, Mario: 2636
Prazakova, Klara: 2078, 2184, 2185, 2186, 2187
Prevost, Francis: 347
Pribilla, M. S. J.: 2843
Price, William Thompson: 1468
Priestley, J. B.: 3198
"Professional Man": 912
"Pure, Simon": 2426, 2844, 2845, 3016
Quimby, Harriet: 814
R.: 2

Index

TITLES OF SECONDARY WORKS

Titles of articles in periodicals and chapters in books are in quotation marks; book titles are in upper case; translations of article titles originally appearing in a foreign language are in parentheses, without quotation marks, and in lower case; translations of book titles originally appearing in a foreign language are in parentheses and in upper case. Numbers after each title refer to the item in the bibliography where the title appears.

386
"Bernard Shaw in Portrait and Caricature": 659, 683
BERNARD SHAW IN SEINEN DRAMATISCHEN WERKEN: 1923
"Bernard Shaw in Shakespeare's Shoes": 726
"Bernard Shaw in the Orient": 2119
(Bernard Shaw: Intellectual Superman): 3271
"Bernard Shaw Intime": 982
"Bernard Shaw is Ill": 727
"Bernard Shaw: Jeanne d'Arc": 2801
"Bernard Shaw: John Bull's Other Island and Major Barbara": 631
"Bernard Shaw kao dramaticar": 439
"Bernard Shaw kein Vampyr?" 678
"Bernard Shaw kenkyu": 3006
"Bernard Shaw Lectures on an Errant World": 2886
"Bernard Shaw Makes a Discovery": 497
"Bernard Shaw. Man and Superman": 1066
(Bernard Shaw, Mineral Water Drinker and Misanthropist): 3143
"Bernard Shaw Moves": 3036
"Bernard Shaw—Musician": 1717
"Bernard Shaw Nearer in Spirit to Americans than to Englishmen": 498
"Bernard Shaw ni tsuite": 775
"Bernard Shaw no Akugeki": 681
"Bernard Shaw no genjitsushugi": 2578
(Bernard Shaw No Vampire?): 678
(Bernard Shaw: Nobel Prize):

2763
"Bernard Shaw, o el sentido común": 3445
"Bernard Shaw ó la crítica funambulesca": 1531
BERNARD SHAW OG HANS VERKER: 2708
"Bernard Shaw on American Women": 499
"Bernard Shaw on Art in the Schools": 1299
"Bernard Shaw on Films": 3174
(Bernard Shaw, on His Realism): 2578
"Bernard Shaw on Incomes": 191
"Bernard Shaw on Statesmen": 2220
(Bernard Shaw: On the Occasion of the First Night of Candida at the National Theatre): 1997
"Bernard Shaw on the Problem of Children (My Friend Bernard Shaw: VII)" 2968
"Bernard Shaw on the War": 1341
(Bernard Shaw on Us and Himself): 3484
"Bernard Shaw on Vegetarians": 2221
"Bernard Shaw on Women and Children": 3347
"Bernard Shaw on Women (My Friend Bernard Shaw: VI)": 2969
(Bernard Shaw, or Common Sense): 3445
(Bernard Shaw or Funambulist Criticism): 1531
(Bernard Shaw, Orator): 749
"Bernard Shaw otthon": 884
"The Bernard Shaw Philosophy": 284
(Bernard Shaw. Portrait of the English Playwright): 761
"Bernard Shaw. Portret

and Equal Pay in Ideal State":
2671

"Shaw Sees Liberalism Still
Active in Britain": 3472

"Shaw Sees Peace in Danger":
2448

"Shaw Sells Rights to Film His
Plays": 3636

"Shaw Seriously Ill; Wife Calls
in Doctor": 3473

"Shaw Sets Conditions Talkies
Must Meet": 3474

"Shaw Shows How to Impersonate Shaw": 2863

"Shaw Silent on Birthday":
2886

"Shaw Silent on Tunneys": 3466

"Shaw Sketch Good But a Trifle
Late": 1898

"Shaw Smiles at Jones": 2533

"Shaw Starts Trouble": 2526

"Shaw Strikes Back at Reproach
from Pulpit; Says Preacher
Misquoted Him on His
Father": 3626

"Shaw Styles War 'Highest of
Sports'": 1164

"Shaw Sues Page for Using
Letters": 3048

"Shaw Taken Ill as His Play
Fails": 827

"Shaw Takes A Dig at Curious
Americans": 3234

"Shaw Takes a Hand in Waist
Strike": 918

"Shaw Takes Honor, But Not
Nobel Cash": 2877

"Shaw Tells British to Seek a
Dictator": 3047

"Shaw Tells Critics They're
Never Good": 3448

"Shaw Tells Labor How to Win
Defeat": 3637

"Shaw Tells the World": 3176

"Shaw-Terry Letters to be
Published Soon": 3638

"Shaw Testimonial Leaves Him

Cold": 3552

"Shaw Thanks Germany for
Recognizing Him While
'Dangerous and Disreputable'
in Britain": 2886

"Shaw: The Later Plays": 3126

"Shaw, the Maid, and American
Folk Drama": 2427

[Shaw the Puritan] : 398

"Shaw, the Show, and the
Shawm or What's Wrong with
the Theatre?": 1873

"Shaw the Talker": 3436

"Shaw the Youthful Pictured by
Shaw": 3528

"Shaw Threatens Suit Over
Letters": 3048

"Shaw to Appear in Film": 3235

"Shaw to Comstock: You Can't
Scare Me": 271

"Shaw to the Life in Play WILD
OAT": 2863

"Shaw to Write on Doctors":
3639

"Shaw Turns Banter on Morrow
and Reed": 3640

"Shaw Turns His Microscope on
Democracy": 3459

"Shaw Turns Wrath Against
Dean Inge": 3236

"Shaw und Mussolini": 3049

"Shaw Unrepentant in Reply to
Critics": 1498

"Shaw Upheld in Suit Here Over
Film Rights": 2887

"Shaw Urges a League of White
Civilization": 1635

"Shaw Urges an Election": 1636

"Shaw vs. Chesterton in a Hot
Debate": 1041

"Shaw versus Chesterton: II:
Mr. Shaw and the Danger of
Living": 1851

"Shaw Versus Roosevelt on
Birth Control": 2672

"Shaw v. Shakespeare and
Others": 43

STUDI DI LETTERATURE
   MODERNE: 1543
STUDIE DI LETTERATURE
   STRANIERE: 3298
STUDIES AND APPRECI-
   ATIONS: 1102
STUDIES IN EUROPEAN
   LITERATURE: 3580
(STUDIES IN FOREIGN
   LITERATURE): 3298
(STUDIES IN MODERN
   LITERATURE): 1543
"Studies in Sin: Sinning at
   Long Range": 2259
STUDIES IN STAGECRAFT:
   1389
STUDIO AND STAGE: 2368
"Studio and Street": 3056
STUDY & STAGE: A YEAR-
   BOOK OF CRITICISM: 72
"Study and Stage: America
   and Mrs. Warren": 249
"Study and Stage: Mr. Shaw
   and Mr. Pinero": 154
(A Study of Bernard Shaw):
   3006
A STUDY OF THE MODERN
   DRAMA: A HANDBOOK
   FOR THE STUDY AND
   APPRECIATION OF THE
   BEST PLAYS, EUROPEAN,
   ENGLISH, AND AMERICAN,
   OF THE LAST HALF
   CENTURY: 2523
"Sturgis Blast Stirs Shaw": 3057
THE SUBTLETY OF GEORGE
   BERNARD SHAW: 3524
"Suffragist's Income-Tax": 1169
"Suffragists Work Ruin in Kew
   Gardens": 1323
"Sugar and Spice: Major
   Barbara": 1719
"Suggests Curb for Shaw": 1509
SUMMER MOTHS: 55
"Summer Schools": 3654
"Sunday Opening of Theatres":
   2095

[A Super-Flapper]: 2352
"The Superman at Seventy!":
   2793
"Super-Man or Super-Society?":
   836
(Superman's Love—A Review of
   Shaw's Man and Superman):
   1280
THE SUPPLANTERS: 1338
A SUPPLEMENT TO
   ALLIBONE'S CRITICAL
   DICTIONARY OF ENGLISH
   LITERATURE AND BRITISH
   AND AMERICAN AUTHORS:
   Volume II: 78
"The Sur-Passing Shaw: An
   Account of Major Barbara":
   371
"Surprising News for G. B.
   Shaw": 1510
A SURVEY OF SOCIALISM:
   3239
A SURVEY OF SOCIALISM:
   ANALYTICAL, HISTORI-
   CAL, AND CRITICAL: 3346
"Suteiji Sosaiechi": 802
"Svata Janá": 2682
"Sviâtaiâ Ioanna": 2463
SYBIL THORNDIKE: 3492
SYMPOSIUM: 639
"Synge and Shaw": 1788
TABLE-TALK OF G. B. S.:
   CONVERSATIONS ON
   THINGS IN GENERAL
   BETWEEN GEORGE
   BERNARD SHAW AND HIS
   BIOGRAPHER: 2567
"The Tailteann Festival": 3244
(Takashi Iba Company): 1181
TALKING THE CURTAIN
   CALL: THE LIFE AND
   LETTERS OF HENRY
   ARTHUR JONES: 3576
TALES FROM BERNARD
   SHAW: 3406
"Talk of Honor for Shaw": 3487
"A Talk with George Bernard

(Theatre Aiming at
Enlightenment): 1649
THE THEATRE AND THINGS
SAID ABOUT IT: 1035
"Le Théâtre anglais": 2188
LE THEATRE ANGLAIS:
HIER-AUJORD'HUI-DEMAIN:
44
"The Theatre: Arms and the
Man": 23
"The Theatre: Army Orders":
3303
"Theatre Arts Bookshelf": 2101
(Theatre. Berlin First Nights):
2583, 2797
(The Theatre: Bernard Shaw's
Great Catherine): 2927
"The Theatre: Better than
Shakespeare?": 3531
"The Theatre: Brieux and
Bernard Shaw": 419
(The Theatre: Caesar and
Cleopatra by G. Bernard
Shaw): 3269
"The Theatre: Candida": 183
THEATRE: ESSAYS ON THE
ARTS OF THE THEATRE:
2979
"The Theatre: Everyman
Theatre, Hampstead—The
Shaw Season": 2099
"The Theatre: Fanny's First Play
at the Little Theatre": 1048
"The Theatre: Getting Married":
666
(Theatre Gossip: French
Criticism and Bernard Shaw's
Saint Joan): 3266
"Theatre Gossip: You Never Can
Tell at the Strand Theatre":
106
"Theatre Guild to Give Cycle of
Shaw Plays": 2683
"Theatre Guild to Give Shaw's
Latest Play": 3490
"The Theatre: Heartbreak House
at the Court Theatre": 2100

(The Theatre in Madrid: The
1928-1929 Season): 3308
[The Theatre: John Bull's
Other Island]: 184
"The Theatre: John Bull's Other
Scold": 3304
"Le Théâtre: La Grande
Catherine de M. Bernard
Shaw": 2927
"The Theatre: 'Leaving
Aristotle Out'": 925
"The Theatre: Major Barbara":
3359
"The Theatre: Mr. Bernard
Shaw's New Skit": 752
"The Theatre: Mr. Forbes-
Robertson's Farewell": 1218
"The Theatre: Mr. Shaw's Sour
Apples": 3305
THE THEATRE NEWS OF
GIOVANNI POZZA: 1029
"The Theatre: 1910 and—
1890?": 3671
(Theatre of Art and the Art of
the Theatre: Directions to
Candida): 3438
(THE THEATRE OF THE
TOWN): 725
THE THEATRE OF TO-DAY:
1430
THE THEATRE OF
TOMORROW: 2056
"The Theatre: Play, Player, or
Producer?": 2700
"The Theatre: Pygmalion at
His Majesty's Theatre": 1417
(Theatre Repertory and German
Drama): 2817
"Theatre Royal: Mr. Forbes
Robertson's Visit": 627
"Theatre Royal: The Admirable
Bashville": 368
"The Theatre: Shaw as a
Lover": 3187
"The Theatre: Shaw's
Heartbreak House: 1975
"The Theatre: Some Moral

Index

393, 403, 424, 437, 467,
514, 553, 560, 573, 585,
587, 605, 607, 610, 611,
630, 669, 702, 703, 719,
744, 799, 811, 816, 831,
840, 841, 864, 903, 913,
937, 946, 970, 1005, 1038,
1089, 1092, 1119, 1130, 1139,
1142, 1173, 1180, 1219, 1220,
1232, 1296, 1297, 1329, 1435,
1437, 1469, 1559, 1713, 1757,
1767, 1802, 1819, 1862, 1922,
2017, 2018, 2020, 2033, 2058,
2135, 2167, 2214, 2279, 2313,
2342, 2357, 2419, 2423, 2424,
2512, 2573, 2614, 2615, 2652,
2717, 2755, 2825, 2854, 2913,
2932, 2963, 2998, 3017, 3092,
3277, 3292, 3293, 3380, 3511,
3546, 3557, 3594, 3621
LA ESFERA: 1924, 2004, 2391,
2746
ETHICAL WORLD: 836
ETUDES: 2655
EUGENICS REVIEW: 3193,
3296
L'EUROPE NOUVELLE: 2604,
3289
EVENING EXPRESS (Liverpool):
1718
EVENING STANDARD (Lond):
2574
EVERYBODY'S: 1110
EZHEGODNIK
IMPERATORSKIKH
TEATROV: 875, 909
DIE FACKEL: 167, 2387, 2798
LA FIERA LETTERARIA:
2636
LE FIGARO: 527, 1079, 1988,
2532, 3286
FINSK TIDSKRIFT: 983
FLACĂRA LITERARĂ: 2147
FLEURON: A JOURNAL OF
TYPOGRAPHY: 2571
FORTNIGHTLY REVIEW:
22, 35, 382, 430, 540, 753,

1201, 1244, 1409, 1609,
2217, 2374, 2375, 2376,
2496, 2629, 2693, 2785,
2816, 3530
FORUM (NY): 762, 948, 988,
1036, 1190, 1619, 2105,
2835, 3350
FRANKFURTER ZEITUNG:
581, 2496
FREEMAN: 2386, 2418
FREETHINKER: 691
GAELIC AMERICAN: 1071
GAKUTO: 889
GERMANISCH ROMAN-
ISCHE MONATSSCHRIFT:
3523
GINDIREA: 3022, 3440, 3441
GOLDEN BOOK MAGAZINE:
3347, 3348, 3349
GOOD HOUSEKEEPING:
545
DER GRAL: 2312, 3388,
3409, 3450
LA GRANDE REVUE: 3447
GRAPHIC (Lond): 741,
742, 769, 1021, 1233, 1470,
1823, 2328, 2329, 2892,
2953, 3135, 3136, 3291,
3334, 3335, 3462, 3553,
3564
GREEN BAG (Bost): 835
GREEN BOOK MAGAZINE:
1146, 1465, 1466, 1592,
1613, 1663, 1719, 1771,
1804
HAMPTON'S MAGAZINE:
781
HARPER'S BAZAAR: 304
HARPER'S MONTHLY: 303,
2376
HARPER'S WEEKLY: 228,
285, 293, 434, 548, 668,
993, 1127, 1198, 1367, 1383,
1475, 1585, 1654, 1688
HARVARD GRADUATES
MAGAZINE: 3263
HEALTH AND STRENGTH:

2822, 2904, 2981, 3096, 3132,
3238, 3240, 3333, 3359, 3396,
3574, 3575
SPRINGFIELD REPUBLICAN:
1418, 1933, 1990
STAGE: 14, 34, 52, 54, 81,
101, 113, 149, 178, 202,
205, 231, 273, 274, 300,
318, 319, 320, 321, 325,
370, 445, 446, 447, 555,
556, 557, 588, 595, 597,
598, 676, 685, 720, 737, 812,
832, 837, 892, 893, 894, 997,
1000, 1001, 1002, 1129, 1132,
1251, 1252, 1253, 1254, 1298,
1363, 1404, 1439, 1590, 1800,
1811, 1829, 1877, 1950, 1973,
2045, 2046, 2047, 2154, 2155,
2156, 2157, 2158, 2215, 2257,
2258, 2280, 2282, 2393, 2394,
2395, 2396, 2397, 2398, 2522,
2543, 2595, 2596, 2597, 2637,
2807, 2808, 2809, 2810, 2989,
2993, 2994, 3086, 3167, 3168,
3169, 3170, 3369, 3370, 3429,
3513, 3583, 3584, 3585, 3586
STAGE SOCIETY NEWS: 188
STANDARD (NY): 2127, 2360,
3009
STAR (Lond): 36
STIMMEN UND ZEIT: 2826,
2843
STUDIES IN PHILOLOGY:
3669
LA SUISSE: 2087, 2290
SUN (NY): 174, 206, 262, 263,
313, 332, 356, 400, 473,
521, 576, 609, 994, 1162,
1163, 1279, 1434, 1502, 1535,
1576, 1632, 1633, 1659, 1670
1683, 1797, 1807, 1898, 1970,
1975, 2008, 2122, 2151, 2181,
2182, 2197, 2277, 2281, 2481,
2553, 2554, 2701, 2774, 2960,
2980, 3201, 3582
SUNDAY CHRONICLE
(Manchester): 2035, 2967,

2969, 2973
SUNDAY EXPRESS
(Lond): 3066
SUNDAY OBSERVER
(Charlotte, NC): 2971
SUNDAY TIMES (Lond):
29, 94, 216, 217, 297, 298,
427, 428, 535, 536, 537,
538, 672, 693, 759, 845,
879, 880, 981, 1108, 1234,
1385, 1386, 1773, 1828,
2002, 2003, 2305, 2306,
2487, 3427
SURVEY: 951, 1007, 1897,
3260
TAIYO: 641, 764, 876, 1120
TATLER: 240
TEATORU: 2714, 2794
POLNOE SOBRANIE P'ES
V SHESTI TOMAKH: 1694
TEIKOKU BUNGAKU: 930,
931
IL TEMPO: 1899, 1900, 1977
LE TEMPS: 181, 376, 647,
716, 2645, 2933
THEATRE MAGAZINE (NY):
408, 410, 547, 780, 1072,
1442, 1455, 1463, 1603,
1618, 1689, 1710, 1712,
1737, 1752, 1755, 1782,
1790, 1803, 1826, 1840,
1958, 1972, 2020, 2061,
2140, 2144, 2165, 2233,
2379, 2515, 2793, 2955,
3124, 3181, 3517,
THEATRE ARTS MAGAZINE:
1914, 2101, 2163, 2837,
3109, 3127, 3325, 3572
THEATRE GUILD BULLETIN:
2568
TIME AND TIDE: 3608, 3609,
3610, 3611, 3612, 3613
TIMES (Lond): 8, 13, 18,
27, 77, 102, 114, 115, 118,
121, 125, 136, 143, 155,
169, 204, 214, 236, 247,
248, 270, 279, 280, 281,

Index

FOREIGN LANGUAGES

Included here are the languages in which articles and books listed in the bibliography originally appeared. Numbers under each language refer to the items in the bibliography where the foreign language title is given. English language items are not listed.

3013, 3049, 3091, 3103, 3107,
3114, 3117, 3142, 3157, 3159,
3166, 3173, 3179, 3209, 3214,
3215, 3216, 3261, 3273, 3280,
3281, 3282, 3288, 3297, 3326,
3339, 3342, 3344, 3361, 3362,
3363, 3364, 3388, 3390, 3409,
3439, 3446, 3450, 3502, 3523,
3555, 3665

Hungarian: 244, 884, 1114,
1292, 1393, 2248

Italian: 950, 1029, 1178, 1327,
1330, 1517, 1543, 1648, 1743,
1760, 1761, 1845, 1899, 1900,
1906, 1977, 2000, 2636, 2687,
2715, 2899, 3298, 3505

Japanese: 641, 681, 697, 775,
801, 802, 803, 843, 850,
876, 889, 890, 908, 930,
931, 933, 1120, 1126, 1181,
1280, 1326, 1394, 1396, 1400,
1445, 1484, 1523, 1606, 1649,
1943, 2578, 2580, 2714, 2767,
2794, 2796, 3006, 3023, 3401,
3568, 3573

Norwegian: 1742, 2708, 2800,
2801

Polish: 1511, 3156

Roumanian: 954, 1066, 1850,
1859, 1861, 1893, 2106,
2124, 2147, 2175, 2210,
2467, 2521, 2544, 2617,

2618, 2761, 2762, 2829,
3022, 3069, 3379, 3410,
3411, 3440, 3441, 3481,
3493, 3503, 3657, 3660

Russian: 631, 875, 898, 909,
975, 1151, 1525, 1694, 2264,
2463, 2464, 2600, 2606,
3171, 3185

Serbian: 397, 2278, 2903,
3391, 3484

Spanish: 161, 246, 328, 504,
505, 506, 725, 730, 749,
1531, 1532, 1584, 1607,
1759, 1818, 1890, 1891,
1924, 1961, 1966, 1979,
2004, 2308, 2314, 2391,
2406, 2453, 2502, 2534,
2545, 2566, 2605, 2742,
2743, 2746, 2756, 2763,
2814, 2815, 2856, 2890,
2946, 2964, 3007, 3020,
3072, 3073, 3074, 3082,
3083, 3084, 3099, 3100,
3101, 3143, 3149, 3158,
3175, 3212, 3248, 3266,
3268, 3269, 3271, 3290,
3308, 3340, 3356, 3358,
3376, 3389, 3402, 3426,
3438, 3445, 3482, 3495,
3497, 3506, 3510, 3666

Swedish: 3267

Index

Included here are all titles by Shaw occurring in titles of articles or books or in the abstracts. Numbers after each title refer to the item in the bibliography where the title appears.